William J Fay 724

O9-BTI-787

# GALATIANS

# HOUSEHOLDER COMMENTARIES

*The series will interpret books of the New Testament in the light of the Old (and vice versa), in the spirit of Mt 13 : 52*

*Volume 2, on the Sermon on the Mount, will consider the beginnings of the Christian moral tradition in its relation to the law and the prophets.*

# GALATIANS

## A Discussion of St Paul's Epistle

## John Bligh

Heythrop College, England.
University of Detroit, U.S.A.

LONDON
ST PAUL PUBLICATIONS
1969

NIHIL OBSTAT:
    Rt. Rev. R. J. Foster, S.T.L., L.S.S.

IMPRIMATUR:
    + George Patrick Dwyer
        Archbishop of Birmingham.
Birmingham, 4th February 1969.

ST PAUL PUBLICATIONS,
LANGLEY, SLOUGH, BUCKS.

ST PAUL PUBLICATIONS,
57 KENSINGTON CHURCH STREET, LONDON W.8.


FIRST EDITION © 1969 ST PAUL PUBLICATIONS


PRINTED IN ENGLAND BY SOCIETY OF ST PAUL, LANGLEY, SLOUGH, BUCKS.

# FOREWORD

After giving five courses of lectures on the Epistle to the Galatians, three in America and two in England, I am publishing a revised version of the fifth course, given at Heythrop in 1966. In the lecture room a certain amount of repetition is necessary and desirable, but I have reduced it to a minimum in this volume; on the other hand I have added a few discussions which were not included in the lectures. Several features of the resulting commentary call for a word of explanation.

First, out of deference to the adult students whom I hope to teach through these pages, I have preserved the dialogue form of question and answer in which I gave the lectures. I do not expect my readers to accept passively and uncritically every opinion which I propose. They must form their own minds, by considering whether I have omitted any important questions, whether they disagree with or can improve upon the answers I have given, and whether my answers are all consistent with one another. No one will ever say the last word on this Epistle. Probably in fifteen years' time I shall want to revise what I have said here, adding new questions and modifying the old answers. Meanwhile, I trust that the present discussion will give its users a good start in their study of this important Epistle and at the same time teach them a method: Look carefully at the text for a long time; list the questions which it raises in your mind; then try to find consistent answers to all the questions.[1] Some of the questions I have discussed are of particular interest to theological students preparing for the priesthood, but I trust they will be of some interest to others as well.

Secondly, philological discussions (on the meaning of the Greek words used by St Paul, and on the construction of his sentences) have been excluded as far as possible. I have dealt with them separately in the companion volume, *Galatians in Greek*.[2] Students who know Greek are recommended to use both volumes concurrently; but those who do not will find that this volume is complete in itself.

Thirdly, I have made much more extensive use of the writings of Philo than have my predecessors. Time and again, while studying

---

[1] The dialogue form is also a safeguard against some of the pitfalls mentioned in my review of J. Héring's valuable commentary on 1 Cor; see HJ 5 (1964), pp. 442-443.

[2] Published in America by the University of Detroit Press, 1966; available in England from St. Paul Publications, Slough.

the Epistle, I have found that words, phrases and whole arguments used by St Paul became clearer to me in the light of parallel passages from Philo. [3] The main issue between St Paul and his adversaries in Galatians can be expressed in the question: 'Who are the heirs of Abraham?' This is the very question discussed at length by Philo in his treatise *Who is the heir of divine things?*, which is a midrash on Gen 15:2-18. [4] But many other treatises too contain helpful parallels. Direct influence of Philo on St Paul is usually denied on the grounds that St Paul's Epistles contain no verbal echoes of Philo. The observation is true — stylistically, St Paul does not depend upon Philo. But the inference based on this observation may not be sound. It cannot be a coincidence that so many passages in Philo cast light on the Epistles. Critics have been content to say that St Paul and Philo moved in the same intellectual climate; Jowett attributes the resemblances between their writings to 'the widely spread diffusion of the same habit of thought.' [5] This presumably means that the exegesis of Philo [6] and of others like him [7] created the spiritual atmosphere of the synagogues of the Diaspora (and perhaps of Palestine too) in which Paul worshipped and taught before and after his conversion. But it is difficult to believe that a learned man like Paul had no direct acquaintance with a body of literature which *ex hypothesi* exercised so much influence on the spiritual atmosphere of his day. Probably at some time in his life he read some of the works of Philo. [8]

Fourthly, this commentary makes systematic use of a method of investigation which has hitherto been used only sporadically. It may

---

[3]  Philo of Alexandria, born about 25 B.C., a member of a rich and powerful Jewish family, became a philosopher and Scripture scholar. He writes for Jews of the Diaspora who may be tempted to think that the wisdom of the Greek philosophers outshines the revelation contained in the Bible. By means of allegorical interpretations, he attempts to show that Greek wisdom is contained in the Bible and may even have been borrowed by the Greeks from the Bible. In A.D. 39, he represented the Jews of Alexandria on an embassy to Rome (described in his *Embassy to Gaius*). He died a few years later.

[4]  Text and translation in the Loeb *Philo*, Vol. IV.

[5]  Cf. Jowett's long excursus on 'St Paul and Philo' at the end of his commentary on Gal. The words quoted above are on p. 454. Cullmann, *Christology*, p. 150, thinks that St Paul was probably acquainted with Philo's theory of the two Adams, though not directly (cf. p. 167).

[6]  Jowett, Gal., p. 459, says: 'The worst extravagances of mystical interpretation among the Fathers, combined with the most tedious platitudes of a modern sermon, will convey an idea of the manner in which Philo "improves" Scripture.' But he adds, p. 462: 'Still he leaves the impression of a great and good man.'

[7]  Philo was probably not a lone wolf. He is the sole extant representative of his type. He refers to others in his treatise *On Joseph*, 151 (Loeb, VI).

[8]  See the essay by Professor Henry Chadwick, 'St Paul and Philo of Alexandria', in *The Bulletin of the John Rylands Library*, 48 (1966), pp. 286-307. He ends by endorsing a remark of Coleridge: 'Philo has not been used half enough.'

be called 'structural analysis'. Most commentaries give a 'plan of the Epistle', but then make little use of it. The whole arrangement of this commentary rests on and incorporates the analysis worked out at the beginning of *Galatians in Greek*, according to which the entire Epistle is a carefully constructed symmetrical composition. For some time now, scholars have recognised that St Paul made use of the literary figure known as 'chiasmus' or 'chiasm'; but no one seems to have any idea of the complexity of his chiastic patterns or of their importance as a tool for exegesis. [9]

In its briefest form, the chiasm is a simple criss-cross, resembling the Greek letter *chi* (x) — hence its name. For example:

| The *sabbath* is for *man* | A B |
|---|---|
| not *man* for the *sabbath*. | B A |

Words or ideas, introduced in the order A - B or A - B - C, are repeated in the reverse order B - A or C - B - A, and so on. An American writer, N. W. Lund, in an important book, *Chiasmus in the New Testament*, published in 1942, pointed out that large chiastic structures are found in many parts of the Old Testament and in several of St Paul's Letters, [10] but he did not draw any examples from Galatians. The work of this pioneer has not yet met with proper recognition.

Some of the reviewers of *Galatians in Greek* expressed doubts as to whether the symmetrical patterns there set forth may not be projections of my ingenuity rather than creations of St Paul's. For my part, I am convinced that the patterns are there in the text, waiting to be discovered. If they are not, how are we to explain that the text is so readily receptive of these patterns, and that the resulting analysis is so fertile in fresh questions and fresh insights? There is a problem here for logicians, comparable to the long-standing dispute between positivists, idealists and realists over the relation of scientific theories to natural objects. However, too much importance should

---

[9] Chiastic structures in the Epistle to the Hebrews have been pointed out by A. Vanhoye, *La structure littéraire de l'Epître aux Hébreux*, Paris-Bruges, 1963. But a glance at this author's "Traduction structurée de l'Epître aux Hébreux", Rome, 1963, will show that the patterns which he finds in Hebrews are far less complex than those which St Paul uses in Galatians. For my criticisms of Vanhoye's valuable thesis see HJ 5 (1964), pp. 170-177.

[10] See also J. J. Collins, 'Chiasmus, the "ABA" Pattern and the Text of Paul,' *Studiorum Paulinorum Congressus Internationalis Catholicus* 1961, (Analecta Biblica, 17-18), t. II, Rome 1963, pp. 575-583; K. Grobel, 'A Chiastic Retribution-Formula in Romans 2,' *Zeit und Geschichte* (Bultmann-Festschrift, 1964, ed. E. Dinkler), Tübingen, 1964, pp. 255-262.

not be attached to this question; structural analysis is only an aid to the discovery of the right questions and possible answers. The value of the commentary depends on the value of the questions and the correctness of the answers.

This discussion of Galatians is at the same time an introduction to the theology of St Paul. Before reading synthetic presentations of the Apostle's thought such as the excellent *Theology of St Paul* by D. E. H. Whiteley, students should patiently study the exegesis of some at least of the Epistles. Galatians is probably the best to begin with — for reasons which will become plain to the reader as he proceeds. [11]

The translation on which I comment is my own. In making it, I tried, on the whole, to turn the Greek into readable English; but I refrained from concealing the ruggedness of some passages (e.g. 2:1-10), and I preferred not to resolve the ambiguities of the original, since these were often the very points which called for comment. The result is an unpretentious version intended for study, not for the liturgy.

In the footnotes I have acknowledged my indebtedness to numerous writers of commentaries, articles and *instrumenta*. Let me here add my gratitude to them and my respect for their labours. A glance at the Index at the end of this volume will show that I owe most to Chrysostom and Jerome among the ancients, to Thomas Aquinas among the medievals, to Luther among the reformers, and to Lightfoot and Lagrange among the moderns. While studying at the Pontifical Biblical Institute in Rome, I attended the courses of Fr S. Lyonnet and Fr K. Prümm on several of St Paul's Epistles. It is hard to say what exactly I owe to these two, but certainly a great love of this fascinating Epistle, with its challenge to faith in Paul and faith in Christ. I have willingly fallen under the spell cast by the Apostle in 6:17.

I am grateful to Fr P. Cooper S.J., for help in typing the manuscript, and to the Fathers and Brothers of the Society of St Paul for the great care they have taken over the printing. May the Lord reward them!

John Bligh s.j.

Heythrop College,
Oxon, England,
1969.

---

[11] Cf. McKenzie, *The Power and the Wisdom*, p. 202: 'There is scarcely any point of Pauline theology which is not directly or indirectly a response to the Judaizers.'

# SELECTED BIBLIOGRAPHY

COMMENTARIES:

Theodore of Mopsuestia, *In Epistolam ad Galatas*, in Swete, H.B., *Theodore of Mopsuestia on the Epistles of St Paul*, Vol. I, Cambridge, 1880, pp. 1-111.
Chrysostom, St John, *Commentarius in Epistolam ad Galatas*, PG 61, 611-682.
Theodoretus, *Interpretatio Epistolae ad Galatas*, PG 82, 459-504.
Pelagius, *Expositio in Galatas*, in Texts and Studies, IX, Cambridge, 1931, pp. 306-343.
Jerome, St, *In Epistolam ad Galatas Libri III*, PL 26, 331-468.
Augustine, St, *Expositio Epistolae ad Galatas*, PL 35, 2105-2148.

\* \* \*

Thomas Aquinas, St, *Expositio in Epistolam ad Galatas*, in *Opera Omnia*, t. XIII, Parma, 1862, pp. 382-442.
Luther, M., *Die erste Vorlesung über den Galaterbrief, 1516-17*, in *Luthers Werke*, t. LXVII, Weimar, 1939.
Luther, M., *Lectures on Galatians 1535*, in *Luther's Works* (Concordia edition) St Louis, Missouri, Vol. 26, 1963, and Vol. 27, 1964.
Amiot, F., *Saint Paul. Epître aux Galates* (Verbum Salutis), Paris, 1946.
Bonnard, P., *L'épître de saint Paul aux Galates* (Commentaire du Nouveau Testament, IX), Paris-Neuchatel, 1953.
Bring, R., *Commentary on Galatians*, Philadelphia (U.S.A.), 1961.
Burton, E. de Witt, *A Critical and Exegetical Commentary on the Epistle to the Galatians* (International Critical Commentary), Edinburgh, 1921.
Buzy, D., *Epître aux Galates* (La Sainte Bible, Pirot et Clamer), Paris, 1948.
Cornely, J., *Commentarius in Epistolam ad Galatas*, Paris, 1892.
Guthrie, D., *Galatians*, Edinburgh, 1968.
Jowett, B., *The Epistles of St Paul to the Thessalonians, Galatians, Romans*, Vol. I, London, 1859.
Lagrange, M.-J., *Saint Paul. Epître aux Galates* (EB), ed. 2, Paris, 1925.
Lake, K., *The Earlier Epistles of St Paul*, ed. 2, London, 1930.
Lietzmann, H., *An die Galater*, ed. 2, Tübingen, 1923.
Lightfoot, J.B., *St Paul's Epistles to the Galatians*, ed. 8, London, 1884.

Lyonnet, S., *Les épîtres de saint Paul aux Galates et aux Romains* (BdeJ), ed. 2, Paris, 1959.

MacEvilly, J., *An Exposition of the Epistles of St Paul*, Vol. I, London, 1855.

Oepke, A., *Der Brief des Paulus an die Galater*, ed. 2, Berlin, 1957.

Orchard, B., 'Galatians' in CathComm.

Ramsay, W.M., *An Historical Commentary on St Paul's Epistle to the Galatians*, ed. 2, London, 1900.

Sanders, J.N., 'Galatians' in *Peake's Commentary on the Bible*, revised ed., Edinburgh, 1962.

Schlier, H., *Der Brief an die Galater* (Kritisch-Exegetischer Kommentar über das Neue Testament), ed. 12, Göttingen, 1962.

Viard, A., *Saint Paul. Epître aux Galates* (Sources Bibliques), Paris, 1964.

Zahn, T., *Der Brief des Paulus an die Galater*, ed. 3, revised by F. Hauck, Leipzig-Erlangen, 1922.

In the footnotes, the commentaries of Chrysostom, Theodoretus, Jerome and Augustine are referred to by the volume and column in Migne. Other commentaries are referred to by the author's surname followed by 'Gal'. In referring to St Thomas's commentary, which is printed on folio pages in double columns, I have added A or B or C or D after the page number, to indicate whether the passage in question is in the first, second, third, or fourth quarter of the page.

OTHER USEFUL BOOKS:

Colson, F.H., and Whitaker, G.H., *Philo* (with an English Translation), 11 vols, (Loeb Library), London, 1949-1953.

Danby, H., *The Mishnah*, Oxford, 1933.

Sutcliffe, E.F., *The Monks of Qumran* (with translations of the Scrolls into English), London, 1960.

\* \* \*

Althaus, P., *The Theology of Martin Luther*, Philadelphia (U.S.A.), 1966.

Anderson, B.W. (ed.), *The Old Testament and Christian Faith*, London, 1964.

Baum, G., *The Jews and the Gospel*, London, 1961.

Bläser, P., *Das Gesetz bei Paulus*, Münster, 1941.

Bultmann, R., *Theology of the New Testament*, London, 1952.

Bultmann, R., *Das Evangelium des Johannes*, 14 Aufl., Göttingen, 1956.

Clements, R., *Abraham and David* (SBT 2nd Series, 5), London, 1967.

Cullmann, O., *The Christology of the New Testament*, London, 1959.

Cullmann, O., *Peter, Disciple, Apostle, Martyr*, ed. 2, London, 1962.

Daniélou, J., *The Theology of Jewish Christianity*, London, 1964.

Daube, D., *The New Testament and Rabbinic Judaism*, London, 1956.

Davies, W.D., *Paul and Rabbinic Judaism*, London, 1948.

Dibelius, M., *Studies in the Acts of the Apostles*, London, 1956.

Dodd, C.H., *New Testament Studies*, Manchester, 1953.

Dubarle, A.M., *The Biblical Doctrine of Original Sin*, London, 1964.

Easton, B.S., *Earliest Christianity*, London, 1955.

Filson, F.V., *A New Testament History*, London, 1965.

Fitzmyer, J., *Pauline Theology*, Englewood Cliffs, 1967.

Freud, S., *Civilization and Its Discontents*, and *The Future of an Illusion*, in *The Complete Psychological Works*, London, 1961, Vol. XXI.

Gaechter, P., *Petrus und Seine Zeit*, Innsbruck, 1957.

Galot, J., *La Rédemption, Mystère d'Alliance*, Paris-Bruges, 1965.

Goulder, M.D., *Type and History in Acts*, London, 1964.

Héring, J., *The First Epistle of St Paul to the Corinthians*, London, 1962.

Hooker, M.D., *Jesus and the Servant*, London, 1959.

Jackson, F. and Lake, K., *The Beginnings of Christianity*, Part I, Vols IV and V, London, 1933.

Jeremias, J., *The Parables of Jesus*, revised ed., London, 1963.

Jeremias, J., *The Central Message of the New Testament*, London, 1965.

Karrer, O., *Peter and the Church*, Edinburgh, 1963.

Knight, G.A.F., *A Christian Theology of the Old Testament*, London, 1964.

Knox, J., *Chapters in a Life of Paul*, London, 1954.

Knox, W.L., *St Paul and the Church of Jerusalem*, Cambridge, 1925.

Knox, W.L., *St Paul and the Church of the Gentiles*, Cambridge, 1939.

Lindars, B., *New Testament Apologetic*, London, 1961.

Lohfink, G., *Paulus vor Damaskus* (Stuttgarter Bibelstudien, 4), Stuttgart, 1966.

Lund, N.W., *Chiasmus in the New Testament*, University of North Carolina, 1942.

Manson, T.W., *On Paul and John* (SBT, 38), London, 1963.

Marcus Aurelius, *Meditations*, trans. by C.R. Haines, (Loeb Library), London, 1941.

McKenzie, J.L., *The Power and the Wisdom*, London, 1965.

Moule, C.F.D. (ed.), *Miracles*, London, 1965.

Munck, J., *Paul and the Salvation of Mankind*, London, 1959.

Richardson, A., *An Introduction to the Theology of the New Testament*, London, 1958.

Schmithals, W., *Paul and James* (SBT, 46), London, 1965.

Schnackenburg, R., *Baptism in the Thought of St Paul*, Oxford, 1964.

Schnackenburg, R., *The Moral Teaching of the New Testament*, London, 1965.

Spicq, C., *L'Epître aux Hébreux*, 2 vols, Paris, 1953.

Turner, N., *Grammatical Insights into the New Testament*, Edinburgh, 1965.

Wainwright, A.W., *The Trinity in the New Testament*, London, 1962.

Weiss, J., *Earliest Christianity*, 2 vols, New York, 1959.

Westermann, C. (ed.), *Essays on Old Testament Interpretation*, London, 1963.

Whiteley, D.E.H., *The Theology of St Paul*, Oxford, 1964.

Wilcox, M., *The Semitisms of Acts*, Oxford, 1965.

Williamson, G.A., *Eusebius, The History of the Church*, Harmondsworth (Penguin), 1965.

Wolfson, H.A., *Philo*, 2 vols, Harvard-London, 1947.

Zedda, S., *L'Adozione a Figli di Dio e Lo Spirito Santo*, (Analecta Biblica), Rome, 1932.

The above works are referred to by the author's name and a short title only. For further bibliography, see the footnotes throughout this volume, and R. Schnackenburg, *New Testament Theology Today*, London, 1963. For the periodical literature since 1956, see NTA (*New Testament Abstracts*), published at Weston College, Weston Mass., U.S.A.

# ABBREVIATIONS

| | |
|---|---|
| ANET | Pritchard, J.B., *Ancient Near Eastern Texts Relating to the Old Testament*, London, 1950. |
| BAC | Bibliotheca Auctorum Christianorum, Madrid. |
| BZ | *Biblische Zeitschrift.* |
| CathComm | *A Catholic Commentary on Holy Scripture*, Edinburgh, 1953. |
| CBQ | *Catholic Biblical Quarterly.* |
| Denz | H. Denzinger et A. Schönmetzer, *Enchiridion Symbolorum*, Ed. 34, Barcelona, 1967. |
| EB | Etudes Bibliques. |
| ETL | *Ephemerides Theologicae Lovanienses.* |
| G in G | Bligh, J., *Galatians in Greek*, Detroit, 1966. |
| HJ | *The Heythrop Journal.* |
| HTR | *Harvard Theological Review.* |
| JB | *The Jerusalem Bible* (English translation of BdeJ). |
| JBL | *The Journal of Biblical Literature.* |
| JES | *Journal of Ecumenical Studies.* |
| JTS | *The Journal of Theological Studies.* |
| LXX | The Septuagint. |
| NEB | *The New English Bible.* |
| NTA | *New Testament Abstracts.* |
| NTS | *New Testament Studies* (Note: Professor C.H. Dodd has a collection of his essays under this title). |
| PG | Migne, *Patrologia Graeca.* |
| PL | Migne, *Patrologia Latina.* |
| RechScRel | *Recherches de Science religieuse*, Paris. |
| RB | *Revue Biblique.* |
| RSV | *The Revised Standard Version.* |
| SB | Strack, H., and Billerbeck, P., *Kommentar zum Neuen Testament aus Talmud und Midrasch*, Munich, 1926. |
| SBT | Studies in Biblical Theology, London. |
| TAPA | *Transactions of the American Philological Association.* |
| TDNT | *Theological Dictionary of the New Testament* (English translation of TWNT). |

| TLZ | *Theologische Literaturzeitung*, Leipzig-Berlin. |
| TWNT | Kittel, *Theologisches Wörterbuch zum Neuen Testament*. |
| TU | Texte und Untersuchungen zur Geschichte der altchristlichen Literatur, Berlin. |
| ZATW | *Zeitschrift für die alttestamentliche Wissenschaft.* |
| ZNTW | *Zeitschrift für die neutestamentliche Wissenschaft und die Kunde der alten Kirche.* |
| ZKT | *Zeitschrift für Katholische Theologie*, Innsbruck. |

\*    \*    \*

Quotations from the Old Testament are from the RSV. For the New Testament I have used my own translation.

# ACKNOWLEDGEMENTS

Texts from Philo are given in the translation of Colson and Whitaker, by kind permission of William Heinemann Ltd. Fr Sutcliffe's translation of the Dead Sea Scrolls is quoted by kind permission of Messrs Burns and Oates. Danby's translation of the Mishnah is quoted by kind permission of the Oxford University Press. The Midrash Rabbah is quoted by kind permission of the Soncino Press. E. Goodspeed's translation of the *Shepherd* of Hermas is used by kind permission of the Independent Press Ltd. Professor H. Chadwick's translation of Origen, *Contra Celsum,* is quoted by kind permission of the Cambridge University Press. For Marcus Aurelius the Loeb version of C.R. Haines is used by kind permission of William Heinemann Ltd. Luther's 1535 Commentary is quoted from *Luther's Works,* edited by Jaroslav Pelican, by kind permission of the Concordia Publishing House, St Louis, Missouri.

# CONTENTS

# GALATIANS

# INTRODUCTION

*When was the Epistle written?*

In Gal 2:1-10, St Paul describes a visit which he made to Jerusalem in the company of Barnabas; he went up in obedience to a revelation to discuss the question whether Gentile converts to Christianity should be circumcised. In Acts 11:29-30, Paul and Barnabas make their 'Famine Visit' to Jerusalem, in response to a revelation, to take alms to the poor of the city; and in Acts 15 they make a further visit to place the circumcision-question before the apostles and elders of Jerusalem. The Famine Visit appears to have taken place in A.D. 45 (shortly after the death of Herod Agrippa I), and the Council of Acts 15 was in A.D. 49. [1]

Commentators who identify the Council of Gal 2 with the Famine Visit of Acts 11 place the writing of the Epistle before the Council of Acts 15, hence about 48/49, and declare that it is the earliest of the Pauline Epistles. [2] But if the Council of Gal 2 is identified with the Council of Acts 15, the date will be much later. After the Council was over, St Paul revisited Antioch twice — immediately in A.D. 49/50 (cf. Acts 15:35), and again between the second missionary journey and the third — about A.D. 54 (cf. Acts 18:22). As the 'Antioch incident' in which Paul rebuked Peter (Gal 2:11-21) is not likely to have occurred immediately after the Council, [3] it must have occurred on the occasion of St Paul's last visit to Antioch, in about 54 A.D. Then the Epistle, which mentions the incident, must be dated later still. As it bears strong resemblances in thought and language to 2 Corinthians and Romans, it was probably written about the same time as these Epistles, i.e., in A.D. 57. [4]

The later dating is almost certainly correct, for the following reasons. First, the Council of Gal 2 ought to be identified with that

---

[1] This date is fixed by reckoning back from the time of St Paul's appearance before Gallio at Corinth. The date of Gallio's governorship of Achaea is fixed by an inscription printed and discussed by Lake in Jackson-Lake, *Beginnings*, 5, pp. 455-464. Lake himself held that Acts 11 and Acts 15 both describe the same visit (ibid., p. 201). Against this see B. Orchard, 'The Problem of Acts and Galatians,' CBQ 7 (1945), p. 386.

[2] Cf. D. Round, *The Date of St Paul's Epistle to the Galatians*, Cambridge, 1906; Orchard, Gal, CathComm 1953, p. 1112.

[3] Gaechter, *Petrus und seine Zeit*, p. 222, thinks otherwise.

[4] For details of these resemblances see Lightfoot, Gal, pp. 45-52; C. H. Buck, 'The Date of Galatians,' JBL 70 (1951), pp. 114-116; K. Prümm, 'Gal und 2 Kor—Ein lehrhaltlicher Vergleich,' *Biblica* 31 (1950), pp. 27-72.

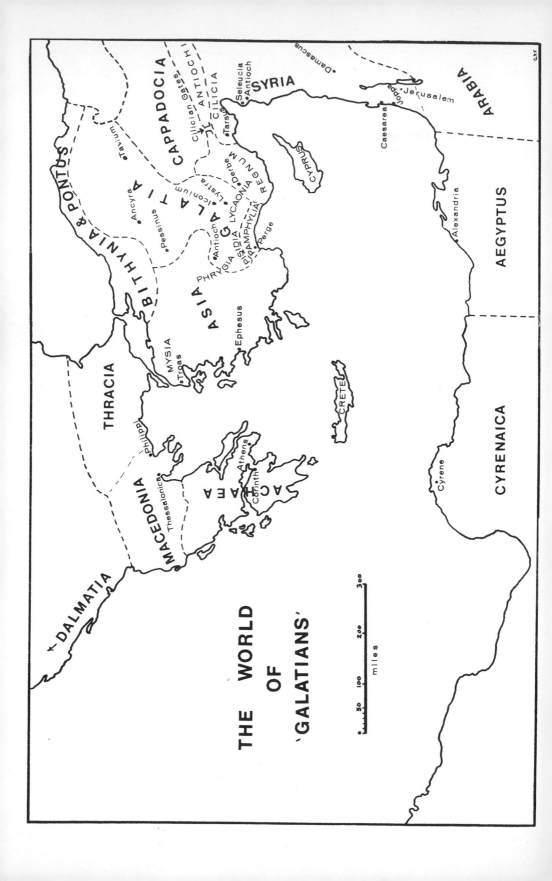

THE WORLD OF 'GALATIANS'

miles
50 100 200 300

DALMATIA

MACEDONIA
Thessalonica
Philippi

THRACIA

ACHAEA
Athens
Corinth

BITHYNIA & PONTUS

Tavium

CAPPADOCIA

Ancyra
Pessinus

GALATIA

Iconium
Lystra
Derbe
Antioch
PISIDIA
LYCAONIA
PAMPHYLIA REG⁻
Perge
PHRYGIA

ASIA

MYSIA
Troas

Ephesus

CRETE

Cilician Gates
Tarsus
CILICIA
ANTIOCH

SYRIA
Seleucia
Antioch
Damascus

CYPRUS

Caesarea

Joppa
Jerusalem

ARABIA

AEGYPTUS

Alexandria

CYRENAICA

Cyrene

G.P.F.

of Acts 15. The same persons (Paul and Barnabas) discuss the same matter (the treatment of Gentile converts) with the same apostles (Peter and John) at the same place, and the outcome is substantially the same. [5] Secondly, a convincing argument against dating Galatians before 1 and 2 Thessalonians can be drawn from the prologues of the Epistles: after his apostolic authority has been challenged, St Paul introduces himself in letters to the churches as 'Paul the Apostle'. He does not do this in 1 and 2 Thessalonians. [6] Thirdly, it is very hard to believe that if St Paul had written the Epistle on the way to the Council of Jerusalem, he would have forestalled the Council's decision by anathematizing his adversaries as he does in Gal 1:8-9.

The composition of the Epistle can, then, be assigned to the year 57. But this date is of no great importance, if, as will be shown below, the body of the Epistle (2:15—5:13) was composed some years before — at the time of the Antioch incident or even earlier — and merely incorporated, with a few revisions and additions, into the Epistle in the year 57. It is equally misleading to date the Epistle to the Romans to A.D. 58, since some sections of it (notably chapters 9-11) were probably composed long before and used many times in preaching before being incorporated in the Epistle.

### Where were the 'churches of Galatia'?

There has been a long, indecisive and fruitless controversy as to whether the 'churches of Galatia' to which the Epistle is addressed (1:2) were in 'South Galatia' or 'North Galatia'. Is St Paul writing to the churches, situated in the south of the sprawling Roman province of Galatia, which he founded at Antioch, Iconium, Lystra and Derbe during his first missionary journey (about 47 A.D.)? Or is he writing to a group of churches in Galatia proper, at such cities as Ancyra, Pessinus and Tavium? (See the map on p. 2).

The view adopted in this commentary is that the churches addressed must be the South Galatian churches — because in all probability there were no Pauline churches in North Galatia in A.D. 57. The existence of Pauline churches in North Galatia is an hypothesis introduced by commentators who have thought that St Paul could not address the churches founded on his first journey as 'the churches of Galatia'.

---

[5] See Lightfoot, Gal, p. 124, and below, on 2:6.
[6] See below, pp. 55-56.

C

If St Paul *did* found churches in North Galatia, he must have done so in the course of the journey described in the following passage of Acts (15:39—16:10): [7]

> *15 : 39* Paul chose Silas and set out on his [second missionary] journey, *40* after the brethren had commended him to the grace of the Lord. *41* He went through Syria and Cilicia bringing new strength to the churches. *16 : 1* He passed on to Derbe and then to Lystra. Here there was a disciple named Timothy *2* who was held in high esteem by the brethren of Lystra and Iconium; his mother was a converted Jewess, but his father was a Greek. *3* As Paul wished Timothy to come with him on his journey, he took him and circumcised him, because there were Jews in those parts, and they all knew that his father was a Greek. *4* Then they went from city to city, and instructed the brethren to observe the decisions reached by the apostles and presbyters in Jerusalem. *5* So the churches grew strong in the faith, and their numbers increased day by day. *6* They travelled through the Phrygian and Galatian country, but were not allowed by the Holy Spirit to preach the word in Asia. *7* When they came level with the borders of Mysia they tried to enter Bithynia, but the Spirit of Jesus did not allow them to do so. *8* So they passed through [8] Mysia and came down to Troas. *9* Here Paul saw a vision during the night: a Macedonian standing appealing to him and saying: 'Cross over into Macedonia and help us!' *10* After he had seen the vision, we concluded that God had called us to preach the gospel in Macedonia, and at once sought means of going there. [9]

As far as 16:5, St Paul's route is clear enough: from (Syrian) Antioch he goes through Syria into Cilicia, probably to Tarsus, then north through the Cilician Gates (a pass in the Taurus range of mountains [10]), then west to Derbe and Lystra, where he circumcises Timothy. Then he goes on 'from city to city' — probably to Iconium, Laodicea and (Pisidian) Antioch. So far so good. But where did he go from Antioch?

Defenders of the North Galatian theory take 16:6 to mean that Paul was prevented by the Holy Spirit from even entering the province of Asia and therefore went through Phrygia [11] and Galatia (proper) to Ancyra. [12] But this is ruled out by 16:7, for by

---

[7]  In 18:23, when St Paul passes through the 'Galatian country' again, he is not founding churches, but 'confirming the brethren'.

[8]  The reading *dielthontes* (D) must be correct, since it is impossible to get to Troas without going through Mysia.

[9]  This text is discussed by Lake in *Beginnings*, 5, pp. 233-239.

[10]  See the photograph in L. H. Grollenberg, *Atlas of the Bible*, Edinburgh, p. 135, plate 399.

[11]  Phrygia is not the name of a province or of any precise region—as can be seen by comparing various maps. The cartographers write PHRYGIA over an undefined area overlapping the provinces of Asia and Galatia.

[12]  The Greek can but need not bear this meaning; cf. G in G, p. 203.

travelling north to Ancyra the missionaries would not 'come level with Mysia'. A much more probable interpretation of 16:6 is that Paul and Silas took the road north from Pisidian Antioch into Asia and went quickly through Asia, not being allowed by the Holy Spirit to stop and preach there. They continued north until they had the Mysian border on their left and the Bithynian border directly ahead. As the Holy Spirit did not allow them even to enter Bithynia (v. 7), they went down through Mysia to Troas. If this is correct, St Paul did not pass through North Galatia on his second missionary journey. 'Phrygia and the Galatian country' in 16:6 must mean 'South Galatia', the region evangelized on the first journey.

In Acts 15:39—16:10 there are three interventions of the Holy Spirit, all directed to the same end: Paul is prevented from *preaching* in Asia (v. 6); he is not allowed even to *enter* Bithynia (v. 7); he is summoned to cross into Macedonia (v. 9). Surely St Luke's purpose is to show why St Paul hurried on to preach in Macedonia and Greece without stopping to complete the evangelization of Asia Minor. There is no room for the founding of North Galatian churches on this journey. St Paul is guided by the Spirit to travel quickly across Asia Minor from Lystra to Troas. A visit to Ancyra would have taken him far out of his way.

Another strong argument against the supposition that St Paul founded churches in North Galatia during his second journey can be drawn from the Epistle. If by the time of writing it (A.D. 57) St Paul had founded two clusters of Galatian churches, one in the south in A.D. 47 and one in the north in A.D. 51, he would not have addressed the northern group alone as 'the churches of Galatia', for the southern group too were within the province of Galatia. Moreover, it seems highly unlikely that the Judaizers, coming up from the south, would have confined their propaganda to the north. If, then, there were North Galatian churches in A.D. 57, the Epistle 'to the churches of Galatia' must have been sent to both groups of churches together. But this is ruled out by Gal 4:12-20, where St Paul is obviously writing to a compact group of churches founded on one particular occasion which he recalls to their mind. Therefore in A.D. 57 there is still only one group of churches in the province of Galatia. It must be the group founded during the first missionary journey in about A.D. 47.

To elude this argument from 4:12-20, defenders of the North Galatian theory would have to argue that the churches of Antioch, Iconium, Lystra and Derbe would not have considered themselves, and would not have been considered by St Paul, as 'churches of

Galatia'. For Iconium at least such a demonstration is impossible. It was a Roman colony and belonged to the province of Galatia. In an inscription of A.D. 54, the people of Iconium speak of their governor L. Publius Praesens as 'governor of the province of Galatia'. [13] If, then, St Paul wrote a letter in A.D. 57 to 'the churches of Galatia', the people of Iconium at least would regard it as addressed to them, and it is reasonable to suppose that St Paul knew this.

Defenders of the North Galatian theory have often argued that it would have been extremely tactless of St Paul to call the Pisidian and Lycaonian inhabitants of the southern churches 'foolish Galatians' (cf. 3 : 1) or even 'Galatians'. However, after seventy-five years of Romanization they may not have been as sensitive as modern writers imagine. The province, established in 25 B.C., now included Galatia proper, Pisidia, Phrygia, Lycaonia, Isauria, Paphlagonia and various other odds and ends. It was convenient to refer to this conglomeration as 'the Galatian province' or 'the Galatian country' or simply 'Galatia'. If St Paul wanted a common designation for his group of churches in Pisidia (Antioch), in Lycaonia (Iconium and Lystra), in the Kingdom of Antiochus (Derbe) [14] and in Pamphilia (Perge?), it is hard to think of a more suitable title than 'the churches of Galatia'. [15] Galatia was a melting-pot of several nationalities, like the mid-western cities of America, where within a generation immigrants can forget their national differences, thanks to the English language and the American way of life. In the Publius inscription, the Iconians name their city 'Claudia' (after the emperor Claudius) and describe themselves as 'Claudians' or 'Claudiconians'. Such people would hardly resent being called 'Galatians'. They might not like being called 'foolish Galatians', but nor would the inhabitants of the north of the province.

Finally, defenders of the North Galatian theory can argue that 'the churches of Galatia' is too high-sounding a title for a little group

---

[13] Cf. *Corpus Inscriptionum Graecarum*, no 3991 (G in G, p. 226); R. K. Sherk, *The Legates of Galatia from Augustus to Diocletian*, Baltimore, 1951, p. 94.

[14] See the inscription published by M. Ballance in *Anatolian Studies* 7 (1957), pp. 147-151. For this reference and the last I am indebted to an article by E. Yarnold, 'North Galatians or South?' printed (not published) in *Bellarmine Commentary* (Heythrop) 1 (1958), pp. 167-174.

[15] For readers interested in the history of the North v. South controversy: The South Galatian theory was defended by E. Renan, *Saint Paul*, Paris, 1869, pp. 51-56. Renan's arguments were subjected to powerful criticism by J. B. Lightfoot in his commentary on Colossians, London, 1886, pp. 24-28. The South Galatian theory was again defended by W. M. Ramsay in 'The "Galatia" of St Paul and the "Galatic Territory" of Acts,' in *Studia Biblica et Ecclesiastica*, IV, Oxford, 1896, pp. 15-57, and in his commentary on Gal; also by Orchard, Gal. But Schlier, Lyonnet, and Viard agree with Lightfoot.

of churches in the southern regions of the province. To this one can reply, first, that Antioch and Iconium were important cities, and secondly, that a certain measure of exaggeration is quite in St Paul's manner. One of his foibles was to exaggerate the magnitude of his missionary achievements. His adversaries accused him of writing commendatory letters for himself (cf. 2 Cor 3:1). In Rom 15:19 he surprises his readers by declaring that he has completed the preaching of the gospel from Jerusalem right round to Illyricum; and in 15:23 he adds that there is no further scope for his apostolic activity in the Eastern Mediterranean. He may have underestimated the extent both of Illyricum and of Galatia.

### How does Acts 13-14 compare with the Epistle?

The importance of the North v. South controversy can easily be overestimated. The theological interpretation of the Epistle is unaffected by this dispute. [16] Yet it is not a complete waste of time. For if the Epistle was addressed to the South Galatian churches, we are fortunate enough to have in chapters 13-14 of Acts a history of their foundation written by a disciple of St Paul.

St Luke describes how, through an intervention of the Holy Spirit in the church of Antioch (in Syria), Paul and Barnabas were sent out on a missionary journey. They visited Cyprus, crossed to Pamphilia, went inland to found the South Galatian churches, then returned to Antioch, having completed the task which the Holy Spirit had set them to do. Barnabas was, therefore, known personally to the Galatian churches (cf. Gal 2:13).

The narrative of this first journey is (like everything else in Acts) arranged in chiastic patterns. One primary pattern contains within itself three secondary chiasms, thus:

A    Departure from Antioch in Syria, 13:1-2.
B    Prayer and Fasting, 13:3.
C    Ministry in Cyprus, 13:4-13 (1st secondary chiasm).
D    *Paul's Discourse at Pis. Antioch* (2nd secondary chiasm).
C¹   Ministry in Galatia, 13:43—14:22 (3rd secondary chiasm).
B¹   Prayer and Fasting, 14:23.
A¹   Return to Antioch in Syria, 14:24-26.

Here, first of all, are the framework passages, AB and B¹A¹, for comparison:

---

[16]  Ramsay himself admits this, Gal, pp. 1-2.

**A**   *13 : 1* The prophets and teachers in the church of Antioch at this time were: Barnabas, Symeon (called Niger), Lucius of Cyrene, a member of the court of Herod the tetrarch called Manaen, and Saul. *2* While they were worshipping the Lord and fasting, the Holy Spirit said to them: 'Set apart for me Barnabas and Saul to do the work for which I have called them.'   **B**   *3* Then, after fasting and prayers, they laid their hands on them and bade them go.

(Here follow C—D—C¹.)

**B¹**   *14 : 23* They also appointed presbyters for the disciples in every church, and with prayer and fasting commended them to the Lord in whom they believed. ¹⁷   **A¹**   *24* Then they passed through Pisidia and into Pamphilia, where, *25* after preaching the word of God at Perge, they went down to Attalia. *26* From there they returned by ship to Antioch, the place where they had been entrusted to the grace of God for the work which they had now completed.

13:2 and 14:26 taken together imply that the Holy Spirit indicated a definite task for the missionaries — otherwise they would not have known when they had completed their assignment. Unhappily, St Luke does not specify the task. Were the apostles told to make a circular tour from Antioch to Cyprus, from Cyprus to Pamphilia, and from Pamphilia back to Antioch? Or were they told from the start that they must go up into Pisidia and Lycaonia in the province of Galatia? The first alternative makes the defection of John Mark more excusable: he could say that they had no charge to go and preach in the inland districts. But as St Paul strongly disapproved of John Mark's defection, the second alternative must be correct: they planned from the start to go up into Galatia, and John Mark's courage failed. (Anyone who has travelled in the Middle East will understand. Little groups of silent Levantines standing watching with unsmiling faces can have an unnerving effect on the foreign tourist.) But if they planned from the start to go into Galatia, it is impossible to accept Sir William Ramsay's explanation of Gal 4:13: 'You know

---

¹⁷ The link between B and B¹ is of special interest as showing that the author intends the laying-on of hands in 13:3 to be compared with the ordinations in v. 23. In both cases the laying-on of hands is part of the rite of 'commending to the Lord' persons who are set aside for a particular task. As the task assigned to Paul and Barnabas is of limited duration, the laying-on of hands is not an 'ordination'. We have here two types of commendation ceremony, one of which is an ordination.

W. Telfer, 'The Didache and the Apostolic Synod of Antioch,' JTS 40 (1939), p. 270, observes that 'in Acts the appointment of presbyters is only mentioned in contexts relating, not to the first foundation of churches, but to the moment when apostolic superintendence begins to be withdrawn.'

H. Küng, *The Church*, London, 1967, p. 405, accuses St Luke of making 'an unhistorical addition' in Acts 14:23. He thinks there were no presbyters in the Pauline churches. But cf. Phil 1:1.

that it was through bodily illness that I preached the gospel to you on the former occasion.' Ramsay took this to mean that the missionaries had not planned to enter Galatia, but did so on account of Paul's ill health: they sought the fresh air in the higher regions and, while there, preached to the Galatians. [18] Some other explanations must be found for Gal 4:13. [19]

The first secondary chiasm (C) is concerned mainly with events on the island of Cyprus. It is arranged thus:

A    Journey to Salamis, 13:4-5a.
B    John Mark present as assistant, 13:5b.
C    Arrival at Paphos, 13:6a.
D    The Proconsul is well disposed, 13:7.
E    Opposition from Elymas, 13:8.
F    *Paul rebukes Elymas, 13:9-11a.*
$E^1$    Elymas is blinded, 13:11b.
$D^1$    The Proconsul believes, 13:12.
$C^1$    Departure from Paphos, 13:13a.
$B^1$    John Mark returns to Jerusalem, 13:13b.
$A^1$    Journey to Pisidian Antioch, 13:14a.

V. 6b, omitted from the above analysis, upsets the pattern and looks like an insertion. Its purpose is to inform the reader that Elymas was a Jew. Here is the text:

A *13:4 Barnabas and Saul, then, sent out by the Holy Spirit, went down to Seleucia, and sailed from there to Cyprus. 5 When they arrived at Salamis, they proclaimed the word of God in the Jewish synagogue.* B *They had John with them as their minister.* C *6 They traversed the whole island to Paphos, and there came upon (a Jewish magician and would-be prophet called Bar-Jesus, 7 who was attached to) the proconsul Sergius Paulus.* D *Sergius, being a man of intelligence, sent for Barnabas and Saul, and said he would like to hear the word of God.* E *8 Elymas, however, the magician, ('magician' is what his name means) opposed them, and tried to turn the proconsul away from the faith.* F *9 But Saul (or Paul) filled with the Holy Spirit, fixed his eyes on him, 10 and said: 'You spawn of the devil, replete with guile and mischief, you enemy of all virtue, will you never give up making crooked the straight ways of the Lord? 11 Now look! The hand of the Lord is upon you: you will be blind for a time and will not see the sun.'* $E^1$ *At once gloom and darkness descended upon him, and he groped for someone to take him by the hand.* $D^1$ *12 When the proconsul saw what had happened, he was struck with reverence for the Lord's teaching, and became a believer.* $C^1$ *13 Paul and his companions sailed from Paphos and went to Perge in Pamphilia.*

---

[18]  Cf. Ramsay, Gal, pp. 420-421.
[19]  See below, pp. 16-17.

**B¹**  Here John left their company and returned to Jerusalem.  **A¹**  *14*
The others went on from Perge and reached Pisidian Antioch.

The second secondary chiasm (B) consists of St Paul's discourse
at Pisidian Antioch placed within two framework-passages:

*14b* On the sabbath, they went into the synagogue and sat down.  *15* After
the readings from the law and the prophets, the president of the synagogue
sent a message to them: 'Brethren, if you have in you any words of encouragement for the people, you may speak.'  *16* Paul came forward,
raised his hand for silence, and spoke as follows.

(Here follows the discourse.)

*42* As they were leaving the synagogue, they were asked to speak again
on the same matter on the next sabbath.

In each of the framework-passages, St Paul receives an invitation to
preach in the synagogue. His discourse, as it stands in Acts 13, has
one sentence which is almost certainly out of place — here in italics:

*22* God removed Saul and raised up David as king; and to him he bore
this testimony: 'I have found David, a man after my own heart, who
will do all that is my will.'  *23* From this man's posterity God, as he
promised, has brought to Israel a Saviour (*Sôtêra*) who is Jesus.  *24* John
went before him preaching a baptism of repentance to the whole people
of Israel,  *25* and when he was nearing the end of his course, he said:
'I am not what you suppose me to be; but there is coming after me one
whose shoe I am not worthy to untie.'  *26 Brethren, sons of Abraham's
line, and you fearers of God, to you the word of this salvation* (tês
sôtêrias tautês) *has been sent out.*  *27* For the people of Jerusalem and
their rulers, having refused to recognise him — or the sayings of the
prophets that are read out every sabbath — condemned him and fulfilled
the prophecies.

In v. 26, as it stands, 'the word of this salvation' appears to refer to
the saying of John the Baptist quoted in v. 25 — which is clearly
inappropriate, since the word of salvation is the good news that God
has sent the promised Saviour in the person of Jesus. Probably,
therefore, v. 26 ought to stand after v. 23, and v. 27 should begin
with 'but'. Then vv. 24-25 coalesce very smoothly with v. 27: in
spite of the clear testimony of the Baptist (vv. 24-25) the people of
Jerusalem refused to recognize Jesus (v. 27). If this transposition is
made, the whole discourse is symmetrical:

A   God's wondrous work for Israel in the past, vv. 16b-19.
B   An unsatisfactory interim preceded the first David, 20-21.
C   God's promise to David is fulfilled in Jesus the Saviour, 22-23.
D   This word of salvation is now sent to you, 26.
E   John the Baptist bore witness to Christ, 24-25.

F   Yet the people of Jerusalem condemned him, and so fulfilled the Scriptures, 27,

G   *and had him crucified,* 28.

F¹   Having fulfilled the Scriptures, they buried him, but God vindicated him by raising him up, 29-30.

E¹   His disciples are now his witnesses, 31.

D¹   And we are bringing you the good news, 32,

C¹   that God's promise to David is fulfilled in Christ, 33-37.

B¹   An unsatisfactory interim preceded the second David, 38-39.

A¹   God's wondrous work for Israel in the present, 40-41.

## Here is the text:

A  *13 : 16b* Men of Israel and fearers of God, give us your attention! *17* The God of this people Israel chose our fathers, and made our people great during their sojourn in the land of Egypt, and brought them out of Egypt with uplifted arm. *18* For some forty years he bore with their ways in the desert. *19* Then he destroyed seven nations in Canaan and gave our people the land of these nations to be their inheritance for some four hundred and fifty years.  B  *20* After this he appointed judges for them down to the time of the prophet Samuel. *21* Then they asked for a king, and God gave them Saul, the son of Cis, of the tribe of Benjamin, and he reigned for forty years.  C  *22* Then God removed Saul and raised up David as king; and to him he bore this testimony: 'I have found David, a man after my own heart, who will do all that is my will.' *23* From this man's posterity God, as he promised, has brought to Israel a Saviour, who is Jesus.  D  *26* Brethren, sons of Abraham's line, and you who fear God, it was to us that this message of salvation was sent.  E  *24* (For) John had gone before him preaching a baptism of repentance for the whole people of Israel, *25* and when he was nearing the end of his course, he said: 'I am not what you judge me to be; but there is coming after me one whose shoe I am not worthy to untie.' F  *27* (But) the people of Jerusalem and their rulers failed to recognise him; they did not understand the sayings of the prophets which are read out every sabbath; but they fulfilled them by condemning him.  G  *28* Although they could find no ground for a sentence of death, they asked Pilate to have him put to death.  F¹  *29* When they had done all that the Scripture had foretold of him, they took him down from the wood of the cross and laid him in a tomb. *30* But God raised him from the dead. E¹  *31* And for many days he showed himself to those who had come up with him from Galilee to Jerusalem. These men are now his witnesses before all the people.  D¹  *32* And now we bring to you the good news that God, who made the promise to our fathers, has fulfilled it for us their children,  C¹  *33* by raising up Jesus, as it stands written in the second psalm: 'You are my Son; this day I have begotten you.' *34* The proof that he raised him up from the dead to return no more to corruption is this word of his: 'I shall give you the holy and sure blessings promised to David'; *35* and in another of the psalms he said: 'You will not allow your Holy One to see corruption.' *36* Now David served the will of God in his own generation and then fell asleep in death and was gathered to his fathers, and saw corruption; *37* but the one whom God has raised up did not see corruption.     **B¹** *38* Therefore, be it known to you, brethren, that it is through him that you are promised forgiveness of your sins. *39* Whoever believes in him is made a just man, freed from all the sins from which you could not be freed under the law of Moses.     **A¹** *40* Therefore take care that this saying of the prophets is not applied to you: *41* 'Behold, you scoffers, and marvel — and then perish! For in your days I shall do a work — a deed that you will never believe when you are told of it!'

Scepticism about the pauline character of this sermon is ill-founded. A comparison of its contents with the Epistle to the Galatians shows that this is exactly the kind of sermon which St Paul must have preached when founding his 'churches of Galatia'. Here, first of all, are the resemblances:

1.  In Gal 3:1 St Paul says that he 'placarded' Christ crucified before the eyes of the Galatians. In the sermon, the crucifixion is placed at the centre (vv. 27-30). Neither the sermon nor the Epistle contains any allusion to the events of the public ministry.

2.  In Acts 13:38, as in Gal 1:4, forgiveness of sins is offered through Christ risen from the dead.

3.  In Acts 13:39 justification is offered to all who believe in Christ, as in Gal 3:10-14. This is the only place in Acts where the specifically pauline verb 'to justify' is used. [20] Acts 13:39 contains in a nutshell one of the main theses of Galatians, and it is repeated in a different form in the quotation from Habakkuk in 13:41. Whereas the Epistle insists that believers are not saved by their own 'works', 13:41 teaches that they are saved by the wonderful 'work' of God.

4.  According to Acts 13:38-39, Christ does for us what the law failed to do. This is the doctrine of Gal 3:10, and more clearly still of Rom 3:19-20.

5.  In the sermon in Acts, vv. 20-21 compared with vv. 38-39 strongly suggest that the period of the law was an unsatisfactory interim like the period of the Judges and Saul before the coming of the first David. In Galatians this idea is expressed by means of the pedagogue-image (3:24).

6.  The discourse at Antioch emphasizes that Christ died in fulfilment of the Scriptures, and vv. 20-21, 33-37 imply that Jesus,

---

[20] Cf. Ramsay, **Gal**, p. **400.**

like David, fulfilled the will of God — a point made explicitly in
Gal 1:4.

7. In Acts 13:33 St Paul treats the resurrection as the day when
Christ entered upon his sonship — an idea which probably under-
lies Gal 4:1-2.

There is only one important difference between the discourse and the
Epistle, and this is not a contradiction. Whereas in the Epistle Christ
is presented as the fulfilment of the promise made to Abraham
(cf. 3:16), in the discourse he is the fulfilment of the promise made
to David, and the title 'sons of Abraham' is given to Jews only (v. 26).
But this divergence lends no support to the common view that the
Epistle is by St Paul and the sermon by St Luke. St Paul undoubtedly
saw many theological connections between the Old Testament and
the gospel which he does not develop in his extant Epistles. In 2 Cor
1:19-20 he says that *all* God's promises received the Yes of fulfilment in Christ, and in Rom 1:1 he gives a passing hint that he did
attach theological significance to Christ's Davidic descent. [21]

It has sometimes been argued that in vv. 30-31 St Luke makes
St Paul say something which in fact he would never have said: 'God
raised him from the dead, and he was seen during many days by those
who had gone up with him from Galilee to Jerusalem; *they* are now
his witnesses.' It is suggested that St Paul himself would not have
spoken this way; he would have included himself among the primary
witnesses of the resurrection (cf. 1 Cor 15:8). [22] But this argument
is unsound. V. 31 is the first half of an antithesis: '*They* are his
witnesses before the people (in Jerusalem and Judaea); but *we* are announcing the good news to you.' St Paul *is* placing himself on a level
with the Twelve, and he is describing the division of labour which
was to be formally agreed upon at the Council of Jerusalem (cf. Gal
2:9).

This comparison shows, then, that the sermon probably represents
very accurately the content of St Paul's kerygmatic preaching in
Galatia. There is no reason why the discourse should not be one
composed by St Paul himself and compressed by St Luke. Or, if St
Luke is held to be its author, we should admit that he understood
St Paul's thought far better than some of his critics allow.

---

[21] Perhaps he would have said that God's covenant with David (2 Sam 23:5) was
a renewal of the gratuitous promise made to Abraham, and not of the law-
covenant made at Sinai. Under the monarchy, the Sinai-covenant receded into
the background of Jewish thinking. Cf. G. E. Mendenhall, 'Covenant Forms in
Israelite Tradition,' *The Biblical Archaeologist* 17 (1954), p. 72.
[22] Cf. J. Knox, *Chapters in a Life of Paul*, p. 120.

After the discourse the narrative is resumed. Again it is arranged in a symmetrical pattern:

A     Paul encourages believers, 13:43.
B     Jewish opposition, 13:44-45.
C     Paul's discourse in reply, 13:46-47.
D     Gentiles believe, Jews stir up enmity, 13:48-50.
E     Paul and Barnabas depart to Iconium, 13:51(52).
F     Conflicts at Iconium, 14:1-2.
G     *Preaching and miracles at Iconium,* 14:3.
F¹    Conflicts at Iconium, 14:4-5.
E¹    Paul and Barnabas depart to Lystra, 14:6-7.
D¹    A Gentile believer is cured; enthusiasm of Gentiles, 14:8-13.
C¹    Paul's discourse in reply, 14:14-18.
B¹    Paul is stoned by the Jews, 14:19-20.
A¹    Paul encourages believers, 14:21-22.

Here again, a sentence seems to be out of place: v. 52 should probably come before v. 51. The text is as follows.

A   *13:43* When the meeting dispersed, many of the Jews and God-fearing proselytes went after Paul and Barnabas, who spoke to them and urged them to remain faithful to God's grace.    B   *44* On the following sabbath, almost the whole city assembled to hear the word of God.   *45* But when the Jews saw the crowds, they were full of jealousy and blasphemously contradicted what Paul was saying.   C   *46* Paul and Barnabas replied boldly: 'The word of God had to be preached to you first; but since you reject it and condemn yourselves as unworthy of eternal life — very well! we turn now to the Gentiles.   *47* For that is the Lord's command to us, in the words: 'I have appointed you to be a light for the Gentiles, to bring salvation to the ends of the earth.'   D   *48* The Gentiles rejoiced to hear this and glorified God's word; those who were destined for eternal life became believers,   *49* and the word of the Lord spread through the whole country.   *50* But the Jews incited the more distinguished of the God-fearing women and the leading men of the city to stir up enmity against Paul and Barnabas, and they expelled them from their territory.   *52* Nevertheless, the new disciples were filled with joy and with the Holy Spirit.   E   *51* So they shook the dust off their feet as a warning to them, and went to Iconium.   F   *14:1* At Iconium too they went into the Jewish synagogue and preached, with the same result, namely, that a large number of Jews and Greeks believed,   *2* but the Jews who did not believe stirred up the Gentiles and poisoned their minds against the brethren.   G   *3* They stayed there a long time and preached with bold confidence in the Lord, who confirmed their preaching of his grace by allowing signs and wonders to be wrought by their hands.   F¹   *4* However, the populace was divided: some sided with the Jews and some with the apostles.   *5* A move was made by both Gentiles and Jews, with the support of their rulers, to maltreat them and stone them.   E¹   *6* But they saw what was coming and escaped to the Lycaonian cities of Lystra and Derbe and the surrounding country, *7* where they continued to preach the gospel.    D¹    *8* At Lystra lived a man with crippled feet; he had been lame from birth and had never walked.    *9* This man was once sitting listening to a sermon of Paul's, when Paul turned his gaze on him, saw that he had sufficient faith to be cured,    *10* and said to him in a loud voice: 'Stand up on your feet.' He leapt up and started walking about. *11* The crowd saw what Paul had done, and shouted out in Lycaonian: 'The gods have come down to us in human form.'    *12* They called Barnabas Zeus and Paul Hermes (because Paul took the lead in speaking).    *13* The priest of the temple of Zeus outside the walls brought oxen and garlands to the city gates and wanted to offer sacrifice with the people.    C¹    *14* When the apostles Barnabas and Paul heard of this, they tore their clothes and rushed among the crowd crying:    *15* 'Citizens, what is this you are doing? We are only men like yourselves, and we are calling you to give up these meaningless sacrifices and turn to the living God who made heaven and earth and sea and all they contain.    *16* In past generations he let every nation go its own way;    *17* yet even then he did not leave you without evidence of himself, for he blessed you by sending you bounty from heaven, giving you rain and fruitful seasons, with food in plenty and joy in your hearts.'    *18* With these words they just succeeded in preventing the people from offering sacrifice to them.    B¹    *19* However, some Jews arrived from Antioch and Iconium and won over the people to their side. They stoned Paul, and dragged him out of the city — dead, as they thought.    *20* But when the disciples gathered round him, he rose up and went back into the city. The next day he left with Barnabas for Derbe. A¹    *21* After preaching the gospel in that city and gaining a large number of converts, they returned to Lystra, Iconium and Antioch, *22* strengthening the spirit of the disciples, urging them to stand firm in their faith, and warning them that we must pass through many tribulations on our way into the kingdom of God.

There are several places in which this narrative agrees remarkably well with the reminiscences of his Galatian ministry which St Paul inserts in his Epistle.

1.  Acts 13:48-52 and 14:14-18 describe the exuberant joy with which the Galatians received the gospel according to Gal 3:1 and 4:15. Never again in Acts is the gospel greeted with such demonstration of joy.

2.  The cure of the cripple who had faith may well be one of the miracles of faith referred to in Gal 3:5.

3.  The attempt to offer sacrifice to Paul as Hermes the messenger of the gods (14:12-13) may have suggested to St Paul the expression which he uses in Gal 4:12: 'You received me as a messenger of God.' On reflection, he probably saw that their homage, which he

had repudiated with horror, contained an element of truth: an apostle is a Christian Hermes.

4. St Paul's summons to the Galatians to give up their 'meaningless sacrifices' (14:15) is matched by the warning against returning to the 'weak and beggarly elements' in Gal 4:9.

5. St Paul's apparent death and resurrection in 14:19-20 may be alluded to in Gal 3:1. [23]

6. When St Paul revisited Lystra, Iconium and Antioch on his way back from Derbe (14:21), he was doubtless still bruised and ill from the stoning. This may well be what he refers to in 4:13-14 and 6:15.

These coincidences do not of course *prove* that the Epistle was written to these churches, but they do confirm the conclusion reached by the arguments given on pp. 2-7.

Here, then, is the chronological outline which results from the above discussion:

| | |
|---|---|
| ca 45 | Famine Visit to Jerusalem. |
| ca 47/8 | Founding of 'the churches of Galatia' in S. Galatia during the First Missionary Journey. |
| 49 | Council of Jerusalem. |
| 50 | Paul at Antioch parts from Barnabas. |
| | Paul revisits the churches of Galatia on the Second Missionary Journey. |
| ca 54 | Brief Visit to Jerusalem (Acts 18:22). |
| | Paul at Antioch rebukes Peter. |
| | Paul revisits the churches of Galatia on the Third Missionary Journey. |
| ca 57 | Paul writes the Epistle to the Galatians. |

It remains to indicate how this chronological scheme can accommodate the texts in Galatians which have been thought to favour the North Galatian theory.

1:6 *I am astonished that you are so quickly abandoning the one who called you.* This might mean that only a very short time has elapsed since the first founding of the Galatian churches. But more probably 'so quickly' here means 'so easily', i.e. with so little pause for reflection, so soon after the appearance of the Judaizing teachers.

---

[23] Cf. Goulder, *Type and History in Acts,* pp. 48-49: 'The crucifixion was placarded (*proegraphê*) before their eyes. Since they were not present at Calvary, it must mean that the crucifixion was re-enacted before their eyes, in the passion of Jesus Christ's apostle.' For other possibilities see G in G on 3:1, and below, p. 490, n. 26.

Nothing, therefore, can be safely inferred as to the length of time that
has elapsed between the founding of the churches and the writing of
the Epistle.

2:5 *Not for a moment did we yield to their demand — in order
that the truth of the gospel might remain with you,* or, *might remain
(to be brought) to you.* If the latter translation is correct, this verse
implies that the Galatians were evangelized after the Council of
Jerusalem, hence on the second journey. But it is probably incorrect,
since it involves a violent and unnecessary ellipse.

4:13 *You know that it was through weakness of body that I
preached to you on the former occasion.* If 'through' is taken in a
strictly causal sense, the meaning will be that St Paul was forced by
ill-health to stop in Galatia and took the opportunity to preach the
gospel there — in which case he must be referring to churches founded
on the second journey, since it is unlikely that on the first journey he
went up into Pisidia and Lycaonia for the good of his health. [24] But
the structure of the passage in which this sentence occurs (4:13
matches 4:19) shows that St Paul is contrasting two occasions when
he *evangelized the Galatians,* not when he *visited* them. He evangelized
them for the first time when he formed Christ in them by his kerygmatic preaching on the first journey, and for the second time when
he wrote this Epistle to form Christ in them anew. The phrase
'weakness of the body' probably refers to the effects of the stoning at
Derbe, a trial to their spirit in Paul's flesh. In the second half of the
same passage St Paul implies that the present trial to their spirit is
making him physically ill again. [25]

### What occasioned the Epistle?

There is no hint in Acts 18:23 that when St Paul revisited the
Galatian churches at the beginning of his third journey he found them
already upset by the propaganda of the false teachers. It is therefore
unlikely that as soon as he arrived in Ephesus, he sat down and wrote
this letter by way of comment on what he had seen in Galatia on the
way through. [26] If the date 57 A.D. is correct, he had already been
in Asia a long time when he received news, either by letter or by
messenger, that the Galatian churches were wavering in their loyalty
to his gospel.

---

[24] See above, pp. 8-9.
[25] See below, p. 381. On the meaning of the preposition 'through' in 4:13, see
G in G, p. 169.
[26] Cf. Bonnard, Gal, p. 14.

The false teachers who had arrived in Galatia were apparently going about telling his Gentile converts that if they wished to be saved, they must 'judaize', that is to say, they must adopt the Jewish way of life by submitting to circumcision and following the law of Moses as expounded by the scribes. [27] This doctrine implied that Christianity, which had begun as a movement within Judaism, should always remain within Judaism: if a Gentile wished to be a Christian, he must become a Jew — just as a Gentile who wished to become a Pharisee would have to become a Jew. If the view of the Judaizers had been allowed to prevail, Christianity would have remained a sect within Judaism. [28]

St Paul judged this judaizing doctrine to be a fundamental distortion of the gospel, resting on a misunderstanding of the efficacy of Christ's death and on a misinterpretation of the Old Testament. When he revisited the Galatian churches in 51 and 54, no doubt he attempted to forearm them against the arguments which he knew the Judaizers were using elsewhere. But when they arrived in Galatia, their arguments made a deep impression. Word was brought to the apostle, we do not know by whom, that his work was being undone (cf. 4:11). Perhaps some of his converts had already submitted to circumcision (cf. 5:3). He responded to the challenge by sending the Epistle to the Galatians, in which he reproaches his converts for their inconstancy, anathematizes the false teachers, and gives a theological and Scriptural justification of his own position — or rather of the gospel as he received it from Christ — according to which Gentile converts should remain Gentiles and should not be allowed to submit to circumcision or to adopt the Jewish way of life. The new communities which he was founding were not to be synagogues of proselytes to Israel according to the flesh; they were the true 'Israel of God' (Gal 6:16), a body of spiritual adults who had no need of the restraints which God had placed upon the Jews in the period of their spiritual immaturity. Christ was not the founder of a new sect within

---

[27] Cf. A. Wikenhauser, *New Testament Introduction*, Edinburgh, 1958, p. 380, and below, p. 345, n. 25.

[28] Cf. Filson, *New Testament History*, p. 114. In discussing Galatians, it is customary to call St Paul's opponents the 'Judaizers'. The word is fully appropriate only to Gentile Christians who had adopted or were about to adopt or felt they ought to adopt the Jewish way of life (cf. 2:14). But it is also applied to the Jewish teachers who were trying to persuade Gentile Christians that they ought to judaize. These teachers were not themselves, properly speaking, Judaizers, since one who is already a law-observing Jew cannot be said to judaize. When the Jewish propagandists won over a Gentile Christian to their way of thinking, such a man would doubtless urge other Gentile Christians to adopt the same view. Hence it is convenient to describe as 'Judaizers' both those who propagated and those who listened favourably to the view that Gentile Christians should judaize.

Judaism (like the Teacher of Righteousness who founded the Qumran community); he had initiated an entirely new era or aeon in the relationship of all mankind to God (cf. 1:4); his work was a new creation (cf. 6:15).

The whole destiny of the Church was at stake in this controversy between St Paul and the Judaizers. The question was: Should the disciples of Christ remain a group of Jews centred upon the earthly Jerusalem, or should the Church break through the wall of separation and become a world-religion looking to the heavenly Jerusalem as its mother (cf. 4:26)? It is to St Paul's everlasting credit that he understood, far more clearly than anyone else in the Church, that the second of these alternatives was God's will, and that he adhered resolutely to this conviction in the face of misunderstanding and opposition from other Christians (cf. Acts 21:20). It is impossible to study his Epistles closely without recognising certain defects in his character (he can be too emotional, touchy, boastful[29]), but these are of small account in a truly great man whom all Gentile Christians should hold in veneration.

In order to justify his view of the relationship between the Church and Israel, St Paul has to give an interpretation of the Old Testament. He and his adversaries were agreed that Christ is the fulfilment of the Scriptures, but they disagreed over the interpretation of the Old Testament. To the Judaizers, Moses was the central figure of the Old Testament, and Christ was the new Moses. But for St Paul, Abraham is the key figure, and Christ is the 'seed (or issue) of Abraham' to whom the great promises of the Old Testament were made. This brief Epistle, therefore, contains an attempt to discern the unity of salvation-history and the mutual relations of its principal periods. Another mark of St Paul's greatness is the broad sweep of his theological vision, playing over the whole panorama of God's dealings with man from the beginning to the consummation.

Some commentators have thought that no sooner had St Paul heard of the Galatian crisis than 'quivering with indignation' he dictated this Epistle 'at a furious rate' to a secretary who could hardly keep up with him. [30] More probably, as St John Chrysostom conjectured, he wrote the whole Epistle, slowly and laboriously, with his own hand. [31] He planned it with immense care and skill, and incor-

---

[29] There is a good comment on Paul's boasting in E. W. Hunt, *Portrait of St Paul*, London, 1968, p. 62: 'It is egocentric, and no amount of apologizing can vindicate it.'

[30] Cf. Orchard, art. cit., CBQ 7 (1945), p. 382.

[31] See below on Gal 6:11.

porated into it arguments which he had first formulated some years earlier (e.g. at Antioch). He knew the contentions of the Judaizers long before he heard that they were at work in Galatia. This Epistle does not contain hasty thoughts produced on the spur of the moment, but the fruits of direct personal encounter with judaizing teachers at Antioch and Jerusalem and of mature reflection on their theological position. It is incorrect to say that St Paul thought out his own characteristic theological position in the heat of the Galatian crisis. The Galatian crisis was only one of a long series of incidents in which the protracted debate with the Judaizers was fought out. The view developed in this commentary is that the theological arguments proposed in 2:15—5:13 were nearly all formulated at the time of the Antioch incident. That was the real crisis.

One of the main sources of our difficulty in understanding the Epistle to the Galatians is that it represents an advanced stage in a controversy, the earlier phases of which we have difficulty in reconstructing. From the discourse in Acts 13 and from the Epistle we can form a fair idea of how St Paul first put the gospel to the Galatians. But we do not know how far he went, on his second and third visits, in forewarning them against the propaganda of the Judaizers. We cannot be sure how much, if anything, he told them about his conflict with Peter. We cannot be quite sure whether the Judaizers who appeared in Galatia were extremists who held that circumcision was necessary for salvation, or middle-of-the-road men who said that it was necessary for perfection (in other words, that Gentile Christians were second-class citizens in the kingdom of God). We do not know exactly what arguments they advanced against St Paul's position when they appeared in Galatia. And we do not know why the Galatians, in spite of St Paul's warnings, so quickly succumbed to the Judaizers' arguments. We can, however, arrive at a set of probable opinions on all these matters, and the Epistle becomes much more meaningful if we do. The remaining sections of this Introduction offer a set of opinions for the reader's appraisal. They will be qualified again and again by the word 'probably' or its equivalents. This is tiresome, but the alternative would be to adopt a dogmatic tone which the state of the evidence does not warrant.

### How did St Paul first put the gospel to the Galatians?

St Paul had probably worked out his own characteristic theological position before he began preaching in Galatia. There are hints of this in the discourse at Pisidian Antioch (cf. Acts 13:38-39), but the chief

reason for thinking so is that before embarking on the Gentile mission
he must have considered carefully whether or not he would require
his converts to be circumcised, and whether or not he was at liberty
to enter the houses of Gentiles and eat with them, in spite of the
prohibitions of 'the law'.

As will be shown below, it is probable that St Paul realized from
the time of his conversion that he was at liberty to preach to the
Gentiles — that he could abandon the law in order to do so, and
hence that he was not obliged to lay upon them the law which he
had abandoned himself. When he went into Arabia (Gal 1 : 17), he
probably preached to Gentiles as well as to Jews. [32]

In any case, before Paul and Barnabas set out on the 'first missionary journey', they must have discussed in detail what obligations
they should impose on their prospective converts. We can be sure
that discussions about circumcision and the law were held in the
church of Antioch before the missionaries were allowed to depart; [33]
and if any members of that church remained doubtful, at least Paul
and Barnabas must have been fully convinced of the rightness of the
missionary policy pursued by them in Galatia and later defended by
St Paul in the Epistle. That is why St Paul says that in the Antioch
dispute (which occurred after the founding of the Galatian churches)
'even' Barnabas was led astray — even Barnabas, one of the two
pioneers of the Gentile mission.

There is, however, some reason to think that while Paul and
Barnabas were agreed about the policy to be pursued in practice, they
were not in full agreement about its theological justification. Probably
Barnabas believed that the policy of not circumcising Gentile converts
was justified by the precedent of what St Peter had done in the case
of Cornelius: he had baptized his household and admitted them to
the Church without circumcision. But St Paul's conviction rested on
his own conversion-experiences rather than on Peter's treatment of
Cornelius. This would explain the different behaviour of Barnabas and
of Paul in the Antioch incident: the missionary activity of Barnabas
had been based on the example of Peter; when he saw that Peter
was withdrawing from contact with the Gentiles at Antioch, he again
took Peter's example as his law. But Paul did not; his thinking and
his conduct were controlled not by Peter's example but by the revelation which he had received at the time of his conversion.

---

[32]   See below, on 1 : 17, p. 135.
[33]   J. Weiss, *Earliest Christianity*, I, p. 265, thinks otherwise.

There are at least three good arguments in favour of the view that when St Paul first evangelized the Galatians, and still more when he revisited them in 51 and 54, he must have dealt explicitly with the question of circumcision and the law. First, a kerygmatic reason: to St Paul's mind, it was the most wonderful 'mystery' of the gospel that salvation was now offered to Jew and Gentile alike on the same terms. [34] His mind was full of this thought; how could he keep silent about it? Secondly, a didactic reason: after his departure, his Gentile converts would be reading the Jewish Scriptures, 'the law and the prophets', at their liturgical gatherings; they would hear strict, clear and emphatic precepts enjoining circumcision under pain of rejection, [35] and fearsome curses upon non-observers of the law. [36] St Paul must have explained before leaving them that the ceremonial laws contained in the Torah were not binding upon them, and he must have tried to explain why not. And thirdly, there was an apologetic reason: he knew that there were some Christians who strongly disagreed with his missionary policy and felt it their duty to tell his converts that he was misleading them. This meant that he had to forewarn his converts of what other teachers might say. [37]

In the missionary partnership of Paul and Barnabas, it was Paul who did most of the speaking (cf. Acts 14:12), but Barnabas was not dumb. No doubt it was left to Barnabas to narrate the conversion of Cornelius by Peter, for Paul preferred to narrate his own conversion experience, which, he believed, implied the same lesson: that Christ was the end of the law for all who believed. Unfortunately, we do not know just how he showed that this essential part of his message was implied in the Damascus-vision, for he does not repeat the demonstration in the Epistle. But he does reaffirm that he received his gospel of Gentile freedom 'by revelation' (cf. 1:12 and 1:16, just before mention of Damascus in 1:17).

It seems, then, that in large measure the contents of the Epistle were not new to the Galatians. They had probably already heard the Scriptural arguments set forth in 3:5-14 and the explanation of the temporary character of the law given in 3:23—4:11. In the auto-

---

[34]  Cf. Eph 3:6-9; Col 1:27.
[35]  Cf. Gen. 17:9-11, quoted below, p. 26.
[36]  Cf. Deut 27:26, quoted in Gal 3:10.
[37]  I describe as 'kerygmatic' the arguments which a preacher uses when he takes the initiative and proclaims the gospel to those who have not heard it before; 'didactic' arguments are those used for the further instruction of those who have accepted the initial kerygma; 'apologetic' arguments are those designed to defend the truth against the attacks of unbelievers and the doubts of believers.

biographical section (1:11—2:19), the story of his conversion was certainly known to them and therefore receives only passing mention (1:15-16). The passages describing the Council of Jerusalem and the Antioch incident are fuller, not because St Paul is reporting them for the first time (he must have reported on the Council during his second visit to Galatia, and on the incident during his third), but probably because the Judaizers had circulated strongly anti-Pauline versions of both. In Galatians, St Paul narrates both incidents, not as interesting pieces of news, but as important items in his self-justification. [38]

In general, then, it seems safe to say that St Paul had worked out the substance of his theology before his first visit to Galatia, and that he had developed it further in the controversies at Antioch and Jerusalem in the intervals between his journeys (i.e. in A.D. 49/50 and *ca* 54). Hence most of the theological arguments incorporated in the Epistle were already known to the Galatians before A.D. 57, and conversely much of the Epistle is a repetition of St Paul's preaching in Galatia and elsewhere.

## Did St Paul provide the Galatians with a written gospel?

It would be interesting to know when a written gospel first reached the Galatian churches. St Paul appears to have carried with him a written collection of the Lord's sayings (cf. 1 Cor 7:10-12, 25), which may have been the Aramaic Matthew, or possibly Q, if Q ever existed. [39] But from the way he talks in 1 Cor 7:25 it seems that he did not allow this collection to be translated and kept by his converts. This is readily understandable if it included such sayings as Mt 5:17: 'Do not imagine that I have come to abolish the law or the prophets,' and Mt 23:2: 'Upon the chair of Moses sit the scribes and Pharisees; you must therefore heed and do all they say to you.' It seems, then, that the only written statements of the gospel which St Paul gave to his churches were the Epistles. Both Galatians and Romans contain the gospel, though they have not the literary form which we call a 'gospel'.

Written gospels may have been introduced into Galatia by the Judaizers. St Matthew's gospel and St Luke's Infancy Narratives would have suited them well.

---

[38] Cf. J. Weiss, *Earliest Christianity*, I, pp. 258-259.
[39] See my diagram in HJ 5 (1964), p. 289.

Before investigating the arguments of the Judaizers, let us discuss
a preliminary question:

*How should we define 'the theology of Jewish Christianity'?*

From A.D. 30 to 70, the principal Christian church was the
church of Jerusalem. Its members spoke for the most part Aramaic
and Hebrew, and they practised circumcision and the law. Undoubtedly this community produced its own theology and its own
books; but the whole of this literature perished in the flight to Pella
and the gradual extinction of the Pella community.

For the most part, historians of the Church have almost completely ignored the theology and history of the early Aramaic-speaking
church. They begin with St Paul and trace the history of Christianity
within the Roman Empire. In the last few years, an attempt has been
made to fill this gap in our knowledge. Just recently there has appeared in English *The Theology of Jewish Christianity* by Père Jean
Daniélou. He begins by proposing various possible meanings which
can be attached to the phrase 'the theology of Jewish Christianity',
and the choice which he makes is perhaps unfortunate: it leads him
away from the real centre of interest to certain peripheral matters,
and from the canonical sources to apocrypha and heretical writings.
He chooses to define Jewish Christian theology as 'a type of Christian
thought expressing itself in forms borrowed from Judaism.'[40] One
disadvantage of this definition is that Daniélou has to classify St Paul's
theology as belonging to the theology of *Jewish* Christianity, whereas
in fact a large part of his theology is devoted to the justification of
Gentile Christianity. According to Daniélou's definition, Gentile theology does not begin until the Church produces Gentile thinkers who
reflect upon the Christian revelation in the light of a body of literature
of non-Jewish origin. If Daniélou's definition is accepted, one cannot
speak of the controversy between Paul and the Judaizers as a clash

[40] Op. cit., p. 9. He gives a summary explanation of what he means by these
'forms' in his Introduction (p. 4): 'The distinguishing marks of this theology
will become clearer in the following chapters. Fundamentally it is characterised
by the fact that its imagery is that of the dominant Jewish thought-form of
the time, namely apocalyptic. It is conceived in terms of the revelation of
cosmic secrets; of the dwelling-places of angels and demons and the souls of
men; of the secrets of history written beforehand in the book of God; of the
mystery of the Cross of glory, and of the pre-existent Church, at once old and
yet young and beautiful. The heart of its faith is the affirmation that Christ
alone has penetrated beyond the veil, and opened the seals of the heavenly
scroll, achieving Paradise for those who bear the Name of the Son of God.'

between a Jewish-Christian theology and a Gentile-Christian theology, and yet, in an obvious sense of the words, that is what it was.

It is not good to quarrel over definitions, but from our point of view, it might be better to define 'Jewish-Christian theology' as the theology of the Jewish-Christian community of Jerusalem in the years 30-70. Correspondingly, 'Gentile-Christian theology' will be the theology of the Gentile-Christian communities. For both, the main problem was presented by the law of Moses. For theologians of the Jewish, law-observing community the question was: 'Why are we continuing to observe the law, if justification does not depend upon it?' And for theologians of the Gentile, non-observing communities the question was: 'Why should we not observe the law, if Christ and his apostles did?' These questions have wide ramifications. They affect the whole interpretation of Christ's public ministry: Did he come to teach the Jews the definitive, Messianic interpretation of the law of Moses? [41] Or did he come to make an end of the law for all who believe? They also affect the question of how the Old Testament is related to the New: Is Christ to be thought of as the Issue of Abraham, or as the New Moses, or as both together? and so on.

The theology of Gentile Christianity has never been homogeneous. The Author of Hebrews agrees with St Paul that Gentile Christians should not follow the law of Moses, but he gives different reasons. So too with Marcion — he gave reasons which the Church had to reject as heretical.

On the Jewish side as well, there were almost certainly wide theological divergences from the start. For example, St James, the brother of the Lord, would probably not have agreed with some of the things said by St Stephen in his discourse in Acts 7. And we know from Acts 15 that there was a party of Pharisaic converts within the Church who still considered circumcision and fulfilment of the law to be necessary for salvation, though Peter and James did not. We must not suppose that the Jewish Christians had one monolithic theology. The Jews who came into the Church in those early years did not come with their minds a complete blank. Some had been Pharisees, some had been publicans, some had been Zealots, some disciples of John the Baptist, some may have been drop-outs from the community at Qumran, and so on. They absorbed the Christian revelation into the framework of their previous thought, so far as they

---

[41] This is the view of St Matthew the Evangelist, according to G. Barth, 'Matthew's Understanding of the Law,' in G. Bornkamm et al., *Tradition and Interpretation in Matthew*, London, 1963, pp. 58-159. See below, p. 345, n. 25.

were able. That is why at the Council of Jerusalem, no less than at Vatican II, there were progressives, conservatives, and extremists.

The opponents of St Paul in Galatians are almost certainly Jewish-Christians from Jerusalem. [42] Our problem is to try and discover what shade of opinion they represented, what practical policy they urged, and what arguments they proposed to commend and justify it. So now let us come directly to the question:

## How did the Judaizers present their case?

Some of the arguments which the Judaizers could bring forward were very strong. Indeed, if the controversy had been settled by the criterion of 'Scripture alone' (Scriptura sola), they would have come off best, because they could appeal to the literal sense whereas St Paul had to fall back on the 'fuller sense' (sensus plenior) and on some rather difficult typological exegesis. St Paul's position was really based on the revelation he had received from Christ. His arguments from Scripture were only confirmatory. [43] In this sense, St Paul's own theology was not really a Biblical theology. He had received a 'tradition' from Christ, [44] and one of his tasks as a theologian was to square this tradition with the inspired Scripture of the Old Testament. Even St Paul was faced with the problem of Scripture and Tradition. For him, tradition (what he had received from Christ) was primary. His adversaries were the Protestants — it was they who gave primacy to the literal sense of Scripture. So it is incorrect to call St Paul 'the father of Protestantism' — in spite of the way in which he treated St Peter at Antioch. [45]

The Judaizers who upset the church of Antioch in A.D. 49 were Pharisaic extremists (cf. Acts 15: 1-5), who maintained that circumcision and observance of the law were necessary for salvation. St Luke does not record their arguments, but it is not difficult to guess. They could say: 'Paul agrees that in Christ are fulfilled the promises made to Abraham. But when God makes the promises to Abraham in Gen 17: 9-11, he says:

You shall keep my covenant, you and your descendants after you throughout their generations. This is my covenant which you shall keep, between you

---

[42] Two other views are considered and rejected below, pp. 31-35.
[43] Cf. W. Gutbrod in TWNT, IV, p. 1067.
[44] In Scriptural language, a doctrine or practice is a 'tradition' as soon as it is 'handed over'; the word does not imply that the doctrine or practice was handed over long ago.
[45] Cf. T. Zahn, 'Petrus in Antiocheia,' Neue Kirchliche Zeitung, 5 (1894), p. 448; K. Holl, Gesammelte Aufsätze, III, Tübingen, 1928, pp. 134ff.

and me and your descendants after you: Every male among you shall be circumcised... If any male have not the flesh of his foreskin circumcised, that person shall be cut off from his people; he has broken my covenant.

'There,' they could say, 'is the will of God. Christ did not repeal this law. What, then, is Paul doing repealing it? Moreover, Paul admits that the covenant granted to Abraham is still valid; but this covenant included the demand "Walk before me and be perfect." The Sinai-covenant was simply a renewal of the covenant made with Abraham: the Mosaic legislation specifies how the sons of Abraham must walk before God and be perfect. In other words, the law is an essential part of the covenant. St Paul cannot keep the covenant and reject the law. He himself has become a sinner by abandoning the law in order to preach to Gentiles.

'Again, Paul must admit that the promises were made "to Abraham and his issue". But "the issue of Abraham" means "the Jews". If anyone wishes to share in the blessings promised to Abraham, he must, therefore, become a Jew; then as a Jew, he must obey the law of Moses.' Such, no doubt, were the Scriptural arguments of the Pharisees.

The Council of Jerusalem, by deciding in St Paul's favour, implicitly rejected these Scriptural arguments. They seem to have argued: 'God has purified the hearts of the Gentiles by faith (cf. Acts 15:9); if they are already circumcised in their hearts, they have no need of circumcision of the flesh. Because they have the Holy Spirit, they possess the reality of which physical circumcision was the symbol — and this reality makes them parties to the covenant.' [46]

After the Council, the Judaizers may have modified their position and held that, while circumcision is not necessary for salvation, no one can be a perfect Christian, like the apostles, unless he is circumcised. If so, they must have abandoned the Scriptural argument from Gen 17. When in Gal 2:14 St Paul accuses Peter of 'compelling the Gentiles to judaize', he means that Peter's conduct is making the Gentile Christians feel that unless and until they are circumcised they must remain second-class Christians, i.e., Peter is treated as an exponent of the mitigated form of the judaizing doctrine. The mitigated form was adopted in some parts of the Church, as we can see from the *Didache* (6:1-3): 'If you are able to bear the whole yoke of the

---

[46] There is probably an anticipation of this argument in the words of Christ in Jn 7:22: 'This is the reason why Moses gave you the law of circumcision (not that it began with Moses—it goes back to the patriarchs) and you circumcise a man on the sabbath.' C. K. Barrett, *The Gospel according to St John*, London, 1956, p. 264, comments: 'The reason is probably . . . a positive one— Moses gave the command of circumcision to serve as a type of the complete renewal of human nature which Jesus effects.'

Lord, you will be perfect; if you are not, do what you can. As regards food, bear what you can, but avoid at all costs meat that has been offered to idols; for it is the worship of dead gods.' The *Didache* may be a product of the church of Antioch. [47]

Lagrange, however, maintains that the Judaizers attacked by St Paul in Galatians are still Pharisaic extremists. [48] He says St Paul gives no hint in the Epistle that he is now dealing with a mitigated form of a heresy which he had previously encountered in a more virulent form, but argues as if the Judaizers were propagating in Galatia the 'virulent' form of the doctrine.

Perhaps Gal 5:3 can be made to cast some light on this problem. St Paul there says: 'Once again I assure every man who has himself circumcised that he is obliged to fulfil the whole of the law' — which seems to imply that the Judaizers placed far more emphasis on circumcision than on anything else (the sabbath, for example). If so, they cannot be the 'moderate Judaizers' postulated by Lightfoot, Cornely and Loisy. In fact, Gal 5:3 may perhaps mean that the Judaizers were saying: 'We grant that observance of the law of Moses is no longer necessary for salvation, but circumcision is not really a part of the Mosaic law; it is a part of the original Abraham-covenant (cf. Jn 7:22). If a Gentile Christian wants to be a party to this covenant, he *must* be circumcised, but he need not, strictly speaking, obey the whole of the law — though if he wants to be perfect, he should do his best.' [49] If the mark of the extremist Judaizer is insistence on circumcision as necessary for salvation, St Paul's adversaries in Galatians must be labelled extremists.

Besides their arguments from Scripture, the Judaizers had some other powerful arguments. They could point to the example and teaching of Christ during his earthly life and argue like this: 'His parents obeyed the law in his regard: he was circumcised on the eighth day and brought up according to the law. In his public preaching he never condemned circumcision, and he did not preach against the law as Paul does. On the contrary, he said: "Do not imagine that I have come to abolish the law or the prophets" (Mt 5:17), and "Every scribe instructed in the kingdom of heaven is like a householder who brings out from his storehouse things both new

---

[47] Cf. W. Telfer, 'The *Didache* and the Apostolic Synod of Antioch,' JTS 40 (1939), pp. 133-146; 258-271.
[48] Cf. M.-J. Lagrange, 'Les judaïsants de l'Epitre aux Galates,' RB 14 (1917), p. 151.
[49] St. Paul's answer is: 'If a Gentile Christian chooses to be circumcised, he becomes a member of Israel according to the flesh, and then the only way of justification open to him is to fulfil the whole of the law.'

and old" (Mt 13:52) — both baptism and circumcision, both the Sermon on the Mount and the laws of the Pentateuch.' It is possible that some form of St Matthew's gospel was the Judaizers' most powerful weapon. They could also point out how Christ himself observed the law even in performing miracles — for example, by sending a leper whom he had cured to show himself to the priest and offer the gift laid down by Moses (Mt 8:1-4).

Thirdly, the Judaizers could point to the example of the apostles in Jerusalem, especially Peter, James and John, the 'pillars of the Church', who were still obeying every jot and tittle of the law. Theodore of Mopsuestia pictured them as arguing thus: [50]

> They (the apostles) were disciples of Christ, they were with him throughout his ministry, and they were accurately instructed by him in what to teach; but Paul had no opportunity to see him or learn from him; he is a disciple of the apostles — for from what other source could he have learned the truth after Christ had ascended into heaven? Therefore one should by no means heed Paul's teaching, but rather learn from the apostles — and they are very careful about observance of the law.

By this kind of talk they would make the Galatians feel that if they did not judaize they would hardly be followers of Christ at all.

Fourthly, the Judaizers launched a direct attack on St Paul. They said: 'He is not an apostle and has no right to the title or authority of an apostle. Christ appointed twelve; Judas fell away, and his place was taken by Matthias; Paul is a late-comer, and not a member of the apostolic college. He was not with Christ and is ignorant of the events of the public ministry — that is why he makes no use of them in his preaching. [51] Further, as he is circumcised himself, his own salvation is not at stake in this dispute. Moreover, as you Galatians very well know, he has had at least one of his Gentile assistants circumcised, namely Timothy — which shows that privately he is convinced of the value of circumcision. [52] Moreover, he is inconsistent in his teaching on this matter. When he was in Judaea, and whenever he is addressing Jews, he says that circumcision is of value and

---

[50]   Theodore, Gal, p. 2.
[51]   St Paul does not reply to this in Galatians. The difficult passage 2 Cor 5:14-17 probably contains his answer: 'One died for all, therefore all died.' The death of Christ was the end of the old order; the resurrection is the beginning of a new creation. The relationships of the old order, Jew and Greek, slave and free, are now irrelevant. The resurrection made such a completely new beginning that even the relationships which the Twelve had with Christ himself before his resurrection are now of no account. For other views on this passage see E. B. Allo, *Seconde Epître aux Corinthiens* (EB), Paris, 1956, pp. 179-182.
[52]   As Chrysostom observes (PG 61, 413 B), the Judaizers had probably accused Paul of hypocrisy. He throws the charge back in Gal 2:13.

that it is an advantage to be a Jew (cf. Rom 3:2), but when he is among Gentiles he changes his tune (cf. Gal 6:15). [53] He says whatever will please the people whom he happens to be addressing. Moreover, he is an ambitious man and would like to overthrow the authority of Peter himself. He goes up to Jerusalem and boasts of his missionary successes, taking all the credit to himself without a word of praise for Barnabas, and at Antioch he even dared to find fault with Peter in public — in contravention of Christ's express command in Mt 18:15-17:

> If your brother sins, go and charge him with his fault privately between yourselves. If he listens to you, you will have won back your brother. If he does not, take one or two others with you, so that everything said can be vouched for by one or two witnesses. If he disregards them too, report him to the church.

According to these rules, Paul should have spoken to Peter privately instead of creating a scene in public. Further, in the clash at Antioch, Barnabas took the side of Peter. He used to agree with Paul, but now he thinks Paul has gone too far. Their partnership broke up almost immediately after the Council, and since the clash with Peter, it is not clear whether Paul and Barnabas are on speaking terms.'

Such, it seems, were the arguments of the Judaizers. Commentators through the centuries have done less than justice to the strength of their position. [54] The Judaizers may have been knaves — this will be considered below — but they were not fools. The controversy over the treatment of Gentiles was not simply a clash between irascible personalities. The strength of the Judaizers (as of the sixteenth century reformers) was that they had a theology of their own. We cannot understand St Paul's side of the argument unless we take seriously the arguments of his opponents — as he did.

*Were the Judaizers knaves?*

St Paul attributes the activities of the Judaizers to discreditable motives. [55] Here are some of the things he says of them:

1. They want to overturn the gospel of Christ (1:7).
2. They are false brethren and want to enslave us (2:4).

---

[53]   This apparent inconsistency is resolved by St Thomas, Gal 413 B, thus: before conversion the Jew is much better off than the Gentile; after conversion both are in the grace of God and neither is the better off.

[54]   Cf. Chrysostom, PG 61, 613. A notable exception is Filson, *New Testament History*, p. 215: 'The opponents of St Paul must be given credit for honest and intelligent thinking.'

[55]   So too does John Chrysostom, PG 61, 413 A.

3. They are courting you with dishonourable intentions, designing to make you honour them instead of Christ (4:17).

4. They are preaching this doctrine only in order to escape persecution and to win social prestige (6:12).

In brief, St Paul says to the Galatians: 'The Judaizers have no love of Christ or of you; they are seeking their own interests.' It is a severe judgment, but perhaps not quite as harsh as it sounds. St Paul does not say that they are consciously and deliberately acting from these evil motives. He acknowledges that before his Damascus vision, when God opened his eyes, he himself acted from the same selfish motives (cf. 1:10). At the time, his conscience did not reproach him (cf. Acts 23:1); he was acting from bad motives without realizing it. Probably he would have admitted that the same was true of the Judaizers — he is uncovering their real motives, which they would recognize if they would examine their conduct more closely (cf. 6:4).

The Judaizers had taken the initiative by attributing bad motives to Paul (cf. 1:10). So he was giving tit for tat. We of the twentieth century, surveying the controversy from afar in the spirit of ecumenism fostered by John XXIII, may be disinclined to see here a contrast of black and white. Theologically and exegetically, there was a great deal to be said on both sides. In the reign of Elizabeth I, the Jesuit Henry Garnet expressed the feeling of many Catholic priests of his day when he described the Anglican clergy as worshippers of Baal. [56] One can admire both Garnet and Paul while regretting some of the things they said about their adversaries.

*Where did the false teachers come from?*

The great majority of commentators have held that the false teachers were Christian Jews from Jerusalem, probably converted Pharisees. This view is almost certainly correct, but in recent years it has been challenged by two scholars of repute, whose views must be considered. Johannes Munck thinks that they were Gentile members of the pauline churches who had concluded from their own reading of the Septuagint that St Paul's presentation of the gospel was incorrect because incomplete. [57] Walther Schmithals thinks they were

---

[56] Cf. P. Caraman, *Henry Garnet and the Gunpowder Plot*, London, 1964, p. 110.
[57] Cf. Munck, *Paul and the Salvation of Mankind*, pp. 87-134. His views are analysed and rejected by W. D. Davies, *Christian Origins and Judaism*, London, 1962, pp. 179-198. Munck's view is accepted by M. Barth, 'Was Paul an anti-Semite?' JES 5 (1968), p. 93: 'It is against ritualistic, pagan born distorters of the Gospel, not against Jews or Jewish Christians that Paul blasts away.'

'Jewish Christian Gnostics'. [58] Thus while the two agree in rejecting the established view, they do not agree with each other. On the contrary, Schmithals has described Munck's reasoning as being 'often positively fantastic'. [59]

Their arguments against the established view are unconvincing:

1. Munck's main argument is from Gal 6:13: 'The Judaizing opponents in Galatia are Gentile Christians. That emerges from 6:13, which reads, "For even those who receive circumcision do not themselves keep the law, but they desire to have you circumcised in order that they may glory in your flesh" '.[60] Munck's contention is that 'those who receive circumcision' (a present participle in Greek) must be 'Gentile Christians who become circumcised under Judaistic demands.' This is probably not what the Greek means. [61] St Paul is saying: 'These intruders from Jerusalem who put their faith in circumcision are not urging you to judaize in order that you may keep the law and so please God. Why, even they themselves do not keep the law! They simply want to go back to Jerusalem and boast of what they have done'. [62]

2. Munck's other argument is so fragile that it must be left in his own words for fear of misrepresentation: 'The Judaizing movement presupposes Paul's idea of his mission. As long as the mission is only to Israel, the conditions for the admission of Gentiles into the Church present no problem; it is not till Christianity goes to the Gentiles and asks for faith in the gospel that the question arises whether that is the right message. And that is exactly what the texts show us: after the Gentiles have received Paul's gospel, they begin to doubt its truth and validity. They therefore reject Paul as an independent "apostle" and want to live in the same way as the Jewish Christians in Jerusalem.' [63] To this one may reply first of all, *a priori*, that when Gentiles were admitted to the Church without circumcision, it was much more likely that ob-

---

[58] Cf. W. Schmithals, 'Die Häretiker in Galatien,' ZNTW 47 (1956), pp. 26-67. The possibility that the Galatian Judaizers were Gnostics was considered and rejected by Lagrange in RB 14 (1917), pp. 163-164. He agreed, however, with Lightfoot that the Colossian Judaizers were probably Jewish Gnostics.

[59] Cf. Schmithals, *Paul and James*, p. 14.

[60] *Paul and the Salvation of Mankind*, p. 87. C. F. D. Moule, *An Idiom Book of N. T. Greek*, Cambridge, 1953, p. 107, and W. D. Davies, op. cit., p. 194, concede Munck's argument from Gal 6:13.

[61] Cf. G in G, p. 218.

[62] Cf. G in G, p. 219, on the tense of the subjunctive *kauchêsôntai*. Munck places far too much weight on a controversial use of the participle, and does not take account of the context.

[63] *Paul and the Salvation of Mankind*, p. 130.

jections should come from the Jews than from the enthusiastic Gentile neophytes themselves (cf. Gal 4:14); and *a posteriori*, that when St Peter admitted Cornelius without circumcision, he met with immediate criticism in Jerusalem (cf. Acts 11:2). [64]

The arguments of Schmithals are not much more convincing:

1. There was no Christian splinter-group in Jerusalem, he says, which was more extreme than James. [65] Answer: Acts 15:1, 7, 12, 24 shows that there was. In Acts 15:24 the authorities in Jerusalem disown the extremists. In Acts 21:20 James still has to warn Paul that many thousands of believers among the Jews are hostile to him.

2. If there was such a party in Jerusalem (*dato, non concesso*), they were hostile to Gentile missions. Hence they would not appear as far afield as Galatia. [66] Answer: The extremists were not opposed to the admission of Gentiles to the Church, but only to their admission without circumcision (cf. Acts 15:1).

3. The view that apostleship is the criterion of right doctrine which St Paul attributes to his adversaries in 1:1, 11-12 was not held in Jerusalem. [67] Answer: Acts 2:42 and Jn 12:20-22 prove the opposite. The passage in John expresses the idea dramatically: the Greeks can approach Jesus only through the apostles Philip and Andrew. [68]

4. Missionaries who were themselves dependent on Jerusalem would not have criticized Paul on the grounds that he was dependent on Jerusalem. [69] Answer: This was only one half of the charge; the whole charge was that having received the gospel from the apostles in Jerusalem, he was not teaching what the apostles taught but diluting the gospel to please the Gentiles (cf. 1:10).

Schmithals' own view is that the false teachers were Jewish-Christian Gnostics. But St Paul does not call them 'Gnostics' and we

---

[64] Munck's theory, if acceptable, would provide a strong argument against the Tübingen view that there was a deep theological cleavage between Peter and Paul. His contention is that St Paul was in full agreement with the church of Jerusalem. The truth seems rather to be that while Peter and Paul were in agreement about principles, they disagreed at Antioch about the conduct which should follow from these principles. Paul thought that Peter's conduct was at variance with his principles, hence sinful, for any action which does not square with a man's belief is sinful, according to Rom 14:23.

[65] ZNTW 47, p. 27.
[66] ZNTW 47, p. 28.
[67] ZNTW 47, p. 34.
[68] Cf. R. Bultmann, *Das Evangelium des Johannes*, Göttingen, 1953, pp. 321-323.
[69] Cf. ZNTW 47, p. 35.

have no reason to think that they gave themselves this title. Schmithals' arguments are not convincing:

1. The idea that an 'apostle' must be independent of any chain of human tradition is 'typically Gnostic'. [70] Answer: If this proves that St Paul's adversaries were Gnostics, it also proves that Paul was a Gnostic, since he accepts the idea (cf. 1 Cor 9:1).

2. The false teachers insisted on circumcision but did not add that circumcision carried with it the obligation to observe the whole of the law. It was left to St Paul to tell the Galatians this in 5:3. The false teachers themselves did not observe the whole of the law (cf. 6:13). Hence they can hardly have been Pharisaic Jewish Christians. On the other hand, Jewish Christian Gnostics, like Cerinthus, did insist on circumcision. [71] Answer: St Paul is simply saying that if his converts judaize, the only way to justification remaining to them will be to observe the whole of the law, as he said in 3:10 — a thing which no one can do (cf. 3:11), not even the Jewish teachers themselves (cf. 6:13). He does not admit that even the strictest Pharisees succeed in doing all that the law demands. If the Galatian Judaizers were Pharisees, they may have been intellectuals who had already become dissatisfied with the bloody sacrifices and material rites of Judaism. [72] They were making their own synthesis or 'syncretism' of Pharisaism and Christianity, and they *may* have absorbed ideas and practices from other religions as well. But as these other elements are not mentioned in Galatians, there is no good reason for calling them 'Gnostics'.

3. Gal 4:10 does not mean that the false teachers demanded observance of the Jewish calendar, but that they warned against the baneful influence exerted by the heavenly elemental powers on certain days. Thus Gnostic speculations about demonic powers lie behind this verse. [73] Answer: St Paul himself admitted the existence of these demonic influences and taught that Christ delivers the believer from their servitude. Thus again, if this argument proves anything, it proves that St Paul too was a Gnostic. [74]

---

[70] Cf. ZNTW 47, p. 38.
[71] Cf. ZNTW 47, pp. 42-45.
[72] Cf. Lagrange in RB 14 (1917), p. 164.
[73] Cf. ZNTW 47, pp. 48-49.
[74] Cf. H. A. Kelly, *Towards the Death of Satan*, London, 1968, p. 27: 'Much of what St Paul says about the angelic archons or rulers of this age could almost be characterized as gnostic or at least protognostic.' Ibid., p. 28, Kelly makes a helpful attempt to define 'Gnosticism'. See further below, pp. 365-367.

4. When St Paul calls the Galatians 'pneumatics' (i.e. 'spiritual men')
   in 6:1, he is adopting a self-designation which they have learned
   from the Gnostics — who probably called St Paul a 'sarkic' (i.e.
   a 'fleshly man'). [75] Answer: There is no evidence in Galatians
   that St Paul's adversaries had called him 'sarkic'. It is unlikely
   that 'pneumatics' in 6:1 is meant sarcastically, since the passage
   is not argumentative but hortatory. If the distinction between
   those who walk according to the flesh and those who walk according to the spirit is the mark of a Gnostic, again it is St Paul
   himself who is the Gnostic.


In support of the customary or traditional view, that the Judaizers
were Jewish Christians who came into Galatia from outside, and
probably from Jerusalem, the following arguments can be adduced:

1. St Paul introduces the matter in Gal 1:6 by saying 'I am astonished that you are so quickly going over from the one who called
   you, to another gospel.' This is surely not what he would have
   said if the Galatians themselves had thought up the new gospel.
   He accuses them of 'changing sides' — of giving up their allegiance to himself and going over to join his adversaries. [76] The
   'other gospel', he adds, 'is not another gospel, but certain persons
   are upsetting you.' He does not say 'Some of you are upsetting
   the rest.'

2. The anathemas in 1:8-9 and the severe warning in 5:10 imply
   that St Paul held some very exalted person responsible for the
   disturbance in Galatia.

3. Before the Galatian crisis blew up, St Paul had encountered the
   judaizing error at Antioch and had discussed it in Jerusalem. That
   the same error produced itself by spontaneous generation a few
   years later among the Gentile Christians of Galatia is unlikely.
   The Galatians crisis was one more battle in the long conflict
   between Paul and the Jewish-Christian defenders of the law.

4. In Gal 4:21-31, Sinai is bracketed with the earthly Jerusalem,
   'a slave and the mother of slaves'; the earthly Jerusalem is
   bracketed with Agar who represents the Judaizers; and the final
   word of the allegory is: 'Send away the slave-woman and her
   children.' St Paul means: 'Send these Judaizers packing — back
   to Jerusalem, where they belong.'

---

[75]  Cf. ZNTW 47, pp. 50-52.
[76]  Cf. G in G, pp. 81-82, on 1:7.

D

## Why were the Galatians so quick to succumb?

Lightfoot, who believes that the Galatians were inhabitants of Galatia proper, thinks that fickleness was their nature. They were closely related to the Gauls (*Galatai* in Greek) of France, and spoke, in addition to Greek, the same language as their kinsmen on the Rhine. [77] In other words, they were fickle because they were French. That the French were fickle even in St Paul's day is proved by the witness of Caesar, who says in his *Gallic Wars* (IV, 5): 'Fearing the weakness of the Gauls — for they are inconstant in counsel and lovers of change — he decided to leave nothing to them.' However, this is not a very satisfactory explanation of the success of the Judaizers in Galatia, since it is quite uncertain whether *these* Galatians were of Gallic stock, and anyway not all Frenchmen are fickle. [78] The French nation has adhered to the gospel with greater fidelity than most.

More probably they succumbed because the Judaizers brought against them such a formidable battery of arguments, while on the other hand St Paul's explanations, so far as they remembered them, were none too clear.

Secondly, in the Galatians' eyes Barnabas may have been a greater authority than Paul. When the two first preached in Galatia, Barnabas was the senior partner. The people of Lystra expressed the relationship aptly by calling Barnabas 'Zeus' and Paul 'Hermes'. When they heard that in the Antioch incident Barnabas and Paul had taken different sides, they may have felt it safer to follow Zeus rather than Hermes — especially as Zeus was in agreement with Peter, and, apparently, had the backing of the church of Antioch as a whole (which the Galatians probably regarded as their mother-church). Unfortunately, we do not know whether Barnabas revisited South Galatia between 47 and 57 A.D. Acts 15:39-41, where Paul and Barnabas part, may perhaps imply that an agreement was made, comparable to the one described in Gal 2:9, that each would keep out of the other's sphere of influence. There is no positive evidence that St Paul ever returned to Cyprus or Barnabas to South Galatia. But even so, the name of Barnabas will have retained its authority in Galatia. It is not surprising if the Galatians, presented by the Judaizers with a

---

[77] St Jerome, in the preface to his commentary on Galatians, Book II, says (PL 26, 382): 'In addition to the Greek language which is used throughout the Levant, the Galatians have a language of their own, almost identical with that of the (Gallic) Treveri.'
[78] Ramsay, Gal, p. 255, remarks rather pointedly: 'We must try to understand the reason of a notable religious movement in Galatia, and not delude ourselves by misleading and superficial talk about Galatian fickleness.'

choice between Peter, Barnabas and the church of Antioch on the one side and Paul on the other, were inclined to 'abandon' Paul and 'go over to' his adversaries (cf. 1: 6).

Thirdly, the Galatians may have been becoming a little disillusioned with Paul's gospel. His method of proposing Christian morality by contrasting two ways of life, the way of the flesh and the way of the Spirit, though it was an excellent method of clarifying what was expected of those justified by God's grace, had the disadvantage of suggesting that the gift of the Spirit would transform their lives overnight and rid them at once of sin and mediocrity. But no doubt the sinful lives they had led in their pagan days had left behind memories and desires which remained sources of grave temptation and sin. Hence when the emotional excitement of conversion had passed and could not be recaptured, they may have felt some discontent with the teaching they had received from St Paul. If so, it is easier to understand why they were willing to listen to new teachers who professed to be filling up the shortcomings of pauline Christianity.

Fourthly, if I may make a guess from my own experience, the Galatians may well have been moved to reverence by the deep religiousness of the Jewish Christians. It was once my good fortune to take part in a dialogue between Jews and Catholics at Oxford, at which I read a paper on Rom 9-11. It seemed to me that the centuries had fallen away, and here was I, the Christian, the newcomer, confronting the bearers of a tradition two thousand years older than our own and steeped in their tradition as few of us Christians are in ours.

## The Symmetrical Structure of Galatians

Bishop Lightfoot observed in his commentary that in Gal 4: 4-5 St Paul uses the figure known to grammarians and rhetoricians as 'chiasmus' or 'chiasm'. On v. 5 he says: 'The two clauses correspond to those of the foregoing verse in an inverted order by the rhetorical and grammatical figure called chiasm: "The Son of God was born a man, that in him all men might become sons of God; He was born subject to law, that those subject to law might be rescued from bondage" '. Before reading this, I had already reached the conviction that the whole of 'Aramaic Matthew' (or whatever one chooses to call the source-gospel which lies behind all four canonical gospels) [79]

---

[79] See my chart of gospel relationships in HJ 5 (1964), p. 289. For some specimens of the evidence on which this view is based, see my article, 'Matching Passages in the Gospels,' *The Way* 8 (1968), pp. 306-317 and 9 (1969), pp. 59-73.

was arranged chiastically throughout. I had also observed a number of significant links between the prologue (1:1-12) and the epilogue (6:12-18) of Galatians (see p. 488). It therefore occurred to me that the whole of Galatians might be a large chiasm centred upon the small one pointed out by Bishop Lightfoot. [79a] I soon found that the whole of 4:1-10 is a chiasm. Its component parts balance thus:

A *4 : 1* What I mean is: so long as the heir to a property is a minor, he is no different from a slave, B though he is the lord of all. C *2* But he is subject to guardians and trustees until the date fixed by his father. D *3* So too with us: so long as we were minors, we were subject to the elements of the world, enslaved to them. E *4* But when the fulness of time arrived, God sent forth his own Son, F who was born of a woman G and became subject to the law, G¹ *5* in order to redeem those under the law, F¹ in order that we might receive the adoption promised to us. E¹ *6* And as a proof that you are his sons — God sent forth the Spirit of his Son into our hearts, crying: 'Abba, Father!' D¹ *7* So then you are no longer a slave but a son; and if a son, then also an heir, thanks to God. C¹ *8* But formerly, not knowing God, you were the slaves of beings who by nature are not gods; B¹ *9* but now that you have come to know God, or rather to be known by God, A¹ how can you turn back to the weak and grasping elements? Do you wish to be enslaved to them all over again, *10* observing days and months and seasons and years?

In A and A¹ St Paul says that in the period of the law men were subject to something like slavery; any Christian who judaizes will be returning to that slavery. In B and B¹ he insinuates that the knowledge of God (which is more a matter of being known than of knowing) enobles a man, making him lord of all. In C and C¹ he says that Jews and Gentiles practising material rituals do not really know God; they are subject to guardians and trustees (angels in the case of Jews, and demons in the case of pagans). In D and D¹ he says that Christians were once slaves but have now been liberated by God. In E and E¹ he describes the two temporal missions of the Son and of the Holy Spirit. F-F¹ and E-E¹ are connected as Lightfoot explained.

I next observed that this central chiasm is sandwiched between two further passages which correspond to each other, thus:

*3 : 5-29* Arguments from Scripture: Who are the heirs of Abraham? Not those who follow the law of Moses, but those who have faith in Christ.

(4:1-10 Central Chiasm)

*4:11-30* Arguments from Scripture: Who are the heirs of Abraham? Spiritual sons of Sarah, not fleshly sons of Agar.

---

[79a] Dare I quote here the saying of a great scientist that 'no discovery is ever made without a bold guess'?

In these two passages St Paul defends his position with arguments from the law and the prophets. In the first he teaches that a man becomes Abraham's heir through incorporation in Christ, and in the second he insinuates that he himself is Sarah suffering birth-pangs (4:19) while re-forming the image of Christ in his Galatian children by correcting their faith.

These two Scriptural passages are again sandwiched between a pair of matching paragraphs:

A    2:11—3:4   Justification is by faith, not by works.
B                       Arguments from Scripture.
C                       *Central Chiasm.*
B¹                      Arguments from Scripture.
A¹   5:1—5:13   Justification is by faith, not by works.

In 2:11—3:4 St Paul narrates how and why he had to condemn the behaviour of Peter and Barnabas at Antioch, then he sets forth the substance of his own theological position. In 5:1-13 he first repeats the summary of his own position (vv. 2-6), then adds a warning that anyone, however exalted, who teaches otherwise, will 'bear the condemnation' (v. 10).

Thus the structural pattern of the whole Epistle appears to be as follows:

A    Prologue, 1:1—1:12.
B    Autobiographical Section, 1:13—2:10.
C    Justification by Faith, 2:11—3:4.
D    Arguments from Scripture, 3:5—3:29.
E    *Central Chiasm,* 4:1—4:10.
D¹   Argument from Scripture, 4:11—4:31.
C¹   Justification by Faith, 5:1—5:10.
B¹   Moral Section, 5:11—6:11.
A¹   Epilogue, 6:12—6:18.

The correspondence between the Autobiographical Section and the Moral Section is not immediately obvious; but, as will be shown in the appropriate section of the commentary, the Moral Section is a description of Two Ways of living, or rather, of the Way of Life and the Way of Death, here called 'walking according to the Spirit' and 'walking according to the flesh'. If, then, St Paul means this passage to be compared with 1:13—2:10, he must have intended the Autobiographical Passage to demonstrate that before his conversion he walked according to the flesh, and since his conversion, whatever his adversaries may say, he has walked according to the Spirit. This structural analysis of the Epistle suggests, therefore, that the main purpose of the Autobiographical Passage is not, as has often been supposed, [80] to prove by an elaborate alibi that Paul did not receive the gospel from the other apostles, but rather to show that throughout his Christian life he has been obeying the promptings of the Holy Spirit. Readers familiar with the literature of the subject should welcome this fresh insight with relief, for the supposed alibi is notoriously incomplete, and in English law an alibi which fails is as incriminating as flight.

Surveying the structure of the Epistle as a whole, one can see how St Paul is defending his apostolic authority, his personal conduct, his missionary policy, and his own presentation of the gospel: at the very centre, he says that Christ has released Jews like himself from the law of Moses so that they can extend the gospel to the Gentiles and thus enable them to become heirs of the covenant made by God to Abraham and his Issue. That great promise is now being fulfilled for Jew and Gentile alike: whoever believes in Christ is one with Christ and is justified through Christ's death. Justification depends, not on perfect fulfilment of the Mosaic law, but on faith in Christ. Paul does not hesitate to propose his own life as an example. [81] In order to convert the Gentiles, he has adopted the Gentile way of life, and it has done him no harm; the service of Christ has not made a sinner of him. Gentile converts need not fear to accept the liberty which he preaches and practises. What is required of Christians is not circumcision of the flesh but crucifixion of the flesh — which means, in practice, turning away from fornication, impurity, idolatry, enmities, strife, jealousy, and the rest of the 'works of the flesh', in order to lead a life of charity, joy and peace. The material rituals of paganism and Judaism are now obsolete; mankind has now come of age in Christ; henceforth true religion consists in 'faith working through charity'. Such is the gospel which Paul was authorised to preach in his vision on the road to Damascus, and if anyone, even an angel from heaven, or St Paul himself, or anyone else, however exalted, should preach any other gospel, let him be anathema!

Having found that the whole Epistle forms one symmetrical pattern centred on 4:4-5, I looked for smaller symmetries within the large one. I soon found that the whole Epistle falls into three main parts, each of which is chiastic in structure:

      A   1:1—3:4    First Main Division.
      B   3:5—4:31   Second Main Division.
      C   5:1—6:18   Third Main Division.

---

[80] Cf. e.g. St Thomas, Gal, 388 B.
[81] Cf. D. M. Stanley, ' "Become imitators of me": The Pauline Conception of Apostolic Tradition,' *Biblica* 40 (1959), pp. 275-293.

The internal structure of each will be indicated at the appropriate place in the commentary. I also found that each of these main *divisions* falls into three *sections*, and these again are chiastic in structure. [82] But this is not all. Each of the nine sections contains within itself smaller symmetrical patterns. Readers making their first acquaintance with chiastic analysis will probably feel inclined to expostulate that such complexity is fantastic, or they may object that if the pattern were really there, it would have been noticed long ago. To which I can only reply that the proper task of a commentator is to direct the reader's attention to what he might otherwise have missed. The ability to recognize patterns and analogies is what is tested by IQ tests. If we are slow to recognize the patterns which St Paul has created, the reason may be that his IQ was far higher than our own.

In another connection, New Testament scholars have recently been pointing out that all historical thinking is analogical. That is to say, we can accept an account of past events as probable only if it represents men of the past as having behaved in ways known to us from our own experience of human existence and activity. [83] This principle has an application here: the modern reader may find it hard to believe that St Paul deliberately composed his Epistles in elaborate symmetrical patterns, simply because modern writers do not use this technique. Students instinctively ask: Are there any other examples of this kind of writing? The answer is that the Old Testament is full of them [84] — two examples are given below, pp. 371-372. From outside the Biblical tradition a good example is Catullus, Carmen 64. [85]

Experience has shown that students become much more interested in these structural patterns as soon as they have worked out a few for themselves. So before proceeding further, the reader is recommended to work out for himself the structure of Gal 3:5-14, moving out from v. 11b, 'The just man will live by faith,' which is its centre. Then he can compare his analysis with the one given below on pp. 238-239. Students who know no Greek have found that this method gives them, for the first time, a method of working on the text for themselves and making discoveries of their own. [86] In this way they

[82] For the sake of clarity, throughout the commentary the words 'division' and 'section' will be used as in this sentence.
[83] Cf. J. Moltmann, *Theology of Hope*, London, 1967, pp. 175-180.
[84] Cf. Lund, *Chiasmus in the N.T.*, pp. 51-134.
[85] Cf. C. Murley, 'The Structure and Proportion of Catullus LXIV,' TAPA 68 (1937), pp. 305-317; P. W. Harkins, 'Autoallegory in Catullus 63 and 64,' TAPA 90 (1959), pp. 102-106.
[86] For further practice take the Epistle to the Philippians. The centre of the whole is 2:25-29a. There are two main divisions, centring on 1:21-22 and 4:2-3. The first division falls into six sections, centred on 1:7, 1:16; 1:21-22; 2:5-6; 2:21;

have come to see that the sequence of St Paul's thought is not as erratic as it sometimes appears. He is simply employing an unfamiliar technique.

Many a layman listens to a Bach fugue and takes great delight in the sound without having any idea of the elaborate structure of the composition. If a professional musician shows him with some of the visual aids now available, how the subject, countersubject and episodic matter are intertwined, the layman will listen again to the same music with greater appreciation of what is happening and with much greater admiration of the composer's skill. Only a very foolish person would say: 'The pattern cannot be there; the composition flows with perfect spontaneity; the composer cannot have been aware of the structures you have pointed out.' Many commentators on St Paul and St John have borrowed the musical metaphor of 'themes' recurring. They should not find it hard to recognize that these two great Scriptural composers were no less capable than the musicians of following rules, and of transcending them. [87]

---

2:27a; and the second falls into five sections centred on 3:5; 3:10-11; 3:20; 4:8-9; 4:20. Philippians is another splendid feat of symmetrical composition. Yet most Introductions see no order in it. Cf. W. Marxsen, *Introduction to the New Testament*, Oxford, 1968, p. 61: 'The somewhat disjointed train of thought has raised the question of its original unity.' He regards 3:2—4:3 as an insertion or interpolation.

[87]  For an analysis of the symmetrical structure of Jn 3 see HJ 8 (1967), pp. 40-42.

# NARRATIVE SECTIONS OF THE EPISTLE

The Judaizers had evidently made great play with their version of the incident at Antioch. [1] One of St Paul's principal concerns in the Epistle is, therefore, to explain to the Galatians what happened there, why he felt obliged to rebuke Peter publicly, why he was justified in doing so, and what exactly he said. As the crisis in Galatia was a repetition of the trouble at Antioch, the arguments used at Antioch needed to be repeated for the Galatians.

St Paul allows us to see that the Galatians had been badly shaken by the propaganda of the Judaizers. By means of structural links within his carefully constructed paragraphs, he insinuates that Peter was in some way responsible. In the second section (see below, p. 121), there is a link between 1 : 7 and 2 : 9 :

B    1:7 Certain persons are shaking you, and trying to overturn the gospel of Christ.

B¹   2:9 James, Cephas and John, who are thought to be 'pillars'.

And in the third section (see below, p. 174) 2 : 11 is linked with 3 : 1 :

A    2:11 When Cephas came to Antioch, I withstood him to his face, because he was (self-) condemned (*kategnôsmenos*).

A¹   3:1 Foolish Galatians, who has bewitched you — you before whose eyes was placarded Jesus Christ the Crucified (*estaurômenos*)?

The implication of the second link is that the Galatians have ceased to look upon Christ the Crucified because they have been distracted by Cephas the self-condemned, while the first link insinuates that Cephas who is supposed to be a pillar of the Church is in fact shaking the faith of Paul's converts. — That may have been Paul's view of the matter; but perhaps a detached observer would have said that what had really shaken them was the account which they had heard from the Judaizers of *Paul's* behaviour at Antioch. [2] The Antioch incident is the climax of the series of events narrated in the first main division of the Epistle. Immediately after giving his own account of it, St Paul makes a direct appeal to the Galatians in 3 : 1-5.

As he writes the Epistle, St Paul is still emotionally upset over what has happened in Galatia and over what has been said against himself. He does not admit for a moment that he was in the wrong,

---

[1]  See above, p. 30.
[2]  Cf. P. Gaechter, 'Petrus in Antiochia,' ZKT 72 (1950), pp. 177-212, reprinted in *Petrus und seine Zeit*, pp. 213-257.

either at Antioch or in his earlier relations with St Peter. The first two chapters offer a vindication of his own conduct, particularly at Antioch; but he goes back to the beginning to show that he was in a position to call Peter back to the truth of the gospel, that his public denunciation of Peter was preceded by a private interview (1:18), and a semi-private discussion (2:2), and that throughout his years as a Christian he has not sought popularity at Peter's expense by going on preaching tours in the churches of Jerusalem and Judaea.

While defending himself, St Paul is at the same time defending the gospel as he first preached it to the Galatians. He does this, first, by showing that his own doctrine is apostolic, both because he is himself an apostle and because his doctrine has been formally approved by the 'pillar-apostles' in Jerusalem; and secondly, by showing that the doctrine of the Judaizers is false — this refutation extends beyond the first division, since it runs from 2:1—3:14.

The structure of the first main division of the Epistle is as follows:

A   Paul addresses the Galatians, reminds them of Christ Risen from the dead, and calls down upon them the gifts of the Spirit (grace and peace), 1:1-3.

B   Why Christ died, 1:4-5.

C   Anathema on any false teacher, however exalted.
Paul is not pleasing men, 1:6-10.

D   Paul's avoidance of Jerusalem after receiving the gospel by revelation, 1:11-17.

E   Paul's journey to Jerusalem to visit Peter:
avoidance of publicity, 1:18-19.

F   *Paul's oath: all this is true,* 1:20.

E¹   Paul's return from Jerusalem:
avoidance of publicity, 1:21-24.

D¹   Paul goes to Jerusalem in obedience to a revelation, and speaks to Peter in the presence of a few others, 2:1-10.

C¹   Paul rebukes Peter publicly at Antioch.
Peter was pleasing men, 2:11-19.

B¹   Christ did not die for nothing, 2:20-21.

A¹   Paul addresses the Galatians, reminds them of Christ Crucified, and of the gifts of the Spirit, 3:1-4.

Hitherto commentators have not been able to explain why St Paul suddenly takes an oath in 1:20. The statement which he has just made in 1:19 ('I saw no other apostle — unless you count James the brother of the Lord') hardly seems to warrant the taking of an oath. The above analysis provides a satisfactory solution: the oath is the centre of the whole composition and is meant to cover every statement in the section.

The message of the whole division can be summed up in these propositions:

1. St Paul's conduct has been blameless throughout; it is Peter who was blameworthy. Paul has consistently sought to please God, but the same cannot be said of Peter — he has acted from human respect.

2. St Paul himself learned by a spiritual experience (the Damascus-vision) that justification depends on belief in Christ crucified and risen, not on obedience to the law of Moses. The Galatians, if they would only be sensible, would learn the same lesson from their experience.

3. Any teacher, however exalted, who teaches a different gospel is to be anathema. St Peter is not openly accused of teaching a different gospel, but he is accused of compelling the Gentiles to judaize. St Paul explicitly applies the anathema to himself in case he should ever preach a different gospel — this is his answer to the charge of inconsistency in preaching one thing in one place and another thing in another.

Although there is no open antipathy between St Paul and St Peter, there is some hidden tension. The patristic commentators, who were understandably reluctant to admit this, found two ways of smoothing the matter out. Clement of Alexandria maintained that the 'Cephas' mentioned in Galatians is not St Peter but one of the seventy-two disciples of Lk 10: 1 [3] — a solution which was revived in 1958. [4] Origen proposed the more reasonable but still indefensible view that the public dispute was pre-arranged by Peter and Paul, in order to enable Paul to teach the Jewish Christians a lesson. [5] Something like this view is to be found in Chrysostom, Jerome, and even in Augustine — though, as will be seen below, Augustine strongly disapproved of Jerome's solution.

Nowadays, the seriousness of the Antioch incident is admitted by commentators of all denominations. There was no *doctrinal* disagreement between Peter and Paul — the Tübingen theory finds no support in this Epistle. But Paul believed that Peter was failing to act up to his convictions in a matter of great importance, and that through weakness he was leading the Gentiles away from the truth of the gospel. What St Paul attacks is the theology which he sees or believes

---

[3]   He is quoted by Eusebius, *H.E.*, I, 12, 2.
[4]   Cf. C. M. Henze, 'Cephas seu Kephas non est Simon Petrus!' *Divus Thomas* 61 (1958), pp. 63-67 [NTA 3-160]; J. Herrera, 'Cephas seu Kephas est Simon Petrus,' *Divus Thomas* 61 (1958), pp. 481-484 [NTA 3-662].
[5]   Cf. Jerome, Ep. 112 (PL 22, 923).

to be implicit in Peter's action — the theological opinions which Peter would hold if his actions were consistent with his beliefs.

Here, for comparison, are the matching passages of the first division of the Epistle, set alongside of each other.

**A** *1 : 1* Paul, an apostle — not from men, nor through a man, but through Jesus Christ and God the Father who raised him from the dead — *2* I and all the brethren with me (greet) the churches of Galatia: *3* grace to you and peace from God our Father and the Lord Jesus Christ,

**A¹** *3 : 1* O foolish Galatians, who has bewitched you — you before whose eyes Jesus Christ was placarded crucified? *2* I would have you tell me this one thing: was it after doing the law that you received the Spirit, or after hearing the faith? *3* Are you really so foolish? Having begun with the Spirit, will you now end with the flesh? *4* Have all your great experiences been useless — or worse than useless?

**B** *4* who gave himself for our sins, in order to rescue us from the present evil age, according to the will of God our Father; *5* to whom be the glory for ever and ever. Amen.

**B¹** *2 : 19* I am crucified with Christ crucified. *20* It is no longer I who live, but Christ is alive in me. So far as I now live, while in the flesh, I live through faith in * God and Christ who loved me and delivered himself for me. *21* I do not set aside the grace of God; for if justice comes through the law, Christ died for nothing.

**C** *6* I am astonished that you are so quickly deserting the one who called you in the grace of Christ and going over to another gospel — *7* which is not another gospel, but certain persons are shaking you and would like to turn Christ's gospel upside down. *8* But if anyone, even ourselves or an angel from heaven, preaches to you a gospel other than the one you received, let him be anathema! *9* We warned you before, and now I say it again: if anyone preaches to you a gospel other than the one you received, let him be anathema! *10* For am I

**C¹** *2 : 11* But when Cephas came to Antioch, I resisted him face to face, because he was self-condemned. *12* For before the arrival of certain persons from James, he had been taking his meals with the Gentiles; but after their arrival, he began to draw back and set himself apart, fearing those of the circumcision. *13* The other Jews played the hypocrite along with him — so much so that even Barnabas was swept along with them by their hypocrisy. *14* But when I saw that they were not walking steadily according to the truth of the gospel, I said to

---

* On the reading adopted here, see below, p. 215.

now seeking the favour of men or of God? Or am I trying to please men? If I were still trying to please men, I should not be a servant of Christ.

Cephas in the presence of them all: 'If you, who were born a Jew, live as a Gentile and not as a Jew, how can you compel the Gentiles to judaize? *15* We by our birth are Jews and not sinners of Gentiles; *16* but because we knew that a man is not justified by works of the law but through faith in Jesus Christ, we too believed in Christ — in order to be justified by faith in Christ and not by works of the law, for by works of the law no man shall be justified. *17* But if through seeking to be justified in Christ, we have turned out to be sinners ourselves — has then Christ become a servant of Sin? Heaven forbid! *18* For if I rebuild what I tore down, I make myself a sinner. *19* For it was through the law that I died to the law, in order that I might live to God.

**D** *11* For I inform you, brethren, that the gospel preached by me is not according to man, *12* nor did I receive it by instruction from any man, but by a revelation of Jesus Christ. *13* For you have heard the way of life I once followed in Judaism — how I was going to extremes in persecuting the Church of God and making havoc of it, *14* how I was making greater progress in Judaism than many of my contemporaries among my own people, and showing greater zeal for the traditions of my forefathers. *15* But when he who had set me apart from my mother's womb and graciously called me was pleased *16* to reveal his Son to me, that I might preach him to the Gentiles, there and then, instead of consulting flesh and blood *17* or going up to Jerusalem to those who had been made apostles before me, I went off

**D¹** *2 : 1* Then, after fourteen years, I again went up to Jerusalem with Barnabas, taking Titus with me too. — *2* I went up in obedience to a revelation — and I laid before them the gospel I preach to the Gentiles, but privately before those held in regard: Was I perhaps running or had I run my course in vain? *3* But even my companion Titus, Greek as he is, was not compelled to be circumcised. *4* But on account of intruders — false brethren who had wormed their way in to spy on the liberty we have in Christ Jesus, in order to enslave us. *5* But not for a moment did we yield to their demand — in order that the truth of the gospel might remain with you. *6* As for those held in regard — what they were once makes no difference to me, God is no respecter of human persons — those held in regard laid down

to Arabia. From there I returned to Damascus.

no further requirements. *7* On the contrary, seeing that I had been entrusted with the gospel of the uncircumcised, as Peter had been with that of the circumcised, (*8* for he who had made Peter's apostleship to the circumcision effective had made mine effective among the Gentiles) *9* and recognizing the grace that had been given to me, James, Cephas and John, the ones regarded as pillars, gave to me and to Barnabas the right hand of fellowship, with the understanding that we should preach to the Gentiles, and they to the Jews. *10* They only asked that we should remember the Jewish poor — and this very thing I took care to do.

**E** *18* Then, three years later, I went up to Jerusalem to see Peter, and I stayed with him for fifteen days. *19* But not one of the other apostles did I see — unless you count James the brother of the Lord.

**E¹** *1 : 21* Then I went into the countries of Syria and Cilicia, *22* but I remained unknown by sight to the Christian churches of Judea — *23* though they kept hearing: 'The man who once persecuted us is now preaching the very faith he formerly tried to destroy.' *24* And they gave glory to God because of me.

**F** *20 I declare before God that what I am writing is the truth.*

# PROLOGUE

The symmetrical structure of the first section centres upon the doxology, thus:

A    Paul is an apostle of Christ, sent not by men but by God, 1:1-2.
B    A blessing for the Galatians, 1:3.
C    Summary of the gospel of Christ, 1:4.
D    *Glory be to God,* 1:5.
C¹   Warning against defection from the gospel of Christ. There is no other gospel, 1:6-7.
B¹   A curse upon false teachers, however exalted, 1:8-9.
A¹   Paul is a servant of Christ, taught the gospel by Christ himself; he pleases not man but God, 1:10-12.

Here is the text:

A   *1:1* Paul, an apostle — not from men, nor through a man, but through Jesus Christ and God the Father who raised him from the dead — *2* I and all the brethren with me (greet) the churches of Galatia: B  *3* grace to you and peace from God our Father and the Lord Jesus Christ, C  *4* who gave himself for our sins, in order to rescue us from the present evil age, according to the will of God our Father, D  *5* to whom be the glory for ever and ever. Amen. C¹  *6* I am astonished that you are so quickly deserting the one who called you in the grace of Christ and going over to another gospel — *7* which is not another gospel, but certain persons are shaking you and would like to turn Christ's gospel upside down. B¹  *8* But if anyone, even ourselves or an angel from heaven, preaches to you a gospel other than the one we preached, let him be anathema! *9* We warned you before, and now I say it again: if anyone preaches to you a gospel other than the one you received, let him be anathema! A¹  *10* For am I now seeking the favour of men or of God? Or am I trying to please men? If I were still trying to please men, I should not be a servant of Christ. *11* For I inform you, brethren, that the gospel which was preached by me is not according to man. *12* Nor did I receive it from any man, nor was I taught it by any man; I received it through a revelation of Jesus Christ.

This section is the 'Introduction' to the Epistle, in the sense that it introduces the main themes which are to be elaborated throughout the following chapters. In A and A¹ St Paul affirms the authenticity of his apostolic commission and of the gospel which he has preached. He received from God and not from men the office and duty of preaching this particular gospel and no other. Here, as in the three narratives of his conversion in Acts (chapters 9, 22 and 26), the revelation by which he received his gospel is identified with the revelation by which he was made an apostle. [6] As he is sent, not by men, but by God the Father and by the Lord Jesus Christ, his duty is to please God and not men. He does not seek his own glory. To emphasize this, in the centre of the section he attributes all glory to God. In B and B[1] he uses his apostolic authority to bless the Galatians and to anathematize anyone who attempts to overturn their faith. In C and C[1] he repeats, in summary form, the gospel of Christ, and warns the Galatians not to go over to any other (so-called) gospel, because there is no other gospel but the one he himself has already preached to them. Even if he himself should one day preach another gospel, he is to be anathema.

*How do vv. 1-5 compare with Apoc 1:4-6?*

A Greek letter normally began with the name of the writer in the nominative, then the name of the addressee in the dative, then a brief greeting — for example: 'Paul to John greetings!' This formula was christianized by the substitution of the religious concepts 'grace and peace' for the secular 'greetings', and by mention of God the Father and of Christ — for example: 'Paul to John grace and peace from God the Father and from our Lord Jesus Christ!'

In Galatians, this formula is further elaborated. After his own name, St Paul places his title 'apostle' and a justification of it. After the name of Christ he gives a summary of Christ's work. And at the end he adds a doxology addressed to God the Father.

An interesting parallel has been pointed out in the prologue to the Apocalypse of St John. [7] Here again there is a description of the work of Christ and a closing doxology:

| | |
|---|---|
| *Paul,* an apostle — not from men, nor through a man, but through Jesus Christ and God the Father who raised him from the dead — I and all the brethren with me | *John* |
| *to the churches of Galatia* | *to the seven churches in Asia* |
| *grace to you and peace* | *grace to you and peace* |

---

6   This is right and proper. The great difference between an ordinary preacher and an apostle is that the apostle has *seen* the risen Lord. His conviction and his witness rest not on faith alone but on direct vision. But the vision still leaves room for faith—cf. Mt 28:17.

7   Cf. A. Farrer, *The Revelation of St John the Divine,* Oxford, 1964, pp. 60-62.

*from God our Father*

*from him who is and was and is to come,* and from the seven spirits that are before his throne,

*and the Lord Jesus Christ,*
who gave himself for our sins, in order to rescue us from the present evil age, according to the will of God our Father;

*and from Jesus Christ,* the faithful witness, the first of the dead to be reborn, the ruler of the kings of the earth, who has so loved us as to free us from our sins with his own life's blood, and has made of us a kingdom and a priestly people for God his Father;

*to him be glory for ever and ever. Amen.*

*to him be glory* and power *for ever and ever. Amen.*

St John describes the work of Christ in terms which imply that he achieved a new deliverance from Egyptian bondage, and created a new 'people of God', that is, a new Israel. There are clear allusions to Exod 19: 5-6:

Now therefore, if you will obey my voice and keep my covenant, you shall be my own possession among all the peoples; for all the earth is mine, and you shall be to me a kingdom of priests and a holy nation.

the ruler of the kings of the earth... who has made of us a kingdom and a priestly people for God his Father.

St Paul too describes Christ's work as a liberation ('to rescue us from the present evil age'), and later he describes the Church as 'the Israel of God' (Gal 6: 16), but he makes no direct allusion to the Exodus from Egypt as a type of the Redemption. From one point of view, the Exodus typology would have suited his purpose well: many of the things which Philo and other Jews have said of the Exodus are transferred by St Paul to the death and resurrection of Christ. [8] For Philo, the end of Israel's slavery and the beginning of

---

8   It is interesting to see how a modern rabbi explains 'freedom' to Jewish boys preparing for Bar Mitzvah. Rabbi Henry A. Cohen, in his excellent book, *A Basic Jewish Encyclopedia*, Hartford, Connecticut, 1965, pp. 82-83, writes as follows: 'The God of Israel is the God of freedom. The Ten Commandments begin, "I am the Lord, your God, who brought you out of the land of Egypt, out of the house of bondage" not, "I am the Lord, your God, who created heaven and earth." Freedom, Judaism teaches, must come and will come for all men and all peoples, for the God of Israel, the God of freedom, is the God of all mankind. . . . Freedom, however, does not mean license, the freedom of the jungle, doing what one pleases and when one pleases. "Let my people go" was the demand that Moses made in the name of God, but then the word of God continued, "that they may serve Me." It was not until the people of Israel received the Torah with its moral obligations that they learned the real mean-

the period of freedom came at the Exodus from Egypt. According to St Paul, Moses did not free Israel: the period of slavery lasted till the coming of Christ; it is he who leads the true Israel to freedom. But St Paul avoids explicit use of the Exodus-typology in Galatians — probably because he wishes to avoid the suggestion that Christ is a second Moses. But he may perhaps have had the Exodus typology in mind when he wrote the phrase 'in order to rescue us from the present evil age' (1:4). The parallel passage in Col 1:13 is even more reminiscent of the Exodus from Egypt: 'He has rescued us from the domain of darkness and transferred us into the kingdom of his beloved Son, through whom we have redemption, the forgiveness of our sins.' In both these passages, salvation is described as a divinely guided migration from one kingdom to another — of which the proto-type is surely the Exodus from Egypt to Canaan. So St John has brought into the open an idea which was lurking at the back of St Paul's mind.

The most remarkable divergence between the two texts is the mention of the 'seven spirits' in the Apocalypse, between the Father and Christ. They are not to be thought of as seven angels, but rather as the sevenfold Spirit of God — sevenfold both because seven is a perfect number connoting fulness, and because the spirits named in Isa 11:2 (LXX) are seven:

> The Spirit of the Lord shall rest upon him:
> the spirit of *wisdom* and *understanding,*
> the spirit of *counsel* and *strength,*
> the spirit of *knowledge* and *piety,*
> the spirit of *fear of the Lord* will fill him. [9]

St John's reason for introducing the Spirit of God may be that he felt the Spirit should be mentioned along with the Father and the Son; but perhaps his main concern was to prepare for mention of the Spirit in the second half of his introduction — for his composition too is symmetrical. [10] This structural consideration also explains why the Spirit is mentioned *between* the Father and the Son. Here is the text of Apoc 1:4-11.

A   4 John to the seven churches of Asia: grace to you and peace
B   from the One who is and was and is to come,     C   and from the

---

ing of freedom. He only is free, the Rabbis tell us, who follows and practises the Torah.' (Quoted by kind permission of the publisher, Hartmore House Inc.)

[9]   The RSV, following the Hebrew, omits 'piety' and thus reduces the seven to six.

[10]   Cf. N. W. Lund, *Studies in the Book of Revelation,* Chicago (Covenant Press), 1955.

seven spirits before his throne, **D** *5* and from Jesus Christ, the faithful witness, the first of the dead to be reborn, the ruler of the kings of the earth. To him who has so loved us as to free us from our sins with his own life's blood, *6* and who has made of us a kingdom and a priestly people for God his Father, **E** to him be glory and power for ever and ever. Amen. **D¹** *7* See, he is coming with the clouds: every eye will see him, even those who pierced him; and all the tribes of the earth will lament at the sight of him. So it shall be. Amen. **C¹** *9* I, John, your brother and your companion in affliction, in kingship, and in patient waiting for Jesus, was on the island of Patmos for having preached the word of God and borne witness to Jesus, when, on the Lord's day, I was rapt by the Spirit, *10* and I heard from behind me a voice as loud as a trumpet, which said: **B¹** *8* 'I am the alpha and the omega, says the Lord God, who is and was and is to come, the almighty. **A¹** *11* Write down in a book what you see, and send it to the seven churches — to Ephesus, Smyrna, Pergamum, Thyatira, Sardis, Philadelphia, and Laodicea.'

In speaking of the Spirit, St John is again making explicit something which he saw lurking in St Paul's mind. If, having studied St John's text, we ask why St Paul does not mention the Holy Spirit in his prologue, the answer probably is that he does. When he speaks of 'grace and peace', he is thinking of all the gifts of the Spirit. The proof of this is that at the other end of the first main division of the Epistle he speaks explicitly of the gift of the Spirit (cf. 3:1-4). So his prologue does allude, though not in so many words, to the Holy Spirit as well as to the Father and the Son. St John has simply made the reference a little more explicit.

A further point of comparison concerns the doxology. In the Apocalypse it is almost certainly addressed directly to Christ, in Galatians it seems to be addressed to God the Father, and therefore, from the Christological point of view, St John's text looks more 'advanced' than St Paul's. But here again St John may have taken his cue from St Paul: he may have noticed that St Paul has associated Jesus Christ so closely with the Father in vv. 1-3 that the relative pronoun 'to whom' in 1:5 can well refer to both.

### Why does St Paul insert his title of 'apostle'?

By proclaiming himself an 'apostle', St Paul was exposing himself to the charge of vainglory. So far as we can see from the Catholic Epistles of James, Peter, Jude and John, it was not the practice of the other apostles to give themselves high titles when introducing themselves. The seer of the Apocalypse introduces himself in v. 4

simply as 'John', then later gives himself some unassuming titles: 'your brother and your companion in affliction, in kingship, and in patient waiting for Jesus.'

In his earliest letters, St Paul gives himself no title. The Thessalonian Epistles both begin: 'Paul, Silvanus and Timothy to the church of the Thessalonians.' Presumably he decided to add the title 'apostle' after his adversaries had begun to say that he was not an apostle (cf. 1 Cor 9: 1) — that he was usurping the title and authority of an apostle without any right. In these circumstances it is understandable that he felt it necessary to insist on this title: he needed to retain it in order to safeguard his teaching authority. This was especially necessary in the Epistle to the Galatians, since he has to explain how in the Antioch incident he had dared to correct Peter in public and call him back to 'the truth of the gospel'. Undoubtedly Peter was held in great veneration: he had lived through the public ministry with Christ, he had denied him in his passion, he had been forgiven, and he had been made shepherd of the whole flock. Through these experiences God had made him a faithful and compassionate High Priest, and we must picture him as such in the fifties — an old man by the reckoning of those days, loved and venerated by his people. It must have been extremely painful for the members of the Church of Antioch to see him publicly reprehended by Paul. One can imagine the feeling of Peter's loyal supporters: 'Who is Paul to rise up against Peter? Peter we know, and James we know; but who on earth is Paul?' Paul's reply to such criticism is that he is an apostle no less than Peter: 'God who has worked in Peter to make him apostle of the Jews, has worked in me to make me apostle of the Gentiles' (2: 8). If Paul had been less than an apostle, it would have been outrageous for him to insist so resolutely on his own interpretation of the gospel and of its implications for the Gentiles. Some critics think that even granted that he was an apostle, his conduct was still outrageous. [11]

An 'apostle' is a plenipotentiary envoy of Christ, endowed with full authority to speak in his name. A notable feature of chapters 1 and 2 of Galatians is the way in which the whole argument assumes that St Paul's doctrine has no claim to acceptance unless it is apostolic. Apostolicity is the canon of orthodoxy. This arises from the nature of Christianity as a revealed religion: only the official recipients of the revelation are in a position to specify its content.

---

[11] Gaechter, *Petrus und seine Zeit*, p. 256, asks how Paul could so forget himself, and offers as excuse that he was still suffering the nervous after-effects of the stoning at Lystra.

St Paul's standing as an apostle of equal rank with the Twelve was not entirely secure in the early Church. St Luke calls him an 'apostle' only twice, and each time brackets him with Barnabas (Acts 14:4, 14). It has been inferred, with a reasonable degree of probability, that St Luke regarded Paul as an 'apostle' in the sense in which Barnabas could be called an apostle, that is, as an emissary of the church of Antioch. Eusebius, in his *History of the Church*, takes much the same view. [12] St Augustine, while conceding St Paul's right to the title, saw the difficulties, and expressed them amusingly in his exposition of psalm 118. After quoting 1 Cor 6:3, 'Do you not know that we shall judge angels?', he pictures Paul's hearers as replying: [13]

> What do you mean by boasting that you will be the judge? Where will you sit? The Lord appointed twelve seats for the twelve apostles. One fell — Judas. St Matthias was ordained to fill his place. So all twelve seats are occupied. First find somewhere to sit; then you can boast that you will be judge.

*How does St Paul introduce himself in other Epistles?*

No doubt St Paul thought carefully about the way in which he should introduce himself in his letters. If the surviving Epistles are arranged in the probable order of their composition, it is possible to discern the development of his thought on this point.

1 Thes    Paul, Silvanus and Timothy (no title)

2 Thes    Paul, Silvanus and Timothy (no title)

Phil [14]    Paul and Timothy, servants of Jesus Christ

Gal    Paul, an apostle — not from men nor through a man but through Jesus Christ and God the Father... and all the brethren with me

1 Cor    Paul, called to be an apostle of Jesus Christ by the will of God, and the brother Sosthenes

2 Cor    Paul, an apostle of Jesus Christ through the will of God, and the brother Timothy

Rom    Paul, the servant of Jesus Christ, called to be an apostle, set apart for God's gospel...

---

12 Cf. Eusebius, *H.E.*, I, 12.
13 This text is used in the Roman Breviary for the Common of Apostles out of paschal time.
14 Phil is placed here on the assumption that it was written during an 'Ephesian

Col    Paul, an apostle of Jesus Christ through the will of God, and the brother Timothy

Phm    Paul, a prisoner of Christ Jesus, and the brother Timothy

Eph    Paul, an apostle of Christ Jesus through the will of God

1 Tim    Paul, an apostle of Jesus Christ by order of God our Saviour and of Christ Jesus our hope

2 Tim    Paul, by God's will an apostle of Christ Jesus, sent to preach the promise of life which is in Christ Jesus

Tit    Paul, a servant of God and an apostle of Jesus Christ, charged to bring God's chosen ones to faith and to knowledge of the truth of our religion with its hope of eternal life

When writing to the Thessalonians and Philippians, St Paul modestly refrains from using any title of dignity. If Galatians was written before the Corinthian Epistles, it is easy to understand why it begins with the most emphatic claim of all to the title of apostle: this is the first letter written since his authority has been openly challenged. In writing his First Epistle to the Corinthians, although his authority has not yet been openly flouted at Corinth, he uses the title 'apostle', both because the Corinthians already know that his right to it has been challenged elsewhere (cf. 1 Cor 9:1-3), and because he sees that the growth of factions is already undermining his position at Corinth (cf. 1 Cor 1:12). In Second Corinthians, written after his authority had been flouted in Corinth, a more emphatic claim to the title of apostle might have been expected; but he *begins* this letter in a mood of exuberant joy and consolation. [15]

The extended form used in Romans looks as though it was designed to meet the charge of self-advertisement which Paul had incurred (cf. 2 Cor 3:1): he gives himself first the title of humility, 'servant', and only then the title of honour and authority, 'apostle'. In Colossians and Ephesians the neat formulation of Second Corinthians is resumed. Since the Epistle to Philemon is, ostensibly at least, a private communication, St Paul does not use a title of authority. The more elaborate formulations used in the Pastorals (1-2 Tim and Tit) probably betray the hand of a reviser or imitator. It is hard to believe that St Paul, writing to his own familiar and trusted lieutenants, would have introduced himself with such a fanfare.

---

captivity'. Cf. T. W. Manson, 'The Date of the Epistle to the Philippians,' in *Studies in the Gospels and Epistles*, Manchester, 1962, pp. 150-167.

[15] The tone changes at 10:1, and to such an extent that many critics believe chapters 10-13 to be part of another Epistle.

*Why did God choose a thirteenth Apostle?*

When we stop to think of it, how strange it is that after Christ had chosen, formed and commissioned twelve apostles to be the patriarchs of the renewed Israel (cf. Gal 6:16), he should then have called another 'unformed' man,[16] who had not witnessed his public ministry, to carry the gospel to the Gentiles! And why, after giving twelve apostles to the small nation of the Jews, did he give just one to the Gentiles? According to Lk 10:1, after appointing the Twelve, Christ appointed another seventy-two, corresponding, in the view of many commentators, to the seventy-two nations of the world. But the seventy-two seem to have left the task to Paul.

We cannot fathom the councils of God. St Paul, when contemplating a mystery such as this, exclaimed: 'How unsearchable are his judgments and how inscrutable his ways!' (Rom 11:33), but he said this only after he had made great efforts to understand the mystery in question. So we may follow his example.

Could it possibly be that Christ chose St Paul to take the gospel to the Gentiles, not in spite of, but because of his ignorance of the details of the public ministry? Perhaps the incidents and preaching of the public ministry were designed specially for the Jews, who were living under the law, in order to release them from the law, and Christ did not wish the gospel to be preached in exactly the same way to the Gentiles who had not lived under the law. Perhaps he did not wish the Gentiles to know too much about his life within the restraints of the law or about his bitter conflicts with the exponents of the law. (St Mark, writing for the Gentiles, omitted most of these things.) We have no reason to think that St Paul believed it his duty to instruct his Gentile converts in the details of the public ministry or to teach them Christian morality in the wording of the Sermon on the Mount. It was conjectured above that he did not furnish his Gentile churches with written gospels. The broad diffusion of the 'Two Ways', known to us chiefly from the *Didache, The Epistle of Barnabas,* and *The Apostolic Constitutions, Bk VII,* shows that the Sermon on the Mount was not found to be the ideal code for the instruction of Gentile converts. Does 'Give to all who ask' leave no room for discrimination in almsgiving? And does 'Judge not and you will not be judged' exempt every vagrant prophet and speaker in tongues from scrutiny? Some of the oriental modes of expression

---

[16] This is the probable meaning of the rare Greek word *ektrôma* (an unformed fetus) in 1 Cor 15:8. Cf. Gal 4:19.

used by Christ could not be transplanted into the Gentile world
without causing difficulties. They are causing difficulties to this day. [17]

This speculation leads to the question: 'What then? Would it be
better for us Gentiles not to have the four gospels?' One's first
impulse is to draw back from the question and abandon this line of
thought. But it is a real question how St Paul would have answered
it. And St Peter too appears to have had his doubts. According to
Clement of Alexandria, when he found out that St Mark had written
his gospel, 'he neither forbade it nor actively encouraged it'. [18] And
the Second Epistle of Peter, which purports to be Peter's spiritual
testament, contains no commendation of any written gospel.

But perhaps another line of speculation is better. Did God wish
to give the Gentiles as their apostle one in whom he had given a
truly staggering display of his power? Paul before his conversion was
the arch-persecutor of the Church — at all events the persecution
stopped when he was converted. It is hard to think how Christ could
have produced a more effective witness to his lordship than by converting the arch-persecutor. Paul himself offers this reason in 1 Tim
1:12-17 — or, if 1 Timothy is not from the hand of Paul, here is
the answer given by one of his disciples to the question why God
chose Paul:

> I give thanks to Christ Jesus our Lord, the source of my strength, for
> having shown his trust by setting me in this ministry, although previously
> I had been a blasphemer and had persecuted and ill-treated his followers.
> In spite of this, I was treated mercifully — because I had acted through
> ignorance in the time of my unbelief — and an abundance of our Lord's
> grace filled me with faith and Christian charity. It is a trustworthy saying,
> deserving of wholehearted acceptance, that 'It was to save sinners that
> Christ Jesus came into the world.' And the chief of sinners is myself.
> But I was treated with mercy, because Christ Jesus wanted to give a first
> demonstration in his dealings with me of the full extent of his patience,
> so as to set me up as an example for the encouragement of others who
> were to believe in him and gain eternal life. To the King of ages, the
> immortal, invisible and only God, be honour and glory for ever and
> ever. Amen.

This leads on to a further speculation, not unrelated to the first.
St Paul's kerygmatic argument was based not on any written gospel,

[17] Thus the problem of 'hermeneutics' arose within the first generation of the
Church's history. Just as the mental presuppositions of the modern secular
world differ from the presuppositions of the Greek civilization in which St Paul
preached, so the Greek civilization in which he preached was very different
from the Jewish, law-observing civilization in which Christ preached.
[18] Quoted by Eusebius, H.E., VI, 14. The Greek is curious: *protreptikôs mête
kôlusai mête protrepsasthai.*

or on the oral narrative of the events of the public ministry, but on the revelation granted him at the time of his conversion, confirmed by the witness of the other apostles (cf. 1 Cor 15: 4-5). It would be possible, and it might perhaps be better, for a preacher of today to follow this pauline method: to start from the conversion of Paul, and then to appeal to the gospels as confirmatory witnesses.

### Did St Paul think of himself as a new Joseph?

In Gen 50: 18-19, after the death of Israël, his sons the patriarchs came to Joseph 'and fell down before him and said, "Behold, we are your servants." But Joseph said to them, "Fear not, for *am I in the place of God?*" ' Instead of this last clause, the Septuagint has 'for I am of God' (i.e. 'I am a servant of God'), which Philo explained thus: 'He declared that he had not received his commission at the hands of men, but had been appointed by God' [19] — a remarkable parallel to Gal 1 : 1.

There is little likelihood that St Paul had read the work of Philo in which this passage occurs. But the parallel suggests the question whether St Paul saw in himself another Joseph. The apostles in Jerusalem are the patriarchs of the new Israel, and Paul claims to be their brother. He sought them out in Jerusalem, and for a while worked with them, but when he stirred up trouble, they packed him off, not to Egypt, but at least to the Gentiles (cf. Acts 9: 26-30). Later, when his brethren in Jerusalem were suffering famine, the brother whom they had sent abroad was able to supply their wants. The patriarchs of the old Israel failed to make Canaan their own, but Joseph who was sent abroad became master of all the land of Egypt (cf. Gen 41: 41); and in the same way the patriarchs of the New Israel failed to convert the Jews of Palestine, but Paul who was sent abroad established flourishing churches.

It has been suggested that St Luke saw the resemblance between Paul and Joseph, because Acts 20: 37 sounds like a deliberate reminiscence of Gen 50: 1: [20]

| Then Joseph fell on his father's face and wept over him and kissed him. | All wept much, and falling upon Paul's neck, they kissed him. |

If the allusion is deliberate, it is better to identify Paul with Israel (Jacob), and the presbyters of Ephesus with Joseph and his brothers.

[19]  *The Migration of Abraham,* 22 (Loeb IV).
[20]  Cf. M. Wilcox, *The Semitisms of Acts,* London, 1965, p. 67.

If Gal 1:1 does contain a typological reference to Gen 50:19, the point will be that Paul, being like Joseph a servant of God, will not harm his brothers and will forgive them the offence they have committed against him (cf. 4:12). [21]

### *The source of St Paul's apostleship — what views does he exclude?*

St Paul appears to reject two possible explanations of his apostleship: he is 'sent' [22] (1) 'not from men' and (2) 'not through a man'. If he has in mind things said about him by his adversaries, the former will mean 'I am not simply a missionary sent out by the members of the church of Antioch,' and the latter will mean 'I am not self-appointed' [23] (for his adversaries cannot have been saying that he received his commission from St Peter or St John).

But in view of the structural link with 1:10a (A and A¹ on p. 49), it is much more likely that Paul has in mind no particular group of men and no particular man. [24] He means that the source of his authority is not human but divine (thus he distinguishes himself from false apostles); and that his authority was not mediated to him by any of the apostles, or by a prophet such as Ananias (cf. Acts 9:10-18) or by anyone else, but came to him directly from Christ (thus he distinguishes himself from his lieutenants, Timothy, Titus, etc., who received their authority from him and carried letters of commendation from him [25] ).

It seems, then, that the phrase 'not from men nor through a man' was introduced, not primarily to exclude any particular misrepresentation of his authority by adversaries, but rather to emphasize by contrast the divine origin of his apostolate. St Paul constantly thinks in contrasts — in this section there are contrasts between human and divine authority, blessing and cursing, the true gospel and a false gospel, this age and the age to come, the glory of God and the glory of man.

---

[21] Joseph in Egypt feigned anger and accused his brothers of having come to spy on him (cf. Gen 42:9-12). Is there perhaps a typological allusion to this in Gal 2:4?

[22] The prepositions depend on the verbal idea contained in the noun 'apostle' which means 'one sent'.

[23] Cf. Jn 7:18.

[24] For this reason, among others (see G in G), there is much to be said for reading 'not from men nor through men'—with Origen, Chrysostom (PL 61, 611), Cyril of Alexandria, and some of the lesser mss.

[25] Cf. 2 Cor 3:1.

But if the Galatians were South Galatians, they knew very well that St Paul had been sent out from Antioch and had returned to Antioch. Inevitably, therefore, when they heard Paul describe himself as an 'apostle not from men', they would think of Antioch, and understand that he was disowning any special link with that church. [26] This is more understandable if, after the incident, the church of Antioch had sided with Peter and disowned Paul. His adversaries may have been saying: 'Paul was previously an apostle of the church of Antioch; now that Antioch has disowned him, he has no authority at all.' If so, St Paul is replying that the disapproval of the church of Antioch makes no difference, since his authority comes directly from Christ. This may have been slightly offensive to the Galatians, if Barnabas had taught them to look to Antioch as their mother church.

*Why does St Paul not say 'through Jesus Christ and from God the Father'?*

If the 'from' had been added, the words would form a neat chiasm:

not *from* men nor *through* a man
but *through* Jesus Christ and *from* God the Father.

To one who loved symmetry as much as Paul did, it must have been painful to omit the second 'from'. No doubt he did so for a good theological reason, and what can this be but that he did not wish to subordinate Christ to the Father by a distinction of prepositions? He decided to use one preposition for both, and chose the preposition 'through' rather than 'from' — perhaps because Christ was in some sense the Mediator between God the Father and mankind (cf. 1 Tim 2:5). Then, having decided not to use a distinct preposition for 'the Father', he allows 'the Father' too to be governed by the preposition 'through' although the Father is not in any sense a mediator. [27]

The choice of these prepositions was certainly not made carelessly and without reflection, for in the very next verse St Paul reintroduces 'God the Father' and 'Jesus Christ', in reverse order, and this time unites them under the preposition 'from'. This is most instructive. St Paul has in mind the mystery of the relation between God the Father and his Son, and finds that the prepositions which we use in discourse about ordinary human relationships do not fit. Christ was

---

[26] Cf. Bonnard, Gal, p. 19.
[27] Similarly in 1:10 he allows 'God' to be the object of the verb *to persuade*, though strictly God is not open to persuasion.

in some sense a Mediator, but he was not an intermediary like Moses (cf. Gal 3 : 19), for in Christ God deals *directly* with man: 'God was in Christ, reconciling the world to himself' (2 Cor 5 : 19; cf. Col 2 : 9). The position of Christ *before* the Father in v. 1 was dictated by the pattern of the section. [28] Lest anyone should suppose that Paul is exalting the Son above the Father, he immediately repeats their names in v. 3 in the reverse order. Dogmatic theologians are justified in using this as evidence that he taught the coequality of the Son with the Father.

St Jerome points out that, strictly speaking, St Paul's words in 1 : 1-2 and 1 : 10-12 imply that Christ is not a man: [29]

> If the gospel of Paul is not according to man, and he did not receive it or learn it from man, but through a revelation of Jesus Christ, then Jesus Christ, who revealed the gospel to Paul, is not a man.

St Augustine too made a comment of the same sort: Paul, he says, was sent by Jesus Christ who after his resurrection was 'wholly God' (*per Jesum Christum totum iam Deum*) because no longer mortal. [30] But he clarified his meaning in his *Retractations*: [31]

> In respect of his immortality, Christ who is God is no longer man; but in respect of the substance of the human nature in which he ascended to heaven, even now Christ Jesus, the mediator between God and men, is a man (1 Tim 2 : 5), for he will come just as those saw him who watched as he went into heaven (Acts 1 : 11).

Augustine perceives that 'men' and 'man' have a pejorative sense here. Paul is not sent by 'men' who are infected with death, therefore with weakness, therefore with sin, but by one who having risen from the dead has passed out of the realm of death and weakness and sin in which 'every man is a liar'. [32]

## *Why is the Resurrection mentioned in verse 1?*

The reference to the resurrection at the end of the parenthesis in v. 1 may seem superfluous, but is not. Both St Paul and St John teach that Christ did not receive power to communicate the Holy Spirit

---

[28]  The position of Cephas in Gal 2 : 4 may also be due to the chiasm. In such a pattern the centre is the place of honour.

[29]  PL 26, 446 C; cf. 336 D.

[30]  Cf. PL 35, 2107-8.

[31]  *Retractationum*, I, 24, 1 (PL 32, 623 A).

[32]  Cf. Pelagius, Gal, pp. 8-9: 'Wherever Scripture speaks of "man" without qualification, the word has a pejorative sense, as in Ps 115 : 2: "Every man is a liar," and Mk 8 : 27: "Who do men say that I am?"'

until after the resurrection (cf. 1 Cor 15 : 45; Jn 7 : 38). It is the risen
Christ who has power to invest his apostles with the great spiritual
powers which Paul is conscious of possessing. That is why both here
and in the opening verses of Romans he traces his apostolic powers
from the Father through (or rather in) the *Risen* Christ to himself.
He holds that an apostle is one through whom the Risen Lord exercises his powers of giving life (cf. v. 3) and pronouncing judgment
(cf. vv. 8-9).

Probably, too, St Augustine is right in thinking that the phrase
'who raised him from the dead' contains the reason why Christ is not
reckoned as a 'man' in v. 1 : because he has been raised from the
dead to die no more, he has entirely escaped from death, weakness
and mortality.

## *'All the brethren who are with me'* — *Who are these persons?*

Ramsay understands this phrase to mean that Paul is writing 'in
the name of a whole great Christian community'. He then asks what
community this can be, and, on his own (early) dating, there are only
two possible answers: Jerusalem or Antioch. As Jerusalem is for many
reasons out of the question, he decides it must be Antioch. Then he
suggests that before the letter was despatched, it must have been
publicly read and approved, either by the whole church of Antioch
or more probably by its representatives. This view, he thinks, has the
advantage of explaining why there is no mention of Antioch in the
body of the letter.

> The Epistle is apt to produce on the modern reader a certain painful
> impression, as not recognising the right of Antioch to some share in the
> championship of freedom. Antioch had taken a very prominent and
> honourable part in the struggle for freedom; yet, on the ordinary theory
> of origin, [33] it is not alluded to in his letter, except to point out that
> every Jew in Antioch betrayed on one occasion the cause of freedom.
> Considering what Antioch had done for Christianity and for Paul, every-
> one who follows the ordinary theory must, I think, feel a pang of regret
> in Paul's interest that he did not by some word or expression give more
> generous recognition to her services. In a letter, in which he speaks so
> much about the actual details of the struggle, he seems, on that view, to
> speak only of his own services, and hardly at all to allude to the services
> of others. But when all Antiochian Christians are associated with the
> Apostle as issuing this authoritative letter, we feel that the Church of
> Antioch is placed in the honourable position which she had earned. [34]

---

[33]  I.e., that it was written from Ephesus or Philippi.
[34]  Ramsay, Gal, pp. 242-244. The quotation is from p. 244.

Unfortunately, Ramsay's reasoning is weak at various points and cannot be accepted. For reasons given above, his dating places the Antioch incident and the writing of the letter much too early. By 57, there were other great Christian communities — Ephesus, Thessalonica, Philippi, Corinth. And anyway, 'all the brethren who are with me' does not imply a great Christian community. Nor is it likely that after the painful incident at Antioch all the brethren of that church would have been willing to endorse this Epistle. Nor does Ramsay's theory really explain why Antioch is not mentioned — St Paul could easily have written 'I and all the brethren of the church of Antioch'. Nor can we be sure that St Paul read out the Epistle for the approval of all the brethren who were with him. A man who has such absolute certainty as is expressed in Gal 1:8-9 is not likely to submit his writing to the censorship of his inferiors. As apostle of all the Gentile churches, St Paul felt he could send greetings in their name without needing to consult them. Hence he can write in Rom 16:16: 'Greet one another with a holy kiss. All the churches of Christ greet you.'

It must, therefore, be admitted that, as Ramsay has tactfully pointed out, St Paul is less generous to his former associates at Antioch than we could have hoped. From the Acts of the Apostles we know that Peter, Barnabas and the Church of Antioch played a great part in winning liberty for the Gentiles. St Paul gives them less credit than they deserve.

The same phrase, 'the brethren who are with me', is used at the end of the Epistle to the Philippians, where it seems to mean, not all the brethren who are in the place where St Paul is living, but only his immediate entourage (4:22): 'The brethren who are with me greet you, and so do all the saints, especially those of Caesar's household.' Since in Galatians there is no mention of a community of 'saints' (i.e. Christians) in addition to the brethren who are with St Paul, it is a reasonable conjecture that at the time of writing either he is on his travels with a small group of associates, or if he is in a large church such as Ephesus, he has not chosen to discuss the Galatian crisis at public meetings of that church. Lightfoot, who places Galatians between the composition of Second Corinthians and Romans, conjectures that St Paul wrote it while travelling through Macedonia or Achaea. Those who date it just before Second Corinthians can hold that it was written at Ephesus. In favour of the latter view is the word 'all' which is probably emphatic (implying 'many'). [35]

---

[35] Cf. G in G, p. 184, on 4:26.

St Paul cannot have had many companions with him on his journey
through Macedonia.

*'To the churches of Galatia' — Why is there no mention of pres-
byters or bishops?*

According to Acts 14:23, at the end of the first missionary
journey, before returning to Antioch, Paul and Barnabas 'appointed
presbyters for the disciples in every church'. One of their principal
tasks was to watch over the faith of the disciples (cf. Acts 20:29-31).
It is therefore surprising that St Paul does not make special mention
of them in the introductory verses of Galatians.

The only Epistle in which the introduction contains mention of
the local hierarchy is Philippians:

> From Paul and Timothy, servants of Christ Jesus, to all God's people at
> Philippi in Christ Jesus, with their bishops and deacons: grace and
> peace to you from God our Father and from our Lord Jesus Christ (1:1-2).

The reason for this exception may be that in this Epistle St Paul has
to thank the Philippians for a gift of money, collected no doubt by
the bishops and deacons. But this does not really explain the omission
of the local hierarchy in the other Epistles.

Could the explanation perhaps be that St Paul did not wish to
encourage bishops [36] and deacons to think themselves in any way superior to God's people? If the clergy are but the servants of God's
people, there is no reason why they should be singled out for honorific
mention. [37]

*The Blessing (v. 3) — Is this formula taken from the liturgy?*

Although Paul is indignant with the Galatians, he begins and ends
the letter with a blessing:

> Grace and peace be upon you from God our Father and our Lord Jesus
> Christ. (1:3)
> The grace of our Lord Jesus Christ be with your spirit, brethren.
> Amen. (6:18)

Both formulae sound as though they are taken from the liturgy.
Probably St Paul intended the Epistle to be read out during the

---

[36] St Paul does not distinguish between 'bishops' and 'presbyters'.
[37] See below on 4:2, pp. 336-337.

liturgical gatherings of the Galatian churches. Vv. 3-5 are written from beginning to end in the language of the liturgy.

A very high Christology is implied in these formulae. In 1:3 Christ is named alongside of the Father as the source of blessings. His role is not distinguished from the Father's by means of a separate preposition; on the contrary, any such distinction is avoided.

It has been suggested that the apostolic Church found itself worshipping Christ as God before it had any clear formulation and explanation of the divinity of Christ and of his coequality with the Father. [38] The clearest expressions of Christ's divinity are very closely related to the liturgy (cf. Rom 9:5; Heb 1:8; Jn 1:18).

## What does St Paul mean by 'grace and peace'?

St Thomas Aquinas has an attractive explanation of the formula 'grace and peace': [39]

> The blessings he wishes them are two which include all spiritual goods. The first is 'grace' which is the beginning of spiritual life, for the Gloss attributes to 'grace' the forgiveness of sins, which is the first stage in spiritual life. For no one can live a true spiritual life unless he first dies to sin. The second is 'peace', which is the quiescence of the mind in its end — this is said in the Gloss to be reconciliation with God. Thus when he wishes them the beginning and end of all spiritual goods, the Apostle includes, as it were between two extremes, the desire that every kind of good may come to them.

But in Galatians, the words 'grace' and 'peace' both take on a special significance: St Paul's converts are in danger of setting aside the grace of God (cf. 2:21) in favour of the law, and the peace of the Galatian churches is seriously threatened by bitter theological disputes (cf. 5:15).

## Why does St Paul place a summary of the gospel in his prologue (1:4-5)?

Immediately after the initial greeting, St Paul reasserts the central doctrine of the gospel, which he believes to be threatened by the

---

[38] Cf. Wainwright, *The Trinity in the New Testament*, pp. 58-60.
[39] St Thomas, Gal, 383 D. He refers, not to the *Glossa Ordinaria* (i.e. the brief 'Commentary in Common Use') by Walafrid Strabo (PL 114, 560-588), but to the *Glossa Interlinearis* by Anselm of Laon, which was often placed between the lines of the Vulgate in medieval texts.

propaganda of the Judaizers: that the forgiveness of sins comes to us from Christ's death on the Cross, and is not the reward of any efforts which we ourselves might make. Sinful men are caught in a slavery from which they cannot escape by their own efforts; a divine intervention was necessary and has been granted. Christ has taken away our sins and liberated us from our former slavery by his death on the Cross. This doctrine is repeated at the centre of the Epistle (4:4-5) and again at the end (6:14-15).

It also reappears at the other end of the first main division (3:1-4), where St Paul says that when he evangelized the Galatians he 'placarded' Christ crucified before their eyes. The word translated 'placarded' is ambiguous; it also means 'to write at the head of' (e.g. of a list). So 3:1 can also refer back to 1:4-5. The Epistle repeats the pattern of Paul's kerygma: he starts by placarding Christ's death before the eyes of his reader.

The purpose of the Epistle is to evangelize the Galatians all over again (cf. 4:19). That is why St Paul keeps reiterating the substance of his gospel: justification is through faith in Christ's cross; what matters is not circumcision but being created anew by the gift of the Holy Spirit. If, as was suggested above, St Paul began with the Antioch Discourse already made and composed the first and third divisions of the Epistle to frame it, the contents of the opening verses were to some extent dictated by the contents of 3:1-4.

*The First Subsection, 1:1-5*

## THE CHURCHES OF GALATIA

The first section of the Epistle divides into two subsections, vv. 1-5 and vv. 6-12, in each of which the usual symmetry of construction can be observed. The first is as follows:

**A** *1 : 1* Paul, an apostle — not from men nor through a man, but **B** through Jesus Christ and God the Father who raised him from the dead *2* (and all the brethren who are with me)   **C** to the churches of Galatia:   *3* grace and peace   **B¹** from God our Father and the Lord Jesus Christ *4* who gave himself for our sins,   **A¹** in order to rescue us from the present evil age, according to the will of God our Father; *5* to him be glory for ever and ever. Amen.

E

The preposition 'from' and 'through' introduced in A are repeated in reverse order at the beginning of B and of B¹. The names of Jesus Christ and God the Father introduced in B are repeated in the reverse order in B¹. In B there is a relative clause referring to God the Father and speaking of the resurrection; in B¹ there is a relative clause referring to Christ and speaking of his crucifixion. [40] C speaks of 'grace and peace', gifts of the Holy Spirit (cf. 3:1-5 at the end of this division). The link between A and A¹ is not immediately obvious but becomes fairly clear when the phrase 'the present evil age (or generation)' is recognized as a synonym for 'men' (i.e. sinful men). The point is this: Christ died for our sins and was raised by the Father in order to take us out of the evil 'generation' of sinful 'men'. Paul, the apostle, is God's servant in carrying out this plan. His commission is not from 'men', nor is he obeying the will of any 'man'. He is working for the glory of God.

This subsection casts precious light on St Paul's way of thinking about 'the churches': a church is a community of men whom God has 'called out' and rescued from their evil generation into the new world which receives grace and peace (gifts of the Holy Spirit) from the Father through or in his Son risen and glorified.

### What is meant by 'the present evil age'?

Jewish rabbis often contrast 'the present age' and 'the age to come', but they think of the age to come as following after the end of the present age. [41] St Paul cannot be using the phrase in this simple way. At least we must say that he regards the two ages as overlapping: the unregenerate remain in 'the present age' while at the same time believers have been transferred to 'the age to come'. But St Paul does not say that 'the age to come' is already here. [42] Hence it is probably wiser to explain the phrase 'the present evil age' by itself, without reference to 'the age to come'. (The division of history into two ages, B.C. and A.D., is too simple: the evil age continues, and the age to come is here only in an anticipatory sense.)

---

[40] In the Greek these are two matching aorist genitive participles. See G in G, p. 12.
[41] Cf. Sasse, TDNT, s.v. *aiôn*, I, p. 206.
[42] He does not say, for example, 'Christ has transferred us into the age to come.' The nearest approach to such a statement is Heb 6:5: 'having experienced the word of God and the powers of the age to come'; but even here the age to come remains future—all that is given in the present is a foretaste. Cf. Mt 12:28.

At the other end of the Epistle occurs the sentence 'through whom the world is crucified to me and I to the world' (6 : 14). St Paul means that through baptism into union with Christ he has 'died out' of this present 'world', or out of this present 'age'. Strictly speaking, 'age' refers to time, and 'world' refers to space; but both words are used to signify the present world-order as a whole, without particular reference to time or space. And they refer, not directly to the space-time framework of this world order, but to the men who live in it. Almost invariably they have a strong pejorative connotation: this 'age', or this 'world', is evil because the men who live in it are evil and corrupt. This pejorative note is clear in such texts as 1 Cor 2 : 6: 'We do make known a kind of wisdom to the spiritually mature, but it is not the wisdom of this world, or of the rulers of this world, who are passing away'; and 2 Cor 4 : 3-4: 'If our gospel is veiled in any way, it is veiled only from the sight of men who are on the way to perdition; the God of this world has blinded their unbelieving minds within them'; and Lk 18 : 8: 'the sons of this world are shrewder than the sons of light'. So in Gal 1 : 4 the adjective 'evil' simply emphasizes something which is implicit in the noun 'age' (aiôn) anyway.

In the gospels there is a third word which has almost exactly the same sense as 'age' and 'world', namely 'generation' — for example, in the phrase 'an evil and adulterous generation' (Mt 12 : 39). In Col 1 : 26 this word occurs in parallelism with 'age': 'The mystery that has been hidden from the ages and from the generations'. Perhaps the most remarkable use of this word is in Mk 9 : 19, where Jesus is told that his disciples have failed to cure an epileptic boy. He exclaims: 'O unbelieving generation, how long shall I be with you? How long shall I endure you? Bring him to me.' Here Christ seems to be looking forward to the day when he will depart from the present world, the present age, or the present generation, and ascend into the world to come, where there is no unbelief, and into the kingdom of heaven, where the power of God reigns supreme.

So when St Paul says in Gal 1 : 4 that Christ offered himself for us 'to rescue us from the present evil age', he means that Christ was opening up the way for us to escape from the present generation of evil 'men' (cf. 1 : 1) into the kingdom of God. This happens in an anticipatory sense while we still remain physically 'in this world', through the gift of the Holy Spirit, whereby the powers of the world to come (cf. Heb 6 : 5) are already at work within us. And the process will be completed at the resurrection of the body.

If 'age' in 1:4 is synonymous with 'generation', St Paul may be deliberately echoing Ps 11:8 where the Septuagint, literally translated, has:

> Thou, O Lord, wilt guard us,
>     and wilt preserve us from this generation
>         and unto the age (i.e. for ever).

Here the Targum adds the word 'evil', [43] giving an even closer parallel to St Paul's words.

Theodore of Mopsuestia has a particularly fine theological comment on this v. 4. He draws into a synthesis several important strands in St Paul's thought: [44]

> If the first man (Adam) had remained immortal as he was, there would be no 'present' life, for life would have no end. But since he became mortal (thnêtos) through sin, this life of ours is called 'the present life' in contrast to the other which is to come hereafter. In this life, we are able to sin and therefore we have need of laws; but in the life to come we shall have no need of any commandments, since we shall be preserved from all sin by the grace of the Spirit.

'Mortal' is not a fully satisfactory equivalent for the Greek thnêtos, which means not simply 'able to die in the future' but also 'infected with death here and now'. The Hebrew mind does not make a sharp disjunction between 'life' and 'death', as we do. As a rule when we say that a man is alive, we mean that he is not dead, and when we say that he is dead, we mean that he is not alive — though we do sometimes say that a man is 'more dead than alive'. But to the Hebrew mind, there is no sharp disjunction: sickness and physical danger are the beginnings of death. To be physically ill or at the mercy of one's enemies is like standing in the sea with the water rising. So the psalmist can pray (Ps 69:14-15):

> Deliver me out of the mire,
>     and let me not sink.
> Let me be delivered from them that hate me,
>     and out of the deep waters.
> Let not the waterflood overwhelm me,
>         neither let the deep swallow me up;
>             and let not the pit shut her mouth upon me.

To the Semitic mind, water is an image of death in the active sense (Death, the demonic power), and baptism is a suitable image for death

---

43  Cf. Wilcox, *The Semitisms of Acts,* p. 30.
44  Theodore, *Gal,* p. 7. Cf. G in G, p. 12.

in the passive sense, that is of succumbing, suddenly or gradually, to the powers of Death. [45]

Theodore is using this Semitic, Biblical notion of 'death'. He means that as a result of Adam's sin his posterity is infected with death throughout its 'life'. This spiritual deadness manifests itself in moral weakness and in sin. If man were not infected with it, there would be no need of the law. Thus law belongs essentially to the present death-infected age, and Christians, in so far as they share in the risen life of Christ, have passed out of the present evil age into a realm where there is no need of law. So Theodore's comment reveals the connection in St Paul's thought between liberation from sin, liberation from death, liberation from this world, and liberation from law.

To go one step further, Theodore's comment helps us to see how perceptive St John was in introducing into his paraphrase of Gal 1 : 1-5 the title 'first-born of the dead'. [46] This world or this age is the world of the spiritually dead. Christ was the first to die out of this world of death and be born into the world of everlasting life.

Very good sense is obtained, therefore, by taking 'age' in v. 4 as a synonym for 'generation'. But perhaps the word 'age' has other associations for St Paul, which 'generation' has not. It may belong to the family of words in which he expresses his ideas about angels and demons. There is a parallel passage in Eph 2 : 2-5 :

> You who were once dead by reason of your transgressions and sins, in which you walked according to the age of this world (*kata ton aiôna tou kosmou toutou*), according to the prince of the powers of the air, of the spirit that now works in the sons of unbelief — you who were dead by reason of your transgressions he restored to life with Christ.

The parallelism between 'the age of this world' and 'the prince of the power of the air' strongly suggests that for St Paul 'the age' is the name of a demonic power. Must we, then, complicate the interpretation of Gal 1 : 4 by reading in it a reference to liberation from the demonic powers? [47] This is a difficult question. When St Paul describes the redemption in Col 2 : 14-15, he explains it in terms of the overthrow of demonic powers. These powers are also mentioned in Galatians, but they are far less prominent. The difficulty is: should we read Galatians assuming that the demonology of Colossians is

---

[45] Cf. Goulder, *Type and History in Acts,* pp. 36-37.
[46] See above, pp. 50-53.
[47] The last petition of the Our Father presents a similar problem: 'Deliver us from evil' or 'from the Evil One'?

already in St Paul's mind? Or should we regard his demonology as a later development of his thought, stimulated by the peculiar character of the false doctrine attacked in Colossians?

Since the two Epistles are separated by only a few years (57-62), since Galatians is far too brief to be a full account of St Paul's thought at the time of writing, and since there are some hints in Galatians of the cosmology and demonology of Colossians, it seems wiser not to postulate any important development in St Paul's thought between the writing of the two Epistles, and therefore to use Colossians to amplify the arguments sketched in Galatians.

Let us then consider (1) how Christ's death dealt with our sins, and (2) how he delivers us from the present evil age.

## How did Christ's death deal with our sins?

The expression 'deal with' is deliberately vague, because St Paul's phrase 'who gave himself *for* our sins' is vague too. He must mean: Christ offered himself as a sacrifice for our sins, to remove our sins, or to expiate our sins. The phrase is concerned, not with the prevention of future sins, but with the expiation or wiping out of sins already committed. How, then, did Christ's death produce this effect?

Before attempting to answer the question, it is as well to observe that the efficacy of faith in the Cross (or in Christ's death) is not dependent on our ability to explain the exact nature of the connection between Christ's death and the forgiveness of sins. When we switch on an electric light or fire, we do not need to know how electricity is generated or how it works; it suffices to know that *here* is a source of power, and *this* is the way to draw upon it. [48] Similarly we do not need to know how Christ's death liberated the purifying power of the Holy Spirit; it suffices to know that it did, and that the way to draw upon this power is to believe.

Some Jewish teachers have refused to speculate about the way in which sacrifice effects forgiveness or obtains forgiveness, on the grounds that theirs is a revealed religion and the means of expiation are to be accepted humbly and unquestioningly. To speculate about

---

[48] This illustration, proposed by L. Hodgson, *The Bible and the Training of the Clergy*, London, 1963, pp. 89-95, is in perfect agreement with St Paul's argument and even with his vocabulary in Galatians. The verb *katargeisthai* in 5:4 expresses exactly what happens to an electric circuit when the plug is pulled out of the power-point: it 'goes dead'. (5:4-6 is another important summary of St Paul's gospel.)

*how* it works is an impertinence; it suffices to know *that* this is what
divine providence has disposed. One must admire the reverence and
obedience implied in this attitude. But it is an attitude which, in
many things, St Paul did not share. Therefore if we wish to understand his letter we must try to find out what explanation he had in
mind when he made such statements as Gal 1: 4-5; 4: 4-5; 6: 14-15.

The Jews believed that death has power to expiate sins. A condemned man had to say before his execution: 'May my death expiate
all my sins.' [49] If the death of a criminal, willingly accepted as a fitting
punishment, expiates his sin, what will be the efficacy of the death
of a just man? The Jews had a strong sense of the solidarity of the
family, of the race, and of mankind as a whole. It was understood,
at least from the time of Second Isaiah, that the death of a just man,
freely accepted, can expiate the sins of others — or, looking at it
from God's point of view, that God will accept the sufferings and
death of the innocent in expiation of the sins of his guilty brethren.

> He was wounded for our transgressions,
>     he was bruised for our iniquities;
> upon him was the chastisement that made us whole,
>     and with his stripes we are healed.
> All we like sheep have gone astray;
>     we have turned every one to his own way;
> and the Lord has laid on him
>     the iniquity of us all.          (Isa 53 : 5-6)

It is disputed whether this should be called 'substitution'. The theory
of 'penal substitution', according to which Christ became a sinner
(or the Sinner) and was punished as such, is certainly to be rejected;
Jesus, while bearing the burden of other men's sins, remained sinless,
and he was not 'punished', because he was not guilty. But in another
sense, Isaiah 53 does announce the substitution of Christ for sinners:
the Lord has laid sufferings on him instead of laying punishment on
us all. [50] But 'substitution' is a misleading word, since Christ's sufferings do not dispense believers from the duty of joining their
sufferings to his. [51]

The commentators who think that the phrase 'for our sins' in
Gal 1: 4 is a deliberate allusion to Isa 53: 6, 11-12, are probably

---

[49] Sanh. VI, 2; cf. J. Jeremias, *The Central Message of the New Testament*,
p. 48; also Rom 6:7, on which see K. G. Kuhn, 'Rm 6, 7', ZNTW 30 (1931),
pp. 305-10; G. F. Moore, *Judaism*, I, pp. 517-552.
[50] Cf. the excellent discussion of 'substitution' and 'solidarity' in Galot, *La
Rédemption*, pp. 249-280.
[51] See below, on 3:4, pp. 223-224.

right. [52] St Paul uses the same phrase 'for our sins' in 1 Cor 15:3:

> I handed on to you what I had myself received:
>> that Christ died for our sins, according to the Scriptures;
>> that he was buried;
>> that he rose again on the third day, according to the Scriptures.

In both cases, the phrase 'according to the Scriptures' probably qualifies the whole of the clause to which it is attached. That is to say: the Scriptures foretold not only that Christ would die, but that he would die for our sins; and they foretold not only that he would rise again, but also that he would rise on the third day. In the latter case, the passage from 'the Scriptures' is most probably Hosea 6:2:

> After two days he will revive us,
>> and on the third day he will raise us up,
>> that we may live before him.

This is the only O.T. text which refers to resurrection on the third day. [53] In the former case, the reference must be to Isa 53, which is the only passage in the Old Testament containing the idea that 'he died for our sins'. [54] So the phrase 'for our sins' in Gal 1:4 is probably to be understood in the same way: Christ as the Suffering Servant made vicarious satisfaction for our sins.

In Col 2:14, St Paul says that Christ 'cancelled the invoice of debts to the law which stood against us, by nailing it to the cross'. He means that Christ died with a tablet or *titulus* nailed to his cross, declaring that he was guilty of treason. He was innocent of that crime, and his death did not expiate it. The crimes which his death did expiate are: our sins, our violations of God's law. St Paul means that to understand Christ's death, we must picture the Cross with Pilate's *titulus* removed, and the list of our transgressions in its place — stuck on a nail like a butcher's bill that has been paid. [55]

In the very next verse, Col 2:15, St Paul goes on to speak of the demonic powers: 'Having stripped off the powers and principalities, he made a public spectacle of them, having triumphed over them

[52] E.g. Schlier, Gal, p. 8. Miss M. D. Hooker, *Jesus and the Servant*, pp. 118-119, disagrees with this view. She maintains that 1 Cor 15:3 is a summary of the primitive kerygma, of which we have a fuller version in St Paul's speech at Pisidian Antioch (Acts 14:27-30), and that 'according to the Scriptures' in 1 Cor 15:3 refers to all the Scripture passages prophesying and prefiguring the crucifixion and resurrection. 'There is thus no justification for believing that the words "according to the Scriptures" have special reference to "for our sins", and do not refer simply to the fact of Christ's death.'
[53] Cf. my review of Lindars, *New Testament Apologetic*, in HJ 4 (1963), p. 186.
[54] Cf. J. Jeremias, *The Central Message*, p. 39.
[55] Cf. Jeremias, ibid., p. 37.

on it (i.e. on the Cross).' This brings us to the second question: Does 'the present evil age' mean the present period of salvation history in which the evil powers still retain control? [56]

## How does Christ deliver us from 'the present evil age'?

The phrase 'in order that he might rescue us from the present evil age' depends directly on 'who gave himself for our sins'. Hence the subject of 'that he might rescue' is 'Christ' (not 'the Father'), and it is tempting to say that St Paul connects our 'rescue' or 'redemption' directly with Christ's death (not with the resurrection). However, account must be taken of the chiastic structure of these verses. There is obvious and deliberate parallelism between:

>       through Jesus Christ    and    God the Father,
>            who raised him from the dead

and:

>       from God the Father    and    the Lord Jesus Christ
>            who gave himself for our sins.

This is an artistic way of saying that the blessings of salvation come to us from Jesus Christ who gave himself for our sins and from God the Father who raised him from the dead. The purpose both of Christ's death and of his resurrection by the Father was that Christ might rescue us from the present evil age. Probably St Paul does not mean that by his death Christ *ipso facto* rescued us from the present evil age. [57]

If we place ourselves at the moment of Christ's death, there is a sense in which he has completed his task, since he says in Jn 19:30: *Tetelestai* — 'It is consummated'; he has completed the laborious part of his task, by making expiation for past sins. But in another sense he has not yet completed his task: he has not yet enabled the men whose past sins have been expiated, to avoid sin in the future. If they remain infected with death, weak, unable to fulfil the law, they will inevitably relapse into sin. Therefore at the moment of Christ's death, the rescue operation is not complete.

To complete it, the Father raises him from the dead and gives him power to communicate his own risen life to others (cf. Rom 1:4; Jn 7:38). By communicating his own life or his own Spirit, Christ strengthens the spirit of believers and makes them capable of

---

[56] Cf. Bonnard, Gal, p. 21.
[57] This is not what St Thomas means when he says (Gal, 384 A): 'The death of Christ itself is the efficient cause of grace.'

resisting sin for the future. The man who believes that God the Father has raised Christ crucified from the dead, will himself be raised to a new level of life and of spiritual strength through the same power of God exercised through Christ.

The man to whom Christ has communicated 'the power of his resurrection' (Phil 3:10), that is, a share in his risen life, no longer belongs to the present death-infected generation or 'age'. He has already begun to live the life of the world to come. He has been set free.

So far, this explanation of how Christ liberates us from the present evil age has been straightforward. [58] But St Paul sometimes describes this liberation as a liberation from demonic powers, and this is not so easy to understand. In Col 2:15 he says that Christ triumphed over the demonic powers on the cross. This may be simply a pictorial or 'mythological' description of man's liberation from sin and its lethal effects. If St Paul intends his words to be taken literally, he probably means that the demonic powers, acting through the human rulers of this world (cf. 1 Cor 2:8), secured Christ's crucifixion, and believed that this was the moment of their triumph — when in fact Christ was triumphing over them! If we ask how this is to be understood, there may be a sketch of St Paul's view in Gal 3:13, where he says that Christ delivered us from the curse of the law by himself becoming accursed. That is to say, by allowing the law to place its curse on him, Christ allowed the 'angels' of the law (cf. 3:19) to make themselves guilty of cursing the Lord of glory. By doing so, they put themselves completely in the wrong; they lost the right to cast stones at others; their power was broken, and they were overthrown. [59]

There is another parallel in Jn 14:13-31, where Jesus says: 'The ruler of this world is coming; he has no power over me (or, no claim against me); but to show the world that I love the Father and do only as he has commanded me, rise up, let us go from here.' Here, as in Galatians and Colossians, the death of Christ is seen as a cosmological event, in which Christ clashes with the ruler or rulers of this world, overthrows them, and so ushers in a new period or aeon. One reason why St Paul's doctrine of redemption is difficult

---

[58] Cf. Chrysostom in PG 61, 618 C. He aptly quotes Jn 17:11.

[59] Their power, though broken, is not utterly extinguished. They can still pronounce their curse on those who obey them. But since the death of Christ no one *need* obey them any more. For by faith and baptism a man can share in Christ's death (cf. 2 Cor 5:14): he can pass through death out of the evil aeon where these powers rule, into the new aeon where Christ is king.

for us to understand is that we dissociate it from his demonology and cosmology. [60] He thinks within the framework of Jewish cosmology, which is a prescientific or mythological cosmology. [61] He seems to personify the Law, the Flesh, and Sin, and then to treat these personifications as demonic powers vanquished by Christ. It is not clear that he regarded this simply as a pictorial way of speaking — probably he did not.

Here the problem of demythologizing presents itself in an acute form. [62] If parts of St Paul's explanation of how Christ's death produced its saving effect rest on prescientific cosmological presuppositions which we can no longer accept, have these parts of his theology of the redemption become entirely obsolete? Or can we separate out the prescientific (mythological) elements and present what is left over in terms more acceptable to modern man? In particular, if St Paul believed that the Mosaic law was imposed by angelic-demonic powers of dubious allegiance to God and of minimal benevolence to men (cf. 3 : 18), and that the Redemption consisted primarily in liberation from these powers, what is a modern Christian to do if he does not think that these powers intervened between God and Moses and doubts whether they exist anyway?

It is often supposed that we have only to find out exactly what St Paul thought and taught and we shall have a pure, Scriptural kerygma which will stir the hearts of men today as it stirred the Galatians, Philippians and Corinthians. But it turns out that this is not so. St Paul thought and expressed himself in terms of a three-decker cosmology, with the upper air full of powers, principalities, thrones, dominations etc., some of whom control the elements, earth, air, fire and water, while others regulate the movements of the heavenly bodies and thereby control the calendar (cf. Gal 4 : 9-10). It was all very well for him to do this, because his hearers lived in the same world of thought, at least if they were Jews. The apocalyptic literature of the intertestamental period (200 B.C. to A.D. 50) shows that during this period a great development of demonology and

---

[60]  Cf. M. Werner, *The Formation of Christian Dogma,* London, 1957, pp. 73-76.

[61]  Already in the time of the Greek Fathers, St Paul's ways of speaking had become an embarrassment to preachers. Theodoretus, PG 82, 464 A, is at pains to show that St Paul did not regard the present life as evil through and through: 'That this life is not in every aspect harmful, the Apostle himself teaches, for he says (Phil 1 : 22): "If to live on in the flesh means that I shall do fruitful work, then I do not know which to choose. I am pulled in two directions. . . ." '

[62]  The debate on demythologizing was launched by Rudolf Bultmann's paper, 'New Testament and Mythology,' which is included in H. W. Bartsch (ed.), *Kerygma and Myth,* I, London, 1954, pp. 1-44.

angelology took place. In part this was a development of traditions indigenous to Judaism, but the Hellenistic environment and the religions of Babylonia and Persia also exercised some influence. [63] This 'cosmos' or 'age' was popularly believed to be in the power of demonic rulers, who were responsible for the evil in the world. We of the twentieth century may say that these 'powers' were purely imaginary; nevertheless they exerted power, and a baneful power, because they were believed in. One purpose of St Paul's preaching was to liberate his hearers from this baneful influence. Theoretically, he could have done it in either of two ways: he could have declared that these powers simply do not exist, or he could declare that they have been defeated and reduced to impotence and therefore are as good as non-existent. As Paul was a man of his own day, he naturally adopted the second of these methods.

For the preacher of today, the situation is quite different. His hearers live in a secular culture which does not postulate angelic controllers of the elements and does not attribute the evil of the world to demonic intervention. It would be absurd for a preacher of today to treat his audience as if they still shared the cosmological belief of Paul's contemporaries. A congregation which has seen the far side of the moon and contemplated the good earth from outer space, will stop listening if a preacher starts explaining the redemption in terms of the overthrow of demonic powers. What then is the preacher to do? This is the problem of 'hermeneutics': how to present the essential gospel message to men and women of our day. [64]

The simplest and probably the wisest solution is to follow the example of St John Chrysostom, who passes lightly over St Paul's references to the demonic powers and explains 'liberation from this evil age' in moral terms, that is, as liberation from the bondage of sin through the power of the Holy Spirit. As students of St Paul, we must try and think our way into the unfamiliar background of the apostle's thought; then we must distinguish, as we do when handling the first chapter of Genesis, between the religious message which the inspired author is formally teaching and the prescientific cosmological framework which he has used to express it.

The same problem presents itself in a much simpler form in 1 Cor 11:10, where St Paul says that women in church must wear

---

[63] Cf. D. S. Russell, *The Method and Message of Jewish Apocalyptic*, London, 1964, pp. 254-62; G. von Rad, *Old Testament Theology*, II, Edinburgh, 1965, p. 349.

[64] Cf. G. Ebeling, *Word and Faith*, London, 1963, pp. 110 and 263; also my review of this book in HJ 5 (1964), pp. 212-3.

a veil 'on account of the angels'. The Scripture scholar may investigate what peculiar views about angels lie behind this odd remark, but he need not pass on his findings to the faithful. One can accept the rule, that women should have their heads covered, without accepting the mythological cosmology which St Paul brought in to justify it (especially as he admits, in 1 Cor 11 : 16, that his arguments have not been fully convincing).

Hitherto preachers have in fact followed the example of John Chrysostom, but in future it may be less easy for them to do so. The *Constitution on the Sacred Liturgy* of the Second Vatican Council prescribes that in future the selection of Scripture readings in the liturgy is to be 'more abundant, more varied, and more appropriate' (§ 35,1), and that 'the treasures of the Bible are to be opened up more lavishly, so that richer fare may be provided for the faithful at the table of God's Word; in this way a more representative portion of the holy Scripture will be read to the people over a set cycle of years' (§ 51). However, the compilers of the new lectionary will probably avoid assigning any difficult passages of Galatians to the Sunday liturgy. So the faithful may hear even less of the doctrinal part of this Epistle than they do at present. There is little likelihood that they will hear about what happened at Antioch.

*Why is 'the will of God our Father' mentioned here (v. 4)?*

The phrase 'through the will of God our Father' is best taken with both of the two preceding verbs, 'he offered himself' and 'to rescue us'.

Taken with 'he offered himself', it shows (a) that there was no conflict between Christ and the Father. Christ is not to be pictured as placating an angry Father, or as wrestling against the Father's will on man's behalf (like another Prometheus). On the contrary, he is obediently carrying out the Father's will or plan for man's liberation. [65] God the Father is the subject of the central affirmation of Galatians (4 : 4-5): 'When the fulness of time arrived, God (the Father) sent forth his Son....to deliver those under the law.' (b) It also shows that during his passion Christ was not really in the power of the ruler of this age, although he appeared to be. The devil, working through Judas and Caiaphas, seemed to have Christ in his power, but in fact

---

[65] 'Will' is not a purely formal concept here. It means the particular plan which God has chosen to realize; cf. Col 1 : 9.

Christ submitted only because it was his Father's will (cf. Jn 14: 30-31).

Taken with 'to rescue us', the phrase means that the whole plan of our redemption (of which Christ's death was a part) proceeds from the Father's will. Because the whole initiative proceeds from the Father's will, the whole glory of its achievement belongs to him, and St Paul fittingly rounds off the sentence with a doxology: 'to him be the glory for ever.' Once the cross is rightly understood, it becomes a glorious revelation of the love of God the Father. [66] St Paul would have appreciated Salvador Dali's picture, 'The Christ of St John of the Cross'.

### How is the doxology connected with the rest of the section?

Since the doxology is placed at the very centre of the section, it must be of major importance in the argument (for the main idea in a chiasm is usually placed in the centre). It is not simply a pious refrain, rounding off the summary of the gospel.

St Paul begins the section by proclaiming himself an apostle. He feels that he must do this, for the reasons indicated above. But being aware that his adversaries may accuse him of boasting, he closes with the protestation that he is Christ's servant, seeking the approval of God and not of men; and in the emphatic central position he insists that the glory belongs to God. St Augustine, though he had no structural analysis to help him, recognized the connection between the doxology and v. 10 at the end. Here is his comment: [67]

> How much the more should men refrain from arrogating to themselves the credit if they do some good, when the Son of God himself, in the gospel, said that he did not seek his own glory (Jn 8:50), and that he had come to do, not his own will, but the will of the one who sent him (Jn 6:38)? The apostle mentions the will and glory of the Father here, so that he too, following the example of the Lord by whom he is sent, may show that he does not seek his own glory nor do his own will in the preaching of the gospel — as he says a little later: 'If I were pleasing men, I should not be the servant of Christ.'

---

[66] Cf. Rom 5:8; Jn 3:16, 1 Jn 4:10; Phil 2:11 (where the Vulgate version, *in gloria Dei Patris*, misrepresents the Greek—it should be *in gloriam Dei Patris*). St Thomas, Gal, 441 B, comments on Rom 5:8: 'Nothing so revealed God's love for us as the death of Christ; hence Gregory's words, O inaestimabilis dilectio caritatis! Ut servum redimeres, Filium tradidisti!' (More probably the *Exultet* is a work of Ambrose. Cf. B. Capelle, 'L'*Exultet* paschal, oeuvre de saint Ambroise,' *Miscellanea Mercati*, I [Studi e Testi, 121], pp. 199-218.)

[67] Augustine, PL 35, 2108 B.

A further reason for the prominence of the doxology is that in Paul's view the doctrine of the Judaizers takes the glory away from God and gives it to man. If justification comes from the law, Christ died for nothing, and the Jew has something to boast about. But if forgiveness and justification are free gifts, given to those who believe in Christ's death, the just man has nothing to boast about. The glory belongs to God. These two basically conflicting religious attitudes are portrayed in our Lord's parable of the Pharisee and the Publican. [68] Galatians 1 : 4-5 can easily be turned into a prayer of thanks for the use of converted publicans:

> We give thanks to our Lord Jesus Christ, who offered himself as a sacrifice for our sins, to deliver us from this present evil age, through the will of God our Father; to him be glory for ever and ever. Amen.

## Is the doxology addressed exclusively to God the Father?

It is simplest to suppose that the antecedent of 'to whom' is the nearest masculine noun, namely 'God our Father'. But since the phrase 'according to the will of God our Father' is only a subordinate part of the long sentence which proclaims the glorious redemption wrought by Christ, the doxology can also be referred to Christ as the main subject of discourse. St Paul certainly cannot intend to *divert* from Christ the glory of the redemption. As he has gone to such trouble to associate Christ as closely as possible with the Father in the parallel phrases 'through Jesus Christ and God the Father' and 'from God the Father and the Lord Jesus Christ', he probably means the doxology to be addressed to both the Father and Christ. Since the redemption is the work of Christ who offered himself and of the Father who raised him, the glory of it belongs to both alike.

A possible objection is that if such had been St Paul's meaning, he could have said 'to *them* be the glory'. But he never uses a plural pronoun for referring to the Father and the Son. God is one. [69]

---

[68] Cf. Lk 18:14. This is probably not dependent on Paul; cf. Jeremias, *Parables* (1963), pp. 141-2.
[69] See on 3:19, below, pp. 308-309.

*The Second Subsection, 1:6-12*

# ANATHEMA

**A**  *1 : 6* I am astonished that you are so quickly deserting from the one who called you  **B**  in the grace of Christ,  **C**  to another gospel,  *7* which is not another,  **D**  but certain persons are shaking you,  **E**  and would like to turn Christ's gospel upside down.  **D¹**  *8* But if anyone, even ourselves or an angel from heaven,  **C¹**  preaches to you a gospel other than the one we preached,  **B¹**  let him be anathema [9-10].  **A¹**  *11* For I inform you, brethren, that the gospel which was preached by me is not according to man.  *12* Nor did I receive it from any man, nor was I taught it by any man, but through a revelation of Jesus Christ.

A and A¹ both begin with formal, official words: 'I am astonished' and 'I inform you'. B and B¹ are linked as contraries, for to be anathema is to be out of the grace of Christ. C and C¹ both contain the idea that a distorted gospel is not a gospel at all — 'gospel' is not a purely formal concept like 'message'. D¹ suggests that the 'certain persons' in D are persons of consequence. E, at the centre, has satisfactory links with the end (A¹) and with the beginning (A). Vv. 9-10 overload the second half of this passage. Perhaps St Paul first composed it without these verses, and inserted them when incorporating this symmetry within a larger one.

*Why is St Paul astonished at the Galatians' conduct?*

Instead of the congratulations and thanksgivings which usually follow his initial greetings, [70] St Paul administers a reproof, beginning with: 'I am astonished', the equivalent of the Latin *Miramur* which is still employed by curial stylists for the same purpose: 'We are astonished to hear...' The formula implies that the writer expected something better of the recipient — who, if he takes the letter in good part, will feel ashamed that he has not lived up to the writer's expectations of him.

St Paul is astonished at the Galatians, first, because they are deserting from 'the one who called them in the grace of Christ'. This is almost certainly an allusion to the manifest workings of Christ's grace through Paul among the Galatians at the time of their 'call' and conversion. St Paul is amazed that after the truth of the gospel has been so clearly confirmed for them, they can think of going over

---

[70]  Cf. e.g. Rom 1:8; 1 Cor 1:4.

to another gospel. Thus he introduces a theme which reappears in
3:1-4 and 4:13-14: if the Galatians would only remember the days
of their first fervour, they would remain loyal to his gospel. He is
reproaching them with disloyalty.

Secondly, he is astonished because they are succumbing 'so quickly'
to the propaganda of the false teachers. As was pointed out above, [71]
this does not necessarily mean 'so soon after your conversion'. More
probably it means: 'so soon after the appearance of the false teachers',
i.e., 'with so little pause for reflection or consultation'. St Paul had
forewarned them against these teachers when he visited them on his
second and third journeys and expected them to stand firm if and
when the Judaizers arrived. Instead, they have succumbed at the first
attack, or rather, as Chrysostom says, 'at the first skirmish' without
putting up any serious defence at all. [72]

## Who is 'he who called you in the grace of God'?

The phrase contains two difficulties: Who is 'the one who called
you'? and how is the prepositional 'in the grace of Christ' related to
'he who called you'?

'He who called you' must be God the Father or Paul himself.
Most commentators choose the former alternative, on the grounds
that St Paul usually attributes the 'calling' of Christians to God the
Father. [73] This sense is certainly not to be excluded here. But St Paul
frequently uses ambiguous phrases intentionally, in order to profit by
the ambiguity. [74] In the present context (vv. 6-7), he probably intends
to contrast himself with the Judaizers who are shaking the faith of his
converts. The phrase 'him who called you' occurs again in Gal 5:8,
where it stands in contrast to 'Who has put obstacles in your way?'
There again St Paul is contrasting himself with the Judaizers.

He is, therefore, rebuking the Galatians in terms which can imply
that he regards their defection from the gospel as a failure in loyalty
to himself. The reason why he uses this studied ambiguity is that he
does not wish to be accused of going round building up a party of
Paul (cf. 1 Cor 1:12); all glory must be given to God (v. 6). He
therefore charges the Galatians with defection from himself while at
the same time forestalling criticism by the ambiguity of his language.

[71] See above, pp. 16-17.
[72] Cf. Chrysostom, PG 61, 620 CD.
[73] Cf. Rom 11:29; Phil 3:14; 2 Tim 1:9.
[74] See below on 2:20. For this reason, even the best translations fail to say all
that the Greek says.

This was not dishonesty. St Paul realizes that the first act of faith he had to ask for was an act of faith in his own witness. His witness, like that of John the Baptist, would in time be superseded by the direct witness of the Holy Spirit; but even then it would be unreasonable to *reject* his own witness. St Paul can see that he should have a permanent place in the faith of the churches he has founded. [75] (His name deserves its place in the first subsection, which defines the nature of the Church — see above, p. 68).

The phrase 'in the grace of Christ' is again ambiguous, and again it is not a question of either-or. St Paul probably intends his words to bear both of the possible meanings. He means: 'When I called you, I was in the grace of Christ, and I called you to be in the grace of Christ.' Hence if they desert him and go over to the party of his adversaries, they will be departing out of the grace of Christ, for Paul has not changed his gospel in the meanwhile. The proof that 'in the grace of Christ' refers to Paul (as well as to the Galatians) is that in the corresponding place in the second half of the first main division of the Epistle St Paul shows that he was formally declared to be in communion with James, Cephas and John by means of 'the right hand of fellowship'. And in the subsection 1:6-12, 'in the grace of Christ' stands in contrast to 'anathema'. See C - C¹ on p. 46, and B - B¹ on p. 82 above.

*'They want to turn Christ's gospel upside down' — Is St Paul making a mountain out of a molehill?*

When he says that the Judaizers want to turn the gospel upside down, presumably he means that while he is teaching that justification is by faith and not by works, they are teaching (at least by implication) that justification is by works and not by faith; while he is teaching that the gospel liberates Jewish believers from the law, they are using the gospel to subject Gentile believers to the law. [76]

Even if the Judaizers were extremists, still maintaining, in spite of the Council, that circumcision was necessary for salvation, they probably thought that St Paul was being very unreasonable. One can imagine them replying like this: 'You intelligent Galatians must not allow Paul to scare you. You have seen this kind of thing in party

---

[75] This raises the question whether kerygmatic preaching should not *always* include the element of personal witness. In the case of modern preachers, this will of course mean witness to the gifts of the Holy Spirit (cf. Gal 4:6). See further below, pp. 512-513.

[76] Cf. Pelagius, Gal, p. 308.

politics: just before the election one side tries to frighten the public with fearful threats of what will happen if the other party gets into power. But you "foolish Galatians" are not so foolish as Paul imagines. He is making a mountain out of a molehill. We do not want to overthrow the gospel. Just as Paul believes that one who has believed must nevertheless be baptized, so we maintain that one who has believed must nevertheless be baptized and circumcised. If one is a material rite, so is the other. What is all the fuss about?'

If the Judaizers were of the moderate variety who merely recommended circumcision to those who wished to be perfect Christians, they would find St Paul's intransigence even more unreasonable. They would say: 'We are not upsetting the gospel of Christ; we are merely recommending you to imitate Christ, who was circumcised on the eighth day, like Paul himself.'

St John Chrysostom evidently felt this difficulty. After quoting the phrase 'they would like to turn the gospel upside down', he adds the comment: [77]

> And yet they were only introducing one or two commandments — circumcision and the observance of certain days! But Paul wishes to show that a small distortion ruins the whole — that is why he uses the phrase 'to turn the gospel upside down'. It is the same with the imperial coinage: the man who chips away a small part of the image renders the whole coin counterfeit. In the same way, one who upsets even the smallest part of the sound faith, is completely ruined, for he goes on from this beginning to worse and worse.

This is probably the best view to take. St Paul recognizes in both forms of the judaizing doctrine the seeds of serious trouble in the future. If the Gentiles are allowed to have themselves circumcised, they will soon attach less importance to baptism than to this painful rite and its humiliating consequences. [78] They will think they are justified by what they have done and suffered. Then they will fail to attach due importance to Christ's death. And if they lose hold of the central truth of Christ's death, they will doubt whether Christ is the Son of God. The true doctrine of the Atonement and the true Christology stand or fall together. If Christ is the Son of God, his death must have some great significance for all mankind; if it has no greater significance than the death of any just man, can it be true that he is the Son of God?

---

[77] Chrysostom, PG 61, 622 C. A little later he says (623 B) that because small beginnings have been left unchecked, 'the Church is torn into a thousand pieces and has become ridiculous in the eyes of the Jews and Greeks alike.'
[78] Philo, *The Special Laws*, I, 1 (Loeb VII), shows that circumcision occasioned much ridicule.

To some extent, therefore, — it is hard to say to what extent — Paul was arguing against implications and dangers which he could see in the doctrine of the Judaizers, but they could not. He saw these implications even in the conduct of St Peter. Many of his readers, including St Peter, probably thought he was making too much of the issue.

History vindicated St Paul, for at least some Jewish Christians later adopted a very low Christology. Eusebius, writing of the time of Trajan, says that the sect of the Ebionites

> regarded Christ as plain and ordinary, a man esteemed as righteous through growth of character and nothing more, the child of a normal union between a man and Mary; and they held that they must observe every detail of the law — by faith in Christ alone, and a life built upon that faith, they would never win salvation. [79]

The Judaizers of St Paul's day are not full-blown Ebionites, since he does not accuse them of questioning whether Christ was the Son of God. Probably they were still unclear in their own minds as to the full implications of their own position.

### Who are the 'certain persons' referred to in v. 7?

When St Paul says 'certain persons', he means 'men whom I refrain from naming, though I could do so'. He does not believe it wise to name his adversaries, for by doing so he would only encourage ambitious teachers who wish to get themselves talked about. [80] A passage of Hegesippus (*floruit* c. 175 A.D.), preserved by Eusebius, shows the wisdom of St Paul's reticence about names: [81]

> When James the Righteous had suffered martyrdom like the Lord and for the same reason, Symeon the son of his uncle Clopas was appointed bishop. He being a cousin of the Lord, it was the universal demand that he should be the second. They used to call the Church a virgin for this reason, that she had not yet been seduced by listening to nonsense. But Thebuthis, because he had not been made bishop, began to seduce her by means of the seven sects (to which he himself belonged) among the people. From these came Simeon and his Simonians, Cleobius and his Cleobians,

---

[79] Eusebius, *H.E.*, III, 27 (trans. G. A. Williamson, p. 137).

[80] Cf. Rom 3:8; 1 Cor 4:18; 15:12; 2 Cor 3:1; 10:2; Phil 1:15 etc. Chrysostom, PG 61, 667 B, says: 'He never gives the names of his adversaries, so that they will not become even more shameless.' The naming of Hymenaeus, Alexander and Philetus in 1 Tim 1:20; 2:17 is exceptional—one reason for thinking that the Epistle is not from the hand of St Paul himself.

[81] Euseb., *H.E.*, IV, 22, 4 (trans. Williamson, pp. 181-2). This passage is also relevant to the problem of how 'James the brother of the Lord' was related to Christ.

Dositheus and his Dositheans, Gorthaeus and his Gorathenes, and the Masbotheans. From these were derived the Menandrianists, Marcionists, Carpocrations, Velentinians, Basilidians, and Saturnilians, every man introducing his own opinion in his own particular way.

In the structure of the first main division, the passage about the 'certain persons who are shaking you and who want to overturn the gospel of Christ' is balanced by the description of the Antioch incident (see above, p. 46); and in the second section (below, p. 121) it balances 2:9 where James, Cephas and John are described as 'those who seem to be pillars'. These connections suggest that the unnamed trouble-makers may be no other than the pillar-apostles. Since, however, it is quite incredible that any of these three went to Galatia and preached the necessity of circumcision, St Paul must have in mind certain lesser figures who claimed to be disciples and perhaps even emissaries of Peter, James and John. In this case, St Paul could say that 'the pillars' were shaking the churches of Galatia through their uncontrolled disciples. In the decretal letter of Acts 15, the apostles disown the Judaizers who claimed to be acting in their name (v. 14). The connection between 1:6-8 and 2:11-19 seems to show that in St Paul's view the pillars *were* responsible for the disturbances in Galatia, through not instructing and controlling their disciples as they should have done.

### Why does St Paul utter this anathema here?

The purpose of the anathema is to bring home to the Galatians the gravity of the threat to their faith. St Paul regards the doctrine of the Judaizers as a radical misrepresentation of the gospel. He tells the Galatians here that anyone who preaches it is outside the Church. In 5:4 he adds that anyone who obeys it is outside the Church.

Secondly, he wishes to rebut the charge that he is a respecter of persons and says whatever he thinks will ingratiate himself with the audience which he happens to be addressing. As John Chrysostom observes, the immediate sequel shows that Paul is demonstrating that 'when the truth is at stake, he has no regard for the dignity of human persons'. [82] Substantially, he is doing again what he did at Antioch, by way of showing that he has no regrets.

Thirdly, by including himself in his conditional anathema, St Paul is rebutting the charge of inconsistency: if he himself ever makes additions or alterations to the gospel, he is to be anathema. A con-

---

[82] PG 61, 625 A.

ditional self-cursing of this kind is equivalent to a promisory oath [83]: Paul will not, on pain of damnation, ever preach a different gospel.

## Why is the angel mentioned in the anathema?

V. 8 mentions an angel, and raises the usual problem: how seriously are we to take St Paul's references to the 'angels'? (In the Scriptures, 'angels' are not always loyal servants of God, confirmed in grace — Christ can speak of 'the devil and his angels'. Nor is there a sharp division between 'good angels' confirmed in grace and 'bad angels' confirmed in malice, for in Col 1:20 St Paul speaks of Christ as 'reconciling' the heavenly powers through his death.)

In Gal 1:8, it is possible that St Paul seriously intends to include angels in his conditional anathema. Since he believes that the Mosaic law was given by or through angels (cf. 3:19-20), he may be considering the possibility that these angels resent man's liberation by Christ and try to reimpose their yoke of slavery. He saw his apostolic struggles as battles against invisible spiritual powers (cf. Eph 6:12), and therefore could regard the crisis in Galatia as being not simply a clash between himself and a few Jewish-Christian preachers, but rather a battle between the Holy Spirit working through himself and angelic-demonic powers working through the Judaizers. St Paul moved in a world full of spirits, and believed himself to have powers over angels (cf. 1 Cor 6:3). [84]

St Thomas Aquinas takes the reference seriously and suggests that the inclusion of angels in the anathema is to be explained in the light of 3:21: as the gospel does not come from any man or angel, it cannot be altered or corrected by any man or angel — and God will not go back on his own word. Therefore the gospel is absolutely immutable. [85]

But further, if the false teachers whom St Paul attacks in Galatians are the same as those he attacks in Colossians, [86] there is reason to

---

[83] Cf. G. E. Mendenhall, 'Covenant Forms in Israelite Tradition', *The Biblical Archaeologist*, 17 (1954), p. 52.
[84] It is possible that St Paul's audacity in cursing the angels (though only conditionally) was imitated by others in the early Church. There is a strange passage in the Epistle of Jude (vv. 9-10) which condemns false teachers who insult the glorious spirits: 'When the archangel Michael was in conflict with the devil in the dispute over the body of Moses, he did not venture to utter any insulting judgment on him, but simply said: "May the Lord rebuke you!" But these men insult what they do not understand.'
[85] Cf. St Thomas, Gal, 386 A.
[86] Most commentators suppose they are not. But the question requires a thorough re-examination. See my paperback, *Colossians* (Scripture for Meditation, 4), London, 1969.

think that they attempted to support their teaching by narrating visions of angels (as St John does in the Apocalypse). The text, unfortunately, is obscure and difficult; it appears to mean (Col 2:18):

> If anyone claims to have had visions and therefore, with affected self-abasement, advocates the worship of angels, he must not be allowed to impose his will on you. He is in fact puffed up with the futile conceits of his own natural mind.

The last clause seems to imply that St Paul regards the 'angelic visions' not as temptations of the devil but as natural illusions. So the 'angel' in v. 8 may simply mean 'any alleged angel'.

The above interpretation may perhaps read too much into St Paul's words. But to go to the other extreme and regard v. 8 as nothing more than a playful allusion to the title of 'Hermes' given to Paul at Lystra (cf. Acts 14:12) does not suit the seriousness of the passage. Perhaps it is best to take a middle course and regard the reference to the angel here (as in 4:14) as a rhetorical device. Then St Paul's meaning is: 'If anyone, however exalted he may be, dares to preach a gospel at variance with mine, let him be anathema.' St John Chrysostom perceived that he had in mind the apostles at Jerusalem:[87]

> Since they (the Judaizers) were appealing to authorities, namely James and John, he (St Paul) speaks of angels: 'Do not talk to me of James,' he says, 'or of John; even if one of the foremost angels or someone from heaven is corrupting the gospel, let him be anathema.'

Chrysostom omits to name St Peter, no doubt from reverence. But as was mentioned above, in the structure of the first division of the Epistle this anathema-passage balances the Antioch-incident. Therefore, while St Peter is not named, he is included in this (conditional) anathema. 'If anyone, however exalted' means 'If anyone, even Peter himself.'

This raises the question whether St Paul believed himself to have authority over everyone including St Peter. The answer depends upon the meaning which is to be attached to the clause 'let him be anathema'. In the Old Testament, to declare a thing anathema means to set it apart for utter destruction; when God declares the Israelites anathema, he means that he is withdrawing his divine protection and exposing them to the assaults of the enemy (cf. Josh 10:7-12). It would seem, then, that in Gal 1:8-9 St Paul is pronouncing a conditional judgment which will come into effect *ipso facto* upon anyone (even St Peter) who breaks his law that circumcision is not to be preached in the Gentile Churches. St Paul is doing, in defence of freedom, almost

---

[87] PG 61, 624 **B**.

exactly what the angels of the law did in defence of the law (cf. Gal 3:10). If anyone disobeys St Paul's law, he will come under a curse. This faces the Judaizers with a radical decision: whose threats will they heed, those of the angels of the law or those of Paul?

St Paul seems to be exercising a conditional judgment over St Peter, but he is not really doing so. He is quite sure that in fact neither an angel from heaven, nor St Peter, nor himself is going to preach another gospel to the Galatians. He is using a canonical form,[88] but combining it with impossible suppositions.[89] He is not really, therefore, exercising or claiming the right to exercise jurisdiction over angels or St Peter here.

But while he is not claiming universal jurisdiction, he is making the most absolute claim to infallibility that one could imagine. He is sure not only that he is right, but also that God will not send an angel from heaven with any alteration or addition to the gospel.[90] The possibility of an addition is ruled out in 3:15; the possibility of an alteration or correction by the manner in which he received the gospel (cf. 1:11-12).

### How often did Paul pronounce this anathema?

There is an unfortunate ambiguity in the opening phrase of v. 9: 'as we warned you before'. This may simply refer back to v. 8. Then the sense is: 'I have said it once, and now I say it again for emphasis.' There is another example of repetition for emphasis in 5:1-2. However, in view of St Paul's use of this same word 'forewarn' in Gal 5:21 and 2 Cor 13:2, it is better to suppose that he is referring to an oral proclamation of this anathema on his last visit to Galatia at the beginning of the third missionary journey. This makes three proclamations in all. Thus the anathema is given all possible solemnity, and Peter, who will doubtless hear of all this, is given a threefold warning.[91]

---

[88] The word 'canon' occurs in the corresponding section at the end of the whole Epistle, in 6:16.

[89] St Thomas, Gal, 386 B, gives a different solution: 'The apostle uttered this sentence not on his own authority, but on the authority of the evangelical teaching of which he was a minister. The authority of this doctrine is such that all who speak against it are to be secluded and repelled. Cf. Jn 12:48: "The word which I have spoken will be their judge on the Last Day." '

[90] It is hard to believe that St Paul would have been so vehement if he wrote this Epistle on the way to the Council of Jerusalem, as some commentators think. His vehemence is more understandable after the Council had decided in his favour.

[91] Cf. P. Gaechter, 'Das dreifache "Weide meine Lämmer",' ZKT, 69 (1947), pp. 328-344.

*Is the anathema equivalent to an excommunication?*

As was pointed out above (p. 81), the formula of blessing in v. 3 probably comes from the liturgy. Perhaps the anathema does too. [92] At the end of First Corinthians, an anathema is placed between a liturgical kiss and a blessing (16: 20-24), and the formula used ('If anyone does not love the Lord, let him be anathema') is probably pre-pauline and liturgical in origin. [93] The Eucharistic liturgy of the *Didache* (10: 6) has a similar warning to the unholy to keep away. [94]

It does not seem likely that St Paul wishes his anathema to be used as a liturgical formula (e.g. in the revised form: 'If anyone preaches a gospel other than what we received from Paul, let him be anathema'); but since anathemas were used in the liturgy, he probably means that the Galatians must not allow Judaizing teachers to partake of their Eucharist. Whoever is 'anathema' is not 'in the grace of Christ'.

No doubt one purpose of the liturgical anathema was to impress upon Christians what a blessing it is to be a member of the Church and how perilous it is to be outside. It was a way of saying *Extra ecclesiam nulla salus* (outside the Church no salvation): either a man is in the grace of Christ, or he is anathema. The abandonment of the liturgical anathema may have helped to weaken the sense of privilege which Christians ought to feel. Nowadays, most Christians probably take too cheerful a view of the prospects of those outside — which is bad in the end both for those outside and for themselves. There is a severe warning at the end of the Sermon on the Mount (Mt 7: 13-14):

> Enter by the narrow gate.
> For the gate that leads to destruction is wide,
>     the road is broad,
>         and many go that way;
> but the gate that leads to life is narrow,
>     the road is hard,
>         and those who find it are few.

To judge from Apoc 22: 15, the anathema was also a means of deterring Christians from post-baptismal sin. It warns the congregation that a Christian who commits certain grave sins must not approach the Eucharist and is excluding himself from the kingdom of God.

[92]  St Thomas, Gal, 385 C, treats the anathema as an excommunication.
[93]  Cf. G. Bornkamm, 'Das Anathema in der urchristliche Abendmahlsliturgie,' TLZ, 65 (1950), cols 227-236; J. A. T. Robinson, 'Traces of a Liturgical Sequence in 1 Cor 16:20-24,' JTS, 4 (1953), pp. 38-41. On the connection between *Maranatha* and *anathema*, see C. F. D. Moule, 'A Reconsideration of the Context of *Maranatha*,' NTS 6 (1958), pp. 307-310.
[94]  Cf. also Apoc 22:15.

*To what charge is St Paul replying in vv. 10-12?*

St Paul's adversaries had evidently accused him of 'pleasing men', that is, of fabricating a special form of the gospel to suit the wishes of Gentiles. They mean that according to the true gospel (as they preach it) Christians must be circumcised, but St Paul knows that circumcision is repulsive to the Gentiles, and therefore declares it unnecessary and pours scorn on it, though privately he believes it is of value. Therefore, they say, Paul is not a true servant of Christ, but a 'man-pleaser' (*anthrôpareskos*). In their eyes, St Paul was a here-siarch. [95]

Since St Paul himself used the contrast between being a 'man-pleaser' and being a 'slave of Christ' in Col 3:22-25 and Eph 6:6-8, he was also being accused of failing to live up to his own teaching.

*How does St Paul reply to these charges?*

The first point of St Paul's reply is made in the angry verse 10, which, like its counterpart in the first half of the section (v. 1b), is parenthetic. Realizing that the vehemence of his language will shock some readers and offend others, he refuses to apologize for his reck-lessness, but points to it as a proof that he is not out to please men: '*Now* whom am I seeking to please — men or God?' The anathema-passage is a demonstration that he is no respecter of persons.

Secondly, he introduces a contrast between his conduct before and after his conversion: 'If I were *still* seeking to please men, I should not be a servant of Christ.' He concedes that in his pre-conversion days, when he was walking according to the flesh, he was sent 'by men', for example to Damascus (cf. Acts 9:1-2), and was really, though unconsciously (cf. Acts 23:1), seeking the favour of the chief priests and other influential Jews. V. 10b contains his answer to Christ's question: 'Saul, Saul, why are you persecuting me?' He had thought, at the time, that he was persecuting the disciples of Christ in order to do honour to God (cf. Jn 16:2), but after the revelation he re-cognized that his real motive had been the desire to win social prestige as a zealous young Pharisee. To the charge made by his opponents in Galatians, that he was still acting from basically the same motive, [96]

---

[95] Cf. J. L. McKenzie, *The Power and the Wisdom*, London, 1965, p. 117: 'To his own people he was the great renegade, fit to take his place in Jewish history with Ahab, Manasseh, and Jehoiachim.'

[96] There was perhaps a grain of truth in this. Even after his conversion, Paul felt the need to excel. Cf. Dodd, *New Testament Studies*, p. 73.

he retorts that if he were still bent on pleasing men, he would still be with the Jews — still persecuting the Church. [97] He would not be a servant of Christ, sharing in the sufferings which Christ himself endured at the hands of the Jews.

Thirdly, St Paul simply states, in v. 11, that the gospel which he has preached is not 'according to man'. This rather vague phrase does not refer exclusively or primarily to the *origin* of his message, but chiefly to the motives that have dictated his preaching of it. The whole of the biographical section which follows (1 : 13—2 : 21) is designed to justify the protestation made in v. 11.

Fourthly, St Paul rejects the charge that his gospel is a human invention, created by himself or any other man: 'I received it through a revelation of Jesus Christ.' This too is amplified in the following section.

The structure of the first main division shows that while St Paul is defending himself, he wishes to insinuate a contrast between himself and St Peter: while he himself is no regarder of persons and seeks only to please God, Peter at Antioch failed to live up to his own convictions, and withdrew from association with the Gentile Christians in order to conciliate the circumcision party (cf. 2 : 12).

*Should a preacher try to please men?*

St Paul himself realized that the Christian preacher has a duty where possible to please both God and men. This is implied in his acceptance of the Jewish missionary maxim: 'Become all things to all men.' [98] And since the gospel is by definition 'good news', the preaching of it should in the nature of things be pleasing both to God and to men.

What St Paul means in v. 10 is of course that when it is impossible to proclaim the truth according to God's will without offending men, he is willing to offend men. St Jerome, who did not give the best example in this matter, at least gave an excellent maxim: [99]

> If it is possible to please both God and men as well, we should please men as well; but if we cannot please men without displeasing God, we should please God rather than men.

---

[97] Cf. Chrysostom, PG 61, 625 C.

[98] Cf. 1 Cor 9:22, on which see Daube, *The New Testament and Rabbinic Judaism*, p. 336.

[99] St Jerome, PL 26, 345 C. St Thomas, Gal, 386 D, solves this little problem by saying that we should not seek to please men for their own sake but in order to draw them towards God.

This can be illustrated from Acts 4:13-20 where the chief priests forbid Peter and John to preach or teach in the name of Jesus, and they reply: 'Judge for yourselves whether it is right before God that we should obey you rather than God; as for us, it is not possible for us to keep silence about what we have seen and heard.'

*Would St Paul say that every Christian is a 'servant' or 'slave' of Christ?*

In Galatians, St Paul describes himself as a 'servant' or 'slave' (*doulos*) of Christ, but he does not say the same of all Christians. Perhaps he deliberately refrained from doing so. His main thesis in this Epistle is that Christianity means liberation from slavery to sonship. When the believer passes out of the old aeon in which the Mosaic law was binding, he passes into a new aeon where Christ's law of charity must be obeyed and (thanks to the gift of the Spirit) can be obeyed. The new situation can be described by saying that the believer becomes a 'servant of Christ'; but this has certain disadvantages: the Greek word *doulos* has strong overtones of constraint. [100]

On the other hand, there were disadvantages in talking too much about Christian liberty. Immature Christians would draw the conclusion that actions previously sinful were no longer sinful for them. To counteract such 'libertinism' or 'antinomianism', St Paul sometimes tells all Christians that they are 'slaves of Christ'. There is an example in 1 Cor 7:22: 'A man who was a slave when called by the Lord becomes the Lord's freedman; and one who was free when called becomes Christ's slave.' But a much closer parallel to Gal 1:10 is Col 3:22-24, which contrasts 'pleasing man' and 'serving Christ':

> **A** Servants, obey in all things your human lords, **B** not with eye-service like man-pleasers, but in the simplicity of your heart (i.e. with single-mindedness) fearing the Lord. **C** Whatever you do, do it with a will, **B¹** for the Lord and not for men, knowing that you will receive from the Lord an inheritance as reward. **A¹** Be servants to the Lord Christ.

Both in 1 Cor 7 and in Col 3, St Paul starts from the thought of ordinary human slavery. It is unlikely that he intends any special allusion to the Servant Songs of Isaiah.

---

[100] W. Zimmerli and J. Jeremias, *The Servant of God* (SBT, 20), London, 1965, p. 40, observe that from Exodus to Judges the LXX avoids the harsh word *doulos* when translating *'ebhed*.

# THE CONVERSION OF ST PAUL

In Gal 1:12 St Paul says that he received his gospel 'through a revelation of Jesus Christ'. The context shows that he is referring to the vision which he saw on the road to Damascus. [1] But he cannot mean that he received the whole content of his preaching during this vision, since his preaching included details of Christ's resurrection appearances to the other apostles and disciples and of the institution of the Eucharist, which he is not likely to have learned direct from Christ on the road to Damascus. [2] In Gal 1:12, he must be referring to the doctrines which were characteristic of his own presentation of the gospel, namely, that God justifies Gentiles through the faith, that circumcision is not necessary for salvation, and that Christ is the end of the law for all who believe. He must have learned at least these things, and perhaps much more, from the vision. It will be profitable to examine the three narratives of the Damascus incident given in Acts 9, 22 and 26, to see how far they contain, at least implicitly, the characteristic theses of St Paul's theology.

The first narrative, in Acts 9, is an account of St Paul's conversion such as Ananias or some other member of the church of Damascus might have given. There is no attempt to describe what St Paul saw or heard (apart from the essential self-disclosure: 'I am Jesus, whom you are persecuting'). This narrative seems to say quite clearly that St Paul first heard of his mission to the Gentiles from Ananias, not directly from Christ himself. The structure of the narrative is as follows:

A   Paul plots against the Christians in Damascus, 9:1-2.
B   Paul sees the vision, is blinded, fasts, 9:3-9.
C   Ananias sees a vision and is commanded to go to Paul, 9:10-14.
D   *Paul's mission is foretold by Christ, 9:15-16.*
C¹   Ananias goes to Paul and reports his vision, 9:17.
B¹   Paul's sight is restored, he is baptized, and eats again, 9:18-19a.
A¹   Paul preaches Christ in Damascus; the Jews plot to kill him, 9:19b-25.

Here is the text:

A   *9:1* Saul, who was still uttering threats of slaughter against the Lord's disciples, went to the High Priest *2* and asked him for letters to the synagogues in Damascus, authorizing him to bring to Jerusalem as pris-

---

[1]   This has been called in question by A. Fridrichsen, *The Apostle and his Message*, Uppsala, 1947; cf. Whiteley, *Theology of St Paul*, p. 11.
[2]   Cf. 1 Cor 11 and 15. The wording is almost identical in Gal 1:11a and 1 Cor 15:1a. For various views on what St Paul learned in his Damascus vision, see A. Goffinet, 'La prédication de l'évangile et de la croix,' ETL 41 (1965), pp. 412-413.

oners any followers of the Way, whether men or women, whom he might find there.   **B**   *3* He was on his journey and approaching Damascus, when suddenly a light from heaven flashed about him.   *4* He fell to the ground, and heard a voice saying to him: 'Saul, Saul, why are you persecuting me?'   *5* Saul said: 'Who are you, Lord?' and he replied: 'I am Jesus, whom you are persecuting!   *6* But rise up and go into the city, and you will be told what you must do.'   *7* The men who were making the journey with him stood there speechless, for they heard the voice but saw no one.   *8* Saul rose from the ground, and when he opened his eyes, he had lost his sight; so they led him by the hand into Damascus.   *9* For three days he could not see, and took no food or drink.   **C**   *10* In Damascus there was a disciple called Ananias. The Lord called him in a vision: 'Ananias!' He replied: 'Here I am, Lord!'   *11* The Lord said to him: 'Rise up and go to the street called The Straight, and inquire at the house of Judas for a man named Saul of Tarsus. He is now praying *12* and has seen a man called Ananias coming in to lay his hands on him to restore his sight.'   *13* Ananias replied: 'Lord, I have heard many accounts of all the wrongs this man has done to your people in Jerusalem. *14* And now he has authority from the chief priests to take prisoners all who call on your name.'   **D**   *15* But the Lord said to him: 'Go! For this man is a vessel whom I have chosen to carry my name to the Gentiles and their kings, and to the children of Israel.   *16* I shall reveal to him how much he himself must suffer for my name's sake.'   **C¹**   *17* So Ananias went. He entered the house, and laid his hands on him and said: 'Brother Saul, the Lord has sent me — Jesus, who was seen by you on your way here — so that you may recover your sight and be filled with the Holy Spirit.'   **B¹**   *18* At once what looked like scales fell from his eyes and he recovered his sight. He rose up and was baptized, and afterwards *19* took food and regained his strength.   **A¹** Paul spent a few days with the disciples in Damascus,   *20* and then began at once to preach Jesus in the synagogues, declaring: 'He is the Son of God.'   *21* All who heard him were amazed and asked: 'Is not this the man who in Jerusalem caused devastation among those who call on this name? And did he not come here expressly to take them as prisoners to the chief priests?' *22* But Saul went from strength to strength, and confounded the Jews of Damascus with his proofs that Jesus was the Messiah.   *23* After many days had passed, the Jews made a plot to kill Saul,   *24* but their plans were made known to him. They were watching the gates night and day, in order to kill him;   *25* but his disciples took him by night and lowered him down over the wall in a basket.

In the second narrative, in chapter 22, the announcement of Paul's mission is again placed at the centre. Ananias tells Paul that he is to be Christ's witness 'before all men' — with no explicit mention of the Gentiles here.

The whole speech is addressed to an audience of Jews in Jerusalem. Probably the crowd included large numbers of *Christian* Jews (cf.

Acts 21 : 20) who disapproved of St Paul's Gentile missions. The speech appears to be planned so as to answer the criticism that he should have stayed in Jerusalem and Judaea to convert his own people first. The impassioned profession of loyalty to Israel in Rom 9 : 1-5 was probably occasioned by the same criticism:

> I am speaking the truth in Christ, I am not lying, my conscience bears me witness in the Holy Spirit, that I have great grief and unceasing pain in my heart; indeed I could wish myself to be anathema from Christ for the sake of my brethren, my kinsmen according to the flesh. They are the Israelites; to them belong sonship, the glory, the covenants; theirs are the law, the liturgy, the promises; theirs are the patriarchs, and from them Christ is descended according to the flesh — he who is exalted above all things, God blessed for ever. [3] Amen.

He means that it was not through indifference to the fate of his fellow-Israelites that he turned to the Gentiles. In Acts 22 he tells his fellow-Israelites that when God appointed him to be 'witness before all men', he chose Jerusalem as the place where he thought his witness would be most effective (vv. 19-20), but Christ told him that his word would not be accepted in Jerusalem; he must go to the Gentiles. Therefore it was not by his own choice or inclination that he had embarked on the Gentile mission.

Such being Paul's argument, it is understandable if he paraphrases Ananias's words so as to omit explicit reference to the Gentiles. It is also understandable that he omits mention of his preaching in Arabia. [4] The plan of the discourse is as follows:

A    Paul comes from the Gentile world to Jerusalem, 22:3.
B    Paul persecuted the Christians, vv. 4-5a.
C    Paul's journey from Jerusalem to Damascus, v. 5b.
D    Paul's vision on the road to Damascus, vv. 6-11.
E    Ananias restores Paul's sight, vv. 12-13.
F    *Ananias tells Paul of his mission, vv. 14-15.*
E¹    Ananias urges Paul to receive baptism (*phôtismos*), v. 16.
D¹    Paul's vision in Jerusalem, vv. 17-18a.
C¹    Paul is commanded to leave Jerusalem, v. 18b.
B¹    Paul speaks of his days as a persecutor, vv. 19-20.
A¹    Paul is sent from Jerusalem to the Gentiles, v. 21.

Here is the text:

A    *22 : 3* I am a Jew. I was born at Tarsus in Cilicia, but brought up in this city. I was carefully trained in the law of our fathers at the feet of

---

[3]    On the translation here, see Wainwright, *The Trinity in the New Testament*, pp. 54-58.

[4]    St. Luke may have omitted mention of Arabia after 9:20 so as not to introduce a discrepancy between ch. 9 and ch. 22.

Gamaliel, and became full of zeal for God as you all are today.  **B**  *4* I
persecuted followers of this Way even to death, and had men and women
thrown into prison and chains,  *5* as the High Priest and the whole body
of elders can bear me witness.   **C**  Equipped with letters from them to
the brethren in Damascus, I had set out to put the Christians in bonds
and bring them back to Jerusalem for punishment.   **D**  *\*6* But in the
course of my journey, when I was approaching Damascus, suddenly about
mid-day a great light from heaven shone all round me.  *7* I fell to the
ground and heard a voice saying to me: 'Saul, Saul, why are you persecuting me?'  *8* I asked: 'Lord, who are you?' He replied: 'I am Jesus
of Nazareth, whom you are persecuting.'  *9* My companions saw the light
but did not hear the voice speaking to me.  *10* I asked: 'What am I to
do, Lord?' And the Lord replied: 'Rise up and go into Damascus. There
you will be told about all that you have been appointed to do.'  *11* As I
had lost my sight through the brilliance of that light, my companions led
me by the hand, and in that way I came into Damascus.   **E**  *12* And a
man named Ananias, a devout observer of the law, a man held in esteem by
all the Jews living in Damascus,  *13* came to me and stood beside me, and
said: 'Brother Saul, receive back your sight!' That very instant I recovered
my sight and looked at him.   **F**  *14* He said: 'The God of our fathers
has chosen you to know his will, to see the Just One, and to hear words
from his own lips,  *15* because you are to be his witness before all men
of what you have seen and heard.   **E¹**  *16* And now why delay? Make
haste and be baptized, call on his name, and have your sins washed away!'
**D¹**  *\*17* After I had returned to Jerusalem, I was once praying in the
temple, when I fell into ecstasy  *18* and saw the Lord saying to me:
**C¹**  'Bestir yourself, and leave Jerusalem quickly, for here they will not
accept your witness about me.'   **B¹**  *19* I replied: 'Lord, they know
themselves how I used to imprison those who believe in you and how I
had them beaten in the synagogues;  *20* and when the blood of your
witness Stephen was shed, I was standing by, and showed my approval
by keeping the clothes of those who were killing him.'   **A¹**  *21* But he
said to me: 'Go! I shall send you to Gentile nations far away.'

The third narrative, in chapter 26, is again a selective account of
what happened, designed to meet the needs of Paul's immediate situation: he is explaining himself to King Agrippa, to show him why the
Pharisees are seeking his death. He has no need to mention Ananias,
and in fact omits him altogether. Nor does he need to defend his
mission to the Gentiles. The purpose of his speech is to bear witness
to the resurrection, and to preach the gospel to this Jewish and Gentile
audience. Accordingly, this time the words of the risen Lord about
himself are placed at the centre of the whole passage: 'I am Jesus,
whom you are persecuting.'

---

\*  V. 6, literally translated, begins: 'It happened to me as I was walking and
   approaching Damascus,' and v. 17 begins: 'It happened to me as I had returned
   to Jerusalem.'

In this account, Jesus himself appears to tell Paul of his mission
to the Gentiles. But this is not a falsification, only a simplification, of
what happened. There is no mention of Ananias, and the two visions
of chapter 22 are combined into one. This is the only account in which
Jesus promises to protect Paul from his persecutors — but the point
is appropriate here, since Paul can show that the promise has been
fulfilled in a remarkable way. The structure is as follows:

A    Agrippa is familiar with Jewish ways and controversies, 26 : 2-3a.
B    Paul asks for a patient hearing, and speaks of his Pharisaic training,
     vv. 3b-5.
C    Paul is defending faith in resurrection, vv. 6-8.
D    Paul once persecuted the Christians, vv. 9-11a —
E    in foreign cities and Damascus, vv. 11b-12a.
F    He had authority from the High Priest. He saw the great light,
     vv. 12b-13.
G    All fell to the ground. Christ asked: 'Why are you persecuting me?'
     vv. 14-15a.
H    *The self-disclosure of Jesus*, v. 15b.
G¹   Paul is told to stand up. Christ explains why he has appeared, and
     promises to protect Paul from persecutors, vv. 16-17a.
F¹   Christ gives authority to Paul to lead the Gentiles to the light,
     vv. 17b-18.
E¹   Paul preaches in Damascus and among the Gentiles, vv. 19-20.
D¹   The Jews have persecuted Paul, but God has protected him, vv. 21-22a.
C¹   Moses and the prophets foretold the death and resurrection of Christ,
     vv. 22b-23.
B¹   Festus grows impatient, interrupts, mocks Paul's learning, vv. 24-25.
A¹   Agrippa understands these matters, v. 26a.

## Here is the text:

A    *26 : 2* 'I consider myself fortunate, King Agrippa, that it is before you,
*3* who are so familiar with Jewish customs and controversies, that I am
to make my defence against all the accusations brought against me by
the Jews.    B    I beg you, therefore, to give me a patient hearing.    *4* The
manner of life which I follow (I adopted it from my earliest youth, when
living among my own nation at Jerusalem) is known to all the Jews.
*5* They know me from of old and could testify, if they wished, that I
lived by the rules of the strictest sect of our religion, I mean as a
Pharisee.    C    *6* And now I am standing trial because of my trust in
the promise made by God to our fathers,    *7* a promise which our twelve
tribes, by earnest worship night and day, hope to see fulfilled. For that
hope, sir, I am now being accused by the Jews.    *8* Why do you Jews
deem it incredible that God should raise the dead?    D    *9* At one time,
I myself thought it my duty to oppose the name of Jesus of Nazareth,
*10* and I did oppose it, vigorously, in Jerusalem: I received authorization
from the chief priests and threw many of God's people into prison, and
my vote helped to bring them to their death.    *11* I went from synagogue

F

to synagogue, and used torture on many occasions to make them blaspheme. E  In the excess of my fury against them, I would even go to foreign cities and track them down.  *12* I was on one of these journeys to Damascus,  F  with authority and permission from the chief priests, *13* and at mid-day we were going along, sir, when a light more dazzling than the sun shone out of heaven all round me and my companions. G  *14* We all fell to the ground, and I heard a voice saying to me in the language of the Jews: 'Saul, Saul, why are you persecuting me? It is no good kicking against the goad.'  *15* I said: 'Who are you, Lord?' H  He replied: 'I əm Jesus, whom you are persecuting.  G¹  *16* But rise up, stand on your feet. The reason why I have appeared to you is to appoint you to be my minister and to bear witness that you have seen me, as you have seen me and will see me again.  *17* I shall rescue you both from your own people and from the Gentiles.  F¹  To them I send you,  *18* to open their eyes, and to lead them from darkness to light, from the domain of Satan to the kingdom of God, that they may receive forgiveness of their sins and an inheritance among those who are sanctified through faith in me.'  E¹  *19* And so, King Agrippa, I did not disobey the heavenly vision.  *20* First in Damascus, then in Jerusalem and throughout Judaea, and also to the Gentiles, I preached repentance and conversion to God, and urged men to give active proof of their conversion.  D¹  *21* And my reward was that the Jews arrested me in the temple and tried to take my life.  *22* But I have enjoyed God's protection to this present day, and still stand here to bear my witness before both high and low.  C¹  Nor do I depart in the least from what Moses and the prophets foretold:  *23* that the Messiah would suffer, that he would be the first of the dead to rise, and that he would bring a message of light both to Israel and to the Gentiles.'  B¹  *24* Festus here interrupted Paul's defence by exclaiming: 'You are raving, Paul! Too much learning is making you mad!'  *25* Paul replied: 'Not so, your Excellency, I am not mad; I am speaking words of sober truth.  A¹  *26* The king understands these matters, and it is to him that I am addressing these plain words of mine.'

## Can these three texts be harmonized?

As is well known, there are a few minor discrepancies between the three narratives (e.g. between 9:7 and 22:9). It has even been said that the three texts present a 'synoptic problem' in miniature. But it is not difficult to combine them into one consecutive history by taking them in the following order:

1. Christ appears to Paul and sends him to Ananias:  9:3-5
   26:16-18
   9:6-9

2. Christ appears to Ananias and sends him to Paul:  9:10-16

3. **Ananias goes to Paul**
                     restores his sight:               9:17-18a
                     delivers the message:           22:14-15
                     invites Paul to be baptized:    22:16
                     Paul is baptized:                9:18b-19

4. Paul preaches in Damascus:               9:19b-25

5. Paul returns to Jerusalem and sees Christ in the
                                  temple:      22:17-21.

Gal 1:23 implies that the story of St Paul's conversion was well known in the churches of Judaea, and there can be no doubt that it was well known in the Gentile churches founded by Paul himself. It is, therefore, most unlikely that St Luke himself created the details of his three narratives. If he is recording tradition, it is reasonable to try to harmonize his three narratives, and such attempts should not be condemned as 'conservative'. The composite text will run as follows.

> *9 : 3* He was on his journey and approaching Damascus, when suddenly a light from heaven flashed about him. *4* He fell to the ground, and heard a voice saying to him: 'Saul, Saul, why are you persecuting me?' *5* Saul said: 'Who are you, Lord?' and he replied: 'I am Jesus, whom you are persecuting!' *26 : 16* But rise up, stand on your feet. The reason why I have appeared to you is to appoint you to be my minister and to bear witness that you have seen me, as you have seen me and will see me again. *17* I shall rescue you both from your own people and from the Gentiles. To them I send you, *18* to open their eyes, and to lead them from darkness to light, from the domain of Satan to the kingdom of God, that they may receive forgiveness of their sins and an inheritance among those who are sanctified through faith in me. *9 : 6* But rise up, and go into the city, and you will be told what you must do.' *7* The men who were making the journey with him stood there speechless, for they heard the voice but saw no one. *8* Saul rose from the ground, and when he opened his eyes, he had lost his sight; so they led him by the hand into Damascus. *9* For three days he could not see, and took no food or drink.

> *9 : 10* In Damascus there was a disciple called Ananias. The Lord called him in a vision: 'Ananias!' He replied: Here I am, Lord!' *11* The Lord said to him: 'Rise up and go to the street called The Straight, and inquire at the house of Judas for a man named Saul of Tarsus. He is now praying *12* and he has seen a man called Ananias coming in to lay his hands on him to restore his sight.' *13* Ananias replied: 'Lord, I have heard many accounts of all the wrongs this man has done to your people in Jerusalem. *14* And now he has authority from the chief priests to take prisoner all who call on your name.' *15* But the Lord said to him: 'Go! For this man is a vessel whom I have chosen to carry my name to the Gentiles and their kings, and to the children of Israel. *16* I shall reveal to him how much he himself must suffer for my name's sake.'

*9 : 17* So Ananias went. He entered the house, and laid his hands on him and said: 'Brother Saul, the Lord has sent me — Jesus, who was seen by you on your way here — so that you may recover your sight and be filled with the Holy Spirit.' *18* At once what looked like scales fell from his eyes and he recovered his sight. *22 : 14* He said: 'The God of our fathers has chosen you to know his will, to see the Just One and to hear words from his own lips, *15* because you are to be his witness before all men of what you have seen and heard. *16* And now why delay? Make haste and be baptized, call on his name, and have your sins washed away.' *9 : 18b* He rose up and was baptized, and afterwards *19* took food and regained his strength.

*9 : 19b* Paul spent a few days with the disciples in Damascus, *20* and then began at once to preach Jesus in the synagogues, declaring: 'He is the Son of God.' *21* All who heard him were amazed and asked: 'Is not this the man who in Jerusalem caused devastation among those who called on his name? And did he not come here expressly to take them as prisoners to the chief priests?' *22* But Saul went from strength to strength, and confounded the Jews of Damascus with his proofs that Jesus was the Messiah. *23* After many days had passed, the Jews made a plot to kill Saul, *24* but their plans were made known to him. They were watching the gates night and day, in order to kill him; *25* but his disciples took him by night and lowered him down over the wall in a basket.

*22 : 17* After I had returned to Jerusalem, I was once praying in the temple, when I fell into ecstasy *18* and saw the Lord saying to me: 'Bestir yourself, and leave Jerusalem quickly, for here they will not accept your witness about me.' *19* I replied: 'Lord, they know themselves how I used to imprison those who believe in you and how I had them beaten in the synagogues; *20* and when the blood of your witness Stephen was shed, I was standing by and showed my approval by keeping the clothes of those who were killing him.' *21* But he said to me: 'Go! I shall send you to Gentile nations far away.'

This composite narrative brings to light a remarkable similarity between the appearance of Christ to Ananias in Damascus and the appearance of Christ to Paul in the temple: in each, Christ announces his will and the recipient of the vision raises an objection on the ground of Paul's past; in each, the objection is overruled and the recipient obeys. In a book like Acts, which makes such extensive use of chiastic patterns, there is a strong probability that two matching passages of this kind will be structural counterparts. But if the two visions are counterparts, the appearance of Christ to Ananias ought to precede the appearance to Paul on the road. As the appearance to Paul in the temple is certainly the end of the whole narrative, the vision which is its counterpart must be the beginning. If this transposition is made (i.e., if the appearance to Ananias in Damascus is placed before the appearance to Paul on the road), the composite text is almost symmetrical. The only defect is that there is nothing in the first half to match St Paul's preaching at Damascus in the second half. To fill the gap, one must introduce Acts 9:1-2 (the counterpart of Paul's Damascus-preaching in chapter 9 as it stands — see above, p. 95).

It seems, then, that St Luke compiled his three narratives of St Paul's conversion by breaking down an earlier and larger composition which had this form:

A     Christ appears to Ananias, overrules his protest, 9:10-16.
B     Paul plans a persecution at Damascus, 9:1-2.
C     Christ appears to Paul, 9:3-6 <26:16-18> 7-9.
C$^1$    Ananias cures Paul, gives message, 9:17-18a <22:14-16> 18b.
B$^1$    Paul preaches Christ at Damascus, 9:19-25.
A$^1$    Christ appears to Paul in Jerusalem, overrules his protest, 22:17-21.

The narrative thus reconstructed bears certain resemblances to the story of the conversion of Cornelius. The two begin in the same way:

| There was a man in Caesarea by name Cornelius. | There was a disciple in Damascus by name Ananias. |

Each sees a vision: in the one Cornelius is told to send men to a certain house where they will find Peter; in the other Ananias is told to go to a certain house where he will find Paul. In each case the house is identified by the name of the owner. Then, in each narrative, the scene changes to the principal character. Again similar wording is used:

| On the next day, while they were on their way and approaching the city. | While they were going along and approaching Damascus. |

Then in each case the Lord speaks.

Then Peter goes to Cornelius and tells him his vision, and Cornelius in reply tells his. But in the reconstruction given above, Ananias comes to Paul and narrates his vision, but Paul does not narrate his. Probably he ought to, for in both narratives Christ grants two complementary visions to two persons, so that words of each will confirm the objectivity of the other's vision. Cornelius and Peter confirm each other; Ananias and Paul should confirm each other. [5] This defect in the reconstruction can be remedied by introducing Acts 22:6-11 after 9:18, thus:

A     Christ appears to Ananias, 9:10-16.
B     Paul plans a persecution at Damascus, 9:1-2.

---

[5]   Perhaps there was a similar relationship between John the Baptist and Christ. Cf. J. Bligh, 'Did Christ live by Faith?' HJ 9 (1968), pp. 414-419.

C     Christ appears to Paul, 9:3-6 <26:16-18> 7-9.
D     *Ananias visits Paul*, 9:17-18.
C¹    Paul narrates his vision; Ananias gives message, 22:6-11,14-16.
B¹    Paul is baptized, preaches at Damascus, 9:18b-25.
A¹    Christ appears to Paul in the temple, 22:17-21.

The most striking thing which emerges from a comparison of the Cornelius-incident and the conversion of St Paul is that whereas Peter's vision contains the lesson that the Gentiles are clean, Paul's does not. And yet, according to Gal 1:12, *Paul* was taught this by revelation during the Damascus vision! Probably the explanation is that *the vision of the sail-cloth was originally part of the narrative of the conversion of St Paul*, and St Luke transferred it to St Peter for his own good reasons. To test this hypothesis, let us examine three questions.

## (1) *Was the Vision of the Sail-Cloth seen by Peter?*

There are various reasons for thinking that it was not:

1. According to Mk 7:14-23, Jesus taught Peter and the others during the public ministry that 'nothing which enters a man from the outside can defile him,' and explained in private that this has reference to the food laws. In Acts 10, St Peter appears to have forgotten all about this. St Luke probably foresaw this difficulty; he omits Mk 7:14-23 (it is part of his 'Great Omission').

2. It is hard to believe that Peter, the Galilean fisherman, had observed the food laws so strictly that he could say he had never eaten anything unclean. We do not know the occasion on which Jesus gave the teaching recorded in Mk 7:14-23;[6] it is a fair guess that he did so when he and the apostles ate something 'unclean'.

3. It is hard to believe that St Peter would have refused to obey the thrice repeated command to take and eat.

## (2) *Does the Vision of the Sail-Cloth belong to the Cornelius-story?*

The vision is directly concerned with clean and unclean *foods*. It was meant to show that the apostle would not be defiled by eating 'unclean animals' and hence could eat with Gentiles without defile-

---

[6]   The setting provided in Mk 7:1-5 is only loosely connected with the discourse on cleanliness (cf. 7:14). According to the *Epistle of Barnabas*, V, 9, the apostles, before Christ called them, were 'supersinners' (literally 'lawless beyond

ment. Eating with Gentiles was forbidden, not because the Gentiles themselves were unclean, but rather because their food was presumed to be unclean.

The vision did not teach that God has made all men clean — there were no men in the sail-cloth. God cleanses the Gentiles from their sins by baptism.

In the narrative of the conversion of Cornelius (ch. 10), there is no mention of any meal taken by Peter with Cornelius. Of course he did eat with Cornelius during the few days of his stay after baptizing him. But presumably Cornelius did not serve 'unclean animals' for Peter to eat. The vision, therefore, has no direct relevance to the Cornelius story. [7]

When the servants of Cornelius arrived to invite him, Peter naturally felt scruples about accepting — not because he foresaw that he might have to eat unclean food, but because of the general prohibition against entering the houses of Gentiles. The Holy Spirit ordered him to go without scruple (10:20). This was sufficient by itself, without the vision of the sail-cloth to support it. It meant that Peter could enter *this particular* Gentile house; it did not necessarily imply that henceforth he could enter any house he pleased. [7a] Thus, by removing the sail-cloth vision from the Cornelius-narrative, we have a reason why St Peter did not afterwards consort regularly with Gentiles.

Chapter 11, in which St Peter is made to repeat the vision of the sail-cloth, contains further anomalies. [8] Cornelius before conversion had been a highly-respected God-fearer, and Peter did not eat with him until after he and his household had been baptized. It is hard to believe that the Jewish Christians of Jerusalem would have objected to this, without any mention of Cornelius's remaining uncircumcised.


## (3) *Was the Vision of the Sail-Cloth seen by Paul?*

The vision of the sail-cloth fits into St Paul's conversion-story immediately after Acts 9:1-2. Paul had just received authorization

---

all sin'). This wild exaggeration may be due to a misunderstanding of Gal 2:6, on which see below, pp. 159-160.

[7] Dibelius, *Studies in the Acts of the Apostles*, pp. 111-2, adopts this view but for different reasons.

[7a] A similar question arises from the story of the Rich Young Man: is the word of Jesus (Mk 10:21) universally applicable? Cf. H. von Campenhausen, *Tradition and Life in the Church*, London, 1968, p. 93.

[8] Cf. Dibelius, *Studies in the Acts of the Apostles*, p. 109.

to go to Damascus and arrest Christians as being disloyal to Jewish law and tradition. The next day, he saw a vision in which a voice from heaven told him to abandon the Jewish food laws. He stoutly refused three times — presumably telling himself that it was a demonic temptation. But he cannot have been sure, and must have wondered whether God was indeed commanding him to abandon the Jewish 'tradition' on this important point. (There was nothing specifically Christian about this vision — the speaker did not identify himself.)

If Paul had obeyed the vision, he would have had to abandon his projected journey to Damascus. But he stifled his misgivings and set out. This will explain why, when Christ has appeared, he says: 'It is no good kicking against the pricks.' As a result of the vision of the sail-cloth, Paul was far from sure that he was doing right, yet he was stifling the pricks of conscience and persisting like a mule that kicks back at its driver's goad.

It is much more likely that Paul, the Pharisee of the Pharisees, could and would boast that he had never eaten anything unclean. He disobeys the thrice-repeated command, in order not to spoil his own fine record.

Further, if this vision belongs to Paul, it is easier to see how he could claim that the gospel for the Gentiles was revealed to *him*.

It seems, then, that the vision of the sail-cloth was originally a part of the narrative of St Paul's conversion-experience. If Acts 10:9-17a is inserted after 9:1-2, the sail-cloth let down from heaven will counterbalance the basket in which Paul is let down, and the saying about 'what God has cleansed' will be linked with baptism. But if Acts 10:9-17a belongs to this chain of events, probably the repetition of it in Acts 11 does too. St Luke appears to have divided up this long narrative between Peter and Paul in order to represent the two apostles as co-founders of the Gentile missions. The reconstructed narrative now has this form:

A   Christ appears to Ananias, 9:10-16.
B   Paul plans a persecution at Damascus, 9:1-2, and
    Paul sees the vision of the sail-cloth, 10:9-16a.
C   Christ appears to Paul, 9:3-4 <26:14b-18> 7-9.
D   *Ananias visits Paul,* 9:17-18a.
C¹  Paul narrates his vision, Ananias gives message, 22:6-11,14-16.
B¹  Paul is baptized, preaches at Damascus, 9:18b-25, and
    Paul is criticized, narrates vision of sail-cloth, 11:1-10,18. [9]
A¹  Christ appears to Paul in the temple, 22:17-21.

---

[9]  If 11:1-10, 18 is given to Paul, the vision of the sail-cloth is relevant. He is accused of *eating* with Gentiles (unconverted ones) and defends himself by reporting the vision which bears on *food*.

Here is the reconstructed narrative:

### Christ appears to Ananias (9:10-16)

*9 : 10* In Damascus there was a disciple called Ananias. The Lord called him in a vision: 'Ananias.' He replied: 'Here I am, Lord.' *11* The Lord said to him: 'Rise up and go to the street called The Straight, and inquire at the house of Judas for a man named Saul of Tarsus. [...] *13* Ananias replied: 'Lord, I have heard many accounts of all the wrongs this man has done to your people in Jerusalem. *14* And now he has authority from the chief priests to take prisoner all who call on your name.' *15* But the Lord said to him: 'Go! For this man is a vessel whom I have chosen to carry my name to the Gentiles and their kings, and to the children of Israel. *16* I shall reveal to him how much he himself must suffer for my name's sake.'

### Paul plans a persecution at Damascus, sees vision (9:1-2; 10:9-16a)

*9 : 1 For* Saul, still uttering threats of slaughter against the Lord's disciples, had gone to the High Priest *2* and asked him for letters to the synagogues of Damascus, authorizing him to bring to Jerusalem as prisoners any followers of the Way, whether men or women whom he might find there. *10 : 9* On the following day, [...] at mid-day *Paul* went up on to the roof to pray. *10* He felt hungry and asked for something to eat. While it was being prepared, he fell into an ecstasy, *11* and saw heaven opened and something like a large sheet being let down by its four corners on to the earth; *12* in it were all the beasts and reptiles of the earth and all the birds of the air. *13* Then a voice said to him: 'Rise up, *Saul*, kill and eat.' *14* But *Saul* said: 'No, Lord! Never have I eaten anything defiled or unclean.' *15* And the voice spoke to him a second time: 'What God has declared clean, it is not for you to declare unclean.' *16* This happened three times, and then the sheet was taken up into heaven.

### Christ appears to Paul (9:3-4; 26:14-18; 9:7-9)

*9 : 3* He was on his journey and approaching Damascus, when suddenly a light from heaven shone about him. *4* He fell to the ground, and heard a voice saying to him: 'Saul, Saul, why are you persecuting me?' *26 : 14* 'It is no good kicking against the goad.' *15* Saul said: 'Who are you, Lord?' And he replied: 'I am Jesus, whom you are persecuting. *16* But rise up, stand on your feet. The reason why I have appeared to you is to appoint you to be my minister and to bear witness that you have seen me, as you have seen me and you will see me again. *17* I shall rescue you both from your own people and the Gentiles. To them I send you, *18* to open their eyes, and to lead them from darkness to light, from the domain of Satan to the kingdom of God, that they may receive forgiveness of their sins and an inheritance among those who are sanctified through faith in me.' *9 : 7* The men who were making the journey with him stood there speechless, for they heard the voice but saw no one. *8* Saul rose from the ground, and when he opened his eyes, he had lost his sight; so they led him by the hand into Damascus. *9* For three days he could not see, and took no food or drink.

### Ananias visits Paul (9 : 17-18)

*9 : 17* Then Ananias entered the house, and laid his hands on him and said: 'Brother Saul, the Lord has sent me — Jesus, who was seen by you on your way here — so that you may recover your sight and be filled with the Holy Spirit.' *18* At once what looked like scales fell from his eyes and he recovered his sight. <Then Ananias asked what had happened.>

### Paul narrates his vision, Ananias gives message (22 : 6-11; 22 : 14-16)

<Paul said> *22 : 6* When I was approaching Damascus, suddenly about midday a great light from heaven shone all round me. *7* I fell to the ground and heard a voice saying to me: 'Saul, Saul, why are you persecuting me?' *8* I asked: 'Lord, who are you?' He replied: 'I am Jesus of Nazareth, whom you are persecuting.' [*9* My companions saw the light, but did not hear the voice speaking to me.] *10* I asked: 'What am I to do, Lord?' And the Lord replied: 'Rise up and go into Damascus. There you will be told about all you have been appointed to do.' *11* As I had lost my sight through the brilliance of that light, my companions led me by the hand, and in that way I came into Damascus...' *14* Ananias said: 'The God of our fathers has chosen you to know his will, to see the Just One, and to hear words from his lips, *15* because you are to be his witness before all men of what you have seen and heard. *16* And now why delay? Make haste and be baptized, call on his name, and have your sins washed away.'

### Paul is baptized, preaches at Damascus, is criticized (9 : 18b-25; 11 : 1-10,18)

*9 : 18b* He rose up and was baptized, and afterwards *19* took food and regained his strength. He spent a few days with the disciples in Damascus, *20* and then began at once to preach Jesus in the synagogues, declaring: 'He is the Son of God.' *21* All who heard him were amazed and asked: 'Is not this the man who in Jerusalem caused devastation among those who call on his name? And did he not come here expressly to take them as prisoners to the chief priests?' *22* But Saul went from strength to strength, and confounded the Jews of Damascus with his proofs that Jesus was the Messiah. *23* After many days had passed, the Jews made a plot to kill Saul, *24* but their plans were made known to him. They were watching the gates night and day, in order to kill him; *25* but his disciples took him by night and lowered him down over the wall in a basket.

*11 : 1* The apostles and brethren in Judaea heard that the Gentiles too had received the word of God. *2* When, therefore, *Paul* returned to

Jerusalem, those of the circumcision party fought with him, *3* because, they said, 'you have been visiting men who are uncircumcised and have sat at table with them.' *4* So *Paul* began from the beginning and explained everything point by point: *5* 'I was in the city....praying, when I fell into ecstasy and saw a vision of something like a large sheet being let down from heaven; it came close to me, *6* and I looked inside and saw the animals and beasts and reptiles of the earth and the birds of heaven, *7* and I heard a voice saying to me: "Rise up, *Paul,* kill and eat." *8* But I replied: "No, Lord. Never have I eaten anything defiled or unclean." *9* Then the voice from heaven spoke to me a second time: "What God has declared clean, it is not for you to declare unclean." *10* This happened three times, then it was all drawn back up to heaven...' *18* When they heard this their objections were silenced. They gave glory to God, and said: 'So then God has given life-giving repentance to the Gentiles too.'

### *Christ appears to Paul in the temple* (22: 17-21)

*22 : 17* 'After I had returned to Jerusalem, I was once praying in the temple, when I fell into ecstasy *18* and saw the Lord saying to me: "Bestir yourself, and leave Jerusalem quickly, for here they will not accept your witness about me." *19* I replied: "Lord, they know themselves how I used to imprison those who believe in you and how I had them beaten in the synagogues; *20* and when the blood of your witness Stephen was shed, I was standing by, and showed my approval by keeping the clothes of those who were killing him." *21* But he said to me: "Go, I shall send you to Gentile nations far away." ' '

## *The Pattern of Acts 10*

When the vision of the sail-cloth has been restored to St Paul, the remaining sections of Acts 10 form a coherent and consistent narrative, as can be seen from the following analysis. The vision of the sail-cloth is superfluous in Acts 10. The revelation of the Holy Spirit is enough to remove Peter's scruples.

**A** *9 : 43* Peter stayed in Joppa for some days, at the house of a tanner called Simon.  **B** *10 : 1* There was a man in Caesarea called Cornelius, a centurion of the Italian cohort. *2* He was devout and God-fearing, as were all his household; he gave alms generously to the Jews, and he prayed to God continually. *3* One day about three o'clock in the afternoon, he saw an unmistakable vision, in which an angel of God came to him and called him by name: 'Cornelius!' *4* He looked at the angel and said to him with awe: 'What is it, lord?' He replied: 'Your prayers and works of mercy have gone up to keep your name before God's sight. *5* Now therefore send to Joppa and invite here a man called Simon, surnamed Peter, *6* who is staying with Simon the tanner, the one whose house is close to the sea.'   *7* When the angel who had spoken to him had gone, Cornelius called two of his servants and a devout soldier who was one of his own staff,   *8* explained everything to them, and sent them off to Joppa.   **C**   *9a* On the following day (vision of sail-cloth omitted here) *17b* the men sent by Cornelius had asked their way to Simon's house and now stood at the door,   *18* and called out: 'Is Simon Peter lodging here?'   **D**   *19* As Peter was wondering (...), the Spirit said to him: 'There are three men here looking for you.   *20* Rise and go down to them, and do not hesitate to go with them, for it is I who sent them here.'   **C¹**   *21* So Peter went down to the men and said: 'Here I am! I am the man you are looking for. What has brought you here?'   **B¹**   *22* They replied: 'A certain Cornelius, a centurion, a just and God-fearing man, who is held in esteem by the whole Jewish people, has been told by an angel to invite you to his house and to listen to what you say.'   **A¹**   *23* So Peter invited the men in and gave them lodging.*

**A**   *23* So Peter invited the men in and gave them lodging.*   **B**   The next day he set out with them, accompanied by some of the brethren from Joppa.   **C**   *24* On the day following, they arrived at Caesarea, where Cornelius was waiting for them, with his relatives and closest friends, whom he had called together.   *25* As Peter came in, Cornelius went to meet him and fell at his feet and worshipped him.   *26* But Peter raised him up: 'Stand up,' he said, 'I am a man like yourself.'   *27* Then he conversed with him and went inside. There he found a large gathering of people.   *28a* He said to them: 'You know that it is unlawful for a Jew to associate with a Gentile or to enter his house. <But the Spirit has revealed to me that I should not hesitate to come to you.>   *29* That is why I made no difficulty about coming when you sent for me. May I ask, therefore, why you sent for me?'   **D**   *30* Cornelius replied: 'Three days ago, at about this time of day, I was reciting afternoon prayers in my house, when suddenly there stood before me a man dressed in a bright garment,   *31* who said to me: 'Cornelius, your prayer has been heard and your works of mercy set on record before God.   *32* Therefore send to Joppa and invite a certain Simon Peter to visit you. He is staying in the house of a tanner called Simon, close to the sea.'   *33* So I sent for you at once, and you have been so kind as to come. Now all of us are here in God's presence to hear what commands have been given you by the Lord.'   **C¹**   *34* Then Peter began to speak: 'I now see,' he said, 'how true it is that *God is not a respecter of persons,   35* and that every God-fearing man who leads a good life is welcomed, no matter what nation he belongs to.   *36* God *sent his word* to the children of Israel, *to bring them glad tidings of peace* in Jesus Christ, who is the Lord of all.   *37* You have heard of the movement through Judaea, starting from Galilee after the baptism preached by John.   *38* You know how Jesus of

---

\*   V. 23 is both the end of the first section and the beginning of the second. Chiastic patterns often overlap in this way.

Nazareth was anointed by God with *the Holy Spirit* and endowed with
power, and went about doing good and curing all who were oppressed by
the devil; for God was with him.   *39* We are witnesses to all that he did
in the country of the Jews and in Jerusalem. Yet they put him to death
by *hanging him on a tree.*   *40* But God raised him up on the third day
and allowed him to appear,   *41* not to the whole people, but to witnesses
whom God had chosen beforehand, namely ourselves, who ate and drank
with him after his resurrection from the dead.   *42* And he charged us
to preach to the people that it is he who has been appointed by God judge
of the living and the dead.   *43* All the prophets bear witness to him,
that through his name everyone who believes in him will receive forgiveness
of his sins.'   *44* While Peter was still speaking, the Holy Spirit came
upon all who were listening to the word.     B¹  *45* The circumcised
believers who had come with Peter were astonished that the gift of the
Holy Spirit had been poured out even on Gentiles;   *46* for they heard
them speaking in tongues and giving glory to God. Then Peter said:
*47* 'Can anyone refuse these men the water of baptism, when they have
received the Holy Spirit no less than we have?'   *48* And he gave instruction for them to be baptized in the name of Jesus Christ.    A¹   Then
they asked him to stay with them for some days.


## The lesson of St Paul's Visions

To return now to the question raised at the beginning of this
Excursus: How much of St Paul's gospel was revealed to him in the
Damascus vision? If the above reconstruction is correct, the question
must be broadened: How much did he learn from the three visions
surrounding his conversion?

In Gal 1:12, he claims that *the gospel which he preached to the
Gentiles* was revealed in these visions, hence that Gentile Christianity
is rooted in his conversion experiences. The gospel comes to the
Gentiles from the Father through (or in) the Son, by means of Paul,
and not from the Father through the Son by means of Peter and
Peter's envoy Paul. For the Gentiles Peter is only a confirmatory
witness, guaranteeing the truth of the gospel which Christ has sent
to them through Paul.

Gal 1:12 cannot mean that the Damascus vision convinced St Paul
that the gospel preached by St Peter, which he had previously regarded
as false and blasphemous, was in fact true, and that thereafter he
preached the gospel of Peter. What is said in Gal 1:12 is that the
revelation itself contained the gospel which Paul later preached. The
doctrines which he had previously rejected were, it is true, presented
to him in a new light and in a new way, so that they no longer seemed

a set of disjointed and foolish propositions but partial expressions of a great mystery which he was allowed to see. But that was not all. What he was allowed to see in the revelation included something fresh, which he had not heard before — something in virtue of which he could talk about 'my gospel'.

Let us examine ten pauline doctrines to see how it was possible for St Paul to learn them from his conversion experiences.

1. Jesus has risen from the dead.
2. He is the Messiah and Son of God.
3. He is Lord over the heavenly powers and principalities.
4. He is the pre-existent Son of God, operative in creation.
5. He identifies himself with believers and them with him, so that they too are God's sons.
6. His death was a redemptive sacrifice.
7. The Cross is a revelation of God's 'justice'.
8. Justification is through faith, and is entirely gratuitous.
9. Those who are united with Christ by faith are free from the Mosaic law.
10. Salvation is open to the Gentiles as Gentiles (without becoming Jews).

It is not to be supposed that St Paul immediately understood all these things with equal clarity. In a well-known passage of the *Literal Explanation of Genesis,* St Augustine points out that the recipient of a vision does not always understand its meaning forthwith: [10]

King Balthasar saw the fingers of a hand writing on the wall, and at once through his bodily sense the image of this bodily reality was printed on his spirit; and when the vision was over and gone, the image remained in his thought. It was <now> seen in spirit and not yet understood. Nor had this sign been understood when it was taking place in bodily reality (*corporaliter*) and manifesting itself to bodily eyes. It was, however, already understood to be a sign, having this character <of sign> from the mind's activity. And because its interpretation was lacking, the mind also started the search for it. It was not found. Then Daniel came, his mind illuminated by the prophetic spirit, and explained to the anxious King what the sign portended. Daniel was the prophet, by reason of this type of vision which belongs to the mind alone — rather than the King who had seen the bodily sign with his bodily eyes, and afterwards continued to see its image in his spirit when he thought about it, and yet with his intellect could do nothing about it except recognize it as a sign and ask for its meaning.

Peter saw in ecstasy a vessel tied by four cords let down from heaven full of various kinds of animals, and he heard a voice saying: 'Kill and eat.' When he had returned to his senses and was wondering about the vision, the Spirit announced to him the men sent by Cornelius: 'Behold

[10]   *De Genesi ad literam,* XII, 23-24 (PL 34, 462).

men are looking for you; rise, go down and accompany them, for it is I who sent them.' When he arrived at Cornelius's house, he himself indicated what he had understood by the words of the vision: 'What God has made clean, do not call common,' for he said: 'God has shown me that I must call no man common or unclean.' Thus when he saw the vessel in a state of separation from his bodily senses, he also heard in spirit the words: 'Kill and eat' and 'What God has cleansed, do not call common.' When restored to his bodily senses, he continued to see in the same spirit by means of his thought what he had seen and heard and preserved in his memory. These were not bodily realities but images of bodily realities, both when they were first seen in ecstasy, and afterwards when remembered and thought about. While Peter was wondering and seeking to understand these signs, his mind was active, but to no effect, until the envoys of Cornelius were announced. Aided by this bodily vision, when he heard the Holy Spirit say to him 'Go with them,' he heard this in the same spirit in which the Holy Spirit had shown him the sign and imprinted his former words, and with divine assistance understood the significance of all these signs.

If the vision of the sail-cloth really belongs to St Paul, the point remains valid. He did not at once perceive its meaning, or he would have abandoned his journey to Damascus.

It is no longer possible for us to trace the stages by which St Paul's thought developed at the time of his conversion. Often a man cannot even retrace the paths of his own thoughts, let alone anyone else's. If he is asked to explain his position, he will describe a short cut by which he could have arrived at it. Similarly with the thought of another man, and of Paul in particular: we cannot say by what circuitous routes he arrived at the ten propositions listed above, but perhaps we can show how he could have arrived at them, starting from his vision. At all events let us try.

## 1.

On the road to Damascus, it seems that St Paul first saw the figure of Christ in glory (cf. 1 Cor 9: 1; Acts 9: 17), then fell on his face in adoration [11] — as Peter, James and John had done at the Transfiguration (cf. Mt 17: 6). But Paul did not know who the figure was. The vision (as a visual experience) did not interpret itself. As is usual in the visions of the Bible, the interpretation was given in words. [12] Paul found himself asking: 'Who are you, lord?' the word 'lord' (*kyrie*) does not itself imply the answer. It was a suitable form

---

[11]  However, St Augustine, *Enarratio in Ps 67:28* (PL 36, 835), may be right in thinking that after Paul's bodily eyes had been blinded by the light, he saw Christ in a spiritual vision.

[12]  Cf. W. Bulst, *Offenbarung*, Düsseldorf, 1960, p. 23.

of address for an angel, as can be seen from Acts 10:4, where Cornelius sees an angel and calls him 'lord'. The answer to Paul's question was given by Christ himself: the glorious figure said: 'I am Jesus, whom you are persecuting.'

At once Paul knows that Jesus who was crucified has risen from the dead and is now a figure of power and glory. The resurrection of the dead has begun; Jesus is 'the firstborn of the dead' (Col 1:18). For him 'the world to come' or future 'aeon' is already present.

## 2.

Within a very short time, St Paul recognized that Jesus was Messiah and Son of God, since this was the message he preached in Damascus (cf. Acts 9:20-22). No doubt he knew that during the trial before Caiaphas Jesus had claimed to be Messiah and Son of God. When he saw Jesus in glory, he knew that God the Father had vindicated these claims, and that he himself was now seeing the glory of the only begotten Son (cf. Jn 1:14).

## 3.

Whenever St Paul speaks of Jesus as 'Lord', he thinks of his superiority to all angelic and demonic powers (cf. e.g. Phil 2:6-11). In the Damascus-vision, as it is described in Acts, no angels appear. But if Paul thought at first that he was seeing an angel, the contrast between 'angel' and 'Son' was brought into his mind in the course of the vision. Reflecting on it afterwards, he could see that his first conjecture had been far below the truth: he had seen not an angel but God's Son — not a servant, but the 'Lord of the whole property' (cf Gal 4:1).

Further, if it was St Paul who saw the vision of the sail-cloth, he could infer from it that if Christ has power to make an end of the prohibitions imposed by the angels of the law, [13] he must be superior to these angels.

## 4.

How did St Paul go on from here to gather that Christ existed before creation and was active in creation? [14] This is a difficult ques-

---

[13]  See below, on 3:19.
[14]  The practical relevance of the doctrine that Christ is our Creator is that as such he is the author of the law of our nature; the law of charity written in the hearts of believers by his Holy Spirit is a renewal of the law of our nature. This is a possible justification from Scripture of the Church's claim to pronounce in matters of natural law.

tion to answer. He may perhaps have known that the Jews had accused
Jesus of making himself equal to God and that Jesus had not rejected
the accusation. Or he may have known that Jesus had said: 'Before
Abraham was made, I am.' But if he learned this part of his Christology *from the vision itself*, he must somehow have seen the actual
dependence of created things on the glorious figure of his vision —
as some later saints have seen visions in which created beings appeared
as the terminations of streams of being flowing forth from God.
Perhaps Paul saw Christ, not as a sort of inset, isolated from the
world, like a picture within a picture, but as the very heart and
centre from which being radiates out. For that is what the Christology
of Colossians means: God the Father did not create the world separately, then give it to his Son; rather, by communicating the whole
of his power to his Son, he empowered him to create the world, so
that all creatures have a natural obligation to obey him. He is the
'Lord' of all things in the fullest possible sense, both as creator and
as redeemer (cf. Col 1 : 15-20). [15]

## 5.

The words, 'Why are you persecuting me?' and 'I am Jesus whom
you are persecuting,' taught Paul that Christ identifies himself with
those who believe in him, and them with him, to the point where he
regards their sufferings as his own. Through their faith they have
entered into a real sharing of life with their Risen Lord. Paul is not
simply persecuting individual men and women who believe in Christ;
he is persecuting Christ who lives in them and gives them strength
to resist persecution. Christ is the source, not only of their natural
being, but also of their supernatural life and strength. [16] It is he who
has put the new Spirit into men like Stephen and Ananias. The words
of Christ, then, contained the truth which Paul was later to express
in terms of the Body of Christ. [17] In Galatians he does not use the

---

[15] See further McKenzie, *The Power and the Wisdom*, p. 136; E. W. Hunt,
*Portrait of Paul*, London, 1968, pp. 185-195. Both these authors think that
Christ's pre-existence was seen to be implicit in the unique Sonship of Jesus. It
is unlikely to have been inferred from the supposition that the beginning of
history (*Urzeit*) must match its End (*Endzeit*)—that if God is to judge all men
through Christ at the end, he must have created all things through Christ at
the beginning. Cf. E. Käsemann, *The Testament of Jesus*, London, 1958, pp. 21
and 51.

[16] Cf. Easton, *Early Christianity*, p. 132.

[17] This is questioned by Whiteley, *The Theology of St Paul*, p. 194, on the
grounds that the Church is not explicitly described as Christ's Body in the
earliest Epistles. But as even the earliest of the Epistles is separated from the
vision by about eighteen years, the objection has little force. It is not to be
supposed that St Paul discovered the doctrine of 'the Mystical Body' (a phrase
which he never uses) between the writing of 1 Thes and 1 Cor.

image of the Body, but the doctrine is clearly present in Gal 2:20: 'It is no longer I who live, but Christ lives in me.'

From the identification of believers with Jesus it follows that they too are sons of God.

## 6.

Next, how did St Paul come to know that Christ's death on the Cross was the means of our salvation? No other New Testament writer lays as much emphasis on this doctrine as does St Paul. It was not revealed to him explicitly in the Damascus-vision, but it is easy to see how the vision would lead him to recognize Christ's death as a sacrifice. Before his conversion, he had shared the view that the Cross was the final proof that Jesus could not be the Messiah (cf Mt 27: 41-42). According to Deut 21:23 (quoted in Gal 3:13), a man hanged upon a tree is accursed of God. But it was inconceivable that the Messiah should be accursed of God. Therefore Jesus was not the Messiah. The argument seemed inescapable.

But now the vision revealed that the same Jesus, far from being accursed of God, was the Son of God, reigning in glory. This knowledge compelled St Paul to find another interpretation of the crucifixion. If Jesus was the Son of God, his death could not have been like the death of any ordinary man; it must have had some further significance — and what could this be but to bear the sins of others?

Or perhaps St Paul started from the words: 'Why are you persecuting me?' and reasoned that if Christ so far unites himself with those who believe in him as to regard their sufferings as his own, it will follow that conversely his sufferings and death are their own. Therefore all suffered and died in him. 'One died for all, therefore all died' (2 Cor 5:14). He *did* become anathema, but for the sake of others, to release them from the curse of the law.

## 7.

Continuing a little further along this same line of reflection, St Paul could easily come to see that the Cross is a revelation of the love and 'justice' of God the Father, for it was evidently with the Father's consent, or by his will, that his Son was born of a woman and bore the sins of disobedient men (cf. Gal 1:4). In a word, God proved his love for us by this: that while we were still sinners, Christ, his Son, died for us.

Then St Paul must surely have asked why God in his love allowed his Son to die for us. His answer in Romans appears to be that God wished to display, not only his mercy or his 'saving justice' — he could have done that by a pure condonation — but also his retribuitive justice. [18] He wished to judge men according to their merits and to acquit them according to their merits, and therefore provided in his Son, dead and risen, a store of merits, so that all who are united to him through faith can be acquitted through the collective merits of the Body to which they belong.

## 8.

Once St Paul had recognized that sinners are to be saved by the merits of Christ, and not by their own personal merits, it must have become plain to him that salvation is to be attained by that act which unites a man to Christ and enables him to share in his merits. This is simply the act of faith expressed in reception of Baptism. By Baptism a man enters into union with Christ, becomes a part of his Body, shares in his merits, and is sanctified by his Spirit. When he comes before God for judgment, he will not be judged solely by his personal observance or non-observance of the Mosaic law or of the law of God made known to him by his conscience. If he were judged in that way, he would be condemned. But he will be judged as a member of Christ and therefore acquitted or justified. The Christian is not an isolated individual before God; he is a member of a Body, and will be judged as such.

But there is also another sense in which faith justifies a man. St Paul appears to have found in himself a new mastery over sin after his conversion. Whereas previously he had struggled with the law, and tried with imperfect success to obey the commandment not to covet, or not to lust (*ouk epithumêseis*), after his conversion he found a new spirit within him (cf. Rom 7 : 7). He had become capable of controlling his evil desires, and thus found, by experience, that he had been made a just man. What all his zeal for the law had failed to do because of the weakness of his flesh, God had done by revealing his Son in glory. [19]

---

[18] This view is based on Rom 3 : 26, which is a paradox: God is just in the very act of acquitting the sinner who believes in Christ.

[19] In spite of K. Stendahl's fine article, 'The Apostle Paul and the Introspective Conscience of the West,' HTR 56 (1963), pp. 199-215, St Paul's description of the struggles of the unconverted man and of the effects of the Holy Spirit in the life of the baptized must surely owe something to his own personal experience. When 'kicking against the pricks', he was trying to silence misgivings about the value of his Pharisaism. He came to Christianity from the strictest form of Judaism—somewhat as Luther came to his Protestant position from a strict form of monastic Christianity. Cf. Fr. Lau, *Luther*, London, 1963, pp. 29, and 67: 'Luther's development into a reformer came out of his monastery

St Paul sometimes speaks (and St Luke still more so) as if belief in the gospel were simply a necessary condition of receiving the Holy Spirit — as if there were no psychological or causal connection between the condition and the gift. But elsewhere he attributes justification to faith as its *cause* (e.g. Rom 5:1). It is possible to point to several psychological causes of his new mastery over sin after his conversion. First, whereas knowledge of the law had failed to make the objects of his evil desires seem less desirable, the knowledge of God's love for him revealed in the Cross did reduce their fascination (cf. Gal 3:1). In other words, the love of God poured out in his heart so strengthened his willingness to obey as to make it effective: in the struggle with the flesh it now has the upper hand (cf. Rom 7:22-23; 8:13). Secondly, St Paul felt a new sense of dignity. He was God's son now, and obliged to act up to his nobility (cf. Eph 4:1). Thirdly, he had been given a new mission: to take the gospel to the Gentiles. This put an urgency and a purposefulness into his life. He felt that he was filling a major role and achieving something great (cf. Col 1:23), and the sacrifices involved in his ministry therefore seemed slight. And fourthly, he had been granted a glimpse of the glory which is in store for the faithful. This too would help him to govern selfish and fleshly desires (cf. 2 Cor 4:17). In other words, the content of the faith or the knowledge imparted by the gospel was itself a health-giving body of doctrine (cf. 1 Tim 1:10 etc.). Once assimilated and made part of a man's habitual thought-processes, it would by psychological necessity help to make a just man of him. Faith itself, by reason of its content, helps to justify a man. In Bultmann's view, the efficacy of the gospel is entirely independent of its content (if indeed, after demythologizing, it can be said to have any 'content'). This makes justification by faith an impenetrable mystery. The fact is that the gospel once believed becomes a source of hope and of love; but both hope and love are powers; they give strength and enable the believer to persevere in obedience to God's will. [20]

## 9.

At the same time and in the same way, St Paul learned that the Mosaic law is not the divinely appointed way to salvation. The law

---

struggles, and not out of the offence that he took at abuses in church practices.' A scientist sometimes receives 'a blinding flash of revelation' (Sir L. Bragg)— but only when his mind has been prepared by patient searching.

[20] Cf. W. L. Knox, *St Paul and the Church of Jerusalem*, p. 100. According to Plutarch, *Coriolanus*, xxii, 3-7 (Loeb IV), Homer embodies a view like this in the Iliad. (I owe this reference to B. S. MacKay, 'Plutarch and the Miraculous,' in Moule, *Miracles*, p. 96.) See further J. Bligh, 'Salvation by Hope,' *The Way* 8 (1968), pp. 270-280.

had seemed to promise him mastery over sin, and it had failed him.
His zeal for the law had so completely misled him that he had ended
up persecuting the Lord himself. There can be no doubt that the
Damascus vision caused St Paul completely to revise his ideas about
the law. In the name of the law he had persecuted the Christians as
being disloyal to the law, and now he found that in this dispute God
was on the side of his adversaries. Stephen had been right: the law
and the temple were not the divinely appointed means of justification;
God had opened up the much simpler and humbler way of faith.

St Paul may also have reasoned that since Jesus now reigns as
Lord, he is no longer subject to the law imposed by angels. But those
who believe in him are so far united with him that they too reign with
him. They share in his kingship (*basileia*, cf. Apoc 1 : 9). Therefore
they too are no longer subject to the law.

This revelation completely upset the theology which St Paul had
learned in the school of Gamaliel. He needed to change his views
about the law and about the place of Moses in the history of Israel.
The law was not, as he had supposed, the ultimate and unchangeable
expression of God's will for men. [21] St Paul did not react to the point
of abandoning the law in his personal life, however; when living among
Jews, he continued to observe it. [22] But when he retired into Arabia
shortly after his conversion, no doubt he did so partly in order to
reconsider his theology — to try and discover what after all had been
the real purpose of the law and what value it still retained. To judge
from Galatians, he was not able to find an entirely satisfactory solution. Even in Romans, which is the charter of freedom for the Gentile
churches, he offers no completely satisfying proof that the law is obsolete. His religious intuitions were in advance of his theological
reasons. [23]

## 10.

It is not easy to show from any of the accounts of St Paul's
conversion, taken singly, how he learned that salvation is open to the
Gentiles as Gentiles. But in the narrative reconstructed above, the

---

[21] Cf. H. G. Wood, 'The Conversion of St Paul: Its Nature, Antecedents, and
Consequences', NTS 1 (1954), pp. 276-282.
[22] Cf. Héring, *First Corinthians*, pp. 81-82.
[23] Wainwright, *The Trinity in the New Testament*, pp. 68-69, makes a similar
observation in another sphere of St Paul's thought: 'The reluctance of Paul and
the author of the Epistle to the Hebrews (to commit to writing the confession
that Jesus is God) may have been caused by this inability to give an account
of the relationship of this confession to the Jewish monotheism to which they
continued to subscribe. *Their faith outstripped their reason*' (my italics).

lesson is clear. The Lord tells Paul that he has made all animals clean — the food laws are no longer binding. So one barrier to the evangelization of the Gentiles is removed. True, the animals do not include or symbolize the Gentiles. But Paul learns a little later that he himself, who has lived as a strict Jew, still needs to have his sins washed away by baptism. It is not, therefore, observance of the law that justifies a man, but baptism. According to the law, Paul was just, but not before God, for he still needed baptism. This effective washing was as applicable to Gentiles as to Jews. So Paul began at once to mix with Gentiles and preach to them.

If, on the other hand, the vision of the sail-cloth belongs to Peter, it is hard to avoid the conclusion that St Paul received the doctrine of Gentile freedom from Peter through Barnabas. For Barnabas is in Jerusalem when Peter makes the speech in Acts 11, and goes thence to Antioch and summons Paul. But if Paul learned the doctrine of Gentile freedom from Peter through Barnabas, his claim in Gal 1:12 is, to say the least, extremely tendencious.

# ST PAUL AND ST PETER

The second section overlaps with the first (as the penultimate does with the last[1]). Its symmetrical structure centres upon St Paul's oath confirming the truth of the history which he is narrating, thus:

A    At your conversion you were in the grace of Christ, 1:6.

B    Certain persons are shaking your faith and corrupting the gospel, 1:7.

C    Paul is no respecter of persons; he condemns a false gospel. He received his own gospel direct from Christ, 1:8-12.

D    Paul's previous attempts to force the law upon Christians, 1:13-14.

E    He received by revelation both his gospel and his mission to the Gentiles. He did not then go up to Jerusalem, 1:15-17.

F    On his first visit to Peter, he avoided publicity in Jerusalem, 1:18-19.

G    *He swears all this is true,* 1:20.

F¹   On his return journey, he avoided publicity in Judaea, 1:21-24.

E¹   In obedience to a revelation he went up to Jerusalem and explained his gospel and his mission, 2:1-2.

D¹   He defended the liberty of Christians against those who would have forced the law upon them, 2:3-5.

C¹   God is no respecter of persons. James, Cephas and John approved the gospel entrusted to Paul by Christ, 2:6-8.

B¹   The 'pillars', who are perhaps not what they seem to be, recognised Paul's apostleship, 2:9a.

A¹   They acknowledge Paul as being in communion with them, 2:9b.

As this section is long, the corresponding passages are here set out in parallel columns, to facilitate comparison.

A  *1:6* I am astonished that you are so quickly deserting the one who called you in the grace of Christ and going over to another gospel,

A¹ *2:9b* gave to me and to Barnabas the right hand of fellowship, with the understanding that we should preach to the Gentiles, and they to the Jews.

B  *7* which is not another gospel, but certain persons are shaking you and would like to turn Christ's gospel upside down.

B¹ *2:9a* and recognizing the grace that had been given to me, James, Cephas and John, the ones regarded as pillars,

C  *8* But if anyone, even ourselves or an angel from heaven, preaches to you a gospel other than the one we preached, let him be anathema! *9* We warned you before, and now I say it again: if anyone preaches

C¹ *2:6* As for those held in regard — what they once were makes no difference to me, God is no respecter of persons — those held in regard made no further requirements. *7* On the contrary, seeing that I

---

[1]    See the diagram in G in G, p. 3, and below, p. 478.

to you a gospel other than the one you received, let him be anathema! *10* For am I now seeking the favour of men or of God? Or am I trying to please men? If I were still trying to please men, I should not be a servant of Christ. *11* For I inform you, brethren, that the gospel which was preached by me is not according to man. *12* Nor did I receive it from any man, nor was I taught it by any man; I received it through a revelation of Jesus Christ.

**D** *13* For you have heard the way of life I once followed in Judaism — how I was going to extremes in persecuting the Church of God and making havoc of it, *14* how I was making greater progress in Judaism than many of my contemporaries among my own people, and showing greater zeal for the traditions of my forefathers.

**E** *15* But when he who had set me apart from my mother's womb and graciously called me was pleased *16* to reveal his Son to me, that I might preach him to the Gentiles, there and then, instead of consulting flesh and blood *17* or going up to Jerusalem to those who had been made apostles before me, I went off to Arabia. From there I returned to Damascus.

**F** *18* Then, three years later, I went up to Jerusalem to see Peter, and I stayed with him for fifteen days. *19* But not one of the other apostles did I see — unless you count James the brother of the Lord.

had been entrusted with the gospel of the uncircumcised, as Peter had been with that of the circumcised, (*8* for he who had made Peter's apostleship to the circumcision effective had made mine effective among the Gentiles)

**D¹** *2 : 3* But even my companion Titus, Greek as he is, was not compelled to be circumcised. *4* But on account of intruders — false brethren who had wormed their way in to spy on the liberty we have in Christ Jesus, in order to enslave us. *5* But not for a moment did we yield to their demand — in order that the truth of the gospel might remain with you.

**E¹** *2 : 1* Then after fourteen years, I again went up to Jerusalem with Barnabas, taking Titus with me too — *2* I went up in obedience to a revelation — and I laid before them the gospel I preach to the Gentiles, but privately before those held in regard: Was I perhaps running or had I run my course in vain?

**F¹** *1 : 21* Then I went into the countries of Syria and Cilicia, *22* but I remained unknown by sight to the Christian churches in Judaea — *23* though they kept hearing: 'The man who once persecuted us is now preaching the very faith he formerly tried to destroy.' *24* And they gave glory to God because of me.

**G** *20* I declare before God that what I am writing is the truth.

The greatest difficulty here is to determine the purpose of the section. At first sight the answer seems plain enough: St Paul is demonstrating the divine origin of his gospel by showing, first, that before his conversion he was not a disciple of the apostles, secondly, that at his conversion he received a direct revelation from God, and thirdly, that after his conversion he had virtually no contact with the apostles until the 'Council' at Jerusalem seventeen years later, when they taught him nothing new. But on closer inspection, this argument proves to be so weak that one is loth to attribute it to St Paul. For, first, in the days before his conversion he must have known the content of the Christian gospel, even though he did not believe it; secondly, immediately after his conversion he associated with Ananias and other Christians at Damascus for at least a few days, during which there must have been talk about the gospel; and thirdly, after his conversion, by his own admission he spent fifteen days with Peter, which was surely long enough to make full enquiries about his teaching; and, as we know from Acts, he had long and intimate contact with Barnabas and other members of the church of Antioch, from whom he would get to know the teaching of the Twelve. If Gal 1 : 13-21 is an elaborate alibi, to show that Paul could not have learned the gospel from any of the Twelve, it is a failure.

It is better, therefore, to regard the whole passage as St Paul's justification of the claim which he makes in 1 : 12: 'the gospel preached by me is not according to man' — a sentence which contains two ambiguous terms. First, the noun 'gospel', as used by St Paul, can mean not only 'the good news' (the divine message) but also 'the preaching of the gospel'. Perhaps the clearest example of this usage is Rom 15 : 19, where St Paul claims to have 'completed the gospel of Christ from Jerusalem right round to Illyricum' — where he must mean: 'I have completed *the preaching of* the gospel from Jerusalem to Illyricum.' Almost equally clear examples are Rom 1 : 1, where he says he is 'set apart for the gospel of God' (i.e. to preach the gospel of God), and Rom 1 : 9, where he says: 'God is my witness to whom I render spiritual service in the gospel of his Son' (i.e. by preaching the gospel of his Son). [2] In Gal 1 : 12 the commoner sense (namely, 'the gospel message') is the one primarily intended, but the other is not to be excluded.

Secondly, 'according to man' is ambiguous. St Paul is not simply saying that his gospel is not of human origin. The preposition

---

[2]    This sense also fits well in 1 Cor 4 : 15; 9 : 14 (to live by *preaching* the gospel); 2 Cor 2 : 12; 8 : 18; 10 : 14; Phil 1 : 5; 2 : 22; 4 : 3; 4 : 15; 1 Thes 1 : 5; 3 : 2; 2 Thes 2 : 14.

'according to' (*kata*) does not refer to origin; it indicates a standard of comparison. [3] So the sense is: 'My gospel (and my preaching of the gospel) do not belong to the purely human level of existence: the gospel message did not come to me through human channels — it was not mediated to me through any man; and my preaching of the gospel has not been guided by human motives and ambitions.'

In 1:13-17 St Paul explains that the gospel was not mediated to him through any man: he never received instruction from Peter, James and John or any of the other apostles. If they received the gospel direct from Christ, so too did he. [4] Then in 1:18—2:10 his main concern is to show that his preaching was not guided by human motives, and in particular that he was careful not to cause embarrassment to Peter, James and John, or to steal the limelight from them. In 2:1-10, he tells how *he* expounded his gospel to Peter, James and John, and they recognized its divine origin and made no addition to it; at the same time he shows why he did this — his decision to go to Jerusalem was not according to man, but was the result of a divine revelation.

Thus the whole section, 1:6—2:10, must be regarded as a defence, not only of St Paul's gospel, but of his conduct in the preaching of it.

*The First Subsection, 1:10-24*

## FROM PERSECUTOR TO PREACHER

The second section, like the first, divides into two symmetrical subsections. The first is as follows:

A  *1:10* For whose favour do I now try to win, man's or God's? Or am I seeking to please men? If I were still seeking to please men, I should not be a servant of Christ.   B   *11* For I inform you, brethren, that the gospel preached by me is not according to man,   C   *12* nor did I receive it by instruction from any man,   D   but by a revelation of Jesus Christ.   E   *13* For you have heard the way of life I once followed in Judaism:   F   how I was going to extremes in persecuting the Church of God and making havoc of it,   E[1]   *14* how I was making greater progress in Judaism than many of my contemporaries among my

---

[3]   Cf. Lagrange, Gal, ad loc.: 'Dans Paul, *kata anthrôpon* ou *anthrôpinon* indique la sphère des possibilités humaines, avec des modalités à discuter dans chaque passage.'
[4]   Cf. G in G, pp. 88-90, on 1:12.

own people, and showing greater zeal for the traditions of my forefathers. D¹ *15* But when he who had set me apart from my mother's womb and graciously called me was pleased *16* to reveal his Son to me, that I might preach him to the Gentiles, C¹ there and then, instead of consulting flesh and blood *17* or going up to Jerusalem to those who had been made apostles before me, I went off to Arabia. From there I returned to Damascus. B¹ *18* Then, three years later, I went up to Jerusalem to see Peter, and I stayed with him for fifteen days. *19* But not one of the other apostles did I see — unless you count James the brother of the Lord. *20* I declare before God that what I am writing is the truth. A¹ *21* Then I went into the countries of Syria and Cilicia, *22* but I remained unknown by sight to the Christian churches of Judaea, *23* though they kept hearing: 'The man who once persecuted us is now preaching the very faith he formerly tried to destroy.' *24* And they gave glory to God because of me.

Here St Paul contrasts his behaviour before and after conversion. He speaks of his pre-conversion activity as a persecutor at the beginning (v. 10), middle (vv. 13-14), and end (v. 23). In those days, he was acting 'according to man' in the sense that he was seeking the approval not of God but of men; he was attacking and attempting to destroy the faith which God had revealed, in the name of human traditions (v. 14). [5]

After conversion, his preaching was not 'according to man' in two senses: first, he was no longer seeking human applause — not even the applause of those within the Church; and secondly, he was preaching a gospel which was not a bundle of human traditions transmitted by a chain of human teachers, but a direct revelation from Jesus Christ. This revelation taught him so much that he felt no need to go up to Jerusalem and consult the other apostles. He did go up after three years to see Peter, but he did not seek out any of the other apostles. The purpose of that journey was not to seek information or instruction.

*Why does St Paul speak of his persecuting days here?*

As we have just seen, St Paul wishes to show that his preaching is 'not according to man' in two senses: he is not impelled by human motives, and his message is not of human origin. The reference to his persecuting days helps both arguments.

---

[5]   In the light of Gal 6:4, v. 14 probably means that in his Jewish days Paul was (unconsciously) following the way of the flesh in so far as he strove to outdo his contemporaries—in order to be able to 'boast' of his superiority; after conversion he did not enter into rivalry with the other apostles, but went away to other mission fields.

First, by persecuting the Christians, he was advancing in Judaism beyond many of his contemporaries. Thanks to his zeal for Jewish traditions, he was an up-and-coming young rabbi, with splendid prospects of advancement. If he had been bent on pursuing his own interests, he would have continued to persecute Christians. His transformation into a preacher of Christianity ruined his career as a Jew. It was therefore absurd for the Judaizers to say that he was preaching his gospel of Gentile freedom for purely human motives.

Secondly, by emphasizing his hostility to the Church at the time of his conversion, St Paul gives the reader a strong reason for believing in the reality of the divine intervention which made him an apostle (vv. 15-16).

These are St Paul's two chief reasons for mentioning his pre-conversion conduct. He may also have wished to point to himself as an example of God's sovereign liberty in dealing with men and of the gratuitousness of his interventions. God is no respecter of persons, if he will choose a persecutor to become his apostle (cf. 2:6). And further, the structure of the section shows that in St Paul's view the Judaizers are now doing essentially the same as he himself had done in his persecuting days: they are trying to force Jewish traditions on Christian believers (compare 1:13-14 with 2:3-5). Judaism and Christianity are two distinct traditions; [6] to force Judaism on Christians is to obliterate the Christian tradition.

St Paul does not say that he was persecuting the Church out of zeal for the law, but out of zeal for the traditions of his forefathers. St Jerome may be right in thinking that he intends to insinuate a contrast between these man-made Jewish traditions (cf. Mk 15:7) and the divine tradition which he had received by revelation (v. 12). [7] Within St Paul's own experience the contrast must have been enormous: he was no longer the purveyor of a mass of book learning: ' Rabbi A says in the name of Rabbi B, etc.' He speaks of what he has himself seen and heard. What was said of Christ could be said of Paul after his conversion: he taught as one having authority, and not like the scribes (piling up human authorities). In this subsection, he is trying to bring home the contrast to his readers.

[6] Cf. Augustine, PL 35, 2110 A: 'If by persecuting and devastating the Church of God he was making progress in Judaism, it is plain that Judaism is contrary to the Church of God.' Contrast W. D. Davies, 'Torah and Dogma: A Comment,' HTR 61 (1968), p. 103: 'There can be little question that Paul remained throughout his life, in his own mind, within the pale of Judaism.'
[7] Cf. Jerome, PL 26, 349 A. At the time, Paul doubtless thought of himself as a defender of the law and regarded Christians as disloyal to the law. Schmithals, Paul and James, p. 28, thinks that he was persecuting the 'Hellenists' only, as being antinomians.

*'He who set me apart from my mother's womb'* — *Why does St Paul refer to God in this particular way?*

St Paul probably chooses this expression to answer some argument of his adversaries. They may have said: 'Paul is a newcomer; Peter and the others were apostles long before he appeared on the scene; it is better to follow Peter than Paul.' If so, Paul's reply is that his vocation dates from long before the calling of the Twelve during the public ministry.

But more probably the adversary's argument was: 'If God had meant Paul to be an apostle, he would have converted him much sooner and made him a disciple of Jesus during the public ministry.' Paul replies that throughout the whole of his life, from his very birth, God has been preparing him for his mission to the Gentiles. He allowed him to advance so far in Judaism as to become the arch-persecutor of the Church, in order to reveal his power in converting him. By this providential disposition, God fortified Paul with a powerful kerygmatic argument. He could say, as he does here: 'I was in full activity as a persecutor, when God suddenly intervened and showed me the truth; the gospel I preach is not a theology which I worked out, but a revelation which God thrust upon me.'[8]

The wording of the phrase 'he who set me apart from my mother's womb' is probably an intentional allusion to Isa 49:1. If so, it is meant to inform the reader that God's treatment of Paul is prefigured in the passage of Isaiah which these words introduce (49:1-6):

> Listen to me, O coastlands,
>     and hearken, you peoples from afar.
> The Lord called me from the womb,[9]
>     from the body of my mother he named my name.
> He made my mouth like a sharp sword,
>     in the shadow of his hand he hid me;
> He made me a polished arrow,
>     in his quiver he hid me away.
> And he said to me, 'You are my servant,
>     Israel, in whom I will be glorified.'[10]
> But I said, 'I have laboured in vain,[11]
>     I have spent my strength for nothing and vanity;
> yet surely my right is with the Lord,
>     and my recompense with my God.'[12]

---

[8]  V. 24 shows that God *effectively* revealed his glory in this way.
[9]  Cf. Gal 1:15.
[10]  Cf. Gal 6:16.
[11]  Cf. Gal 2:2; 4:11.
[12]  Cf. Gal 1:20.

And now the Lord says,
   who formed me from the womb to be his servant,
to bring back Jacob to him,
   and that Israel might be gathered to him, [13]
for I am honoured in the eyes of the Lord,
   and my God has become my strength —
he says:
   'It is too light a thing that you should be my servant,
     to raise up the tribes of Jacob
      and to restore the preserved of Israel.
   I will give you as a light to the nations, [14]
     that my salvation may reach to the end of the earth.'

St Paul saw in this passage a description of himself. He was sharing with Christ in the vocation of the Servant by carrying Christ's gospel to the nations and his salvation to the end of the earth. [15] He is an arrow whom God set aside and kept secretly until it was time to send him shooting into the Gentile world.

The further phrase, 'and called me through his grace,' is added to show that it was not through any merit of Paul's that God called him to the dignity of the apostolate. Throughout this section, while describing events which might be reckoned to his credit, St Paul is careful to give the glory to God and avoid praising himself. God did not choose him because of his exact observance of the law. [16] His own human choices led in one direction, and the will of God overruled them to lead him in another direction. He probably has in mind the contrast between being set apart by God as an apostle and setting oneself apart as a Pharisee. [17] Paul became a Pharisee through human decisions of his own, which led him to persecute the Church (cf. Phil 3:5-6); but God had already set him apart for another task — to preach the gospel and propagate the Church; and God's decision had prevailed, for he has power to compel even rebel wills.

St Paul thought deeply about the mystery of divine predestination. In chapters 9-11 of Romans he tries to discern the wisdom which he knows must somehow lie behind God's apparent rejection of his own

---

[13] Cf. Gal 6:16.
[14] Cf. Gal 1:16; 2:7.
[15] Cf. L. Cerfaux, 'Saint Paul et le "Serviteur de Dieu" d'Isaïe,' *Receuil Lucien Cerfaux*, II, Gembloux, 1954, pp. 439-454; Hooker, *Jesus and the Servant*, p. 115.
[16] In Gal 2:6 it is probably implied that Peter, James and John, before their conversion and vocation, were *not* strict observers.
[17] The Greek verb translated 'set apart' (*aphorisas*) has the same radicals as the Hebrew *paras*, from which 'Pharisee' is derived. Cf. J. W. Doeve, 'Paulus der Pharisäer und Galater 1:13-15,' *Novum Testamentum* 6 (1963), pp. 170-181 [NTA 8-1063].

people Israel in favour of the Gentiles. He argues that this rejection
is only temporary, and is serving God's purpose. In the same way,
reflecting on God's treatment of himself, he sees that God had his
own good reasons for allowing him at first to reject and persecute the
Church; his rejection of it was only temporary, and it has worked
together unto good, for now the Jewish Christians are giving glory
to God because of him (v. 24). Probably all his thinking about predestination springs from his Damascus vision. As J. Jeremias observes,
'people who have experienced such a violent break in their lives know
better than others that God alone has done everything.' [18]

If one asks whether St Paul thought that God predestined him
*ante* or *post praevisa merita* (i.e., before or after 'foreseeing his
merits'), it seems obvious that the answer should be *ante* (before), for
God is not a respecter of persons but exercises sovereign liberty in
choosing whom he wills. Nevertheless, St Jerome thought otherwise. [19]

### *Was St Paul's Damascus-vision a purely interior experience?*

The strictly literal, word-for-word translation of 1 : 15-16 is: 'When
he who had set me apart from my mother's womb was pleased to
reveal his Son *in* me that I might preach him *in* the Gentiles.' The
prepositional phrase 'in me' then suggests that the Damascus-vision
was a purely interior, mystical experience. But this was not St Paul's
view. In 1 Cor 15 : 5-8, he reckons the Damascus-vision as the last
of the resurrection appearances — which were not interior experiences,
since Christ ate fish and made a fire; and in 2 Cor 12 : 1-6, where
Paul speaks of the visions and revelations which he has received from
the Lord, he does not mention the Damascus-vision.

Probably the preposition 'in' (*en*) has the same sense in both its
occurrences in verse 16. The same preposition is repeated to mark
the successive stages of revelation: 'When (God)....was pleased to
reveal his Son to me, that I might preach him to the Gentiles.' [20]
There is another example of this non-classical use of 'in' in 2 : 2, [21]
where the word-for-word translation would be 'the gospel which I

---

[18]  J. Jeremias, 'The Key to Pauline Theology', *Expository Times* 76 (1964), p. 29.
[19]  Cf. PL 26, 350 B: 'Hoc ex Dei praescientia evenire, ut quem scit iustum
      futurum, prius diligit quam oriatur ex utero: et quem peccatorem, oderit
      antequam peccet.'
[20]  In other words, the preposition *en* is pleonastic. The meaning would have been
      much plainer if it had been omitted. But Hellenistic Greek writers prefer to
      'specify' oblique cases with a preposition of some sort.
[21]  In the second section 1 : 16 matches 2 : 2, see above, p. 122.

preach *in* the Gentiles', and the sense is 'the gospel which I preach to the Gentiles.'

*Why does St Paul describe the vision as a revelation of the Son by the Father?*

In view of the descriptions given in the Acts of the Apostles, we might have expected St Paul to say: 'When it pleased the Lord Jesus to reveal himself to me.' If we had not the Acts of the Apostles, we should infer from vv. 15-16 that St Paul had a vision, similar to the Transfiguration, in which he heard a voice from heaven saying: 'This is my beloved Son; preach him to the Gentiles,' rather than one in which he heard the risen Lord say: 'I am Jesus whom you are persecuting.'

It is remarkable that the account of the Transfiguration contains more of the pauline gospel than do the accounts of the Damascus-vision as they stand in Acts. St Paul's doctrine of freedom from the law can easily be shown to be implicit in the Transfiguration narrative: Jesus is seen with Moses and Elijah, who represent the law and the prophets. Then the law and the prophets disappear, and the heavenly voice says: 'This is my beloved Son — hear *him*.' As was shown above, it is much harder to explain how St Paul learned his doctrine of Gentile freedom from the Damascus-vision, unless one allows that the vision of the sail-cloth was part of his conversion experience.

One is tempted to think that the abbreviated accounts of the Damascus-vision attributed to St Paul in Acts (22 and 26) may be rather different from the account which he himself would have given. However, as the narrative of his conversion must have been extremely well known in the Gentile churches some other explanation must be found of the curious way in which he describes the vision in 1:16.

The reason why he attributes the revelation to the Father may be that he has in mind the saying of Christ to Peter in Mt 16:17: 'It was not flesh and blood that revealed this to you, but my Father in heaven.' St Paul implies that he is in no way inferior to Peter: just as God the Father revealed his Son directly to Peter, and not through flesh and blood (that is, not through any human intermediary), so too with Paul: God the Father revealed his Son to Paul, and Paul did not, even afterwards, seek further enlightenment from flesh and blood.

*Is St Paul dependent on the Synoptic Tradition in 1:15-16?*

In 57 A.D., when St Paul wrote to the Galatians, probably none of our four canonical gospels had been compiled; but they are the four surviving products of a *tradition* of gospel-making (cf. Lk 1 : 1), which probably began in the forties. The question is, therefore, whether St Paul was acquainted with some pre-canonical stage (or stages) of the tradition which produced our synoptic gospels.

There are some remarkable points of contact between 1 : 15-16 and a group of passages dispersed through St Matthew's gospel, namely:

a. the Transfiguration, Mt 17 : 1-8,
b. Peter's Confession, Mt 16 : 13-17,
c. Jesus' Prayer of Thanksgiving and Offer of the Easy Yoke, Lk 10 : 21, Mt 11 : 25-30,
d. the Sending of the Twelve to all nations, Mt 28 : 18-20.

In the canonical gospel according to St Matthew, the first three pericopes are placed in the public ministry and are unrelated to one another. But in content they form a closely connected group: Peter confesses at Caesarea what he has learned at the Transfiguration; then Jesus thanks his Father for having granted the revelation to his 'little ones', and expands the words 'hear ye him' into his Offer of the Easy Yoke.

St Peter's confession of Christ's divine Sonship probably belongs to the post-resurrection period, [22] and the same may well be true of the other pericopes listed above. Here are the texts in sequence:

*a. The Transfiguration* (Mt 17 : 1-8)

After six days, Jesus took Peter and James and John his brother, and led them up a high mountain alone; and he was transfigured before their eyes: his face shone like the sun, and his clothes were as bright as light. And Moses and Elijah appeared before them, conversing with Jesus. Peter cried out to Jesus: 'Lord, it is good for us to be here! If you wish, I will make three tabernacles here, one for you, one for Moses and one for Elijah.' While he was still speaking, suddenly a cloud of light overshadowed them, and a voice came from the cloud saying: 'This is my beloved Son in whom I am well pleased: hear him!' When the disciples heard this, they fell on their faces, stricken with fear. But Jesus came near and touched them and said: 'Rise up, and do not be afraid.' Then they looked up and saw no one but Jesus alone.

---

[22] Cf. E. Sutcliffe, 'St Peter's Double Confession,' HJ 3 (1962), pp. 31-41, and below, pp. 359-360.

G

### b. Peter's (second?) Confession (Mt 16:13-17)

Jesus went also to the district of Caesarea Philippi. There he asked his disciples:....'Who do you say that I am?' Simon Peter answered: 'You are the Messiah, the Son of the living God.' Jesus replied: 'Simon bar Jonah, you are blessed indeed! For it was not flesh and blood that revealed this to you, but my Father in heaven.'

### c. Jesus' Prayer of Thanksgiving (Lk 10:21; Mt 11:25-30)

At that time, Jesus was filled with the joy of the Holy Spirit and said: 'I thank you, Father, Lord of heaven and earth, because while concealing these things from the wise and prudent, you have revealed them to the simple; yes, Father, I thank you, because this has been your good pleasure. Everything has been delivered to me by my Father, and no one knows the Son except the Father, nor does anyone know the Father except the Son, and those to whom the Son chooses to reveal him. Come to me, all who are weary and overburdened, and I will give you rest; for I am meek and humble of heart. Take my yoke upon you and learn from me, and you will find rest for your souls; for my yoke is easy, and the burden light.'

### d. The Mission to the Gentiles (Mt 28:18-20)

Then Jesus drew near and addressed them: 'All power has been given to me in heaven and on earth,' he said, 'Go then, and teach all nations; baptize them in the name of the Father and of the Son and of the Holy Spirit; and teach them to observe all the commandments I have given you. And be sure, I am with you always, even to the end of the world.'

The points of contact between this group of pericopes and Gal 1:15-16 are as follows. First, both speak of a revelation of Jesus as Son of God granted by God the Father to chosen apostles — Peter, James and John in the one case, Paul in the other. Secondly, in each case it is said that the revelation comes, not from 'flesh and blood', but from God the Father. Thirdly, in each case there is mention of God's 'good pleasure' as the principle of his choice. Fourthly, each vision is described as a 'revelation' or 'apocalypse'. Fifthly, each contains a revelation about the law: in Matthew the 'easy yoke' of Jesus is substituted for the burden of the law as taught by the Pharisees, and in Galatians St Paul implies that he, the former Pharisee, was taught his doctrine of freedom from the law in this vision. And sixthly, each contains a mission to the Gentiles.

Some recent writers have maintained that Matthew is directly dependent on Galatians here. [23] But this is unlikely. The words and phrases ('revelation', 'good pleasure', 'little ones') which Matthew has

---

[23] Cf. A. M. Denis, 'L'investiture de la fonction apostolique par "apocalypse". étude thématique de Gal 1:16,' RB 60 (1957), pp. 335-362; 492-515; and F. Refoulé. 'Primauté de Pierre dans les évangiles.' RechScRel 38 (1964). pp. 1-41.

in common with St Paul are probably taken straight from the Book of Daniel, not from Galatians. In the earliest gospel tradition, typological references to the story of Daniel in the lions' den (Dan 6) and to the glorification of the Son of Man (Dan 7) ran right through the passion narrative into the resurrection narrative. [24]

It is much more likely that St Paul knew the synoptic pericopes grouped together in a resurrection narrative, and that he deliberately described his own vision and apostolic mission in words reminiscent of the gospel, in order to emphasize that what God had done for Peter he had also done for Paul (cf. Gal 2:8).

If St Paul expected the Galatians to recognize these allusions, they must have been in possession of a synoptic gospel of some kind. Probably, as was conjectured above, such a gospel had been introduced by the Judaizers. But there is also the possibility that this Epistle, though addressed to the Galatians, was intended by St Paul as a lesson for the Jews of Jerusalem and elsewhere. As a result of the agreement recorded in 2:10, he was hardly at liberty to address a dogmatic letter to the Jews in Jerusalem directly. But he must have foreseen that his letter to the Galatians would find its way to Jerusalem, and it is possible that while nominally writing to the Galatians, he was thinking chiefly of the Jewish Christians in Jerusalem. As will be pointed out below, there are places in this Epistle where St Paul seems to forget that he is talking to Gentile converts, and uses 'we' and 'us' as if he were writing to Jews (e.g. in 4:1-5). Perhaps, then, he was not much concerned as to whether the Galatians could recognize his allusions to the synoptic tradition; the Christians of Jerusalem would recognize them, and that was enough. [25]

### What did St Paul do 'immediately' after the vision?

In v. 16 the adverb 'immediately' is in a curious position: 'Immediately I did not consult flesh and blood....but went off to Arabia.' The adverb goes with the verb 'went off'. Hence 'I did not

---

[24] Cf. J. Bligh, 'Typology in the Passion Narratives: Daniel, Elijah, Melchisedek,' HJ 6 (1965), pp. 302-309; B. Gerhardsson, *Memory and Manuscript*, Uppsala, 1961, pp. 269-270; J. Dupont, 'La révélation du Fils de Dieu en faveur de Pierre (Mt 16:17) et de Paul (Gal 1:16),' RechScRel 52 (1964), pp. 411-420.

[25] Dibelius, *Studies in the Acts of the Apostles*, p. 118, makes a similar observation on St Peter's speech to the people assembled in Cornelius' house (Acts 10: 28-29): 'The hearers can hardly suspect the significance of these ideas, far less their motivation. It is, rather, for the reader to appreciate their significance— and *also for those Jewish Christian witnesses from Joppa*' (my italics).

consult flesh and blood' must be parenthetic. St Paul begins to say: 'Immediately I went off to Arabia,' but interrupts himself to reject the idea that he went to Jerusalem and consulted the apostles. Evidently his adversaries had been saying that this is what he did.

The effect of the parenthesis is to throw great emphasis upon 'immediately'. [26] It is curious that the same word 'immediately' receives similar emphasis in St Matthew's account of the vocation of Peter and Andrew, James and John (4: 18-22):

> While walking beside the sea of Galilee, he saw two brothers, Simon who is called Peter, and his brother Andrew, both fishermen, casting a net into the sea. He said to them: 'Come, follow me, and I will make you fishers of men,' and *immediately* they left their nets and followed him. Then he went on and saw another pair of brothers, James son of Zebedee and his brother John, in a boat with their father Zebedee, putting their nets in order. He called them, and *immediately* they left the boat and their father and followed him.

If St Paul is alluding to this story, his adversaries must have been saying that whereas Peter, James and John responded immediately to their vocation, Paul did not. Paul retorts that he did respond immediately — by going off into Arabia. The parenthetic clause is usually translated 'I did not *consult* flesh and blood' — a sense which the word can certainly bear. [27] But when the same verb recurs in 2: 6, it means 'they did not impose any additional burden on me.' Hence in 1: 16 it may mean 'I did not impose an additional burden on them.' St Paul's presence would undoubtedly have been an embarrassment to the apostles, if he had returned to Jerusalem immediately after his conversion. The chief priests and Pharisees would have persecuted him as a renegade, and the whole Church would have been involved in the commotion. So once again we have an ambiguous phrase which must be taken in both senses: 'I did not consult flesh and blood, and I did not inflict myself as a burden on the Jewish Christian community.' [28] This interpretation has two advantages: it shows that 'flesh and blood' stands in antithesis to 'Arabia'; and it renders intelligible St Paul's omission to specify the purpose of his journey to Arabia — he mentions it to confirm his assertion that he did not encumber the community in Jerusalem.

---

[26] Words which belong together normally go together. When separated (by 'hyperbaton'), they acquire special emphasis by reason of their unusual positions.

[27] This brings v. 17 into line with the view that the whole section is concerned with the origin of St Paul's gospel.

[28] This brings v. 17 into line with the view that he is also defending his conduct in the preaching of the gospel.

Perhaps he is also insinuating a criticism of the other apostles here: when sent by Christ to teach all nations (Mt 28: 19-20), they did not immediately go to the nations but remained with their own flesh and blood and relied upon them for their support.

### Why did St Paul go to Arabia?

If the above interpretation of v. 17a is correct, St Paul avoided Jerusalem so as not to be a burden or an embarrassment to the Christian community there. He went 'immediately' to Arabia in obedience to his divine vocation. Presumably, therefore, he went to Arabia to preach to the Arabians. He may perhaps have confined his preaching to the synagogues of Jews; but the contrast between 'flesh and blood' and 'Arabia' seems to imply that already in these early days he was preaching to the Gentiles. (This is confirmed by the structural link between 1: 16b-17 and 2: 6-7 in the first main division of the Epistle.)

Some commentators think that St Paul withdrew into Arabia for a period of reflection: as his conversion experience had upset all his previous theological opinions, he felt the need to reread his Bible in the light of his new knowledge, to find out what Moses and the prophets really meant. Thus St Jerome says: [29]

> As soon as Paul believed, he turned to the law, to the prophets, to the mysteries of the now obsolescent Old Testament, and sought in them Christ, whom he had been told to preach to the Gentiles; and having found him, he did not remain there long, but returned to Damascus.

No doubt St Paul was rereading his Bible at this time, but if the illumination he had received on the road to Damascus was enough to equip him to preach in the synagogues of Damascus, [30] it was also enough to enable him to preach to the Arabs. It is likely that Christianity spread into Arabia at a very early date. The Jews of Jerusalem and Damascus were in contact with Petra and Edessa — places much closer at hand than Iconium and Lystra. [31]

It has been conjectured that St Paul may have penetrated as far into Arabia as Mt Sinai, [32] and that in this way he learned that 'Agar is a mountain in Arabia.' He may have wished to imitate Elijah in going back to Sinai — especially if his Damascus vision was even more

---

[29]   Jerome, PL 26, 353 D.
[30]   Cf. Acts 9 : 19-20.
[31]   Cf. Williamson, *Eusebius*, p. 70.
[32]   Cf. Lightfoot, Gal, pp. 88-89.

like the Transfiguration than the accounts given in Acts allow us to see, for if Paul too saw Moses and Elijah, it would be natural for him to retrace their paths. But all this is conjecture.

Against the view that St Paul went to Arabia to preach to the Arabians, it might be objected that according to Acts 22:17-21 he did not learn that his mission was to the Gentiles until his first visit to Jerusalem:

> After I had returned to Jerusalem, I was once praying in the temple, when I fell into ecstasy and saw the Lord saying to me: 'Bestir yourself, and leave Jerusalem quickly, for here they will not accept your witness about me.' I replied: 'Lord, they know themselves how I used to imprison those who believe in you and how I had them beaten in the synagogues; and when the blood of your witness Stephen was shed, I was standing by, and showed my approval by keeping the clothes of those who were killing him.' But he said to me: 'Go! I shall send you to Gentile nations far away.'

This can be reconciled with Gal 1:15-16 and Acts 26:17 by assuming that St Paul did not understand at once that his mission was to be permanently or even primarily among the Gentiles (cf. 22:15). He may have thought that God was sending him to the Gentiles first, because for the time being he could not safely return to Jerusalem and preach — he might have been lynched as a turn-coat. After three years, he thought it safe to return, and it was during this visit that God told him that the Jews would still refuse to accept his witness, and he must go to the Gentiles far away. [33]

### What did St Paul do at Damascus (1:17-18)?

St Paul does not say how long he remained in Arabia. It may have been only a matter of months. Then he says: 'I returned to Damascus' — meaning 'I did not go to Jerusalem.' The 'three years' mentioned in 1:18 include both the sojourn in Arabia and the following period at Damascus, which may therefore have been two years and more.

In Acts 9:20-25, St Luke omits the journey into Arabia, but says that Paul preached in the synagogues:

> Paul stayed a few days with the disciples in Damascus, and then began immediately [34] to preach in the synagogues that Jesus is the Son of God.

---

[33] For some speculations as to why St Luke omits to mention Paul's activities in Arabia, see Goulder, *Type and History in Acts*, p. 70.
[34] See above, p. 134.

All who heard him were amazed and asked: 'Is not this the man who at Jerusalem made havoc among those who call on his name? And did he not come here expressly to take them as prisoners to the chief priests?' But Saul went from strength to strength, and confounded the Jews at Damascus with his proofs that Jesus was the Messiah. After many days had passed, the Jews made a plot to kill Saul, but their plans were made known to him. They were watching the gates night and day in order to kill him; but his disciples took him by night and lowered him down over the wall in a basket.

## St Paul himself mentions the escape in 2 Cor 11:32:

At Damascus, when an agent of King Aretas placed an ambush round the city in hopes of catching me, I was let down in a basket through a window in the wall, and so escaped his hands.

Since Damascus was in Syria, not in Nabatean Arabia, St Paul must have incurred the displeasure of Aretas by his activities in Arabia, and must have fled back to Damascus when persecuted. Presumably Aretas sent agents to extradite him illegally.

It is not altogether clear why St Paul bothers to mention the basket in 2 Cor 11:32. It seems such an anticlimax after the persecutions and perils he has catalogued. Surely he cannot mean that the final degradation of all was being let down in a basket. When a man's life is at stake, it is no time for him to stand on his dignity and make a fuss about getting into a basket. When the scene was enacted on TV (in the series 'Paul of Tarsus'), the basket made a perfectly decorous descent. One possibility is that in this incident St Paul saw himself as an antitype of Moses who also was saved from a king's hatred in a basket (cf. Exod 2:3-5). Earlier in 2 Cor (3:7-12) St Paul has explicitly compared himself to Moses. Just as Stephen in Acts 7 regards both Joseph and Moses as types of Christ, so, it seems, St Paul regarded both Joseph and Moses as types of himself — he is sharing in the life and history of Christ. [35]

Another possibility, not incompatible with the one just mentioned, is that St Paul introduced the basket incident in order to fill out a symmetrical pattern. 2 Cor 12:1 (which is the centre of a section running from 10:1 to the end of the Epistle) is immediately followed by the account of how Paul was taken up to the third heaven, and it is immediately preceded by the story of how he was let down from the walls of Damascus in a basket. This suggests that the rapture occurred soon after the basket incident and was seen by St Paul as a reward or compensation: he was let down in a basket, *propter quod et Deus exaltavit illum*. Here is the text:

---

[35] See above, pp. 59-60.

A *11 : 30* If boast I must, I shall boast of my weakness. *31* The God who is Father of the Lord Jesus (he who is blessed for ever) knows that I am not lying.   B *32* At Damascus, when an agent of King Aretas placed an ambush round the city in hopes of catching me, I was let down in a basket through a window in the wall, and so escaped his hands. C   *12 : 1* Must I boast? It is not a good thing, but still I will go on and mention the visions and revelations I have had from the Lord.   B¹   *2* I know a man who is in Christ, who, fourteen years ago, was suddenly taken up into the third heaven — whether he was in or out of his body, God knows, I do not.   *3* But I do know that this man — let me repeat that whether he was in his body or out of it God knows, I do not — *4* this man was taken up into paradise and heard secret words which man is not allowed to utter.   A¹   *5* About such a man as that I will boast, but all the boasting I will do about myself is to display my weaknesses. *6* If I consent to make a boast about such a man as that, I shall not be raving, but telling the truth.

## *Why does St Paul mention his first visit to Peter (1:18-19)?*

'After three years I went up to Jerusalem to see Peter, and I stayed with him fifteen days.' As has already been pointed out above, it does not make sense to treat this as part of an argument to show that Paul did not receive his gospel from Peter or any of the other apostles. Attempts have been made to interpret v. 18 in this sense. Pelagius, for example, says: 'Paul shows that he received a friendly welcome from Peter, and that in such a brief time he could not learn anything.' [36] But for teaching a man the gospel, or for discussing disputed points in the presentation of it, fifteen days is not a brief time; we have no reason to suppose that the Council of Jerusalem of Acts 15 and Gal 2 took anything approaching fifteen days.

It is more reasonable to suppose that in v. 18 St Paul is still rebutting the charge that after his conversion he became a burden and an embarrassment to the apostles in Jerusalem. He replies (a) 'I did not go to Jerusalem until after three years' — when the emotions aroused by my defection from the Jewish cause had subsided and my presence was less likely to cause trouble. (b) 'I stayed with Peter only fifteen days' — and therefore put him to little expense. [37] (c) 'As for the other apostles, I did not even see them — unless you count James the brother of the Lord as an apostle.'

---

[36] Pelagius, Gal, p. 311: 'et susceptum se ab illo in caritate demonstrat, et in brevi tempore nihil discere potuisse.' Schlier, Gal, p. 30, says much the same.
[37] The early Church found it necessary to make rules about the length of time a guest could stay. Didache 11 : 4 is amazingly strict.

A further reason for the mention of this visit is that St Paul wishes to show that before denouncing Peter publicly at Antioch, he spoke to him privately (1 : 18), and in the presence of a few witnesses (2 : 2).

## *What was the purpose of St Paul's first visit to Peter?*

St Jerome remarks that St Paul did not go to Jerusalem 'to look at Peter's eyes, cheeks and face, to see if he was fat or thin, whether his nose was hooked or straight, whether he had a fringe of hair across his brow or was bald (as Clement says in his *Periodi*).' [38] Jerome thinks that it was a courtesy visit, whereby St Paul paid respect to an older apostle. [39] Chrysostom says much the same: 'It was not that he wished to learn anything from him....but simply to see him and honour him with his presence.' [40]

A courtesy visit would not have been out of place; and if St Paul felt some curiosity about Peter, to see his appearance and demeanour, and to hear from his own lips some reminiscences of Christ's ministry, this was at least pardonable, if not positively laudable. But surely the two apostles must have held serious conversations during the fifteen days; and if St Paul had already preached to the Gentiles in Arabia, they must have discussed the treatment of Gentile converts. According to the reconstruction of St Paul's conversion set forth above, on this occasion he explained why he had considered himself free to enter the houses of Gentiles and eat with them. Presumably St Peter found no fault with Paul's reasoning and approved of his missionary policy.

Acts 22 : 17-21 appears to imply that St Paul went to Jerusalem in order to preach, thinking that his witness would be more effective there than anywhere else:

After I had returned to Jerusalem, I was once praying in the temple, when I fell into ecstasy and saw the Lord saying to me: 'Bestir yourself, and leave Jerusalem quickly, for here they will not accept your witness to me.' I replied: 'Lord, they know themselves how I used to imprison those who believe in you and how I had them beaten in the synagogues; and when the blood of your witness Stephen was shed, I was standing by, and showed my approval by keeping the clothes of those who were killing him.' But he said to me: 'Go! I shall send you to Gentile nations far away.'

In view of this text, one must conclude that although Paul went up to Jerusalem 'to see Peter', this was not his only purpose. He would have stayed longer, if God had not told him to go off to the Gentiles.

---

[38]  Jerome, PL 26, 354 A.
[39]  'Honoris priori apostolo deferendi (causa)'—354 B.
[40]  Chrysostom, PG 61, 631 C.

*Can Gal 1:18-21 be harmonized with Acts 9:26-30?*

These two texts both describe St Paul's first visit to Jerusalem after his conversion. St Luke's version of what happened is as follows:

> When he (Saul) arrived back in Jerusalem, he tried to attach himself to the disciples there, but they were all afraid of him and did not believe that he was a disciple. Only Barnabas gave him a welcome; he took him to the apostles and told them that he had seen the Lord on his journey, that the Lord had spoken to him, and that he had boldly preached at Damascus in the name of Jesus. So he remained with them, appearing publicly in Jerusalem, and preaching boldly in the name of the Lord. He also held debates with the Greek-speaking Jews, until they plotted to kill him. When the brethren discovered this, they accompanied him down to Caesarea, and set him on his way to Tarsus.

There is no denying that this narrative gives the impression that after Barnabas's intervention St Paul associated freely with at least a few of the other apostles, and that his presence eventually became an embarrassment to them.

In order to harmonize the two texts, one must suppose (a) that when St Luke says: 'He took him to the apostles' he is using a plural of category, [41] and means in fact 'to Peter and James the brother of the Lord'; (b) that when St Paul says 'I stayed with Peter fifteen days,' he does not mean that his whole stay in Jerusalem lasted only fifteen days, or that his whole stay in Jerusalem was spent in private conversation with Peter.

Neither of the two texts tells the whole truth; they are written from different points of view. St Paul does not say whether his original intention was to stay in Jerusalem for only fifteen days; to judge from Acts 22:17-21, until he had the vision in the temple, he intended to settle there. Nor does he say in Gal 1:21 why he left Jerusalem. It would not have suited his purpose to admit that through his debates with the Greek-speaking Jews he had become an embarrassment to the apostles and that they had sent him away.

St Luke's version is not anti-pauline, but it enables us to see how St Paul's adversaries were able to profit by these events. They could say that when St Paul went up to Jerusalem, the apostles were prudently lying low, but Paul thought them timid and tried to put them to shame by preaching much more boldly; when this threatened to unleash a persecution, Peter and James had to send Paul away.

---

[41] Cf. Mt 26:8: 'the disciples were annoyed, saying, What is the good of this waste?' According to Jn 12:4-6, it was Judas who murmured.

*Why was 'James the brother of the Lord' so called?*

The James in question is presumably to be identified with the James mentioned in Mk 6:3, where the people of Nazareth say of Jesus: 'Is not this the carpenter, the son of Mary, the brother of James and Joses and Jude and Simon?' Protestant commentators who do not accept the tradition of Mary's perpetual virginity suppose James the brother of the Lord to be a child of Mary and Joseph and younger than Jesus. Catholic commentators seek some other solution. [42]

Some of the Greek Fathers thought that James was a child of St Joseph by a previous marriage. [43] But the Infancy narratives do not give the impression that Joseph already had a family of small children to look after. [44]

According to Mk 15:40, the mother of James and Joses was called Mary. Presumably St Mark is not here speaking of Mary the mother of Jesus. Therefore, if the 'James and Joses' in this passage are identical with the James and Joses of Mk 6:3, James is not the brother of Jesus, but at the closest his first cousin. Probably the two Marys were closely related to each other (though not as sisters[45]), and the words 'brothers' and 'sisters' are used loosely in Mk 6:3 of the children of related families, perhaps sharing the same home.

From Mk 6:3 and still more from Jn 7:5 ('even his own brothers did not believe in him') it is probable that during the public ministry James was not even a disciple. He may have shared the view that Jesus had gone mad (cf. Mk 3:21). After the resurrection, Jesus appeared specially to James (cf. 1 Cor 15:7), and thus converted him as he converted Paul. James, therefore, had the same claim to the title of 'apostle' as Paul had — which may account for the peculiar form of words used in Gal 1:19. The translation will be: 'I saw none of the other apostles — unless you count James the brother of the Lord.' [46]

On the view adopted above, Alphaeus and his son James may not have been related to Jesus at all. But if 'Alphaeus' is another form of

---

[42] Cf. J. Bligh, 'The Virgin Birth,' HJ 6 (1965), pp. 190-197; P. Gaechter, 'Die "Brüder" Jesu,' ZKT 89 (1967), pp. 458-459.

[43] Cf. U. Holzmeister, 'Quaestiones biblicae de S. Ioseph,' *Verbum Domini* 24 (1944), pp. 170-183.

[44] Cf. S. Shearer, 'The Brethren of the Lord,' CathComm, 673a.

[45] Joachim and Anna are not likely to have called both their daughters Mary—though C. Lattey, 'The Apostolic Groups,' JTS 10 (1908-09), pp. 107-115, does not think it impossible.

[46] According to Eusebius, *H.E.*, IV, 5, 3-4, this James was the first of fifteen members of Christ's kindred who held the position of 'bishop' in Jerusalem. It was far from Christ's own intention to found a caliphate of this sort. Cf. Mk 3:31-35, and above, p. 86, n. 81.

'Cleophas', he was close to Jesus in some way. On the road to Emmaus, Jesus appeared to Cleophas and another disciple (probably his wife, Mary of Cleophas). [47] It is possible that there were two Cleophases, but it is not likely, since no patronymic is added to distinguish one from another. [48]

## How much of the autobiographical section is covered by the oath in v. 20?

Lagrange observes that if St Paul's protestation applied to the whole of the narrative section, it ought to be at the beginning or at the end. [49] But in a chiastic composition the place of particular emphasis is the centre. Since this oath stands at the centre of the section 1:6—2:10, there is no reason why it should not cover the whole. However, as it comes immediately after St Paul's first visit to St Peter, it may perhaps have special reference to this — in which case a false account of the first visit must have been used by the Judaizers in their polemic against Paul. They may have been saying: 'Immediately after his conversion, Paul returned to Jerusalem, where he remained for a long time, was taught the gospel by the apostles — and then tried to eclipse them; now he has invented a new version of the gospel, distorting the true gospel which he learned from them, and he is trying to make out that their version is wrong!' Paul replies: 'I was taught the gospel by Christ himself, and for three years I did not show my face in Jerusalem — surely you do not suppose that for three years I remained in ignorance of the gospel? When I did go to Jerusalem, at the end of three years, I saw only Peter and stayed only fifteen days with him. I swear that *this* is the true account of what actually happened.'

## Had not Christ forbidden such oaths?

In the Sermon on the Mount (Mt 5:33-37), Christ says: 'You have heard that the men of old were told, *You shall not swear false oaths...* I tell you not to swear oaths at all... Let your word be plain Yes when you mean Yes, and No when you mean No. Anything

---

[47] Cf. G. B. Caird, *St Luke*, Harmondsworth (Penguin), 1963, p. 259.
[48] On the Brethren of the Lord, see further F. Prat, 'La parenté de Jésus,' RechScRel 17 (1927), pp. 127-138; J. B. Lightfoot, *Dissertations on the Apostolic Age*, London, 1892, pp. 3-45: 'The Brethren of the Lord.'
[49] Cf. Lagrange, Gal, p. 19.

beyond this is from the evil one.' How then could St Paul permit himself to take the oath in 1:20? The answer is that in the Sermon on the Mount Christ is giving rules of *private* morality. Those in public authority may sometimes kill, they may resist evil, and by the same token they may sometimes take and demand oaths, namely, when the public good is seriously threatened. Gal 1:8-9 shows that St Paul considers the public good of the Galatian churches to be seriously jeopardized by the propaganda of the Judaizers.

## *What do vv. 21-23 contribute to the argument?*

If the purpose of the whole section were to prove by an alibi that St Paul did not receive the gospel from men, vv. 20-23 would have to be interpreted as meaning that he did not learn the gospel from the apostles *indirectly* by visiting the churches of Judaea in which the apostles had preached. This would be a very poor argument in itself (since the doctrine of the apostles was known in Damascus and at Antioch which he did visit), and entirely superfluous after Paul has admitted that he spent fifteen days with Peter himself.

It is much better, therefore, to regard these verses as completing St Paul's demonstration that he did not cause embarrassment to the apostles in Jerusalem. 'On the contrary,' he says, ' I went away to the regions of Syria and Cilicia, and the success of my missionary work gave joy and edification to the churches of Judaea, when they heard what I was doing.' [50]

In the structure of the second section (see pp. 121-22), this passage balances the account of St Paul's first visit to Jerusalem. There he says that he did not even see most of the apostles; here he says that he remained unknown to the churches of Judaea. [51] In both passages he is showing that he did not seek notoriety in the churches of Judaea which the other apostles had founded. That this is the main point is confirmed by the closing sentence: 'They gave glory to God because of me' — not 'They gave glory to me because of what God had done for me.'

---

[50] Schmithals, *Paul and James*, p. 24, infers from 1:23 that the churches of Judaea knew that at this time Paul was preaching his gospel of Gentile freedom. If so, he is saying in v. 23 that before the Council of Jerusalem the Jews accepted a favourable hearsay account of his preaching, and since the Council they have accepted an unfavourable account of it, again on hearsay. Cf. E. Bammel, 'Galater 1:23,' ZNTW 59 (1968), pp. 108-112.

[51] Chrysostom, PG 61, 634 A, thinks this is mentioned as proof that Paul did not preach circumcision in Judaea.

*What did St Paul do in the 'silent years'?*

When St Paul says that he went 'into the regions of Syria and Cilicia', he probably means that he returned home by way of Antioch in Syria to Tarsus in Cilicia. [52]

It is uncertain whether he means to imply that during the next fourteen years (or ten, if the fourteen of 2:1 includes the three of 1:18) his activities were confined to 'the regions of Syria and Cilicia'. According to the chronology adopted above, it was during these years that he visited Cyprus, Pisidia and Lycaonia (i.e. South Galatia). Perhaps he intends to include Pisidia and Lycaonia in 'the regions of Syria and Cilicia'. This is surprising, but St Luke appears to have done the same, for he reports that St Paul published in the churches of Pisidia and Lycaonia the apostolic letter addressed 'to the brethren of Antioch, Syria and Cilicia' (cf. Acts 15:23; 16:4).

During this period, St Paul may also have visited Crete in the company of Titus (cf. Tit 1:5). At all events, he was not idle, for the churches of Judaea 'kept on hearing' that he was preaching the gospel which he had previously persecuted.

*The Second Subsection, 2:1-10*

## THE COUNCIL OF JERUSALEM

Here is the text as it stands. The sense is obscure, and the syntax rugged. A revised version will be given below (see pp. 152-53).

A   *2:1* Then, after fourteen years, I again went up to Jerusalem with Barnabas, taking Titus with me too — *2* I went up in obedience to a revelation — and I laid before them the gospel which I preach to the Gentiles,   B   but privately before those held in regard:   C   Was I perhaps running or had I run my course in vain?   D   *3* But even my companion, Titus, Greek as he is, was not compelled to be circumcised.   E   *4* But on account of intruders — false brethren who had wormed their way in to spy on the liberty we have in Christ Jesus,   F   in order to enslave us.   G   *5* But not for a moment did we yield to their demand — F¹   in order that the truth of the gospel might remain with you.   E¹   *6* As for those held in regard — what they were once makes no difference to me, God is no respecter of human persons — those held in regard   D¹   laid down no further requirements.   C¹   *7* On the con-

---

[52] Acts 9:30 does not exclude a visit to Antioch on the journey to Tarsus.

trary, seeing that I had been entrusted with the gospel of the uncircumcised, as Peter had been with that of the circumcised, (8 for he who had made Peter's apostleship to the circumcision effective had made mine effective among the Gentiles) 9 and recognizing the grace that had been given to me, B¹ James, Cephas and John, the ones regarded as pillars, A¹ gave to me and to Barnabas the right hand of fellowship, with the understanding that we should preach to the Gentiles and they to the Jews. 10 They only asked that we should remember the Jewish poor; and this very thing I took care to do.

## Does this passage describe the same Council as Acts 15?

Most commentators identify the meeting of Paul and Barnabas, James, Peter and John, described in Gal 2:1-10, with the Council of Jerusalem described in Acts 15. [53] The arguments in favour of this identification are strong: the same persons meet in the same place, to discuss the same matter, in the face of the same opposition, and the outcome is substantially the same in both cases.

Nevertheless, some scholars of note have proposed to identify the meeting of Gal 2:1-10 with the 'Famine Visit' described in Acts 11:27-30: [54]

During this time some prophets came down from Jerusalem to Antioch. One of them named Agabus rose up and was moved by the Holy Spirit to predict that the whole world would suffer a severe famine (this was verified in the reign of Claudius). So the disciples decided to contribute, each according to his means, to furnish relief for the brethren living in Judaea; this they did, and sent it to the elders through the hands of Barnabas and Saul.

I shall first give the arguments offered in support of this view and reply to them (1); then I shall give an argument against it (2).

### (1)

*First argument:* In Gal 1:6—2:10 St Paul is recording his relations with Jerusalem under oath (v. 20). He places a gap of fourteen (or

[53] Cf. Lake in *The Beginnings of Christianity*, V, pp. 195-211; Lightfoot, Gal, p. 102; Lagrange, Gal, p. 23; Schlier, Gal, pp. 70-71; Filson, *A New Testament History*, p. 220; P. Parker, 'Once More, Acts and Galatians,' JBL 86 (1967), pp. 175-182.
[54] Cf. Orchard, Gal, 893 cd; R. G. Hoerber, 'Galatians 2:1-10 and the Acts of the Apostles,' *Concordia Theological Monthly* (St Louis, U.S.A.), 31 (1960) pp. 482-491; S. D. Toussaint, 'The Chronological Problem of Gal 2:1-10,' *Bibliotheca Sacra* (Dallas, U.S.A.), 120 (1963), pp. 334-340. [NTA 5-476; 8-668.]

perhaps eleven) years between his first visit and his second. But if the visit described in Gal 2: 1-10 is identical with the Council of Acts 15, he has concealed the visit which, as we know from Acts 11, he made about the middle of this fourteen year period. Hence, to secure St Paul against a charge of perjury, the visit of Gal 2 must be identified with that of Acts 11. *Reply:* This argument rests on the assumption that in Gal 1 : 6—2 : 10 St Paul is proving by an alibi that he did not receive the gospel from the apostles in Jerusalem, and therefore that he is giving a complete record of his relations with the church of Jerusalem during the seventeen (or fourteen) year period after his conversion. But this assumption is incorrect. St Paul is proving that throughout this period his conduct has not been dictated by human motives. The incidents which he discusses are those which his adversaries had turned into arguments against him. He can pass over the Famine Visit, because his adversaries had not used it as evidence against him.

*Second argument:* In Gal 2:2, St Paul emphasizes that the meeting was a private one with the rulers of the church; Acts 15 describes a more public meeting of 'the apostles and presbyters'. These cannot be one and the same meeting. *Reply:* There is no real discrepancy here. St Paul does not say that James, Peter and John were the only 'important people' present — his narrative leaves room for some presbyters; and Acts 15 does not imply that other apostles were present over and above the three named by St Paul. Moreover, the account in Acts shows that there was an informal meeting (v. 4) before the Council itself; and if v. 12 is out of place (see below, pp. 149-50), Paul and Barnabas did not address the public meeting until after the apostles and presbyters had reached their decision. It is, in fact, very easy indeed to harmonize the two accounts: when addressing the large assembly, Barnabas and Paul narrated the events of their mission among the Gentiles; they discussed the theological implications of their missionary policy in private with a few leading members of the church of Jerusalem. The two texts would be irreconcilable only if Acts 15 represented St Paul as explaining his gospel of Gentile freedom to a public meeting of the church of Jerusalem — which it does not.

*Third argument:* According to Acts 15, the Council settled the dispute with a formal decree in which Gentile Christians were required to abstain from certain kinds of meat. St Paul says that no ritual requirements were laid upon him after the meeting described in Gal 2 (cf. v. 6); and if the Council of Gal 2 did settle the matter with a

decretal letter, it is embarrassingly difficult to explain why Galatians
contains no reference to this decretal. [55] *Reply:* If it is difficult to
explain why the decretal is not mentioned in Galatians, it is equally
difficult to explain why it is not mentioned in 1 Cor 8:1-13; 10:14-33,
and in Rom 14, texts on the same subject, which were certainly written
after the Council of Acts 15. If St Paul's silence about the decretal
in 1 Cor and Rom is not a sufficient reason for dating these Epistles
before A.D. 49, it is not a good reason for dating Galatians to that
period either.

There is no conflict between the letter of Acts 15 and St Paul's
statement in Gal 2:6 that the apostles 'added nothing' to what he
himself had been requiring of Gentile converts. At the common meals
in pauline churches ordinary courtesy must have made it a custom
or tradition to refrain from serving ham and other sorts of pork, or
meat that was known to have been sacrificed to idols. The decretal
of Acts 15 did not require anything beyond what must have been
already established practice in the churches founded by St Paul. 'He,
too, no doubt led his mixed groups in a way of life that used many
common Jewish practices, not to force Gentiles to keep the law to be
saved, but simply because it was the familiar pattern and enabled
Jewish and Gentile Christians to eat and worship together without
offending long-standing Jewish feelings.' [56]

St Paul's reason for not explicitly quoting the letter can easily be
guessed. If St Luke has given anything like the exact wording, the
letter could be interpreted to mean that Gentiles *need* not observe
anything beyond the few 'necessary prohibitions', but *could* adopt
more of the law if they chose. In other words, the letter could have
been used in support of the mitigated form of the judaizing doctrine. [57]
St Paul appears, therefore, to have chosen to promulgate its substance,
but not its actual wording, its spirit, not its letter (cf. 2 Cor 3:6).

The above solution seems the best. Those who do not like it may
prefer to think that the decree was sent out by James on a later occasion and has been attached to the Council by St Luke because it
deals with the same topic as the Council. There are other examples
of such 'telescoping' or 'foreshortening' in St Luke's work. In Lk
24:36-53, for instance, he telescopes the appearance of Christ to the
apostles on the evening of Easter Sunday with his Ascension into
heaven, so that Christ seems to ascend into heaven on Easter Sunday
evening. Then at the beginning of Acts, he tells us, without any sign

[55] Cf. Orchard, Gal, 893 c.
[56] Filson, *A New Testament History*, p. 221: cf. Ramsay, Gal, p. 253.
[57] See above, pp. 27-28.

of embarrassment, that Jesus appeared to his disciples during forty days between the Resurrection and the Ascension (cf. Acts 1:3). Another example is Lk 4:16-30, the Rejection of Jesus at Nazareth, which combines accounts of at least two visits to Nazareth. [58] It is, therefore, in accordance with St Luke's known literary habits, if he has combined with the narrative of the Council of Jerusalem a decree on the same subject issued by the authority of James some time later. In support of this view, it can be pointed out that in Acts 21:25 James tells Paul about this decree as if Paul had not heard of it. But this may be just a small defect in St Luke's dramatic art: he makes James tell Paul what he already knows in order to remind the reader of what he may have forgotten.

(2)

*An argument against the identification:* After the Famine Visit of Acts 11, Paul and Barnabas remain in partnership for about five years, during which they evangelize South Galatia together. But there is a strong hint in Gal 2:10 that immediately after the meeting of 2:1-10 Paul and Barnabas parted: 'Only *we* were to remember the poor — which very thing *I* took care to do.' The change from 'we' to 'I' implies that Paul and Barnabas did not cooperate in fulfilling the apostles' request. [59] St Paul organized the relief fund during his second and third journeys without Barnabas's help. In Acts, Paul and Barnabas separate almost immediately after the Council of Jerusalem in Acts 15. Hence Gal 2:1-10 should be referred to the Council of Acts 15, and not to the visit of Acts 11 (where there is no mention of a Council, nor of any theological discussion).

## The Council of Jerusalem as described in Acts

The narrative in Acts consists of two framework passages enclosing a pair of symmetrical paragraphs. V. 12 is probably out of place. [60]

A    Barnabas and Paul are sent from Antioch to Jerusalem, 14:27—15:3.
B    Barnabas and Paul report miracles in Galatia, 15:4.

---

[58] See the note in JB ad loc.
[59] Perhaps this argument is not as strong as it looks. St Paul seems to regard the agreement of the three 'pillars' with himself and Barnabas as an agreement between St Peter and himself. He goes on at once to show (a) how he himself kept the agreement, and (b) how Peter did not—see below, p. 179. (There is another curious switch from 'we' to 'I' in 1:9.)
[60] Irenaeus, *Adversus Haereses*, 11, 12, 14, does not retain Acts 15:12; cf. Dibelius, *Studies in the Acts of the Apostles*, p. 116, n. 11.

C    Pharisees insist on the law, 15:5.
D    Peter refers to the conversion of the Gentile Cornelius, 15:6-7.
E    God has given the Spirit to the Gentiles as to us, 15:8-9.
F    *Therefore the law must not be imposed,* 15:10.
E$^1$   Our faith is the same as the Gentiles', 15:11 [v. 12].
D$^1$   James supports Peter and refers to the same events, 15:13-14.
C$^1$   James argues from Scripture, 15:15-18.

G    James suggests certain prohibitions, 15:19-20.
H    Moses has his preachers everywhere, 15:21.
I    Choice of Paul and Barnabas, Jude and Silas, 15:22.
J    *The Judaizers are repudiated,* 15:23-24.
J$^1$   Choice of Paul and Barnabas, Jude and Silas, 15:25-27.
H$^1$  'It has seemed good to the Holy Spirit and to us', 15:28a,
G$^1$  to impose only these prohibitions, 15:28b-29.

B$^1$  Barnabas and Paul report miracles in Galatia, <15:12>.
A$^1$  Barnabas and Paul return to Antioch from Jerusalem, 15:30-35.

V. 12, where it stands, upsets the first symmetry, since there is nothing in the first half to correspond to it. If it is transferred to the end of the passage, as above, it exactly fills a gap. The effect of this transposition is that Paul and Barnabas first report their ministry in Galatia to the apostles and presbyters (15:4) — this, before the Council meets. At the Council, in the first paragraph Peter speaks on the doctrinal issue, and receives the support of James; then in the second paragraph James repudiates the view of the Judaizers and suggests a practical policy. Only after these matters have been settled do Barnabas and Paul narrate to the whole Council the wonders of their ministry in Galatia. Here is the opening framework, A and B:

> A  *14:27* On their arrival (at Antioch), they gathered the church together, and reported all that God had enabled them to do, and told how he had opened the door of faith to the Gentiles. *28* And they stayed no little time there with the disciples. *15:1* Then some teachers came down from Judaea and began saying to the brethren: 'Unless you are circumcised and live according to the custom of Moses, you cannot be saved.' *2* Paul and Barnabas vigorously opposed them and argued against them, but in the end it was decided to send Paul and Barnabas and some others from Antioch to put this problem before the apostles and presbyters in Jerusalem. *3* They were set on their way by the church, and went through Phoenicia and Samaria, where they reported the conversion of the Gentiles and brought great joy to all the brethren.

> B  *4* When they arrived in Jerusalem, they were welcomed by the church and by the apostles and presbyters, and reported to them all that God had done through them.

And here is the closing framework, B$^1$ and A$^1$:

**B¹** *12* The whole assembly fell silent and listened to Barnabas and Paul describing all the signs and wonders that God had done through them among the Gentiles.

**A¹** *30* So the messengers set off, and went down to Antioch, where they gathered the people together and delivered the letter. *31* The reading of it brought joy and consolation. *32* Judas and Silas, who were themselves prophets, made long discourses of exhortation and encouragement. *33* After spending some time with the brethren there, they took their leave of them in peace and returned to those who had sent them. *35* But Paul and Barnabas remained in Antioch, where, along with many others, they preached the word of the Lord.

## Here are the two paragraphs enclosed by the above framework:

**C** *5* But some who had been converted to the faith from the sect of the Pharisees rose up and said: 'The Gentiles must be circumcised and told to keep the law of Moses.' **D** *6* The apostles and presbyters held a meeting to consider the matter, *7* and after a long discussion, Peter stood up and addressed them as follows: 'Brethren,' he said, 'in the early days, as you know, God made his choice among you and decreed that from my lips the Gentiles should hear the word of the gospel and believe; **E** *8* God who knows men's hearts testified his approval of them by giving the Holy Spirit to them just as to us; *9* he made no distinction between them and us, but cleansed their hearts by faith. **F** *10* Why, then, would you now tempt God by laying a yoke on the disciples' neck which neither we nor our fathers have been able to bear? **E¹** *11* It is through the grace of the Lord Jesus that we trust to be saved, and so do they.' *12* **D¹** *13* When he had finished, James spoke as follows: 'Brethren,' he said, 'listen to me. *14* Symeon has narrated how God first visited the Gentiles, to choose out of them a people to bear his name. **C¹** *15* And the words of the prophets are in agreement with him, for they say: *16* "Afterwards I shall return and rebuild the fallen dwelling of David; I shall rebuild its ruins and establish it once more, *17* that the rest of mankind may seek the Lord, all the Gentiles upon whom my name is invoked. *18* Thus says the Lord, who made these things known from of old."

**G** *19* Therefore my judgment is that we should not disturb those of the Gentiles who are converted to God, *20* but only write and tell them to abstain from anything contaminated by idols, from fornication, from meat killed by strangling, and from meat with blood in it. **H** *21* As for Moses, from early times he has had his preachers in every city, and is read every sabbath in the synagogue.' **I** *22* Then the apostles and presbyters, with the approval of the whole church, decided to choose men from their number and send them to Antioch with Paul and Barnabas. They chose Judas (known as Barsabbas) and Silas, both leading men among the brethren, *23* and entrusted them with a letter which run thus: **J** 'The apostles and presbyters send brotherly greetings to the Gentile brethren in Antioch, Syria and Cilicia. *24* Since we have heard that some of our number, without authorization from us, have caused confusion among you and unsettled your souls with their talk,     $I^1$     *25* we have held a meeting and decided to send chosen delegates to you with our beloved Barnabas and Paul, *26* men who have dedicated their lives to the cause of our Lord Jesus Christ. *27* The men we are sending you are Judas and Silas, who will confirm this message by word of mouth:     $H^1$     *28* it is the will of the Holy Spirit and our will     $G^1$     to lay no other burden on you than these necessary prohibitions: *29* you must abstain from meat offered to idols, meat with blood in it, and meat killed by strangling, and likewise from fornication. Keep yourselves from these and it will be well with you. Farewell.

### Why does St Peter in Acts 15 refer only to the conversion of Cornelius?

It may seem a little strange that at the Council of Jerusalem, when the real issue is the legitimacy of St Paul's mission, St Peter should argue, not from the gift of the Spirit granted to St Paul's converts, but to the conversion of Cornelius which had occurred several years before. [61] But really it is not so strange. St Peter's argument in the public assembly is that Paul's missionary policy is nothing new or unheard of; the principle on which it was based had been revealed long before to himself and his companions (cf. Acts 10:45). He could now see that the purpose of the intervention of the Holy Spirit in the Cornelius-episode was not simply to secure the conversion of a particularly deserving God-fearer, but also to prepare the church of Jerusalem in advance to accept the work of Paul and Barnabas.

The rest of St Peter's speech (vv. 8-11) is pauline through and through — as pauline as anything that Paul is allowed to say in Acts. A simple explanation of this phenomenon is that St Paul *had*, as he says, explained his gospel to Peter, James and John in private, and that in the public meeting Peter gave a summary of Paul's arguments, with which he was fully in agreement. He does not make any reference to the vision of the sail-cloth, [62] but only to the conversion of Cornelius, in which he now recognizes that Paul's gospel of justification by faith was implicit.

It is also surprising that in resolving this difficult problem Peter and James make no reference to anything that Jesus did or said during

---

[61] This question is discussed by Dibelius, *Studies in the Acts*, pp. 117-122.
[62] See above, pp. 104-106.

his public ministry. They might have referred to Jesus' table-fellowship with publicans and sinners, to his prophecy that many would come from East and West and sit down with Abraham, Isaac, and Jacob in the kingdom of heaven (Mt 8:11), and especially to his teaching on inner purity: 'Nothing that enters a man from outside can defile him; it is what comes out of a man that defiles him' (Mk 7:15). Instead, the apostles seem to look directly to the guidance of the Holy Spirit in the period since the Ascension. Probably this is simply the result of St Luke's selection of material. Much more was said at the Council than is recorded in Acts 15.

Incidents such as the cure of the Syrophoenician Woman's Daughter were clearly used by both sides. In St Matthew's version (15:24-26) Jesus says: 'I am sent only to the lost sheep of the house of Israel,' and when the woman insists, he adds: 'It is not right to take the children's bread and throw it to the dogs.' But in the Marcan version (7:27) he says nothing about the restriction of his ministry to Israel, and the second saying has the significant alteration: '*First* let the children be satisfied; it is not right to take the children's bread and throw it to the dogs.' Here we catch echoes, if not of the Council itself, at least of the controversies that preceded and followed it.

*Has the text of Gal 2:1-10 suffered dislocations?*

The text of Gal 2:1-10, as it stands in the manuscripts and printed editions, is extremely confused (see above, pp. 144-45). It is not clear whether the false brethren intruded themselves at Antioch or at Jerusalem, whether St Paul had or had not begun to doubt the validity of his preaching, whether he did or did not make a temporary concession to his adversaries, whether Titus was or was not circumcised, and whether Paul does or does not intend to imply that the 'pillars' were not what they seemed to be or thought they were.

Some commentators think that St Paul's syntax has gone to pieces because he is extremely embarrassed over what happened. But this explanation (or excuse) is not much to his credit. Surely he did not imagine that he would strengthen his case by giving such an obscure and embarrassed account of the Council. It is much more likely that the text has been upset — that St Paul's account of the incident was written with no less care than the rest of the Epistle, and was originally free from the difficulties which now encumber it. Probably it is no coincidence that the passage contains all the material needed for the construction of an excellent pattern. Blass suggested, on grounds of

sense, that v. 3 (about the circumcision of Titus) is out of place. [63]
If it is transferred to follow v. 9, the symmetry is immediately improved: Paul, Barnabas and Titus appear both at the beginning and
at the end (in A and A[1]). After this transfer has been made the structure still has a defect: C (v. 2c) is too short to balance C[1] (vv. 7-8-9).
If the parenthetic verse 8 is transferred to follow 2b, not only is the
balance of the passage improved, but the text no longer contains
the (improbable) implication that St Paul had begun to have doubts
about the validity of his preaching. A confirmatory proof that v. 8 is
out of place is that once it is removed, vv. 6b, 7, 9 and 10 form a
significant pattern:

A  *6b* 'Those who seemed' laid no further requirements upon me,    B  *7*
but on the contrary, seeing that I had been entrusted with the gospel of
the uncircumcision, as Peter had been with that of the circumcision,
C  and recognizing the grace that had been given to me,    D  James
E  Cephas    D[1]  and John [those who seemed to be pillars]    C[1]  gave
to me and to Barnabas the right hand of fellowship,    B[1]  with the understanding that we should go to the Gentiles, and they to the circumcision
—  A[1]  <those who seemed to be pillars!> [64]  —  only we were to
remember the Jewish poor.

It seems, therefore, that the original order of the text was as follows:

A  *1* Then, after fourteen years, I again went up to Jerusalem with
Barnabas, taking Titus with me too —  *2* I went up in obedience to a
revelation — and I laid before them the gospel which I preached to the
Gentiles — but privately, before those held in regard:    B  'Was I
perhaps running, or had I run, my course in vain? [3] *8* For he who
made Peter's apostleship to the circumcision effective made mine effective
among the Gentiles.'    C  *4* (I did this) on account of intruders —
false brethren who had wormed their way in to spy on the liberty we
have in Christ Jesus, in order to enslave us.    D  *5* Not for a moment,
however, did we yield to their demand; (we resisted) in order that the
gospel might remain with you in its purity.    C[1]  *6* As for those held
in high regard — what they were once makes no difference to me, God
is no respecter of persons — those held in regard laid down no further
requirements;    B[1]  *7* on the contrary, seeing that I had been entrusted
with the gospel of the uncircumcised, as Peter had been with that of the
circumcised, [8] *9* and recognizing the grace that had been given to me,
A[1]  James, Cephas and John gave to me and to Barnabas the right hand of
fellowship, with the understanding that we should preach to the Gentiles
and they to the Jews — they who were regarded as the pillars.  *3* Even
my companion Titus, Greek as he is, was not required to be circumcised.

---

[63]  Cf. Funk-Blass-Debrunner, *Greek Grammar of the New Testament*, Cambridge, 1961, 448 (6).
[64]  The transference of this phrase improves the structure, but is not strictly necessary.

*10* They only asked that we should remember the Jewish poor; and this very thing I took care to do.

The transference of the verse about Titus was probably not accidental. It may be the work of Paul himself. The contrast between the agreement between Peter and Paul at Jerusalem (2:10) and their disagreement at Antioch (2:11) stands out more sharply in the canonical text than in the suggested original. Perhaps St Paul originally composed the passage with Titus mentioned at the beginning and end, and decided to transfer the second sentence about him elsewhere only when he was joining this paragraph to the next. However, it is difficult to believe that he put it where it stands in the canonical text, since in that position it badly upsets both the grammar and the argument.

## *Why did St Paul make this journey to Jerusalem?*

According to Gal 2:2, St Paul went to Jerusalem to lay his gospel before the authorities. The dislocated text has given some commentators the impression that he had begun to wonder whether his gospel of Gentile liberty was after all a mistake. [65] But this is inconsistent with his claim in 1:12-17 that he is absolutely certain of the correctness of his gospel because he received it directly from Christ. If the revelation did not give him certainty at the time of the visit to Jerusalem, it could not make him certain at the time of writing the Epistle. There is no need to attribute this inconsistency to St Paul. It is sufficient to suppose that in v. 2c he suddenly switches into direct speech (just as he did in 1:22): 'I laid before them the gospel which I preach to the Gentiles, (and put the question): "Is it possible that I am running [66] or have run my course in vain?"' — a question expecting the answer 'Of course not!' [67]

In the reconstructed text, v. 8 can be regarded as a continuation of the direct speech. Paul asks: 'Is it possible that I am running or have run my course in vain, seeing that God has blessed my mission to the Gentiles just as he has blessed the mission of Peter to the Jews?'

---

[65] Cf. Schlier, Gal, p. 37.

[66] 'Running' is simply a metaphor for apostolic effort. St Thomas's comment (Gal, 392 B) is unintentionally amusing: 'He describes his preaching as "running" on account of the speed of his teaching, for in a short time he preached the gospel from Jerusalem to Illyricum and even to Spain.' At the time of the Council, of course, he had run only as far as Derbe.

[67] Cf. Chrysostom, PG 61, 653-54: 'He himself had no need to learn that he had not run in vain; his purpose was the correction of his critics.' Lagrange, Gal, p. 27: 'He was certain beforehand what the answer would be—it could only be negative.'

In the uncorrected text, v. 4 is a problem. Either it explains why
St Paul allowed Titus to be circumcised — if Titus *was* circumcised;
or, if he was not, it explains why St Paul has stopped to mention that
he was not circumcised. Both explanations are awkward. In the reconstructed text v. 4 explains why, although St Paul himself had no
doubt whatever that his preaching had been fruitful and effective, it
was nevertheless God's will (and his own) to submit the matter to the
apostles in Jerusalem: 'on account of certain intruders...'

In the reconstructed version, since these intruders occasioned the
journey to Jerusalem, they must have intruded elsewhere, and presumably at Antioch. [68] Then the Epistle is in agreement with Acts
15:1-2:

> Some teachers came down from Judaea and began saying to the brethren:
> 'Unless you are circumcised and live according to the custom of Moses,
> you cannot be saved.' Paul and Barnabas vigorously opposed them and
> argued against them, but in the end it was decided to send Paul and Bar-
> nabas and some others from Antioch to put this problem before the
> apostles and presbyters in Jerusalem.

It is true that in Gal 2:2 St Paul says that he went up to Jerusalem
'in accordance with a revelation'. But this is not inconsistent with his
being sent by the church of Antioch. If the deputation to Jerusalem
was suggested *before* the revelation was given, St Paul had good reason
to oppose the idea: the sending of such a deputation would be taken
to imply that there was serious doubt as to whether his preaching had
been in vain. [69] If circumcision was necessary for salvation, his preaching had been substantially wrong, and the salvation of his converts
was not assured. Even to admit the semblance of doubt on such an
important matter would be bad for the Gentile Christians. Moreover,
if Paul consented to be one of the delegates, he would seem to admit
that the primitive apostles had a right to censor his theological views
— which he did not admit. [70] In these circumstances, probably
nothing short of a revelation would have made Paul willing to go up
to Jerusalem.

God gave him the revelation. Evidently it was his good pleasure
that the pauline churches and later generations of Gentile Christians
should have the assurance that St Paul's gospel was not defective and
that it had the full approval of St Peter.

---

[68] Goulder, *Type and History in Acts,* p. 199, adopts this view, on grounds of
sense. Similarly, Munck, *St Paul and the Salvation of Mankind,* p. 96.
Lagrange, however, thinks that the deputation from Antioch lodged together in
Jerusalem, and the false brethren feigned friendship with this little group to
spy on them (Gal, p. 32).
[69] Cf. Filson, A *New Testament History,* p. 217, n. 33.
[70] Cf. J. Weiss, *Earliest Christianity,* I, p. 267. O. Linton, 'The Third Aspect,'

Before the revelation was given, St Paul probably felt that there was no need for him to go to Jerusalem — it was up to St Peter to take the initiative and teach the Jewish Christians not to criticize his work among the Gentiles. He may well have expressed this point of view at the private meeting and admonished Peter to speak out more boldly in the matter. But there is no hint of any friction, since according to Acts 15 Peter did speak out boldly at the Council.

## Were the 'false brethren' of v. 4 in any sense Christians?

St Paul's words could mean that the persons in question were non-Christian spies, posing as Christians. But more probably *they* considered themselves Christians and St Paul disagreed. [71] In his view their doctrine made Christ's death fruitless and meaningless; since they were virtually rejecting the central doctrine of justification by faith in Christ's cross, they were not true brethren at all.

St Paul's strictures are intelligible and perfectly just, if the false brethren were tending towards the views which Eusebius attributes to the Ebionites. [72] However, it is unlikely that the Judaizers explicitly held a low Christology, or St Paul would have attacked them on this point. But by failing to do justice to the saving efficacy of Christ's death they showed that they had a poor grasp of the essentials of the gospel and hardly deserved to be reckoned as Christians. [73]

## Was St Paul the leader of the deputation?

Acts 15:2 simply says that the church of Antioch decided that 'Paul and Barnabas and certain others' should go to Jerusalem. But Gal 2:1 shows that St Paul regarded himself as the leader. He says: 'I went up with Barnabas, and I also took with me Titus' — that is 'I took Titus in addition to Barnabas.' If he had regarded Barnabas and himself as equals, he would presumably have said: 'and *we* took Titus with us.' Then he adds: 'I laid before them the gospel which *I* preach to the Gentiles' — not which *we* preach; and in vv. 7-8 he compares Peter's apostolate to his own, with no mention of Barnabas.

This was probably one of the causes of the split between Paul and Barnabas after the Council. If Barnabas was still the senior of the

---

*Studia Theologica* III/2 (1951), p. 95, remarks that in Acts 15 'Paul is described as more conciliatory than he really was.'

[71] Cf. Lagrange, Gal, p. 32; and 1 Jn 2:19.
[72] Cf. Eusebius, *H.E.*, III, 27, quoted above, p. 86.
[73] Cf. R. Bultmann, *Theology of the New Testament*, Vol. 2, London, 1955, p. 135: 'The proponents of directions of thought which were later rejected as heretical considered themselves completely Christian.'

pair, it was for him to decide whether they should take John Mark on the second journey. Paul apparently thought either that the decision was his, or that it should be made on theological principles (as he saw them). John Mark was the occasion of the split, but trouble had been brewing for some time before. [74]

### Why did St Paul take Titus with him?

If the delegation to Jerusalem was chosen by the church of Antioch, it was natural for them to include an uncircumcised Gentile as one of the delegates. But St Paul seems to imply that Titus was his choice: 'I went up... taking Titus with me.' And in v. 3 he speaks of 'my companion Titus.' So perhaps it is safe to infer that it was St Paul's idea to take Titus, and that he was meant to be a test-case: Paul would make it known that he was lodging with an uncircumcised Gentile convert, and the authorities in Jerusalem would have to pass not only a theoretical judgment on the necessity of circumcision in general but also a practical judgment on the case of Titus in particular: did he require circumcision for salvation? and was it right for Paul to associate with him?

Both Barnabas and Titus would also be witnesses, to report back to the church of Antioch what Paul said to the apostles and what the apostles said to him. [75] 'On the testimony of two or three witnesses every word shall stand.' [76]

### Is St Paul disrespectful to the pillar-apostles?

In vv. 2, 6 and 9, St Paul uses an idiomatic Greek phrase which changes its colour like a chameleon, according to its context. It can mean:

> They seem to be (and are).
> They seem to be (and are not).
> They think they are (and are).
> They think they are (and are not).
> They are thought to be (and are).

---

[74] Later on, St Paul relented and forgave Mark, as can be seen from Col 4 : 10: 'Mark, the cousin of Barnabas, sends greetings. You have received instructions about him: if he visits you, make him welcome.'

[75] Jerome, PL 26, 357 B, Augustine, PL 35, 2111 B, and St Thomas, Gal, 391 C, recognise that Barnabas and Titus were *witnesses*, the one a Jew, the other a Gentile.

[76] Deut 19 : 15; cf. Mt 18 : 16.

> They are thought to be (and are not).
> They are regarded as...
> They are held in regard.
> They are famous.
> They are powerful.
> They are rulers.

The phrase occurs in a saying of Christ in Mk 10:43: 'You know that those who seem to rule (or 'are the powerful rulers', or 'are held in regard as rulers', or 'claim to rule') the Gentiles lord it over them.'[77]

This ancient idiom was already a puzzle in the time of Christ and the apostles,[78] as can be seen from Philo's treatise *On the Cherubim*, where he gives a pious meditation on it: human rulers do not really rule, they only seem to rule, for God is the one true ruler: 'no mortal can in solid reality be "lord" of anything; when we give the name of "master" we speak in the language of appearance, not of truth.'[79]

The ambiguous phrases which St Paul uses in vv. 2, 6 and 9 need not imply any disrespect, but they can be heavily loaded.[80] Once again, St Paul probably wishes to take advantage of the ambiguity of the words he uses. He is making insinuations and yet at the same time covering his traces. *First,* in v. 2 James, Cephas and John are described as 'those who seem' — which might mean 'those held in high regard, and rightly so.'[81] *Secondly,* in v. 6 they are called 'those who seem to be something'; but the phrase could equally well mean 'those who think they are something' — with an undertone of disparagement. It is no accident that in this carefully planned letter one of the moral maxims which St Paul considers specially suitable for the Galatian situation is (6:3): 'If anyone thinks he is something, he is deceiving himself, for he is nothing.' *Thirdly,* in v. 9 St Paul specifies what Peter, James and John seem to be or think they are: 'pillars'.[82] He probably insinuates that while they believe themselves to be the pillars of the Church and are revered by others as such, in fact they are not what they seem, for they have left it to St Paul to defend 'the truth of the gospel', and at Antioch in Paul's judgment Peter was actually 'compelling the Gentiles to judaize' — shaking their faith in the

[77] Cf. T. W. Manson, *The Teaching of Jesus*, pp. 313-315.
[78] It is used by Euripides, *Hecuba*, 294, and Plato, *Gorgias*, 472 A.
[79] Philo, *De Cherubim*, 63-83 (Loeb, II); cf. Epictetus, *Discourses*, I, 9. See further J. Bligh, 'Matching Passages in the Gospels,' *The Way* 8 (1968), pp. 316-317.
[80] Cf. 2 Cor 11:5: 'the super-apostles'.
[81] Compare the English idiom 'very important persons'.
[82] Similar imagery was used at Qumran, e.g. in the Manual of Discipline, V, 5 and Hymns 2, 9-10. See J. Murphy-O'Connor, 'La vérité chez saint Paul et à Qumran,' RB 72 (1965), p. 69: 'It is precisely as the concrete incarnation of perfect fidelity that the Essenes are "a foundation of truth".'

gospel preached by Paul and turning it upside down. Paul regards
the pillars as enjoying an undeserved reputation for being what he
himself really is. It is he, Paul, who has defended the truth of the
gospel and the freedom of the Gentile Christians, whereas Peter at
Antioch was guilty of 'hypocrisy' and of departing from 'the truth of
the gospel' (2:13-14). It is possible for personal antipathies to exist
between holy men, and at the time of writing this Epistle, St Paul
was not altogether well disposed to St Peter.

St Augustine recognises the implication that Peter, James and
John were not really pillars, and gives an explanation which is reminiscent of the passage of Philo quoted above. (Philo's influence
probably came to Augustine through Origen.)

> Nor were they truly pillars, but they 'seemed' to be. For Paul knew that
> Wisdom had built herself a house, and had set up not three pillars but
> seven (cf. Prov 9:1). This number refers either to the unity of the Church
> (for seven represents completeness...) or else to the sevenfold working of
> the Holy Spirit....by which the house of the Son of God, that is the
> Church, is held together. [83]

*How is the parenthesis relevant in v. 6?*

The parenthesis in v. 6 again contains an ambiguity, and again
St Paul probably intends to profit by it. The two possible translations
are:

(1) 'As for those held in regard — what they really *were* makes no difference to me...' (*qualescumque revera erant*)
(2) 'As for those held in regard — what they *once* were makes no difference to me...' (*quales aliquando fuerint*).

In the second subsection (p. 144), this sentence balances v. 4
which is about the false brethren. The connection is stronger if the
first of the above alternatives is adopted: the false brethren pretended
to be what they were not, the pillar apostles were thought to be what
perhaps they were not. In the latter case, Paul refrains from judging
since the judgment is irrelevant. If God is no respecter of persons
and entrusts authority to men who are not all that they seem, it is
not for Paul to be a respecter of persons — he must recognize the
authority of Peter, James and John whether or not they are showing
themselves worthy of it.

But in the structure of the whole section (p. 121), v. 6 balances
1:12-14 where St Paul speaks of what he himself once was — a

---

[83]  Augustine PL 35, 2113 A.

persecutor of the Church. [84] This connection is stronger if the second alternative is adopted. Peter and John had been illiterate fishermen; James the brother of the Lord may have been another carpenter; probably none of them was a strict observer of the law before his conversion. Nevertheless, God chose them and entrusted authority to them. Paul, who had been a learned, law-abiding Pharisee, might well feel a *natural* disinclination to laying his gospel before them for their approval. But he is now walking according to the Spirit. So he humbled himself and submitted to their judgment.

### Was Titus circumcised?

In the unrevised text (see above, p. 144), St Paul appears to speak of a dispute as to whether Titus should be circumcised. He seems to attach great importance to the point, and yet commentators have never been able to agree as to whether he means that Titus was circumcised or that he was not. V. 3 can be taken in two ways, either (1) 'Even my Greek companion Titus was not *forced* to submit to circumcision' — with the implication that he submitted as a conciliatory gesture; or (2) 'Even *Titus*, a Greek, who was there with me, was not compelled to be circumcised' — with the implication that he was not circumcised. V. 5, too, is ambiguous. It can mean either (1) 'We did not yield and obey'; or (2) 'We did yield, but not by way of obedience' — with the implication that a concession was made for the sake of peace.

Those who think that Titus was circumcised have two principal arguments. First, according to Gal 5:11, St Paul's adversaries said that he was 'still preaching circumcision'. Presumably they accused him of inconsistency in that he admitted the value of circumcision when among Jews and denied it when among Gentiles. The charge would be a little easier to understand, if he did in fact give way at Jerusalem and allowed Titus to be circumcised. (But this is not a strong argument. St Paul's critics could just as easily have argued from the case of Timothy.)

Secondly, it is pointed out that the syntax of this passage is exceptionally irregular. It is a jumble of parentheses and anacolutha. The explanation might well be that St Paul is embarrassed over the incident. F. C. Burkitt's comment has appealed to many: 'Who can doubt that it was the knife which really did circumcise Titus that has cut the syntax of Gal 2:3-5 to pieces?' [85]

---

[84]  St Thomas, Gal, 394 B, observes this connection. And see above, p. 104.
[85]  *Christian Beginnings,* London, 1924, p. 118; cf. Bo Reicke, 'Der geschichtliche

If this view is correct, the pillar-apostles recommended St Paul to conciliate the opposition by circumcising Titus, and he did so. There is a similar incident in Acts 21:22-23, during St Paul's last visit to Jerusalem, when James proposes a conciliatory measure and Paul accepts.

However, Burkitt's wisecrack must not be allowed to sweep the board. There are stronger arguments on the other side. At the centre of the subsection 2:1-10 stands St Paul's boast: 'Not for a moment did we yield to the slavery [86] (which they wished to impose) — in order that the truth of the gospel might remain with you.' The passage is ruined if the central statement is an embarrassed admission that Titus was as a matter of fact circumcised. Moreover, in the unrevised text, v. 3, 'Titus was not compelled to be circumcised,' has as its counterpart v. 6, 'they added nothing' (made no further demands, but accepted my gospel as sufficient).

In the revised text (see above, p. 153), Titus is mentioned at the beginning and at the end. The dispute at the centre is not a dispute as to whether Titus should be circumcised; it is the dispute as to whether all Gentiles should be circumcised. Not for a moment did Paul yield to *this* tyrannical demand — in order that the truth of the gospel might remain with the Gentile Christians.

When transferred to its proper place at the end, v. 3 is no longer ambiguous. St Paul says: 'The pillar-apostles laid down no further demands — why, even Titus who was there with me was not required or urged to be circumcised!'

The syntax of vv. 3-5, as they stand, has been ripped to pieces; but this is not the fault of St Paul, unless he is the person who dislocated the text.

## *Why does St Paul insist that the meeting was a private one?*

St Jerome raises this question and replies that Paul may have discussed these matters privately or 'secretly' (*abscondite*) 'on account of the large numbers of Jewish believers who could not yet endure to hear that Christ was the fulfilment and end of the law, and who, in Paul's absence, had put about the saying that he was running and

Hintergrund des Apostelkonzils und der Antiochia-Episode Gal 2:1-14,' in *Studia Paulina* (Festschrift de Zwaan), 1953, pp. 184-87; J. Weiss, *Earliest Christianity*, I, p. 271.
[86] Cf. Chrysostom, PG 61, 656 B: 'He does not say "to their words" but "to their slavery", for their aim was not to teach anything useful but to subject and enslave.'

had run his course in vain because he thought that the old law should not be followed.' [87] And in his letter to Augustine: [88] 'Why "separately" and not in public? Lest scandal be given to the Jewish faithful, who believed that the law should be observed and that faith should be placed in Christ as Saviour on this basis.' He means, apparently, that St Paul was in agreement with St Peter that there was no chance of convincing the church of Jerusalem as a whole that the law was obsolete, and therefore conspired with Peter at Jerusalem (as later at Antioch [89]) to confirm both Jewish and Gentile Christians in their previous views.

This is a possible explanation of why the meeting was private, but it does not explain why, in writing the Epistle, St Paul thought it important to interrupt his sentence to emphasize that the meeting was a private one. The explanation may be that he wishes to show that he followed the evangelical rule and admonished Peter semiprivately before doing so publicly. But he intended his viewpoint to be made known to the church of Jerusalem. St Luke is doubtless right in representing St Peter as passing on the substance of St Paul's reasoning in the more public assembly.

Perhaps St Paul also wishes to show that while he recognizes Peter, James and John as having authority to judge whether his doctrine has been right or wrong, he does not acknowledge that the church of Jerusalem as a whole has any such *magisterium*. He did not go up to Jerusalem to discover the *sensus fidelium* or to consult the laity on a point of doctrine. If the decision had been left to a democratic vote of all the Jewish Christians in Jerusalem, it might have gone against St Paul (cf. Acts 21:20).

### What happened at the private meeting in Jerusalem?

First, St Paul laid before James, Cephas and John the gospel which he had been preaching to the Gentiles. Then he put to them the question: 'Have I been running my course in vain?' and (according to the reconstructed text) summed up the evidence which should enable them to give a decision: God who had worked for Peter and in Peter to effect the conversion of Jews had worked for Paul and in Paul to effect the conversion of Gentiles. [90] Probably he meant

---

[87]   Jerome, PL 26, 358 B.
[88]   Jerome, Ep. 112, 8.
[89]   Cf. Jerome, PL 26, 364 B.
[90]   On the meaning of v. 8 see G in G, p. 110; and Abbot Chapman, 'St Paul and the Revelation to St Peter,' *The Downside Review* 55 (1937), p. 434.

that just as God had prepared Peter for his apostolate by the Trans-figuration, so he had prepared himself (Paul) for his by the Damascus-vision; and just as God had visibly poured out the Holy Spirit upon Peter's converts among the Jews (cf. Acts 2: 42-47), so he had blessed Paul's among the Gentiles (cf. Gal 3: 1-5).

Probably St Paul next explained why he was asking the 'pillars' to pass judgment: not because he was in any doubt, but on account of the false brethren who had upset the church of Antioch. There is no indication that these were present at the private meeting. St Paul resisted them precisely by seeking this private meeting with the apostles.

As was suggested above, St Paul may also have reproached Peter, James and John for having failed to take a firm line against the Pharisaic extremists. In Paul's view, the apostles ought to have used their authority to control these trouble-makers and to condemn their doctrine. Even apart from the question whether Gentile converts should be circumcised, many of the Jewish Christians in Jerusalem thought that Paul ought not to have gone off preaching to the Gentiles before the Jews had been converted. The children should be fed before the dogs. In St Paul's view, Peter, James and John, by failing to speak out against this opinion, were giving the impression that they did not really approve of what he was doing. He asked them, therefore, to give formal and explicit approval not only to his doctrine but also to the very existence of Gentile missions at a time when Israel remained unconverted. We see in v. 9 that they did so, and to us it may appear that they could not conceivably have done otherwise. But for the early Jewish members of the Church it was a serious problem. What had become of the privilege of Israel, if the Church was to be full of Gentiles and almost empty of Jews? [91] St Paul himself conceded that there was something in what his critics said. Twice in Romans he says that the gospel is to be preached 'to the Jew first, then to the Greek' (1: 16 and 2: 10); and when evangelizing Greek cities, he always went to the synagogue first. In Jerusalem, too, in A.D. 58, he had to defend himself on this point, as can be seen from his speech in Acts 22, [92] where he shows that he would not have gone to the Gentiles but would have remained in Jerusalem, if he had not been explicitly told, in his vision in the temple, to go to Gentile nations far away.

So, at the private meeting, Paul asked for formal approval both of his doctrine and of the continuance of his work among the Gentiles.

---

[91] Rom 9-11 is St Paul's fullest treatment of this problem.
[92] See the analysis given above, pp. 97-98.

H

The authorities may not have liked this *démarche*. When ecclesiastical rulers are asked to make such a judgment, there are usually some who declare it 'inopportune'. There were probably inopportunists at Jerusalem, complaining that Paul was causing the apostles unnecessary embarrassment. But visitors who bring substantial alms to the Holy City can usually obtain a hearing. Paul and Barnabas had brought alms on a previous occasion, and probably did so on this visit too — this supposition renders more intelligible the words '*which very thing* I took care to do (or, I had taken care to do).'

In the revised version of the text, the apostles make no attempt whatever to have Titus circumcised. The question does not even arise. St Paul says that 'they laid down no further requirements' which he should impose on Gentile converts. They agreed that Gentile Christians should not be circumcised or made to observe the law.

'On the contrary', says St Paul at the beginning of v. 7. St Jerome took this to mean: 'They taught me nothing — on the contrary, it was I who taught them and confirmed them in their understanding of the gospel.' [93] But the view of St John Chrysostom is better: 'They did not find fault with me — on the contrary, they congratulated me and shook hands.' [94]

The apostles' favourable judgment was based partly on Paul's own witness to the Damascus vision, partly on the corroborating witness of Barnabas (cf. Acts 9:27, a similar intervention), partly on their joint testimony to the success of their work among the Gentiles. In so far as they judged Paul's mission by its success, Peter, James and John were relying on the principle given in Mt 7:16: 'By their fruits you shall know them.' In St Paul's words, the success of his mission was the 'seal' authenticating his apostolate. [95]

*Who is the James mentioned in v. 9?*

St Augustine thought that the 'James, Cephas and John' mentioned in v. 9 were the Peter, James and John who witnessed the Transfiguration: [96]

---

[93] Cf. Jerome, PL 26, 361 A.

[94] Chrysostom, PG 61, 637 C. Schmithals, *Paul and James*, p. 52, regards as 'well-grounded' the conjecture that in Gal 2:7-9 St Paul is quoting an official record of the outcome of the discussion. But if the meeting was private, it is unlikely that there was any official communiqué or a written contract.

[95] Cf. 1 Cor 9:3; 2 Cor 3:2. In our own day this principle has been used to authenticate the mixed ministry of the church of South India.

[96] Augustine, PL 35, 2113.

Peter, James and John were the most honoured among the apostles because
the Lord showed himself to them on the mountain as a sign of his kingdom
(or, 'in the manifestation of his kingdom'), when six days earlier he had
said: 'There are some of those standing here who will not taste death before
they see the Son of Man in his Father's kingdom.'

But, as James the son of Zebedee was put to death by Herod Agrippa
I, who himself died in A.D. 44, Augustine must be mistaken about
James.

Peter and the two sons of Zebedee, James and John, were the
original three 'pillars'. When James was executed, his place was taken
by another James, namely, James the brother of the Lord, who, although he had not seen the Transfiguration, had been granted a special
appearance of the risen Lord (cf. 1 Cor 15:7). [97]

### Why is James named before Cephas in v. 9?

St Paul surprises us by placing the pillar-apostles in the order
James-Cephas-John. The explanation cannot be that he regards James
as the most important, [98] since in vv. 7-8 he acknowledges Peter's
primacy among the apostles of the circumcision. Several other reasons
suggest themselves.

Perhaps St Paul is *picturing* the three apostles as three pillars
and therefore places the chief pillar or 'rock' (Cephas) in the middle.
Just as he himself is flanked by Barnabas and Titus, so Peter is flanked
by James and John. Perhaps James is named first as being the resident
head of the church of Jerusalem and the president of this private
meeting. (His position may be compared to that of Linus and Anac-
letus at Rome, while Peter was still alive.) Perhaps James is named
first as being the one who was most attached to the law and therefore
most likely to find fault with St Paul's doctrine; [99] or perhaps because
his authority was recognised by the Judaizers. [100] Or perhaps St Peter
is placed in the middle because the centre of a chiasm is the place
of honour. [101] As was observed above (p. 153), if the parenthetic v. 8

[97] See above, p. 141.
[98] Cullmann, *Peter*, p. 43, thinks that Peter had resigned the primacy in favour
of James.
[99] Thus P. Benoit, 'La Primauté de Pierre,' *Exégèse et Théologie*, II, Paris, 1961,
p. 255, n. 1.
[100] Thus Karrer, *Peter and the Church*, p. 41.
[101] Cf. the position of the chief priests in the structure of Mk. 8:31-32: 'The Son
of Man must A suffer many things, B and be rejected, C by the elders D and
chief priests C¹ and scribes, B¹ and be put to death, A¹ and rise again after
three days.'

is omitted, vv. 6-10 form a symmetrical pattern centring on the name 'Cephas'.

### *What was the significance of the handshake?*

Peter, James and John recognized the grace that had been given to Paul and Barnabas by giving them a formal handshake. This was not an established religious usage among the Jews, [102] and it has not been widely used in the Church. [103] It was, however, a common and natural practice in political and civil life. Images of clasped right hands were used as symbols of friendship and loyalty. [104] When St Paul says that James, Cephas and John gave to Barnabas and himself the right hand of fellowship, what he excludes is perhaps as important as what he affirms. There was no question of ordination by the laying-on of hands. St Paul's authority was not derived from the Twelve by ordination; they recognized that he had already received his commission and authority from Christ in the vision. There is a passage in Exodus (24:9-11) which shows that the vision of God renders ordination superfluous. After Moses had offered the covenant sacrifice and sprinkled the people with the blood of the covenant,

> Moses and Aaron, Nadab and Abihu, and seventy of the elders of Israel went up, and they saw the God of Israel; and there was under his feet as it were a pavement of sapphire stone, like the very heaven for clearness. And he (Moses) did not lay his hand on the chief men of Israel; they beheld God, and ate and drank.

There was no need for Moses to mediate the Holy Spirit to the seventy elders by the laying-on of his hands, because they had already come into direct contact with his power and glory in the vision. So too with Paul.

In the ceremony of clasping hands, the pillar apostles appear to have made no distinction between Paul and Barnabas. If they accepted them as equal to each other, they can hardly have accepted them as equal to themselves, for Barnabas did not claim to have received a revelation like Paul's. But according to vv. 7-9, St Paul thought that the pillars had recognized his own pre-eminence in the Gentile mission. He implies that just as Cephas was the chief missionary to the Jews,

---

[102] There is one instance in Ezra 10:19 (LXX, 1 Ez 9:20).

[103] But in the Ordinal of the Church of South India, immediately after ordaining a presbyter, 'the Bishop gives him the right hand of fellowship and says: "We give you the right hand of fellowship, and receive you to take part with us in this ministry." '

[104] Cf. Lightfoot, Gal, ad loc.

and therefore superior to James and John, so he was the chief missionary to the Gentiles and therefore superior to Barnabas.

## *What was the nature of the agreement mentioned in 2:9?*

The two sides shook hands on an agreement which is briefly described in 2:9: 'that we to the Gentiles, they to the circumcision.' It appears to have been a rather vague, unwritten, gentlemen's agreement, of the sort that often leads to disputes. In general, it meant that while the pillar apostles would continue to observe the law in order to be able to carry on their apostolate among the Jews (cf. 4:4-5), Paul and Barnabas would abandon the law so far as their missionary work among the Gentiles would require them to do so. It certainly meant that Paul and Barnabas would leave Jerusalem and Judaea to the pillars; but it did not necessarily mean that James, Peter and John would confine themselves to Jerusalem and Judaea, for there were large communities of Jews living abroad, for example, in the three great cities of Rome, Alexandria and Antioch. Paul may have understood the agreement to mean that Peter would refrain from exercising his authority outside Palestine, but Peter may not have intended this. And Peter may have understood Paul to mean that he would go and preach directly to the Gentiles; in fact, whenever Paul entered a Gentile city he preached first to the Jews and then to the Greeks. [105] If the agreement was as ill-defined as Gal 2:9 suggests, it was bound to lead to disputes. For example, to which mission field did Rome and Alexandria belong? So far as we know, St Paul never visited Alexandria, where there were about a million Jews. At Rome there was a colony of thirty to forty thousand Jews, and the first Christian community in Rome was probably Jewish. [106] In spite of the agreement referred to in Gal 2:9, St Paul felt obliged to apologize for visiting this church which he had not founded (cf. Rom 15:20).

The agreement reached at Jerusalem was, to some extent, an agreement to differ. There was probably a discussion at this meeting about the way in which the apostles ought to go about their task of evangelizing the whole world. By the year 58, when he wrote Romans, and probably much earlier, St Paul had reached the conclusion that it was God's will to bring in the Gentiles first and then

---

[105] Cf. Rom 1:16; 2:9, 10; Acts 13: 5, 14; 14:1; 16:13; 17:2, 10, 17; 18:4. Schmithals, *Paul and James*, p. 60, rejects all this evidence: 'It is almost impossible,' he says, 'to imagine Paul beginning his preaching in the synagogues.'

[106] Cf. Cullmann, *Peter*, p. 80.

move Israel to repentance by spiritual jealousy. [107] After quoting Deut 32:21, 'I shall make you jealous of a nation that is no nation,' he goes on to say (Rom 11:25-26): 'The partial hardening of Israel is to last only until the full number of Gentiles has come in, but after that all Israel will be saved.' It is quite possible that St Paul proposed this view in his discussion with the pillar-apostles, and called upon them to come out and preach to the Gentiles. But they seem to have taken the view that Israel must be converted first. [108] Gal 2:9 probably means that a compromise was reached: the three pillar-apostles would continue to work for the conversion of Israel, but they did not disapprove of the establishment of Gentile missions even before Israel was converted. Paul and Barnabas were therefore free to continue their work among the Gentiles. Understood in this way, the agreement would not forbid Peter and John to change their minds at a later date and go to the Gentiles — that was what Paul had really wanted, and *volenti non fit iniuria.*

From our modern point of view, this division of the world into two spheres of influence, the tiny land of Israel for Peter and the rest of the five continents for Paul, looks absurd. The geographical horizons of Peter, James and John were doubtless limited; but it is hard to believe that they thought they were keeping the lion's share for themselves and yielding to Paul and Barnabas only the 'periphery'. [109] More probably they realized the immensity of the task to be done in the Gentile world, but thought the conversion of the little nation of Israel a necessary preliminary. After Israel had been converted, it would be time to preach to the Gentiles. If this is what was in the apostles' minds, the agreement was necessarily a temporary arrangement: the pillars would remain with the Jews until their conversion only. In the year 49, they probably hoped and expected that Israel would be converted within a generation. St Paul's arguments in Rom 9-11 seem to show that he still clung to this expectation even in A.D. 58. [110]

---

[107] Here again, St Paul may be drawing upon his own experience. The fortitude of St Stephen may have awakened pangs of spiritual jealousy in Paul's breast. See above on 1:15.

[108] Cf. Munck, *Paul and the Salvation of the Gentiles*, p. 303; Gaechter, *Petrus und Seine Zeit*, p. 225; Baum, *The Jews and the Gospel*, p. 136.

[109] Cf. Gaechter, *Petrus und Seine Zeit*, p. 225.

[110] Schmithals, *Paul and James*, pp. 53-54, thinks that St Paul went up to Jerusalem to persuade the pillar-apostles to undertake a mission to the Jews of the Diaspora parallel to his own mission to the Gentiles of the Diaspora, and that the agreement in 2:9 'laid upon the Jewish Christians of Jerusalem the obligation to carry the gospel to the Jews in those places in which Paul preached to the Gentiles.' On this view, Peter's presence at Antioch was in fulfilment of the agreement, though he should not have been eating with Gentile Christians (p. 55)—he should have been organizing a separate Jewish Christian mission. Against this: (1) the structure of vv. 9b-11 (p. 169) implies that in Paul's

## How did the agreement work out?

The unsatisfactory vagueness of the agreement quickly revealed itself when St Peter visited the mixed community at Antioch. The church of Antioch was a Jewish foundation (cf. Acts 11:19), and no doubt all its members, Gentiles as well as Jews, *wanted* to see and hear Peter as much as every church would today if he were still alive. St Peter did not consider himself bound by the Jerusalem agreement to stay away from such a church. St Paul, however, seems to have thought that Peter's presence there was from the beginning (i.e., even before he went off with the Pharisaic extremists) a breach of the agreement. This is not clearly stated but is implied in a small antithetical structure which ties the end of the second section to the beginning of the third (2:9b-11):

A    They gave to me and Barnabas the right hand of fellowship:
B    we were to go to the Gentiles, they to the Jews —
C    only, we were to remember the (Jewish) poor,
$C^1$    which very thing I took care to do.
$B^1$    But when Cephas came to Antioch,
$A^1$    I withstood him face to face.

Here St Paul contrasts his own fulfilment of the contract with St Peter's breach of it, and balances the agreement at Jerusalem against the disagreement at Antioch.

Peter, James and John may have been equally dissatisfied with the working out of the agreement. They probably understood Paul to have agreed that he would go away and preach directly to the Gentiles, without causing disturbances among the Jews. But on his second and third journeys he continued to preach in the synagogues, his preaching continued to shake and upset the Jewish communities of the Diaspora, and these disturbances reverberated in Jerusalem. When he arrived in Jerusalem after the third journey, James said to him (Acts 21:20-21):

> You see, brother, what vast numbers of believers there are among the Jews. All are zealous defenders of the law, and they have been informed that you are teaching all the Jews who live among the Gentiles to apostatize from Moses, telling them not to circumcise their children and not to follow our traditional customs.

The accusation was unjust in so far as St Paul did not tell Jewish Christians in the Diaspora to abandon the law (cf. 1 Cor 7:17), but

---

view Peter should not have visited Antioch at all; (2) Paul certainly did not want a wall of separation running through the church in every city of the Diaspora; and (3) he himself always preached 'to the Jew first, then to the Greek'—he always began in the synagogue where there was one (see above, p. 167, n. 105).

it was justified in so far as Paul's theoretical arguments went beyond his own practical position and would have justified any Jewish Christian father who decided not to circumcise his son. The authorities in Jerusalem probably thought that St Paul had adhered neither to the spirit nor to the letter of their agreement.

It was an impracticable agreement, and contained the seeds of future discord.

## *Why was the collection necessary?*

The poverty of the church of Jerusalem was well known to the Christians of Antioch, for when Agabus prophesied a famine, they at once saw the necessity of sending alms to Jerusalem (cf. Acts 11:28-29).

If poverty was more acute in the Jerusalem community than elsewhere, this may have been due in part to the general economic situation of Judaea, a country badly irrigated and heavily taxed. The problem had, however, been aggravated by the persecution which the church had endured at the hands of Paul and others, and perhaps too by the early attempts to establish a sharing of goods through the sale of capital and distribution of the proceeds (cf. Acts 4:32). This sharing of goods was not obligatory (as at Qumran,[111] or in later monastic life); nor was it at all widespread. The only Jew who is known to have sold property (apart from Ananias and Sapphira) is Barnabas (cf. Acts 4:36-37). St Paul never boasts that he has done so.[112] Probably the sharing of goods was found to be an unsatisfactory basis for the life of a non-monastic community. Paul and Barnabas did not attempt to establish this kind of sharing (*koinônia*) in the Gentile churches,[113] except in so far as they expected the rich to provide for the poor at the common meals of the churches (cf. 1 Cor 11:21).

---

[111] Cf. Schnackenburg, *The Moral Teaching*, p. 210.

[112] Probably he had no property to sell. He had simply the money he could earn by the work of his own hands, and this he did use for the support of others (cf. Acts 20:34; 1 Cor 4:12; 1 Thes 2:9), in fulfilment of his own counsel or exhortation in Eph 4:28: 'If anyone has been a thief, he must steal no longer, but work instead; with what he earns by the honest work of his hands, he will then be able to help his neighbour in need.'

[113] St Thomas, Gal, 394-5, discusses this point and offers a very curious explanation: 'The reason why the primitive custom of selling possessions was observed in the Jewish church but not in the Gentile church is that the Jewish faithful congregated in Jerusalem and in Judaea, which were destined to be destroyed by the Romans soon afterwards, as the event proved, and therefore the Lord wished that possessions should not be kept where they were not destined to

The word which St Paul uses for 'the poor' in Gal 2:10 means literally 'the beggars'. The same word is used in Christ's first beatitude: 'Blessed are the beggars, for theirs is the kingdom of heaven.' Probably some members of the church of Jerusalem took this quite literally and chose, for religious reasons, not only to be poor but also to be beggars, that is, to live by begging alms of others. [114] From Gal 2:10 it appears that James, Cephas and John fully approved of this group and were willing to solicit alms for its members. St Augustine has an interesting comment on this verse: [115]

> The apostles shared in common the care of the poor among the Christians of Judaea who had sold their goods and laid the money at the feet of the apostles (Acts 4:35). Thus Paul and Barnabas were sent to the Gentiles with the understanding that the Gentile churches which had not done this (i.e. had not sold up their property) should be moved by their exhortations to supply the needs of those who had done it. Hence St Paul says to the Romans: 'At present I am going to Jerusalem to do a service for God's people there; for Macedonia and Achaea have generously collected a fund for the poor among God's people at Jerusalem. It was generous of them, and yet it was also an obligation; for Gentile Christians who have shared in the spiritual goods of the Jews ought to render them assistance with their material goods' (Rom 15:25-27).

The interpretation placed upon Rom 15:25-27 is debatable. St Augustine seems to think it means that since Gentile Christians are receiving spiritual blessings through the merits of the voluntary poverty of the Jewish Christians, they should in return supply the material wants of these Christians. But the interesting point is that St Augustine regards the giving of alms to those who are voluntarily poor as a substitute for selling one's property and becoming a mendicant oneself. This may well have been the view of Peter, James and John. But it was probably not the view of St Paul. He would not have allowed that his Gentile Christians were following a way of life which was only a second-best by comparison with the thorough-going, hundred-percent Christianity of the Jerusalem community.

*Why was St Paul so zealous in promoting the collection?*

No doubt his first motive was simple charity. He had lived in Jerusalem and seen the poverty of the Christian community with his

---

remain. But the church of the Gentiles was to be strengthened and increased, and hence by the counsel of the Holy Spirit possessions were not sold.' This would seem to imply that the Jewish churches had an interim ethic of their own.
[114] Cf. Schnackenburg, *The Moral Teaching*, pp. 131-132.
[115] Augustine, PL 35, 2113 C.

GALATIANS 172

own eyes. Secondly, he felt partly responsible for it. Before his conversion he had persecuted the Church and 'laid it waste'. He probably felt some obligation to make amends. [116]

To judge from Rom 15:26-27, the motive which he set before the Gentiles was gratitude: having shared in the spiritual wealth of the Jews, they should make repayment from their material wealth — a surprising argument. It seems to imply that the Jews had a proprietary right over the gospel and over God's grace, and that they have shown great generosity in preaching the gospel to the Gentiles and giving them access to Christ's grace. Since the Jew who had shown this generosity was, as it happens, Paul himself, he is almost suggesting that the Gentiles can repay *his* kindness by giving alms to the poor of Jerusalem. St Paul could claim that he was not transgressing Christ's precept, 'What you have received as a gift, give as a gift' (Mt 10:8), because he was not raising the money for his own advantage, but as alms for others.

Modern writers emphasize that the collection was valuable as a means of strengthening the bond of charity between the Gentile churches and the mother church in Jerusalem. [117] But it is hard to find a text where St Paul commends the relief fund to his Gentile churches for this particular reason.

Another explanation of St Paul's great concern to make the collection a success is that once he had been asked to make it, he feared that if it proved a fiasco, it would be worse than useless. If the sum sent to Jerusalem was small, the Jews might even take offence. This will explain St Paul's otherwise puzzling request, in Rom 15:31, for prayers that his collection may prove acceptable:

> The inference appears to be that the Hebrews regarded themselves as having a quite definite claim to it, and would be offended if it were not large enough. If it were a piece of purely unsolicited generosity on the part of the Gentiles, the Hebrews could hardly be offended however small it might be, and St Paul would not be so anxious to ask the Romans to pray that it might prove acceptable. [118]

The simplest explanation of Gal 2:10 and Rom 15:31 is that St Paul agreed with Peter, James and John that the church of Jerusalem had some kind of right or claim to the alms of the Gentile churches and could reasonably take offence if the money was not forthcoming. [119]

---

[116] Thus Theodore, Gal, p. 20.
[117] Cf. e.g. Schnackenburg, *The Moral Teaching*, p. 182; Viard, Gal, p. 48.
[118] W. L. Knox, *St Paul and the Church of Jerusalem*, p. 287, n. 22.
[119] K. Holl, 'Der Kirchenbegriff des Paulus in seinem Verhältnis zu der Urgemeinde,' *Sitzungberichte der Akademie der Wissenschaften zu Berlin*, 1921,

Perhaps what lay behind this view was the belief that the Messianic age had arrived and that it was time for the fulfilment of the prophecy of Isa 60:5-6: 'The abundance of the sea shall be turned to you; the wealth of the nations shall come to you.' St Paul may even have hoped that a really large collection from the Gentile churches would help to convince the still unconverted Jews of Jerusalem that the Messianic times had indeed arrived. [120] He probably hoped to see the conversion of Israel in his own day, and may have thought that his relief fund, 'the wealth of the nations', would spark off a mass conversion movement in Jerusalem. If so, he must have been bitterly disappointed.

*What is St Paul's main purpose in reporting the Council?*

The whole of the narrative leads up to the agreement in vv. 9-10. The punch-line of the story is: 'We were to preach to the Gentiles, they to the Jews.' Immediately after v. 10 comes the Antioch incident. It seems, then, that one of St Paul's main purposes in narrating the Council was that in his view the Antioch incident should be judged in the light of the Jerusalem agreement. The contrast between v. 9, in which Peter and Paul are shaking hands in mutual congratulation and agreement, and v. 11, where they clash face to face, is deliberately planned. The narrative of the Council is to a large extent subordinated to the narrative of the dispute at Antioch. All through the autobiographical section 1:10—2:10, St Paul is setting the scene for the Dispute at Antioch. In Gal 2:15-21 he gives a summary of his gospel, which he unfolds in the remaining sections of this Epistle, and again at greater length in the Epistle to the Romans. [121] It can therefore be said that the whole of the Epistle to the Galatians is about the Antioch incident, to justify the stand which St Paul there took against Peter.

---

pp. 920-947, maintained that the church of Jerusalem claimed a legal right to the money. St Paul would not have admitted this. See below on 6:7.

[120] Cf. Munck, *Paul and the Salvation of Mankind*, ch. 10, especially p. 303.

[121] O. Modalsli, 'Gal 2:19-21; 5:16-18 und Röm 7:7-25,' TZ 21 (1965), pp. 22-23, points out the following correspondences:

| Gal 2:15 | : | Rom 1:20-2:29 |
| Gal 2:15-17a | : | Rom 3-5 |
| Gal 2:17b | : | Rom 6:1, 15 |
| Gal 2:19 | : | Rom 7:7-25 |
| Gal 2:20 | : | Rom 6-7; 8:1ff |

# THE INCIDENT AT ANTIOCH

The third section is the end and climax of the first main division of the Epistle. It is again symmetrical. The matching elements become shorter towards the centre, where St Paul proclaims emphatically and even repetitiously that justification is through faith in Christ. Here is the text, in which St Paul gives his version of the Antioch incident, to show why his own conduct was right and proper.

**A** *2 : 11* But when Cephas came to Antioch, I resisted him face to face, because he was self-condemned. *12* For before the arrival of certain persons from James, he had been taking his meals with the Gentiles; but after their arrival, he began to draw back and set himself apart, fearing those of the circumcision. *13* The other Jews played the hypocrite along with him — so much so that even Barnabas was swept along with them by their hypocrisy. **B** *14* But when I saw that they were not walking steadily according to the truth of the gospel, I said to Cephas in the presence of them all: **C** 'If you, who were born a Jew, live as a Gentile and not as a Jew, how can you compel the Gentiles to judaize? **D** *15* We by our birth are Jews and not sinners of Gentiles, **E** *16* but knowing that no man is justified **F** from works of the law, **G** but through faith in Jesus Christ, **H** we too put our faith in Jesus Christ, **G¹** in order to be justified from faith in Christ, **F¹** and not from the works of the law, **E¹** for from works of the law *no flesh will be justified*. **D¹** *17* But if through seeking to be justified in Christ we have turned out to be sinners ourselves — has Christ become a servant of Sin? Heaven forbid! **C¹** *18* For if I rebuild what I tore down, I make myself a sinner. **B¹** *19* For it was through the law that I died to the law, in order that I might live to God. I am crucified with Christ crucified. *20* It is no longer I who live, but Christ is alive within me. So far as I now live, while in the flesh, I live through faith in God and Christ who loved me and offered himself for me. *21* I do not set aside the grace of God; for if justice comes through the law, Christ died for nothing. **A¹** *3 : 1* O foolish Galatians, who has bewitched you — you before whose eyes Jesus Christ was placarded crucified? *2* I would have you tell me this one thing: Was it after doing the law that you received the Spirit, or after hearing the faith? *3* Are you really so foolish? Having begun with the Spirit, will you now end with the flesh? *4* Have your great experiences been useless, or worse than useless?

St Thomas Aquinas points out how this section advances beyond what has been said in the previous sections of the Epistle: 'Above, the Apostle showed that he gained no profit from his conference with the aforesaid apostles; here (2 : 11-21) he shows how he himself was of profit to others, and in the first place to Peter, by correcting him.' [1] By juxtaposing the two narratives, St Paul implies: 'Peter did not correct me at Jerusalem; I corrected him at Antioch.'

St Paul is not giving the Galatians the first report they have ever heard of the incident at Antioch. His manner of narrating it shows that they have already heard another version, from the Judaizers. [2] For he does not first narrate the facts and then give his judgment on them. He begins by pronouncing Peter guilty, and then justifies his verdict by a rapid narrative of what happened.

The Judaizers' report of the incident must have set Paul in a very bad light. Even his own version has failed to convince some of his readers that his conduct was right. One recent commentator is moved to exclaim: 'How could he so forget himself?' [3] His opponents probably said something like this: 'When Peter came to Antioch, at first he ate with the Gentiles, but when some disciples of James came to the city, he repented of having abandoned the law; so he withdrew from the Gentiles and lived as a Jew again. The other Jewish Christians did the same, including good men and friends of Paul like Barnabas. Eventually Paul found himself isolated, but instead of bowing to the views of the others, he made a shocking scene in which he virtually told Peter that he did not understand the gospel. He also said that once a man has abandoned the law, he commits a sin if he goes back to the law, which is strange, since he himself goes back to the law when he is in Jerusalem. Paul thought to discredit Peter by this attack, but instead he has discredited himself. It is no longer safe to follow him. You would do well to follow Peter's example and judaize.'

To counteract this propaganda, St Paul gives his version of what happened. The Galatians are hesitating as to whether they should obey Paul and remain free of the law, or follow the example of Peter and judaize. St Paul argues that the choice is not between Peter and Paul, but between Christ the Crucified (*estaurômenos*) and Peter the

---

[1]    St Thomas, Gal, 395 A. As R. Bring, Gal, p. 85, points out, this incident was of great significance to Luther: 'It strengthened his certainty that he had the right and the duty to proclaim the truth of the gospel in opposition to the contemporary leadership of the church.' It still encourages protesters—cf. L. Pyle, *Pope and Pill*, London, 1968, p. 151.

[2]    When St Paul revisited the Galatians at the beginning of his third journey, he probably refrained from telling them much about the Antioch incident. Pelagius, Gal, p. 314, draws an interesting comparison: 'The weakness of the Galatians compels him to narrate how he did not spare even Peter, the prince of the apostles, when he failed to defend the truth of the gospel—just as for the profit of the Corinthians he makes known [in 2 Cor 12:2] a vision which he had kept secret for fourteen years.'

[3]    Gaechter, *Petrus und Seine Zeit*, p. 248. Lagrange too (Gal, p. 41) thinks that St Paul should have shown more deference.

Self-condemned (*kategnôsmenos*). He repeats the arguments which he used against Peter at Antioch, and calls upon the Galatians to judge. Though he does not put it in quite these terms, he is really calling on them to judge who is right, himself or Peter. He tells them they are acting foolishly in abandoning his gospel (i.e. if they go over to Peter by following his example), and hints that just as Peter began well and ended badly, so they are in danger of doing the same. 'Foolish Galatians,' he says, 'who has bewitched you?' The structure of the section points to the answer: Peter.

The centre and substance of this section is the speech addressed by Paul to Peter and now repeated for the benefit of the Galatians. If they can be brought to feel as strongly as Paul felt how indefensible and reprehensible was Peter's conduct, they will lose all desire to obey the Judaizers.

Both at Jerusalem and at Antioch Paul's defence of his gospel against the judaizing opposition takes the form of an appeal to Peter. If the Judaizers keep pointing to Peter's example, the best answer to them is that Peter himself approves of Paul's gospel. He gave his approval formally at Jerusalem, then seemed to withdraw it by his vacillation at Antioch. The only way for Paul to undo the damage was to challenge Peter once more on the principle.

It is surprising that Paul does not say how Peter reacted to this protest. The explanation of this omission may be that by the time Paul reaches v. 21 he thinks he has made his point with such clarity that it is superfluous to say that Peter repented. But more probably, as will be argued below, 2:21 is not really the end of what Paul said to Peter; after the apostrophe to the 'foolish Galatians' in 3:1, Paul is still repeating what he said at Antioch.

2:15—3:4 contains Paul's main argument against the Judaizers. In 3:2 he asks one question which ought to settle the whole issue. Unfortunately there is reason to suspect that the words 'I would have you tell me this one thing' have been displaced. As the text stands, the crucial question is: 'When and how did you receive the Holy Spirit — after doing the law or after hearing the gospel?' But structural considerations suggest that originally the crucial question was: 'Did Christ die for nothing? (For if justification comes from the law, he did.)' [4]

The end of the second section is skilfully combined with the beginning of the third to form an overlapping pattern (1:23—2:14).

---

[4] See below, pp. 226-27.

Once this is spotted, a number of remarkable insinuations come to light. Here is the text:

> A  *1 : 23* They kept hearing: 'The man who once persecuted us is now preaching the very faith he formerly tried to destroy.' *24* And they gave glory to God because of me.  B  *2 : 1* Then, after fourteen years, I again went up to Jerusalem with Barnabas [Titus] —  C  *2* I went up in obedience to a revelation, and I laid before them the gospel I preach to the Gentiles, but privately before those held in regard: 'Was I perhaps running or had I run my course in vain?' *[3]* — *4* this on account of intruders, false brethren who had wormed their way in to spy on the liberty we have in Christ Jesus, in order to enslave us.  D  *5* But not for a moment did we yield to their demand — in order that the truth of the gospel might remain with you.  E  *6* As for those held in regard — what they really were makes no difference to me — God is no respecter of human persons — those held in regard laid down no further requirements.  F  *7* On the contrary, seeing that I had been entrusted with the gospel of the uncircumcised, as Peter has with that of the circumcised,  G  *8* for he who had made Peter's apostleship to the circumcision effective, had made mine effective among the Gentiles,  F¹  *9* and recognizing the grace that had been given to me,  E¹  James, Cephas and John, the ones regarded as pillars, gave to me and Barnabas the right hand of fellowship: we were to preach to the Gentiles, and they to the Jews.  *10* Only, we were to remember the (Jewish) poor — and this very thing I took care to do. *11* But when Cephas came to Antioch,  D¹  I resisted him face to face, because he was self-condemned.  *12* For before the arrival of certain persons from James, he had been taking his meals with the Gentiles; C¹  but after their arrival, he began to draw back and set himself apart, fearing those of the circumcision.  *13* The other Jews played the hypocrite along with him —  B¹  so much so that even Barnabas was swept away with them by their hypocrisy.  A¹  *14* But when I saw that they were not walking steadily according to the truth of the gospel, I said to Cephas in the presence of them all: 'If you, who were born a Jew, live as a Gentile and not as a Jew, how can you compel the Gentiles to judaize?'

This pattern is designed to insinuate a contrast between Paul's own behaviour and that of others in face of the judaizing trouble-makers. In A Paul tells how he preached the faith which he had formerly tried to destroy; in A¹ he accuses Peter of destroying the faith he had formerly approved. In B he describes how at first Barnabas resolutely 'went up' with him to Jerusalem to defend Gentile freedom; in B¹ he describes how even Barnabas was 'swept away'. In C he describes how he himself reacted to the propaganda of the hypocritical Judaizers: he boldly went up to Jerusalem and laid his cards on the table; in C¹ he describes how Peter allowed himself to be intimidated by the same kind of opposition, and how, instead of putting up a bold resistance, he concealed his true opinion. In D Paul describes how he resisted the Judaizers; in D¹ how he resisted Peter when he had associated himself with the Judaizers. In E he hints that perhaps the apostles were not what they seemed to be, but says: 'at all events they laid down no further requirements to be imposed on Gentile converts'; in E¹ he shows how these men who were supposed to be pillars of strength shook hands on a bargain which they did not keep. In F - G - F¹ he shows how the other apostles recognized his own authority.

## Did the Antioch incident occur before or after the Council of Jerusalem?

As the Antioch incident is narrated by St Paul after his account of the Council of Jerusalem, most commentators assume that it took place after the Council. However, the introductory phrase, 'But when Cephas came to Antioch,' does not necessarily imply temporal sequence, and some commentators, beginning with Augustine, [5] have preferred the view that the dispute took place before the Council, and precipitated it. In some ways, this is an attractive view: (1) If the Council occurred first, St Paul does not tell his readers how the dispute ended. If the dispute comes first, it ends with the handshake of reconciliation at Jerusalem. (2) If the Council occurred first, the Judaizers made trouble at Antioch twice: just before the Council, and at the time of the incident. It is more economical to suppose that St Paul has described the same disturbance twice. (This is a much weaker argument than the first.) To defend this view, it would be necessary to explain why St Paul narrated the Council before the incident, if the incident caused the Council. A possible explanation might be that he wished to place the Council in the prominent position at the centre of the overlapping pattern, 1:23—2:14, and that he wished to keep to the end of the autobiographical section the speech which he made at Antioch, so that it would serve as an introduction to the more theological section of the Epistle (3:5—4:31).

In spite of these arguments, the ordinary view remains preferable. [6] St Paul does not tell the story of the Council in order to prove that he *had been* right at Antioch; he tells it to show that Peter was in the wrong when he came to Antioch. As was observed above, there

---

5  Cf. Augustine's letter to Jerome, *Ep. Hieron.*, 116, 11; Munck, *Paul and the Salvation of Mankind*, pp. 100-103; H. M. Feret, *Pierre et Paul à Antioche et à Jérusalem*, Paris, 1955.
6  Cf. J. Dupont, 'Pierre et Paul à Antioche et à Jérusalem,' RechScRel 45 (1957), pp. 42-60; 225-239.

is a strong link between the end of the Council-narrative and the
beginning of the Antioch-narrative:

A    9b  They gave to me and to Barnabas the right hand of fellowship:
B    we were to go to the Gentiles, they to the Jews —
C    10  only, we were to remember the (Jewish) poor,
C¹   which very thing I took care to do.
B¹   11  But when Cephas came to Antioch,
A¹   I withstood him face to face.

The agreement at Jerusalem is contrasted with the conflict at Antioch,
and Paul's fulfilment of his promise to collect alms for Jerusalem is
contrasted with Cephas's interference in a Gentile church. Hence the
particle 'But' (*de*) at the beginning of v. 11 has adversative force.
St Paul considered Peter's presence at Antioch a breach of the agreement. No doubt Peter thought otherwise. As was pointed out above,
the agreement was so vague that it was bound to lead to misunder-
standings. On the other hand, if 2:11-21 is read before 2:1-10, there
is no connection between the end of the Antioch-narrative and the
beginning of the Council; on the contrary, the Antioch-incident seems
incomplete (because St Peter's reaction is not described), and the
Council is separated off by the phrase 'Then after the lapse of fourteen
years.' [7] Further, if Barnabas deserted Paul during the Antioch incident, it is surprising to find him at Paul's side in the Council-narrative.
One might suppose that he allowed himself to be won over by Paul's
words in 2:15-21, but there is no mention of this in the text.

Further, the Epistle cannot be written to deal with a situation
created by reports of the Council, which turned out in Paul's favour.
And if the Antioch incident occurred before the Council, Paul's conduct at Antioch was vindicated by the Council. Therefore if the dispute occurred before the Council, and was settled by the Council in
Paul's favour, it is hard to see how the Judaizers could have used it
to upset the Galatian churches. If it was public knowledge that Peter,
James, John and Barnabas had all acknowledged that Paul was right,
the Epistle itself would have been superfluous.

If, on the other hand, the incident occurred after the Council,
and especially if Paul and Barnabas did *not* capitulate, it is very easy
to see how the Judaizers could upset the Galatians, and why the
Epistle was necessary: its whole purpose is to deal with the situation
created by reports of Peter's conduct at Antioch and of Paul's reaction.
The whole of the autobiographical section has been leading up to this

[7]  This of course can be simply accounted for: 2:11-21 was not designed to stand
before 2:1-10.

incident: first the private admonition, then the semi-private admonition, then the formal agreement, then Peter's violation of it, and Paul's public protest.

Finally, throughout the autobiographical section, Paul has been comparing Peter unfavourably to himself. It is hard to believe that he would have done this if the last stage in his relationship with Peter had been a formal reconciliation in Jerusalem. At the time of writing, St Paul is not well-disposed to Peter. The Epistle contains several unflattering insinuations about Peter, and not one word of praise for him.

## What attitude does St Paul expect the Galatians to take towards St Peter?

He expects them to agree that at Antioch Peter was in the wrong, that he was going back on the agreement made at Jerusalem, and that he was failing to live up to his reputation of being a pillar of the Church. St Paul seems to be inculcating an attitude of disapproval. He does not say or suggest that Peter repented or apologized. Rather, he suggests that the Galatians must follow either Peter or himself. [8]

There is, therefore, something to be said for the view that St Paul was not particularly concerned about the *unity* of the Gentile churches with the Jewish churches; what he cared about was the *liberty* of the Gentile churches. He was quite content that his Gentile churches should regard Peter as being the apostle of the Jews, as having nothing to do with them, and perhaps as not being a very admirable character anyway.

St Paul himself probably felt that he had been badly let down by St Peter and that it would be better for all if he would confine his ministry to the Jews.

These are unpleasant conclusions. It is not surprising that the Greek Fathers almost fell over backward in their efforts to avoid them.

## The Disputes of the Fathers about the Dispute at Antioch.

The philosopher Porphyry used the Antioch incident to impugn the characters of Peter and Paul, and thus to discredit Christianity. St Jerome gives this account of Porphyry's argument: [9]

[8] See above, pp. 175-76.
[9] Jerome, *Ep.* 112, 6.

He accuses Paul of insubordination, in that he dared to rebuke Peter, the prince of the apostles, and argued with him publicly, and tried to prove that he had done wrong— that is, that he was guilty of a misdeed, the same misdeed of which he (Paul) himself was equally guilty.

In other words, Peter was in the wrong, but Paul was doubly in the wrong, for he was impudently condemning Peter for doing what he had done himself.

In reply to Porphyry, Origen proposed the theory that Peter *pretended* to judaize in order to give Paul an opportunity to *pretend* to correct him. (The text of Origen, however, is not extant; we learn of this from Jerome.) There is one phrase in the text which might be used to give colour to Origen's hypothesis, namely, 'I withstood him *kata prosôpon*', which is usually translated 'I withstood him to his face,' but could also mean 'I withstood him to outward appearances', i.e., 'I acted the part of withstanding him.' It is not clear, however, what purpose Origen saw in this play-acting: was it to convert the Jewish Christians, or to confirm both sides in their previous opinions? Origen's hypothesis was used by John Chrysostom:[10]

> It was a pretence (*schêma*). For if it had been a real battle, they would not have rebuked each other in the presence of their disciples; for this would have scandalized them greatly. But as things were, the public contest was profitable.

It is also adopted by Jerome:[11]

> He publicly resisted Peter and the others, in order that their pretence of observing the law, which was doing harm to the Gentile believers, might be corrected by a pretended rebuke, and thus each people would be saved — the admirers of circumcision following Peter, and those who refused circumcision admiring the liberty of Paul.

According to Jerome's view, the purpose of the feigned dispute was not to win over the Jews to a policy of integration, but to confirm both sides in their own views. That is to say, Peter and Paul expected that the Jews would take Peter's side and condemn Paul, while the Gentiles would take Paul's side and condemn Peter.

But later St Jerome seems to adopt the view that Peter and Paul conspired for the correction of the Jewish believers. The text is uncertain here:[12]

> Just as those who have sound feet yet pretend to be limping have nothing wrong with their feet, but have some cause for limping, so Peter, though

---

[10]  Chrysostom, PG 61, 641 C.
[11]  Jerome, PL 26, 364 B. For further quotations see Lightfoot, Gal, pp. 128-32.
[12]  Jerome, PL 26, 367 A.

he knew that neither circumcision nor its absence is anything but only observance of God's commandments, ate at first with the Gentiles, but for a time withdrew from them, lest he should lose the Jews from their faith in Christ. Hence Paul, putting on the same artful pretence, resisted him face to face, and spoke to him in the presence of all, not so much in order to prove Peter wrong, but rather to correct those for whose sake Peter had assumed his pretence — or, to remove the arrogance of the Jews and the despair of the Gentiles.

St Augustine strongly disapproved of Jerome's explanation and wrote to protest: [13]

It is a much more admirable and praiseworthy thing to accept correction willingly than to correct another's error boldly. To my poor judgment, therefore, it seems that it would have been better to reply to Porphyry by defending Paul's freedom of speech and Peter's humility.

Augustine's view eventually prevailed.

*The First Subsection, 2:11-14*

## PETER WITHDRAWS

The third section divides into four subsections, each with a symmetrical structure. The first of the four is slightly irregular, in that it is 'double-centred', having the pattern A-B-C, D-E-F-E¹-D¹, G-H-H¹-G¹, C¹-B¹-A¹. St Paul may have inserted G-H-H¹-G¹ (i.e. v. 13, about Barnabas) after completing the rest of the structure. Without v. 13, the whole subsection would be concerned with the conduct of Peter.

A  *2 : 11* But when Cephas came to Antioch,  B  I resisted him face to face,  C  because he was self-condemned.  D  *12* For before certain people came from James,  E  he was eating with the Gentiles.  F  But when they came,  E¹  he drew back and kept himself apart,  D¹  fearing those of the circumcision,  G  *13* and his hypocrisy was shared  H  by other Jews, H¹  so that even Barnabas  G¹  was swept away by their hypocrisy.  C¹  *14* But when I saw that they were not walking steadily according to the truth of the gospel,  B¹  I said to Peter in the presence of them all:  A¹  'If you who were born a Jew live as a Gentile and not as a Jew, how can you compel the Gentiles to judaize?'

The link between A and A¹ shows that for Paul 'When Cephas came to Antioch' meant 'When the apostle of the Jews came to visit the mother church of the Gentiles.'

---

[13]  Augustine, *Ep. Hieron.*, 116, 22.

'I *resisted* him face to face' is explained by the end of the passage:
Peter was compelling the Gentiles to judaize — he was bringing moral
pressure to bear, by the force of his example. That is why Paul can
describe his protest as 'resistance'. In v. 12, the rather puzzling imperfect tenses used in the Greek (namely, 'he was drawing back' and
'was separating himself') may have been chosen to balance the imperfect 'he was eating'. The link between the beginning and the end
of this verse shows that 'the circumcision party' and the 'certain
persons from James' are to be identified with each other.

*What was the nature of the meals mentioned in v. 12?*

The words used in v. 12 (literally, 'he was eating with the Gentiles')
could mean that Peter was accepting invitations to dine at various
Gentile-Christian houses, somewhat as Christ accepted invitations from
Pharisees and others. If so, the meals were private and presumably
non-liturgical. On this view, 'he began to draw back and set himself
apart' could mean that he accepted such invitations more and more
rarely and fulfilled his engagements unobtrusively.

Alternatively, the meals may be public ones, at which the whole
church gathered, and during which the Eucharist was celebrated.
Such meals were being held at Corinth about three years later (cf.
1 Cor 11:17-21). On this view, 'he began to draw back and set himself apart' has to mean that as soon as 'the people arrived from James',
Peter began *at once* to absent himself from the common meals and
that he continued to do so. It would have been useless for him to
absent himself gradually, for the people from James would have been
scandalized if he was present even once.

The second of these alternatives is the more probable — in view
of v. 13, which says that the other Jews followed Peter's example,
and in view of v. 14, which condemns Peter's withdrawal as a departure from the truth of the gospel. St Paul could hardly have taken
so serious a view of the matter, if Peter was merely declining invitations to private houses.

It seems, then, that St Paul is speaking of common meals to which
Jews and Gentiles took food which they shared with one another and
with their poorer brethren (cf. 1 Cor 11:21), and at which they ate
the bread and drank the chalice of the Lord. Here could be seen in
practice the 'mystery' of the gospel — the wall of division torn down,
Jew and Gentile, slave and free, male and female, sharing the Lord's
table. After centuries of segregation, it was an amazing achievement.

St Peter's conduct threatened to destroy it. The people who came from James did not join in the common meals, and Peter, instead of telling them that it was their duty to do so, went off and joined them at separate meals of their own, and the other Jews followed his example. Thus Peter was reintroducing segregation into an integrated church. If one looks at the matter in this way, it is not difficult to share in Paul's indignation. It is far easier to create divisions than to heal them. However, as will be pointed out below, the conduct of the men from James is understandable, and, in those early days, still pardonable.

### What was the attitude of James, and of 'the people from James'?

James the brother of the Lord, known as 'the Just' on account of his exact observance of the law, probably believed that fulfilment of the law was obligatory for Christian Jews. [14] He held that Gentile Christians need not observe the whole of the law, but he would presumably not have condemned them if they freely chose to become proselytes to Judaism. Probably he held that Jewish Christians were free to associate with Gentile Christians who observed the prohibitions of the Council of Jerusalem, but not that they were obliged to do so.

The 'persons who came from James' or 'people of James's party who came' (it makes no difference) evidently did not consider themselves obliged to associate with the Gentile Christians and would not have approved of Peter's doing so.

St Paul does not say that these disciples were sent by James or that James knew of their visit to Antioch. They may have been unauthorized busybodies like those whose earlier interference at Antioch had occasioned the Council (cf. Acts 15:24). Or perhaps they were in Antioch for business, and caused the trouble without saying anything, simply by what they did.

The separatism of these visitors from Jerusalem should not be judged too harshly. They could appeal to the obvious lesson of the first chapter of the Book of Daniel. In exile among the Gentiles, Daniel is willing to serve the king of Babylon and to learn his language, but he will not eat food from the royal table (which has probably been offered to idols); God shows his approval by protecting Daniel and blessing him. The author of this story was probably one of the Hasidim, and his purpose was to encourage Jews to remain loyal to the food laws during the struggle with Antiochus Epiphanes (cf.

---

[14]  Cf. Lagrange, RB 14 (1917), pp. 159, 163.

1 Mac 1 : 62-63). [15] The Pharisaic descendants of the *Hasidim* had learned the lesson so well that when converted to Christianity they could hardly be expected to unlearn it overnight.

## *What was St Peter afraid of?*

According to St John Chrysostom, Peter was not afraid of any personal danger; rather, 'he feared those of the circumcision, lest they should apostatize.' [16] He was afraid that if these strict, law-observing Jews from Jerusalem saw the chief of the apostles abandoning the law, they might decide to dissociate themselves from the Church. They had become disciples of Christ in the belief that he taught a more perfect observance of the law than the scribes and Pharisees. If in fact the real purpose of the Christian movement was to shrug off the law, they would have nothing to do with it. The formulation of Mt 5 : 17 looks as though it was designed to reassure such people: 'Do not imagine that I have come to abolish the law or the prophets; I have come not to abolish, but to fulfil.' St Peter may, therefore, have been afraid of scandalizing the disciples of James so that they and all their friends in Jerusalem would abandon the Christian faith.

In these circumstances, St Peter may have remembered the incident of the coin in the fish's mouth, when he was told to pay the temple tax to avoid giving scandal. Christ had explained to him that the disciples, being God's sons, are free of the taxes laid upon his Jewish servants or slaves, but that to avoid giving scandal they should pay the temple tax (cf. Mt 17 : 24-27). St Peter may have reasoned that the principle was applicable at Antioch. [17] To avoid scandalizing the disciples of James, he had better return to the Jewish way of life.

The above seems a likely explanation of St Peter's conduct, but it is not what St Paul means when he says that Peter withdrew 'through fear of the circumcision-party'. For Paul is not defending or excusing Peter's conduct; on the contrary, he is showing why he considers it indefensible.

At the Council of Jerusalem, Peter had recognized that God had 'made no distinction between us and them (Jews and Gentiles) but had cleansed their hearts by faith' (Acts 15 : 9); and on his first arrival at Antioch he had acted on this conviction by eating with the Gentiles.

---

[15]  Cf. N. Porteous, *Daniel*, London, 1965, pp. 24-29 and 137.
[16]  Chrysostom, Gal, 641 C; cf. Jerome, *Ep.* 112, 8; St Thomas, Gal, 395 D. For the construction see Gal 4 : 11.
[17]  However, Christ meant 'to avoid scandalizing the *unconverted* Jews' who are not yet sons.

GALATIANS

186

Therefore, when the disciples of James arrived, in St Paul's opinion he ought to have insisted that they too must recognize the Gentiles as clean and give proof of this by coming and eating with them. No doubt he would have liked to do this, but he foresaw stiff resistance, shirked the conflict, and withdrew from association with the Gentiles. His fears were, therefore, partly for himself. He feared that the Judaizers might answer back with theological arguments which he could not refute [18] — in which case he would be made to look foolish before the church of Antioch. Once again, as in the courtyard of the High Priest, he had ventured into a situation which required greater resources of courage and argument than he possessed. When St Paul read the riot act, Peter must have known in his heart that this was what *he* ought to have done.

### What can be said for Barnabas?

Barnabas was not the man to follow Peter's example if he thought his conduct was dictated by moral weakness (cf. Acts 9: 27). [19] Perhaps he simply took the view that it was not for him to judge or condemn the conduct of Peter, and therefore he should follow Peter's example. St Paul does not go so far as to accuse him of hypocrisy. He merely says that he was carried away by the hypocrisy of the others. He can hardly be blamed for following the example of Peter, even if he did not see how it could be justified. He may have found it equally difficult to follow the arguments of Paul on the other side.

### Was St Paul inconsistent in condemning Peter's conduct?

As was mentioned above (p. 180), the philosopher Porphyry accused St Paul of condemning Peter for doing much the same as he himself had done in similar circumstances. St Jerome conceded that the accusation would be justified if St Paul rebuked Peter in all seriousness. [20]

---

[18] W. Foerster, 'Die *dokountes* in Gal 2,' ZNTW 36 (1937), pp. 286-292, and 'Abfassungszeit und Ziel des Galaterbriefes,' in *Apophoreta* (Festschrift für E. Haenchen), Berlin, 1964, p. 140, holds that the Judaizers regarded Peter and James as uneducated men who were unaware of the theological implications of their practical policy.

[19] Gaechter, *Petrus und Seine Zeit*, p. 234, passes a severe judgment on Gal 2:13: 'Here speaks the incensed prosecutor, who does not weigh his words.'

[20] Cf. Jerome, *Ep.* 112, 11. Doubts about Paul's consistency are also expressed by Gaechter, *Petrus und Seine Zeit*, pp. 246-247, Héring, *First Corinthians*, p. 74, and McKenzie, *The Power and the Wisdom*, p. 206.

According to Acts 16:3, St Paul circumcised Timothy 'because there were Jews in those parts and they all knew that his father was a Greek.' In Acts 21:26, at the suggestion of James the brother of the Lord, he gave a demonstration of loyalty to the law by paying the expenses of four men who were under a vow. In 1 Cor 9:20-21 he says: 'With the Jews I have lived as a Jew, to convert Jews; as they lived under the law, I have lived as one under the law, though I am not under the law, to convert some men under the law.' If St Paul could make concessions of this sort, to avoid offending the Jews, why should not Peter do the same?

It might be said in St Paul's defence that he made his concessions in order to convert Jews to the faith, whereas Peter was making concessions to Jews who had already been converted and should not have needed such concessions. But this difference will not suffice. St Paul himself was willing to make concessions to believing brethren who felt scruples about taking full advantage of the liberty which he preached. In 1 Cor 8:13 he says: 'I will give up eating meat altogether, rather than scandalize my brother by what I eat.'

The real issue was whether *in this particular case* St Peter was making a concession which he ought not to have made. St Paul held that (1) in an all-Jewish Christian community the law should still be observed; (2) that in an all-Gentile community the law should not be observed; and (3) that in a mixed community the Jews must abandon their scruples and live as Gentiles. This last was the disputed point. The disciples of James probably said: 'On the contrary, we take precedence in the Church, and we are not at liberty to abandon the law; if the Gentiles will not judaize, we must form a separate community, and we will coexist as two Christian churches.'

St Peter may have taken the view that he should not try to compel the Jews at Antioch to hellenize. He probably saw that it would be a useless effort, and the result might be to drive them out of the Church altogether. In these circumstances, he may have decided that the only practical policy was to have two distinct communities at Antioch, the Gentiles led by Paul and the Jews led by himself. He may have said to Barnabas: 'I do not mean to condemn the Gentile Christians as unclean; I am simply accepting the fact that we have here two social and racial groups with distinct cultural traditions, and they are not yet ready to fuse and integrate.'

St Paul would not accept this policy of coexistence, for two reasons. The first appears in 2:14: 'How can you compel the Gentiles to judaize?' The implication is that the policy of coexistence would not work. If there were to be two Christian communities in the city, one led by himself and the other by Peter, his Gentile converts would be prepared to judaize in order to belong to Peter's group. This means that they held Peter in much higher regard than Paul, and were much surer of Peter's apostolic authority than of Paul's. It seems, then, that there was some element of personal rivalry in this dispute. Already at Antioch, it seems, some were saying 'I am for Paul' and more were saying 'I am for Cephas' (cf. 1 Cor 1:12).

Secondly, St Paul refused to accept the policy of coexistence for a theological reason. The separatism of the disciples of James amounted to a practical denial that the Gentile Christians had been cleansed by the Holy Spirit. They were acting *as if* the Gentile Christians were still sinners, and *as if* they themselves would sin by associating with them. In St Paul's view, this was a serious breach of charity, which Peter should have forbidden at any cost. If Christ was living in these Gentile converts, the disciples of James in rejecting them were rejecting Christ — just as Paul by persecuting Christians had persecuted Christ. In other words, St Paul was not averse to making concessions for the preservation of peace and unity within the Church, but he could not countenance the concession which Peter was making since it contradicted the essence of the gospel as he understood it.

### What charge does St Paul make against Peter in 2:14a?

In the structure of this subsection (p. 182), the allegation in v. 11 that Peter 'was self-condemned' is balanced by v. 14a, which specifies the charge a little more closely: 'I saw that they were not walking steadily along the path of the true gospel.' The rare word which St Paul uses here was used of the unsteady gait of little children. If this association was intended to be felt in the present context, St Paul must mean that Peter and Barnabas were still babes in the faith, [21] and had a long way to go before reaching Christian maturity. This will be the first occurrence of the theme of 'growth to maturity' which becomes dominant in chapter 4.

However, as it seems hard to believe that Paul would use such disrespectful language of Peter and Barnabas, it is better to suppose that the metaphor is borrowed from 1 Kgs 18:21 where Elijah protests to the false prophets who would like to combine the worship of Yahweh with the worship of Baal: 'How long will you go limping with

---

[21] Cf. G. D. Kilpatrick, 'Gal 2:14—*orthopodousin*,' *Neutestamentliche Studien für R. Bultmann*, Berlin, 1957, pp. 269-274.

two different opinions? If the Lord is God, follow him; but if Baal, follow him.' Similarly, in St Paul's view, Peter and Barnabas are limping from side to side, vacillating between Christianity and Judaism; they would like to combine Judaism with Christianity, but this is not possible. [22]

The 'truth of the gospel', which ought to dictate the line of their conduct, is the same as in 2:5, namely, the central mystery that justification is offered to Jew and Gentile alike on the same terms: faith in Christ's cross. To behave as if justification depended on observance of the law of Moses is to teach by example that Christ died for nothing. [23] In the third section (p. 174), v. 14a is balanced by v. 21.

*How could St Paul be so certain that Peter was wrong?*

Most probably St Paul judged the Antioch incident in the light of the Damascus vision, which was always present to his mind. He had then learned that Christ accepts and identifies himself with those who believe in him: 'Saul, Saul, why are you persecuting *me*?' Christ lives in them and suffers in them. St Peter was now refusing to eat with men whom Christ had united so intimately with himself. How could it be a sin for a Jew to associate with Gentiles whom Christ had accepted (cf. Rom 14:3)? The conduct of the disciples of James, and now of Peter and Barnabas, did not square with the basic truth of the gospel that Christ and his disciples are one, that he lives in them (v. 20), and that Gentiles are really cleansed by baptism. The 'weak conscience' which Peter was respecting was in fact the fruit of failure to understand the substance of the gospel (cf. 1:7). A man's status before God no longer depends upon observance or non-observance of the law, and Peter should not act as if it did. If Peter will not instruct the disciples of James in this essential 'truth of the gospel', Paul must do it for him. He does so in 2:14-18.

*On what occasion did St Paul admonish Peter?*

2:14 is usually translated 'I said to Peter in the presence of all' — which sounds as though St Paul made this speech before a general

---

[22] Gal 1:14 shows that St Paul considers himself to be no longer 'in Judaism'.
[23] According to Schmithals, *Paul and James*, p. 76, St Paul 'equates the motive for Peter's decision with what he fears will be the *result* of this decision in the eyes of his churches, namely doubts about justification by faith.' But St Paul does not mean that Peter has begun to doubt the truth of the gospel—only that his conduct does not square with his belief.

meeting of the whole church of Antioch, Jews and Gentiles together. But the Greek could also mean: 'I said to Peter in the hearing of *them all*,' that is, in the hearing of all the Jewish Christians — the disciples of James, Barnabas, and the other Jews who had followed Peter and separated themselves off from the Gentile Christians. This second interpretation is preferable, because it seems unlikely that there were any joint meetings of the Jewish and Gentile sections of the church of Antioch at this time; and it was certainly St Paul's intention to let the adherents of James hear what he had to say. Probably, then, this speech was made at a purely Jewish-Christian gathering, for example, at one of their private meals. If so the 'we' in vv. 15-17 refers not to Peter and Paul only, but to all who are present.

We can picture the occasion in this way. The Jewish members of the church of Antioch are sitting down with the visitors from Jerusalem to a meal of kosher meat, with Peter at their head, and Barnabas at his right, when in comes Paul with thunder on his brow.

## Why did not Paul admonish Peter privately?

Paul may have decided that since he had already spoken to Peter privately (1:18-19) and semi-publicly (2:2) about the treatment of Gentiles, it was now legitimate to admonish him publicly. The semi-public admonition at Jerusalem had failed to settle the matter.

Further, St Paul may have wished to go and admonish the followers of James, to teach them 'the truth of the gospel', and may have felt that in view of the agreement made at Jerusalem, it was not proper for him to do so. If, however, he spoke to Peter publicly, with the followers of James present and listening, they would 'overhear', and might learn a lesson, without feeling that they themselves were the object of direct attack. The discourse in vv. 14-21, though addressed to Peter, is meant quite as much for the instruction of the adherents of James.

The view of the later Antiochene exegetes, that there was some collusion between Peter and Paul, is not entirely beside the point. [24] St Paul was glad to have this opportunity to correct the disciples of James, and Peter cannot have been entirely displeased that they should have this lesson. If each recognized the other's secret wish, there was a kind of tacit collusion in this scene. St Jerome says: [25]

[24] Chrysostom's view, see above, p. 181, was shared by Theodore of Mopsuestia, Gal, p. 22, and Theodoretus (*Bibliotheca Patrum*, Oxford, pp. 337-340).
[25] Jerome, PL 26, 364 D.

Paul had certainly read in the gospel the Lord's precept: 'If your brother
sins against you, go and correct him between yourself and him alone; if
he hears you you will have gained your brother' (Lk 17:3). How then,
when the Lord ordered this to be done even for the least of the brethren,
did Paul dare to correct the greatest of the apostles so boldly and so in-
solently — unless Peter too was glad to be corrected in this way?

The circumstances of the time had forced Peter and Paul to play the
roles of patrons of two conflicting parties, though between themselves
there was no real conflict at all. There is, therefore, some justification
for St Jerome's comparison of the two apostles to two Roman orators
clashing in the courts on behalf of their clients, although there is
really no personal animosity between them.

So the theory of collusion is not just an exegetical subterfuge to
save St Paul's face. Only, one must not go so far as to suppose that
before Peter withdrew from the mixed gatherings, he and Paul agreed
to adopt this stratagem. [26]

*What is the purpose of v. 14? — Is Paul unmasking Peter's 'hypocrisy'?*

St Paul begins as if he were unmasking Peter's hypocrisy: 'If you,
though born a Jew, live in the Gentile fashion and not as a Jew, how
can you compel the Gentiles to judaize?' If the visitors from Jerusalem were unaware that Peter had been associating with Gentiles,
St Paul's words would cause embarrassment to Peter and consterna-
tion among the visitors from Jerusalem. But such cannot have been
the situation. Even if Peter broke off his association with the Gentiles
as soon as the visitors from Jerusalem arrived, Barnabas and the
others did not. They succumbed gradually, and no doubt after much
discussion. So St Paul is not really unmasking Peter's hypocrisy. He
is drawing attention to what is known already.

His charge is that Peter had been inconsistent. He is condemned
by his own past action: if he has been living as a Gentile, how can
he now consistently force the Gentiles to live as Jews? His former
conduct showed that to live as a Gentile is not sinful; but if it is not
sinful, how can he now force the Gentiles to give it up? In v. 18
St Paul returns to this charge of inconsistency: Peter is rebuilding

---

[26] There is a curious parallel in the gospels. In Mt 11:2-6, when John the Baptist
hears about the things which Christ is doing (cf. Mt 9:10-15), he sends his
disciples with a question, and Jesus sends a reply to John, not for the enlightenment of John (cf. Jn 3:22-36), but for the instruction of John's disciples, who
are too attached to their ascetical practices of fasting, avoidance of table-
fellowship with sinners, etc. See also above, p. 133.

the wall of separation which he had previously torn down. If it was right to tear it down, how can it now be right to build it up again?

V. 14 contains a remarkable tribute to St Peter's authority. Without saying a word, simply by what he is doing, he is 'compelling the Gentiles to judaize'. The Gentiles are so anxious to remain in visible union with Peter, to remain in table-fellowship with him, breaking bread with him, sharing the Eucharist with him, that they will even submit to circumcision, if this is necessary. They are not content to let the Church split into a Petrine group of Jewish Christians and a Pauline group of Gentile Christians and to remain with Paul. St Paul himself might have been satisfied with a policy of *apartheid* (2:9 suggests as much), but his Gentile converts were not; they were prepared to desert Paul in order to remain with Peter. They were not prepared to be looked down on by these self-satisfied Jewish Christians as a kind of third order, loosely attached to the Church.

The visitors from Jerusalem were probably less concerned about the visible unity of the Church. They may have reasoned that just as there were at Jerusalem different synagogues for Jews of different language-groups, so there could be different churches at Antioch, each with its own rite, and each with its own vernacular liturgy. But in practice this would not work. The Gentiles would not accept the inferior status assigned to them.

One would like to credit these Gentile converts with a disinterested zeal for the visible unity of the Church. But if St Peter had not been there, it seems very doubtful whether Barnabas and the other Jews would have gone off to join the visitors from Jerusalem. It was Peter's conduct which caused the trouble. In St Paul's view, *he* was not sufficiently careful about preserving the visible unity of the Church. But St Paul's own main concern was much less to preserve the visible unity of the Church than to preserve the freedom of his Gentile churches. [27]

*Why was St Paul so determined to safeguard the freedom of the Gentiles?*

St Paul had several reasons for insisting that Gentile Christians must not be made to judaize, and he himself might have found it hard to say which weighed most with him.

---

[27] Similarly in the U.S.A. at the present time coloured people are not particularly concerned about integration for its own sake. What they want is freedom to live where they choose, to send their children to the schools of their choice, etc.

First, there were practical reasons. Circumcision was repulsive to Gentiles and excited ridicule. In the life of a Greek city, circumcision could only with difficulty be concealed, since men stripped naked at the baths and sports arenas. Insistence on circumcision might have proved an obstacle to many Greeks, especially to the more philosophically minded, who would ask why salvation should depend on a physical operation of that sort.

Secondly, St Paul probably felt that if he had to preach justification through faith, baptism and *circumcision*, in the eyes of most men he would be preaching Judaism. The true nature of his message would have been obscured. He was firmly convinced that the gospel was something completely new — the resurrection had ushered in a new aeon. He was not going about making proselytes to Judaism but winning disciples for Christ who had passed through death into a realm of existence where the law of Moses is not binding. To have preached the gospel and Judaism together would have obscured the message.

Thirdly, St Paul was convinced that Christ did not want these Gentile converts to be turned into Jews. He had learned this in his conversion experience: God cleanses men, even Jews, even Pharisees, of their sins by faith and baptism. If the Gentiles have these things, they have no need of the law.

Fourthly, St Paul may have learned, either from his own conversion experience, or from hearing of Christ's denunciations of the Pharisees, that the law tends to produce the wrong type of character. It tends to produce externalism, formalism, pride and hypocrisy. St Paul never makes this fourth point very clearly. But he does suggest that the law belongs to spiritual childhood, and that the spiritual adult, in other words the Christian, does not need all these observances. It so happens that St Paul's surviving Epistles contain a large measure of religious controversy. But it may be doubted whether that is what he was really interested in. He wanted to build up communities of spiritual adults — men and women of a certain type or character — and he did *not* think that circumcision and the law of Moses would help them to become what they ought to become. Like Christ before him, he wished to eradicate the idea that religion consists in a code of laws enforced by supernatural sanctions. It consists essentially in love, which fulfils the law willingly and goes much beyond the requirements of law.

*The Second and Third Subsections, 2:15-17 and 2:17-21*

# PAUL PROTESTS

The second and third subsections overlap. In other words, the
end of the second symmetrical pattern is used as the starting-point
for the third. [28]

**A**  *2 : 15* We by our birth are Jews and not sinners of Gentiles;  **B**  *16* but
knowing that no man is justified  **C**  from works of the law,  **D**  but
through faith in Jesus Christ,  **E**  we too put our faith in Jesus Christ,
**D¹**  in order to be justified from faith in Christ,  **C¹**  and not from
works of the law,  **B¹**  for from works of the law *no flesh will be justified*.
**A¹**  *17* But if through seeking to be justified in Christ we have turned
out to be sinners ourselves — has Christ become a servant of Sin?

**A**  *17* But if through seeking to be justified in Christ we have turned
out to be sinners ourselves — has Christ become a servant of Sin? Heaven
forbid!  **B**  *18* For if I rebuild what I tore down, I make myself a
sinner.  **C**  *19* For through the law I died to the law in order to live
to God. I am crucified with Christ crucified.  **D**  *20* It is no longer I
who live,  **E**  but Christ lives in me.  **D¹**  So far as I now live while
in the flesh,  **C¹**  I live through faith in God and Christ who loved me
and delivered himself for me.  **B¹**  *21* I do not annul the grace of God.
**A¹**  For if justice comes from the law — did Christ die for nothing?

Vv. 15-21 are not a refutation of the assertion that the Gentiles
ought to judaize, nor are they primarily a demonstration that a Jew
commits no sin when he associates with uncircumcised Gentile Christians. They are a lesson for Jewish Christians, to teach them that
although they are still observing the law, they must not put their faith
in the law. Though living 'as if under the law,' they are not really
under the law (cf. 1 Cor 9:21). Their standing before God — whether
they live in his grace or whether they are sinners — does not depend
on the law any longer. The law may pronounce them sinners for acts
of dishonesty or hatred or unchastity which they have committed; but
if these sins have been washed away by Christian baptism, the law's
condemnation is of no further effect.

As was pointed out above, one reason why St Paul did not want
his Gentile converts to submit to the law was that he saw that ob-

---

[28]  This technique of overlapping is used three times by St Paul in the Christological hymn of Phil 2:5-11. See my analysis in *Biblica* 49 (1968), pp. 127-129.

servance of the law would confuse the issue for them: they would slip unconsciously into the belief that their justification depended on the law. He must also have seen that the law was a constant danger to the faith of Jewish Christians. He did not go so far as to tell them to abandon it. In view of the closeness of the End, he recommended them to continue to observe it (cf. 1 Cor 7:17-18). But at the same time he wanted them to remain spiritually detached from it. They must live as if under the law, though in fact they are not under the law — a difficult posture to maintain. If St Paul pursued his own thoughts to their logical conclusion, he must have concluded that Gentile Christians were much the better off: the unfortunate Jews had to go on practising the rituals of spiritual childhood, though they were in fact no longer children.

The substance of St Paul's speech is, then, a reminder to the Jewish Christians from Jerusalem that they themselves are not justified by the law, however perfectly they may observe it. They have been justified by interiorly renouncing the law and seeking justification from Christ; if they now slip back into their old ways and put their faith in the law again, they are renouncing Christ and making sinners of themselves in the process, for the law itself pointed to Christ.

St Paul goes right to the root of the matter here. He sees that the source of the trouble at Antioch is that the Jewish Christians have a wrong attitude to law — they are still wedded to it as before their conversion. He does not deal with the external symptom, which is their refusal to eat with Gentile Christians. He goes right to the heart of the matter, and tells these Jews that they have not understood the gospel.

*Is St Paul speaking ironically in v. 15?*

If the speech is made in the presence of all members of the church of Antioch, Gentiles as well as Jews, the 'we' in v. 15 will mean 'you, Peter, and I, Paul': 'We by our birth are Jews and not sinners of Gentiles' — which is either ironical or extremely tactless.

But St Paul is not being ironical. In his view, all Jews are born of a holy stock and ought to be holy (cf. Rom 11:16). [29] He can

---

[29] In his review of G in G, Dr Markus Barth (CBQ 30, 1968, p. 77) draws my attention to Luther's suggestion that 2:15 be interpreted, 'We are sinners of Jewish origin, not of Gentile extraction.' But the sentence describes what the

be more easily cleared of the charge of tactlessness, if, as was suggested above, he is speaking at a meeting of Jewish Christians. Then he says, without any trace of irony: 'We, all of us here present, are by our birth Jews and not sinful Gentiles.' He continues: 'But once we had come to know that no man is justified by his observance of the law, we too put our faith in Christ.' The implication is: 'If we are justified now, so too are these sinners of Gentile origin, who share the same faith and baptism as ourselves.'

The argument in vv. 15-17, though ostensibly addressed to Peter, is really meant for the visitors from Jerusalem. In keeping aloof from the Gentile Christians, they are acting as if (a) the Gentile Christians were still 'sinners of Gentiles' — as if they were still unclean, in spite of their baptism, and (b) as if they themselves had not been sinners before their baptism. Their conduct implies a failure to appreciate the efficacy of faith and baptism both in their own lives and in the lives of the Gentiles.

## What, in St Paul's view, is the spiritual status of Gentiles?

Gal 2:15 shows that St Paul regards all unconverted Gentiles as 'sinners'. They deserve this appellation on three scores. (1) As a result of Adam's sin they are all born sinners (cf. Rom 5:19). (2) They habitually follow the example of Adam by doing the works of the flesh (cf. Rom 1-2). (3) They live outside the law of Moses. It is even possible that St Paul regarded all Gentiles as being subject to the curse of the law (cf. 3:10, 13). If so, he must have accepted the midrashic view that the law was offered to all the seventy nations, Israel alone accepted it, and the rest were accursed for rejecting it. However, it will be maintained below that 3:13 was originally addressed to the *Jewish* Christians at Antioch. St Paul appears to have incorporated it into the Epistle without considering whether it was really applicable to Gentile Christians. [30]

persons in question are *physei* (by birth)—they are (1) Jews, and (2) not 'sinners of Gentile origin'. Luther's sense would require *hêmeis ex Ioudaiôn kai ouk ex ethnôn hamartôloi*. The sense is: 'By our birth we are . . . not sinners like the Gentiles (who are born outside the law); have we *become* sinners (by placing ourselves outside the law) through our faith in Christ? Surely not!' K. Kertelge, 'Zur Deutung des Rechtfertigungsbegriffs im Galaterbrief,' BZ 12 (1968), pp. 211-222, observes that v. 15 is a pleonastic expression of the pre-christian Jewish self-understanding which is acknowledged and transcended in the Christian revelation; Paul's aim in vv. 15-16 is 'die Entkräftigung des jüdischen Selbstbewusstseins.' Cf. Mt 3:9.

30  See below, pp. 264-273.

*Did Peter and Paul understand that justification is by faith, before they believed?*

It was argued above that 'we' of vv. 15-16 includes many others besides Peter and Paul. But it certainly does not exclude these two. And yet it is far from obvious how St Paul can say that he and Peter recognised that justification is by faith and then believed, and indeed that they chose to believe *because* they had become convinced that justification is by faith and not by obedience to the law. How, then, is v. 16 to be squared with the biographical information we have about Peter and Paul?

When Peter first responded to Christ's call, he did not know anything about 'justification by faith in Christ'. At least, he did not think of it in those terms. However, if he, like James and John, had heard the Baptist's announcement of one who would baptize with the Spirit, he will have responded to Christ's call in order to experience the promised purification by the Spirit. To desire baptism with the Spirit was to admit, by implication, that the law had proved ineffectual. [31]

Perhaps too, St Paul may have known of the occasion when St Peter said: 'Lord, to whom shall we go? You have the words of eternal life' (Jn 6:68). In the fourth gospel, 'eternal life' is something which is already possessed by the believer in an anticipatory manner even in this world. St Peter had realized that Christ's 'words' could give what no one else's words could give — eternal life both here and hereafter. In the Old Testament, the ten commandments are called the ten 'words'. So St Peter's reply meant that he recognised Christ's words as preferable to the words of Moses. That is why he chose to cleave to Christ, even when the multitudes were drifting away. Therefore it could be said of him that he chose to believe in Christ because he recognised that a sinful man is not justified by observance of the law but only by faithful acceptance of the life-giving words of Christ (cf. Mk 1:27; Lk 5:8).

As for St Paul himself, he did not reason his way to the doctrine of justification by faith and thereupon decide to believe in Christ. He was allowed to see Christ, who told him to go into Damascus where

---

[31] Thus John the Baptist taught 'justification by faith'. Philo too (cf. *The Deca-logue*, 10-13, Loeb VII) had the idea that a man must first be purified before he can receive the law with any hope of fulfilling it—the law itself is not the means of purification. According to Philo the means of purification used by Moses was retreat into the desert. Probably John the Baptist regarded his baptism as a symbol of retreat into the desert—cf. U. Mauser, *Christ in the Wilderness*, SBT 39, London, 1963, p. 58.

he would be told what he must do. He was informed by Ananias that he must be baptized in order to have his sins washed away (Acts 22:16). In this way, Christ taught him that his zeal for the law had not justified him; only baptism could justify him. Because Paul believed this, he submitted to baptism. So he could say that he too had sought justification through faith in Christ *because* he had come to know that one is not justified by the law.

### In v. 16, is St Paul's use of Ps 143:2 legitimate?

Although the quotation from Ps 143 is introduced by the word 'because', St Paul does not mean that he, or Peter, or any of the others present, learned the doctrine of justification-through-faith by reflection on Ps 143. The last clause in v. 16 is added simply as a scriptural confirmation. It is almost an aside, thrown in to remind the hearer (or reader) that this doctrine of justification through faith is not a new-fangled idea of Paul's own devising, but a part of their Jewish tradition, imbedded in the Psalms.

The words taken from the Psalm are: 'No man will be justified.' St Paul amplifies this into 'No man will be justified *by the works of the law*' — which may seem very bold of him. But his addition is a legitimate exegesis of the psalmist's meaning, because the psalmist is saying that if God judges any man by his works, that man will have to be condemned. The whole of the verse in question is:

Do not enter into judgment with thy servant,
　for (if thou dost) no living creature will be justified before thee.

A few verses later the psalmist adds (v. 10):

Lead me to do thy will, for thou art my God;
　thy Spirit shall lead me into a straight path.

St Paul is, therefore, perfectly correct in claiming that the Psalm too teaches both the futility of seeking justification through observance of the law and the possibility of obtaining justification in a different way, namely through the gift of the Spirit.

### What is St Paul's argument in v. 17?

Vv. 15-16 contain St Paul's presupposition rather than the argument itself. V. 17 contains his argument in a highly compressed form. One interpretation takes the meaning to be this: 'You agree that we made our choice and sought justification through faith in Christ. Very well then, to proceed: this faith inevitably brings us into contact with Gentiles, because through faith we are "in Christ" and through the same faith the Gentiles are "in Christ". Jewish and Gentile believers are united in Christ, mystically through his grace, and socially in his Church, especially at the Lord's Supper. Now, if you choose to say that Jewish believers who eat with Gentile Christians thereby become sinners, it will follow that Christ, who brought us together, has led us into sin, that Christ has become the servant of Sin, and that he has done the devil's work for him by making sinners of us. Is that possible?' Because Paul is arguing with Christians, it is sufficient for him to reply: 'Heaven forbid!'

St Paul is arguing from the holiness of Christ. Christ who is the Son of God cannot have become a servant of Sin. He imparts holiness, not sinfulness. St Paul could also have argued that since Gentile Christians are holy by reason of their baptism into Christ, to associate with them cannot possibly be a cause of defilement. The reason why he does not develop this more obvious argument may be that the Jewish Christians held that the Gentile converts were not justified until they had been baptized *and circumcised.* In which case they were what Lagrange calls the 'virulent' type.

But the argument as expanded above contains a serious defect. It makes Paul presuppose that the Jewish Christians will *inevitably* come into illegal contact with Gentiles. But the visitors from Jerusalem held that this was not inevitable — that they could and would avoid it. They did not regard themselves as having died to the law in obedience to the law; on the contrary, they were still obeying the law. Moreover, they could reply that Paul himself had not died to the law in order to seek justification in Christ; he had abandoned the law in order to lead Gentiles to faith in Christ.

So perhaps it is better to understand v. 17 in a different way. St Paul is talking to Jews many of whom have so far avoided social contact with Gentile Christians, and he considers whether even they have become sinners in the process of their conversion to Christ. In order to turn to Christ and seek justification from him, they had to turn their backs on the law — *interiorly,* by acknowledging that the law could not give justification (v. 16). St Paul asks: 'When you abandoned the law to turn to Christ, did you thereby become sinners? If you did, then Christ, who called you away from the law, was acting as the minister of Sin — which is impossible.'

According to this second interpretation, to 'die to the law' (v. 19) means not 'to abandon the law by consorting with Gentiles' but to cease to put any faith in the law, whether one abandons it externally or not. It means an interior act of rejection.

In the eyes of an unconverted Jew, this interior act of rejection will certainly make the Christian Jew a sinner, but not in the eyes of God, and, St Paul claims in v. 19, not in the eyes of the law itself, for the law itself commands the Jew to die to the law and seek justification as a free gift from God. St Paul is telling the visitors from Jerusalem that they must cease to think as unconverted Jews think — they have not yet completed their spiritual detachment from the law. (This was natural enough; they were being asked to perform the psychological feat of fulfilling a divinely instituted law without attaching any religious significance to it.)

According to this second interpretation, St Paul is not directly concerned in v. 17 with the problem of table-fellowship with Gentiles. He is trying to correct the attitude of the Jewish Christians to the law in their own spiritual lives. Once that is put right, the problem of table-fellowship will vanish.

*What does St Paul mean by the verb 'to be justified' in vv. 16-17?*

In vv. 16-17, St Paul uses the verb 'to be justified' (in Greek, *dikaiousthai*) four times. He says:

A man is not justified by works of the law, but by faith in Christ Jesus.
We believe in Christ Jesus in order to be justified.
By works of the law *no flesh shall be justified.*
If through seeking to be justified in Christ we turned out to be sinners...

The fourth example is the most helpful. It shows that 'to be justified' is the opposite of 'to become a sinner'.

The supposition of St Paul's argument is that all men are either 'sinners' or 'just men'. The distinction was used by Christ himself: 'I am come to call not just men but sinners to repentance' — an ironical use of 'just men'. Christ means: 'If you are satisfied that you are already a just man, my preaching will mean nothing to you; but if you recognise that you are a sinner, I have come to call you to repentance' (cf. Jn 9:41). But though the saying is ironical, it shows that St Paul's distinction between 'sinners' and 'just men' goes back to Christ himself.

Christ presupposes, and St Paul makes explicit, that all Jews are sinners. According to St Paul, the Jews are of a holy stock (cf. Rom 11:16) — which means that they *ought* to be just men, and that together they ought to be a holy people (cf. Exod 19:6), but in fact they are all sinners, just as the Gentiles are (cf. Rom 1-2). Before God, no man can boast; all are sinners.

Nevertheless — this is the message both of Christ and of St Paul — it is possible for every man, for the Jew first and then for the Gentile, *to become just, to be made just,* or *to be justified.*

When God justifies a sinner, or makes him just, he does this not simply by forgiving his past sins and reckoning him as if he were just. A just man is one who loves God's will, who wants to do it, and who has the strength to do it. God turns a sinner into a just man by imparting justice to him, so that, thanks to the gift or 'grace' which he has received, the man really is a just man: he does love God's will, he does want to do it, and he has the strength of the Holy Spirit to enable him to do it.

'Justification', then, is the act by which God transfers a man from the flock of goats at his left hand to the flock of sheep at his right hand; but in the process of transferring him he transforms him — 'intrinsically', as Catholic theologians have been fond of saying. So justification is more than forgiveness; it is forgiveness plus transformation. Henceforth, the man, who is a sinner no longer, enjoys God's approval, is looked upon by him with favour, and stands in his grace (these are three ways of saying the same thing). But becoming a just man is not identical with being looked upon by God with favour. Rather, being looked upon with favour is the consequence of becoming a just man — at least from the man's point of view (from God's point of view the two things are simultaneous).

God justifies the sinner, and the sinner is justified. But just as when fire melts ice, the ice remains ice no longer, so when God justifies the sinner, he remains a sinner no longer. He is not, as Luther said, *simul justus et peccator* (simultaneously just and a sinner) — just as if you heat a snowball, you do not end up with a hot snowball. There is a sense in which the Christian can be called *simul justus et peccator* — namely, that even after justification, he remains prone to sin and may succumb. But to admit this use of the phrase obscures the point that the just and the sinners are two distinct categories and no one belongs simultaneously to both. God's word of pardon is really effective: it transfers the sinner to the kingdom of his Son.

The verb 'to justify' (*dikaioun*) often occurs in judicial contexts where it means 'to acquit'. St Paul sometimes uses it in this sense (cf. Rom 8:33-34), but not always, and not in Gal 2:16-17. The word always implies reference to a judgment, but not necessarily to a Court of Judgment. God will hold his court on the Day of Judgment, but meanwhile all men are constantly under his judgment in the sense that he sees the hearts of all men at all times and discerns the just and the sinner.

By what criterion does God discern the just from the sinners? St Paul replies: 'The just are, all of them, former sinners who through God's mercy have become just; they have become just, not by careful observance of the law of Moses, but by reason of their faith in Christ. When God sees that a man believes in Christ, or rather, when he enables him to believe in Christ, he forgives his sins and declares him just. This word of clemency is effective: it imparts justice to the believer — it gives him the strength of the Holy Spirit, which makes him a just man, no longer enslaved to Sin, but henceforth capable of resisting temptation. This imparted strength *is* justice (it is what makes the recipient a just man). It is a free gift — a 'grace' — and the man remains just, so long as he cooperates with this grace (cf. Phil 2:12; 3:9-10).

To start with, all men are sinners, both Jews (A, B, C, D, E...) and Gentiles (K, L, M, N, O...). The Jews, being of a holy stock, ought to be just, but are not. In Christ, God provides the means of justification for Jew and Gentile alike. Some Jews (say A, C, E...) and some Gentiles (say K, N, O...) respond: they believe and are thereby changed into just men. God implants in them the love of his will and the strength to do his will, and these graces make the recipient a just man — or, as St Paul often says, one of 'the saints'. 'Justifying' is 'just-making'.

Here the question inevitably arises: How does it come about that these particular men (A, C, E... K, N, O...) believe, and the rest do not? St Paul does not teach that the believer himself produces faith within his own breast and God then recognizes it (that is the semi-Pelagian error — that grace is not required for the *initium fidei*, i.e. for the very first act of faith [32]). On the contrary, he holds that faith itself is a gift of God. So here we come up against the mystery of predestination: Why does God bestow the gift of faith on some and not on all? It is no solution to say that he *offers* it to all and some accept, for the act of acceptance is not distinct from the act of faith — the act of acceptance is itself a gift of God. All we can do at this point of our speculations is to say that we do not understand the

---

[32] Cf. S. Gonzalez, 'De Gratia,' *Sacrae Theologiae Summa*, III (BAC), Madrid, 1950, s. 18.

ways of God. That is how St Paul ends his discussion of predestination, in Rom 11:33-36.

### A Note on 'the Justice of God'

In Galatians, St Paul does not use the expression 'the justice of
God'; but he uses it in Rom 1:17 — a verse which has been much
debated. 'Justice' is the attribute in virtue of which God justifies
repentant sinners. This is obviously not strict retributive justice, but
rather 'clemency' or 'saving justice'. [33] The word *dikaiosynê* has this
meaning in the LXX, where it is used to translate *sedaqah*, e.g. in
Ps 97:2 (Heb 98:2):

> The Lord has made known his salvation (*sôtêrian*),
> > he has revealed (*apekalypsen*) his justice (*dikaiosynên*)
> > > before all the nations.

The 'justice' which God communicates to the believer also entails
clemency. One of the prime obligations of a Christian is to be ready
to forgive others as God has forgiven him (cf. Mt 18:21-25). Without
this, he is not a just man.

However, the 'justice' of God is also his impartiality: he is no
respecter of persons, and will punish Jewish sinners no less than
Gentiles (cf. Rom 2:11-12, and Philo, quoted below, p. 307).

### Is St Paul speaking of 'the faith of Christ' in v. 16?

The Greek of v. 16 can be translated: 'Because we knew that a
man is not justified by the works of the law but *through the faith of
Christ Jesus,* we too put our faith in Christ Jesus, in order to be
justified *by the faith of Christ,* and not by the works of the law.' [34]
The italicized phrases are deliberately ambiguous. In addition to the
meaning ordinarily assigned to them, they can also mean that we are
saved by Christ's fidelity in the execution of his Father's will or
covenant, and we are saved by our own trusting response — which
is itself a part of his gift in fulfilment of the covenant. Just as our
'justice', our 'glory', and our 'life' are participations in the justice,
glory and life of Christ, so too it is reasonable to say that our faith
is a participation in Christ's faith (cf. Phil 3:9).

---

[33] Cf. J. H. Ropes, 'Righteousness in the Old Testament and in St. Paul,' JBL
22 (1903), pp. 211-227; S. Lyonnet, 'De justitia Dei in epistola ad Romanos,'
*Verbum Domini* 25 (1947), pp. 23-34; 118-144; 193-203; 257-264.
[34] In CBQ 30 (1968), p. 76, Dr. Markus Barth rightly pointed out that I
neglected to discuss this question in G in G. It was first raised by G. Hebert,
"Faithfulness" and "Faith", *Theology* 58 (1955), pp. 373-379.

St Paul delights in these ambiguities, because they help to express the mysterious communion of life between Christ and his disciples. It would be entirely in line with his thinking to suppose the meaning of v. 16 to be: 'We are saved not by *our* works, but by *Christ's* faith,' that is, by what Christ did in obedient fulfilment of his commission. However, strictly speaking, the contrast in v. 16 is not between our works and Christ's faith; it is between the works of *the Law* (which is almost personified here, because in antithesis to Christ) and the faith of Christ. [35] The sense is: 'We submitted to the influence of the Law, and the Law did not justify us; we put our faith in Christ, and the faith of Christ, manifesting itself in charity (cf. 5:6) on the cross (cf. 2:20) did justify us.' See also Rom 1:17; 3:22; Gal 3:22; Phil 3:9. Professor T. Torrance pointed out in an important article that

> in most of these passages the *pistis Iesou Christou* (faith of Jesus Christ) does not refer only either to the faithfulness of Christ or to the answering faithfulness of man, but is essentially a polarized expression denoting the faithfulness of Christ as its main ingredient but also involving or at least suggesting the answering faithfulness of man.

In reply, [36] Professor C. F. D. Moule, while not denying the ambiguity of the phrase *pistis Christou* ('faith of/in Christ') or the polarity of the reality which it names, questioned whether the faithfulness of Christ is the 'main ingredient'.

In the reality itself which is named, undoubtedly the faith of Christ is the main ingredient — otherwise our faith is in danger of becoming a meritorious work. Whether this ingredient was uppermost in St Paul's mind when he wrote Gal 2:16 is open to question, and Professor Moule may be right. But it has recently been pointed out that if *pistis Christou* is taken in the subjective sense, i.e., as meaning 'the faith of Christ', Gal 2:16 and 3:22 are found to be closely linked with the covenant-theology of the Epistle: by his covenant or testament to Abraham and his Seed (singular) God the Father made Christ his heir, with a request or requirement (*fidei commissum*) that he would buy and liberate his brethren who were slaves (cf. Jn 8:36).

---

[35] Luther saw that 'the works of the Law' could mean 'the works which the Law does in us.' Cf. Althaus, *The Theology of M. Luther*, p. 138: 'Whatever we do because we fear the punishment which the law threatens or because we desire the reward which the law promises is not our own work but rather the work of the law which has wrung it out of us with threatening or cajoling.'

[36] Cf. T. Torrance, 'One Aspect of the Biblical Conception of Faith,' *Expository Times* 66 (1956), p. 113; C. F. D. Moule, 'The Biblical Conception of Faith,' in the same volume, p. 157, with a brief reply from Professor Torrance on pp. 221-222. See also G. Howard, 'On the "Faith of Christ",' HTR 60 (1967), pp. 439-484.

Christ faithfully fulfilled this requirement by his death on the cross
(cf. Gal 3:13). [37]

## Does St Paul here teach 'justification by faith alone'?

As was mentioned above, St Paul uses 'to be justified' in two
senses: (1) to be made just here and now by the gift of the Spirit,
and (2) to be acquitted on the Day of Judgment. It is convenient,
therefore, and it saves much confusion, to distinguish between *first
justification* and *final justification*. First justification takes place when
the believer passes over from the state of sin to the state of grace;
final justification will take place when God as Judge declares the
believer just at the Judgment.

In Rom 3:28 St Paul says: 'We reckon a man to be justified
by faith (*pistei*), apart from works of the law.' Luther translated
*pistei* 'allein durch den Glauben', i.e., 'by faith alone', and thereby
provoked a great controversy. But was the addition of *allein* any
bolder than St Paul's addition to Psalm 143: 'No man will be
justified *by works of the law*'?

The controversy can be resolved by means of the above distinction.
In so far as Rom 3:28 refers to first justification, Luther was right:
the initial forgiveness by which a sinner is justified is through faith
alone; our works have nothing to do with it. But if Rom 3:28 refers
also to final justification, it is incorrect to say that a man will be
justified by his faith alone. He will be judged also by his works and
by his words (cf. Mt 12:37). Through faith the sinner becomes a
just man; but then his faith, which is Christ's faith imparted to him,
must bear fruit in charity, as St Paul says in Gal 5:6 and St James
in Jas 2:24.

## How were the saints of the Old Testament justified?

After quoting vv. 16-17, St Jerome says that certain persons
(presumably Jews) object that if Paul's doctrine were true, the
patriarchs, prophets and holy men who died before the coming of
Christ were not justified. He replies: [38]

---

[37] Cf. G. M. Taylor, 'The Function of *pistis Christou* in Galatians,' JBL 85
(1966), pp. 58-76; D. G. Nowell, *Questions and Answers on Roman Law*,
London, 1959, pp. 99-103. Ignatius of Antioch, in the prologue of his Epistle
to the Romans, speaks of 'the faith and charity of Christ'. Some editors omit
'faith and', but cf. O. Perler, 'Ignatius von Antiochia und die römische
Christengemeinde,' *Divus Thomas* (Freiburg), 22 (1944), pp. 414-418.
[38] Jerome, PL 26, 368-369. According to St Thomas, Gal, 396 B, both Jerome
and Augustine agreed that before the passion of Christ the works of the law

We should admonish such people that it is here said that justice is not attained by those who believe that they can be justified by works alone, but the holy men of antiquity were saved by faith in Christ. Thus Abraham saw Christ's day and was glad (cf. Jn 8:36); and Moses thought it greater wealth to share in the humiliation of Christ than to own the treasures of Egypt, for his eyes were fixed on the day of recompense (cf. Heb 11:26); and Isaiah saw the glory of Christ (Isa 6:1, 9), as John the Evangelist mentions (Jn 12:41).

Whether this answer would satisfy the Jewish questioner seems doubtful. He might say: 'Granting for the sake of argument that Abraham, Moses and Isaiah were given some special foreknowledge of Christ, I am still worried about the rank and file of pious Jews throughout the centuries who had no such foreknowledge but put their faith in the law and the sacrifices enjoined by God in the law, and especially in the rites and sacrifices of the Day of Atonement.'

Some at least of the Pharisaic Jews of St Paul's time probably held that on the Day of Atonement God really and effectively justified them — forgave their sins, even grievous ones, and gave them a new start as just men. According to the Mishnah (Shebuoth, I, 6):

> for uncleanness that befalls the Temple and its Hallowed Things through wantonness, atonement is made through the goat whose blood is sprinkled within the Holy of Holies and by the Day of Atonement; for all other transgressions spoken of in the law, venial or grave, wanton or unwitting, conscious or unconscious, sins of omission or of commission, sins punishable by extirpation or by death at the hands of the court, the scapegoat makes atonement.

A Jew of St Paul's day who held this belief would say that justification does come from the works of the law. God has laid down in the law the rituals of atonement, and just as past generations performed these rituals and were justified, so too the present generation can find justification through the works of the law.

There is no answer to this objection in St Paul's own Epistles, but an attempt is made in the Epistle to the Hebrews (7:11, 18-19) to show that the levitical sacrifices were ineffectual; and in the central passage of the whole Epistle (9:11-14), the author says that whereas the animal sacrifices of the levitical priesthood effected only a purification of the flesh, Christ's sacrifice 'cleanses our consciences of deeds of death and fits us to serve the living God.' But the author of Hebrews is talking to Christians. The only argument he gives, to prove that the

---

were living or life-giving (*viva*)—original sin was forgiven by circumcision, and God was placated by sacrifices and victims. St Thomas adds, 397 D, that 'although of old some were justified by observing the works of the law, this was only through faith in Christ.'

levitical sacrifices were ineffectual, is the rhetorical question: 'If perfection could have been achieved through the priesthood of the sons
of Levi, what need would there be for a further priest to arise, a
priest of the order of Melkisedek and not belonging to the line of
Aaron?' (7 : 11). In other words, only in the light of the Cross do we
recognize that the levitical sacrifices were ineffectual. It is impossible
to say whether this argument comes from St Paul, or whether he
would have accepted it. Perhaps he would have agreed that the
sacrifices of the old law, including the sacrifice of the Day of Atonement, were ineffectual *in themselves* but effectual by reason of Christ's
death which they typified (cf. Rom 3 : 25-26). [39] This would mean
that the 'works of the law' were formerly effective, but have ceased
to be so since the coming of Christ.

However, the view expressed in the Mishnah may not have been
at all common in the time of Paul. Neither John the Baptist nor Christ
told the people to seek justification through sincere participation in
the rites of the Day of Atonement. St John the Baptist, though he
was of priestly stock, turned his back on the sacrifices of the temple
altogether, and preached a baptism of repentance to last until it was
rendered obsolete by the coming of the Baptism of the Spirit. Unfortunately, we do not know what St John the Baptist said about the
temple and its sacrifices; but to judge from what he did, he had
decided that they had proved ineffectual and might as well be
abandoned. [40]

### How does Gal 2:16 compare with Jas 2:24?

| | |
|---|---|
| *Gal 2:16* Knowing that no man is justified by works of the law, but through faith in Jesus Christ, we too put our faith in Jesus Christ, in order to be justified by faith in Christ, and not by works of the law. | *Jas 2:24* A man is justified by works and not by faith alone. |

These are both polemic statements, which would never have been
made if there had not been controversy in the early Church about the

---

[39] The view of Lyonnet, in his note on Rom 3:25 in BdeJ, that on the Day of
Atonement God granted 'a half-pardon, a sort of non-imputation', is rejected
by Galot, *La Rédemption,* p. 97. But where the strength of the Spirit is not
given, sin is not effectively dealt with, and the sinner is not, in the full sense,
'justified'.

[40] Cf. Galot, *La Rédemption,* pp. 299-303, on the 'retroactive influence' of the
power of Christ.

relation between faith and works. The two statements represent different points of view, obviously, but not necessarily contradictory or even conflicting points of view. How then, do they compare with each other?

First, *the Epistle of James does not represent the position of the Judaizers.* It does not say that Gentile Christians must be circumcised. It does not say that any Christian, whether Gentile or Jew, must obey the law of Moses. On the contrary, it says that Christians must obey 'the law of liberty' (2:12), which is also called 'the royal law' (2:8). But this is the very same law of charity which St Paul calls 'the law of Christ' in Gal 6:2. So the James who is the author of the Epistle cannot be regarded as the protagonist of the Judaizers, and St Paul in Galatians is not attacking the position of the author of this Epistle.

Secondly, *the Epistle of St James is not attacking the position of St Paul,* though at first sight it may appear to be doing so. The contrast between Jas 2:14-23 and Rom 4:1-3 is particularly striking.

*14* What use is it, my brethren, if a man claims to have faith but has no works? Has his faith power to save him? *15* Suppose some of the brethren or sisters are without clothing and short of their daily bread, *16* and one of you says to them: 'Go in peace, keep yourselves warm, and have a good meal,' but does not give them what their bodies need, what is the good of that? *17* So too with faith: if it has no good works to show for itself, it is barren and dead. *18* If someone objects: 'One person has faith, and another has works,' I reply: 'Show me your faith without works if you can; I for my part will show you my faith by means of my works.' *19* You have faith to believe that God is one? Well and good. But even the demons believe that, and they tremble with fear. *20* Do you want a proof, you empty man, that faith without works is dead? *21* Was it not through his works that our father Abraham was justified, when he offered his son Isaac on the altar? *22* His faith, as you can see, was at work in what he did; his faith was made perfect in and through his works. *23* That is how the words of Scripture were fulfilled which say: 'Abraham believed God and it was reckoned to him as justice'; and again, 'he was called God's friend.' *24* So you see that a man is justified by works and not by faith alone. *25* Then again was not Rahab the harlot justified

*Rom 4:1-3* What then shall we say of Abraham, our forefather according to the flesh, if Abraham was justified by works has he not ground for boasting? Not before God! For what does the Scripture say? 'Abraham believed God, and it was reckoned to him as justice.'

> by her works, when she welcomed
> the messengers and sent them away
> by a different route? *26* As the
> body without breath is dead, so faith
> without works is dead.

However, it is unlikely that James is here making a direct attack on
the doctrine of St Paul. James does not misunderstand St Paul's
position; he seems to be unacquainted with it. St Paul meant that
through faith and baptism a man dies to sin and rises with Christ
into a new sphere of existence. He was talking mainly about first
justification. The believer's heart is cleansed by the Holy Spirit. He
is able for the future to live a life of charity, joy and peace, and in
doing so, he fulfils the law (cf. Gal 5:14; Rom 13:8-10). St James
is not attacking this account of how first justification comes about.

Thirdly, it seems highly probable that *James is attacking a misunderstanding of St Paul's doctrine*. [41] St Paul himself lets us see that
some of his hearers made his doctrine of justification an excuse for
moral laxity (cf. Gal 5:13; Rom 6:15). They did not recognize that
he was talking about first justification, and concluded, apparently,
that at the Last Judgment God would acquit them because of their
faith. Jas 2:18 seems to imply that they also made use of St Paul's
doctrine of the Mystical Body: 'One man has faith and another has
works — God does not expect the same of all of us.' The error of
those who understood 'freedom from the law' to mean 'freedom to do
all that the law forbade' is known as Antinomianism. St James' Epistle
seems to be directed against the Antinomian misunderstanding of St
Paul. The author, who is a good Jew and not a speculative theologian,
replies that a 'faith' which does not express itself in works of justice
and charity is just an empty, futile use of pious-sounding words. It is
like saying to a cold and hungry man: 'Go in peace, keep nice and
warm, have a good meal!' and *doing nothing to help him*. [42]

St Paul's theology, misunderstood, becomes a theology of laziness
— a theological justification for doing nothing whatever apart from
believing. At Thessalonica, some of his converts gave up their em-

---

[41]  Schnackenburg, *The Moral Teaching*, p. 356, rejects this view of the Epistle:
     'Its points are made, not against any teaching, but against negligent Christian
     conduct.' But why not against both? The persons attacked seem to have used
     'justification by faith' as a slogan to justify their negligent conduct. Cf. K.
     Aland, 'Der Herrnbruder Jakobus und der Jakobusbrief,' TLZ 69 (1944),
     97-98.

[42]  There is a famous Peanuts cartoon on this subject. It is reproduced in R. L.
     Short, *The Gospel according to Peanuts*, Richmond (Virginia), 1964, p. 11. See
     further below, pp. 399-400. Rahab is linked with Abraham as a model of
     hospitality—cf. Jn 8:39-40, and R. B. Ward, 'The Works of Abraham',
     HTR 61 (1968), p. 287.

ployment and loafed about waiting for the End of the World. And right through the Middle Ages, some Christians placed perhaps too much emphasis on waiting for the Parousia and singing psalms to kill the time of waiting.

It is unfortunate that James's fine Epistle is stored away in the part of the New Testament which fastidious theologians rarely visit — a shame too that the liturgy does not make more use of it. St Paul's emphasis on freedom from 'law' and 'works' was necessary in his own particular circumstances. But most Christians today probably have greater need of the message of James — which is also the word of Christ: 'It is not those who say to me "Lord, Lord" who will go into the kingdom of heaven, but those who do the will of my Father in heaven' (Mt 7:21). For the student of theology the temptation is to think that when he has performed the difficult task of mastering St Paul's doctrine of justification, he is justified by this 'work' and can rest from his labours — as if the study of the Epistles were itself the way of life which they recommend.

We pass on now to the third subsection (2:17-21), which was printed above, p. 194.


*What does v. 18 add to v. 17?*

V. 18 is a retort or counter-attack. St Paul says: 'Christ does not make me a sinner by calling upon me to renounce my inner allegiance to the law; on the contrary, I make *myself* a sinner if I build up again what I have torn down, that is, if I return to my allegiance to the law.' St Paul cleverly argues *ad hominem* here. He does not say: 'I make myself a sinner by going against the will of Christ,' but 'I make myself a sinner by going against the law, for "it was in obedience to the law that I died to the law" and hence it must be disobedience to the law to return to the law.'

The metaphor which St Paul uses here, of tearing down and building up, shows that he is thinking of the law as a wall, and probably as a wall of separation between Jew and Gentile (cf. Eph 2:14). [43] He means that St Peter's action in withdrawing from contact with Gentile Christians is equivalent to rebuilding the wall of separation, and implies an inner return to the law. If the visitors from Jeru-

---

[43] Possibly St Paul has at the back of his mind the idea that Jesus is the antitype of Joshua (called 'Jesus' in the LXX) who after throwing down the walls of Jericho said (Josh 6:26): 'Cursed before the Lord be the man that rises up and rebuilds this city, Jericho.' In Eph 2:14 it is Christ who tore down the wall of separation.

salem think that Peter was committing a sin by mixing with the
Gentiles, Paul retorts that, on the contrary, he commits a sin by
breaking off contact with the Gentiles — at least if his interior disposition corresponds to his exterior actions.

The Greek words taken above to mean 'I make myself a sinner'
could also mean 'I confess that I was a sinner'. Then the whole sentence
means: 'If I build up what I once tore down I confess that I was a
sinner in tearing it down.' This sense is not applicable to Peter, but
it is applicable to Paul himself. Before his conversion he was doing
his best to tear down the Church (1:13); now he is building it up,
and by so doing he confesses that he was wrong in attempting to
destroy it. [44] However, this application is hardly relevant to the context.


*In what sense did St Paul 'die to the law through the law' (v. 19)?*

There are three possible interpretations of this ambiguous saying,
and the context requires at least two of them. Perhaps St Paul himself
formulated this *dogma*, [45] and then considered the various senses in
which it was true.

First the sentence may mean: 'In obedience to the law of faith
(cf. 6:2) I abandoned the law of Moses.' [46] This is an idea which
St Paul would accept, but it is not appropriate to the context, since
there has been no mention of 'the law of faith' in the preceding
verses. And further, the paradox of 'dying to the law through the
law' is spoilt if the word 'law' means two different things in its two
occurrences.

Secondly, in view of the *preceding* context it is best to take the
sentence to mean: 'In accordance with the law, or in obedience to the
law, I died to the law.' This flows on very well from v. 18: 'If I
return to the law which I abandoned, I make myself a sinner against
the law, because it was *through the law* that I died to the law.'
St Paul means that the law itself tells the Jew to seek justification
elsewhere. The word 'law' is here used in the broad sense of 'Torah'

---

[44] Cf. P. Menoud, 'Le sens du verbe *porthein*,' in *Apophoreta* (Festschrift Haenchen), Berlin, 1964, p. 180.

[45] *Dogmata*, in the Greek philosophers, are axioms or short pithy sayings, which
sum up an important aspect of reality. They are to be recalled to mind
frequently, so that the mind will take its dye from these familiar ideas or
'opinions' (*doxai*). But the word was also used of royal and imperial decisions
or edicts (cf. Lk 2:1). The earliest ecclesiastical use is Acts 16:4, where it is
used of the decisions of the Council of Jerusalem. Dogmatic theology is largely
concerned with the decisions of Councils.

[46] Cf. Lyonnet, Gal, ad loc.

or 'Scripture' (as in Rom 3:19). [47] One place where the Scripture teaches this lesson is the quotation from Ps 143 in v. 16. In that psalm, the law itself declares its own incapacity to justify and bids the Jew seek justification elsewhere. St Paul has done so, in obedience to the law. To retrace his steps would therefore be to contravene the law.

Taken in this second sense, v. 19 has a parallel in Rom 10:1-13, where St Paul again argues that the law itself points to a way of salvation other than the way of works, namely the way of faith. He quotes Deut 30:11-14 and inserts glosses to show that Moses described the appointed means of salvation in terms which exactly fit Christ:

> The justice that comes from faith speaks thus: '*Do not say* in your heart, *Who can go up to heaven* (that is, to bring Christ down)? or *Who can go down into the abyss* (that is, to bring Christ up from the dead)?' But what does it say? It says: *The message is near you, in your mouth and in your heart* — meaning the message of faith which we preach.

In both texts, St Paul is trying to show that the law itself teaches the Jew its own temporary character, and points forward to a régime of salvation other than the régime of the law. The same point is made at greater length and with greater clarity in Heb 8:7-13, where the author quotes the promise of a new covenant from Jer 31:31-34. [48]

There is also a parallel in the Fourth Gospel. In Jn 1:19-34 the evangelist seems to be offering an *apologia pro vita sua*. He shows that in leaving John the Baptist in order to join Christ, he was not being disloyal to the Baptist, but on the contrary was obeying him. Just as John the evangelist would have been disobeying the Baptist if he had left Christ and returned to the Baptist, so St Paul says that if he or any other Jewish Christian abandons faith in Christ to go back to the régime of the law, he is disobeying the law by going against its will. The law, like the Baptist, points forward to Christ. Both St Paul and St John had to defend themselves against the charge of being turn-coats — a charge which St Paul throws at the Galatians in 1:6.

---

[47] The Jews refer to their Scriptures as 'The Law, the Prophets, and the Writings', or more briefly as 'The Law and the Prophets', or more briefly as 'The Law' (the Torah).

[48] If St Paul means, not simply 'The Law said to me: Die to the Law!' but rather, 'The Law said to me: Die to the Law in order to live to God!' it is probable that he had Jer 31:31-34 in mind. For Jeremiah speaks of a time when each man will receive instruction directly from God. St Thomas, Gal, 399 D, points out that the antithesis between 'living to the Law' and 'living to God' is equivalent to 'receiving instruction indirectly' and 'receiving it directly'.

Thirdly, in view of the *following* context, it makes good sense to read v. 19 in the light of 3:13. Then the meaning is: 'The law released me from its servitude by condemning Christ, making itself guilty, and so losing the right to condemn,' or 'The law put Christ to death and in so doing provided for me a way of escape from its servitude, for in baptism I die with Christ, and pass out of this world where the law holds sway.' [49] This interpretation leads smoothly into v. 19b: 'I am crucified with Christ crucified.'

Taken in this third sense, v. 19 has a parallel in Rom 7:4: 'you have died to the law through the body of Christ.' Through faith and baptism, the believer has been incorporated in the crucified body of Christ, and has so passed through Christ's death into a sphere of existence beyond the reach of the law. [50]

*How is v. 20 connected with what precedes?*

In vv. 16-20, St Paul has presented Jewish Christians with an alternative: they must seek justification *either* from Christ *or* from the law, not from both. If they want to seek justification from Christ they must inwardly abandon the law; if they then decide to go back to the law, they are inwardly abandoning the grace of Christ (v. 21a). The pattern of thought in vv. 16-20 is threefold: (1) When the Jew abandons the law to believe in Christ, he does not become a sinner. (2) If the Christian Jew abandons Christ to go back to the law, he does become a sinner. (3) When the Jew abandons the law to believe in Christ, he becomes a just man, because Christ begins to live in him. [51] Thus v. 19 is linked to v. 17 by an antithesis: 'Christ has not become a servant of Sin (v. 17)....for he has become the source of life and holiness.' [52] (The same antithetic pattern is applied, in 3:6-10, to the law: 'The law will not bring you the blessings promised to Abraham; on the contrary it will bring a curse on you.')

Once it is recognised that vv. 19-20 stand in antithesis to v. 17, it becomes clear that the emphatic part of v. 19 is the purpose clause

---

[49]  Cf. Schlier, Gal, p. 62; T. W. Manson, *On Paul and John*, p. 61.
[50]  Cf. O. Modalsli, art. cit., TZ 21 (1965), p. 24.
[51]  It is often said that in vv. 17-21 St Paul gradually ceases to address Peter and thinks more and more of the Galatians (cf. e.g. Schmithals, *Paul and James*, p. 77). According to the above analysis, this is not so. Vv. 16-20 are a lesson for *Jewish* Christians. Gentile Christians who are allowed to overhear, can draw a lesson for themselves, but the argument is framed to meet the spiritual difficulties of Christian Jews who have to observe the law without putting their faith in it.
[52]  St Thomas here aptly quotes Rom 5:19 and 1 Pet 2:22.

at the end: 'For when in obedience to the law I died to the law, it was in order that I might *live* for God — not that I might become a sinner and die!' In these verses St Paul expresses his profoundest religious conviction. Here is the essential lesson of the Damascus vision, which made such a change in his own religious life that he could describe it only as a death and resurrection. Previously he had tried to make himself a just man by self-discipline and strict observance of the law. The vision was a revelation both of the glory of Christ and of the failure of his own personal efforts. In seeking to maintain the law, he had made a sinner of himself and had ended up persecuting the Lord; and the Lord had told him that if he wished to be cleansed of his sins, he must be baptized (cf. Acts 22:16). Thereafter he knew that if he was to be pleasing in God's sight, it must be thanks to Christ — through the glory of Christ reflected on his brow (cf. 2 Cor 3:18); and if he was to be a just man, it must be through the strength of Christ's Holy Spirit controlling the wayward desires and ambitions of the flesh.

In vv. 19-21 St Paul's argument develops like this: 'When I sought justification through faith I was not sinning against the law, but obeying it; through faith I was united to Christ, and in union with Christ dying on the cross I died to this evil world. I am crucified to the world, as he is crucified to the world. [53] The true life which I now have, though I remain in the flesh, is a life which I draw from the Risen Christ. He lives in me and energizes me through the gift of the Holy Spirit, won for me by his self-offering on the cross. *There* is the source of life and of justice for me — in Christ crucified and risen! I do not try to dispense with God's grace by seeking justification from the law. For that is what a man is doing if he seeks justification from the law: he is virtually declaring God's gracious gift superfluous and setting it aside. *For if justification comes from the law, Christ died for nothing!*'

This last thunderbolt of a sentence means that if a Jew needs nothing else in order to become a just man beyond the external guidance of the written law, then as far as he is concerned the cross was useless.

That a Jewish teacher of St Paul's day could speak as if a man can become just simply by a study and observance of the law may

---

[53] Literally, the Greek means 'I am co-crucified with Christ.' But this does not mean 'I hang upon Christ's cross.' The perfect tense expresses a present state resulting from a past action or actions. So the meaning is: 'I *am now* dead to this world because *in the past* Christ died on the cross and I was baptized into his death.'

perhaps be illustrated from Philo's treatise, *Who is the heir?*, which traces the development of the Jew from birth to maturity. [54] In the first seven years, says Philo, very surprisingly, the soul receives no impressions; in the next seven it becomes loaded with sins; in the next, with the aid of philosophy (i.e. study of the law) sin is driven out; in the fourth it returns to good health and becomes the heir of wisdom. In all this, human effort seems sufficient: not the divine Spirit but human philosophy drives out sin. However, Philo does not express the whole of his thought in this passage; elsewhere he recognizes that wisdom is a gift of God; and he condemns those who say that, although the blessings they receive come from the Ruling Mind, they nevertheless have a right to them because they are prudent, courageous, temperate and just, and are therefore deemed worthy by God of his favours. [55]

## What is the correct reading in 2:20?

In 2:20 four important manuscripts, including the Chester Beatty papyrus (P[46]) and Vaticanus, have *en pistei zô têi tou theou kai Christou tou agapêsantos me* — which can be translated in two ways: (1) 'I live by faith in the God and Christ who loved me and gave himself for me.' This would be one of the clearest statements of the divinity of Christ in the New Testament. However, the second translation is preferable: (2) 'I live by faith in God and in Christ who loved me and gave himself for me.' The printed editions (Nestle, Souter, Merk) prefer the reading, 'I live by faith in the Son of God who loved me,' which is certainly simpler. However, in the structure of the first main division of the Epistle, 2:20-21 matches 1:4-5, where St Paul mentions both 'Christ who offered himself for our sins' and the Father by whose will he did this. So probably 2:20-21 should contain explicit mention of both the Father and Christ. Therefore the longer reading is to be preferred, and *tou theou* should be referred to the Father, not to the Son.

## Is St Paul speaking of 'mystical' union with Christ in v. 20?

The word 'mystical' is so vague that the question needs to be reformulated before it can be answered.

---

54  *Who is the heir?* 294-299 (Loeb, IV).
55  Cf. Philo, *The Sacrifices of Cain and Abel*, 54 (Loeb, II).

First, then, is St Paul speaking in v. 20 of a union with Christ which is *experienced*? [56] The answer is Yes, for two reasons: (a) Christ lives and works in Paul through the gifts of the Spirit, which are so clearly experienced that he can appeal to them as a verification of the truth of the gospel (3:2-4); and (b) the Greek phrase normally translated 'Christ lives in me' (*zêi de en emoi Christos*) may also mean 'Christ is fermenting within me' — like a new leaven gradually transforming the whole lump of my being. St Paul feels this ferment going on within him and sees it in others so clearly that he can say to them: 'How did this start? Was it through performing the rituals of the law, or simply by believing the gospel?'

Secondly, is St Paul speaking in v. 20 of an experience which is granted only to a few highly privileged individuals? The answer here is No. St Paul speaks in the first person singular in v. 20, but the continuation in 3:1-4 shows that he thinks his own experience is repeated in the life of every believer. [57]

*'It is no longer I who live'* — *Does St Paul regard the law as an incitement to selfishness?*

It was suggested above that one reason why St Paul was so insistent that Gentile Christians should not accept the law was that he thought it would be a hindrance rather than a help to the formation of Christian character. This is borne out by v. 20. In vv. 18-20 'Christ' and 'I' stand in constant contrast: 'Christ does not make me a sinner by releasing me from the law, I make myself a sinner if I return to the law. Thanks to the law my *ego* died, crucified with Christ. That *ego* no longer lives, but Christ lives in me. I live now in faith, therefore in dependence on God and on Christ who loved me and delivered himself for me, to release me from my sins and make me a just man. I do not try to make myself a just man, I allow Christ who died for me to impart to me the justice of God. Christ is not a minister of Sin, he is a minister of the justice of God. When I submit to him and he takes possession of me, he does not infect me with sin, he transforms me with his grace, or his justice.'

---

[56] Alfred Wikenhauser, in his book *Pauline Mysticism* (Freiburg-Edinburgh, 1960), practically excludes all experience or awareness of grace from pauline spirituality. He maintains that pauline spirituality is 'mystical', but only in the sense that the believer's union with Christ is mysterious. It is mysterious because it lies beyond the range of experience—in other words, because (in the commonest sense of the word) it is non-mystical. Cf. J. Bligh, 'Liturgical Mysticism,' HJ 2 (1961), pp. 333-344.

[57] There is a good example of the exemplary 'I' in Philo, *The Decalogue*, 42-43 (Loeb, VII).

St Paul is here giving to the Jews at Antioch his personal testimony as to what the gospel had meant in his own life. Before his conversion, he used the law as a means of polishing the brass on his own *ego*. Unawares, he was pursuing his own glory and self-advancement (cf. 1 : 10b). His cult of the law was a subtle cult of himself. After his conversion, he realised that he was not at the centre of the universe. 'Jesus is Lord' — a far greater figure than Paul can ever be; the greatest honour to which Paul can attain is to be his servant. So after his conversion, Paul begins to pursue the glory of Christ, by doing *his* will. He puts himself at the disposal of Christ, to allow Christ to live and work in him. At Antioch he assures the Jewish Christians that by placing himself at the disposal of Christ in this way, he has not delivered himself up to Sin, but has opened himself to the workings of the Holy Spirit. He is warning his opponents that Judaism tends to become a subtle cult of the *ego*; Christianity, and especially the Gentile form of Christianity, dethrones the ego and enthrones Christ instead.

Christianity teaches a man to accept the position of a satellite. The Christian is not the centre of his universe; he is the servant of another far greater man, Jesus Christ, who is also the Son of God. There is a useful human analogy in the early history of the Roman Empire: M. Agrippa, a much greater man than many of the later emperors, had the sense to recognize in Augustus an even greater man than himself and to be content with the position of his lieutenant and loyal supporter. Similarly with John the Baptist, and with St Paul.

By teaching men to accept the position of satellites, Christianity creates the possibility of real cohesion. So long as everyone wishes to be first, there is no stable harmony, but only a temporary balance of conflicting ambitions. If all Christians are content to be the servants of Christ, Christ can live in them all and unite them in one compact body. This was what St Paul was trying to realise in the Gentile churches. He saw that the introduction of the Jewish law would not be a help.

Faith, by uniting the individual to Christ, incorporates him into the body of Christ and makes him *ipso facto* a sharer in the 'spirit' of this body. So faith breaks down the isolation of the individual and enables him to become, as a member of the Body, something much better than he could have been as an isolated individual. As an individual son of Adam, he had the life of his ego, which was a living death; as a member of the Body of Christ, he is energized by the life of the whole Body, which flows down, according to St Paul's anatomical ideas, from the Head: 'from which the whole body, through its joints and ligaments, is supplied with nourishment, given solidity, and made to fill out as God would have it grow' (Col 2:19).

## *Was St Paul right in regarding the law as an incitement to selfishness?*

V. 19 contains an implication which must be highly offensive to pious Jews: if one must die to the law in order to live for God, the law must be an obstacle to the service of God; it must be a positive incitement to self-advancement, self-satisfaction and self-admiration. In the life of Paul such had been its effect; but was he right to generalize from his own experience? V. 19, uttered in the heat of controversy, does not contain a carefully balanced estimate of the value of positive law in a man's religious life. [58]

(1) *Abusus non tollit usum.* If some ambitious young men turn the law into a means of self-advancement, this does not justify a wholesale condemnation of law. In the lives of other, better-balanced personalities the law may do much good. There can be no doubt that, thanks to the law, 'the moral level of Judaism was far above the level of the Hellenistic world as a whole.' [59]

(2) A certain measure of self-satisfaction is necessary to the mental health of every man, and especially of the Christian preacher. If a man despises himself, he cannot live at peace with himself; if he cannot live at peace with himself, he will start to murmur against God; and if he is not at peace either with himself or with God, he will become a psychological case. The law, rightly used, by a man who has the aid of the Holy Spirit to enable him to fulfil it, is a positive help towards the preservation of peace with himself and peace with God. As regards the Christian preacher, if he is not at peace with himself, and in some degree satisfied with himself, how can he call upon others to imitate him and to follow him in a way of life which leaves him personally dissatisfied and disgruntled? He may continue to preach from a sense of duty, but he will have no real zeal for the propagation of a doctrine which has led him into a state of self-contempt. An overdose of humility will destroy a preacher's zeal.

## *'Christ lives in me' — In what way does St Paul mean this?*

A man who admires the work of a philosopher, such as Epictetus, or of a religious leader, such as General Booth, might say: 'I have

---

[58] Cf. J. Bligh, 'De munere positivo Legis in oeconomia salutis,' *Verbum Domini* 41 (1963), pp. 186-187.
[59] McKenzie, *The Power and the Wisdom*, p. 19.

learned much from him; I try to live in the spirit which he inculcates; indeed you might say that his spirit lives on in me.' Does St Paul mean something like this? Does he mean: 'Christ lives in me because I accept his teaching about God, about man, about this world, about the next world, about the way I must live in this world'? Does he mean: 'My life is governed by this body of wisdom which Christ set forth in his teaching and by which he lived and died — it is not of my own devising; I accept it on faith from him. He controls my life through his word'?

St Paul does mean this much — and the value of this much should not be underrated. The question is whether he also means a great deal more. He sometimes speaks as if justification took place in two stages: (1) a man believes in the gospel, and (2) God responds by infusing into him the Holy Spirit (cf. 3:2). But perhaps this is not quite what he means, for if it were correct, it would seem to follow that the man is not justified, properly speaking, by faith, but by the gift of the Holy Spirit given on the occasion of the man's faith. Yet St Paul says very clearly in some texts that 'man is justified *by faith*' (cf. Gal 2:16; Rom 3:28; 5:1; Eph 3:16). So faith should not be reduced to a mere disposition.

Since the act of faith is itself a gift of God, may it not be that faith *is* the active presence of the Holy Spirit — so that to say that we are justified by faith and that we are justified by the Holy Spirit come to the same thing? Faith is itself a new source of strength in the believer. It generates hope and love — and these are *powers*, which enable a man to do what he could not do without them.

The act of faith is the response of man's natural powers to God's revelation, but it is a response which these natural powers can make only when they are aided in the act by a supernatural gift of grace. In the act of faith, God and man concur in an act which man's natural powers alone cannot achieve. So one can say that the act of faith by which a man is justified is an act of the Holy Spirit. The believer is justified by faith and by the Holy Spirit in one and the same act.

Theodore of Mopsuestia explains this verse, according to his wont, by means of a contrast between the present life and the life to come. He paraphrases St Paul thus: 'Passing over from the present life, I think of myself as already living that life according to which Christ also lives in me.' [60] That is to say, Christ's living in me depends upon my thinking of myself as sharing in his risen life: his possession of my being is not magical but operates through faith. His power

---

[60]  Theodore, Gal, p. 34. Cf. above, p. 70, and Rom 6:11.

is available to men on condition that they will believe in his power; but the believing is not a *mere* condition. If they do believe, his power works through their faith. [61]

*What is meant by 'the grace of God' in 2:21?*

'Grace' (*charis*) is not yet a technical term in St Paul's Epistles. In secular Greek it has the same ambiguity as the English word 'favour' in the expressions 'to look with favour on someone' and 'to do someone a favour'. When God looks with favour on someone, this looking is effective. Therefore when St Paul says: 'Grace be upon you and peace from God our Father,' he means not only 'May God look upon you with favour,' but also 'May he grant you a favour (or, as we say, a blessing, a grace)!' God's grace, as it is received in us, can also be called a *charisma*.

In 2:21, when St Paul says: 'I do not set aside the grace of God,' he means: 'I do not set aside the grace which I have received (or, the gift which God has graciously given me).' In the third subsection (p. 194), there is a link between this verse and 2:18:

| | |
|---|---|
| If I rebuild what I tore down (viz. the law), I make myself a sinner. | I do not set aside the gracious gift of God. |

St Paul has in mind, therefore, a contrast between setting aside the law and setting aside God's gracious gift. The gift is either Christ himself, or the work of Christ, or the gift of justification, that is, the gift of God's justice imparted to the believer, the life of Christ (v. 20), his Holy Spirit.

St Paul is warning the Jewish Christians that they must put their faith either in the law or in Christ. If they return to the law, they can do this only by renouncing the gift of imparted justice. They will then be setting aside 'the justice that comes through faith in Christ, God's justice, based on faith,' in order to strive after a justice of their own making based on the law (cf. Phil 3:9).

*How do vv. 19-20 compare with 1:4-5?*

In the structure of the first main division, 2:19-20 corresponds to 1:4-5. Both passages speak of the purpose of Christ's death:

| | |
|---|---|
| *1:4-5* ...the Lord Jesus Christ who offered himself for our sins to | *2:19-20* I am crucified with Christ crucified. It is no longer I who live, |

---

[61] This is one of the meanings of Gal 5:6: 'faith energized by (Christ's) charity.'

rescue us from the present evil age, according to the will of God our Father...

but Christ lives in me. So far as I now live while in the flesh, I live through *faith* in God and in Christ who *loved* me and delivered himself for *me*.

The second passage adds three points to the first. It shows (1) that our transference from the present evil age into the kingdom of Christ depends on faith — hence on dying with Christ, hence on baptism. It shows (2) that Christ offered himself for our sins out of love (v. 20), hence that our transference from the present evil age depends on faith in Christ's death as a manifestation of divine love, or on faith in God's love manifested in the cross. And (3) it shows that the individual Christian can say not only 'Christ offered himself for *us*' (1 : 4) but also 'Christ loved *me* and offered himself for me.' On this last point, St John Chrysostom has a good comment: [62]

> What are you doing, Paul, appropriating to yourself what is common to all, and treating as your own what was done for the whole world? — For he does not say 'who loved *us*' but 'who loved *me*'. Yet the evangelist says: 'God so loved *the world*' (Jn 3 : 16), and you yourself say: 'who did not spare his own Son, but gave him,' not for you, but 'for all' (Rom 8 : 32), and again 'in order that he might win for himself *a people* of his own' (Tit 2 : 14). What then is this thing that he says? Observing the abject state of human nature and Christ's ineffable care for us, and the evils of which he rid us, and the blessings which he freely gave, Paul is inflamed with love for him — that is why he speaks in this way. The prophets, too, often make the God of all their own, saying for example: 'O God, *my* God, I watch for you till dawn' (Ps 62 : 1). And further, Paul shows that it is right for each of us to be as grateful to Christ as if he had come for himself alone. For he would not have refused to fulfil this dispensation even for one man, for he loves each man with the same measure of love with which he loves the whole world.

Chrysostom is surely right when he says that in writing v. 20 St Paul's soul took flame with love and longing (*pothos*). When one is studying a text slowly, and carefully examining it phrase by phrase, it is easy to miss the emotional overtones, even when these are very strong. Chrysostom does well to remind us here. These are not cold dispassionate dogmatic statements, but vehement assertions of the apostle's profoundest convictions. His zeal for the true gospel is kindled to flame by the thought of the Judaizers' failure to recognize Christ's love: they have not recognized Christ's death for what it is — the outpouring of God's love for the salvation of mankind. That is why in the next verse Paul breaks out: 'Foolish men, who has bewitched you — who has made you forget the purpose of Christ's death?'

---

[62] Chrysostom, Gal, PG 61, 646-7.

The purpose of Christ's death was discussed above, in the comment on 1:4-5. Here are some further reflections on that important subject.

## Why did Christ suffer?

The nineteenth century Quest of the Historical Jesus was an attempt to discover Jesus' *intentions* at the beginning of his ministry and in the course of its development: What did he set out to do? Did he foresee his rejection and crucifixion from the beginning? In spite of the failure of the nineteenth century Quest, we cannot leave this question alone. It is impossible to follow Christ intelligently without having some idea of his intentions.

From the outset of his ministry, Jesus called his followers to penance: 'Repent, for the kingdom of heaven is at hand.' This implied that the law had failed to justify Israel; for if the law had succeeded there would have been no need of the call to repentance. The call for repentance was a call for works of penance, especially almsgiving. Jesus himself set an example by a life of homelessness and poverty, and he called upon others to take up their cross after him.

If, as seems likely, he regarded his own baptism as a symbolic death and resurrection (cf. Mk 10:38) and as a 'baptism into death' (cf. Rom 6:3), he foresaw from the outset that he would be rejected and killed. [63] The decision, therefore, to expose himself to the hatred of his enemies and to death at their hands was not a desperate remedy adopted when he found that his call to penance fell on deaf ears. He intended from the start to set a great example of suffering voluntarily accepted, in order to reinforce his call to repentance by his example — by leading the way. The cross was, therefore, foreseen as a demonstration of the seriousness of the call to penance and, by implication, of the failure of the law. Jesus says, as it were, 'The law has not made you just men; come, do penance by voluntary acceptance of suffering, and I will lead the way!' As St Peter says in his First Epistle (2:21): 'Christ suffered for you, and left you an example, that you should follow his footsteps.'

But while Christ intended his death to be an *example to others* to animate them to take up their cross and follow him, he also foresaw that his death would be *a sacrifice for others*. Since he himself was sinless, his death could be of profit only to others — 'a ransom for the

---

[63] For a different view see A. Vögtle, 'Exegetische Erwägungen über das Wissen und Selbstbewusstsein Jesu,' in *Gott in Welt* (Rahner-Festschrift), Freiburg, 1964, I, pp. 624-634.

many' (Mk 10:45). St Peter combines Christ's two intentions when he says: 'Christ suffered (1) for you — on your behalf — and (2) left you an example.' [64] St Paul places so much emphasis on the first of these intentions that the second almost disappears from view. Dogmatic theologians have done the same.

The danger of a pious overemphasis of the superabundance of Christ's merits is that there no longer seems to be any reason why we should follow Christ's example. If the satisfaction made by Christ was superabundant, and indeed infinite, what need is there for his followers to try to make satisfaction themselves? Is it not better humbly to receive the fruits of his sacrifice? Do we not call in question the sufficiency of Christ's sacrifice if we try to add something of our own? [65]

So we must ask, not only how Christ viewed his own suffering, but also how he viewed the relationship of his sufferings to those of his disciples. Although he intended to offer his life as a ransom for them, he did not intend to exempt them from carrying the cross behind him. He must, therefore, have regarded their sufferings and his own as being in some way complementary. But how so? St Paul gives us his explanation in the difficult passage, Col 1:24: 'I am helping to pay off in my person, on behalf of his body which is the Church, the amount by which we fall short of the sufferings of Christ.' St Paul appears to mean that in God's design the sufferings of the Head were intended to be completed by corresponding sufferings of the body. It was not God's will that the Head alone should suffer, but rather that the whole body should suffer in all its members, the suffering of every part being for the expiation of the whole ('on behalf of his body which is the Church').

---

[64] It is hard to say which was Christ's 'first intention', and which his 'second intention'. But from our point of view, Christ's sufferings are easier to understand, if we start by considering his intention to set an example.

[65] The first principle of Luther's theology is that it is impossible to exaggerate the glory of Christ. He says in his 1535 Commentary on Galatians, p. 66:

I recall that when my movement first began, Dr. Staupitz, a very worthy man and the Vicar of the Augustinian Order, said to me: 'It pleases me very much that this doctrine of ours gives glory and everything else solely to God and nothing at all to men; for it is as clear as day that it is impossible to ascribe too much glory, goodness, etc., to God.' So it was that he consoled me. And it is true that the doctrine of the Gospel takes away all glory, wisdom, righteousness, etc., from men and gives it solely to the Creator, who makes all things out of nothing. Furthermore, it is far safer to ascribe too much to God than to men.

One of the present writer's teachers, Fr K. Prümm, once remarked in this connection that Luther's doctrine sounds very pious and is therefore difficult to argue against. We must give all glory to God for what he has done for us in Christ, but we must not go to the extreme of holding that Christ's work was so perfect and complete that no work is expected of his disciples, or that the sufferings and labours even of St Paul are of no account.

This passage of Colossians shows a reason why Christ's sufferings should not be described as a substitute for the sufferings of others. They are not a substitute, because God did not ordain that they should be. He disposed that the Church should be saved as a body, each member making some expiation, not for itself alone, but for the whole, and in union with the Head.

Faith incorporates the individual into Christ's body, makes him a sharer in Christ's merits, and opens him to influences coming down from the Head. But it is then his duty to become conformed to the Head by bearing his share of the sufferings of the whole Christ. In a word, it is not God's plan that the Head should be crowned with thorns and the rest of the body go scot-free (cf. Acts 14:22). St Thomas' verse,

cuius una stilla salvum facere          One drop of His blood
totum mundum quit ab omni scelere,    could save the world from all sin,

requires the distinction: absolutely speaking, Yes; in this order of providence, No.

If we ask the further question, Why did God so dispose?, St Paul furnishes no answer. But it would be in agreement with the lines of his thought to say that God in his goodness willed that man's redemption should be effective through a covenant, hence not by a unilateral act of condonation, but by an alliance in which man should cooperate with God (cf. Phil 2:12). [66] God shows greater love by calling men to cooperate with him. 'So great is his goodness that he wills that his gifts should be merited by us' (*tanta est Dei bonitas, ut nostra velit esse merita quae sunt ipsius dona*). [67]

*The Fourth Subsection, 2:21—3:4*

# THE CRUCIAL QUESTION

A  *2:21* Did Christ suffer death for nothing?  B  *3:1* O foolish Galatians, who has bewitched you — you before whose eyes Jesus Christ was placarded, crucified?  *2* I ask you this one thing:  C  Was it from works of the law  D  that you received the Spirit,  C¹  or from hearing the faith?  B¹  *3* Are you so foolish? Having begun with the Spirit, will you now end with the flesh?  A¹  *4* Have you suffered (or, experienced) so much in vain?

---

[66]  Cf. Galot, *La Rédemption,* pp. 235-236 and 277-280.
[67]  From the *Indiculus* of Pope St Celestine, Denz. 141.

As Lightfoot observes, the thought arrived at in 2:21 provokes the indignant remonstrance in 3:1. [68] Can Christians be so foolish as to imagine that Christ died for nothing? Who has bewitched them? But there is also a close connection between 3:2-4, which speaks of the working of the Spirit in believers, and 2:20, which speaks of the activity of Christ working in the believer. Further, the structure of the third section (p. 174) shows that 3:1-4 forms a literary unit with what precedes. It is therefore incorrect to place a major break in the argument between 2:21 and 3:1. [69] St Paul's discourse is certainly incomplete without 3:1-4. After setting forth his dogmatic argument in 2:15-21, he must have appealed to the Jewish Christians to adopt his way of thinking. One has only to drop the word 'Galatians' from 3:1 to see that 3:1-4 is the continuation of St Paul's admonition to the Jewish Christians at Antioch, who were visitors from Jerusalem, for, first, the phrase 'before whose eyes Christ was placarded, crucified' is applicable in a special sense to them. They had seen the crucifixion with their own eyes. [70] And secondly, it was more appropriate to ask Jewish Christians whether they received the Holy Spirit by fulfilling the works of the law or by hearing and believing, for they *had* done the works of the law before their conversion. It seems, then, that 3:1-4 belongs to St Paul's Antioch discourse, and has been revised by him to serve as an appeal to the Gentile Galatians. He has inserted 'Galatians' in v. 1, and has added v. 3b, 'having begun with the Spirit, will you now end with the flesh?' The original ending used at Antioch was probably something like this:

A   Did then Christ suffer death for nothing? — I would have you tell me this one thing.   B   O foolish men, [71] who has bewitched you — you before whose eyes Jesus Christ was placarded, crucified?   C   Was it through works of the law   D   that you received the Spirit,   C¹   or was it through hearing the faith?   B¹   Are you so foolish? Having suffered yourselves at the hands of your fellow Jews, will you now fall away? [72]   A¹   Have all your sufferings been useless — or worse than useless?

---

[68]   Cf. Lightfoot, Gal, p. 133.
[69]   As is done, for example, in the JB and NEB.
[70]   Cf. Goulder, *Type and History in Acts*, p. 48; and 1 Jn 1:1.
[71]   St Jerome, PL 26, 372 AB, has an amusing passage in which he suggests that foolishness was the national characteristic of the Galatians. As the Cretans are liars, the Moors vain, the Dalmatians ferocious, the Phrygians timid, the Athenians clever, the Greeks fickle, and the Jews stiff-necked, so the Galatians were foolish. But cf. Lk 24:25.
[72]   The Greek may have been, e.g., *pathontes kai hymeis hypo tôn idiôn symphyletôn, nyn parapeseisthe?* Cf. 2 Thes 2:14. Presumably St Paul altered this part of the text because at the time of writing the Galatians had not suffered persecution.

The link between A and A¹ would be even stronger if St Paul had written, not *apethanen* ('suffered death') but *epathen* ('suffered'). The meaning would then be: 'Did Christ suffer for nothing? Did his sufferings fail to teach you anything?'

His sufferings ought to have taught the Jewish Christians that the law had not justified them, for they should have reasoned: 'The death of the Messiah and Son of God must have had some great purpose; it was not to expiate his own sins; therefore it was to expiate the sins of others. If he gave his life to the profit of no one, he died for nothing. But this is not possible. Therefore he died in order that others might receive forgiveness as a free gift.'

If 3:1-4 is a revision of the original ending, 2:15—3:4 is a literary unit consisting of the three overlapping subsections:

A    *2 : 15-17*  We Jewish Christians abandoned the law in order to seek justification through faith in Christ.

B    *2 : 17-21   The effect of this conversion from the law of Christ was not to make us sinners, but to give us life.*

A¹   *2 : 21—3 : 4*  An appeal to Jewish Christians: Do not be so foolish as to turn back from Christ to the law! Has not experience confirmed your initial belief that justification comes through faith?

Without the third of these passages, both the argument and the literary pattern would be incomplete. (2:14, in which Peter is accused of inconsistency, does not belong to the pattern.)

*What is the 'one question' which St Paul asks?*

In the canonical text, the one question is: 'Was it from works of the law that you received the Spirit, or was it from hearing the faith?' Thus the argument which should clinch the whole matter is a direct appeal to personal experience. At Antioch St Paul wished the Jewish Christians to recall how they first received the Holy Spirit, and now he puts the same question to the Galatians. Let them remember how this new Spirit began to seethe and ferment within them, or in other words, let them recall how Christ began to live in them. Was it through fulfilling the requirements of the Mosaic law? Both the Jews from Jerusalem and the Gentiles of Galatia must reply that it was not. It was simply through believing in the gospel of Christ's cross.

However, the sentence, 'This one thing I would learn from you,' may be out of place. If it is transferred to follow 2:21, as in the above reconstruction, the link between A and A¹ is improved — both now contain the idea of learning by experience, or learning by suffering, a favourite conjunction of concepts in Greek, because the two verbs rhyme: *pathein* is 'to suffer' and *mathein* is 'to learn'. And as there is nothing in B¹ corresponding to 'This one thing I would learn from you,' the link between B and B¹ is not impaired by the transfer.

The result of the transfer is that the one crucial question is: 'Did Christ die for nothing?' — and the answer is 'Certainly not, he died in order that we might receive the Holy Spirit.' This shows that the dislocation, if there has been one, is not of great importance, for the two questions converge on the same point: 'Did Christ die for nothing, or to give the Holy Spirit to those who believe in him?'

*'Who has* bewitched *you?' — Why does St Paul use this strange word?*

The Greek verb represented by 'bewitched' is *baskainô*. It is probably a loan-word borrowed by the Greeks from the Thracians. The Romans in turn borrowed it from the Greeks, and gave it the form *fascinare* ('to fascinate' or 'bewitch'). [73]

Greek authors use the word in several cognate senses: to envy, to nurse a grudge against someone, to malign him, to bewitch him by means of spells or by casting the evil eye upon him. [74] It was popularly believed in antiquity that the look emitted by the evil eye of a jealous person could harm the person looked at. St John Chrysostom in his commentary warns his hearers not to conclude from this verse, or from Christ's saying in Mt 6:23, that 'the look of an evil eye harms those who see it.' [75]

St Jerome adds the interesting information that children too young to walk steadily were believed to be most vulnerable to the evil eye. [76] He quotes as evidence a line from Virgil's third *Eclogue*: 'Nescio quis teneros oculus mihi fascinat agnos' ('I know not whose eye is be-witching my tender lambs').

St Paul is, therefore, implying that the Galatians, instead of keep-ing their eyes fastened on the cross so as to receive again and again its salutary influence, have deflected their eyes and allowed themselves to fall under the evil influence of men who envied their good fortune. He implies too that they are vulnerable because they are still children

---

[73] Cf. J. H. Moulton and G. Milligan, *The Vocabulary of the Greek Testament Illustrated from the Papyri and other Non-Literary Sources*, London, 1930, s.v.
[74] Cf. H. G. Liddell and R. Scott, *A Greek-English Lexicon*, Oxford, 1940, for references.
[75] Cf. Chrysostom, PG, 61, 648 C.
[76] Cf. Jerome, PL, 26, 373 A. Thus he connects 3:1 with 2:14.

J

in the faith. If they had been grown-ups, walking steadily along the path of the true faith, they would not have succumbed to this fascination. The question was applicable to the Jewish Christians of Antioch, because they too were tottering like tiny tots (cf. 2:14).

St Paul is of course speaking playfully here. He does not mean that a Christian, to preserve his faith, must keep looking at a painted or carved representation of Christ on the Cross, and he does not mean that the Judaizers are doing their damage by nasty looks. To show that the 'looking' is metaphorical, he quickly substitutes a reference to 'hearing' in v. 3: 'Was it from works of the law you received the Spirit, or from hearing the faith?' St Jerome took this too literally and asked how, then, the deaf could be saved. [77] But the hearing too is metaphorical. St Paul is speaking of seeing with the eyes of faith and hearing with the ears of faith.

In the Epistle, where the question is addressed to the Galatians, the most obvious answer is: 'The Judaizers have bewitched you,' and the implication is that their motive is jealousy (cf. 4:17). It pains them to see that these Gentiles, who have not borne the burden of the law through the heat of the day, are now receiving the Holy Spirit as a free gift. Their jealousy implies that they imagine they themselves have established a right to it by their observance of the law.

But if the question was addressed to the Jews at Antioch, the answer might be: 'It is the devil who has bewitched you. Just as he envied the felicity of Adam and Eve at the beginning and set himself to undermine their faith in God (cf. Wis 2:24), so through envy of your felicity, he is trying to undermine your faith in Christ.'

However, the structure of the third section (see p. 174) shows that at Antioch it was Peter the self-condemned who had cast his spell upon the Jewish Christians and distracted them from Christ crucified. Perhaps, therefore, the answer to be supplied by the Galatians too is: 'Peter!' He has bewitched them without even visiting them, simply through the Judaizers' report of his conduct.

## How did St Paul picture 'Christ crucified'?

In one sense, Christ was *estaurômenos*, 'crucified', throughout the three hours when he hung on the cross. In another sense, he is still *estaurômenos* — he is one who has died out of this world by crucifixion.

---

[77]  Cf. Jerome, PL 26, 374 C.

It is not clear which sense St Paul has in mind when he says that Christ crucified was placarded before the eyes of the Galatians. His words *may* mean that in his preaching in Galatia he painted vivid verbal pictures of Christ 'stripped naked, transfixed, nailed to the cross, spat upon, reviled, given vinegar to drink, mocked by thieves, pierced by the lance,' as Chrysostom thought. [78] But there is nothing of this kind in St Paul's letters, which are doubtless a fair reflection of his preaching. Nor does St Paul mean that images of Christ on the cross were painted up in the Galatians' houses or shrines. This was never done until after the Emperor Constantine had prohibited execution by crucifixion.

Probably, therefore, St Paul intended *estaurômenos* to be taken by the Galatians in the second of the two senses distinguished above. He set before their eyes Christ who is now Lord of the world to come because he overthrew the thrones and dominations by his death on the cross (cf. 1 : 4-5; Phil 2 : 6-10). St John provides an imaginative picture embodying almost the same conception when he sees in heavenly vision 'a Lamb standing as it had been slain', that is, slaughtered yet standing on its feet again, surrounded by angelic beings who cry: 'Thou wast slain and hast purchased unto God with thy blood men of every kindred and tongue and people and nation, and made them unto our God a kingdom and priests, and they shall reign on the earth' (Apoc 5 : 6-9). However, there is a shift of emphasis here. When St Paul speaks of *Christos estaurômenos,* though he thinks of both suffering and glory, the emphasis is certainly on Christ's suffering. He means that the cross itself, in the mental picture evoked by the word *estaurômenos,* is a revelation of the glory of God. Once the Galatians had recognized that on the cross the Son of God himself was suffering 'for me' (2 : 20), their eyes should have been drawn to this great revelation of the lovingkindness of God like a moth to a flame. They should be impervious to any other fascination. For the believer, the cross is a far greater manifestation of God than any sunset; the very thought of it arouses awe, self-abasement, exultation and wonder. The centurion on Calvary saw the glory, and gave glory to God (cf. Mk 15 : 39). From that moment the cross has been the object of Christian worship — the supreme revelation of God's hatred of sin and of his merciful concern to save sinners (cf. Rom 1 : 17).

Therefore, when St Paul says: 'I am crucified with Christ crucified' (6 : 14), he means: 'Through incorporation into Christ, and imitation of Christ, I have passed out of this evil world, and out of the realm of the demonic powers; already the powers of the world to come are

---

[78]   Chrysostom, PG 61, 649 A.

at work in me through faith. I stand at the horizon of the two worlds
and share in Christ's *deadness* to this world and *risenness* to the world
to come; and my glory, if there is any in my life, is to suffer in the
service of others.'

*Why did St Paul add v. 3b?*

In the original Antioch Discourse, according to the reconstruction
given above, the folly of the Jewish Christians consisted in their refusal
to learn the lesson of the sufferings and other spiritual experiences
which God had granted them: *pathos* had failed to produce *mathos*,
a sure sign of stupidity and dullness.

When revising the discourse for the benefit of the Galatians, St
Paul puts in v. 3b: 'Having begun with the Spirit, will you now end
with the flesh?' Not only have they failed to learn the lesson of their
spiritual experiences but they now hope for some greater gift as a
result of a surgical operation on their private parts. How foolish can
they get? [79]

In the structure of the third section (see p. 174), this passage
balances 2: 11-12 where St Paul describes how at Antioch Peter began
well and ended badly. [80] St Paul was well aware that the main difficulty in the life of faith is perseverance. To begin to believe is not
too difficult; but when the first charismatic enthusiasm has worn off
and the long haul begins, the temptation is to let faith slip away and
return to a religion of exterior ritual. While St Paul was present in a
church, he could sustain its faith by his preaching and example, but
he feared what could happen in his absence. Hence his exhortation to
the Philippians:

> My dear friends, who have always been obedient, let it not seem that
> your obedience depends on my presence; but now much more in my
> absence, continue in fear and trembling the work of your salvation; for
> God is at work in you, enabling you both to will and to accomplish his
> loving purpose.

This passage draws a valuable corollary from Gal 2: 20. The presence
of Christ living in the Gentile believer is a reason for holding the
Gentile believer in reverence and treating him with love and respect.
Phil 2: 12-13 adds that the presence of Christ living in oneself is a

---

[79] St Thomas, Gal, 403 B, aptly quotes Jn 6:64: 'It is the Spirit that gives life;
the flesh is of no avail,' and refers to the vision of Nabuchadnezzar in Dan 2,
where the golden-headed image has feet of clay.
[80] St Augustine, PL 35, 2118 A, links 3:3 with 1:7 where the Judaizers are said
to be 'turning the gospel upside down.'

reason for reverence towards oneself: each one must work out his salvation in fear and trembling because God is at work within him, and this reverence will ensure his perseverance.

If the supernatural presence and assistance of the Holy Spirit is a motive for self-reverence, so too is the natural presence of God who concurs in all our actions. This was recognised by the Stoics. Marcus Aurelius says: [81]

> It is the characteristic of the good man to delight in and to welcome what befalls him and what is spun for him by destiny; and not to sully the divine 'genius' that is enthroned in his bosom, nor yet to perplex it with a multitude of impressions, but to maintain it to the end in a gracious serenity, in orderly obedience to God, uttering no word that is not true and doing no deed that is not just.

It seems, then, that the three dangers to perseverance are: neglect of the divine presence within oneself; lack of a preacher to sustain the true faith; and the presence of misguided teachers who propagate the wrong kind of religion (cf. 3 : 1; 4 : 17). St Paul is keenly aware that a Christian is not 'an encapsulated unit, hermetically sealed against outside influences' but is constantly subject to divine and human influences to which he must respond with discrimination. It has been correctly observed that 'the error of Pelagius lay partly in this, that he seems to have taken it for granted that each human being is more independent and less "open" than is actually the case.' [82]

## What reply could the Judaizers make?

The position of the Judaizers was perhaps not quite as absurd as St Paul tries to make out. They could reply: 'You may think that it is absurd that God should want his sons circumcised, but this is a revealed religion. If it is not absurd for a man like Cornelius, who has already received the Holy Spirit, to be baptized with water, why should it be absurd for him to undergo circumcision? Our view is that faith and baptism are the beginning of the Christian life, but what is begun in baptism must be completed by fulfilment of God's positive laws, including the law of circumcision. [83] In order to be justified at the Judgment, a man must not only believe and be baptized; he must also fulfil the law. Faith without works is useless.'

---

[81] Marcus Aurelius, *Meditations*, III, 16.
[82] Cf. Whiteley, *The Theology of St Paul*, pp. 92-93.
[83] St Paul's terminology ('initiation' and 'completion') in 3 : 3 may be borrowed from his adversaries, as Schlier suggests, Gal, p. 83; cf. Jas 2 : 22 (on which see above, pp. 208-210).

When heat is generated in theological debate, it is often a sign that good men are talking at cross-purposes and using the same words in different senses. Looking *backwards* to his conversion, a Christian can agree with St Paul that he was justified by faith in Christ and not by any works of his own; but looking *forward* to the Judgment, he can agree with the Judaizers that if he is to be justified then, it will be through 'works' which he has been enabled to do through the gift of the Spirit. For God will judge every man according to his works (cf. Rom 2:6).

The real question at issue was: Which 'works' must Gentile Christians do? Must they fulfil the whole of the law (including its demand for circumcision)? There were three possible answers: (1) The Judaizers (probably) said: 'Yes, they must fulfil the whole of the law.' (2) St Paul said: 'No, the law of Moses does not bind them at all; but they are subject to the law of Christ.' (3) St Peter probably said: 'When Christ gave me the power of binding and loosing (cf. Mt 16:19), he left it to me to determine which precepts of the Mosaic law the Gentiles should obey and which they should not, and I declare them released from circumcision and most of the food laws. [84] The decalogue of course still holds.' The second and third answers were different ways of arriving at the same practical conclusion. But the Petrine way had the great advantage of leaving no excuse for Antinomianism.

## *Does v. 4 contain a threat?*

In v. 4 St Paul has in mind the Greek saying *pathei mathos*: 'One learns by suffering (or, by experience).' If experience fails to teach, it has been wasted. So St Paul asks the Galatians in v. 4a: 'Have all your spiritual experiences been wasted (for they do not seem to have taught you anything)?' 'Has your experience of the Holy Spirit been useless?' Then in v. 4b he adds: 'if indeed useless.' [85] So the whole verse can be translated: 'Has your experience of the Spirit been useless — or even worse than useless?' St Paul means that if a man receives the gifts of the Holy Spirit and fails to profit by them, his last state is worse than his first; for one who fails to live according to the Spirit will live according to the flesh, and who-

---

[84]  Acts 15:10 shows that Peter considered the Council to have power to determine what yoke should be laid on Gentile believers, i.e., how much of the positive law of Judaism. See further below, pp. 421-422.

[85]  Chrysostom, PG 61, 650 B, takes this clause as an invitation to repentance: 'Have you suffered so much in vain—if it is really possible that you have suffered in vain.' But this does not do justice to the intensive *kai*. St Thomas, Gal, 403 C, agrees with Chrysostom, and adds: 'This shows that *opera mortificata reviviscunt.*'

ever does the works of the flesh excludes himself from the kingdom (cf. 5 : 11). The same warning is given, in fuller form, in Heb 6 : 4-6 :

> It is impossible to lead back to repentance men who have once been en-lightened, who have tasted the heavenly gift, who have shared in the Holy Spirit, who have had experience of the goodness of God's word and of the powers of the world to come, and after all this have fallen away. It is impossible, I say, to lead them back to repentance; for they are again rejecting God's Son, as at his crucifixion, and making a mockery of him.

## *What was the outcome of the Antioch incident?*

This is a much more important question than the hoary old North v. South Galatians controversy. Lightfoot thinks that St Peter im-mediately repented. He points out how this scene resembles Peter's denial of Christ during the Passion — the same impulsive courage is followed by the same shrinking timidity. Then he adds: [86]

> And though St Paul's narrative stops short of the last scene of the drama, it would not be rash to conclude that it ended as the other had ended, that the revulsion of feeling was as sudden and complete, and that again he went out and wept bitterly, *having denied his Lord in the person of these Gentile converts.*

These closing words are exactly to the point, for St Paul's argument has shown that Christ is living in the Gentile converts, and therefore to turn away from them is to turn away from Christ.

Nevertheless, it seems more probable that on this occasion St Peter did not repent, for the following reasons.

(1) The whole of the autobiographical part of the Epistle builds up towards the Antioch incident. The Epistle itself is a part of the aftermath of the incident. It is designed to vindicate Paul's conduct and to remove the scandal caused in Galatia by anti-pauline versions of what happened. If the incident had ended with Peter shedding tears of repentance, the Epistle would probably never have been written, for the Judaizers could have made no use of the incident. On the other hand, if Peter remained unconvinced, if he felt that the construction which Paul was putting on his conduct was unwarrantable, if he was offended by the manner of Paul's protest, and if he went away without conceding victory to Paul, it is easy to understand how the propaganda of the Judaizers could continue, [87] and why Paul found it necessary to write the Epistle in self-defence.

---

[86]  Lightfoot, Gal, p. 129, my italics. R. Bring, Gal, p. 82, agrees: 'the text implies that Peter accepted Paul's rebuke.'

[87]  The position of the anathema in the first main division of the Epistle implies that the Judaizers were still appealing to the authority and example of Peter.

(2) If Peter gave way, St Paul would surely have said so. This would have been another powerful argument in favour of the correctness of his doctrine and a vindication of his conduct. — This, of course, is only an argument from silence. [88] One who shares the view of Lightfoot might reply that St Paul may have omitted the end of the story out of deference to Peter. But St Paul does not show much deference to Peter in this Epistle (cf. 2:11-13); and it would not have reflected discredit on Peter to say that he admitted having been in the wrong.

(3) If the incident occurred in A.D. 54 (see above, pp. 178-80), St Paul never returned to Antioch after the incident. The reason may be that the church of Antioch as a whole did not approve of his public attack on Peter's conduct. [89]

It seems, then, that in spite of St Paul's arguments, St Peter did not give way. Presumably it was not pride or stubbornness that prevented him from yielding. It is not difficult to imagine how he could have replied — though the reply is not one which he would have wished to make in public: 'My dear brother Paul,' he could say, 'I have no desire to compel the Gentiles to judaize; but equally I do not wish to compel these Jews to hellenize. If I press them too hard, they will abandon the faith. I do not disown the Gentile Christians as unclean; I recognize, as you say, that Christ lives in them. But I also accept the fact that we have here two social groups with distinct cultural traditions, and for the present at least, they are not ready for fusion and integration.' Perhaps Peter did say something like this to Paul in private and then went away from Antioch, leaving behind an atmosphere of uncertainty. This would explain Paul's obvious dissatisfaction over the conduct of Peter.

If Peter left Antioch at once, the Judaizers may have concluded that he was still uncertain what to do in the whole matter, and that the concessions granted by him at the Council of Jerusalem had been only an expression of his uncertainty. They may have felt even more strongly than Paul that Peter had hardly lived up to the title of 'pillar'. Neither apostle was entirely blameless in this unfortunate incident.

[88] It is accepted and used by E. Haenchen, *Die Apostelgeschichte*, Göttingen, 1957, p. 422, and by Schmithals, *Paul and James*, p. 77.
[89] An obscure passage in the *Didache* (11:11) may contain a condemnation of St Paul's conduct at Antioch: 'Every prophet who is approved and true, and acts as he does for the universal mystery of the Church, but does not teach others to act as he does, shall not be judged by you; his judgment is with God.' The Didachist probably means that if a Jewish apostle, working for the conversion of the Gentiles, keeps the whole of the Jewish law himself, but does not require his Gentile converts to do the same, no one is to find fault with him.

# ARGUMENTATIVE SECTIONS OF THE EPISTLE

The second main division of the Epistle continues and develops the argument begun in 2:14-21.

It was shown above that St Paul's Antioch Discourse did not end at 2:21, but continued at least as far as 3:4. But even 3:4 does not make a fully satisfactory ending to the Discourse. One still expects a direct appeal to the Jewish brethren to stop compelling the Gentiles to judaize and to be faithful to the pauline gospel. Vv. 5-7 take a step in this direction, but do not arrive at the point of drawing the practical conclusion. Thus the question arises whether the Antioch Discourse does not run on much further. The Scriptural arguments proposed in 3:5—4:10, which assume familiarity not only with the text of the Old Testament but also with the midrashic traditions based on it, would be much more intelligible to Jewish Christians from Jerusalem than to Gentile converts in Galatia; and the first person pronouns 'we' and 'us' in 3:13, 3:24 and 4:4 are more easily intelligible if their meaning is 'we Jews' and 'us Jews'. [1] Probably, then, the Discourse at Antioch runs on at least as far as 4:10.

The next paragraph, 4:11—4:20, cannot be part of the Discourse, since it contains reminiscences of St Paul's work in Galatia, [2] not at Antioch. But 4:10 cannot be the end of the Antioch Discourse. It is far too abrupt. Moreover, the allegory of Sarah and Agar, 4:21-31, is required to complete the Scriptural argument begun at 3:5. Far from being an afterthought, the allegory is the climax of St Paul's discussion of the question, Who are the heirs of Abraham?, and contains, in allegorical language, the practical conclusion towards which the whole Discourse has been driving: 'Send away the slave-woman and her children!' (i.e., Send away the Judaizers).

4:30 is a possible end, but probably the Discourse continued still further. 5:7-10 contains just the kind of hortatory conclusion which the whole Discourse requires, and, as will be shown below, the whole section 4:31—5:13 contains many links with the beginning of the Discourse — in other words it rounds off the symmetry, in St Paul's manner.

However, just as St Paul revised 3:1-4 when incorporating the Discourse into the Epistle, so too he has revised this closing section 4:31—5:13. [3] It is unlikely that the Discourse ended with 5:13 —

---

[1]  Cf. St Thomas, Gal, 414 D.
[2]  See above, pp. 5-6 and 15-16.
[3]  For the text of this passage, see below, p. 414.

Once a covenant has been ratified — even a human covenant — no one sets it aside or adds conditions to it. *16* Now the promises were made to Abraham 'and to his Issue'.   **F**   It does not say 'and to his issues', in the plural, but uses the singular 'and to his Issue' — and this is Christ. **G**   *17* What I mean is this: when the covenant had been ratified by God,   **H**   the law, made four hundred and thirty years later, does not invalidate it,   **I**   so as to render the promise void. **J**   *18* For if from the law   **K**   comes the inheritance,   **L**   it is no longer from the promise. **M**   But to Abraham   **L¹**   it was by way of promise   **K¹**   that God made the gift.   **J¹**   *19* What then was the purpose of the law?   **I¹**   It was added on account of sins,   **H¹**   until the Issue should come, to whom the promise had been made.   **G¹**   It was drawn up by angels by the hand of a mediator.   **F¹**   *20* Now a mediator does not mediate between one party, and God is one.   **E¹**   *21* Is then the law opposed to the promises? Heaven forbid!   **D¹**   For if a law had been given with power to give life, truly justice would be from the law.   **C¹**   *22* But the Scripture has delivered up all to sin, in order that the promised blessing may be given to all through faith in Jesus Christ.   **B¹**   *23* But before the coming of faith we were locked up in custody until the faith should be revealed. *24* So the law was our pedagogue to Christ, that we might be justified through faith. *25* Now that faith has come, we are no longer under a pedagogue.   **A¹**   *26* For you are all God's sons through faith in Jesus Christ.   *27* For when you were all baptized in Christ, you put on Christ. *28* There is no longer Jew or Greek, there is no longer slave or free, there is no longer male and female; for you are all one, in Christ Jesus.   *29* But if you belong to Christ, then you are the Issue of Abraham, and heirs according to the promise.

*The First Subsection, 3:5-14*

## COVENANT AND FAITH

As usual, the section divides into two symmetrical subsections. The first runs from 3:5 to 3:14, and centres upon St Paul's favourite text, Hab 2:4 (cf. Rom 1:17). The analysis is as follows:

A   The Spirit is given to those who are sons of Abraham through faith (Gen 15:6 quoted), 3:5-7.
B   Scripture promises that the blessing of Abraham will be extended to the Gentiles (Gen 18:18 quoted), 3:8-9.
C   Those who are under the law are under a curse; for it is written: 'Cursed is every man...' (Deut 27:26), 3:10.
D   By the law no one is justified before God, 3:11a.
E   *For 'the just man will live by faith'* (Hab 2:4), 3:11b,

**D¹**   and the law is not a matter of faith but of works (Lev 18 : 5 quoted),
3 : 12.
**C¹**   Christ has delivered us from the curse of the law; for it is written:
'Cursed is every man...' (Deut 21 : 23), 3 : 13.
**B¹**   Thus the blessing of Abraham is extended to the Gentiles, 3 : 14a.
**A¹**   And we receive the promised gift of the Spirit through faith, 3 : 14b.

After raising the crucial question of the meaning of Christ's death
and appealing to the experience of his hearers in 3 : 1-5, St Paul
passes quickly into this passage which contains no less than six quotations from the Old Testament. These verses should not be regarded
as an academic demonstration from Scripture that justification is by
faith. St Paul is reassuring his hearers and readers that they are all,
by reason of their faith, sons of Abraham and sharers in the blessings
promised to Abraham. Vv. 6-9 contain two arguments, the conclusions of which are: first, 'The men of faith — *these* are the sons of
Abraham' (v. 7), and secondly, 'It is the men of faith who are blessed
along with faithful Abraham' (v. 9). These are polemic utterances,
which imply that the Judaizers held a different view. At Antioch,
if they were not openly saying, at least their conduct was implying,
that the Gentile Christians are not yet sons of Abraham; if they wish
to be sons of Abraham, they must be circumcised and follow the
law; only those who are circumcised and follow the law can share in
the blessings promised to Abraham.

St Paul replies: 'Christians are sons of Abraham, and heirs of
the promises made to him, by reason of their *faith*. No one receives
the blessings promised to Abraham through obeying the law; the law
brings not a blessing but a curse.'

Thus the question at issue is: *Who are the heirs of Abraham?*
St Paul was not the first to write on this subject. Philo discusses it
in his treatise, *Who are the heirs of things divine?* But the question
was raised first of all by Abraham himself, in Gen 15 : 2-3.

*What arguments did the Judaizers use?*

As was pointed out in the Introduction (p. 27), the Judaizers in
Galatia probably argued thus: 'In Christ God has fulfilled his great
promises to Israel. [5] Now the greatest of the promises were made to
our father Abraham and to his Issue. But God formally declared to
Abraham that no man would be recognised as his issue unless cir-

---

[5]   With this premise St Paul agreed; cf. 2 Cor 1 : 20.

cumcised. Gen 17:9-11 could not be more explicit: "If any male have not the flesh of his foreskin circumcised, that person shall be cut off from his people; he has broken my covenant." From this text it follows that if any Gentile wishes to become a party to the Abraham-covenant, he must be circumcised; and having become a party to it, he must keep the law of the covenant as defined and specified by Moses and the Jewish tradition.'

Thus the Judaizers had a powerful argument from Scripture taken in the literal sense, and they could confirm it by pointing out that Jesus himself was circumcised, that he said he had not come to abolish the law (cf. Mt 5:17), and that a Christian teacher should bring forth both old things and new (cf. Mt 13:52). This was probably the main argument used by the Judaizers. St Paul, therefore, as soon as he has set forth his own main argument, attacks the main argument of his opponents.

### How does St Paul reply?

In 3:5-14, St Paul does not deal directly with the literal sense of Gen 17:9-11; he gives a hint of how he circumvents this text in 6:15-17 (see p. 494), and develops the point in Col 2:11, where he says that in baptism the Colossians have received 'a spiritual circumcision, not a surgical operation for the removal of bodily flesh, but Christ's circumcision — you have been buried with him in baptism.' In other words, baptism is the reality of which circumcision is but a symbol. He who has the reality no longer needs the symbol. [6] It is surprising that St Paul does not develop this argument in Galatians. Perhaps he saw that it would open him to a retort: if the man who has the spiritual reality no longer needs the material symbol, he whose heart has been cleansed by faith has no need of baptism.

Instead, St Paul argues from other texts (a) that since Abraham himself was justified, not by circumcision and observance of the law, but by faith, the same will be true of the sons of Abraham: they will be justified by faith; (b) that when Abraham was promised that 'all the Gentiles' would be blessed in him, the promise was so worded as to imply that the Gentiles would still be Gentiles when they received the blessing; (c) that the Gentiles who are blessed in Abraham will therefore be Gentiles who have become his sons through faith —

---

[6]    Philo too recognised circumcision as a symbol, but maintained that the symbol should not be rejected by those who claim to have the reality symbolized. Cf. *The Migration of Abraham*, 89-92 (Loeb IV), quoted below on 6:15-17, p. 492.

v. 9; (d) that the law is not a means to the attainment of the blessings promised to Abraham, for it brings upon its subjects not a blessing but a curse; and (e) that Christ's death, by removing the curse of the law, has brought about the fulfilment of the great promises made to Abraham, for Jew and Gentile alike.

In this passage, it begins to become manifest that the clash between St Paul and the Judaizers was a clash between two different interpretations of the Old Testament. St Paul would not have conceded that it was a clash between two *Christian* interpretations of the Old Testament. He regarded the interpretation proposed by his adversaries as depriving the death of Christ of all meaning (cf. 2 : 21), and as overturning the gospel (cf. 1 : 7). His own interpretation shows that while the law did not bring about the fulfilment of the promises made to Abraham, the death of Christ did (cf. 3 : 13-14; Rom 8 : 3).

## How should 3:5-6 be punctuated?

V. 6 can be read as a subordinate clause dependent on the preceding sentence:

He then who bestowed the Spirit upon you and worked wonders in you — was it through works of the law? or was it through hearing and believing, just as 'Abraham believed God and it was reckoned to him as justice'?

Alternatively, v. 6 can be separated off as an independent sentence:

5 He then who bestowed the Spirit upon you and worked wonders in you — was it through doing the law, or was it through hearing the faith? 6 It was the same with Abraham: 'He believed God, and it was reckoned to him as justice.' 7 Recognize, then, that those who rely on faith — these are the sons of Abraham.

The second alternative is better, because at the end of v. 5 St Paul completes his own argument, and at the beginning of v. 6 he begins to attack the argument of his adversaries. Moreover, the conclusion drawn in v. 7 follows from v. 6 alone, rather than from vv. 5-6 together.

## How was Abraham justified?

St Paul starts from the sentence in which the Scripture describes the justification of Abraham. God said to him (Gen 15 : 5-6):

'Look towards heaven, and number the stars, if you are able to number them.' Then he said to him: 'So shall your descendants be.' And he believed the Lord; and it was reckoned to him as righteousness (or, justice).

St Paul develops his position more fully in the parallel passage in Rom 4:9-12. Abraham, he argues, at the time when God spoke to him, was a Gentile, the uncircumcised son of heathen parents; God made a promise to him, and *he believed God's word* — he put his faith in the fidelity of God. That is all he did, and straightaway he was reckoned a just man. He was justified by the act of faith which he made when he accepted God's word as faithful and true. He was justified by faith and not by works.

Clearly St Paul is here talking about the *first* justification of Abraham, that is, about how Abraham came to stand in God's grace. He does no violence to the text of Genesis, because Gen 15:5-6 is likewise talking about Abraham's first justification. As interpreted by St Paul, this text means that the first demand which God made of Abraham was for an act of faith. Abraham obeyed and was thereupon reckoned a just man: he had done what God had demanded of him so far. He had set his feet on the way of obedience, and so long as he remained on this way, he would remain a just man. Circumcision was not a part of the process by which he became a just man. He was first justified, then received circumcision as a covenant-sign, or 'as a seal upon the justice which he had through faith' (Rom 4:11).

It is interesting to consider how the Judaizers could have replied to this argument. First, they may have argued that according to Gen 17:9-11 circumcision was more than a sign of the covenant; the essential stipulation of the covenant was that every descendant of Abraham should wear the sign of the covenant: 'This *is* my covenant which you shall keep... every male among you shall be circumcised.'

Secondly, they may have argued, as St James does in his Epistle (2:21-24), that Gen 15:6, 'Abraham believed God,' refers to belief shown in action, particularly in the sacrifice of Isaac. James interprets 15:6 in the light of a later passage, 22:16-17, 'By myself I have sworn, says the Lord, because you have done this, and have not withheld your son, your only son, I will indeed bless you, and I will multiply your descendants as the stars of heaven.' The Judaizers may have reasoned that the sacrifice demanded of Abraham was not an offering for the expiation of past sins; it was 'a test to which God put his faithful servant before confirming the promises already made to him.' [7]

---

[7]    Dubarle, *Original Sin*, p. 214.

But thirdly, it was also open to the Judaizers to reply like this: 'Paul is concentrating too much on the very beginnings of justification. It is true that Abraham was first justified by his faith, as Gen 15 : 6 says; but he would not have remained a just man if he had not performed the works which God required of him — and one of the works which God required of him was that he should circumcise himself and his son and all the males in his household — which he did (Gen 17 : 22-27). So too the Gentiles have now been justified by faith, but that is not the end of the matter. God now requires of them certain works — they must be circumcised and must do the 'works of the law' which God has laid down for the sons of Abraham. Our position is not as foolish as St Paul makes out. He says it is folly to begin with the Spirit and end with the flesh. But is not that just what happened in the case of Abraham? He was first justified by faith and then told to circumcise his flesh. [8] St Paul might well reflect on his own observation that the folly of God is wiser than man!'

It is difficult to avoid the conclusion that St Paul was trying to establish *a priori* a conclusion which could in fact only be established by an exercise of the power of binding-and-loosing: that the divine positive law of circumcision is not binding on Gentile converts. [8a]

### How does v. 7 follow from what precedes?

From Gen 15 : 6, 'he believed God, and it was reckoned to him as justice,' St Paul leaps at once to the conclusion that 'those who are justified by faith (or, who rely on faith for their justification) are the sons of Abraham.' The hidden premises, which he takes for granted, as points equally presupposed by his adversaries, are two. The first is that there is a connection between imitation (or assimilation) and sonship, so that one who imitates Abraham (or is unconsciously assimilated to him) becomes a son of Abraham. — Christ himself makes this supposition in the Sermon on the Mount, when he says: 'Love your enemies and pray for your persecutors; then you will be sons of your heavenly Father; for he makes his sun rise on good and bad alike' (Mt 5 : 44-45), and in Jn 8 : 44, where he says to the Jews: 'You are of your father the devil' — meaning that the devil was a murderer from the beginning, and the Jews are imitating him by plotting against Christ. The second presupposition is that 'sons of

---

[8]  St Augustine, PL 35, 2118 C, remarks that circumcision was given to Abraham as a *signaculum fidei*—a covenant sign, to remind him to keep faith (cf. Rom 4 : 11). The Judaizers could argue that Christians still need such a reminder.

[8a]  Cf. p. 232 above.

Abraham' in the religious sense are those who resemble Abraham in respect of that which constituted him a just man. St Paul's argument in vv. 6-7 is, then, that it was faith, not circumcision and the law, which first made Abraham a just man and thereafter was the basis of his familiarity with God; and therefore Gentiles who are justified by faith without circumcision or the law are, in the religious sense, 'sons of Abraham'.

Once again, it was easy enough for the Judaizers to reply: 'You are concentrating too much, brother Paul, on the first moment of justification. [9] If the question had been asked later in Abraham's life, "Why is Abraham justified before God?", the answer would be: "Because he has obeyed God in all things: in addition to the obedience of his initial act of faith, he has obeyed the command to circumcise himself, and he has obeyed the command to sacrifice Isaac." In the same way, what God requires of the Gentile convert is not only the obedience of faith — that is only the beginning — he also requires certain works: the man must submit to baptism, he must submit to circumcision, and he must obey the law of Moses. If he stops short at the act of faith, he ceases to be a son of Abraham, because Abraham did not stop short.' We have no reason to suppose that the Judaizers were proposing a theory about first justification. According to Acts 15:1, they taught that circumcision and observance of the law were necessary for 'salvation'. They could reasonably claim that St Paul does not refute their position by showing that the very first step towards salvation is the act of faith. Their theology was not concerned solely with the very first step, but with the whole process of salvation. They could concede all that St Paul says about first justification and still maintain that the works of the law are necessary for final salvation.

*What is the literal sense of Gen 15:6?*

The Hebrew of Gen 15:6 contains three ambiguities. 'He believed' may refer to Abraham's initial act of faith or to his abiding and per-

---

[9] Luther goes even further. In his 1535 commentary, p. 247, he says: 'It was certainly an outstanding ground for boasting that Abraham accepted circumcision when God commanded it, and that he was provided with brilliant virtues, and that in everything he was obedient to God. Thus it is a laudable and happy thing to imitate the example of Christ in his deeds, to love one's neighbours, to do good to those who deserve evil, to pray for one's enemies, and to bear with patience the ingratitude of those who requite good with evil. *But none of this contributes to righteousness in the sight of God*' (my italics). Reply: None of this contributes to first justification, *concedo;* to final justification, *nego.* Luther

severing state of faith. 'Justice' (*sedaqah*) may mean 'a just act' or the quality of justice. And 'it was reckoned to him' may or may not imply a fiction, or a reference to the ledger of the recording angel.

Probably the author of the passage wished to answer the question how Abraham, who had not known the law or worshipped the true God, came to be a just man. His answer is that God revealed himself to Abraham, and Abraham put his faith in him, and on the strength of this faith God reckoned him a just man (i.e. forgave his past sins and treated him for the future as a just man). Abraham's initial act of faith was a just act, but the author is not thinking exclusively of that. He is thinking of how Abraham came to enjoy the privileged position of God's friend. He sees that it was freely conferred on him through God's initiative. All Abraham was required to do was to co-operate with God by believing. This he did, and God did the rest. He was then 'reckoned' a just man, not by a fiction, but certainly by a favour (*kata charin*). He had not earned the status of a just man, but he had responded to the one demand God made on him — by the 'obedience of faith' (Rom 1 : 5).

There is probably no reference to a divine account-book in Gen 15 : 6 — this interpretation of 'it was reckoned' would require 'justice' to be taken in the sense of 'a just act'. But that can hardly be the author's meaning, since he would then have no answer to the question how Abraham came to be reckoned God's friend: the act of faith is not reckoned as a 'good work' on the credit side outweighing the 'evil works' on the debit side of a ledger.

The word 'reckoned' has been a source of much difficulty and dispute. If it is taken to mean that Abraham, though not in fact a just man, was *deemed* to be just, the road is wide open to the Lutheran doctrine of extrinsic justification, according to which the sinner who believes in Christ remains intrinsically a sinner, but is reckoned as just, by a legal fiction, because of his faith. But if, as suggested above, the author means that God reckoned Abraham just because of his faith, the sense is that because of his faith God truly forgave him his past sins and gave him justice. The author of Genesis is not trying to explain how Abraham came to be *deemed* just.

Similarly, the Christian who renders to God 'the obedience of faith' is thereby placed in a right relationship to God. It is as if he had fulfilled the whole of the law. And indeed he *has* fulfilled the

---

talks as if the Abraham who has faith and the Abraham who does works were two distinct men. The Christian who is first justified by faith is the same person who will be finally judged by his works.

whole of the law, not personally but vicariously — because he is now united through his faith, to Christ who has faithfully fulfilled the whole of the law for his sake. Through his faith he is associated with the one work of expiation which is truly effective. It is not a work of his own, performed in obedience to the law; it is the work of redemption which Christ performed for the justification of all who adhere to him in faith. By his faith, the disciple receives justification or forgiveness as a free gift, and at the same time commits himself to live according to the teaching of Jesus, which demands a higher standard of justice than the law as interpreted by the Pharisees (cf. Mt 5:20).

## What was the object of Abraham's faith?

Most modern commentators take vv. 5-7 to mean: 'We are justified in the same way as Abraham, for he believed in God and was justified, and we believe in Christ and are justified.' But probably St Paul meant more than this. [10] His argument is stronger if he means: 'Just as Abraham believed in the gospel of Christ, so too we believe in the gospel of Christ.' This is the interpretation of many of the Fathers, and it is justified by the text. In 3:8, St Paul says that God announced the gospel to Abraham beforehand (*proeuengelisato*), when he promised the coming of Christ in whom all the nations would be blessed. [11] In Rom 4:17, the point is pressed still further: Abraham's faith was faith in resurrection of the body.

Thus, just as the author of Genesis 15 makes Abraham a disciple of Moses by anticipation, so St Paul makes him a Christian by anticipation.

## How did St Paul understand Gen 15:6?

In Rom 4:1-9, St Paul explains 'it was reckoned to him as justice' with the aid of Ps 32:1-2:

> Blessed are those whose iniquities are forgiven,
>> and whose sins are pardoned.
> Blessed is the man whose sin the Lord will not reckon.

The two quotations are linked by the common word 'reckon'. When God forgives a man's sins, he no longer 'reckons' his sin; on the con-

---

[10] Cf. A. V. Longworth, '"Faith" in Galatians. A Study in Galatians 2:16—3:29,' *Studia Evangelica* II (TU, 87), Berlin, 1964, p. 607; Althaus, *The Theology of Luther*, pp. 98-99.
[11] Cf. Jn 8:56; 1 Cor 10:4.

trary, he reckons the man just. The 'reckoning' of justice is the same as the 'not-reckoning' of sin, and both these phrases describe the forgiveness of sin.

Presumably, therefore, St Paul took Gen 15:6 to mean that when Abraham believed the good news announced to him, his sins were forgiven and he was given the Holy Spirit. St Paul does not explicitly say that Abraham 'received the Holy Spirit', but he regards the justification of Abraham as setting the pattern for the justification of all who believe.

### Was Abraham's faith praiseworthy?

The text of Gen 15:6 seems to record Abraham's faith as something praiseworthy. But how, then, can his justification be an act of pure grace on God's part? Philo attempts an answer in *Who is the heir?*, 90-93. Scripture records Abraham's faith as something praiseworthy by contrast to the incredulity of most men, yet in the eyes of God he was simply doing what was fitting:

> The words 'Abraham believed God' (Gen 15:6) are a necessary addition to speak the praise due to him who has believed. Yet, perhaps it may be asked: 'Do you consider this worthy of praise? When it is God who speaks and promises, who would not pay heed, even though he were the most unjust and impious of mankind?' To such a questioner we will answer: 'Good sir, do not without due scrutiny rob the Sage of his fitting tribute, or aver that the unworthy possess the most perfect of virtues, faith, or censure our claim to knowledge of this matter. For if you should be willing to search more deeply and not confine yourself to the mere surface, you will clearly understand that to trust in God alone and join no other with him is no easy matter, by reason of our kinship with our yokefellow, mortality, which works upon us to keep our trust placed in riches and repute and office and friends and health and strength and many other things... This act of justice and conformity with nature has been held to be a marvel because of the untrustfulness of most of us. And it is in re-proof of us that the holy text tells us, that to rest on the Existent only, firmly and without wavering, though it is a marvel in the sight of men who have no hold of good things unsullied, is deemed no marvel at the judgment-bar of truth, but simply an act of justice and nothing more.

But this reply is too simple for our purposes. If faith in its continuation (i.e. perseverance) is praiseworthy and meritorious (before God), it must also be praiseworthy at its inception. Faith is a theological virtue, and all acts of faith are good, admirable and praiseworthy.

To safeguard the gratuitousness of justification, it is sufficient to insist that the prevenient and concomitant grace, which renders possible the act of faith, is a gift of God. The man who believes is accepting God's offer of cooperation; he is accepting God's gracious gift. His action is praiseworthy in as much as he does this freely. As Philo observed, to make this act of faith is an act of simple justice, not a work of supererogation; but it is not only works of supererogation which are praiseworthy.

It appears, then, that even the very first act of faith is a praiseworthy 'work' (cf. Jn 6: 29), but it is a work which is rendered possible by God's prevenient and concomitant grace. It is 'a work which our heavenly Father has *given* us to do' (cf. Jn 17: 4). It is at once our work and God's gift. As Pope St Celestine says in the *Indiculus*: [12]

| | |
|---|---|
| Tanta enim est erga omnes homines bonitas Dei, ut nostra velit esse merita, quae sunt ipsius dona, et pro his quae largitus est, aeterna praemia sit donaturus. | God wills in his goodness that what is of his giving should also be of our deserving; and in return for what he has given us, he will grant us eternal rewards. |

In Rom 4: 4-5, St Paul may appear to say that faith is not a work at all; but vv. 6-7 show that what he means is that forgiveness and justification are not wages owed in justice to the man who believes: the act of faith is not a work commensurate to what he receives. [13] St Paul does not mean that the believer is completely inactive, or that his action is in no sense meritorious. He is showing that the man who is truly justified before God has nothing to boast about. He is just because of his faith. But he cannot boast of his faith as if it were all his own work. It is the work of God within him; all he can do is to cooperate 'in fear and trembling' (cf. Phil 2: 12). [14]

## How then shall we interpret Gen 15:6?

Perhaps the thought of Genesis and of St Paul can be expressed in this way. In God's eyes all men are divided into two categories, the just and the sinners. The former category are characterized by 'justice' (*dikaiosunê*) and the latter by 'sin' (*hamartia*). As a result of the Fall in Gen 3 all men were sinners; then in Gen 12 God called Abraham and began the work of restoration. Abraham was at first a sinner like the rest, but 'he believed God, and it was reckoned to him as justice.' He was transferred to the category of the just by the for-

---

[12] Denz. 248.
[13] In technical language: 'fides non meretur iustificationem, sicut opera merentur mercedem, i.e. de condigno'—H. Lange, *De Gratia*, Freiburg im Breisgau, 1929, p. 130.
[14] Cf Lange, *De Gratia*, p. 131: 'Paulus videtur fidei relate ad iustificationem eam efficaciam adscribere quam nos vocamus meritum de congruo.'

giveness of his sins and by the imparting or infusion of justice, which, as was mentioned above (p. 219), is not really distinct from faith itself. Through this infusion of justice he is transferred into the category of the just — of which he is the first member. He is now reckoned as just by a favour (through the forgiveness of his sins, and in spite of his lack of just acts), but not by a fiction, for he now has the root and substance of all just acts implanted in his soul — namely, faith. Faith is the principle from which just actions will spring (cf. Gal 5 : 6).

By reason of his faith Abraham is reckoned as a just man, that is, as one who loves the will of God and habitually does just acts. But it still remains for him to become in fact what he is in principle. He is just in principle because he has the root of justice, namely faith; he must now become just in action by doing just acts. [15] This explains the curious conjunction of indicatives and imperatives in St Paul: we are just, but we must become just; we are holy, but must become holy, and so on.

The act of faith is the beginning of justification; it is the act through which first justification comes about. But St Paul does not mean that faith is the only thing a man has to do in this world — that he can leave the rest to Christ. Man has his task (his *ergon*), just as every other creature has. Faith is not his task. Rather, faith enables him to fulfil his task, which is the service of others in charity (cf. Gal 5 : 13).

*In what sense is a Christian 'simul iustus et peccator'?*

According to Luther: [16]

On account of my faith in Christ God does not see the sin that still remains in me. For so long as I go on living in the flesh, there is certainly sin in me. But meanwhile Christ protects me under the shadow of his wings and spreads over me the wide heaven of the forgiveness of sins, under which I live in safety. This prevents God from seeing the sins that still cling to my flesh. My flesh distrusts God, is angry with him, does not rejoice in him etc. But God overlooks these sins, and in his sight they are as though they were not sins...

---

[15] Luther, Gal, 1535, p. 231, says: 'Two things make Christian righteousness perfect: the first is faith in the heart, which is a divinely granted gift and which formally believes in Christ; the second is that God reckons this imperfect faith as *perfect righteousness* for the sake of Christ' (my italics). But St Paul does not say or imply that all who are justified are reckoned perfectly or equally just. Some sinners are worse than others, and some just men are more just than others.

[16] Luther, Gal, 1535, p. 231. Cf. H. Küng, *Justification*, London, 1964, pp. 225-236.

Thus a Christian man is righteous and a sinner at the same time (*simul iustus et peccator*), holy and profane, an enemy of God and a child of God. None of the sophists will admit this paradox, because they do not understand the true meaning of justification.

But perhaps it is Luther who has underestimated the sincerity of divine forgiveness. When a man is justified, his conscience is no longer burdened by past sins; these are truly forgiven and he stands in God's grace. What remains in him is concupiscence, the impulse of sin; but concupiscence is not formal sin, and in the just man it is controllable. The believer who has been justified by his faith does not find himself under an inner compulsion to distrust God and to be angry with him. Luther's description of the habitual state of a Christian believer is markedly different from the one given by St Paul in Rom 5: 1-11:

> Through our faith, then, we have been justified, and are at peace with God, through our Lord Jesus Christ. Through him we have obtained admission, by faith, to the grace in which we stand, and through him we find joy in the hope of seeing God's glory. What is more, we find joy in our tribulations...

Luther interprets St Paul in the light of his own spiritual experience as a monk, which was quite unlike the experience of Paul the Apostle. His interpretation of Paul differs widely from that of St Augustine, whose experience was much closer to that of St Paul. As a recent biographer of Luther has observed, 'Augustine came to feel a total transformation in himself, and praised the grace that had transformed him; Luther comforted himself with the grace of God, even though sin, incurvedness upon himself, self-seeking, still remained in him.' [17]

The Lutheran picture of the Christian as *simul iustus et peccator* obscures the important fact that men divide into two categories, the sinners and the just, and no man belongs to both categories (cf. Col 1: 13-14). This is a truth of revelation. The baptized Christian is a man whose sins have been truly forgiven and who seriously intends with the aid of the Holy Spirit to keep the whole of God's law as interpreted by Christ. His will is to live a life of obedience to God's will and to repent of his occasional lapses and failures. He is relieved of anxious strain. His confidence in God gives him the assurance of a son in his Father's house.

The pharisaic Judaizer expects to be judged by his own works. At the Judgment, he will be able to catalogue on the one hand his sins, and on the other hand his good works, including those pre-

---

[17] Franz Lau, *Luther*, London, 1963, p. 64. On St Paul's 'robust' conscience see K. Stendahl, 'The Apostle Paul and the Introspective Conscience of the West,' HTR 56 (1963), pp. 199-215.

scribed by the law for the expiation of his sins. He is confident that, on balance, he will be found a just man — the 'works of the law' will cancel out his sins. St Paul replies that if this is the case Christ died for nothing (cf. 2 : 21). The Christian believes that at his judgment his sins, of which he has repented, will be seen to have been expiated by Christ; and he hopes that the works which the Holy Spirit has enabled him to do will be found sufficient, i.e., that he will not be held guilty of serious omissions, like the people in Mt 25 : 41-46. [18]

*What is the literal sense of Gen 18:18?*

The Hebrew of Gen 18 : 18b can be translated in two ways: 'Shall I hide from Abraham what I am about to do, seeing that Abraham shall become a great and mighty nation, and *in him* all the nations of the earth shall bless themselves' *or* 'all the nations of the earth shall be blessed.' Both in the Hebrew and in the Greek, the phrase 'in him' too is ambiguous: it can refer either to Abraham or to the great nation which his descendants will become. (The nation has in fact been called by the name not of Abraham but of his grandson, Israel. We talk of 'the people of Israel' not the 'people of Abraham', but the sense would be the same.)

If the verb in v. 18b is taken as a reflexive, the sense will be: 'All the nations of the earth will bless themselves by saying "May God do to us as he has done to Abraham (or, to the people of A-braham)!"' If the verb is taken as passive, the sense will be 'All the nations of the earth will receive a blessing through Abraham (or, more probably) through the people of Abraham.' [19]

Both interpretations strain the phrase 'in you' (or, 'in it'). The second of them, which is the one adopted by the Septuagint, is preferable, because the first hardly does justice to the elevated, pro-grammatic tone of the passage. Moreover, the context in which the promise to Abraham is first recorded is highly significant. Gen 11 describes the dispersal of the human family from the tower of Babel;

[18] According to Luther (quoted by Althaus, *The Theology of M. Luther,* p. 29), 'it is impossible for a person not to be puffed up by his good works unless he has first been deflated and destroyed by suffering and evil until he knows that he is worthless and that his works are not his but God's.' Luther here assumes that the experience of every Christian will conform to the pattern of his own. But cf. Mk 10 : 14. See further below, p. 423.
[19] Cf. Jn 4 : 22. The parallel passage in Gen 22 : 18 has: 'and all the nations of the earth will be blessed in your issue.' Hence Chrysostom, PG 61, 654 B, says: 'He promised Abraham that the nations should be blessed through his issue.' Cf. G. von Rad, *Genesis,* London, 1961, on Gen 18 : 18.

then in Gen 12 Abraham is called to become the centre of a new humanity. The promise that all the nations of the earth will be blessed in him is a promise that one day God will restore the unity of mankind through the Issue of Abraham. [20]

*What fuller sense does St Paul see in Gen 18:18?*

St Paul follows the interpretation of the Septuagint, but in the light of the fulfilment of the promise, he is able to attach a precise meaning to the obscure phrase 'in you' (or, 'in it'). He takes the words in an ultra-literal sense: 'All the Gentiles will be blessed in your posterity — they will become a part of your posterity, and that without ceasing to be Gentiles — therefore without circumcision. They will become Gentiles in you, sons of Abraham who are nevertheless Gentiles; and they will be blessed in you — as part of your posterity, they will share in the blessings promised to you.' The Scripture personified, or the Holy Spirit who speaks in the Scripture, foreseeing that God would justify the Gentiles by faith and not by circumcision, framed the promise in these particular words, which have become clear only after their fulfilment: 'all the Gentiles (as such) will receive a blessing in you (when they have been incorporated into your spiritual posterity through faith).'

*Is St Paul's exegesis of Gen 18:18 defensible?*

St Paul's manner of arguing in 3:8-9 is one which no modern Scripture scholar would venture to imitate. But Christ himself had set an example in his argument with the Sadducees. He quoted 'I am the God of Abraham, of Isaac and of Jacob,' and added that God is the God of the living — that is, to be 'God of' is a relationship which requires a living term. It implies protection, love and guidance. Therefore, when God says: 'I *am* the God of Abraham, Isaac and Jacob,' he implies that he is here and now extending his protection and love over the patriarchs (cf. Mk 12:26-27).

Another important Old Testament text which the early Church interpreted in an ultra-literal sense is Hosea 6:2-3: 'He will strike us and he will cure us. He will revive us after two days; on the third day he will raise us up, and we shall live in his sight.' This is probably the text referred to in 1 Cor 15:4, where St Paul, summarizing the

---

[20] Cf. Dubarle, *Original Sin*, pp. 86-87. St Paul sees the fulfilment of this promise in the growth of the Gentile churches.

gospel, says that Christ 'was raised from the dead on the third day according to the Scriptures.' In the literal sense, 'after two days, on the third day' is probably an idiom meaning 'after a short time'. If so, the prophecy was fulfilled in an ultra-literal sense, for Jesus rose on the third day. [21]

Other texts which St Paul treats in this same curious way will be pointed out below. It would be rash to suppose that he received a special revelation in each case to inform him that the Holy Spirit intended from the start to fulfil the promise in the fuller sense which he discerns. Rather, St Paul is arguing with men who believe as he does that in Christ all God's promises are receiving the Yes of fulfilment. He points back to the enigmatic promise in Gen 18:18 and invites his adversary to consider how remarkably the Christian fulfilment matches it. Or, to put the same in a slightly different way, he regards Gen 18:18 as an obscure oracle, the meaning of which has been revealed by the event. The oracle did not explain (a) how the Gentiles were to share in the promised blessing, or (b) how the Gentiles could be said to be 'in Abraham'. The spread of the gospel among the Gentiles has disclosed the answers: (a) the Gentiles will share in the promised blessings through sharing Abraham's faith (v. 9), and (b) the Gentiles will be 'in Abraham' while remaining Gentiles, because their faith will make them 'sons of Abraham' and thus members of his corporate personality.

Here again, the Judaizer could reply with an appeal to the literal sense. He could say: 'Later books of Scripture, in particular Isaiah and Daniel, show that the prophecy is to be fulfilled in quite a different way: when Israel has been converted, the kingdom of the Son of Man will succeed the bestial world-empires that have ruled hitherto; then out of Zion will go forth the law and the word of the Lord from Jerusalem, and all the nations will share in the great blessing of gentle rule by the saints of the Most High.' St Paul seems to have in mind exactly this objection, when he goes on to say in v. 10 that the Gentiles will *not* share in the blessings by being brought under the law, for the law brings only a curse.

*Does the divine initiative exclude human cooperation in first justification?*

In v. 8, St Paul does not say that the Gentiles will be justified by their faith, but that God will justify them by (or, as a result of) faith.

---

[21]  Cf. Lindars, *New Testament Apologetic*, p. 61.

From this it has been inferred that 'faith is not man's contribution to justification but the means which God chooses to justify pagans gratuitously.' [22] But in St Paul's view faith is both man's 'contribution' and God's contribution: in this work man cooperates with God (cf. Phil 2:12). Faith is wholly a gift of God, since man can only believe through God's grace or strength; but it is also man's action — the response which God enables him to make to the gospel.

The gift of faith is not merited by any previous works, or it would not be a grace. But the act of faith which the gift enables the recipient to make is, through the goodness of God (*kata charin*), meritorious. [23] We have no right to work in the Lord's vineyard, but in his goodness he takes us on, and allows us to earn a reward. The reward is God's gift and our merit; but the magnitude of the reward is out of all proportion to our merit. Therefore we can be said to merit it only in an analogous sense (*de congruo*).

*What was the content of the promise, according to St Paul?*

In Gen 12:1-3, Abraham is promised a land, which remains un-named, and a great posterity. In Gen 15:17-21 and 17:21, the land is specified as Canaan. This promise was already fulfilled in the time of Joshua (Josh 21:43-45):

> The Lord gave Israel all the land which he had sworn to their fathers to give them; they occupied it and settled down in it, and the Lord gave them peace on every side, just as he had sworn to their fathers; not one of all their enemies could withstand them, the Lord having delivered all their enemies into their power. Not one of the good promises which the Lord made to the house of Israel failed, all being fulfilled.

But Israel had not yet reached the numerical strength and power implied in Gen 15:5: 'Look toward heaven, and number the stars, if you are able to number them... So shall your descendants be.' Nor were all the nations blessed in Israel (as was promised in Gen 22:18). Therefore the final fulfilment still lay in the future.

From Rom 4:13 we learn that St Paul believed that Abraham was promised the whole world as his possession. This was not Paul's own private fancy, but a common opinion among the rabbis, [24] based, apparently, on the blessing given to Abraham by Melkisedek in Gen 14:19-20:

---

[22] Bonnard, Gal, p. 66.
[23] See above, pp. 247-248.
[24] Cf. SB, III, pp. 208-209, and 2 Esdras 6:53-59, with the comment by M. Hooker, *The Son of Man in Mark*, London, 1967, pp. 50-51.

> Blessed be Abraham by God Almighty:
> the possessor of heaven and earth!

If 'possessor' is here referred to 'Abraham', the text means: 'Blessed be Abraham, possessor of heaven and earth, by God Almighty.' Confirmation of this universalistic interpretation was read into the promise made by God to Abraham in Gen 28:14: 'Your descendants shall be like the dust of the earth, and you shall spread abroad to the west and to the east and to the north and to the south.' This passage may have been in the psalmist's mind when he addressed to the Davidic king the words (2:8):

> Ask of me and I will make the nations your heritage,
> and the ends of the earth your possession.

In the same tradition, Dan 7:14 promises that the Son of Man will be given 'dominion and glory and kingdom, that all peoples, nations and languages should serve him.' [25] Philo too believed that what God had promised Abraham was something far greater than the land of Canaan. His view is based on the wording of the promise in Gen 15:5: the descendants of Abraham were to be not merely as numerous as the stars, but as great and glorious as the stars. Anyone believing that the stars were angelic beings [26] who control terrestrial events, could quickly infer that the descendants of Abraham were to be rulers of the world. [27]

Thus the Jews of St Paul's day, or some of them, believed that in the days of the Messiah the seed of Abraham would inherit the whole of earth and heaven. St Paul claims that the promise has already been fulfilled. Already Christ reigns at God's right hand over the whole of creation. [28] Those who are incorporated into him by faith and baptism already reign with him in spe, [29] and one day, after the renewal of all things, will reign with him visibly. [30]

In Gal 4:26-28, the inheritance is described as citizenship in the heavenly Jerusalem: the Jerusalem that is above belongs to those who are sons of Abraham by faith. When a man is born into the new world of which Christ is king, his name is inscribed on the citizen-rolls of the heavenly city. Every ancient city revised its citizen-rolls from time

---

[25] Cf. A. Vanhoye, 'Christologia a qua initium sumit epistola ad Hebraeos,' *Verbum Domini* 43 (1965), p. 7.
[26] Cf. Job 38:7: 'the morning stars sang together, and all the sons of God shouted for joy.'
[27] Cf. Philo, *Who is the heir?*, 76, 86, 315-6 (Loeb IV).
[28] Cf. Phil 2:10-11; Col 1:15-20; Eph 1:20-22; Heb 1:2.
[29] Cf. Apoc 1:9. Althaus, *The Theology of Martin Luther*, p. 118: 'His lordship consists in the fact that he makes those who are his become what he is.'
[30] Cf. Eph 2:6; Col 3:1-4, 24.

to time, and the names of malefactors were struck off. So too with the heavenly city: those who commit the works of the flesh will not enter into their inheritance (cf. 5:21). Thus the land of Canaan gives place in the hope of Israel to the kingdom of God, and the earthly Zion and Jerusalem give place to their heavenly counterparts.

St Paul was probably confirmed in his view about the content of the promise to Abraham, by the knowledge that the Issue, when he came, was God's own Son. An heir, in ancient systems of law, was thought of as continuing the personality of the testator, taking over the great majority of his rights and liabilities, and charged with the duty of continuing his family. Accordingly, an heir could not normally be instituted to a part of the testator's estate. [31] St Paul may have reasoned that if Christ, the Son of God, has been given an inheritance, it cannot be anything less than the universe (cf. Heb 1:2). Hence, what was promised to Abraham and his Issue was, from the beginning, ownership of the universe.

*What is the literal sense of Deut 27:26 (quoted in 3:10)?*

At the end of the cursing ceremony prescribed in Deut 27:11-26, the levites are to say (according to the Hebrew, as rendered by the RSV):

Cursed be he who does not confirm the words (= commands) of this law by obeying them! And all the people shall say: Amen.

The Chicago Bible has:

Cursed be he who does not give effect to the provisions of this code by observing them.

The Septuagint makes it more emphatic:

Cursed be every man who does not abide by all the commandments of this law so as to fulfil them! And all the people shall say: So be it!

The purpose of the whole cursing ceremony is to call down divine punishment on anyone who is guilty of secret crimes which do not come to the cognisance of human courts and therefore escape legal punishment: secret worship of idols, dishonour to father and mother, removal of a neighbour's landmark, misleading a blind man on the road, oppression of foreigners, orphans and widows, incest, bestiality, secret murder. The purpose of the last, comprehensive curse (quoted above) is not clear. Moses cannot have expected every Israelite to call down

---

[31] There were exceptions, however, in Roman law in the case of military wills.

a curse upon anyone, including himself, who might infringe even the lightest of the commandments. Perhaps the idea is: 'Cursed be anyone who is fundamentally disloyal to the law — anyone who does not, by his actions, show that he is on the side of the law and anxious to "make the law stand".' If so, this final curse may be compared to St Paul's anathema in 1:8-9: 'Cursed be any man who is fundamentally disloyal to the gospel.' But more probably the final curse in v. 26 is inserted to make the transition to the blessings and curses of Deut 28, which were written by the Deuteronomist in full knowledge of the melancholy course which Israelite history had taken.[32] He knows that the curses of the law have come into effect, not its blessings; and so, by dilating on the curses, he is not merely providing a deterrent for the future, but also explaining the past history of Israel.

> And if you obey the voice of the Lord your God, being careful to do all his commandments which I command you this day, the Lord your God will set you high above all the nations of the earth. And all these blessings shall come upon you and overtake you, if you obey the voice of the Lord your God. Blessed shall you be in the city, and blessed shall you be in the field...
>
> But if you will not obey the voice of the Lord your God or be careful to do all his commandments and his statutes which I command you this day, then all these curses shall come upon you and overtake you. Cursed shall you be in the city, and cursed shall you be in the field...
>
> Because you did not serve the Lord your God with joyfulness and gladness of heart, by reason of the abundance of all things, therefore you shall serve your enemies whom the Lord will send against you, in hunger and thirst, in nakedness, and in want of all things; and he will put a yoke of iron upon your neck, until he has destroyed you. The Lord will bring a nation against you from afar, from the end of the earth, as swift as the eagle flies, a nation whose language you do not understand, a nation of stern countenance, who shall not regard the person of the old or show favour to the young, and shall eat the offspring of your cattle and the fruit of your ground, until you are destroyed...

### How does St Paul interpret Deut 27:26?

St Paul gives a paraphrase of the Septuagint version of Deut 27:26: 'Cursed be every man who does not abide by all the commandments written in the Book of the law so as to fulfil them!' It was probably a favourite text with zealous law-observing Pharisees such as Paul had been before his conversion. He took it in the strictest

[32] Cf. Jerome, PL 26, 386 A: 'prophetico spiritu his qui peccaturi erant, ea quae eis ventura sunt, nuntiantur.' Also M. Noth, *The Laws in the Pentateuch and other Essays*, Edinburgh, 1966, pp. 118-131.

possible sense as meaning that any Jew who broke any written law came under this curse. Rom 7:14-21 probably shows that he knew in his heart of hearts that he himself had failed to keep the commandment 'Thou shalt not covet (or lust).'

### How does St Paul argue from this text?

St Paul merely sketches his argument here; he does not develop it. He adds to Deut 27:26 the further promise that no Jew has ever succeeded in keeping every part of the written law (cf. Rom 3:9-20), and he concludes that all Jews are under the curse of the law.

The premise that no Jew has ever succeeded in keeping every part of the law may be a generalization from his own experience: if he himself, who had outstripped most of his own generation in his efforts to keep the law, had nevertheless failed, he had no reason to think that anyone else had succeeded. This opinion was confirmed for him by the witness of Scripture (cf. vv. 11-12); and, he probably felt, it accounted for the melancholy condition of Israel — oppressed by the idolatrous power of Rome. This was what they had come to through their cult of the law!

The relevance of this argument to the whole section is that since the cult of the law has certainly not brought about the fulfilment of the promises for the sons of Abraham according to the flesh, it is absurd to suppose that his spiritual sons among the Gentiles can enter into the promised inheritance only by submitting to this law. If they do that, they too will fall under the curse.

### Is St Paul's use of this text defensible?

In 1:6, St Paul accuses the Judaizers of turning the gospel upside down. By his argument in 3:10 he exposes himself to the charge that he is turning the law upside down. His opponents could say: 'Paul is indulging in sophistry. He must know perfectly well that the words of Deuteronomy were never meant in the rigorous sense he attaches to them. Has he never read the prophets — Ezekiel 18, for example? The prophets do not say that as soon as any Jew commits some minor infringement of the law, he is excluded, helplessly and irrevocably, from the blessings promised to Abraham and his issue. On the contrary, the law and the prophets teach that even if a man commits grave sins, God will forgive him, if he repents. It is absurd, therefore, to suggest that the whole Jewish people is under a curse. Many of our people lead sincere and holy lives, falling occasionally into sin, but quickly repenting, and using the means of expiation laid down in the law. It is outrageous to suggest that all God's people have been under a curse since the time of Moses!'

St Jerome raised a difficulty on this score, and thereby earned a severe castigation at the hands of Luther:[33]

> Let us not rave with Jerome, who was so deceived by his precious Origen that he understood almost nothing in Paul; they both regarded him as a political legislator. 'Does this mean,' Jerome asks, 'that all the patriarchs were accursed, even though they were circumcised, offered sacrifices, and observed the law?' Thus he rushes into Paul without any judgment and does not make a distinction between the true doers of the law who are justified by faith and the doers who rely on the works of the law.

St Jerome does raise such an objection, but only in order to answer it:[34]

> It might be objected: 'So then, Moses and Elijah and the other prophets who were under the works of the law, were under a curse?' But a man will not fear to admit this, if he has heard the Apostle saying: 'Christ redeemed us from the curse of the law, being made for our sake a curse.' He will not fear to admit that each of the saints was at one time made accursed... If Christ died for all (2 Cor 5:14-15), then he died for Moses and all the prophets.

This is a much better answer than the one Luther gives. The reformer thinks that St Paul means: 'Those who rely on their own works are accursed, not for their failure to keep the law, but for the very attempt to find justification by keeping the law.' Such people, he says, 'do not actually say with their mouths, "I am God; I am Christ." Yet in fact they arrogate to themselves the divinity of Christ and his function. In fact, then, they do say: "I am Christ. I am the Saviour — not only my own but for others as well".'[35] He says that 'God loathes these people who disregard his mercy and think they can make themselves just.' This is a forced and violent interpretation. St Paul is clearly speaking of those who are cursed for their failure to keep the law, not for their *attempt* to keep it perfectly. The patriarchs, prophets and holy men of the Old Testament observed the law; but they put their faith, not in these observances, but in God who had commanded them and who forgives the penitent transgressor.

St Paul does not mean that all the Jews who lived before the coming of Christ lived and died under a curse. Throughout the

---

[33] Luther, Gal, 1535, p. 275. In this part of his commentary, his language is somewhat intemperate. On p. 263 he speaks of the 'filthy swine' who 'think that righteousness is something moral.'
[34] Jerome, PL 26, 383-384.
[35] Luther, Gal, 1535, p. 258.

K

while their enemies maltreat them, is a sign that his faith in the goodness, justice and fidelity of God are flagging. In these circumstances an exhortation to faith in God is not necessarily, or even probably, an exhortation to exact fulfilment of the works of the law.

The second text is Lev 18:5:

> And the Lord said to Moses, 'Say to the people of Israel, I am the Lord your God. You shall not do as they do in the land of Egypt, where you dwelt, and you shall not do as they do in the land of Canaan, to which I am bringing you. You shall not walk in their statutes. You shall do my ordinances and keep my statutes and walk in them. I am the Lord your God. You shall therefore keep my statutes and my ordinances, by doing which a man shall live: I am the Lord.

There is a veiled threat here: he who obeys the statutes and ordinances of the law shall live, and he who does not shall die. The statutes which follow are prohibitions of incest. At the end, the threat is made explicit (18:26, 28-29):

> Do none of these abominations... lest the land vomit you out, when you defile it, as it vomited out the nation that was before you. For whoever shall do any of these abominations, the persons that do them shall be cut off from among their people.

Both Hab 2:4 and Lev 18:5 speak of 'life' on this earth, and promise a happy life in the land of Israel. St Paul reads a deeper sense in both: the texts promise spiritual life, or life in communion with God.

Both texts may have been first used in this controversy by the Judaizers. They could say that the text in Habakkuk promises 'life' to the man who is faithful to the law, and the text of Leviticus promises life to those who obey the Lord's statutes and ordinances.

*How does St Paul use these texts?*

As St Thomas observes, St Paul's argument is a syllogism of the second figure, but it is not set forth in the order major, minor, conclusion. [41] Rearranged, it would have this form:

> He who is just by faith will live.
> But the law does not enjoin faith.
> Therefore no one is justified by the law.

In other words, Scripture promises, in the prophecy of Habakkuk, that the man who seeks justification by faith shall live. But the law does not tell a man to seek justification by believing; on the contrary,

---

[41]   St Thomas, Gal, 406.

it promises that he who does certain works will live. Therefore, if Habakkuk is right, the law does not lead where it promises — it does not lead the way to life.

## Is St Paul's exegesis of these texts legitimate?

The Judaizers could reply that Hab 2:4 does not refer to first justification and Paul is doing violence to it in so applying it. The prophet meant: 'The just man will continue to live if he remains faithful to God,' and the proof of fidelity to God is fulfilment of the works of the law.

They could also reply that the law *is* on the side of faith, because Hab 2:4 is part of the law (the Torah), and it enjoins faith — faith which is to be manifested in works, but nevertheless faith.

Thirdly, they could reply that when God promised the Israelites in Lev 18:5 that the man who fulfilled the commandments would live, he was not mocking them with a false promise. He was laying down the works which as parties of the covenant they must fulfil. Probably Lev 18:5 was first introduced into the controversy by the Judaizers, since in its literal sense it suits them much better than it suits St Paul, who tries to neutralize it by means of Hab 2:4.

St Paul might have replied to these criticisms by saying: 'Look more closely at the text of Habakkuk. He does *not* say that the just man will live by fidelity to the law; he has just referred to God's promise that the day of retribution, even if it seems slow, will nevertheless come (Hab 2:3). When he goes on to say: "the just man will live by his faith," he means the just man who believes this divine promise will live. The faith in question is a faith in God's word of promise — as Abraham's was too. From this faith will spring fidelity to the law, no doubt; but the source and origin of the man's justice is his acceptance of God's word. Lev 18:5 is concerned with the regulation of a man's conduct after he has been justified; it says nothing about faith, because faith is presupposed. A man must first be justified by faith; afterwards he can think about the law. But our present controversy is about how a man is first justified.'

In reply to the objection that the law does enjoin faith, St Thomas observes that as a generalization it remains true that [42]

> the precepts of the law are not about things to be believed, but about things to be done, even if they do announce something to be believed.

---

[42] St Thomas, Gal, 406: 'Praecepta Legis non sunt de credendis sed de faciendis, licet aliquid credendum annuntient.'

Hence the efficacy of the law comes not from faith, but from works. The proof of this is that when the Lord wished to confirm the law, he did not say 'He who believes them' but 'He who does them will live.' By contrast, the new law is a law of faith: it says: 'He who believes and is baptized will be saved.'

If we allow the Judaizers the last word, they might say: 'Once again, we are not interested in first justification alone, but in what a man must do in order to be saved. He must fulfil the new law, if you like; but the new law is not exclusively concerned with what to believe. Listen to Lk 10:25-30 again:

Once a lawyer rose and put a question to test him: 'Master,' he asked, 'what must I do to gain eternal life?' Jesus replied: 'In the law what is written? What do you read there?' He answered: 'You shall love the Lord your God with your whole heart, and with your whole soul, and with your whole strength, and with your whole mind, and your neighbour as yourself.' Jesus said to him: 'You have answered rightly; do this and you will live.'

## Whom did Christ redeem from the curse of the law?

Since St Paul is writing to the Galatians, it is natural to suppose that when he says 'Christ redeemed *us* from the curse of the law,' he means 'you Galatians, myself Paul, and all other believers,'[43] just as in 1:4, when he says that Christ 'offered himself for our sins, to rescue us from this present evil age,' he cannot wish to exclude the Galatians from the group denoted by 'us' and 'our'.

But on the other hand, since the Galatians have not been subject to the law, they cannot have incurred the curse of the law, for, as St Paul himself says in Rom 3:19: 'Whatever the law says, it says to those who are subject to the law.' So it seems that 'Christ redeemed us from the curse of the law' must mean 'Christ redeemed us Jews from the curse of the law.' This is very awkward, for St Paul has not mentioned the Jews (at least, not in such a way as to identify himself with them)[44] since 3:1, where he was speaking to the Galatians by name.

The same awkwardness occurs in 3:24, where St Paul says to the Galatians: 'The law was *our* pedagogue unto Christ,' and in 4:1-5,

---

[43] This is the view of Whiteley, *The Theology of St Paul,* p. 84.
[44] 'Those who rely on the works of the law' in 3:10 are Jews, but not a group of Jews with whom St Paul would identify himself as 'we' or 'us'.

where again 'we' seems to refer to Jewish Christians, not to the Galatians. As was suggested above (p. 235), the most likely explanation of this anomaly is that 3 : 6—4 : 7 is the continuation of St Paul's speech at Antioch, which was addressed to Jewish Christians. He has incorporated this speech almost verbatim (with slight revisions in 3 : 1-5), leaving the reader to guess from the context that by 'us' he must mean 'us Jewish Christians'.

*In what sense(s) did Christ redeem Jewish Christians from the curse of the law?*

The most obvious meaning of the words is: 'Christ redeemed us Jewish Christians from the curse of Deut 27 : 26 which we had brought upon ourselves by failing to abide by all that is written in the book of the law.' But St Paul does not mean that Christ destroyed the curse itself. V. 10 shows that those who put their trust in the works of the law are still under the curse of the law. So the sense is not: 'Christ has released all Jews from the curse of the law.' Only Jewish *Christians* have been effectively redeemed.

Secondly, St Paul also means, as the sequel shows (v. 14a): 'Christ has altogether removed us Christian Jews from the law's sphere of influence, so that we are no longer even under the shadow of the law's *conditional* curse ('If in the future you disobey, you will be accursed'). Therefore, in the future, the curse of the law will no longer fall upon us if we do what the law forbids — for example, if we enter the houses of Gentiles and eat with them, or if we do not do what the law enjoins — for example, if we do not observe its sabbaths and new moons. Christ has released us from the *possibility* of becoming accursed, by transferring us, through the mystical death of baptism, into a new aeon where the law is no longer binding. Now, therefore, a Christian Jew can associate freely with Gentiles without incurring the curse of the law.'

Perhaps St Paul intended his words to bear a third meaning, too. The genitive in the phrase 'the curse of the law' may be an explanatory or defining genitive. If so, the phrase means 'the curse which is the law', that is, 'the accursed law' (just as in 3 : 14 'the promise of the Spirit' means 'the promised blessing which is the Spirit'). Then St Paul is practically saying: 'Christ saved us from the accursed law of Moses.' Before his conversion, Paul had an exaggerated zeal *for* the law (cf. 1 : 13); his conversion brought about a violent reaction. He felt that he had moved into a new era in which law was a thing of the past. He looked back at the law of Moses with distaste, sometimes almost with hatred, as an instrument of tyranny, to which he had been subject far too long. There is probably a studied ambiguity in the phrase 'the curse of the law' comparable to that in 'those held in regard' (2:6, etc.). In both cases, St Paul seems to wish to mock his adversaries while at the same time covering his tracks, for neither phrase *need* necessarily have any offensive overtones. In interpreting this Epistle, allowance must be made for the atmosphere of polemic debate in which it was written. There is an element of exaggeration in 3:13, which is not corrected until 6:2, where St Paul mentions at last that the Christian has not passed into an age where law has disappeared altogether, but must still fulfil 'the law of Christ'.

Unfortunately, many of St Paul's interpreters have not made allowance for the peculiar atmosphere of post-conversion enthusiasm and of polemic debate in which it was written, and have failed to keep clearly before them the distinction between first justification and final justification. The result has been an over-sharpening of the antithesis between gospel and law [45] — as if law were really something sub-Christian from which the gospel ought to deliver us — and between kerygma and didachè, kerygma being the proper subject of theology, while didachè can be left to the elementary school teacher. This lack of balance has been most pronounced in protestant writers of Lutheran tradition, with their gospel of justification by faith alone. But it has affected Catholic writers too.

In his recent book on the Sermon on the Mount, Professor W. D. Davies points out an instructive parallel between the peculiar atmosphere in which Galatians was written and an early phase of the Marxist revolution in Russia: [46]

> Parallels between Communism and Christianity have frequently been drawn, but it has seldom been noted how similar is their dealing with the question of 'law'. Marx, and other socialist theorists, approached this in two ways. First, they regarded the traditional Russian legal system, like all existing legal systems, as a cloak for class interest, a device which reflected the claim of the bourgeoisie over against the propertyless masses... Secondly, in consonance with this, the same theorists looked forward to a future in which law, like the state, would vanish....There would be a 'glorious transition to a new order of equality and freedom *without* law.' Communism would be the end of law: it reveals on the question of law what a

---

[45]  Cf. Luther, Gal, 1535, p. 313.
[46]  W. D. Davies, *The Setting of the Sermon on the Mount*, Cambridge, 1964, pp. 437-438 (quoted by kind permission of the publishers, Cambridge University Press).

historian has referred to as a 'kind of New Testament foolishness'. It is not surprising, therefore, that Soviet Russia, after 1917, passed through a period of legal nihilism....And at first, after the Revolution, in accordance with Communist theory, law did tend to die out. But not for long could such a position be held.

In the same way, sayings such as Gal 3 : 13, 'Christ has redeemed us from the curse of the law,' reflect the atmosphere of a particular phase in the history of the early Church — a phase which it is neither possible nor desirable to perpetuate. Law itself, in the Bible, is an expression of the prophetic spirit.

*How did St Paul think of 'the curse'?*

St Paul often hypostatizes 'the Law' or 'Sin' or 'Death'. He may well be doing the same with 'the Curse', since others had done this before him. [47] Zechariah regards the Curse as a punitive, destructive power which goes through the air in the form of a scroll and enters the houses of the wicked to destroy them (5 : 1-4):

Again I lifted my eyes and saw, and behold, a flying scroll! And he [an angel] said to me: 'What do you see?' I answered, 'I see a flying scroll; its length is twenty cubits, and its breadth ten cubits.' Then he said to me, 'This is the curse that goes out over the face of the whole land; for everyone who steals shall be cut off henceforth according to it, and everyone who swears falsely shall be cut off henceforth according to it. I will send it forth, says the Lord of hosts, and it shall enter the house of the thief, and the house of him who swears falsely by my name; and it shall abide in his house and consume it, both timber and stones.'

Another text which illustrates this pictorial way of thinking of blessings and curses is the story of Isaac and his two sons Esau and Jacob. When Isaac pronounces the blessing upon Jacob, it is a word of power which goes out upon Jacob, and Isaac is unable to recall it or divert it. [48] His curse too is a word of power, going out to punish and destroy; but in this case there is a possibility of diverting the curse. When Jacob says to Rebekah: 'Perhaps my father will feel me, and I shall seem to be mocking him and bring a curse upon myself and not a blessing,' Rebekah replies: 'Upon me be your curse, my son,' and Jacob is satisfied (Gen 27: 12-13). She can, as it were, put up a lightning conductor and bring down the curse upon herself; this will exhaust its strength and leave Jacob safe.

[47]   Cf. Viard, Gal, p. 71.
[48]   Cf. Isa 55 :10-11.

St Paul may perhaps be thinking in these pictorial terms. He may mean that Christ said, as it were, 'Upon me be your curse,' and drew down the curse of the law upon himself when he died by crucifixion. But this view suffers from the defect that in respect of the unbelieving Jew the curse is still operative. Christ has not destroyed the law or taken away its power to curse. So let us examine Deut 21:23 in search of a better explanation.

### What is the literal sense of Deut 21:23?

Deut 21:22-23 lays down that if a man has been found guilty and hanged on a tree, his corpse must be taken down before nightfall. The reason given is ambiguous in the Hebrew: *ki qilelath Elohim taluy*. Word for word, this means 'for a curse of God is a hanged man.' The author probably meant either 'a man hanged is an insult to God' (because man is made in God's image), or 'a man hanged is a shocking disgrace (to the land).' [49] But the Septuagint took it to mean that a man who is hanged on a tree is cursed by God, i.e., becomes the object of God's wrath and rejection. This interpretation of the text gave death by crucifixion a special horror in the eyes of the Jews.

It is not unlikely that the unconverted Jews were the first to use this text in controversy with the Christians. [50] Indeed, St Paul himself, before his conversion, may have used it against the Christians — arguing, for example, that Jesus could not possibly be the Messiah and Son of God, since by the manner of his death, he had become accursed of God, and it is unthinkable that God would have pronounced a curse, through the Scriptures, on his own Son dying in agony. [51] By means of Scriptural arguments such as this, he tried to force the Christians to blaspheme Christ — doubtless with some such formula as 'Let Jesus be anathema!' (1 Cor 12:3).

In the *Didascalia Apostolorum*, Deut 21:23 is regarded as the means whereby God blinded the Jews in punishment for their sins: [52]

Because of manifold sins there were laid upon them customs unspeakable; but by none of them did they abide, but they again provoked the Lord. Wherefore he yet added to them by the Second Legislation a blindness

---

[49] For the intensive use of *Elohim* see F. Zorell, *Lexicon Hebraicum et Aramaicum*, Rome, 1956, s.v. II, 1, c (p. 54, col. 2).
[50] Cf. Lindars, *New Testament Apologetic*, pp. 232-233.
[51] Cf. J. Jeremias, 'The Key to Pauline Theology,' *Expository Times*, 76 (1964), pp. 28-29.
[52] R. H. Connolly, *Didascalia Apostolorum*, Oxford, 1929, p. 222. Cf. also p. 230.

worthy of their works, and spoke thus: *If there be found in a man sins worthy of death, and he die, and ye hang him upon a tree; his body shall not remain the night upon the tree, but ye shall surely bury him the same day: for cursed is every one that is hanged upon a tree;* that when Christ should come they might not be able to help Him, but might suppose that He was guilty of the curse. For their blinding, therefore, was this spoken, as Isaiah said: *Behold, I show my righteousness, and thine evils: and they shall not help thee at all.*

This probably implies that Deut 21:23 continued for centuries to be a stumbling-block to the Jews. St Jerome says that the text was still used as an objection by Jews in his days. [53]

### How does St Paul use this text in 3:13?

After his conversion, St Paul had to find answers to his own previous arguments. We might have expected him to revise his interpretation of Deut 21:23 and to conclude that it does not pronounce a curse on every man who dies by crucifixion. St Jerome recommends this way of answering the Jews of his own day who brought up this text against Christians: [54]

It is first to be observed that not everyone who is hanged upon a tree is cursed of God, but only the man who has sinned and who for his crime has been condemned and raised on a cross; and he is not accursed because he has been crucified but because he has incurred such guilt as to deserve to be crucified... A man is not accursed if he is sentenced to crucifixion by the injustice of his judges and the power of his enemies, or through the clamour of a mob, or through envy of his virtues, or through the anger of a king.

St Paul, however, does not argue in this way. He takes the bolder line of saying that Jesus *did* become accursed, and he explains this startling admission by saying that it was a work of love: 'he became *for our sake* accursed.' [55] (In Rom 9:3, when he says: 'I could wish myself to be anathema from Christ for the sake of my brethren,' he is probably desiring to imitate not only Moses in Exod 32:32, but also Christ himself, who became accursed for the sake of his brethren.)

St Paul retains the interpretation of the text given in the Septuagint, except that he does *not* say that Christ became accursed 'of

---

[53] Jerome, PL 26, 387 C.
[54] Jerome, PL 26, 387-388.
[55] The paradox of 'salvation through a curse' is also mentioned in the *Didache*, 16:5. Cf. C. Taylor, *The Teaching of the Twelve Apostles with Illustrations from the Talmud*, Cambridge, 1886, pp. 100-101.

God'. He admits that by the manner of his death Christ became in some sense 'accursed'; but since he deliberately omits the phrase 'of God', he probably means, as St Thomas Aquinas says, that Christ became accursed 'in the opinion of men' — in fulfilment of Isa 53:4:

> We esteemed him stricken,
>> smitten by God and afflicted.
> But he was wounded for our transgressions,
>> he was bruised for our iniquities.

The Jews, when they saw Christ dying by crucifixion, concluded that he was indeed a malefactor, cursed of God and smitten by God (cf. Jn 19:31-37). [56]

But how can St Paul say that Christ 'by becoming accursed' saved Jewish believers from the curse which would otherwise have fallen on them? One explanation, that he drew the sting of the law and took away its power to curse, has been mentioned already and set aside.

A second explanation is that according to Gal 3:19 the law emanates, not from God himself, but from angels acting in relative independence. [57] The curse which Christ allowed to fall upon himself was, therefore, not the curse of God but of these angels. By pronouncing their curse upon Christ, the angels of the law made themselves guilty, and in this way their power was broken, for one who is guilty himself has no right to cast stones at others (cf. Jn 8:7; Rom 2:1-3). Therefore, according to this interpretation, by the manner of his death Christ broke the power of the angels of the law, so that they no longer have any power to curse the guilty. — But against this second explanation one can raise the same objection as against the first: Christ's death has not deprived the angels of the law of all power to curse. The non-Christian Jew is still subject to them. St Paul does not hold that because they made themselves guilty in the death of Christ, they no longer have any power over anyone.

There remains a third explanation. Christ in his death experienced the curse of the law. Therefore every Jew who at baptism is united with Christ in his death, undergoes with Christ the curse of the law, but the pain and shame of it are borne by Christ. That will explain why St Paul says that 'Christ is the end of the law,' not for all Jews, 'but for those who believe' (Rom 10:4). When Christ died, he did

---

[56] St Thomas is willing to admit (Gal, 405) that in a sense Christ was even 'accursed of God'—'quia Deus ordinavit quod hanc poenam sustineret, ut nos liberaret.'

[57] See below on 3:19, pp. 304.

not deliver all Jews *ipso facto* from the law, but he offered to all a way of escape from the curse of the law: through union with himself in faith and through union with his death in baptism they could pass out of the present evil aeon in which the law holds sway, into a new aeon where there is no law and no curse. — This seems to be the best explanation of how St Paul can say: 'Christ redeemed us (believing Jews) from the curse of the law by himself becoming accursed for our sake.'

More precisely, he says: 'by becoming *a curse* for our sake.' His use of the rhetorical figure of metonymy (abstract for concrete) at this point may simply be a rhetorical artifice for the sake of emphasis, [58] but it may also show that he was thinking of the Hebrew noun *qᵉlalah* which lies behind the Greek adjective *epikataratos* ('accursed').

## Is St Paul's use of this text legitimate?

St Paul may have regarded the text of the Septuagint as inspired. Whether he accepted the legend of the seventy translators as told in the *Letter of Aristeas* and elsewhere, we have no means of telling. But he seems willingly to argue from the Septuagint translation, where it suits him.

In the present case, however, he appears to have in mind both the Greek and the Hebrew. So it cannot be said that he has been misled by the Septuagint. He may have reasoned that if the Hebrew means 'a hanged man is an insult to God,' then, since God must look with abhorrence on what men recognize as an insult to him, the hanged man is abhorrent to God — which is as much as to say that he is accursed of God.

A modern reader, who regards the Hebrew as the inspired text and not the Septuagint, may be inclined to say that Deut 21 : 23 does

---

[58] There is a somewhat similar metonymy in 2 Cor 5 : 21—indeed there are two examples in this text: 'Him who knew not sin he made sin for our sake, in order that we might become the justice of God in him.' But this may not be a true parallel to Gal 3 : 13. When Paul says that Christ was 'made sin' he may mean that just as we are deprived of the glory of God by sin (cf. Rom 3 : 23) and this state of deprivation of 'glory' is a state of sin, so Christ in his Incarnation emptied himself of his glory (cf. Phil 2 : 6), and this state of deprivation can analogously be called 'sin'. So Christ emptied himself of his glory in order that we might enter into his glory. (R. de Vaux, *Ancient Israel*, London, 1961, p. 420, suggests that *hamartia* is equivalent to *hattah*, a sin-offering. But this greatly weakens the antithesis between 'sin' and 'justice'.)

not imply that Jesus became 'accursed' but merely that the treatment inflicted on him by his enemies was offensive to God. But this is too easy a way out. It remains a source of amazement that the Scripture should contain this explicit statement that the manner in which Christ died would have been an insult to God even if Christ had not been God. He became obedient to death, even to the death of the Cross, a death in which his own body was sacrilegiously used in a manner insulting to God.

A Jew might object to St Paul's use of this text by saying: 'I agree that when a man dies, he is no longer subject to the law and passes beyond the power of its curse (cf. Rom 6:7). But this is true only of physical death, not of the mystical death which you say a man undergoes in baptism. A baptized Jew remains in this present evil world, and therefore he is still subject to the curse of the law, if his sins have incurred it.'

A direct reply to this objection seems impossible. St Paul would have to begin by convincing his opponent that Jesus was the Christ and Son of God, and therefore that his death was for some great purpose — the redemption of sinners. In Gal 3:13 he is arguing with believers. He presupposes that Christ's death saves his followers from the consequences of their sins, and merely puts this into the language of the law by saying that Christ redeemed Jewish believers from the curse of the law, and that he did so by becoming 'accursed'. Gal 3:13 is not a demonstration of the efficacy of Christ's death; it is rather a description, in terms taken from the law, of what this efficacy means for Jewish Christians.

*How are the two further effects of Christ's death related to each other?*

The two further effects of Christ's death, mentioned in 3:14, are dependent on the redemption of the Jews from the curse of the law. Because Jewish apostles like St Paul were released from the law, it was possible for them to go and evangelize the Gentiles 'that the blessing of Abraham might be extended to the Gentiles' (v. 14a), and in this way both Jews and Gentiles were to receive the promised gift of the Spirit through faith (v. 14b).

The order of the two final clauses is the reverse of what might have been expected. After 'Christ redeemed us (Jews) from the curse of the law' we expect 'in order that we (Jews) might receive the promised gift through faith, in order that thereafter we might extend this blessing to the Gentiles.' Instead, St Paul has put the extension of salvation to the Gentiles first. This arrangement was probably dictated by his belief that the Gentiles must be converted before the Jews (cf. Rom 11 : 25-26). The same order is preserved in Eph 2: 14-18, where the effects of Christ's death are described as being, first, to break down the wall of separation between Jew and Gentile, and secondly, to give both Jew and Gentile access in the one Spirit to God the Father.

### *Does the gift of the Spirit fulfil the promise of the inheritance?*

In 3: 14, St Paul considers the gift of the Spirit to the Gentiles as equivalent to the extension to the Gentiles of the blessing promised to Abraham. Yet Abraham was promised a royal inheritance. Indeed in Rom 4: 13 he is said to have been promised 'ownership of the whole world'. [59] So St Paul seems to regard the gift of the Spirit as the fulfilment of the promise of a kingdom.

A similar substitution of the Spirit for the kingdom occurs in Acts 1: 6-8:

> Once when they were with him, they asked him: 'Lord, is this the time when you will restore the kingdom to Israel?' He answered: 'It is not for you to know the periods and the turning-points of history; the Father has reserved them in his own power. But you are about to receive the power of the Holy Spirit coming upon you; and you are to be my witnesses in Jerusalem, throughout Judaea and Samaria, and to the ends of the earth.'

The connection between the two is that 'kingdom' (*malkuth, basileia*) means 'royal power', and the Holy Spirit is a 'power' (*dynamis, exousia*. [60] The Spirit sent forth by Christ is his royal power. Through this power, according to Acts 1: 8, the apostles were to make the kingdom come, in the life of the Church.

Christ's royal power extends, by right, throughout the whole of the universe; therefore those who receive a share of his power are sharing in his kingship over the universe — which is the blessing promised to Abraham and his Issue. The kingdom of Christ, the Issue of Abraham, 'comes' as the Spirit is extended to the Gentiles; and as this happens, the Gentiles are blessed in Abraham and in his Issue.

---

[59] See above, pp. 254-256.
[60] Cf. H. Conzelmann, *The Theology of St Luke*, London, 1960, pp. 181-183.

*The Second Subsection, 3:15-29*

# COVENANT AND LAW

St Paul continues his discussion of the relationship between the covenant (given to Abraham) and the law (of Moses). The analysis is as follows.

A   God will be faithful to the covenant granted to Abraham and his Issue, who is one, namely Christ, 3:15-16.

B   The law does not annul the covenant, 3:17.

C   The inheritance does not come from the law, 3:18a.

D   The covenant was a free gift from God to Abraham, 3:18b.

E   *The law was a disciplinary measure of limited duration,* 3:19a.

D¹  The law was given to Moses by angels, 3:19b-20.

C¹  Life does not come to us from the law, 3:21.

B¹  The law promotes the fulfilment of the covenant, 3:22-24.

A¹  All who are baptized in Christ are one, hence are the seed of Abraham and heirs of the covenant, 3:25-29.

Here is the text:

A  *3:15* Brethren, I speak in human fashion. Once a covenant has been ratified, even a human covenant, no one sets it aside or adds conditions to it. *16* Now the promises were made to Abraham 'and to his Issue'. It does not say 'and to his issues' in the plural, but uses the singular 'and to his Issue' — and this is Christ.    B  *17* What I mean is this: the covenant had been ratified by God, and the law which was made four hundred and thirty years later does not invalidate it, so as to render the promise void.    C  *18* For if the inheritance is from the law, it is no longer from the promise.    D  But it was by way of promise that God made the gift to Abraham.    E  *19* What, then, was the purpose of the law? It was added on account of sins, until the Issue should come, to whom the promise had been made.    D¹  It was drawn up by angels by the hand of a mediator. *20* Now a mediator does not mediate between one party, and God is one.    C¹  *21* Is then the law opposed to the promises? Heaven forbid! For if a law had been given which had power to give life, truly justice would be from the law.    B¹  *22* But the Scripture has delivered up all to sin, in order that the promised blessing may be given to believers through faith in Jesus Christ. *23* But before the coming of faith we were locked up in custody until the faith should be revealed. *24* So the law was our pedagogue to Christ, that we might be justified through faith.    A¹  *25* Now that faith has come, we are no longer under a pedagogue. *26* For you are all God's sons through faith in Jesus Christ. *27* For when you were all baptized in Christ, you put on Christ. *28* There is no longer Jew or Greek, there is no longer slave or free, there is no longer male and female; for you are all one, in Christ

Jesus. *29* But if you belong to Christ, then you are the Issue of Abraham,
and heirs according to the promise.

### What is the purpose of this passage?

In this passage it becomes fully apparent that the fundamental
disagreement between St Paul and the Judaizers is over the interpretation of the Old Testament. The Judaizers say that according to St
Paul's presentation of the gospel, God has abandoned his chosen
people and therefore broken his covenant (cf. Rom 9:6; 11:1-2); if
justification is offered to Jew and Gentile alike by way of faith alone,
what is the advantage of being a Jew? St Paul retorts, in 3:15-18,
that on the contrary it is the Judaizers who fail to defend the fidelity
of God, for their theology represents him as one who first made a
gratuitous contract of gift, and then later went back on it by adding
a burdensome law. Even men, here in this wicked world, do not behave like that (cf. 3:15).

But this passage is not purely negative. Besides rejecting the
Judaizers' view, St Paul develops his own argument to show that God
*has* been faithful to his covenants. He does this by proposing an
interpretation of the promise to Abraham, the lawgiving at Sinai, the
coming of Christ, and the relationship between these three events —
or, one could say, between the three figures Abraham, Moses and
Christ.

It would, however, be too much to claim that St Paul is here
offering a Christian interpretation of the *whole* of the Old Testament.
He does not here explain his views on the relation between the promise
to Moses in Exod 3:7-8 and the promise to David in 2 Sam 7, or
on the relation of Jeremiah's prophecy of a new covenant (31:31-34)
to the Abraham-covenant on the one hand and to the Sinai-covenant
on the other. [61] He deals with these matters elsewhere: in his sermon
at Pisidian Antioch he presents Christ as the fulfilment of the promise
to David; and in 2 Cor 3 he sees the prophecy of Jeremiah fulfilled
in his own ministry. In Galatians, he concentrates on Abraham and
Moses, that is, on Genesis and Exodus, no doubt because this was
the main area of disagreement between himself and the Judaizers.
They had raised the question: 'Who are the heirs of Abraham?'
Their answer was: 'The disciples of Moses.' St Paul could not refute
this answer by speaking of Christ as the fulfilment of the promise

---

[61] Cf. G. Ernest Wright, in Anderson, *The Old Testament and Christian Faith*,
pp. 215 and 234; also L. Rost, 'Sinaibund und Davidsbund,' TLZ 72 (1947),
cols 129-134, and G. von Rad, *Theology of the Old Testament*, Edinburgh,
1965, II, pp. 323-324.

made to David, but only by showing that the true sons of Abraham are those who imitate the patriarch's faith.

In the last twenty years, Old Testament scholars have devoted much attention to the word 'covenant' (in Hebrew *berith*, in Greek *diathêkê*), and have examined the various kinds of covenant found in the Bible and in the life of the ancient Middle East. They have not, however, achieved complete agreement among themselves. [62] Some of our difficulties, when we try to understand and justify the views developed in Gal 3:15-29, arise because we possess more information than was available to St Paul, and others from our uncertainty as to how we should interpret the information now available.

Moreover, literary analysis of the Pentateuch has shown that in-spired writers within the Old Testament itself had considered the problem of the relationship between the covenant with Abraham and the Sinai-covenant, and had adopted divergent views. As the Old Testament itself does not contain one consistent covenant-theology, it was possible for both St Paul and his adversaries to appeal to dif-ferent strands of Scriptural tradition in support of their different views.

The narratives of the Abraham-covenant in Gen 12 and Gen 15 are the work of the Yahwist (tenth century B.C.), who was interested in relating the Abraham-covenant to the Davidic covenant rather than to the Sinaitic covenant. With an eye on the contemporary *Sitz im Leben* under David or Solomon, he showed by a *vaticinium ex eventu* (no doubt elaborating an earlier tradition) that Israel had a divine right to possess and rule, not only the regions occupied by Joshua, but the whole of the territory of the Davidic kingdom. These covenant passages are, therefore, Israel's title-deeds to possession of the holy land. [63] The Deuteronomic view, by contrast, severed the link between Abraham and David, placed the greatest emphasis on the Sinai-covenant, and regarded the covenant granted to the patriarchs as a mere adumbration of the Sinai-covenant (cf. Deut 5:2-3). Thirdly, the Priestly author (P) in Gen 17 goes back to the view that the Abrahamic covenant is basic — probably as a result of the repeated failures of Israel to live up to the demands of the Sinai-covenant (cf. Ezek 20).

Oversimplifying the matter, one might say that St Paul develops the thought of J and P, while his opponents adhere more closely to D.

---

[62] Cf. D. J. McCarthy, 'Covenant in the Old Testament: the Present State of the Inquiry,' CBQ 27 (1965), pp. 217-240. M. Barth, 'The Kerygma of Galatians,' *Interpretation* 21 (1967), p. 138, remarks that 'it is now necessary that the Old Testament itself and current Old Testament scholarship be used for under-standing Paul.'

[63] Cf. R. Clements, *Abraham and David*, SBT/2, No. 5, London, 1967, p. 81.

However, even D allows a certain preeminence to the patriarchal covenants, for example in Deut 9:26-27, where Moses pleads for mercy
on behalf of Israel saying: 'Remember thy servants, Abraham, Isaac
and Jacob.' This probably implies that (as St Paul was to say)
Yahweh's covenant with the patriarchs was a more immutable and
firmer ground of assurance than the Sinai-covenant. (Later Jewish
tradition regards Deut 9:27 as an appeal to the *merits* of the patriarchs. This, of course, St Paul as a Christian would not accept.)

*What is St Paul's view of the relation between the law and the
covenant?*

St Paul offers a simple, unscientific interpretation of the history
of Israel: in Genesis God gives an unconditional promise to Abraham;
there are no strings attached; Abraham is simply required to believe
that God will do what he says. Then in Exodus, a burdensome law is
imposed on the Jews. If the fulfilment of the promise is made conditional upon the fulfilment of this law, God has in fact set aside the
unconditional promise. But if even a man cannot do such a thing
without breaking faith, *a fortiori* God cannot do it. To safeguard the
fidelity of God, we must keep the promise to Abraham quite distinct
from the law given at Sinai. The covenant-relationship between God
and Israel rests on the gratuitous promises made to Abraham, not on
the law of Moses. The law was not an essential element in the
covenant-relationship; hence the law could be repealed and the covenant left intact. The law was a temporary institution.

The law did, however, in a rather unexpected way, help to lay the
scene for the fulfilment of the promise. Its actual effect in the history
of Israel was to multiply sin, for the Jews were never able to live up
to it. By making sinners of them all, it deprived them of any *claim* to
the fulfilment of the promise made to Abraham. As sinners they could
receive the inheritance only as a pure gift. Christ, whose death brings
the interim period of the law to an end, is now offering them the inheritance, along with forgiveness of their sins, as a free gift, if they
will believe.

Thus for St Paul Abraham is the great figure of the Old Testament, and Moses is an interloper, a 'minister of death' (cf. 2 Cor 3:7).
Genesis is more important than Exodus, and the gospel is a new
Genesis rather than a new Exodus. The covenant made at Sinai was
temporary, conditional, and restricted to Israel. The covenant granted
to Abraham was something far greater: it was a promise of permanent

validity, unconditional, and universal in its scope. All nations were to share in the blessing promised to Abraham and his Issue. The promise was made to Abraham before he became a Jew by circumcision (cf. Rom 4:9-12); and it was made to him, not as ancestor of Israel according to the flesh, but as ancestor of a new humanity according to the Spirit. [64]

## What was the view of the Judaizers?

The Judaizers regarded the Exodus from Egypt and the lawgiving at Sinai as the greatest events of their history, on which their relationship to God was founded. The history of the patriarchs had been nothing more than a prelude; Israel had come into being as God's people at Sinai. The covenant with Abraham was an adumbration of the Sinai-covenant. It contained from the start the moral demand: 'Walk before me and be perfect.' The law given at Sinai was simply an explicitation of this demand. The law itself was created (in the mind of God) before the foundation of the world; it was revealed at Sinai; it is eternal and will never pass away; the Messiah will give his own perfect interpretation of it; he does not abolish it. When Gentiles enter into the covenant-relationship, they must keep the law of the covenant. The law is an essential part of the covenant. If the law were destroyed, the covenant too would cease to be.

## How are we to understand the Sinai-covenant?

Valuable light has been thrown upon the structure of the covenant chapters in Exodus (ch. 19-24) by scholars who have compared them with covenants granted during the second millennium B.C. (ca 1500-1300) by the great kings of the Hittite empire (now Turkey) to their vassals. [65] These were covenants between unequal parties, granted by the stronger to the weaker, and containing stipulations which laid obligations only on the weaker. They have a regular structure. First, the preamble identifies the Hittite king who is granting the covenant by giving his name, titles and ancestry, for example: [66]

---

[64] Cf. T. W. Manson, On Paul and John, p. 45. W. Zimmerli in Westermann, Essays in Old Testament Interpretation, p. 93, points out that the universal reference of the promise to Abraham counterbalances the world-wide curse in Gen 3:11.

[65] The first writer to point out these resemblances was G. E. Mendenhall, 'Covenant Forms in Israelite Tradition,' The Biblical Archaeologist 17 (1954), pp. 50-76. See also W. Moran in Verbum Domini 40 (1962), pp. 1-17.

[66] From Pritchard, ANET, p. 203.

These are the words of the Sun, Mursilis, the great king, the king of the Hatti land, the valiant, the favourite of the storm-god, the son of Supiluliumas, the great king, the king of the Hatti land, the valiant.

Secondly, *the historical prologue* gives a history of the previous relationship between the Hittite kingdom and the vassal, with special emphasis on the benefits conferred on the vassal by the Hittite king. These benefits place the vassal under a moral and legal obligation to remain faithful to the Hittite king and to obey his stipulations. The vassal's fidelity is to spring from gratitude for benefits received. Here is an example: [66]

Aziras was the grandfather of you, Duppi-Tessub. He rebelled against my father, but submitted again to my father...

Nearly the whole document is written in this 'I-Thou' formula. 'The covenant form is still thought of as a personal relationship, rather than as an objective, impersonal statement of law.' [67] Thirdly, *the stipulations* follow. These are laid on the vassal only. The great king undertakes no specific obligations (unless he chooses to make a promise). Examples of typical stipulations are:

not to become vassal of any other power (e.g. Egypt),
not to attack other vassals of the Hittite king,
to take up arms at the call of the Hittite king,
not to listen to rumours against the Hittite king,
to appear before the king at regular intervals and pay tribute.

Fourthly, provision is made for *deposit of the document* in a temple and for periodic public reading. Fifthly, *the gods invoked as witnesses* are listed. The gods of both sides were invoked, on the analogy of the human witnesses of a civil contract. Sixthly, *blessings and curses* are pronounced, the blessings to become operative if the vassal remains loyal, the curses if he breaks faith. Seventhly, *an oath* is taken by the vassal in acceptance of the covenant. And finally, *a ceremony* is held to solemnize the covenant. The purpose of such a covenant was to clarify an unclear legal situation which would otherwise have been fraught with danger to both sides. [68]

The Sinai-covenant, as described in Exodus, conforms fairly closely to the above pattern. Yahweh is thought of as a Great King who is granting a covenant of protection to the little nation of Israel. [69] There

---

66   From Pritchard, ANET, p. 203.
67   Mendenhall, art. cit., p. 59.
68   Cf. G. von Rad, *Genesis*, London, 1969, p. 196.
69   Men cannot think of their relations with God except by means of analogies drawn from their own personal, social and political relationships. 'Redemption' of captives (and slaves) was much commoner in the N.T. world than it is in ours. And St Anselm took his concept of 'satisfaction' from contemporary society.

is an historical prologue recalling the benefits which he has just conferred on Israel (20:2): 'I am Yahweh your God, who brought you
out of the land of Egypt and out of the house of bondage.' The basis
of the covenant is Israel's gratitude for this benefit now in the past,
and hope for similar divine interventions in the future. Israel's primary
obligation is fidelity — to keep faith to the great God of heaven. The
law simply stipulates the forms which this fidelity must take. [70] First
come the general stipulations, then follow corresponding blocks of
particular laws. [71] The covenant is ratified by a sacrifice (ch. 24), and
blessings and curses are attached (cf. Gal 3:10). [72]

Thus the Mosaic religion, as presented in Exodus, rests on faith,
just as Christianity does. Just as the Jews renewed the memory of the
deliverance from Egypt in order to reaffirm their faith in this event
as a divine intervention, so Christians renew the memory of Christ's
death and resurrection in order to reaffirm their faith in these events
as a divine intervention. On the Jew's faith in the Exodus rests his
observance of the law of Moses; on the Christian's faith in the cross
and resurrection rests his observance of the law of Christ. There
seems no reason why the Jews should not have developed a theology
of justification-by-faith with the saving-events of the Exodus occupy-
ing the same position as the death-and-resurrection of Christ in the
theology of St Paul. Such a theology is implicit in the psalms which
constantly remind the worshipper of the events of the Exodus, in order
to renew his gratitude, his hope, and his fidelity. (It is curious that
the Church, which *has* an explicit theology of justification by faith,
has continued to use the psalms which speak of the *Jewish* saving-
events. The Christian worshipper is meant to use these as types of

---

[70]   Contrast Gal 3:12: 'The law is not from faith.'
[71]   Cf. A. E. Guilding, 'Notes on the Hebrew Law Codes,' JTS 49 (1948), pp.
       43-52.
[72]   E. Gerstenberger, 'Covenant and Commandment,' JBL 84 (1965), pp. 38-51,
       criticizes the work of Mendenhall on the ground that the commandments of the
       decalogue have little in common with treaty stipulations: the commandments,
       he says, are not arrived at by previous negotiations, and they are not linked
       directly with the curses; they regulate relationships, not between the Israelites
       and God, but between one Israelite and another; they do not specify what the
       Israelites are to do in particular eventualities; their original *Sitz im Leben* is
       not the vassal-treaty but the instruction given by a father to his son. All these
       points may be conceded; but they do not destroy the resemblance pointed out
       by Mendenhall. In the decalogue, Yahweh is giving instructions to his first-
       born son (cf. Exod 5:22-23), but he is doing so within a framework which is
       alien to the father-son relationship. There have been no previous negotiations,
       because God does not negotiate with men; and if the content of the command-
       ments differs from that of the stipulations of the vassal treaties, that is because
       what God demands of men is not what a human king demands of his subjects.
       The Sinai covenant resembles the Hittite vassal-treaties in form and structure,
       not in content.

the death and resurrection of Christ no doubt; but this is a feat of which few are really capable. So we continue in our prayers to look back to the Exodus instead of the Cross and Resurrection!)

*How are we to understand the Abraham-covenant?*

In Genesis, the relationship between God and Abraham is not thought of as being analogous to that between a Hittite king and his vassal. Abraham is not a king; the only stipulation laid upon him is that he be circumcised; the emphasis is upon God's promise.

The substance of the covenant is the promise of an inheritance and of a great posterity (12:1-3; 15:5; 17:4-8). The promise of a great posterity does not conform to any human pattern, since no man can make such promises. But the promise of an inheritance is comparable to the making of a will. The making of a will is essentially the institution of an heir, to whom the testator promises a gift of property.

The property promised to Abraham in Gen 15:18-21 and Gen 17:8 is 'the whole land of Canaan', and in 17:6 he is promised: 'kings shall come forth from you.' So the inheritance promised to Abraham was in fact a kingdom — a large piece of land to be ruled over by his descendants. The promise received its first fulfilment in the time of David.

*Were the Abraham-covenant and the Sinai-covenant two different types of covenant?*

Even if it is allowed that the writers or editors of the Pentateuch thought of the Abraham-covenant on the analogy of a man's will instituting an heir, and the Sinai-covenant on the analogy of a vassal treaty, it does not follow that the Old Testament knows of two radically different types of covenant, or that the attempts to assimilate the one to the other were mistaken. The Sinai-covenant itself was unlike a vassal treaty in that it did not confirm the vassal in possession of a kingdom but only promised him possession in the future. The substance of both covenants was the same: the promise of an 'inheritance' which was to be a kingdom. [72]

---

[73] This view has recently been defended, most persuasively, by O. Eissfeldt, 'Das Gesetz ist zwischeneingekommen,' TLZ 91 (1966), cols 1-6 (English summary in *Theology Digest* 16, 1968, pp. 135-36). He argues that in the oldest stratum of tradition, represented by Exod 34:10-13, 15-16, the object of the Sinai-covenant is a divine promise, not a law; it is the promise of military victory and conquest of Canaan. Eissfeldt remarks that Gal 3:17, 'the law was inserted, or intruded, four hundred and thirty years later,' *could* be understood as refer-

The chief difference between the two covenants is that in the Abraham-covenant God's moral demands on Abraham are either implict or very briefly stated, whereas in the Sinai-covenant, as it is described in Exodus, they are spelled out in detail. But in both covenants there is the same promise, the same demand for fidelity, and substantially the same moral demand. Both covenants were granted by God by way of gift, but both called for human cooperation. Both were bilateral covenants or alliances. [74]

St Paul, however, maintains that the promise or covenant given to Abraham was different in kind from the Sinai-covenant. The text of Gen 12:1-3 (J) seems to bear out his view that there were no stipulations attached to the promise made to Abraham:

> The Lord said to Abraham: Leave your country, your kinsfolk and your father's house, for the land which I will show you. 2 And I will make a great nation of you. I will bless you and make your name great, so that you will be a blessing. 3 I will bless them that bless you, and curse them that curse you. In you shall all the nations of the earth be blessed.

After Abraham has left his country, his kinsfolk and his father's house, he has no further conditions to fulfil, but God has bound himself in fidelity to give the blessings enumerated in vv. 2-3. [75]

There are other texts, however, which point to a different conclusion. Probably the Judaizers argued from these texts that the Sinai-covenant was a renewal and development of the Abraham-covenant. In Gen 15:1-21, the second account of the covenant with Abraham, the narrator seems anxious to relate the Abraham-covenant to the Sinai-covenant. In 15:7 there is an historical prologue: 'I am the Lord who brought you from Ur of the Chaldeans, to give you this land to possess,' which is clearly an imitation of Exod 20:2: 'I am the Lord your God who brought you out of the land of Egypt, out of the house of bondage.' Secondly, the Abraham covenant is now confirmed by a sacrifice (15:9-10). And thirdly, the phenomena of smoke and fire appear (15:7) to match Exod 19:8. [76]

But in Gen 15 there are still no stipulations. The first steps have been taken in the assimilation of the Abraham-covenant to the Sinai-

---

ring to the four and a half centuries separating the Sinai-covenant from Elijah and the prophets (who in fact 'inserted' most of the pentateuchal legislation). St Paul was not intending to refer to this later period; but his view that the law was a later addition to the covenant is in agreement with Eissfeldt's analysis of the evolution of the Sinai-narratives in Exodus.

[74] Cf. Clements, *Abraham and David*, pp. 33-34; Galot, *La Rédemption*, pp. 36-37.

[75] However, even in Gen 12:1-3 a moral demand is implicit. Since God is a moral being, he cannot be undertaking to curse those who curse Abraham even if his conduct has made him worthy to be cursed.

[76] Cf. Zimmerli, in Westermann, *Essays on Old Testament Interpretation*, p. 91.

covenant, but there is still no law in the Abraham-covenant. Stipulations first make their appearance in Gen 17:1-21, which is part of
the Priestly document. [77] It begins with a moral demand: 'Walk in
my presence and be perfect (*tamim*)'. Abraham is required to be perfect
in fidelity: he must commit himself wholeheartedly and without re-
serve to this relationship. [78] Further, it is stipulated that every male
Israelite must bear the sign of the covenant, namely circumcision.

The promises, too, in the Priestly version have been assimilated
to the promises made by God at Sinai. 'I will make nations of you
and kings shall descend from you' is doubtless intended to anticipate
Exod 19:6: 'You shall be to me a kingdom of priests (or, a priestly
kingdom).' And the promise, 'I will be their God,' anticipates the
very substance of the Sinai covenant. [79]

Thus within the Old Testament itself there are attempts to show
that the Abraham-covenant was an adumbration of the Sinai-covenant
— implying that the two covenants are of the same type.

*How did the Judaizers understand the relationship between the two
covenants?*

The Judaizers held that the Sinai-covenant was a renewal of the
Abraham-covenant, and presumably that the Mosaic law was an explicitation of the demand to walk before God and be perfect. [80] There
is no reason to think that they regarded the two covenants as being
of distinct types, the one a covenant of gift, the other a wage contract.
On the contrary, they regarded the two covenants as being substantially
one and the same, the first being an adumbration of the second, and
the second an explicitation of the first.

Since they held that the two covenants were really one, they could
treat circumcision as a part of 'the law' of the covenant. [81] It was the
earliest of the stipulations embodied in the one covenant.

---

[77] According to Zimmerli, op. cit., p. 94, P puts the covenant right back into
the time of Abraham and 'speaks not a word about a covenant in the time of
Moses.'
[78] Cf. von Rad, *Genesis*, p. 196. In Gen 20:5 *tamim* clearly means 'unreserved'
or 'sincere'.
[79] Cf. von Rad, *Genesis*, p. 195.
[80] Probably they would not have admitted St Paul's charge that they were treating
the law as an addition (*epidiatagma*). They contend that the law was implicitly
there from the beginning. Here St Paul has the stronger case. The ritual legislation was an addition, to stop the Israelites from falling into idolatry. See
below, pp. 294-295.
[81] St Paul, on the other hand, having separated the Abraham covenant from the
law, should logically have given one set of arguments to show that the law is

Since they held that the one covenant was still in force and was to be fulfilled by the return of Christ to establish his kingdom, they naturally held that any Gentile [82] who wished to become a party to the covenant must obey the stipulations embodied in it: 'unless you are circumcised and follow the customs of Moses, you cannot be saved' (Acts 15:1).

## Why did St Paul reject this view?

St Paul refuses to regard the law as being in any way a part of the Abraham-covenant. He speaks of the law as one thing and the covenant (or 'promise') as another, so that if the inheritance comes from the one, it does not come from the other.

Mendenhall tries to justify St Paul's position by contrasting the nature of the two covenants:

> It is not often enough seen that no obligations are imposed upon Abraham. Circumcision is not originally an obligation, but a *sign* of the covenant, like the rainbow in Gen 9. It serves to identify the recipient(s) of the covenant, as well as to give a concrete indication that a covenant exists. It is for the protection of the promise, perhaps, like the mark on Cain in Gen 4.
>
> The covenant of Moses, on the other hand, is almost the exact opposite. It imposes specific obligations on the tribes or clans without binding Yahweh to specific obligations. [83]

No doubt St Paul would have accepted this argument, since he does regard the two covenants as different in kind; but the argument which he uses in 3:15-29 takes a more subtle course. He rejects the Judaizers' view on the ground that it attributes to God a degree of dishonesty and infidelity which is not tolerated even among human beings, bad as they are. Once a man has made a promise or settlement or covenant in due legal form, the civil law holds him to his promise, however freely it was made. The law does not allow him, later on, in a less generous mood, to add conditions, impossible of fulfilment, which would tacitly annul the promise. Even where the law cannot enforce promises, it is universally understood that a man is a scoundrel if he

---

no longer binding and another to show that circumcision is no longer required. In Galatians he talks as if circumcision were a part of the Mosiac law. An Old Testament scholar, who heard the present writer lecturing on this problem, remarked in the discussion afterwards that this shortcoming of St Paul's argument 'sticks out like a sore thumb.' Cf. Jn 7:22.

[82] Cf. Gen 17:13, Ezek 44:9.
[83] Mendenhall, art. cit., p. 62.

evades fulfilment by adding conditions. For example, if a candidate seeking office as magistrate promises that should he be elected he will provide ten acres for every landless man, and then after election, explains that he meant that he would enact a law enabling every landless man to buy ten acres of land at the market price, he would be considered to have broken his promise, for anyone obtaining a holding (in Hebrew 'an inheritance') in this way would obtain it from the law at his own cost, not from the magistrate's election promise as a free gift. Or to take a simpler example: A rich man says to his son aged twelve: 'If you are successful in your studies, I will pay you an annuity of £500 when you leave school.' Then, when his son is in his last year at school and working hard at chemistry and physics, the father adds: 'The test of whether you have succeeded in your studies will be whether you can recite the whole of Homer's Iliad by heart in Greek.' The addition of such a condition, virtually impossible of fulfilment, would in fact nullify the promise.

St Paul's argument against the Judaizers is that according to their theology God's conduct has been as deceptive as that. He made a solemn promise to Abraham, then later added stipulations too burdensome to be fulfilled. This is simply a dishonest way of annulling the promise. An interpretation of the history of Israel which attributes such infidelity and injustice to God cannot be right. One must therefore find some other explanation of the relation of the Mosaic law to the Abraham-covenant: 'What, then, *is* the purpose of the law?' (3 : 19). This question will be discussed later.

The addition of burdensome conditions *could* convert a gratuitous promise into a wage-contract. If a farmer says to a tramp: 'Come to my house and I will give you a meal,' then, when the tramp arrives, adds: 'First of course you must do some work: cut the hedge back all round that field,' the tramp would receive the meal as wages for work done. But presumably St Paul did not think that the Sinai-covenant was of the form, 'Do these works of the law, and you will receive the kingdom as wages.' As there is no proportion between the work and the 'wages', the Sinai-covenant cannot reasonably be regarded as a wage contract.

St Paul's argument is not that whereas the Abraham-covenant was entirely unconditional, the Sinai-covenant was burdened with intolerable conditions, and that these cannot be one and the same contract. His argument is that when a man makes a covenant of promise, fidelity requires that he should state any conditions first, before the covenant is ratified; he cannot add them afterwards, or he would be going back on his promise and proving unfaithful to his word. If this holds for man, *a fortiori* it holds for God, who is more faithful than men.

## Is St Paul arguing from Jewish law or from Roman?

V. 15 has been interpreted above as referring to human covenants in general: once ratified, they cannot be 'renegotiated' by anyone — neither the donor nor any third party can add burdensome conditions which the recipient did not foresee when he accepted the covenant.

Some commentators take the word 'covenant' (*diathêkê*) here in the more restricted sense of a last will and testament. Then the question arises, whether St Paul is referring to Jewish or to Roman law when he says that no one can set aside or add to such a testament. Both views have been held by recent writers, [84] but neither is satisfactory, since in both systems of law a man could annul his will and testament by a later will, or could add codicils to his first will (i.e., directions to the heir, imposing a burden upon him). In both systems, it is claimed, there were *some* forms of testament which the testator was unable to alter. But this observation, if true, is not relevant, since St Paul is not speaking about a particular type of will. He is stating a general principle about 'covenants'. If he has in mind any particular kind of covenant while making this general statement, it would seem to be a covenant of promise made by a father to his son, to come into effect when the son reaches his majority, on the assumption that the father will still be living. [85] If a human father makes a formal covenant of this kind, fidelity requires that he should not, years later, add burdensome conditions. By analogy, therefore, since God is more faithful than man, if God made formal promises to Abraham and his

---

[84] E. Bammel, 'Gottes DIATHEKE (Gal 3:15-17) und das Jüdische Rechtsdanken,' NTS 6 (1960), pp. 313-319, maintains that St Paul is referring to a type of *mattanah* (deed of gift); but his account of the matter does not agree with that to be found in L. N. Dembitz, *The Jewish Encyclopedia*, Vol. 12, New York, 1907, under 'Will'. G. M. Taylor, 'The Function of *Pistis Christou* in Galatians,' JBL 85 (1966), pp. 58-76, maintains that St Paul is arguing from Roman law. He thinks that by a Roman *testamentum* 'the transfer (of property) was thought of as taking immediate effect when the testament was made' (p. 65). This was perhaps equivalently so in the case of an *extraneus heres* (an heir adopted from outside the family). Cf. Ramsay, Gal, p. 353. But it is hardly to be supposed that Gal 3:15 means: 'When a man has made a will in favour of an *heres extraneus,* under Roman law no one can set it aside.' St Paul's proposition is entirely general. Moreover, as a matter of fact, under Roman law such a will could be set aside, e.g., through a successful *querela inofficiosi testamenti* or plaint that the will was 'unduteous'—unfair to the testator's family.

[85] Such a covenant bears some resemblance to a will. But when St Paul develops his argument in 4:1-4, he does not imply that the father envisages his own death. Cf. G in G on 4:2.

Issue, he cannot have added burdensome conditions to this covenant in the time of Moses.

The answer is, then, that St Paul is not referring to any particular code of law but to a principle of conduct accepted by honest men everywhere. The argument would, therefore, be equally intelligible — or equally obscure — whether used at Antioch or in Galatia.

## *Has 3:15 a special message for speculative theologians?*

St Thomas Aquinas generalizes from 3:15 and justifies the use of secular learning by Christian theologians: [86]

> *I speak in human fashion,* that is, in accordance with human reason and human custom. Here we have a proof that we may use any truth from any science in our discussions of the truth of faith. As we read in Deut 21:11, 'If you see among the captives a beautiful woman, and you have desire for her and would take her for yourself as wife, then you shall bring her home to your house' — that is, if secular wisdom and learning please you, you shall bring them within your domain — 'and she shall shave her head and pare her nails' — that is, you shall prune away all erroneous notions. That is why in many places in his Epistles the Apostle uses Gentile authors, for example, in 1 Cor 15:33: 'Bad company ruins good morals.'

St Thomas is of course defending his own theological method. He quotes Aristotle several times in his commentary on Galatians — for example, two pages later, when commenting on 3:19, 'the law was added on account of sins':

> The reason can be taken from the Philosopher (Aristotle) in the Fourth Book of his *Ethics*: men who are well disposed are moved to do good of their own accord; fatherly advice is sufficient for them, hence they have no need of law.

St Paul himself gives the general rule on which St Thomas acts when he says in 1 Thes 5:21: 'Test every coin; keep what rings true.' But he did not make extensive use of it. St Thomas's phrase, 'in many places in his Epistles', is an exaggeration. St Paul shows no familiarity with secular Greek literature. The few tags he quotes were probably proverbial. He may not have known that in 1 Cor 15:33 he was quoting Menander's *Thaïs*.

## *'The Issue is Christ' (v. 16) — How does St Paul know this?*

'The Issue is Christ' may not be a specifically Christian statement. Unconverted Jews who believed that Gen 22:18, 'in your issue shall

---

86   St Thomas, Gal, 408 B.

all the nations of the earth be blessed,' pointed forward to the Messianic era when Israel would enjoy world empire, would agree that the 'issue' in this and parallel texts is the Messiah.

St Paul learned that Jesus was the promised 'Issue' of Abraham when he learned that he was the Messiah, that is, during his Damascus vision. When once he had seen Jesus glorified as Lord, more radiant than any star, he knew that the promise to Abraham had been fulfilled: a descendant of Abraham had entered into possession of the universe as its Lord and Master. Through Isaac Abraham had become the father of the Jews and Edomites; through Jesus risen from the dead he had become the father of men of all nations. [87]

At the same time, St Paul learned that Jesus as Lord identifies himself with those who believe in him. If he suffers in them, they reign in him. Therefore the Christ who is the promised Issue of Abraham is both an individual and a collectivity. At the beginning of the subsection (v. 16b) St Paul points out that he is one; at the end (vv. 26-29) he adds that he is many. St Paul must have been delighted when after his vision, he reread Genesis and noticed that the word 'Issue' is a singular collective noun. Once again, the fuller sense of Scripture is an ultraliteral sense (cf. 3 : 8).

### How does 3:16 compare with 3:7?

In 3 : 7 St Paul said: 'Recognize, then, that the men of faith — these are the sons of Abraham.' But in 3 : 16 he does not argue that as Jesus was preeminently the man of faith, therefore he was the promised Issue of Abraham. He takes it for granted, as a point that will not be questioned by his adversaries, that Jesus was a descendant of Abraham according to the flesh. [88] The proof that Jesus is the promised 'Issue' is not that he particularly resembled Abraham in any respect during his earthly ministry, but simply that the promise to Abraham has in fact been fulfilled in him, since he now sits at the right hand of God as 'Lord' of all things in heaven, on earth, and under the earth.

Yet, it seems, St Paul could have presented Christ as the spiritual son of Abraham par excellence. For Jesus, at God's command, offered not a son but himself as a sacrifice. He knew and believed that his death would ransom the many, and he trusted his Father to raise him from the dead for the sanctification of all the nations. It is probably

---

[87]  Cf. Lindars, *New Testament Apologetic*, p. 226.
[88]  Cf. Chrysostom PG 61, 654 C.

a mistake to attribute so much knowledge to Christ that there is no room for any kind of faith in his spiritual experience. His dying words, 'Father, into thy hands I commend my spirit' (Lk 23:46), were certainly in some sense an act of faith. His faith was vindicated at the resurrection, when, as we read in 1 Tim 3:16, 'he was justified in spirit.' This obscure phrase is the second half of an antithesis:

> He was revealed in flesh;
> he was justified in spirit.

Probably the meaning is that Jesus appeared on earth in a weak, passible, fleshly body, in which he was put to death; but at his resurrection he was justified or vindicated in a 'spiritual body'. [89] It is, therefore, preeminently true of Christ that 'he trusted in God, and it was reckoned to him as righteousness.'

Christian believers who seek justification through faith in Christ are in fact associating themselves with the very act of faith by which Christ himself was justified or vindicated. Through sharing in his act of faith, they share in his justification — they receive a share in the royal spirit with which he was anointed after his resurrection. [90]

From the comparison of 3:7 and 3:16 it also appears that even Gentile 'sons of Abraham' are in some sense sons of Abraham according to the flesh, for Christ is a son of Abraham according to the flesh, and all believers, whether Jews or Gentiles, are united with him by a bond which St Paul compares to marriage. [91] The corporate personality of Christ is the Issue of Abraham according to the flesh, because Christ is a Jew.

*'If the inheritance is from the law, it is no longer from the promise' (v. 18) — How could the Judaizers reply to this?*

The Judaizers could reply: 'God's promise was: "I will grant the kingdom, if Israel will fulfil the law." Christ did fulfil every jot and tittle of the law, and accordingly in him Israel had entered into the promised kingdom. Therefore the inheritance is both from the law and from the promise.'

St Paul would probably reply: 'Christ did not enter into the kingdom and open up the way into the kingdom for us by offering

---

[89] Cf. 1 Cor 15:44; 1 Pet 4:18.
[90] Cf. Rom 1:4. F. J. Schierse, *Verheissung und Heilsvollendung*, Munich, 1955, p. 205, on Heb 12:2: 'Christ is here treated as the highest model of faith.' And see above, pp. 203-204.
[91] See below on 4:18.

the sacrifices laid down in the law. They had been offered over and over again, ineffectually. He opened up the way for Israel to enter into the inheritance by offering another sacrifice, *not* prescribed in the law. If justification had come through the sacrifices prescribed in the law, Christ's sacrifice would have been for nothing. That is why I say that the promise to Abraham had been fulfilled not through the law of Moses but through the death of Christ.'

*What was the basis of obligation in each of the covenants?*

The just actions of Abraham (for example, his obedience when ordered to sacrifice Isaac) rested ultimately on his faith in God — not merely on his faith in God's promise. He trusted God's guidance even when it ran counter to his own prudence. He must have believed in God's power and providence and veracity before he accepted the word of promise in Gen 15:5. Therefore, one can see in him the *pius credulitatis affectus* (devout readiness to believe), to start with. After he had accepted the word of promise, his obedience rested not only on his fundamental trust in the goodness of God, but also on *gratitude* for the promise and *hope* of its fulfilment.

The Sinai-covenant too rested on a prevenient belief in God's power, which had been revealed in the drowning of Pharoah's army and again in the thunder and lightning at Sinai. Here belief was reinforced by *gratitude for blessings already received* (i.e. for the liberation from Egypt), by gratitude for a further promise (Exod 19:6: 'you shall be to me a kingdom of priests and a holy nation'), and by *hope* for further blessings comparable to the wonders of the Exodus.

In both cases it is possible to discern the psychological mechanism which connects faith with fidelity to God's will: faith works through gratitude and hope. But this is not the whole of the story. The *pius credulitatis affectus* which disposes a man to believe God's word of promise also disposes him immediately to obey God's word of command. It is almost identical with charity.

These reflections show that St Paul's formula 'faith working through charity' (5:6) requires a good deal of amplification. If the *pius credulitatis affectus* is largely made up of charity, charity works in faith. And this faith does not work *directly* through charity, but by means of gratitude and hope. Since the Christian liturgy is called 'Eucharistia' (Greek for 'gratitude'), it is surprising that St Paul omits this notion from the theology worked out in Galatians and Romans. It does not come into its own until Colossians. The reason for its absence from Galatians may be that St Paul is almost exclusively concerned, in the dogmatic section of this Epistle, with *first* justification (contrast 1 Cor 10:1-13). The same is true of Romans, and these two Epistles set the pattern for later theological development. As a result, the concept of 'gratitude' has never had the position in our theology which the liturgical use of the word *Eucharistia* suggests that it ought to have.

## How did St Paul work out his theology of justification by faith?

Unfortunately, we know very little about the theological views held by St Paul in his pre-conversion days. It is possible that he had already developed a theology of justification-by-faith, and that after his conversion he simply attached faith to the new saving events (the cross and resurrection) in place of the old (the Exodus). His undoubted zeal for the law before conversion does not necessarily exclude this possibility. His activity as a persecutor does not necessarily prove that in his Pharisaic days he held that a man is justified by his own works. He may have held that every Jew must obey the law as a divine command, and that no one is likely to do so unless he firmly believes in the reality of God's intervention at the Red Sea and at Sinai. There is, however, this important difference, that he understood Christian justification to involve forgiveness, and he did not suppose, even before his conversion, that the events of Sinai mediated forgiveness. [92] But more probably before his conversion he held a theology of justification by works such as he rejects in Phil 3:6-7. In attacking the Judaizers he is attacking his former self and defending the truth of what he learned at the time of his conversion. [93]

## What is St Paul's own view of the law?

Having criticized and rejected the view that the law is an addition to the covenant granted to Abraham, St Paul must offer a positive interpretation of his own. He does this in a brief and obscure passage, 3:19:

> What then was the purpose of the law? It was added on account of sins, to remain in force until the coming of the Issue to whom the promise had been made, and it was given by angels into (?) the hand of a mediator.

---

[92] Cf. G. Vermes, *Scripture and Tradition in Judaism* (Studia Postbiblica), Leiden, 1961, pp. 218-229.

[93] Cf. Luther, quoted above, p. 251, n. 18.

L

Three points are made here, each of which will require examination: first, the law was given 'on account of sins', to multiply sins, and yet not to impede the fulfilment of the promises; secondly, it was given by angels, not by God himself; thirdly, it was a temporary enactment, and its time is over.

### Does 'the law' in v. 19 include the decalogue?

It is hard to believe that St Paul regarded the decalogue as a list of rules for spiritual infants, to be discarded, like animal sacrifices and food-laws, when Israel reached maturity. The Greek Fathers (quoted below) draw a distinction between the moral law and the ceremonial law, and explain St Paul's statements about 'the law' as referring only to the ceremonial law. One feels instinctively that this must be correct, but it is difficult to show that St Paul drew the distinction in question. [94] He never says that a part of the Mosaic law remains in force. The one law which he acknowledges is the 'law of Christ' (6:2). However, according to Rom 13:9 this sums up the moral precepts of the decalogue.

The one indication that 3:19 concerns only the ceremonial law is the statement that 'it was added on account of transgressions.' If, as seems most likely, this means: 'it was added because Israel had fallen into idolatry (by worshipping the Golden Calf) and to prevent further sins of idolatry,' St Paul cannot be talking about the decalogue, which was given before the making of the Golden Calf, but only about the further legislation added after Israel had sinned. Strictly speaking, the decalogue was not 'added' at all; it summed up the religion of the patriarchs. What was added was the positive ritual-legislation concerning sacrifices, forbidden foods, etc.

It is unsafe to suppose that St Paul's view of what happened at Sinai was derived solely from the text of Exodus. He probably ac-

---

[94] Theodore of Mopsuestia, Gal, pp. 30-31, justifies the distinction by appealing as usual to the contrast between the present life and the life to come: in the life to come, the moral commandments, which can be summed up in the one precept of charity, will still be observed. Christians, who already live, by anticipation, in the world to come, must therefore continue to observe the moral commandments. But circumcision, sacrifices and feast days will have no place in the world to come; they belong to the old aeon to which Christians are dead. Theodoretus, PG 82, 474 A says much the same. St Thomas, Gal, 397 D, gives a philosophical explanation: 'Of the works of the law some were moral, some ceremonial. But the moral works, though contained in the law, could not properly be called "works of the law", since man is drawn towards these by natural instinct and by the law of nature; only the ceremonial works are properly speaking "the works of the law".'

cepted midrashic developments of this narrative, as he certainly did of the rock which gushed water in the desert (1 Cor 10 : 4). One such development is preserved by Irenaeus, who says that God himself gave the decalogue, but empowered Moses to make the rest of the legislation after Israel had sinned: [95]

> Moses again says to them: 'Choose life that you and your descendants may live, loving the Lord your God, obeying his voice, and cleaving to him; for that means life to you and length of days' (Deut 30 : 19-20). To instruct men for this 'life', God himself personally spoke the words of the decalogue to all alike; that is why they remain valid for us, for they are not abolished but extended and enlarged through his incarnation. But the precepts of slavery he laid separately upon the people through Moses — precepts designed for their training or their punishment, as Moses himself says: 'And the Lord commanded me at that time to teach you statutes and ordinances' (Deut 4 : 14).

A midrashic tradition similar to this probably lies behind St Paul's all too brief statement about 'the law' in 3 : 19.

*What connection does St Paul make between 'the (ceremonial) law' and sin?*

The statement that 'the law was added on account of (or, for the sake of) sins' is a polemic utterance which has always been offensive to the Jews. It may be a product of St Paul's habit of thinking in antitheses. The Judaizers were saying: 'The law was given to enable us to become just men, to train us to habits of justice by multiplying just acts — in a word, the law was given for the sake of justice.' St Paul retorts: 'On the contrary, the law was given for the sake of sin.' This provocative utterance is not arrived at slowly by a careful process of thought. It is flung out in the heat of debate — and the hearer is left to consider in what sense or senses it is true. Four possible meanings have been suggested, of which the first two go together:

(1) 'The law was added on account of the sins which Israel had committed,' and in particular on account of the making and worship of the Golden Calf. In this sense, St Paul's words cannot refer to the decalogue, for according to Exod 34 : 1 the same commandments were written on the second set of tables, given after the making of the Calf, as had been written on the first set, which Moses

---

[95]  Irenaeus, *Adv. Haer.*, IV, 28.

broke. Moreover, the commandments of the decalogue cannot be regarded as a punishment for sin; they arise from the very nature of man and from his condition as God's creature. But the burdensome ceremonial law could well be regarded as a punishment for sin.

(2) 'The law was added to restrain the Jews from falling into further sins, especially sins of idolatry.' Chrysostom expresses this by saying that the law was a bit put between the teeth of the Israelites to hold them in check. [96] It restrained the Jews partly by its threats of dire sanctions, and partly by preserving them from contact with sinful Gentile idolaters (cf. Lev 20:22-26).

These two explanations are complementary to each other and both should be admitted. Thus Irenaeus says: [97]

> At first, God admonished them through the natural precepts which he had implanted in men from the beginning, that is, through the decalogue (observance of which is necessary for salvation); and he demanded nothing further of them. Thus Moses says in Deuteronomy [5:22 — immediately after the decalogue]: 'These are all the words which the Lord spoke to the whole assembly of the children of Israel at the mountain, and he added nothing more, and he wrote them on two tables of stone and gave them to me' in order that those who wished to follow him might keep the commandments.
> But when they turned aside to make the Calf, and returned in mind to Egypt, desiring to be slaves rather than free men, they received, as their concupiscence deserved, further servile obligations, which did not separate them from God, but did impose upon them a yoke of slavery, as Ezekiel says when he explains why such a law was given: 'Their eyes went after the lust of their heart, and I gave them precepts that were not good, and statutes in which they might not live.'

The *punitive* function of the ceremonial law is emphasized by the author of the *Didascalia Apostolorum*, who warns his Christian readers not to read the Mosaic legislation as if it were meant for them: [98]

> Have this set before thine eyes, that thou discern and know what is the law, and what are the bonds of the Second Legislation... For the law is that which the Lord God spoke before the people had made the calf and served idols, which consists of the ten commandments and the judgments. But after they had served idols, He justly laid upon them bonds, as they were worthy. But do not thou therefore lay them upon thee; for our Saviour came for no other cause but to fulfil the law, and to set us loose from the bonds of the Second Legislation.

---

[96] Cf. Chrysostom, PG 61, 654 C. See further below, p. 316.
[97] Irenaeus, *Adv. Haer.*, IV, 25-26.
[98] Translation (slightly revised) from R. H. Connolly, *Didascalia Apostolorum*, Oxford, 1929, pp. 12-14.

Justin emphasizes the *preventive* purpose of the ceremonial law. He says to the Jew Trypho: [99]

> Your people showed themselves unjust and ungrateful to God, when they made the Calf in the desert. Then God adapting himself to that people, commanded them to offer sacrifices as to his Name, in order that they might not fall into idolatry.

Irenaeus adds that the sacrifices and rituals which God enjoined were not merely preventive; they also had a positive value in so far as they were types of the future sacrifice of Christ: [100]

> Thus God laid upon his people the making of the tabernacle, the building of the temple, the choosing of levites, the sacrifices and offerings, and all the rest of the servitude of the law — not that he himself had need of any of these things, for he is always full of all goods, having in himself every odour of sweetness and every fragrant odour, even before Moses existed; but, as the people were prone to return to idols, he wished to train them, instructing them by many appeals to persevere in the service of God. He called them through the second things to the first, that is, through types to realities and through earthly to heavenly — as Moses was told (Exod 25 : 40): 'See that you make everything after the pattern of the things you saw on the mountain...' Therefore the law was for them both a discipline and a prophecy of things to come. [101]

From Romans (3 : 25) and First Corinthians (10 : 1-12) it is certain that St Paul regarded the sacrifices of the Old Testament as figures of the death of Christ; and from Colossians (2 : 11), that he regarded circumcision as a figure of baptism. It is unlikely, therefore, that he meant to attribute a purely disciplinary function to the law when he described it as a 'pedagogue' (3 : 24).

The other two explanations of v. 19a are again connected. (3) 'The law was added to make the Jews conscious of the sinfulness of their sins.' This is particularly true of the sacrificial laws in Leviticus: they were enacted to make Israel sin-conscious. [102] St Paul certainly held that one function of law is to quicken the conscience, since he says in Rom 3 : 20: 'What comes through the law is full knowledge of sin.' [103] Here he is in agreement with Philo, who says: 'By the sin-

---

[99] Justin, *Trypho*, p. 237.

[100] Irenaeus, *Adv. Haer.*, IV, 25, 3.

[101] In the Latin the last sentence runs: 'Itaque lex et disciplina erat illis et prophetia futurorum.'

[102] Cf. Chrysostom, PG 61, 655 C, who adds that this sin-consciousness should have made the Jews more ready to believe in Christ. They should have recognised him as the Saviour they needed.

[103] Gal 3 : 19 is translated by the NEB: 'It was added to make wrong-doing a legal offence.' But that can hardly be what St Paul means. He is concerned chiefly with the ceremonial parts of the law (circumcision, sacrifices and food laws)

offering Moses warned them (the Jews) against continuing in sin, for he who asks for absolution of the sins he has committed, is not so lost a wretch as to embark on other new offences at the very time when he asks for remission of the old.' [104]

(4) 'The law was added to multiply sins.' In spite of the difficulty of harmonizing this with the second sense accepted above, it must be accepted, because St Paul certainly regarded the law as a provocation to sin. In Rom 5:20 he says: 'The law put in its appearance in order that sin might abound (or, in order that sins might be multiplied).'

All four meanings should be admitted. The problem of how to reconcile the fourth with the second (that is, the problem of explaining how the law can be both a deterrent and an incitement) is resolved when once it is remembered that St Paul did not make the sharp distinction which we make between what God causes and what he permits, between the purpose of the law and the effects of the law. [105] In itself, the law is designed as a deterrent: it distinguishes the way of justice and the way of sin, and attaches promises to the one and dire threats to the other. Nevertheless, in the course of Israel's history the law was often ignored and forgotten. Again and again, the Jews disobeyed and fell under the curse of the law. Historically, St Paul was justified in saying that the effect of the law had been to multiply sin; and because he did not distinguish between divine causality and permission, he could say that the law was given to multiply sin.

## What, then, did St Paul mean by 'the law'?

From the above discussion it seems that the early exegetical tradition (of Justin, Irenaeus, and the *Didascalia Apostolorum*) was correct: in v. 19 St Paul is speaking, not about the whole of the Mosaic law, but only about the ceremonial laws added after Israel had sinned. These laws were not a part of the original covenant granted to Abraham, but a distinct, disciplinary measure.

If so, St Paul must be held guilty of having used this word 'law' with most regrettable ambiguity. Since he draws no clear distinction between the decalogue and the ceremonial law, readers and commentators have naturally supposed that he was speaking of the whole of

---

which prescribed and forbade things not directly pertaining to the sphere of right and wrong.

[104] Philo, *The Special Laws*, I, 193, (Loeb, VII).

[105] Cf. 'Lead us not into temptation,' which means: 'Do not permit us to enter into temptation.'

the Mosaic legislation. This has led to a devaluation of law in general. St Paul may have thought it obvious that he was using 'law' in the restricted sense [106] — because what he says in v. 19 is not applicable to the decalogue: it was not 'added on account of sins', but given *before* Israel had sinned; it was not to last 'only till the Issue should come', for the Issue confirmed its validity (cf. Mt 19:17); and it was not 'given by angels', since Exodus 19 says it was given to Moses by God himself.

Two of the main sources of confusion in the interpretation of this Epistle are St Paul's failure to distinguish between first justification and final justification, and his failure to distinguish at all between the decalogue and the ceremonial law.

### *What place has the law in Christian preaching?*

In his 1535 Commentary, Luther distinguishes a 'double use of the law' (*duplex usus legis*). The exact meaning of this phrase is uncertain. 'Who is the subject of this *using*? God as the author of law? Or man, to whom the law applies? Or the man who preaches the law? Strangely enough, this question has never been discussed in Protestant theology,' says a recent writer. [107]

The scriptural origin of the phrase is 1 Tim 1:8, 'We know that the law is good, provided that one uses it rightly,' where the context shows that the reference is to use of the law by preachers and teachers. But since the preacher speaks as ambassador of God, God may be said to 'use' the law through the preacher when he uses it rightly. And every man is his own preacher, when he reads the law for his own instruction. So there is no need to choose between the three possible alternatives.

Luther gives his doctrine of the 'double use' in his comment on Gal 2:19. [108] As was shown above, St Paul was speaking only of the ceremonial law, but Luther does not draw this distinction. He takes the occasion to propose a doctrine of the use of law in general.

> Here one must know that there is a double use of the law (*duplex usus legis*). One is the civic use. God has ordained civic laws, indeed all laws, to restrain transgressions. Therefore every law was given to hinder sins. Does this mean that when the law restrains sins, it justifies? Not at all.

---

[106] Cf. 1 Cor 5:9-10, where St Paul has to clear up another misunderstanding, which arose from his omission of a distinction which seemed to him obvious.

[107] Gerhard Ebeling, 'On the Doctrine of the Triplex Usus Legis in the Theology of the Reformation,' in his collected essays, *Word and Faith*, London, 1963, p. 75.

[108] Cf. Luther, Gal, 1535, pp. 308-309.

When I refrain from killing or from committing adultery or from stealing, or when I abstain from other sins, I do not do this voluntarily or from the love of virtue but because I am afraid of the sword and of the executioner. This prevents me, as the ropes or chains prevent a lion or a bear from ravaging something that comes along. Therefore restraint from sins is not righteousness but rather an indication of unrighteousness... Thus the first understanding and use of the law is to restrain the wicked...

The other use of the law is the theological or spiritual one, which serves to increase transgressions. This is the primary purpose of the law of Moses, that through it sin might grow and be multiplied, especially in the conscience. Paul discusses this magnificently in Rom 7. Therefore the true function and the chief and proper use of the law is to reveal to man his sin, blindness, misery, wickedness, ignorance, hate and contempt of God, death, hell, judgment, and the well-deserved wrath of God. Yet this use of the law is completely unknown to the hypocrites, the sophists in the universities, and to all men who go along in the presumption of the righteousness of the law or of their own righteousness. To curb and crush this monster and raging beast, that is, the presumption of religion, God is obliged, on Mount Sinai, to give a new law with such pomp and with such an awesome spectacle that the entire people is crushed with fear. For since the reason becomes haughty with this human presumption of righteousness and imagines that on account of this it is pleasing to God, therefore God has to send some Hercules, namely, the law, to attack, subdue, and destroy this monster with full force. Therefore the law is intent on this beast, not on any other.

This is a reasonable account of the use of the law (1) by magistrates, and (2) by preachers when they are addressing the unconverted.

(1) According to Plato and Aristotle, the task of a lawgiver is to train his citizens to virtue. But most political philosophers would agree that all a lawgiver can do is to insist on certain external standards of conduct.

(2) Luther is right in saying that the Christian preacher must use the law to terrify the consciences of the unconverted. St Paul himself does this, very effectively, in Rom 1:19—2:18. He reminds the Gentile that he is condemned by the law of God promulgated by his own conscience, and the Jew that he is condemned by the law of Moses. Every man must first recognise that he is a sinner, by comparing his own conduct with the law under which he stands; only then will he be ready to accept Christ as his Saviour. So the law remains a necessary part of the armour of the Christian preacher in his approach to the unconverted. To use the vigorous language of Luther, the law is the hammer which God has given him to smash the wall of self-complacency which sinful men build round themselves.

In his Commentary on Galatians, Luther speaks only of the use of the law in preaching to the unjustified. Elsewhere, he differentiates within the *usus theologicus*, the effect which the law has on the 'impious' and the 'pious'. [109] Since even the man who has been justified is *simul iustus et peccator*, it is still necessary to preach the law to him in so far as he is a sinner (*in quantum peccator*). Catholic theology can admit this point and profit by it, provided the phrase *simul iustus et peccator* is understood in a Catholic sense. [110] In the man who has been intrinsically justified by grace, there remain inclinations to sin, venial sins, and habitual failings, which self-love can easily persuade him to ignore. Worse still, he can fall into grave sins (as David did with Bathsheba) and fail to condemn himself. Therefore the proclamation of the law is still necessary even for the converted, to enable them to see themselves as they really are. [111] This is probably what St James means when he says (Jas 1:23-24): 'If a man is a hearer of the word but not a doer of it, he is like one who sees in a mirror the face he was born with: he looks at himself and goes away and at once forgets what he is like.' By looking to the law, a man sees himself as he truly is, and how far he falls short of what God requires of him. The law is like a mirror in that it enables a man to see himself as he really is. If he goes away and does nothing about it, he is like a man who has looked into a mirror and seen that he needs a shave or a haircut, and then has forgotten what he saw — the image has vanished. [112]

In the structure of the *Spiritual Exercises* of St Ignatius Loyola, the 'first week' contains the proclamation of the law: the Christian sinner is required to examine his conscience. He does this by going through the ten commandments. The task of the Christian preacher is not simply to proclaim salvation. He must reveal the need of salvation by proclaiming the law, that is, the ten commandments. The law has a permanent place in Christian preaching. It is not superseded by the gospel.

In addition to the ten commandments, the Church has her own ceremonial law. It is far simpler than the Jewish ceremonial law, but serves the same purpose, namely, to foster a sense of sin or a tender

---

[109] Cf. Ebeling, loc. cit., p. 28, for quotations and references.
[110] See above, pp. 249-251.
[111] Cf. Philo, *On the Decalogue*, 98 (Loeb, VII).
[112] Bo Reicke, *The Epistles of James, Peter and Jude*, New York, 1964, p. 22, can hardly be right in saying that the function of the mirror is 'to enable the new man in Christ to appear.' What the man sees is 'the face he was born with', not a new face. Philo, *On Joseph*, 87 (Loeb, VI) describes the virtuous conduct of Joseph as a mirror in which others see their own misbehaviour for what it is and are ashamed.

conscience. There is the command to receive the Holy Eucharist at least once a year and preferably much oftener. This forces the Christian to examine his conscience carefully at least once a year and preferably much oftener, for all Christians know the warning given in 1 Cor 11:28-29: 'A man must examine himself and only then eat the bread and drink from the chalice. If he eats or drinks unworthily, he is eating and drinking his own damnation.' There is also the command to confess all grave post-baptismal sins — an irksome obligation, fulfilment of which brings home to the penitent, painfully, the fact of sin. [113] The two sacraments reinforce each other in this respect: the Eucharist compels the Christian to examine his conscience, Penance enables him to rid himself of his sins, then the Eucharist helps him to avoid sin in the future. These two sacraments, therefore, fulfil the purpose of the old ceremonial law. They are combined in the decree of the Fourth Lateran Council: [114]

> Every Christian of either sex, after coming to the age of reason, must faithfully confess all his sins in private to his own priest and strive to fulfil the penance laid upon him; and he must reverently receive the sacrament of the Eucharist, at least at Paschal time, unless perchance on the advice of his own priest for some good reason he thinks that he should abstain for a time. Otherwise he is to be forbidden entry to the church while alive, and deprived of Christian burial when he dies. Hence this salutary statute must be frequently promulgated in churches, lest anyone should use the blindness of ignorance as a veil of excuse.

In Galatians, St Paul does not compare the Christian ritual law with the Jewish ritual law. On the contrary, he talks as if the Church had no ritual law. There is some reason for the view that the sacraments are not fully integrated into his theology. [115]

*Does St Paul mean to identify the 'law' with the Sinai-covenant?*

In the section 3:15-29, St Paul does not speak of two covenants, but of 'the covenant' and 'the law'. Only in 4:24 does he speak of 'two covenants', when he is allegorizing Sarah and Agar.

---

[113] In the gospels, greater emphasis is laid on the penitent's obligation to forgive those who trespass against himself. Cf. H. Kruse, ' "Pater Noster" et Passio Christi,' *Verbum Domini* 46 (1968), p. 23.
[114] Denz. 802. The 'self-examination' urged in 1 Cor 11:28-29 is not primarily examination of conscience. The communicant must examine whether he is 'discerning the Body of the Lord' by treating it with due reverence. But he is not doing so if he is proposing to receive the sacrament while his will remains wedded to some grave sin.
[115] Cf. J. Bligh, 'Baptism in St Paul,' HJ 7 (1966), pp. 60-62.

If he distinguished between the decalogue and the ceremonial law, the question arises whether he considers that the encounter with Yahweh at Sinai was originally intended to be a renewal of the Abraham-covenant. He may have held that although it began in that way, it ended differently on account of Israel's sin in worshipping the Golden Calf. Then there are two possibilities: either the Abraham-covenant was not renewed, but was suspended, and in its place was put a different, temporary covenant which included the ceremonial law; or the Abraham-covenant was renewed, and the law was added to it as a temporary disciplinary measure. The first alternative has the advantage of explaining how St Paul could speak of 'two covenants', but the second agrees better with the wording of v. 19: 'It was added on account of sins' — it was added to the covenant, not as a condition of the fulfilment of the covenant, but as a temporary disciplinary measure. (The covenant was to be fulfilled, even if the law was not kept.)

To use St Paul's human analogy: in the time of Abraham, the Father by a covenant makes the infant Israel his heir and promises him an inheritance; as the infant grows up, he becomes wayward; the Father, while reaffirming his intention that the boy shall enter into his inheritance, puts him under tutors who are to enforce a code of strict rules. These rules are not meant to render the covenant ineffectual. On the contrary, they are meant to help the child to grow up so as to be worthy of his inheritance. The appointment of tutors and the giving of rules can be regarded either as an addition to the original covenant or as a separate arrangement or covenant. In the latter case it is really a covenant between the father and the tutors. The two points of view can be harmonized by saying that from the point of view of the child (3:19) the law is a temporary addition to the covenant, and from the point of view of the tutors (4:26) it is a distinct covenant.

*Was the Mosaic law foreseen at the time of the Abraham-covenant?*

It was not foreseen by Abraham, but it must have been foreseen by God, who knew how long a time was to elapse before the fulfilment of the promise. God must have intended the law to contribute to the fulfilment of his plan of salvation. But in what way? It might have done so in various ways: first, by making the Israelites conscious of sin, it would make them eager to accept a Saviour from sin, and therefore eager to welcome Christ; secondly, by leading them towards spiritual maturity, it would prepare them to receive Christ; and thirdly, by leading them to think that it contained all wisdom in itself and the power to give life, it would make them *un*prepared to receive Christ, and thus would drive the gospel out to the Gentiles. In Galatians, St Paul assigns a positive function to the law (see below on 'the pedagogue' in v. 24); in Rom 9:33, he describes it as a stumbling-block, which has prevented Israel from recognizing Christ. But this latter idea is also adumbrated in Galatians: the Gentile Galatians too are in danger of becoming so fascinated with the law as to lose sight of the efficacy of Christ's death.

St Paul is in difficulties here. If he says that the law was given to make Israel ready, he is confronted by the fact that on the whole Israel was not ready; and if he says that the law was given to make Israel unready, he exposes himself to the charge of regarding the law as a means of frustrating the promises — as the means whereby God has disowned his chosen people in favour of the Gentiles. In Romans, he boldly adopts the latter alternative when he argues that this rejection is only temporary: God is driving the gospel out to the Gentiles, but ultimately for the benefit of his own people, who will one day be moved by jealousy to accept Jesus as the Christ (cf. Rom 11:11, 26).

## *Was the patriarchal period the time of Israel's infancy?*

St Paul's analogy between the growth of an individual from childhood to maturity, and the spiritual growth of Israel as a whole would seem to imply that the patriarchal period was a period of spiritual infancy. Yet surely it must be admitted that Abraham, Isaac, Jacob and Joseph were spiritually mature.

The explanation may be that St Paul, reading the book of Genesis, saw in the patriarchs a simple, childlike faith and obedience which rendered a written law superfluous for them. Irenaeus adopts this line of explanation when he infers that there was no law in the patriarchal period from Deut 5:2-5:

> The Lord our God made a covenant with us in Horeb. *3* Not with our fathers did he make this covenant, but with us, who are all of us here alive this day. *4* The Lord spoke with you face to face at the mountain, out of the midst of the fire, *5* while I stood between the Lord and you at that time.

V. 3 is almost certainly a cultic addition, inserted to bring home to the worshippers of later days that the commandments are addressed to them. But Irenaeus takes it as a part of the historical narrative, and comments as follows: [116]

> Why, then, did not the Lord lay down a covenant [117] for the patriarchs? Because 'law is not imposed on just men' (1 Tim 1:9); and the just patriarchs had the decalogue inscribed as a power within their hearts and souls, for they loved the God who made them and abstained from injustice towards their neighbours. They had no need to be admonished by corrective writings, because they had within themselves the justice of the law. But when this justice and their love for God had lapsed into oblivion and extinction in Egypt, of necessity God, in his great kindness towards men, revealed himself through a voice, and led forth his people from Egypt in power, in order that once again man might become the disciple and follower of God; and he brought trials of obedience upon them, so that they would not despise the one who made them; and he fed them with manna so that they would receive the food of reason — as Moses says in Deuteronomy (8:3): 'And he fed you with manna, which your fathers had not known, that you might know that not by bread alone does man live, but by every word that proceeds from the mouth of the Lord.'

The patriarchal period was therefore a time both of childhood and of maturity. Both St Paul and Philo (quoted above, p. 215) regard the ascent to maturity as a process whereby the individual slowly and laboriously recovers the justice and innocence of childhood. [118] The same idea is found in the preaching of Christ:

> Let the little children come to me and do not stop them; the kingdom of heaven belongs to such as these. (Mt 19:14)

> If you do not become like little children again, you will not enter the kingdom of heaven at all. (Mt 18:3; cf. Jn 3:5)

There is, however, no indication in these synoptic sayings that Jesus himself equated becoming like children with becoming like the patriarchs.

*Why does St Paul mention the 'angels' in 3:19?*

St Paul is trying to show that the (ceremonial) law is quite distinct from the covenant or promise to Abraham. The structure of the subsection (see above, p. 274) shows that he sees the following contrast:

---

[116] Irenaeus, *Adv. Haer.*, IV, 27, 3.
[117] 'Covenant' here means 'law', as the sequel shows.
[118] This may help to explain how the child's cry of 'Abba' comes to be regarded by St Paul as evidence of spiritual maturity. See below on 4:6.

> D    It was by way of promise that God made the gift to Abraham.
> D¹  (The law was) drawn up by angels (and placed) in the hands of a mediator.

Or more simply:

> D    The promise to Abraham was a deed of gift granted by God himself.
> D¹  The law given to Moses was enacted by angels. [119]

The law is a distinct and inferior institution because it was given, not by God himself, but by his angels (acting in relative independence). As Gal 1:1 shows ('not from men, nor through a man,' etc.), St Paul held that God's personal action confers a special honour and dignity upon the recipient. Abraham in receiving the promise from God himself was more highly honoured than Moses in receiving the law from God's angels.

*Whence comes the idea that the law was given by angels?*

The idea that the law was given by angels is not a theologoumenon invented by St Paul, or he could not have used it in polemic debate. He takes it for granted that his Jewish opponents will not challenge the point.

The same belief is expressed by St Stephen in his speech in Acts (7:38, 53):

> He (Moses) it was who in the congregation in the desert mediated between the angel who had spoken to him on Mount Sinai and our fathers... You received the law at the angels' bidding and have not kept it.

King Herod the Great, too, says in a speech attributed to him by Josephus: [120] 'We learned the finest of our doctrines and the holiest of our laws through angels from God.' This view is a midrashic development of certain details given in the Sinai-narrative in Exodus. The fire, clouds, thunder and trumpets at Sinai (cf. Exod 19:9, 16) were attributed to the presence and activity of the angels who control the elements (*stoicheia* in Greek). In the Book of Exodus itself the angels are not mentioned. They first appear in the midrashic tradition as God's escort, to emphasize his glory and majesty. Later they become mediators or givers of the law — originally in order to emphasize the transcendence of God; but St Paul twists this tradition

---

[119] The structural link shows that St Jerome, PL 26, 393 A, is probably right in regarding the phrase 'in the hand of a mediator' as equivalent to a dative: 'Lex posita est per angelos in manu mediatoris.' However, the law was given to him as mediator; hence it was also given 'through' or 'by' him. See Deut 5:2-5, quoted above, p. 302.

[120] Josephus, *Antiquities*, XV, 5, 3.

to his own purpose, using it as evidence of the inferiority of the law
to acts which God does himself.

There is a similar development in regard to the manna (a symbol
of God's word, according to Deut 8 : 3). In Exod 16, it is a gift from
God himself — 'the bread which the Lord has given you to eat'
(v. 15) — there is no mention of angels. But in Psalm 78 : 25 it is
called 'the bread of angels', which, as Theodore of Mopsuestia wisely
observes, should not be taken to mean that the angels eat manna. [121]
Rather, according to the psalmist's midrash, the manna, like the law,
was given by ministering angels.

*What view did Philo hold about the angels?*

St Paul speaks so briefly about the angels in 2 : 19 that one can
hardly guess what he has in mind. But his older contemporary Philo
has spoken at greater length, and St Paul's argument becomes much
more intelligible on the supposition that he held views similar to
those of Philo. What, then, did Philo hold?

He gave the angelic 'Powers' (*dynameis*) an important place in his
theology of creation and providence, in order to explain the presence
of evil in the world; for he felt it would be irreverent to attribute the
creation of evil directly to God. In his treatise *On the Confusion of
Tongues,* he says: [122]

> God fills all things; he contains but is not contained. To be everywhere
> and nowhere is his property and his alone. He is nowhere, because he
> himself created space and place coincidentally with material things, and
> it is against all right principle to say that the Maker is contained in
> anything that he has made. He is everywhere, because he has made his
> Powers (*dynameis*) extend through earth and water, air and heaven
> [the 'elements' or *stoicheia*], and left no part of the universe without
> his presence, and uniting all with all has bound them fast with invisible
> bonds, that they should never be loosed... [The Greek is defective here]
> ...That aspect of him which transcends his powers cannot be conceived
> of at all in terms of place.

From this passage it is not yet clear that Philo regards the Powers
as distinct from God, but this becomes plain in the sequel:

> God is one, but he has around him numberless Powers which all assist and
> protect created being. Among them are included the Powers of chastise-
> ment. Now chastisement is not a thing of harm or mischief, but a pre-
> ventive and corrective of sin... [123]

---

[121] Cf. Theodore, Gal, p. 48.
[122] §§ 136-137 (Loeb, IV).
[123] § 171.

There is, too, in the air a sacred company of unbodied souls, commonly called angels in the inspired pages, who wait upon the Heavenly Powers (*Ourania*). So the whole army composed of several contingents, each marshalled in their proper ranks, have as their business to serve and minister to the Captain who thus marshalled them, and to follow his leadership, as right and the law of service demand. For it must not be that God's soldiers should ever be guilty of desertion from the ranks. Now the King may fittingly hold converse with the powers and employ them to serve in matters which should not be consummated by God alone... [124]

Thus it was meet and right that when man was formed, God should assign a share in the work to his lieutenants, as he does with the words, 'Let *us* make man,' that so man's right actions might be attributable to God, but his sins to others. For it seemed to be unfitting to God the All-ruler that the road to wickedness within the reasonable fold should be of his making, and therefore he delegated the forming of this part to his inferiors... [125]

Thus the Powers and angels are made to bear responsibility for the tendency to evil which is innate in human beings. Philosophically, this shifting of the blame does not achieve much, since God remains responsible for what he foresaw that the angels would create; [126] but from the religious point of view, at least in unphilosophic minds, the idea helps to safeguard respect for the holiness and benevolence of God. For the same reason, Philo goes on to attribute the chastisement of sinners to the angels: [127]

God is the cause of good things only and of nothing at all that is bad, since he himself was the most ancient of beings and the good in its most perfect form. And it best becomes him that the works of his hands should be akin in nature, surpassing in excellence even as he surpasses, but that the chastisement of the wicked should be assured through his inferiors...

In conformity with these ideas, Philo explains in his treatise on *The Decalogue* that the reason why the ten commandments have no sanctions attached to them is that they were given by God himself and it was unfitting for him to punish. The implication is that the particular laws, which have sanctions attached to them, were given, not by God himself, but by the angels, to whom punishment is deputed: [128]

Next let us pass on to give the reason why He expressed the ten words or laws in the form of simple commands or prohibitions without laying down any penalty, as is the way of legislators, against future transgressors. He was God, and it follows at once that as Lord He was good, the cause of

---

[124] §§ 174-5.
[125] § 179.
[126] Cf. S. Freud, *Complete Psychological Works*, London, 1961, Vol. XXI, p. 120.
[127] §§ 181-2. Cf. *On Flight and Finding*, 66-67 (Loeb, V).
[128] Philo, *On the Decalogue*, 177-178 (Loeb, VII).

good only and of nothing ill. So then He judged that it was most in accordance with His being to issue His saving commandments free from any admixture of punishment, that men might choose the best, not involuntarily, but of deliberate purpose, not taking senseless fear but the good sense of reason for their counsellor. He therefore thought right not to couple punishment with His utterances, though He did not thereby grant immunity to evil-doers, but knew that Justice His assessor, the surveyor of human affairs, in virtue of her inborn hatred of evil, will not rest, but will take upon herself as her congenital task the punishment of sinners. For it befits the servants and lieutenants of God, that like generals in wartime they should bring vengeance to bear upon deserters who leave the ranks of justice. But it befits the Great King that the general safety of the universe should be ascribed to Him, that He should be the guardian of peace and supply richly and abundantly the good things of peace, all of them to all persons in every place and every time. For indeed God is the Prince of Peace while His subalterns are the leaders in war.

## Does St Paul regard the 'angels' of the law as good or bad?

If the angels in St Paul, like the angels in Philo, are made responsible for acts which reverence forbids us to attribute directly to God, it must be allowed that these angels act with a large measure of independence, for if they were simply obedient ministers without any personal initiative, the whole responsibility for their actions would fall upon God.

As was shown above, St Paul held that the law was given 'on account of sins', to punish sins, and yet to provoke further sins. He knew from the history of Israel and from his own personal history that the law had multiplied sins, had placed the Jews under its curse, had brought Christ to his death (cf. 2:19), had misled himself (Paul) into persecuting the Lord of Glory, and many of his contemporaries into rejecting the gospel. It is understandable that he should have felt reluctant to attribute the creation and promulgation of this law to God himself. He is glad, therefore, to be able to make use of the midrashic tradition and attribute the law to angels. But then the question arises whether he is thinking of good or bad angels.

Once again, the answer must be that our sharp distinctions were not present in the mind of St Paul. Just as Philo does not consider the angelic creators of the evil impulse to have been bad angels, so too St Paul does not say or imply that the law was given by demons. He recognizes that its commandments are holy and just and good (v. 21; cf. Rom 7:12). But on the other hand, he does not regard the angels of the law as having been entirely friendly, since they brought God's people into slavery and apparently wished to keep them in slavery. If the angels are required to protect the benevolence and holiness of God, some measure of malevolence must be attributed to them. Probably St Paul thought that they were guilty merely of too much zeal, as he himself had been before his conversion (cf. 1 : 14).

## *How does St Paul show that the law was an interim measure?*

In 3 : 19, St Paul says quite clearly that the law was to remain in force 'until the coming of the Issue (of Abraham) to whom the promise had been made.' But his argument in support of this assertion is not at all clear. Literally it runs: '(The law was) made by angels in the hand of a mediator, but a mediator is not of one, and God is one.'

The principle on which the argument is based, 'a mediator is not of one', must mean that there is never a mediator between one party: there must always be two parties A and B (though A and B may be one person and one person, or one person and a plurality, or two pluralities).

The argument from this principle must be that when the promised Issue comes there will no longer be room for a mediator — which implies that God and the Issue are one. This implication is not *stated*, no doubt because St Paul is arguing with Christians who accept it, but it must be in his mind, or the argument collapses.

The argument is that the law was given through angels and through Moses, so that the pattern of the relationship was:

God → angels → Moses → ISRAEL.

But when the promised Issue comes, the relationship cannot be:

God → angels → Moses → THE ISSUE,

because God and the Issue are one, and it is impossible for the angels and Moses to mediate between one party. St Paul says clearly at the beginning of the subsection that Christ, the Issue, is one (v. 16), and at the centre that God is one (v. 20). [129] Unfortunately, he does not add with equal clarity that Christ and God are one; but this must certainly be what he means, for otherwise the argument is incomplete. There was room for the angels and for Moses between God and the Israelites, because he was one and they were many, but there is no room for a mediator between God and Christ since they are one. The argument rests on a very 'high' Christology, but it is not too high

---

[129] At the end (v. 18), he adds that all believers are one in Christ. See pp. 274-275.

for this Epistle. The first verse of the first chapter separates Christ from 'men' and brackets him with God the Father. [130]

However, this argument from the unity of God is supplementary. V. 19a taken by itself already implies a reason why the law became obsolete at the arrival of the promised Issue: 'the law was added on account of sins, (to remain in force) until the Issue should come to whom the promise had been made.' St Paul understands the content of the promise to be (a) forgiveness of sin, and (b) the gift of the Holy Spirit. Thus v. 19a practically means: 'The law was added to deal with sins until such time as God should deal effectively with sin by sending the promised Issue, who would effectively expiate past sins, and restore liberty from sin (i.e. freedom not to sin, *posse non peccare*) through the gift of the Holy Spirit.' The argument is, then, that the law was an imperfect and ineffectual instrument for dealing with sin, and it became obsolete as soon as God provided an effective instrument in the cross and resurrection of his Son. [131] The types and figures were rendered obsolete by the reality they had prefigured. This argument is developed at length in the Epistle to the Hebrews. [132]

### *When exactly did the Interim end?*

From v. 19, 'it was added until the Issue should come,' it might seem to follow that the period of the law was terminated as soon as the Issue of Abraham 'came', that is, from the very birth of Christ. But the discussion just completed shows that St Paul must be thinking of the whole ministry, death and resurrection of Jesus as his 'coming'. Christ had to become subject to the law in order to redeem those under the law (cf. 4 : 4), and he had to overthrow the angelic-demonic powers by his death (cf. Col 2 : 15). The law did not, like an old soldier, simply fade away; it had to be attacked and overthrown. In St Paul's thought, the angels of the law did not retire gracefully, as soon as Christ appeared.

We cannot be sure how St Paul explained to himself or to others the reluctance of the angels to retire. Probably he knew from his own observation how old men cling to power and authority long after they should have retired. If he shared the opinions of some of his contemporaries among the apocalyptic writers, he probably held that the

---

[130] See above, pp. 61-62 and 81.

[131] One might add 'and in the sacraments which mediate the efficacy of the cross and resurrection', but St Paul does not add this.

[132] For a third argument, see below, p. 311.

angels of the law should have retired when the Issue appeared, but as they had for a long time exceeded their rightful authority, they refused to submit. In the history of Jewish thought, the angels probably began as demoted pagan gods; and in the post-exilic period, angelology developed in a direction not favourable to the angels, through reflection on the problem of evil. [133] This development is traced out by a recent writer on Jewish Apocalyptic, who gives the following summary: [134]

> Ever since the days of the Captivity the problem of suffering had been a great mystery to the Jewish people, especially as it had applied to their own nation and to the righteous men within their nation. Attempts had been made to explain it, but none was wholly satisfactory. The problem of suffering, moreover, was only one aspect of the much bigger problem of moral evil which formed the subject matter of not a few writings of this period. There gradually grew up, no doubt under the influence of foreign thought, the notion that the angels to whom God had given authority over the nations and over the physical universe itself, had outstripped their rightful authority and had taken the power into their own hands. No longer were they simply God's envoys to whom he gave the charge of punishing those who denied his rule; they themselves became part of the rebellious family and took upon themselves the right to reign.

St Paul must have regarded the angels of the law as rebellious, or he would have seen no need of their reconciliation (cf. Col 1:20). [135]

### Why is Moses mentioned at all in v. 19?

Moses is not explicitly named here or anywhere else in the Epistle. But he is referred to as the 'mediator' of the law. This is the aspect of him which has a bearing on the argument. The law is doubly inferior to the promise, because whereas the promise was given directly by God, the law was not even given directly by angels, but only indirectly: they used Moses as their mediator.

It is hardly correct, therefore, to say that Moses is mentioned to show that the Sinai-covenant was a bilateral contract, [136] for Moses' task as mediator was not to negotiate with the angels for better terms, but simply to signify the people's acceptance and to receive the angels' commands. [137]

---

[133] See the quotations from Philo, above, pp. 305-307.
[134] D. S. Russell, *The Method and Message of Jewish Apocalyptic*, London, 1964, pp. 237-238 (quoted by kind permission of the SCM Press Ltd).
[135] Cf. J. Bligh, 'Demonic Powers,' HJ 1 (1960), pp. 314-323.
[136] Cf. P. Démann, 'Moïse et la-Loi dans la pensée de saint Paul,' *Cahiers Sioniens*, 8 (1954), p. 197 (315).
[137] The Jews were uncertain as to Moses' exact function—cf. Philo, *On Moses*, I,

Moses, then, is introduced to emphasize the contrast between the immediacy of God's dealings with Abraham and the circuitousness of his imposition of the law. The Epistle to the Hebrews (2:3) points out that the gospel message of salvation was 'first preached by the Lord himself'. That is to say, in Christ God began again to speak *directly* to his people. Perhaps, therefore, v. 20 is meant to suggest a third proof of the temporary character of the law: as soon as God began again to speak directly to his people, there was no further need of the indirect revelation which had been given through the angels and through Moses. The defect of this argument is, however, that it tends to prove too much: it points to the conclusion (drawn by Marcion) that as we have the words of the Lord himself in the gospel, we have no further need of the many partial revelations given through the prophets, i.e., that the Old Testament can be rejected.

### What view did St Paul take of Moses?

Since St Paul's view of the angels contains a large measure of midrashic development, the same may be true of his view of Moses. Philo identifies Moses with the Logos and describes him as a kind of angel. He is

> ambassador of the ruler to the subject. He glories in this prerogative and proudly describes it in these words 'and I stood between the Lord and you' (Deut 5:5), that is, neither uncreated (*agenêtos*) as God, nor created as you, but midway between the two extremes, a surety to both sides. [138]

Since Christ himself described John the Baptist as a prophet and more than a prophet, even 'an angel' (*angelon*, Mt 11:10), St Paul may have believed that Moses too was no ordinary man but in some sense an angel. If so, he was a 'mediator' by his nature, an angel among the angels and a man among men.

In 1 Tim 2:5, when St Paul describes Christ as 'mediator between God and men', he may be thinking that just as Moses was both angel and man, mediating between angels and men, so Christ is both God and man, mediating between God and unconverted men. (He is not, properly speaking, the mediator between God and believers, because they are one with him, vv. 26-29, as he with God.)

However, Moses is not here treated as a figure of Christ. St Paul does not regard Christ as a second Moses. Even in 1 Cor 10 where

---

1 (Loeb, VI): 'I propose to write the life of Moses, whom some describe as the legislator (*nomothetês*) of the Jews, others as the interpreter (*hermêneus*) of the Holy Laws.' Cf. Paul VI, *Humanae Vitae*, § 18.

[138] Philo, *Who is the heir?*, 206 (Loeb, IV); cf. Schlier, Gal, p. 114.

he explains the events of the Exodus as types of the Christian dispensation, it is not Moses but the rock which is the type of Christ. [139] St John shows a similar reluctance to compare Jesus with Moses, for Jesus transcends Moses as grace and truth transcend law (cf. Jn 1:17). [140]

*Was the law opposed to the promises of the covenant?*

In 3:21 St Paul allows his opponents to raise an objection. What has just been said seems to imply that law, far from being a means towards the fulfilment of the promises, has actually stood in the way of their fulfilment. The Judaizers might well ask: 'Is then law by its nature opposed to God's promises?'

The objection arises from v. 19a ('the law was added for the sake of sins'). But if the objector had listened more carefully to vv. 19b-20, he would have foreseen the answer: the promise is to the Issue of Abraham; when the Issue comes, the law will cease, and the promise will be fulfilled. But St Paul does not repeat this. In v. 21 he adds that law does not of itself cause sin and death. It points the way to justice and life, but it is powerless to give to its subjects those first instalments of justice and life which would enable them to obey its precepts and advance towards the fullness of justice and life. In fact, therefore, though not in intention, the written law delivered all men (and indeed all creation) into the power of sin, by laying upon them a yoke too great for their weakness to bear.

The Greek of v. 21a is usually taken (as above) to mean: 'Does the law work against the promises, in such a way as to frustrate the promises?' To this the answer is given in v. 21b: if the same law had been given in another form, that is to say, not as a written code but as an interior spirit, justification would come from the law. [141] 4:6 shows that such a law has been given to Christians.

But the Greek of v. 21a could also be taken to mean: 'Has the law *in fact* frustrated the promise?' This question is answered in

---

[139] Cf. P. Démann, art. cit., p. 193.
[140] Cf. E. L. Allen, 'Jesus and Moses in the New Testament,' *The Expository Times* 67 (1955-6), pp. 104-106; T. F. Glasson, *Moses in the Fourth Gospel* (SBT 40), London, 1963. At a precanonical stage of the johannine tradition, Jn 1:6 probably said: 'There was a man sent from God whose name was *Moses*.' Not John the Baptist but Moses had been identified with the Logos. The polemic of the Prologue was against Judaism itself.
[141] Cf. Theodore of Mopsuestia, Gal, p. 50. Luther thought otherwise: 'If a man were completely and absolutely to fulfil the law through the power of the Holy Spirit, he would still have to appeal for God's mercy; for God has determined

4:7: in spite of the law and in spite of sin, thanks to your faith 'you are no longer a slave, but a son; and if a son, then an heir, through God.'

*How did the law help to prepare the fulfilment of the promise?*

Because the law which was given was an exterior, written law, unable to give Spirit and life, all who were under the law came to find themselves transgressors of the law, enslaved to the power of Sin, and unable to escape from sin. Yet St Paul can see the wisdom of God at work in all this. It was his will to give the promised inheritance as a free gift to those who believe in his Son, Jesus Christ. By permitting all men to become sinners, God disposed that no man should be able to claim the inheritance by reason of his birth and conduct; the *only* way to salvation for all was to be through faith in Jesus Christ. All who enter the inheritance enter through the grace and favour of Christ. *Finis redemptionis gloria Christi.* [142]

*Were the Jews 'locked up' for their protection or as punishment?*

St John Chrysostom explains v. 23, 'we were kept in custody, locked up,' as referring to protective custody: [143]

The phrase simply points out the security (*asphaleia*) resulting from the commandments of the law. For, as if they were within a wall, the law held them in check through fear and through a life governed by fear, and thus preserved them for faith.

St Jerome, on the other hand, understands the phrase to refer to a prison or house of bondage. [144]

Here again, it is better not to make a choice; the context requires both senses. The subsection 3:15-29 embodies the idea that in childhood a person needs to be protected from evil influences; later, as a full grown man, he must go out and conquer evil by goodness. The exclusiveness forced upon the Jews by the law was all very well while they were children, but now the time has come for them to break down the wall of separation and go out to convert the Gentiles to Christ, to build up a new humanity, in which there will no longer be Jew and Greek.

---

that he will save men through Christ and not through the law' (quoted by Althaus, *The Theology of Luther,* p. 121).
[142] Cf. Council of Trent, VI, 7 (Denz. 1529).
[143] PG 61, 655 D.
[144] Cf. PL 26, 393 C: 'in custodiam, et, ut ita dicam, in carcerem.'

But St Jerome is also right, in saying that under the law the Jews were almost 'in prison'. In 3:4, St Paul says that God sent forth his Son to 'redeem' those under the law — a word which implies release from prison, or from a house of bondage (like Egypt).

The law is not, therefore, pictured as a kindly protector and guardian who willingly hands over his charge when the time comes, like an amiable schoolmaster saying Goodbye to his boys at the end of term. Rather, the law handed over the Jews to Sin. Sin was the gaoler, not the law; and the redemption was won at a high price (cf. 3:13).

To pious Jews, the assertion or insinuation that to be under the law is to be in gaol is offensive, and even absurd. Epictetus has an answer for St Paul when he says: 'A man's prison is the place that he is in against his will, just as, conversely, Socrates was not in prison, for he chose to be there.' [145] It is no wonder that St Paul's apologetic has never made much impression upon the Jews. If he were alive today, they might point out to him that the proportion of Jews in British and American prisons is remarkably low.

### How does the law resemble a 'pedagogue'?

A 'pedagogue' in ancient Greece was a slave charged to keep watch over a boy, to keep him out of mischief and danger, and to take him to school. The law resembled a pedagogue in that (1) it imposed restraints on the son of another, and (2) its office was of limited duration. [146] But there is also a third resemblance, perhaps of greater importance: the law and the pedagogue are alike in their shortcomings. St Paul uses the word 'pedagogue' in one other text, 1 Cor 4:14-16:

> I do not write this to shame you; but you are my beloved children, and I do wish to correct you. For even if you should have ten thousand 'pedagogues' in Christ, yet you will not have more than one father. In Christ Jesus, through his gospel, it is I who am your father. I urge you, therefore: be imitators of me.

The contrast between the pedagogue and the father shows that while the pedagogue imposes restraints which have some positive moral value, he does not embody the ideal which the child must imitate.

The Jews believed that they had, in the law, 'the perfect pattern of knowledge and truth' (cf. Rom 2:20). But St Paul will not admit

---

[145] Epictetus, *Discourses*, I, 12.
[146] Cf. Jerome, PL 26, 393-4; Chrysostom, PG 61, 656 A.

this. The law, he says, belonged to the spiritual childhood of Israel. Its function was strictly limited both in duration and in scope. The Jews are like those pathetic characters who idolize their schoolmasters and tutors to such an extent that they remain schoolboys or undergraduates throughout their lives. St Paul himself escaped from the tyranny of the pedagogue on the road to Damascus. Looking back, he sees that it was then that he put away the things of a child and began to live as an adult son in his father's house. Now he tries to pass on this lesson to the Jews and Judaizers.

There is a passage in Plutarch which shows that boys would sometimes rebel against their pedagogues and beat them up:[147]

> Antisthenes the Socratic, when he saw the Thebans in high feather after the battle of Leuctra, said in all seriousness that they were just like little boys strutting about because they had thrashed their pedagogue.

But St Paul is not behaving like a victorious Theban. He does not say that the law was a *bad* pedagogue. It was the boys under its charge who were bad. The worst he says of the law is that it was *only* a pedagogue. Nor does he suggest for a moment that Israel would have been better off without a pedagogue at all. Philo asks, 'Do not boys who are rebuked by pedagogues turn out better than those who have no pedagogue?'[148] And St Paul would have agreed that they do (cf. Rom 9 : 4).

In general, Philo's views about pedagogues agree closely with those attributed above to St Paul. He allows that they have good intentions, and that they make some positive contribution to the moral formation of their charges:[149]

> Praise is due to one who seems to be using his voice to revile and accuse but is really intending to bless and speak well. Such is the way of proctors (*sôphronistai*), pedagogues, schoolmasters, parents, elders, magistrates, laws. All of these by rebukes, and sometimes by punishments, bring about improvement in the soul of those whom they educate.

On the other hand, because pedagogues have not studied philosophy and therefore are without wisdom, they unwittingly do much harm:[150]

> The instructors to sin are legion, nurses and pedagogues and parents and the laws of cities, written and unwritten, which extol what should be derided.

---

[147] Plutarch, *Lycurgus,* 30, 6.
[148] Philo, *The Worse attacks the Better,* 145 (Loeb, II).
[149] *The Migration of Abraham,* 116 (Loeb, IV). The 'proctors' were an Athenian institution—a special body of police to keep the teenagers in order, particularly in public places.
[150] Philo, *Who is the heir?,* 295 (Loeb, IV).

Much of what has been learned from pedagogues must later be un-learned — in the school of philosophy, according to Philo; [151] in the school of Christ according to St Paul. [152]

## What did the 'pedagogue' achieve for Israel?

It is not St Paul's business to praise the law in this chapter. On the contrary, he is trying to reduce the exaggerated esteem in which it is held by the Jews. One might easily get the impression that the law simply delivered up the Jews to sin, that it failed to lead Israel to maturity, and that maturity came very suddenly when Christ poured out his Holy Spirit upon believers.

But probably this is not quite what St Paul means. He must have seen, as we can see, that the materialistic, ritualistic religion of the law was required by Israel in the early centuries when idolatry and polytheism were real temptations. When the Israelites first settled in Canaan, as the splendid sacrifices and rituals of Baal were a tempta-tion to them, God allowed them to worship him with animal sacrifices and elaborate rituals. [153] But after the Exile, when idolatry was less and less a temptation, the ritual law became more and more meaning-less and superfluous. Israel was growing to maturity, and no longer needed the concessions granted in the law of Moses. Thus the law was already becoming obsolete before Christ came.

It is hard to explain just how the advance to maturity came about. Where the 'wind of change' comes from, no man quite knows. Contact with the critical spirit of the Greeks may have had something to do with Israel's development. And something must be put down to the credit of Israel's pedagogue, the law (of Moses).

But a pedagogue, in the years when he had charge of a boy, never had the sole charge of his education. His main task was to take the boy daily to the schoolmaster. The time of the pedagogue was, there-fore, also the time of the schoolmaster. Unfortunately St Paul does not name the schoolmaster. Perhaps it is legitimate to fill out this gap in his account of Israel's education by drawing upon Heb 1:1. If Moses was the pedagogue, the (later) prophets fulfilled the office of schoolmasters. What Christ did was to bring to completion the work

---

[151] Who is the heir?, 297.
[152] Cf. Rom 6:17.
[153] Cf. St Augustine, In Ioannis Evangelium, X, 2 (PL 35, 1468 D): 'Sacrificia illi populo pro eius carnalitate et corde adhuc lapideo talia data sunt, quibus teneretur ne in idola deflueret.' See above, p. 294.

which God had been carrying out through the prophets — for they frequently attacked the ritual law. [154]


*Was St Paul the first to describe the law as Israel's pedagogue?*

It is possible that the midrashic tradition already contained the idea that while God is Israel's father, Moses is his 'pedagogue'. The Midrash Rabbah on Deuteronomy comments on Moses' intercession with God on behalf of Israel after the making of the Golden Calf in Exod 32:10-12, as follows: [155]

> R. Simon said: It is as if a king and his son were in an inner chamber and the son's tutor was in the vestibule, and the king kept on shouting out 'Let me be while I kill my son,' but in reality he was seeking for someone to plead on his son's behalf. Likewise when God said to Moses: 'Now therefore let me alone, that my wrath may wax not against them, and that I may consume them, and I will make of thee a great nation,' Moses said to himself: 'Am I then to hold back God's hands? If one may say so, He is surely looking for someone to plead on their behalf.'

True, this is a parable, not an allegory. But perhaps the rabbis did not distinguish these literary forms as sharply as we do.

St Paul may be adapting to his own purpose a midrashic idea about Moses, just as he has twisted to his own purpose the midrashic notion that the law was given through angels.

An interesting metaphorical use of 'pedagogue' occurs in the *Meditations* of Marcus Aurelius: [156]

> Do not be disgusted or despondent or downcast, if you do not invariably succeed in acting from right principles. When you have been jolted out of them, come back to them, and rejoice if for the most part your conduct is worthy of a man, and love that to which you come back. Do not come back to philosophy as to a pedagogue, but as the sore-eyed to their sponges and their white of egg. [157]

This shows that though the pedagogue was someone who might do good, he was not a person whom the child was expected to like or love. In this respect the pious Jew of St Paul's day would probably not have admitted that the law was his pedagogue. But, as Luther points out, Moses was not loved by the Jews in the desert: [158]

---

[154] A fine collection of prophetic texts is given by Irenaeus, *Adv. Haer.*, IV, 29.
[155] Midrash R. on Deut, III, 15 (Soncino edition, Vol. VII, p. 85).
[156] *Meditations*, V. 9.
[157] Cf. Apoc 3:18.
[158] Luther, Gal, 1535, p. 345.

Did the Jews love Moses and willingly do what he wanted? Their love and obedience towards Moses were such, as the history shows, that at times they would have been willing to stone him.

## Should there be a pedagogue-period in the life of every Christian?

Vv. 23-24 make good sense if they were originally addressed to the Jewish Christians at Antioch: 'Before the coming of faith, *we* were locked up in custody... the law was *our* pedagogue to Christ.' But the same could not be said of the Gentile Galatians, who had not lived under a positive religious law.

Unfortunately, St Paul does not stop to consider how these ideas can be adapted to the spiritual history of Gentile Christians. According to Philo, in the spiritual development of every individual there should be a 'period of Agar' (high school) before the 'period of Sarah' (university and maturity). [159] But it is not clear whether St Paul would have agreed. He himself had lived through a long pedagogue-period before his conversion. So too had the Jewish Christians. If St Paul attributed any positive value to the pedagogue's influence, he must have seen the desirability of having a pedagogue-period in the life of every Christian. But his own theology makes this difficult, for, if the Gentile convert, whether adult or child, receives at Baptism the gift of the Spirit, and this Spirit is the spirit of adult maturity, there would seem to be no room for the insertion of a pedagogue-period.

The difficulty is particularly obvious in the case of children baptized in infancy. According to St Paul's theology, they have the spirit of adult maturity practically from birth. But they cannot be expected to behave as spiritual adults from their earliest years. They still need the control of a pedagogue, in spite of their baptism. Philo is right in saying that the spiritual history of Israel has to be recapitulated in the life of every individual.

How, then, can St Paul's theology be adapted to what is now the normal case: the child of Christian parents who is baptized within a week or two of birth?

One solution is to treat the children as if in fact they had not yet received the Holy Spirit, and to keep them under a strict religious discipline till school-leaving age, then give them the Holy Spirit by the laying-on of hands in Confirmation, tell them that they are now released from the rules and practices of childhood, and expect them to

---

[159] Cf. *On Mating with the Preliminary Studies* (Loeb, IV).

behave thereafter as spiritual adults. But this solution has two short-comings. First, it rests on a fiction, namely that the Holy Spirit has not been given in baptism. [160] This, however, is not an insuperable difficulty. One might reply (a) that the fiction has a very good precedent in the life of Christ himself; as Gal 4:1-3 says, he was treated as a slave although he was the Lord of all; or (b) one might say that Confirmation confers an 'earnest' of the Spirit, and Baptism gives the infants only an 'earnest' of this 'earnest'; this assertion would clear up theoretical difficulty, but we have no assurance that it is true. The effects of Confirmation are not empirically verifiable. The second difficulty is that Catholic tradition is in favour of administering Confirmation long before school-leaving age. [161] In the early Roman liturgy Confirmation was not separated from Baptism: the two sacraments were given within one ceremony, Confirmation being the completion of Baptism. To defer Confirmation until school-leaving age would weaken even more than hitherto the bond which ought to exist between these two sacraments.

It seems, therefore, that we must do without any tidy correspondence between educational practice and the theology of the sacraments. The discrepancy arises from the interim-character of our present existence: we are what we must become. The sacraments make us spiritual adults in principle before we have become such in our conduct. Religious rules, requiring, for example, regular attendance at public worship, are generally believed by Christian educationalists — and no doubt rightly — to help Christians to become what they are. There is, therefore, room for the pedagogue in the life of every Christian. St Paul seems to imply that the pedagogue has only a limited period of usefulness. But since we never completely become what we are, perhaps we never completely outgrow the pedagogue. In 1 Cor 4:14-16, St Paul seems willing to allow the Corinthians ten thousand 'pedagogues in Christ' if they want them.

*What is the purpose and effect of the 'revelation' of faith (v. 23)?*

It is not sufficient to say that the purpose of revelation is to communicate knowledge. Gal 3:23-25 shows that such an answer is altogether too academic. As St Paul sees it, the purpose of revelation

---

[160] Cf. S. Bailey, 'Baptism and the Outpouring of the Holy Spirit in the New Testament,' *Theology* 49 (1946), pp. 11-14.

[161] Cf. B. Leeming, 'The Age of Confirmation,' *Clergy Review* 41 (1956), pp. 649-662, and especially the quotation from Leo XIII on p. 661: 'When confirmed early, children become more docile in accepting the commandments, they are better able to prepare themselves to receive later the sacrament of the Holy

is liberation. Revelation is the communication of liberating knowledge. As St John says (8:23), 'the truth will set you free.'

If revelation means 'liberating knowledge', the question arises whether St Paul would allow that God 'revealed' himself to Moses. Probably he would not. The effect of the lawgiving at Sinai was not liberation; on the contrary, it created the very bondage from which the Christian revelation liberates. As was pointed out above, this is probably the main reason why St Paul adopted the view that the law was given by angels. He never uses the word 'revelation' in connection with Sinai.

The Christian revelation takes place in three stages. First, God revealed himself in *act*, in the incarnation, in the miracles of the public ministry, and in the death and resurrection of Christ; at this stage the revelation remained wrapped in concealment. Secondly, in the resurrection appearances and in the Damascus vision, Christ revealed to the Eleven and to St Paul that he was now the Lord to whom all power had been given in heaven and on earth. It is particularly plain in the case of St Paul that this *formal* revelation casts its light back over all Christ's previous history. Before his conversion, Saul knew a certain amount about the ministry and death of Jesus. The Damascus vision transformed this 'not-knowing knowledge' into revelation. [162] Then thirdly, St Paul was able to communicate revelation to his hearers, and they in their turn to others, in the preaching of the gospel. Bultmann's apparent desire to restrict the word 'revelation' exclusively to the third stage produced the wisecrack that revelation takes place at 10 a.m. on Sundays when Dr Bultmann ascends the pulpit.

By the initial revelation-in-concealment God changed the whole objective situation in which man lives. He put an end to the law (cf. 4:5-6), raised up a man, his Son, Jesus Christ, to be ruler of heaven and earth, and opened up a way for believers to enter his kingdom. By his formal revelation to the apostles he equipped them for their apostolic task. [163] And through their preaching he 'revealed the faith' to others (cf. 3:25) and extended to others the power to become sons

---

Eucharist, and when they receive it, they draw more abundant fruits from it.' This may be a generalization from pastoral experience, but it may also be an *a priori* inference from the theology of Confirmation.

[162] The phrase 'not-knowing knowledge' is borrowed from R. Bultmann, 'Revelation in the New Testament,' in *Existence and Faith* (ed. S. M. Ogden), London, 1961, p. 65. See also G. O'Collins, *Theology and Revelation*, Cork, 1968, p. 51.

[163] A.-M. Denis, 'L'investiture de la fonction apostolique par "apocalypse". Étude thématique de Gal 1:16,' RB 64 (1957), pp. 335-362 and 492-515, goes too far in identifying the revelation with the commissioning of the apostles. In fact, the commissioning followed soon after the revelation.

of God. The revelation-in-act transforms the objective situation. The believer's acceptance of revelation through his faith transforms his status by conforming it to the new objective situation. On the other hand, the man who rejects the gospel thereby condemns himself to live henceforth in an unreal world. He lives as if God had not sent his Son into the world, when in fact he has; and if he is a Jew, he remains subject to the law, though it is now God's will that he should seek salvation in another, simpler and humbler way.

The Christian revelation is, therefore, God's intervention brought to man's knowledge. It is designed to bring us from spiritual childhood into adulthood and to make us heirs of the kingdom promised to Abraham. That is why it is fitting to thank God in liturgical prayers for his revelation, as the early Christians did: [164]

> Our Father, we thank Thee for the life and knowledge which Thou hast revealed to us through Jesus thy Servant. To Thee be glory for ever.

Any revelation from God is a blessing for which we owe gratitude. But the measure of gratitude owed depends chiefly on the content of the revelation. The content of the revelation given us through Christ far exceeds the manifold revelations given through the prophets of the Old Testament (cf. Heb 1:1).

Natural revelation too takes place in three stages. God first reveals himself in the act of creating. This revelation becomes formal revelation when a human mind recognizes it as revelation — which many do not (cf. Rom 1:20-21). Perhaps here too there are 'natural apostles' whose eyes are opened by a quasi-prophetic gift to recognize creation as a revelation of God. They are then able to impart this revelation to others.

The Christian revelation does not abolish the natural revelation but subsumes it and fulfils it. In the Sermon on the Mount Christ himself performs the prophetic function of bringing to his hearers' mind the natural revelation which was there waiting to be seen all the time (Mt 7:9-11):

> Is there a man among you who will hand his son a stone when he asks for bread, or a snake when he asks for a fish? If then you, bad as you are, know how to give good things to your children, how much more will your Father in heaven give good things to those who ask him?

In principle, any man could make this reflection for himself; he has the necessary experience, and the requisite power of inference. But as few men left to themselves do make it, God raised up a prophet in the person of his Son to make it for them. In religion as in all other

---

[164] Didache, 9:3.

spheres of human life, the many are dependent on the insight and wisdom of the few.

It follows that 'revelation' and 'inspiration' must not be treated as mutually exclusive. When 'inspiration' enables an inspired writer to discern and express some new aspect of God's revelation, whether natural or supernatural, it is at the same time a part of the whole process of 'revelation'. [165]

## *What is the purpose of vv. 25-29?*

In vv. 25-29, St Paul completes his explanation of the way in which God's promises to Abraham are being fulfilled. [166] He shows that God has not used the law to elude his obligations of fulfilling the promises, but has used it in such a way as to enable both Jew and Gentile to become heirs of Abraham on an equal footing, namely, by faith and baptism.

The Judaizers were saying that in order to become heirs of Abraham, Gentile Christians must be circumcised. St Paul replies that in the new aeon or era introduced by Christ's death and resurrection such things no longer have any value. Jewish blood, free birth, and male sex do not give a man any standing before God. The right to inherit the kingdom of God does not depend on any of these things. The only thing that matters is whether a person is 'in Christ'. To the Jews, this levelling-up was a revolutionary idea. In our own day, the Jewish morning service still includes a series of blessings which begins as follows:

> Blessed art thou, O Lord our God, King of the universe, who hast given the cock intelligence to distinguish between day and night.
> Blessed art thou, O Lord our God, King of the universe, who hast not made me a foreigner.
> Blessed art thou, O Lord our God, King of the universe, who hast not made me a slave.
> Blessed art thou, O Lord our God, King of the universe, who hast not made me a woman.

## Here is added, in small print:

> Women say:—
> Blessed art thou, O Lord our God, King of the universe,
> who hast made me according to thy will.

---

[165] Cf. P. Benoit, 'Révélation et Inspiration selon la Bible, chez saint Thomas et dans les discussions modernes,' RB 70 (1963), pp. 321-370 [NTA 8-826].

[166] Being a son of God (v. 26) is certainly something greater than being a son of Abraham (v. 29), as Chrysostom observes (PG 61, 656 B). But vv. 26-29 do not form an anticlimax, since the point at issue in this debate is: Who are the heirs of Abraham?

St Paul teaches that for those who are in Christ such distinctions no longer have any religious significance. (He does not of course deny that they remain political, social and biological realities. When Corinthian women began to abandon the veil, he quickly told them to put it back.) [167] The heirs of Abraham are not free-born male Jews who have been circumcised; they include women, slaves, and Gentiles.

*How is baptism related to faith in vv. 25-27?*

In vv. 25-27 St Paul makes no attempt to distinguish the effects of Baptism from the effects of faith. The effects of faith-and-baptism together are: (1) being clothed with Christ, (2) being God's son, (3) being free from the law (the pedagogue). Now if these effects are produced by faith (cf. 3 : 1-5), it is not clear why Baptism is required, or why a man who has believed and has received the Holy Spirit still needs the material rite of baptism. [168] There is at least a *prima facie* case for the view that the sacrament of Baptism is not satisfactorily integrated into the theology of Galatians and Romans. According to these Epistles, the man who believes in Christ becomes one with him, a member of his body, inhabited by his Spirit; the whole process of justification and sanctification requires on man's part, first, acceptance of God's grace through faith, and secondly, obedience to the law of Christ through charity (cf. 5 : 6). What need is there of the external, material rite of Baptism in a spiritual religion of this kind? For practical purposes, it is of course sufficient to reply that Christ so ordained. It is the task of theology to seek an understanding of why he so ordained, and of Scripture scholars to try to find out why St Paul thought Christ had so ordained.

Albert Schweitzer proposed the view that St Paul found the sacrament of Baptism in existence, instituted by Christ, and knew that the other apostles attributed to the rite of Baptism exactly what, in his own theology, was effected by faith; he therefore attributed justification both to faith and to Baptism without stopping to relate the one to the other, or to explain how it comes about that there is room for such a rite in the régime of justification by faith. [169] It may be that there is a gap in St Paul's theology here — that he had no explanation to offer; at least there is a gap in the written record of it.

---

[167] Cf. 1 Cor 11:2-16.

[168] Cf. the case of Cornelius in Acts 10:44-48. According to Chrysostom, PG 61, 663 BC, the sacramental words form the new Christian in the womb of the waters, just as the word of promise formed Isaac in the womb of Sarah. But according to Gal 4:19 it is the word of the preacher, not the form of the sacrament, which forms Christ in the neophyte.

[169] Cf. A. Schweitzer, *Paul and his Interpreters*, London, 1912, pp. 214-215.

M

In Col 2:11, he describes Baptism as 'the circumcision of Christ'. In Rom 4:11, he says that Abraham received circumcision as a 'seal' upon the justice he had received through faith. Putting these two statements together, one might draw the conclusion that the Christian Baptism is a 'seal' set upon justice received through faith. But 'patchwork-interpretation' of this kind is always dangerous, since we have no reason to think that St Paul himself joined the two propositions or made the inference. Indeed it is questionable whether he would have accepted it, for whereas circumcision leaves a permanent visible sign to remind the bearer of his covenant obligations, baptism does not; and St Paul treats Baptism as something much more than a seal placed on a completed transaction. In Gal 3:27-28 he seems to be comparing it to the dyeing of clothes: when a person is dipped in the bath of baptism, he comes out a changed man: his former colour disappears, he comes out the colour of Christ. [170] Whether the person before dipping was a Jew or a Gentile, a slave or a free man, a man or a woman, no longer matters; once he is baptized, he is a part of Christ. But no explanation is given in Galatians of why an actual dipping or Baptism is required. [171]

It must be admitted, therefore, that Baptism does not fit too comfortably into the theology sketched out in Galatians and Romans. The reason is partly that St Paul could not consistently attack circumcision as a material rite and at the same time defend the necessity of the material rite of Baptism, and partly that Baptism was instituted by a positive law (cf. Mt 28:19-20), whereas St Paul is doing his best in Galatians to present Christianity as a religion which is beyond law. [172]

### 'Putting on Christ' — How is this metaphor to be explained?

Attempts have been made to connect the idea of 'putting on Christ' with the Greek mystery-religions in which it was customary to end the ceremonies by clothing the initiate in the garb of the god and

---

[170] In Greek, the meanings of *baptizô* (to dip or baptize) overlap with those of *baptô* (to dip or dye). The other verb in v. 27 (to put on) is again concerned with clothing.

[171] G. R. Beasley-Murray, *Baptism in the New Testament*, London, 1962, p. 151, supplies the following explanation: 'Through such an alliance of faith and baptism, Christianity is prevented from evaporating into an ethereal subjectivism on the one hand, and from hardening into a fossilized objectivism on the other. The two aspects of Apostolic Christianity are preserved in faith-baptism.'

[172] Cf. J. Bligh, 'Baptism in St Paul', HJ 6 (1965), pp. 60-62. McKenzie, *The Power and the Wisdom*, pp. 157-158, gives this explanation: 'Baptism is a rite of initiation; and in this it can be compared to other rites of initiation in the ancient world, particularly in the mystery cults. There is no obvious dependence on any of the mystery cults; but the idea of ritual initiation was common, and

greeting him as if he were identified with the god. [173] The best known example is from the description by Apuleius of his initiation into the religion of Isis: [174]

> When morning came and solemnities were finished, I came forth sanctified with twelve stoles and in a religious habit, whereof I am not forbidden to speak, considering that many persons saw me at that time... In my right hand I carried a lighted torch, and a garland of flowers was upon my head, with white palm-leaves sprouting out on every side like rays; thus I was adorned like unto the sun, and made in fashion of an image, when the curtains were drawn aside and all the people compassed about to behold me.

However, we have no evidence that in St Paul's time Christian Baptism ended with an investiture ceremony of this kind; [175] and as he regarded pagan religions as worship of demons (cf. 1 Cor 10: 20-21), it is unlikely that he has consciously borrowed their imagery or vocabulary. [176]

Another interesting parallel is the custom whereby the Roman boy put on the *toga virilis* to mark his becoming a man. But again, it is unlikely that St Paul intends to compare baptism to this usage.

He may perhaps have developed this strange expression 'to put on Christ' from the language in which he speaks of circumcision. According to Col 2: 11, circumcision is a 'stripping-off' (*apekdusis*) of sinful flesh; and baptism is the reality of which circumcision is the token. Hence baptism is a stripping-away of the whole sinful body (cf. Rom 6: 6). But the believer is not left naked — he 'puts on' (*enduetai*) the body of Christ, or, more briefly, he 'puts on Christ'.

Another possibility, not incompatible with the last, is that St Paul is adapting the language which some Old Testament writers use of the Holy Spirit. [177] In Jud 6: 34, for example, 'the Spirit of the Lord clothed (LXX: *enedusen*) Gideon, and he sounded the trumpet;' and in 1 Chron 12: 18, 'the Spirit clothed (*enedusen*) Amasai, chief of the thirty, and he said, "We are yours, O David." ' Since in Gal 2: 20—3: 5 the indwelling of Christ is practically identified with the

---

Christianity would have been eccentric if there were no external official cultic act by which members were inducted into the group.'

[173] Cf. O. Casel, *Die Liturgie als Mysterienfeier*, Freiburg, 1923; Josephus, *Ant.*, 19, 8, 2; and F. H. Borsch, *The Son of Man in Myth and History*, London, 1967, pp. 104 and 384.

[174] Apuleius, *The Golden Ass*, XI, 22-26, quoted from C. K. Barrett, *The New Testament Background: Selected Documents*, London, 1958, p. 99.

[175] But baptism by immersion did of course involve the taking-off and putting-on of clothes; cf. McKenzie, *The Power and the Wisdom*, p. 149.

[176] Cf. Schnackenburg, *Baptism in the Thought of St Paul*, p. 147; W. L. Knox, *St Paul and the Church of the Gentiles*, p. 138.

[177] Cf. A. Grail, 'Le baptême dans l'épître aux Galates,' RB 58 (1951), p. 508.

infusion of his Spirit, 'you have put on Christ' in 3:27 is practically equivalent to 'the Spirit of Christ has clothed you.' [178]

The language of 'stripping off' and 'putting on' occurs again in Col 3:8-11, a passage which strongly resembles Gal 3:27-28:

> You must strip yourselves of every vice, of anger, passion, and baseness... Put off your old selves and your evil ways, and put on the new man, the nature that is being progressively restored in the image of its Creator and brought to know him better. In the new humanity there is no discrimination between Greek and Jew, circumcised and uncircumcised, Barbarian, Scythian, slave or free; one thing only matters: Christ is in them all. Since you are God's chosen ones, his holy and loved ones, dress yourselves fittingly: put on the garments of compassion, kindness, humility, gentleness, patience... But above all these virtues put on charity, which gathers them up to perfection.

In the parallel in Eph 6:11-14, the Christian is exhorted to put on virtues as pieces of armour. And in Rom 13:14 he is told to 'put on the Lord Jesus Christ.' The difference between these passages and Gal 3:27 is that they use 'put on' in the imperative, whereas Gal 3:27 uses it in the indicative. In St Paul's thought the imperative presupposes the indicative. We must become in outward conduct what we already are in principle through faith and baptism. The new being received in Baptism renders possible new standards of conduct. The child who has been 'christened' can grow up into a Christ-like character. [179]

### Is St Paul thinking of the Second Adam in 3:26-29?

Professor Alan Richardson observes that 'though in Gal 3:28 the name of Adam is not mentioned, the Adam-typology is not far beneath the surface: "There can be neither Jew nor Greek (as Adam was neither), bond nor free (Adam was God's free man), male nor female ('Adam' is common gender): for you are all one in Christ Jesus."' [180]

The suggestion that St Paul has in mind, without actually mentioning, Christ as the second Adam is a good one; but the choice of the three pairs, Greek and Jew, slave and free, male and female, was not dictated by the thought of Adam. The first is obviously relevant

---

[178] Cf. also 1 Cor 12:12-13.
[179] Cf. Schlier, Gal, p. 129.
[180] Richardson, *An Introduction to the Theology of the New Testament*, p. 246; Whiteley, *The Theology of St Paul*, pp. 112-113, agrees. According to some Jewish rabbis, the first Adam was originally androgynous; cf. J. Bligh, 'Richard of St. Victor's *De Trinitate*,' HJ 1 (1960), p. 121.

to the debate with the Judaizers (and is repeated in 6:15), but so too are the second and third. In human law, the slave as such cannot inherit, and the woman does not inherit except in default of a male heir. St Paul is discussing, Who are the heirs of Abraham? His answer is that the distinctions between Jew and Greek, slave and free, male and female, are irrelevant here. All Christians are equally heirs.

The idea that Christ is the second Adam is quite easily combined with the idea that he is the Issue of Abraham. For the blessing promised to Abraham's issue in Gen 12:3 takes away the curse pronounced upon Eve and her issue in Gen 3. St Paul is here introducing his vision of a new humanity, restored to unity in Christ, and through Christ in God the Father. St Jerome aptly quotes Jn 17:22: [181]

> Since the situation is that every difference of race, social condition, and sex is removed by Christ's baptism and by putting on his livery, we are all one in Christ Jesus, so that 'as the Father and the Son are one, so we are one in them.'

The parallel is particularly apt, if, as we mentioned above, vv. 19-20 at the centre of this subsection imply that Christ and the Father are one.


*'No longer Jew or Greek' — Did St Paul hope for a unification of language?*

In Genesis, the call of Abraham in ch. 12 is the first step, not only towards the removal of the curse imposed in Gen 3, but also towards healing the division of mankind resulting from the sin committed at Babel in Gen 11. Christ not only takes away the sin of the world, but also reunites the human family.

The division of mankind was effected and is perpetuated through the multiplication of languages. Men who cannot talk the same language cannot 'understand' one another; and men who cannot understand one another first shout, then come to blows. The story of the tower of Babel expresses an important truth. 'As soon as a child is integrated into a community by virtue of the language he has learned, he inevitably becomes fatally cut off from other people.' [182]

Since Christ reunites the human family (v. 28), we might expect, *a priori*, that through his Body, the Church, he would propagate a common language. The miracle of Pentecost, as described in Acts 2, may have given rise to hopes that the unification of language would occur miraculously. [183] At all events, neither St Paul nor any of the

---

[181] Jerome, PL 26, 395 B.
[182] Cf. Dubarle, *Original Sin*, p. 37.
[183] Zeph 3:9 seems to promise a unification of language in the Good Time to Come;

other apostles appears to have taken any active steps in the matter. On this, as on other questions, St Paul's thought may have been inhibited by his expectation of a speedy End to this world (cf. 1 Cor 7:17).

In later centuries, the Church has striven to maintain unity of language in her law, liturgy, and official documents. There was a good theological reason for this: it is the Church's duty to reunite and reconcile the divided human family. One way in which Christians can love their enemies is to learn their language. Now that Latin is falling into disuse, we need to look for another common tongue.

*Has 3:28 any bearing on the problem of race-relations?*

Gal 3:28 is often quoted as if it were a direct pronouncement of St Paul against the colour-bar — as if he were saying that Christians should draw no distinction between black and white, since all are God's children and all have the same rights. [184] But St Paul is not talking about *social* or *civil* relationships here. He did not want to abolish the distinction between Jew and Greek; on the contrary, he wished Jews to continue to follow the Jewish way of life and forbade the Gentile Christians to adopt it (cf. 1 Cor 7:17); nor did he seek to abolish the distinction between free citizen and slave even within the Church; and of course he did not attempt to ignore the distinction between men and women or to demand any change in the civil status of women. What he is actually saying is that 'in Christ' Jew and Gentile, male and female, slave and free are all equally heirs of the kingdom of God. There will be no second-class citizens in heaven. He does not say that the Church should try to alter the civil status of women or slaves or other less privileged persons. Hoping, as he most probably did, that the Parousia would occur within a generation, he did not think it important to attempt a revision of social institutions. Those who attempt to derive from Gal 3:28 a policy of civil rights for all inhabitants of the globe are drawing consequences which St Paul himself did not draw from what he said. [184a]

But are such consequences nevertheless legitimately drawn? Strictly speaking, the text attributes a certain equality to all who are baptized

see further G. Bardy, *La Question des Langues dans l'Eglise-ancienne,* Vol. I, Paris, 1948, pp. 1-79.

[184] Theodoretus, PG 82, 494 C, has this comment on 5:6: 'Faith has destroyed the distinction between circumcision and uncircumcision. So too what generals look for in soldiers is not whether they are white or black, but whether they are trained fighters.'

[184a] Cf. W. Rauschenbusch, *Christianity and the Social Crisis,* New York (1907) reprint 1964, p. 102: 'Paul was a radical in theology, but a social conservative.' Cf. Rom 13:1-2.

into Christ. It does not assert that all men are by nature sons of God and therefore equal. One cannot even say that if all men on the globe were to become Christians, their baptism in Christ and consequent divine sonship would give them a right to civil equality. St Paul does not say that baptism in any way alters a man's relationship within the present aeon. Each Christian remains what he was: either a Gentile or a Jew, either a slave or a free man, either a man or a woman. [185]

In Colossians and Philemon, St Paul does urge that being Christians should affect the relationship of slave and master in that the master will be more gentle, and the slave obedient and willing. But this simply means that Christians will exercise justice and charity within the existing pattern of social relationships.

Until the Church had abandoned the expectation of an early Parousia, the Christian conscience did not feel any obligation to ask whether the social relationships themselves were just and charitable.

A much sounder basis for a civil rights programme can be found in the Golden Rule: 'What you would that men should do unto you, do you also to them.' This is a principle of natural law endorsed by Christ. As Harnack observed, 'insufficient and prosaic as the rule may seem, yet, if extended to cover all human relationships and really observed, it contains a civilizing force of enormous strength.' [186] But where deep divisions already exist between racial and social groups, it is far from sufficient, for it is only a variant of the *lex talionis*. [187] It sums up the law and the prophets, but the law and the prophets *unfulfilled*. Christ, the new Elijah, the Apostle of reconciliation (cf. Mal 4: 5), brought this doctrine to completion by teaching that reconciliation must come about through love of enemies. Evil must be overcome by good. He said these things in a country that was restless under the yoke of Roman imperialism. [188]

---

[185] As usual, Theodore of Mopsuestia (Gal, p. 57) interprets v. 28 with the aid of a contrast between the present life and the future risen life: What is said in v. 28 will be fully true after the resurrection and is true now by anticipation. He seems to think that the risen body will be neither male nor female, neither circumcised nor uncircumcised—a prospect which puzzles the imagination. Still, he may be right—cf. Mt 24 : 38.

[186] A. Harnack, *What is Christianity?* ed. 3, London, 1904, p. 78.

[187] Cf. M.-J. Lagrange, *Saint Matthieu*, Paris, 1923, p. 145, on Mt 7 : 2.

[188] For a first-century criticism of Roman imperialism, see the speech of the Scottish freedom-fighter Calgacus in Tacitus's *Agricola*, 30: 'Plunderers of the world! Now that there is no more land to satisfy their passion for universal devastation, they are combing the sea. If their enemy is rich, they lust for wealth; if he is poor, then for power—neither East nor West has sated their craving—alone of all men they look with the same hungry eyes on wealth and poverty. Looting, slaughter, and rapine they cloak with the name of "empire", and where they make a wilderness they call it "peace".' Many in Palestine shared such sentiments; there was never real peace in Israel under the Romans.

*The Fifth Section, 4:1-10*

# LIBERATION

The fifth of the nine sections is the central passage of the whole Epistle. The symmetry both of the section and of its two subsections is constructed with particular care.

**A** *4 : 1* What I mean is: so long as the heir to a property is a minor, he is no different from a slave, **B** though he is the lord of all. **C** *2* But he is subject to guardians and stewards until the date fixed by his father. **D** *3* So too with us: so long as we were minors, we were subject to the elements of the world, enslaved to them. **E** *4* But when the fulness of time arrived, God sent forth his own Son, **F** who was born of a woman, **G** and became subject to the law, **G¹** *5* in order to redeem those under the law, **F¹** in order that we might receive the status of sons. **E¹** *6* And as proof that you are his sons, God sent forth the Spirit of his Son into our hearts, crying: 'Abba, Father!' **D¹** *7* So then you are no longer a slave but a son, and if a son, then also an heir, thanks to God. **C¹** *8* Formerly, not knowing God, you were the slaves of beings who by nature are not gods; **B¹** *9* but now that you have come to know God, or rather to be known by God, **A¹** how can you turn back to the weak and grasping elements? Do you wish to be enslaved to them all over again, *10* observing days and months and seasons and years?

*Was this passage originally addressed to Jews or to Gentiles?*

St Paul cannot be saying that before the coming of Christ the Gentile nations, worshipping their idols, were already God's sons and heirs, though they were treated as slaves. The comparison proposed in vv. 1-3 applies only to the Jews. Israel was from the start (cf. Exod 4: 22) God's son; but during the period of the law the condition of the Israelites was no better than that of the Gentile nations who were slaves. Both were subject to the same 'guardians and stewards', namely the 'angels' of the elements, the Gentiles because they *were* slaves, the Jews because for the time being they were treated as slaves — that is, until the date fixed for their liberation. The opening phrase of v. 3, 'So too with us,' must mean: 'So too with us Jews.' In vv. 4-7, St Paul goes on to speak of the liberation of the Jews from servitude to the law (of Moses). He cannot be speaking of the Gentiles here, since they were not subject to the law of Moses. They were subject to the law written (imperfectly) in their own hearts (cf. Rom 2: 14); but Christ did not redeem them from this interior law, and St Paul is not talking about the law of conscience in vv. 4-5.

4:1-10 is, therefore, fully intelligible only when recognised as a part of the discourse which St Paul addressed to the Jewish Christians at Antioch. Against this view, three objections might be raised.

(1) First, it might be objected: 'In v. 5 St Paul says that Christ became a man and was subject to the law "in order that we might receive *huiothesia*." Now *huiothesia* is the regular word for "adoption". But the Jews had already been made God's sons before the coming of Christ (cf. Exod 4:22; Rom 9:4). Therefore the "we" in v. 5 cannot refer to the Jewish Christians.'

It must be admitted that *huiothesia* does normally mean 'adoption'. But the context shows that here St Paul has something else in mind. He says that during the period of the law Israel 'was in no way different from a slave'. When Christ redeemed the Jews from the law, they ceased to be slaves and entered upon the condition of sons. Etymologically, this is exactly what *huiothesia* means: 'instatement as a son'. According to St Paul (cf. Rom 1:4), Christ himself received 'instatement as God's Son' at his resurrection. There is, therefore, no reason why the same should not be said of Jewish believers when they die and rise with Christ in baptism: through their baptism they receive *huiothesia* — they are given the status of sons of God.

(2) It might be objected that during the period of the law the Jews were not 'subject to the elements of the world, enslaved to them' (v. 3); this must be a description of the Gentiles, whose idolatrous worship enslaved them to the demonic powers.

This argument is refuted by vv. 9-10, where St Paul says that to return to the law of Moses is to become enslaved once more to the weak and grasping elements. He does regard obedience to the law and enslavement to the elements as equivalent to each other.

(3) It might be objected that v. 8 is a description of Gentile converts, not of Jews: 'Formerly, not knowing God, you were the slaves of beings who by nature are not gods.'

It must be admitted that the words apply more strictly to Gentile Christians than to Jewish Christians (cf. 1 Thes 4:5); but St Paul probably means that before the Jewish Christians learned to cry 'Abba, Father', they did not truly know God, and before they had received the Holy Spirit, they were not truly known by God; before their conversion, God did not deal with them directly, but placed them in servitude under the angels of the law.

*Did St Paul think that this argument (4:1-10) was somehow applicable to the Gentiles?*

Since St Paul re-uses this passage in a letter addressed to Gentiles, he must have thought that it applied, though less well, to them. They could regard their pre-conversion days as their childhood, and the demonic powers of their false religions as the stewards and guardians from whom they had been released. Christ could be said to have redeemed them from the law, in as much as he had made expiation for the sins they had committed against the law of their consciences. They had received *huiothesia* in the strict sense of 'adoption'. Before their conversion they had been more 'ignorant of God' than the Jews (v. 8). And the temptation to adopt the Jewish law was a temptation to return to a ritualistic religion similar to the pagan rites which they had abandoned.

So, in a rough and ready way, the argument is applicable to the Gentiles, and St Paul must have been satisfied that the Gentiles should make this rough and ready application. But if they studied it with anything like the care which later generations have lavished upon it, they must have seen that the opening comparison (vv. 1-3) is not really applicable to Gentiles, but only to Jews.

St Jerome attempts to deal with this difficulty by the following comment:[1]

> The little heir, who is no different from a slave, although he is the lord of all, and is subject to guardians and stewards until the date fixed by his father, is *the whole human race* down to the coming of Christ, and, let me add, to the very end of the world. For just as all die, even before they are born, in the first man Adam, so all men, including those born before the coming of Christ, are restored to life in the second Adam (cf. 1 Cor 15:22). Thus we were slaves to the law in the fathers, and they are saved by grace in their sons. This interpretation fits the Catholic Church, which asserts the unity of providence in the Old and New Testament, and does not distingush in time those whom she has united in condition.

This is an extremely ingenious solution to the problem: Gentile converts to Christianity become so truly a part of the Israel of God (cf. 6:16), that the history of Israel becomes their history, and the forefathers of the Jews become their forefathers. They can and must look back to Moses and the lawgiving as part of their own history, so that they too can say, along with their Jewish brethren, 'In the childhood of *our* nation, God made us slaves to the law.'

---

[1] St Jerome, PL 26, 396 A.

It is an ingenious solution, but probably incorrect. The Jewish proselyte was not allowed to say: 'A wandering Aramean was my father.' [2] St Paul is not likely to have taught his Gentile converts to identify themselves with Israel according to the flesh even more closely than the rabbis taught their proselytes to do so. Secondly, if St Paul, when composing the passage, had been thinking of 'the whole human race before the coming of Christ', he would not have compared it to an heir, for the status of heir was then the privilege of Israel (cf. Rom 9:4). And thirdly, in Gal 4:1-10 St Paul is showing how Christ undid the work, not of Adam, but of Moses.

*Is the heir in v. 1 an orphan?*

The introductory phrase in v. 1, 'What I mean is,' introduces this passage as a clarification of what has already been said, hence as an elaboration of the covenant-analogy used in 3:15-16.

4:1-3 is usually read as a description of the condition of an orphaned heir. This view is derived from the customary translation of v. 2 as 'he is subject to trustees (*epitropoi*) and stewards until the day fixed (*prothesmia*) by his father.' Both *epitropos* and *prothesmia* are words used in wills; hence, it is inferred, St Paul is thinking of an heir placed under trustees by his father's will. However, these words are not used exclusively in wills; and a man does not appoint stewards by will. The language is just as appropriate if St Paul is thinking of God as a king or as a great landowner who has several properties and administers them during his own lifetime through procurators (*epitropoi*) and stewards (*oikonomoi*). [3] While his son and heir is a child, he is placed under the control of these agents and stewards and in this respect is no different from the king's servants and slaves. The king may well leave it to his agents to appoint a pedagogue to look after the child. He appoints neither the agent nor the pedagogue by his will.

This is an allegory of the history of Israel. In the time of Abraham, God promised an inheritance to Israel (i.e. to the Issue of Abraham [4]), that is, he made Israel his heir. What happened at Sinai, four hundred and thirty years later, was that God entrusted the growing boy Israel to the care of his agents and stewards (the 'angels' of the elements).

[2] Cf. Daube, *The New Testament and Rabbinic Judaism*, p. 92.
[3] Cf. Mt 20:8, 'The owner of the vineyard said to his steward (*epitropos*) . . .' According to Philo, *On Joseph*, 117 (Loeb, VI), Joseph received the office of steward or procurator (*epitropē*) from the Pharaoh)—while the latter was still living of course.
[4] See above, p. 251.

These agents appointed Moses as pedagogue. He was a faithful servant
in God's household (cf. Heb 3:5), but his office was not permanent.
It was to end when Israel's minority ended, at the date fixed by God
the Father. Then Israel received back the status of God's son, which
had been in suspense during the period of slavery to the law.

## Are vv. 1-2 applicable to Christ?

The liturgy of Christmas applies this passage to Christ. Of him
it is preeminently true that during his earthly life he was 'no different
from a slave although he was the Lord of all.' St Paul may have
chosen his words here so that they would be specially applicable to
Christ, the Lord of all. [5] As was pointed out above (p. 331), St Paul
regarded Christ's divine Sonship as temporarily in abeyance while he
bore the form of a slave (cf. Phil 2:7). If the Transfiguration is a
post-resurrection incident, [6] one might say that the period of abeyance
lasted from the Baptism of Christ to the Transfiguration. The Baptism
was a baptism into slavery (cf. Rom 6:16-23), whereby Jesus took
upon him the office of Servant of Yahweh; and the resurrection was
his formal reinstatement in the glory proper to God's Son.

At one point, the comparison breaks down in the case of Christ.
The heir is required to obey agents and stewards for his own good,
because he is not yet capable of acting with full responsibility. But
Christ became subject to the law and to the angels of the law (cf.
Heb 2:9) for the good of others — 'to redeem us who were subject
to the law, that we might receive the status of sons.'

## What is the purpose of the whole section (4:1-10)?

The purpose of the whole section is to show Jewish Christians
that their spiritual childhood is over, that they must leave behind the
religious practices of childhood, and that having left them behind,
they must not return to them — to return to the law is an infantile
regression. In a word, the message is: 'You are now spiritual adults,
and must behave as such.'

At the same time, St Paul is answering a difficulty which might
arise from the argument proposed in the last section: If the law is an
interim arrangement, which was intended to last only till the coming

[5]    Chrysostom, PG 61, 662 B, applies the phrase 'lord of all' to Isaac, in contrast
to Ishmael. But there is no reason to think that in 4:1 St Paul is already thinking of Isaac and Ishmael.
[6]    See above, p. 131.

of the Issue, why did the Issue, when he came, submit to the law, throughout the whole of his life? Why did he not renounce the law, at least when he became an adult? St Paul's answer is: 'Christ became subject to the law for the very purpose of liberating us from the law; therefore, to imitate his obedience to the law is unintelligent copying, which does not correspond to his own intentions.' [7] In respect of his observance of the law, Christ is not set before us as a model for imitation. He came to lead Israel out of childhood into adult maturity. This he did by his teaching and by his death. In his teaching he re-iterated the prophetic message that God asks for mercy not sacrifice (cf. Mt 9:13; 12:7, where he quotes Hosea 6:6); and by his death he offered a sacrifice which rendered obsolete the animal sacrifices of the old law. In the present passage, St Paul says nothing of the teaching-ministry of Christ, and alludes only indirectly to his death. But he is certainly thinking of his death when he says that 'Christ became subject to the law in order to redeem us who were under the law.'

There is an interesting passage in Philo's treatise *On Joseph* where he describes the transition from each stage of human life to the next as an anticipatory death. After distinguishing the successive stages, Philo asks himself: [8]

> Where are all these gone? Has not the baby vanished in the boy, the boy in the lad, the lad in the stripling, the stripling in the youth, the youth in the man, the man in the old man, while on old age follows death? Perhaps, indeed, each of the stages, as its resigns its rule to its successor, dies an anticipatory death, nature thus silently teaching us not to fear the death that ends all, since we have borne so easily the earlier deaths.

This parallel may cast some light on St Paul's thought in 4:1-10. Christian Jews pass from childhood to maturity when they die with Christ in baptism out of childhood into maturity. This transition or exodus should be as irreversible as the death of Christ.

## Who were the 'guardians and stewards'?

St Jerome proposes three possible identifications: the guardians and stewards are either (1) the prophets, (2) guardian angels, or (3) the priests and kings of Israel. [9]

---

[7]   Heb 11:24-27 suggests an O.T. comparison. Moses could have lived in splendour as the son of Pharoah's daughter. But he preferred to share the status of the Jews in order to redeem them from their Egyptian bondage.

[8]   Philo, *On Joseph*, 128-129 (Loeb, VI). Cf. Marcus Aurelius, *Meditations*, IX, 21: 'Consider the stages of thy life—childhood, boyhood, manhood, old age— each step in the ladder of change is a death.'

[9]   Cf. St Jerome, PL 26, 396 B.

The structure of the section shows that St Paul had chiefly in mind the angels who gave the law. The counterpart of v. 2 is v. 8: 'You were the slaves of beings who by nature are not gods' (i.e. the 'angels' of 3:19). These angels showed excessive zeal in their task, [10] but they intended, as St Jerome says, to act as guardians; he aptly quotes Ps 33:8: 'He will set the angels of the Lord about those who fear him, to deliver them.' St Paul may also have been thinking of the prophets, if, as is likely, he regarded the prophets as mouthpieces of the angels. According to Philo, the angels could appear in human shape as prophets. In discussing the appearance of the three strangers to Abraham and Sarah in Gen 18, he says that when Sarah laughed at the idea that she might bear a son in her old age, the visitors replied: 'Is anything impossible for God?', and he adds the comment: [11]

> It was then, I think, that she first saw in the strangers before her a different and grander aspect, that of prophets, or of angels transformed from their spiritual and soul-like nature into human shape.

If St Paul regarded Moses as a representative of the angels, he probably held similar views about the other prophets.

Perhaps too St Paul would admit St Jerome's third interpretation of his words. The priests and kings of Israel, being instituted by the law, must have been appointed by the angels of the law. St Paul does not emphasize the point, but Christ, by redeeming Jewish Christians from the law, necessarily released them from their obedience to the High Priest and from their obligations to the levitical priesthood. Those Jews who, in Christ, have come of age, are released from the control of the Jewish priesthood. Christ himself became subject to the Jewish religious authorities, but in order to release his disciples from them. In Jn 10:8 he says: 'All who came before me were thieves and robbers.'

## Is the Christian free from the control of guardians and stewards?

Vv. 1-5 have a bearing on the theology of the laity, or at least on the relationship of the laity to the clergy. If Israel is subject to guardians and stewards only in the years of childhood, it would seem to be the mark of an adult Christian to be free from the control of the guardians and stewards. Yet the Church has its guardians and stewards — in the first generation Peter, Paul, Apollos and the rest, of whom Paul himself says: 'We should be regarded as ministers of Christ and

---

[10] See above, pp. 307-308.
[11] Philo, *On Abraham*, 113 (Loeb, VI). This idea may lie behind Heb 1:1, where some commentators have thought that the argument requires the substitution of 'angels' for the manuscript reading 'prophets'.

stewards of God's mysteries' (1 Cor 4:1); and in later generations there have been bishops, priests and deacons.

St Paul's argument points towards the conclusion that bishops, priests and deacons must themselves be mature men, and that Christian laymen will require positive guidance from their clergy only so long as they remain immature — that is, while they are in fact children (say, to the age of fourteen), and then afterwards as long as they fail to become mature Christians. For the most part, the clergy will influence the adult faithful by preaching — and by silent example, for, as the Preface of Ordination to the Priesthood says, they should gently reproach the conduct of others by the example of their holy lives. [12] But further they should have a special care for Christian children and for the spiritually immature. In parochial experience, this is very much what we see happening: the clergy are largely concerned with the instruction of children, in and out of school, and with the running of youth clubs for the teenagers. The adult Christian rarely feels the need to go to the priest for advice. This being so, it is perhaps to be regretted that the clergy are now withdrawing from the field of education in favour of laymen. If this policy rests on the unconscious assumption that once the clergy are relieved of the care of children, the adults will come forward in larger numbers for spiritual guidance, it is doomed to disappointment. Most of the adults who knock on presbytery doors are prospective converts and engaged couples. If in other cases a priest takes the initiative and offers advice unsought, he may find himself rather rudely rebuffed. The average layman feels that he is an adult and knows how to manage his own life. In future, the priest may be more and more concerned with the aged. [12a]

## What does St Paul mean by 'the elements' (4:3)?

The word 'elements' (in Greek *stoicheia*) can mean (1) the four 'elements' out of which, according to the ancient cosmology, the material universe was created, namely, earth, air, fire and water; (2) the heavenly bodies, and (3) the letters of the alphabet and hence 'elementary instruction'.

In the present context, however, St Paul seems to use the word in a fourth sense. The *stoicheia* appear to be identical with the angelic guardians and stewards to whom Israel was subject in the period of the law. This sense is not attested by parallel passages in authors

---

[12] 'Censuramque morum exemplo suae conversationis insinuant.' Cf. J. Bligh, *Ordination to the Priesthood*, London, 1956, pp. 102-108.
[12a] Cf. L. Paul, *The Deployment and Payment of the Clergy*, London, 1964, p. 51.

prior to or contemporary with St Paul. However, as the ancients did not distinguish clearly between the material elements and the angels who were believed to control them, there was no reason why *stoicheia* should not be used of the angels. In Ps 104:4, the Lord is described as 'making his angels winds and his ministers flaming fire' — as if the Lord could and did make his angels and spiritual ministers take on the material forms of wind (air) and fire, two of the elements. [12b]

The reason why St Paul chose to describe the angels of the law as *stoicheia* may be that in the midrashic tradition they originate from the thunder and lightning, fire and smoke of Exod 19:16-18; but further he wishes to imply that subjection to these angels is an 'elementary' situation, like that of infants learning their ABC under schoolmasters and pedagogues. [13]

Perhaps, too, the word *stoicheia* had for St Paul the same connotation of savagery as has the English 'elements' in such phrases as 'exposed to the buffetting of the elements'. In Philo, the 'elements' are the instruments of divine punishment; for example, seven of the Egyptian plagues are attributed by him to the four elements.[14] Perhaps, therefore, St Paul also means: 'You are sheltered now by Christ from the buffetting of the elements; why do you want to expose yourselves to them again?'

*Does St Paul equate Judaism with idolatry here?*

If 'we' and 'us' are understood throughout this passage as including both Jews and Gentiles, it is impossible to avoid the conclusion that St Paul is putting Judaism on a par with the idolatrous religions of the Gentiles and describing both together as 'slavery to the elements of the world'.

However, if the passage was originally addressed to an audience consisting solely of Jews, no comparison was made with pagan religions. St Paul was simply restating what he had said before, namely, that during the period of the law the Jews were subject not to God himself, but to the 'angels' — who are now called 'the elements'.

The implication that Judaism is not much better than idolatry comes in only when the passage is re-used for the instruction of Gentiles. They too were subject to the 'elements' when they offered animal sacrifices to their false gods. They are warned that to adopt Jewish ceremonial practices is tantamount to relapsing into idolatry. St Paul

---

[12b] Cf. Knight, *Christian Theology of the O.T.*, p. 69.
[13] St Jerome has a long discussion of the 'elements' in PL 26, 397.
[14] Cf. Philo, *Moses*, I, 96-97 and 114; II, 53 (Loeb, VI).

was not so tactless as to say this openly to the Jews at Antioch. But
when addressing the Gentiles of Galatia, he lets it be seen that in his
view before the coming of Christ all men were subject to spiritual
powers or angels — the Jews to angelic powers of imperfect obedience
and the Gentiles to demonic powers (since he says in 1 Cor 10:20:
'the sacrifices which the Gentiles offer, they offer to no god, but to
demons'). This does not mean that the same demonic powers which
were worshipped in pagan religions were also at work in the ceremonies
of Judaism. [15] It means that Jewish ceremonial observances are on the
same *material* level as pagan observances. A crass material ritual like circumcision, for example, belongs to the same crude level of religious observance as the self-castration of Phrygian priests alluded to in 5:12. [16]

## *Whence comes the concept of spiritual childhood?*

St Paul appears to have felt that in his own life he had recapitulated
the religious history of mankind. There was first his childhood, when
he was free from the law and innocent (cf. Rom 7:9), then came his
period under the law when Sin enslaved him (cf. Rom 7:9-14), then
came his conversion, when he was delivered from the law, strengthened
by the Spirit, and made a just man. To these stages in his own life
corresponded the periods from Abraham to Moses, from Moses to
Christ, and now the Christian period. It is likely, then, that in 4:3
St Paul is drawing upon his own religious experience.

But probably he is also indebted to literary sources. The influence,
direct or indirect, of Philo may have helped him to see his conversion
as a transition from spiritual childhood to maturity. In his treatise,
*Who is the heir?*, Philo gives a midrash on Gen 15:16: 'In the fourth
generation they shall come back hither.' He explains the four generations as the four periods of seven years in which a man grows from
infancy to maturity. From one to seven is the period of innocence,
from seven to fourteen the period of sin, from fourteen to twenty-one
the period of correction, and from twenty-one to twenty-eight the
period of growth to maturity. [17] Here we have the same combination

---

[15] St Paul himself continued to take part in the Jewish ritual as late as A.D. 58.
St Augustine says in a letter to Jerome (*Ep. Hieron.*, 116, 8): 'He undertook
the celebration of those rites . . . lest he should be believed to condemn as
Gentile idolatry those rites which God had fittingly commanded in earlier times
as figures of things to come.'

[16] Cf. Bring, Gal, p. 190: 'Paul identifies the religious attitude under a law
interpreted as in Judaism with the attitude found in heathen religions.' The
dress of the High Priest, as explained by Philo, *On the Special Laws*, I, 82-97
(Loeb, VII), symbolizes the Jews' servitude to the *stoicheia*. See further, below,
pp. 433-434.

[17] Cf. Philo, *Who is the heir?*, 293-299 (Loeb, IV); cf. above, p. 215.

of ideas as in Gal 4: 1-11 — the linking of periods of salvation-history with periods of the individual's spiritual life, and the conception of growth from spiritual infancy to maturity. St Paul does not distinguish four neat periods, and he reverses the direction of the allegory: he does not use the periods of history to explain the development of the individual, but the periods of the individual's development to cast light on the stages of the religious history of mankind.

*The First Subsection, 4:1-2*

## LIBERATION OF SON AND HEIR

**A**   *4 : 1* So long as the heir to a property is a minor,   **B**   he is no different from a slave,   **C**   though he is the lord of all,   **B¹**   *2* but is subject to guardians and stewards   **A¹**   until the day fixed by his father.

*How was the 'fulness of time' determined?*

In the human situation described in this subsection, the date at which the son's minority is to end is fixed by the father, but not of course without any reference to the anticipated development of the child. So too the spiritual childhood of mankind comes to an end at a time appointed by God the Father, but presumably not without reference to the spiritual development of mankind.

Spiritually, mankind had developed a long way in the centuries between Moses and Christ. The Jewish prophets and the Greek philosophers both played their parts. The writing of Philo can be taken as symptomatic of the times: Jews who were in contact with the best of pagan thought could no longer accept the old material ritual without question. They had to justify it to their own reasoning minds by interpreting it as a pattern of symbols; and once the symbols had been read, the question necessarily arose whether the material ritual was still necessary. [18]

There is always an element of arbitrariness in the fixing of a school-leaving age. The sending of Christ to deliver man from the schoolroom tasks of material ritual could have taken place a generation or two earlier, or a generation or two later. [19] But, with this qualification, we can say that the time was ripe for the redemption of man from legal-

---

[18]   Cf. Philo, *The Migration of Abraham*, 89-92 (Loeb, IV).
[19]   Similarly Christ could have begun his public ministry a year or two earlier or later, but he waited till the 'hour' appointed by his Father. Cf. Jn 2:4; 7:5; St Thomas, Gal, 414 B.

istic religion. [20] Gentiles as well as Jews were ready for a more spiritual religion than they had previously known — in fact the Gentiles were more ready than the Jews, as can be seen from the greater success of the gospel in Gentile lands.

In our own day, we have seen such a turning-point in the development of mankind. In the forties and early fifties of this century, few people thought it unfitting that millions of Africans should be ruled over by a small minority of European 'pedagogues', who addressed them as 'boy'. But in the late fifties and early sixties, world sentiment underwent a period of rapid development as a result of which 'colonialism' has been almost universally abandoned.

Christianity came into the world at such a period: it was carried abroad by the winds of change. Men had outgrown the old religions, and found Christianity something which the adult mind could accept. They welcomed it with feelings of relief and liberation.

The problem of the Church now is this: in the twenty Christian centuries mankind has made further great advances. Can the religion which satisfied our ancestors of two thousand years ago still satisfy us? The answer can be 'Yes', only if Christianity has within itself the power to develop as the human spirit develops. But even if we claim that it has, we can no longer preach the gospel as a message of liberation in the same way as St Paul could. We cannot expect the modern pagan to accept the yoke of the gospel with a sigh of relief. The great appeal of Bishop Robinson's *Honest to God* was that it seemed to offer to the modern Christian a renewal of that sense of liberation, so that he could again sigh with relief — relief, this time, at being freed from out-moded, prescientific forms of *Christian* thought.

The trouble with St Paul's analogy is that it seems to imply that the spiritual development of mankind was complete, or nearing completion, in his own day. This was easy enough to believe when the End was thought to be at hand; but looking back from his present vantage-point, the modern Christian may find it less plausible. There has been a forward movement in the spiritual development of mankind, both outside the Church and within it, whereas his analogy suggests that once the fulness of time had come, no further developments were to be expected. Outside the Church, and largely independently of the Church, there has been a great movement of social reform in the last century. Inside the Church at present, the call for inner renewal is a confession that we need to recapture the vigour of youth.

---

[20] For a different view see McKenzie, *The Power and the Wisdom*, p. 26: 'Any moment for the incarnational intrusion of God into the world is the right moment; any moment is also the wrong moment.'

*The Second Subsection, 4:3-10*

# LIBERATION OF GOD'S SONS

**A** *4 : 3* So too with us: when we were minors, we were subject to the elements of the world, enslaved to them. **B** *4* But when the fulness of time arrived, **C** God sent forth his own Son, who was born of a woman and became subject to the law, *5* in order to redeem those under the law, in order that we might receive the status of sons. **D** *6* And as proof that you are his sons — God sent forth the Spirit of his Son into our hearts, **E** crying: 'Abba, Father!' **F** *7* So then you are no longer a slave but a son, **G** but if a son, then also an heir, thanks to God. **F¹** *8* Formerly, not knowing God, you were the slaves of beings who by nature are not gods, **E¹** *9* but now that you have come to know God, **D¹** or rather, to be known by God, **C¹** how can you turn back to the weak and grasping elements, **B¹** *10* observing days and months and seasons and years? **A¹** *9b* Do you want to be enslaved to them all over again?

*Why does St Paul insert 'who was born of a woman and became subject to the law'?*

In C and C¹ of this subsection, the liberality of God is contrasted with the demands of the 'grasping elements'. The contrast is not enhanced, and the balance in length is spoiled, by the addition of the phrases 'born of a woman' and 'subject to the law'. Moreover, the whole section (see above, p. 330) would have a satisfactory centre without these phrases. It would run as follows:

**E** When the fulness of time had come, God sent forth his Son, **F** in order to redeem those under the law, in order that we might receive the status of sons. **E¹** And because you are his sons, God sent forth the Spirit of his Son...

The two purposes-clauses in F are complementary to each other: the first describes redemption from the curse of the law, the second the bestowing of the blessing of sonship. [21]

Why then did St Paul insert the two phrases? One effect of their insertion is to emphasize that Christ shared the condition of those whom he came to redeem. He became as like us as possible, in order that we might become as like him as possible. He became a man in order to raise us above the level of humanity; he became subject to the law in order to raise us above the law — in other words, so that we

[21] Cf. Chrysostom, PG 61, 657 B ('both the taking away of evil and the giving of good'); Philo, *On Moses*, II, 134 (Loeb, VI).

might share the condition which he had before he abased himself. It is highly appropriate for St Paul to insist on the divine condescension in this context. Only because God has first shown this condescension can we make bold to speak to him with the intimacy implied in 'Abba, Father'.

The idea that Christ became as much like his followers as possible is further developed in the Epistle to the Hebrews, where the author goes so far as to say that Christ was like us in all things 'sin alone excepted' (4 : 15).

### Why did Christ become subject to the law?

Christ came under the law when he was circumcised (cf. 5 : 3). This phrase contains the only allusion in the Epistle to the fact that Christ himself was circumcised. Historically, his parents circumcised him simply because it was what the law required (cf. Lk 2 : 21) and what the angel had taken for granted. But theologically, it must have been an embarrassment to St Paul. According to the argument he is developing, one would expect him to say: 'When we were minors, we were subject to the elements of the world, enslaved to them; but when the fulness of time arrived, God sent forth his Son to abolish the law and set us a pattern of how an adult son should live.' But he could not say this, for Christ had not set the law aside and had submitted to the 'elementary' rules of the Mosaic law.

The problem can be put this way: Why did not Christ himself come among the Jews and say: 'The law was given for the period of Israel's infancy, which is now over; it is time to set aside the traditional ritual of the temple, the priesthood, the animal sacrifices, etc., and practise a more spiritual religion'? [22] The strange thing is that this is very much what St John the Baptist had done. Though he was of priestly stock, he turned his back on the temple, went into the desert, and preached a baptism of repentance for the remission of sins. [23] When he was asked 'What must we do?' he said nothing about the ritual law, but urged charity and justice in social relationships. He warned the Jews not to trust in their descent from Abraham; and by

---

[22] Christ does say something like this to the Samaritan woman in Jn 4 : 21-23. But this may be a post-resurrection utterance. Cf. HJ 5 (1964), p. 293.

[23] J. E. Fison, *The Faith of the Bible*, Harmondsworth (Penguin), 1957, p. 133, observes that 'the greatness of John consisted in the fact that he came from the pious and priestly tradition of Jerusalem and therefore appeared in the wilderness of Judaea not as some eccentric crank, but as a creative pioneer, born into a great tradition and prepared to sacrifice his birthright for a tradition that was even greater. Born to the Temple service, he gave it up and followed the tradition of the tabernacle.' Much the same could be said of St Paul.

preaching a baptism he implied that circumcision and the law do not justify a man. It is probable that many of the themes of St Paul's preaching were already present in the preaching of John the Baptist. There is an obvious continuity between St Paul's preaching in 1-2 Thessalonians and on the Areopagus (Acts 17) on the one hand, and John the Baptist's on the other.

The wonder is that there is not greater continuity between the teaching of Jesus and of the Baptist. Jesus began, like John, preaching and baptizing in the desert. Neither of them openly attacked the ceremonial law, but in the desert it was not applicable — hence they could preach salvation 'apart from the law' (Rom 3 : 21). But Jesus left the desert, went to Jerusalem, took part in the temple ritual, and observed the law. To explain why he did this, St Paul has to fall back on paradox and say: 'He became subject to the law in order to redeem those under the law.' He went in at their door, so as to come out at his own. He joined the Jewish community in order to overthrow its constitution.

Presumably St Paul means that in some sense Christ *had* to submit to the law in order to redeem the Jews from the law. This can be understood in two ways. First, Jesus *did* come to teach the Jews how God's grown up sons should live; but they would not have listened to his teaching if he had openly attacked and renounced the law; even the small incidents in which he *seemed* to break the law were enough to alienate them (cf. Jn 9: 24). However, St Paul does not regard Christ as having redeemed the Jews from the law by his teaching; so it is better to interpret the words in another way. Secondly, then, Jesus submitted to the law, in order to be judged, condemned and executed under the law, so as to bring upon himself the curse of the law and thereby redeem the Jews from the curse of the law. [24] In Baptism they die, symbolically or mystically, a death to which the law attaches a curse.

*Does St Paul reveal the intentions of Jesus during the public ministry in v. 5?*

One of the greatest problems involved in the Quest of the Historical Jesus is: What were the intentions of Jesus during his public ministry? What did he set out to do? And how far did he achieve his aims? Did he attempt to reform Judaism? Did he intend from the start to found a new religious community distinct from Judaism and including the Gentiles? Did he wish to gain acceptance as Messiah?

---

[24] See above on 3 : 13, pp. 270-271.

In Gal 4:4-5, St Paul explains the intentions of God the Father in sending his Son. He does not say, but probably means us to infer, that his Son knew (in his human mind) and accepted these intentions from the beginning of his ministry (at least). It seems, then, that according to St Paul, Christ knew throughout his ministry that his essential task was to redeem the Jews from the law, from the tutelage of the angels of the law, and from the curse of the law which they had incurred by their transgressions, and that he was to do all this through coming under the curse of the law by dying on the cross. No other form of death would have achieved these effects.

We may feel a little reluctant to attribute these intentions to Christ himself. The recorded sayings of his public ministry can hardly be said to reveal that he understood his ministry in this way. If we had only the gospels and not the Epistles, we should never conclude from a study of his sayings that he had come to redeem the Jews from their servitude to the law. There are even places where he seems to say the exact opposite. Moreover, we may feel a little reluctant to admit that he understood his ministry and death in terms of a conflict with the principalities and powers of St Paul's prescientific cosmology.

Nevertheless, St Paul is probably right. If he thought in these prescientific terms, so too could Christ, who thought as a man of his own day. It is quite certain that Jesus did think of his Passion as a conflict with the demonic 'prince of this world' (Jn 14:30), and the gospels contain many hints, recognizable in the light of St Paul's Epistles, that Jesus understood his ministry as a campaign to overthrow the law and the angels of the law. At his Baptism and in the Temptations, he concealed from the devils who he was; throughout his ministry he practised 'Messianic secrecy'. When he prophesied his death, he specified that it would be by crucifixion. When he was delivered to Pilate, St John emphasizes that the Jews *had* to refuse Pilate's offer of jurisdiction ('Take him you and judge him') in order that he might die in the way he had prophesied. All these items of the gospel narrative become more significant when seen in the light of St Paul's theology. Probably the pauline interpretation of Jesus' intentions was incorporated in earlier (pre-canonical) stages of the synoptic tradition and has been obscured in the extant gospels. [25] For example,

---

[25] See my chart of gospel relationships in HJ 5 (1964), p. 289. Gal 4:4-5 has an important bearing on the controversy as to whether Jesus stood within Judaism, and whether Christianity can still be regarded as a schismatic sect of Judaism. St Paul's answer is that Jesus lived 'in Judaism' (cf. 1:14) in order to put an end to this religion of law. Cf. W. D. Davies, 'Torah and Dogma,' HTR 61 (1968), p. 104.

the story of the delivery of Jesus to Pilate would have been much
more significant if it originally ended like this (cf. Jn 18:31-32):

> Pilate said to them: 'You take him then, and deal with him by your law!'
> The Jews replied: 'We are not allowed to put anyone to death.' So it
> came about that Jesus' prophecy about the manner of his death was ful-
> filled; and so it came about that Christ redeemed us from the curse of the
> law by himself becoming accursed for our sakes; for it is written: 'Cursed
> is every man that is hanged upon a tree.' [26]

Again, Jesus says in the Sermon on the Mount (Mt 5:17):

> Do not imagine that I have come to abolish the law or the prophets; I have
> come not to abolish, but to fulfil,

and immediately after the Sermon on the Mount, he cures a leper
and sends him to the temple to show himself to the priest and offer
the sacrifice which Moses laid down (Mt 8:4) — showing that he
accepts and respects the temple, the levitical priesthood, the ceremonial
law of Moses and its sacrifices. At a precanonical stage of the synoptic
tradition, there was almost certainly a structural link between this
passage and the first pericope after the death of Christ. He cries out
*Tetelestai* — 'All is fulfilled!' — and the veil of the temple is at once
rent from top to bottom, to mark the end of the temple, the levitical
priesthood, the sacrifices, and the ceremonial law. Probably, therefore,
at an earlier stage of the gospel tradition it was easier to see that when
Christ said: 'Not one jot or tittle of the law shall pass away, until
all is fulfilled' (Mt 5:18), he was both revealing and concealing his
intentions in regard to the law.

Some of the early revisors of the Synoptic tradition probably
spoiled the materials they handled. It is therefore better not to extend
the grace of inspiration over all who had any hand in the formation
of our gospels. [27]

## Does 4:4 imply knowledge of the Virgin Birth?

If in Gal 4:1-6 St Paul is meditating on the great act of condescension by which God has overcome the chasm between himself and
men and has made himself their Father in a new sense, it can hardly

---

[26] The counterpart of this passage in the structure of the Passion Narrative is the
request of Joseph of Arimathea for permission to remove the body of Jesus from
the cross. One reason for the urgency of this request was that according to Deut
21:23 a hanged body ought to be taken down for burial before night. In other
words, neither of this pair of passages is fully intelligible apart from Deut
21:23, though neither quotes it.

[27] Cf. HJ 5 (1964), p. 285, n. 4, and J. Bligh, 'Matching Passages, 2: St
Matthew's Passion Narrative,' *The Way* 9 (1969), pp. 59-73.

have escaped his notice that the 'woman' whom he mentions was taken into an astonishing intimacy with God. When she cried 'Abba, Father', she was addressing the Father of her own Son. To this day, it is impossible to contemplate the relationship of Mary the Mother of Jesus to God the Father of our Lord Jesus Christ without wonder and amazement.

But did St Paul realize that God's Son was 'born of a woman' in the exclusive sense, that is, that he was born without the cooperation of a human father, and of a woman who was a virgin? On the whole Catholics reply that he did, and Protestants that he did not; but there are exceptions on both sides. [28]

The argument of those who do not admit that v. 4 implies knowledge of Mary's virginal motherhood is that the phrase 'born of a woman' is simply a Biblical way of referring to man as a weak and frail creature. There are three examples in Job (14:1-2; 15:14-15; 25:4-5), one in Ben Sirah (10:6), and finally one in Mt 11:11, where Christ says of John the Baptist:

> I tell you truly, among the *sons of womankind* there has arisen none greater than John the Baptist; yet one who is younger is greater than he in the kingdom of heaven.

However, this last example should be left out of account, since Christ may have chosen the phrase 'sons of womankind' precisely in order to include himself — he is admitting that on the purely human level John is in some (unspecified) respects a greater man than himself. Although the phrase 'son of womankind' does signify 'a weak human being', the speaker or writer who uses it may have other reasons for choosing it in preference to possible alternative phrases. [29]

Why, then, did St Paul choose the phrase 'born of a woman' in v. 4? The symmetry of the centre of the section might have been better if he had written:

> God sent forth his own Son, *who took the form of a servant* and became subject to the law, in order to redeem those under the law, *that we might receive the status of sons.*

The point would be that Christ came down to the level of the servants in order to raise up the servants to the level of sons. There is no clear

---

[28] H. E. W. Turner, 'The Virgin Birth,' *Expository Times* 68 (1956), pp. 12-17, sees a veiled allusion to the Virgin Birth in Gal 4:4-6. A. Legault, 'Saint Paul a-t-il parlé de la maternité virginale de Marie?' *Sciences Ecclesiastiques* 16 (1964), pp. 481-493, not only denies the presence of any allusion in Gal 4:4, but says that at the time of writing Galatians St Paul did not know of the Virgin Birth.

[29] In the parallel passage Rom 8:3 St Paul uses 'in the likeness of sinful flesh.'

link, either of resemblance or of contrast, between being born of a woman and receiving the status of a son, since 'born of a woman' is applicable to the child of either a slave or a free woman.

St Paul probably chose the phrase 'born of a woman' because his argument requires him to emphasize the true humanity of Jesus. He says: 'God sent forth his Son to *redeem* men from the law (not to subject them to it); but in order to do this, his Son had to become subject to the law; and in order to do this, he had to be truly a man.' St Paul expresses the idea of 'truly a man' by saying 'born of a woman.' Probably he chose this phrase in preference to others which he might have used because it is complementary to the preceding phrase which speaks of God's Fatherhood. God is Christ's Father, and Mary is his mother. [30] The phrase probably implies that St Paul knew of the Virgin Birth; but it was not chosen in order to introduce an allusion to the Virgin Birth, since this would be irrelevant to the argument. The point is that just as Christ was Son of God yet became truly man, so thanks to the redemption, we who are men can become truly sons of God. [31]

A further piece of indirect evidence that St Paul knew of the remarkable relationship between Mary and Joseph may be derived from 1 Cor 7:36-38, if this passage is understood as regulating the continuance and discontinuance of spiritual alliances of perpetual betrothal between young Christian men and women. [32]

> If a man finds that his passions are strong and he is not acting honourably in regard to his betrothed, he may do what he wishes, if it is better that it should be so. Let them marry — it is no sin. But if a man is firm in his resolution, feels no compulsion, is master of his own choice, and has resolved in his heart to keep his betrothed a virgin, he does well. He who marries does well, and he who does not will do better.

It is possible that this type of espousal came into existence as an unexpected result of applying to the betrothed St Paul's principle that each convert should remain in the condition he had when he was converted (cf. 1 Cor 7:17, 24); but if it was extended beyond these cases, as seems to be implied in the above passage, this may well have been done in imitation of the marriage of Mary and Joseph. There is some reason for thinking that St Paul himself had such a relationship with Thecla for a time. [33]

---

[30] Cf. Ignatius of Antioch, *Epistle to the Ephesians*, 7:2.
[31] See further E. de Roover, 'La maternité virginale de Marie dans l'interprétation de Gal 4:4,' *Studiorum Paulinorum Congressus Internationalis Catholicus 1961* (Analecta Biblica 17-18), II, Rome, 1963, pp. 17-37.
[32] On 1 Cor 7:36-38 see Whiteley, *The Theology of St Paul*, pp. 218-222.
[33] Cf. S. Baring-Gould, *A Study of St Paul*, London, 1897, pp. 170-174. The

Furthermore, it will be shown below, in the discussion of 4:21-31, that St Paul's statement that Ishmael was born 'according to the flesh' and Isaac 'according to the spirit' is in *prima facie* agreement with the view of Philo that Sarah conceived Isaac solely as a result of the divine promise and not as a result of intercourse with Abraham. If St Paul too held this opinion about the birth of Isaac, he will have had no difficulty in holding the same about the birth of Christ, who, as the true Issue of Abraham, is the antitype of Isaac. However, a parallel passage in Romans (4:19-20) shows fairly conclusively that St Paul did not share Philo's view on this matter (see below, p. 399).

## Does 'adoption' take place by stages?

If *huiothesia* means 'adoption', St Paul either uses the word in three different senses or implies that adoption takes place in three stages.

First, he says in Rom 9:4-5 that 'adoption' (*huiothesia*) is one of the privileges of Israel according to the flesh:

> They are the Israelites; to them belongs adoption (*huiothesia*), the glory, and the covenants; theirs are the law, the liturgy and the promises; theirs are the patriarchs, and from them Christ is descended according to the flesh — he who is above all things, God blessed for ever. Amen.

This means that 'adoption' or 'adoptive sonship' in some sense belongs to the Jew even before he believes in Christ. As soon as he becomes a member of the covenant-people by circumcision, he can lay claim to 'adoption'. The Old Testament justification for St Paul's ascription of adoptive sonship to Israel according to the flesh is Exod 5:22-23, where Moses is sent by God to rescue his son Israel from slavery to Pharaoh:

> You shall say to Pharaoh, 'Thus says the Lord, Israel is my first-born son, and I say to you, "Let my son go that he may serve me"; if you refuse to let him go, behold, I will slay your first-born son.'

'Israel is my first-born son' looks very much like a formula of adoption. It would seem, then, that God adopted the Israelites as his first-born, while they were still in their Egyptian bondage, that is, before the Exodus, and before Sinai. [34]

---

above paragraph is reproduced from my discussion of H. von Campenhausen, *The Virgin Birth in the Theology of the Early Church,* London, 1964, in HJ 6 (1965), pp. 190-197. H. H. Rowley, *Dictionary of Bible Themes,* London, 1968, ends his entry on 'Virgin Birth' with this observation: 'It is perhaps significant that those who do not accept it almost all deny the Resurrection, which is fundamental to NT faith.'

[34] Cf. also Deut 14:1.

Secondly, St Paul says in Gal 4:5 that 'we (Jews) receive adoption (*huiothesia*)', through faith in Christ.

And thirdly, in Rom 8:23, according to most manuscripts, St Paul says that Christians are still awaiting adoption (*huiothesia*) — at the resurrection of the body:[35]

> We ourselves, although we have received the first-fruits of the Spirit, we too groan inwardly, while we wait to receive adoption (or sonship), the deliverance of our bodies.

One way of resolving the apparent inconsistency between the first and the second statement is to say that even under the Old Law the Israelite shared in the privilege of adoptive sonship by reason of his physical membership of the Jewish nation, but that he still had to develop this prerogative by internalizing it through faith in Christ.[36] In the vocabulary of St Paul, this solution would amount to saying that under the Old Law the Jews were sons of God according to the flesh, and that under the New Covenant they become through faith sons of God according to the Spirit. St Paul does not actually say this, though probably he would have admitted it (cf. Gal 4:29).

But perhaps a better solution would be to say that in the patriarchal period before Sinai God adopted Israel as his son through his covenants with Abraham, Isaac and Jacob, and then, in the period of the law, withdrew, not the privilege of adoption itself, but the outward status of sonship — because the condition of the Jews under the law was no better than that of slaves. This being so, as was mentioned above, it is better to translate *huiothesia* as 'instatement as sons' or 'the status of sons'.[37] Then one can say that in Rom 9:4 St Paul means: 'the status of sons belongs to the Israelites as a thing promised, not as a thing enjoyed'; and the reason for his grief is that his own people ought now to be entering upon the status of sonship which had been promised them, but in fact they are not doing so, and others are taking their places.

There remains the third use of *huiothesia* in Rom 8:23. Neither on textual nor on theological grounds is there any need to reject this reading. If Christ's resurrection was his *huiothesia*,[38] there is no

---

[35] In the BJ, the reading *huiothesian* is rejected, chiefly on the strength of its omission by the Chester Beatty Papyrus. Cf. M. W. Schoenberg, 'St Paul's Notion of the Adoptive Sonship of Christians,' *The Thomist* 28 (1964), pp. 51-52.

[36] This is the solution proposed by M. W. Schoenberg, 'Huiothesia: The Adoptive Sonship of the Israelites,' *American Ecclesiastical Review* 143 (1960), p. 273.

[37] Similarly 'resurrection' means either the act of rising again, or the status of one who is risen (cf. Phil 3:10).

[38] See above, pp. 331 and 334.

reason why the final resurrection of Christians should not be described as their *huiothesia*. If so, just as we distinguish between first justification and final justification, so we must distinguish between first *huiothesia* and final *huiothesia*. These distinctions are perfectly in line with what St Paul is saying in Rom 8 : 23 : at first justification, when we receive the status of sons, we receive the first fruits of the spirit into our human spirit; but we still groan inwardly, awaiting the fulfilment and completion of this gift at the resurrection, 'the redemption of our bodies', when we will arise with a spiritual body (*sôma pneumatikon*, 1 Cor 15 : 44).

Corresponding to the two or three senses of *huiothesia*, two or three senses of *klêronomoi* ('heirs') can also be distinguished. [39] During the period of the law, the Jews were 'heirs' in the sense in which a child is 'heir' when subject to guardians and stewards. One might say that they were *heredes in spe*. After the coming of Christ, they could become 'heirs' in the fuller sense: they already enjoy partial possession of their inheritance in the form of the 'earnest of the Spirit'. They will become heirs in the fullest sense only when they rise from the dead — as Christ did (cf. Heb 1 : 2).

### How is v. 6 to be translated?

Two translations are possible: (1) '*Because* you are his sons, God has sent forth the Spirit of his Son into our hearts.' Strictly, this would imply that God first conferred the status of sonship, then imparted the gift of grace corresponding to this status (the *gratia status*), namely, the spirit of sonship. (2) If there is a slight ellipse after the first clause, the translation will be: '*That* you are his sons <is plain, for> God has sent forth the Spirit of his Son into our hearts.' This does not imply that the status in any way (even logically) precedes the grace. It could mean that God confers the status *by* conferring the grace.

Theologically, it may be convenient to think of the status as prior to the grace, but in God's eyes the two are doubtless simultaneous. The distinction between the status (in this case *huiothesia*) and the grace of the status (in this case the spirit of sonship) is useful —

---

[39] According to Schoenberg, art. cit. (*The Thomist*, 1964), p. 60, 'in the Epistle to the Galatians *huiothesia* is introduced not for its own sake but as an adjunct in the description of the character and purpose of the law.' But to judge from v. 7, it is introduced as a middle term to prove that Christians are *heirs*: 'If a son, then also an heir.' The question is still: 'Who are the heirs of Abraham—those who obey the law of Moses, or those who imitate the faith of Abraham?'

especially if it can be legitimately extended to the other sacraments. Sacramental theology can be systematized, if it can be shown that each sacramental *rite* confers a special *grace* corresponding to a particular *status* in the Church. Baptism and Orders fits easily into this system; other sacraments less easily.

But in Gal 4:6, St Paul is not speaking explicitly or exclusively about the *gratia status* — which is present even when the Christian is asleep (cf. Mt 25:1-13). His argument is an appeal to experience. The Holy Spirit, who is habitually present, occasionally bears perceptible witness to our divine sonship by moving us to cry 'Abba, Father'.

*What is the purpose of this appeal to experience in v. 6?*

When St Paul addressed the passage to the Jews at Antioch, he must have meant: 'You know that as Christians you have entered into a new degree of familiarity with God — you now address him as "Abba", which you never did before, and you feel no impropriety in this, since God has taken the initiative in coming close to us, sharing our condition as men, and sharing our condition as Jews. You know by experience, then, that you are now God's sons; it follows that you are also his heirs. If you share Christ's sonship, you also share his heirship' (cf. Rom 8:17; Eph 3:6). For Jews, this is a cautionary argument. St Paul is impressing upon them that their present privileged position depends on their faith in Christ and on nothing else. If they inwardly despise faith and exalt the law, they will lose their position as sons and fall back into the status of slaves.

When addressed to Gentiles, the argument is perhaps less clear, since the Gentiles have not, like the Jews, passed from the use of 'our Father' (*abhînu*) to the use of 'Father' (*abba*) in prayer. But if previously they had not prayed at all, or if they had not been accustomed to using the word 'Father' in prayer, it must have been, for them too, a moving experience to adopt this practice. Now that they are addressing God as 'Father' in the Christian liturgy, St Paul can say: 'This liturgical use is a guarantee that you are already God's heirs. Your use of "Father" implies that you believe yourselves to be God's sons; but if you are his sons, you are also his heirs.' [40] For the Gentiles, this passage, like its parallel in Rom 8:15-17, is one of reassurance and encouragement, highly appropriate as St Paul moves towards the end of the theological section of the Epistle: the Galatians

[40]  Cf. St Jerome, PL 26, 400 A.

must not allow themselves to doubt that they are already God's sons and already heirs to the kingdom. They have no need of circumcision or the law. Already 'the Spirit himself bears witness to our spirit that we are children of God; and if children, then also heirs — heirs of God and coheirs with Christ' (Rom 8: 16-17).

## *Is St Paul speaking of mystical prayer in v. 6?*

In v. 6, as in 3: 1-5, St Paul is appealing to the spiritual experience of his hearers and readers: each one can look into his own soul; if he will reflect on the consolation, and assurance, and hope, and conviction with which he finds himself crying 'Abba, Father', he will recognize that it is not he alone who is praying, but God is praying in him; if God is at work, moving him to cry out 'Father', this must surely mean that he is indeed God's son. St Paul is here speaking of charismatic prayer which may fittingly be called 'mystical', since it is a prayer in which the cooperation of the Holy Spirit is experienced. It is not, however, the dreamy kind of prayer which, according to the old gag, begins in mist and ends in schism. It is a vehement prayer which shakes a man's mortal frame like a shout (cf. 4: 6) or a deep groan (cf. Rom 8: 15-16, 23).

The cry 'Abba, Father' is not only a cry of recognition; it is also a prayer of petition made by God's son and heir, longing to enter into his inheritance, which is the kingdom: 'Father... thy kingdom come!' Before the time of St Paul, Philo had realized that a spiritual man who longs for the kingdom would pray like this. There is a remarkable passage in his treatise, *Who is the heir?*, where he discusses whether one who leads 'the life of the blood' (that is, the life of the flesh) can become the heir to divine blessings. He replies that, on the contrary, only the man who receives the spirit from above can become the heir: [41]

> Can he who desires the life of the blood and still claims for his own the things of the senses become the heir of divine and incorporeal things? No! One alone is held worthy of these, the recipient of inspiration from above (*ho katapneustheis anōthen*)...

Philo goes on to describe the effect of this inspiration from above on the mind of him to whom it is given. It is an inarticulate, wordless longing for the inheritance: [42]

> Who then shall become the heir? Not the man who of his own free will remains in the prison of the body, but the man who has been loosed from

---

[41]  Philo, *Who is the heir?*, 63-64 (Loeb, IV).
[42]  Philo, *Who is the heir?*, 68-70.

his fetters, has been set free, has come outside the walls, and has so to speak left himself behind. 'For he that shall come out of thee,' the Scripture says, 'he shall be your heir' (Gen 15:4). If, then, a yearning comes upon thee, O soul, to inherit the divine blessings, leave behind not only 'thy land' (the body), 'thy kinsfolk' (the senses), 'thy father's house' (speech), but flee from thyself, and leave thyself in ecstasy, frenzied and inspired with a prophetic enthusiasm like dervishes and corybants. For the inheritance belongs to the mind that is filled with God and is no longer in its own power, but is stirred to its depths and maddened by divine love, and led by him who truly is, and drawn upwards towards him, while truth leads the way and removes all obstacles before the feet, that it may follow a smooth path.

Upon reading this passage, a student of comparative religion might be tempted to say: 'St Paul must have read this; then no doubt he argued that a soul which is heir will feel this intense yearning, but Christians are heirs, therefore they must feel the yearning.' If this conjecture were correct, Gal 4:6 would contain a strong element of *a priori* reasoning. But apart from the general uncertainty as to whether St Paul knew any of the works of Philo, there is his own experience to take into account. In his Damascus vision he had seen the glory of the Risen Lord (cf. 1 Cor 9:1). Afterwards, his hope could feed on the memory, as we know from Phil 1:23. No doubt his own longings communicated themselves to his converts. If in his student days he read Philo's treatise *Who is the heir?*, the experience of yearning which it describes may have seemed as strange to him as Gal 4:6 seems to many Christians today. But after his conversion he knew, doubtless far better than Philo himself, the experience which Philo had striven to describe. Thus he found, in Christ, the answer to the finest aspirations of contemporary Jewish mysticism.

There is, therefore, no good reason to doubt that in 4:6 St Paul is writing from his own spiritual experience and is appealing to the spiritual experience of his converts. These experiences may be called charismatic or mystical, but they may also be liturgical. [43] St Paul is probably referring to the *Abba* at the beginning of the Lord's Prayer: 'Father... thy kingdom come!' This is the occasion when the Holy Spirit bears witness to our spirit that we are children of God — or when he should.

Nowadays, he hardly gets a chance. The Lord's Prayer is brief, and the opening words shoot by without having time to produce much effect. Perhaps in St Paul's day things were arranged differently. Gal 4:6 and Rom 8:15 would be more intelligible in a community

---

[43]  Cf. J. Bligh, 'Liturgical Mysticism,' HJ 2 (1961), pp. 333-344.

which still felt that to address God as *Abba* would be presumptuous and shocking, if God had not authorized it himself. In such a church, one can imagine the leader of the liturgy reading the introductory formula (which is almost an apology): 'Bearing in mind the permission granted us by our Lord, we are so bold as to say' — here he takes a deep breath — '*Abba!*' — he pauses while everyone winces — 'Thy kingdom come, Thy will be done!' This must have been a moment of climax and tension in the early liturgy — a moment when the believer *experienced* his sonship, feeling that God was drawing him into an almost frightening intimacy.

To go one step further, perhaps the verb which St Paul uses in both contexts (Gal 4:6 and Rom 8:15: *krazon*) is to be read as a rubric. After a moment of silence, the leader of the liturgy cried out in a loud voice the one word *Abba!* and this was felt, as it were, to rend the heavens and give direct access to God. The charismatic effect of this one word of address will then affect all the petitions which follow — they are all felt to be uttered in the presence of God the Father. This presence is felt to be a benign presence — not the presence of an imperious, censorious Superego, but the presence of a Father who is loved and respected, and whose presence is good for us — the presence of the Father who is revealed in the parable of the Prodigal Son.

*What does* Abba *mean and imply?*

In the prayers of non-Christian Jews, God has never been addressed as 'Abba'. They use 'Our Father' (*abhînu*) or 'My Father (*abhî*), who art in heaven,' but not simple 'Abba' without a pronominal suffix. 'Abba' is a familiar, diminutive form  of address, used by children, as can be seen, for example, from the story about a certain Hanin ha-Nehba, a Jewish holy man of the first century B.C., who had the repute of being able to obtain rain by his prayers: [44]

> When rain was needed, the teachers would send schoolchildren to pluck at the hem of his cloak and say: 'Abba, abba, give us rain!' Hanin would then pray: 'Master of the world, do it for the sake of these children, who cannot yet distinguish between an abba who can give rain and an abba who cannot.'

This is as near as a Jew ever came to calling God 'Abba', and it is not a parallel to the Christian usage. The children address Hanin as

---

[44] Quoted from the Babylonian Talmud, tr. Ta'anith, 23b, by J. Jeremias, *The Central Message of the New Testament*, p. 19, and *The Prayers of Jesus* (SBT II/6), London, 1967, p. 111.

'abba', and Hanin addressed God as 'Master of the world'. No one addresses God as 'Father'. Hanin refers to God as 'a Father', but this is not a departure from Jewish usage. When Jesus began to use 'Abba' as a form of address, he was assuming a degree of familiarity with God which was wholly new in Judaism. [45]

It was a word used by children, but the English word 'Daddy' is very far from being a satisfactory equivalent, because 'Abba' was not used exclusively by children (and who can imagine the priest crying out 'Daddy!' at the climax of the liturgy?). Sons and daughters could continue to use this word when grown up. We find it, for example, in legal texts in the Mishnah, where 'Daddy' would be quite out of place. In the treatise on Oaths it is laid down that children (obviously grown-up children) may not receive payment of a debt owed to their father's estate unless they take an oath saying: 'We swear that *abba* did not enjoin [in his testament], nor did *abba* say to us, nor have we found written in the documents of *abba,* that this bond of indebtedness has been paid.' [46] This is obviously not baby talk. *Abba* is a word which can be used by grown children in the formality of a courtroom. The Greek equivalent which St Paul adds by way of clarification is not a diminutive (*ho Patêr*).

This is a point of some consequence. When we hear that Christ addressed his Father in prayer as 'Abba', it is quite incorrect to think of him as deliberately using baby talk. That is not what he meant by 'becoming like children'. It is seriously misleading to illustrate 'Abba' with the English 'Daddy' or 'Dad'. When St Paul says that the Holy Spirit comes into our hearts and makes us cry 'Abba, Father', he does not mean that the Holy Spirit draws us back into an infantile state of mind in which we cry 'Daddy!'. Such an interpretation is at discord with the whole context. St Paul is saying that Christians are men who have spiritually come of age: they have passed out of the restraints of childhood, they are no longer subject to tutors and guardians, they are adults and free men. It is absurd to suppose that he adds: 'The proof of our arrival at the maturity of manhood is that we cry out "Daddy!" like little children who have just been weaned.'

What was new about 'Abba' was not its association with infancy, but the degree of intimacy which it implied. The feeling that it is almost presumptuous to address God in this way has left a trace or vestige in the Latin liturgy's phrase *audemus dicere* — 'we make bold to say' — which refers, not to the whole prayer, but to the opening word *Pater.* Only a vestige of the original feeling remains, because the

---

[45]  Cf. Kittel, s.v. 'Abba', in ThDNT, I, p. 5.
[46]  Cf. Danby, *The Mishnah,* p. 420.

Jews would not have felt any shrinking from the compound form 'Our Father' (*abhînu*), which is common in their prayers.

It is an amazing disposition of divine Providence that our Lord's most revolutionary innovation in the matter of prayer should be so difficult to render into languages other than Aramaic — a language which was so soon to die out. To judge from Gal 4:6 and Rom 8:15, St Paul himself felt the difficulty and dealt with it by introducing the Aramaic word into the liturgy of his Gentile, Greek-speaking churches. [47]

### Does the New Testament contain a new revelation of the Fatherhood of God?

To begin with: natural reason can arrive at the conviction that 'God is our Father.' It can demonstrate to its own satisfaction that there exists a necessary being, who is creator, provider, teacher, and protector to all men, and it can sum all this up by saying 'God is our Father.' Homer describes the highest god of his mythology as 'father of men and of gods.'

But what natural reason can discover, God can also reveal. Many of the truths and moral precepts which God has in fact revealed are truths and precepts which natural reason could discover and which some (few) men have discovered without revelation. There is no conflict between reason and revelation — but as reason may easily go wrong, revelation may have to correct the conclusions at which men have arrived by their natural reason.

It is an instructive exercise to try and imagine what we would believe about God if we had no revelation. We would probably conclude from the order and beauty of nature and from the astonishing complexity of our own bodily and spiritual being that God exists and God is good. But probably we would also conclude that we have incurred his displeasure and wrath by our misdeeds, that he has turned away from us, that he does not hear our prayers, and that he has abandoned us to the consequences of our own sins. We would believe in the power and goodness of God, but perhaps not in his Providence. We would probably not believe in the resurrection of the body or in the survival of the soul. If recent radio programmes have faithfully reflected popular opinion, there are large numbers of people in England who have some vague belief in God and yet are convinced that they

---

[47] St Thomas, Gal, 417 C, suggests another explanation: 'he (St Paul) uses both the Hebrew and the Greek to show that the grace of the Holy Spirit is the common possession of both peoples.'

themselves will be snuffed out like candles at death, with no survival.
Their conclusion is: 'God exists, but he does not care; this, however,
causes us no resentment, because we do not deserve his care.'

The voice of revelation in the Old Testament and in the New
declares that this melancholy conclusion contains a large mixture of
error. God does care. He has not turned away from mankind. His
will is to save us from the consequences of our sins. Like a good father,
he loves his children in spite of their sins, and will go to amazing
lengths to redeem them.

The prophets of the Old Testament sought to implant this more
comforting doctrine, and we should give them credit for a remarkable
degree of success. One of the hymns from Qumran has the following
ending: [48]

> Many a forgiveness accompanies my steps
> and abundance of mercies,
> when Thou judgest concerning me.
> Unto hoary age Thou wilt support me,
> for my father knows me not
> and my mother has left me to Thee,
> for Thou art father to all Thy faithful [sons];
> and Thou rejoicest over them
> like a woman pitying her child,
> and, as a nurse in his bosom,
> Thou dost cherish all Thy creatures.

A fine expression of the indomitable faith of Israel! Indeed the
fidelity of Israel, after the Exile, is hardly less remarkable than God's
fidelity to Israel — if indeed the history of Israel apart from Christ
can be said to display the fidelity of God at all. The whole panorama
of Israelite history is a succession of bright hopes and disillusionments.
There is a promising beginning with Abraham, but it ends with oppression at the hands of a Pharoah who knows not Joseph. Then there
is a promising beginning with Moses, but it ends with death in the
desert. Then there is a promising beginning with Joshua, but it ends
with the anarchy of the Judges. Then there is a promising beginning
with David, and it ends with Exile in Babylon. Then Second Isaiah
prophesies a glorious restoration, and all that happens is the pitiable
ministry of Ezra and Nehemiah. The Jews remain under the heel of
pagan powers — Persia, Macedon, Egypt, Syria, Rome — until the
final destruction of their city in A.D. 70 and of their national existence
in 135. Read in this way, 'the Old Testament is the history of why it
does not make sense to believe in God; a God ought to be good for

---

[48] Hymn IX (trans. by Sutcliffe, *Monks of Qumran,* p. 200).

something; but in both social and individual life there is only defeat, agony, and suffering.' [49] In Rom 1:20, St Paul claims that God's 'eternal power and divinity' have been disclosed to man's reason since the foundation of the world; but he does not claim that the fidelity or justice of God has been disclosed in past history. On the contrary, God seemed to have abandoned men to their sin; it is only in and through the gospel that the justice of God is revealed (cf. Rom 1:17). Yet the hymns of Qumran show that the faith of Israel had survived the trials of history. Those admirable Essenes were still able to believe that God is more faithful than any human father and more loving than any human mother.

Does the gospel go any further? In part it reaffirms what reason can discover; in part it repeats the teaching of the Hebrew prophets, and in part it does go beyond them. Here are three texts in illustration. First, Christ our Lord is leading his hearers' minds through a path accessible to human reason when he says in the Sermon on the Mount (Mt 7:9-11):

> Is there a man among you who will hand his son a stone when he asks for bread, or a snake when he asks for fish? If then you, bad as you are, know how to give good things to your children, how much more will your Father in heaven give good things to those who ask him?

Secondly, he is reiterating the message of Hosea and other prophets when he teaches in the parable of the Prodigal Son that God the Father still loves his children, even when they are in their sins, and that he wants their return and reconciliation (cf. Lk 15:11-24). But thirdly, there is a further revelation of the Father which is given only through Christ our Lord, for we read in Mt 11:27:

> All things have been delivered to me by my Father,
> and no one knows the Son except the Father,
> nor does anyone know the Father except the Son
>     and those to whom the Son chooses to reveal him.

Unfortunately, this verse is very loosely attached to its context in St Matthew's gospel. We can only conjecture the circumstances in which it was originally spoken by our Lord. A probable conjecture is that it was spoken after the Transfiguration, and that the Transfiguration took place after the resurrection. [50] After his resurrection is the time for Christ to say 'all things have been delivered to me by my Father' (cf. Mt 28:18). He adds: 'No one knows the Son except the Father' — he has passed through his public ministry and Passion unknown,

---

49 J. Dillenberger, 'Revelational Discernment and the Problem of the Two Testaments,' in Anderson, *The Old Testament and the Christian Faith*, p. 166.
50 See above, pp. 131-132.

except to the Father, who has now revealed his knowledge in the voice at the Transfiguration: 'This is my beloved Son, in whom I am well pleased.' He continues: 'Nor does anyone know the Father except the Son and those to whom the Son chooses to reveal him' — of all men Christ was the first to know that God, the God of creation, the God of the Old Testament, has a Son who is eternal and possesses the same divine nature as himself, and that he has sent this Son to live as a man among men, to be the firstborn among many brethren. This deeper sense in which God is a Father was revealed by Christ to those whom he chose. He chose Peter, James and John and led them up the mountain and was transfigured before them. There they received a new revelation of Christ as the Son of God and therefore of God as the Father of our Lord Jesus Christ.

On the road to Damascus a similar vision was given to St Paul; he heard Christ say: 'Saul, Saul, why are you persecuting me?' and he learned that all who are united with Christ through faith share the life of Christ and so become sons of God in a sense of which the Old Testament prophets had never dreamed. He learned that in Christ, the Son of God and Son of a woman, God had closed the great chasm between heaven and earth, between God and man. He had given all men power to become sons of God in the sense of being members of his own family, brethren of Christ, sharers in the divine nature. This was the good news of the gospel: that God the Father so loved the world — that he so loved us men and women — in spite of our sins, that he sent forth his Son to be born of a woman, to die on the cross, to redeem us from our sins, and to give us the grace of divine sonship. When the condescension and mercy and love of God first strike home to a man's heart, what else can he do but cry out 'Father! Abba! Father' — trying to grasp the mystery. Whether this first happens in private or in liturgical prayer, it is in prayer that the believer receives the new revelation of God's Fatherhood — just as it was in a moment of prayer and adoration that St Thomas recognized Jesus as 'my Lord and my God'. The structure of the sub-section 4:3-9 (p. 342) shows that a Christian comes to 'know God' in a new sense, in which previously he did not know God, when he cries out 'Abba, Father'. St Paul is speaking of a new knowledge of God's Fatherhood which is received in prayer. It is in the strict sense received, since God must first know the believer and send the spirit of sonship into his heart before he can cry 'Abba, Father'.

Since this revelation is communicated in and through prayer, it is important that priests and others who instruct converts should instruct and encourage them, from the start, to pray.

*Is the new revelation of the Fatherhood of God the essence of the gospel?*

Adolf Harnack, in his well-known book, *What is Christianity?*, maintained that the teaching of Jesus can be summed up under three heads: the kingdom of God and its coming; God the Father and the infinite value of the human soul; the higher righteousness and the commandment of love. [51] He argues that nothing tells us more certainly what the gospel is than the Lord's Prayer, and that 'the Lord's Prayer shows the Gospel to be the Fatherhood of God applied to the whole of life.' [52] Later he adds: [53]

> Christ takes the publican in the temple, the widow and her mite, the lost son, as his examples; none of them knows anything about 'Christology', and yet by his humility the publican was justified. These are facts which cannot be turned and twisted without doing violence to the grandeur and simplicity of Jesus' message in one of its most important aspects. To contend that Jesus meant his whole message to be taken provisionally, and everything in it to receive a different interpretation after his death and resurrection, nay, parts of it to be put aside as of no account, is a desperate supposition.

And so Harnack arrives at his characteristic thesis, which he prints in italics: *'The Gospel, as Jesus proclaimed it, has to do with the Father only and not with the Son.'* [54]

At the opposite extreme, certain contemporary writers (Bonhoeffer and Bishop Robinson are telling us that we have no knowledge of God apart from Jesus, that he is the only revelation we have of God, and that in fact we should do better to abandon the very concept of 'God' because of its childish associations: 'God is teaching us that we must live as men who can get along very well without him.' [55]

Faced with these extreme views, we are tempted to say: 'Well, of course, the gospel is both a revelation of God as Father of our Lord Jesus Christ and a revelation of our Lord Jesus Christ as the Son of God — and, for that matter, a revelation of the Holy Spirit who proceeds from the Father and the Son; and yet these are not three revelations but one revelation.' This is true, but it does not solve all problems. In the period before the Arian controversy, in practice the Church treated the gospel as a revelation about God the Father, for it addressed its liturgical prayers to him. [56] After the Arian period, it

---

[51]   Third edition, London, 1904, p. 52.
[52]   Ibid., p. 67.
[53]   Ibid., p. 146.
[54]   Ibid., p. 147.
[55]   J. A. T. Robinson, *Honest to God*, London, 1963, p. 39.
[56]   Cf. Don Cupitt, 'What is the Gospel?' *Theology* 67 (1964), pp. 343-347.

became common to address prayers directly to Christ — and sometimes directly to the Holy Spirit. Nowadays we have no fixed principles
in this matter, but pray as the Spirit moves us to the Father, Son or
Holy Spirit. That the addressing of prayers to the Son is a legitimate
development is shown by Jn 5 : 23 : 'It is his will (the Father's) that
all should honour the Son no less than they honour the Father; he
who refuses honour to the Son is refusing to honour the Father who
sent him.' It took the Church centuries to understand the implications
of these words.[57]

Harnack's view that the Church's proclamation of the gospel should
be simply a continuation of the message preached by Jesus sounds
today like the utterance of an extremist among the 'New Questers' of
the Historical Jesus, for their aim is to overcome the great cleavage
created by Bultmann between the preaching of Jesus and the kerygma
of the apostles. [58] Continuity there certainly is, but there is also dis-
continuity. At the beginning of Romans (1 : 2-3), St Paul describes his
gospel as a message from God (euangelion theou) about his Son (peri
tou huiou autou), and Galatians leaves no room for doubt that St
Paul's gospel is the gospel of the Cross (cf. 2 : 19-21).

There is an oft-quoted saying of Tertullian that the Our Father
is a summary of the whole gospel, breviarium totius evangelii. [59] This
is true in so far as the Lord's Prayer is a summary of the preaching
of Jesus during his public ministry; but it is not a summary of the
gospel as preached by St Paul. Christ's main task on earth was his
death, by which he redeemed us from the law and from sin and gave
us the status of sons (Gal 4 : 4-5). Then he was raised from the dead
and 'marked out as God's own Son with power to give the Spirit of
holiness' (Rom 1 : 4). It was the beginning of a new creation. Henceforth neither the incidents of the public ministry nor the instruction
given by Christ during his public ministry could form the centre of
the gospel. The cross and resurrection were now central, and all else
necessarily became less than central. This does not, however, mean
that the doctrine of the Fatherhood of God became peripheral, for
the cross itself is the greatest revelation of the Father's love: 'God
so loved the world as to give his only Son, that whosoever believeth
in him may not perish' (Jn 3 : 16). It is so hard to define the relationship between the new revelation of God the Father and the revelation of his Son, that it will be wisest to retain the formula of St
Paul: the gospel is a message from God about his Son.

[57]   Cf. J. Bligh, 'Jesus in Jerusalem,' HJ 4 (1963), p. 128.
[58]   Cf. J. M. Robinson, A New Quest of the Historical Jesus (SBT, 25), London,
       1959.
[59]   Cf. Tertullian, De Oratione, cap. 1 (PL, 1, 1153).

*How does 'the Spirit of his Son' manifest itself?*

The Spirit of God's Son, or 'the spirit of sonship' (Rom 8:15), manifests itself first of all in the cry 'Abba....Thy will be done.' It bears witness to the believer that he is God's son, gives him knowledge of God as his Father, and enables him to recognize himself as son of this Father in a lived experience. In the first place, then, the spirit of sonship affects the prayer of Christians.

But secondly, it also affects their conduct. The proper response of a son to the love of his father is obedience, fidelity and reverence, as Jeremiah says (3:19-20):

> I thought how I would set you among my sons,
>     and give you a pleasant land,
> a heritage most beautious of all the nations.
> And I thought you would call me 'My Father',
>     and would not turn from following me.
> Surely as a faithless wife leaves her husband,
>     so have you been faithless to me, O house of Israel.

The new interior spirit of sonship granted to Christians confers upon them a new responsibility to be obedient and a new power to obey. The Christian is no longer a wayward child, but an adult son in his Father's house. In the Epistle to the Hebrews (3:1-6) there is an instructive comparison between Christ and Moses, the prototypes of Christianity and Judaism. Moses, the author recognizes, was faithful in God's great household, as a servant is faithful; but Christ was and is faithful as a son is faithful in a house that is his own. The Jew, though he addressed God as 'Our Father', thought of himself as a servant or slave in the household of a great king; [60] he did not venture to think of himself as a son in a household which is his own. But that is just what the Christian *is* encouraged to think. Being united to Christ and sharing in his life, he *is* a son of God and he *belongs* in God's household in the same way as Christ belongs there — or almost. There is, of course, the important difference that Christ could not and cannot sin, and therefore cannot possibly fall from his Father's grace, whereas in this life the Christian still can. But this thought should not destroy the sense of security which an adult son or daughter should feel in the house of a good father. [61] Expulsion and disinheritance are extreme measures which in a normal family need not even be mentioned or thought about. The Christian should feel that since he has been adopted

---

[60] Cf. Philo, *The Special Laws*, I, 57 (Loeb, VII). It must have been much easier to appreciate the privilege of sonship in the ancient world, where there were households comprising two or three sons and three or four hundred slaves.
[61] The whole of Rom 8 is designed to build up this sense of security.

into God's family and household, not by a purely legal adoption, but by an infusion of the life of God's own Son, he really belongs.

This interpretation of the 'spirit of sonship' as the spirit of *adult* sonship is justified by the comparison sketched out in Galatians between the condition of the Jew under the law and the condition of an heir during his minority: the condition of a Christian is that of the same son and heir when he has attained his majority and enjoys the freedom of an adult. The whole context shows that when St Paul speaks of the spirit of sonship, he is thinking of an adult son — of one who respects the memory of his father if he is dead, and respects his presence if he is alive. The Christian should go about in this world as God's adult son, conscious of his Father's affection, aware of the standards of conduct which his Father expects him to maintain, valuing his Father's presence as a restraint and an inspiration — a restraint from dishonourable conduct, and a stimulus to make some worthy use of the talents he has been given. God's influence on his adult sons resembles in several ways the influence of aging parents on their sons and daughters. The parents do not need to *say* much; their very presence and the respect which they command from their children has its restraining and stimulating effect even when the children live at a distance and do not see them often. [62] To take an illustration from the countryside, the influence of one generation on another should be like that of the spruces planted among beech trees: the presence of the spruces forces the beeches to grow up tall and straight; and when the spruces are taken away, the beeches are much finer specimens than they would have been if left to grow unaided. In the spiritual development of a man, reverence for God supervenes upon reverence for his human parents, and it can no doubt lead him beyond the

---

[62] After the death of Jacob, the brothers of Joseph feared that now their father was gone, Joseph would no longer refrain from taking vengeance on them for their attempt to kill him. In Philo's treatise *On Joseph*, 262-265 (Loeb, VI), Joseph reassures them as follows: 'Our father's death has awakened the old fear which you felt before our reconciliation, with the idea that I gave you my pardon only to save my father from sorrow. But time does not change my character, nor, after promising to keep peace with you, will I ever violate it by my actions. I was not watching for the hour of vengeance repeatedly delayed, but I freely granted you immunity from punishment once for all, partly no doubt influenced, for I must tell the truth, by respect for my father, but partly by the goodwill which I cannot but feel towards you. And, even if it were for my father's sake that I acted with this kindness and humanity, I will continue in the same now that he is gone. In my judgment, no good man is dead, but will live for ever, proof against old age, with a soul immortal in its nature no longer fettered by the restraints of the body. But why should I mention that father who is but a creature? We have the uncreated Father, the Imperishable, the Eternal, 'who surveys all things and hears all things' (Homer), even when no word is spoken, he who ever sees into the recesses of the mind, whom I call as witness to my conscience, which affirms that that was no false reconciliation.'

standards of conduct and dedication which respect for parents, however good, can inspire. [63]

## To whom are vv. 8-10 addressed?

In the original context at Antioch, these verses cannot have been addressed directly to the visitors from Jerusalem, since they are not 'returning' (v. 9) to Jewish ritual practices — they have never given them up. The ones who are 'returning' are Peter, Barnabas and the Jewish Christians of Antioch. V. 8 is a description of the religious condition of Jews, which only Christian Jews could possibly accept: 'Formerly, not knowing God, you were the slaves of beings who by nature are not gods.' It is an extremely uncomplimentary description of Judaism. The 'knowledge' on which the Jews prided themselves [64] is declared to be ignorance, and what the Jews describe as 'service of God' is declared to be 'slavery to beings who are not gods' (the angels of the law are meant — cf. 3:19). St Paul expects the Jewish Christians to be able to accept this severe judgment on Judaism, in the light of their Christian experience of the Spirit: 'Now that you have come to know God (as Abba, Father) or rather to be known by him (through the infusion of his Spirit), you can see your previous condition for what it was: a wearisome and unprofitable bondage. How can you turn back to the weak and grasping elements, which cannot give life and indeed cannot give anything at all! They only demand with an ever-open and grasping hand. How can you wish to be enslaved to them all over again?' The argument is virtually a repetition of 3:1-4. St Paul is urging his hearers to compare their religious experience as Jews under the law with their experience as believers in Christ, and to draw the lesson from their own experience. The Jewish ritual achieves nothing, but through faith in Christ a man receives the life-giving Spirit.

In the context of the Epistle, the argument is addressed to the Gentile Galatians. They would readily admit that before their con-

---

[63] Philo observes the close connection between respect for parents and respect for God. Cf. *Moses*, II, 198 (Loeb, VI): 'Upon the heels of disrespect for God follows disrespect for parents, for country, for benefactors.'

[64] Cf. Ps 76:1 and Rom 2:17-20. In so far as St Paul claims that Christianity (as expounded by himself) has a monopoly of saving 'knowledge', it is hard to see why his theology should not be called 'Gnostic'. He offers a liberating knowledge of God (rendered possible by God's prevenient knowledge of man) which can deliver men from slavery to angelic and demonic powers and give them direct access to God. The only reason why this system is not called 'Gnostic' is that this word is usually applied to dualistic systems and hence connotes strong disapproval. But etymologically, there is no reason why only dualistic systems should be called Gnostic.

version they did not know God and were the slaves of beings who by nature are not gods. They are here warned that since Judaism is another form of slavery to the elements, if they adopt Jewish ritual practices, they will be going back from liberty to slavery, and will end up practically where they started from. In this case, all St Paul's efforts will have been wasted (as he goes on to say in v. 11)

## How does St Paul's position compare with Marcion's?

It is only one small step from St Paul's position in vv. 7-9 to the position of Marcion, which the Church condemned as heretical. By way of disparaging the law and discouraging Christians from adopting it, St Paul says in effect, first, that there is not much difference between Judaism and paganism in so far as both are forms of slavery to 'the elements of the world'; secondly, that the Jews think they are serving the one true God, but they are not — they are enslaved to angelic beings who by nature are not gods; and thirdly, that these angelic beings who posture as gods are responsible for the law and for the punishment of sin. These are polemic statements, and must be balanced against St Paul's other utterances on the same subject: that the law is holy and just and good (cf. Rom 7:12), and that God placed the Israelites under angelic guardians for their own good. [65]

What Marcion did was to exaggerate the independence of the angel (or angels) of the law. Like Philo, he held that angels were responsible both for the evil in creation and for the evil aspect of the law. But he made the creator-angel into an almost independent creator-god, differing greatly in his attributes from the one true God. He explained Judaism as service of the creator-god or Demiurge, the god of law and of wrath, and Christianity as service of the one true God, the God of mercy and compassion. Origen reports Marcion's view as follows: [66]

> The members of the heretical sects, reading the passage, 'A fire has been kindled in mine anger'; and 'I am a jealous God, visiting the sins of the fathers upon the children to the third and fourth generation'; and 'It repenteth me that I have anointed Saul to be king'; and 'I, God, make peace and create evil'; and elsewhere, 'There is no evil in a city, which the Lord did not do'; and further, 'Evils came down from the Lord upon

---

[65] H. D. Betz, 'Orthodoxy and Heresy in Primitive Christianity,' *Interpretation* 19 (1965), p. 310, remarks that from the point of view of the history of religions, 'the kind of Christianity in which Paul lived was a very complicated syncretism.' It was an unstable compound, which his disciples and successors could not preserve unaltered. The theology of St Paul was not a timeless system, to be passed on from one generation to another without any modification. The development of Christian theology was necessary and inevitable.

[66] Origen, *Periarchon*, IV, 1.

the gates of Jerusalem'; and 'An evil spirit from the Lord troubled Saul'; and ten thousand other passages like these, have not dared to disbelieve that they are the writings of God, but believe them to belong to the 'Creator' whom the Jews worship. Consequently they think that since the Creator is imperfect and not good, the Saviour came here to proclaim a more perfect God who they say is not the Creator, and about whom they entertain diverse opinions.

Marcion then went on to draw a practical conclusion: since the Old Testament contains the revelation only of the avenging god of justice, whereas the New Testament reveals the true God, the Father of mercy and the God of all consolation, Christians have no need of the Old Testament and are far better off without it. Marcion saw, however, that he could not simply reject the Old Testament and retain the New, because many of the New Testament writers had not (in his opinion) rightly understood the relation between the two Testaments — the apostles themselves had immediately contaminated Christ's teaching with an admixture of Jewish doctrine; Paul was the only genuine preacher of Christ, and even in his Epistles required expurgation. Marcion therefore rejected the Old Testament, and began the work of expurgating the New — the task was to be finished by his disciples. To us, this seems an outrageous project, but in Marcion's day the Church had not yet promulgated a canon of New Testament Scriptures; it was felt unsatisfactory to have *four* gospels containing so many discrepancies, [67] and the Church had not yet achieved stability in her self-understanding vis-à-vis of Judaism. [68]

There is no reason to think that Marcion was a knave. He made a sincere and bold attempt to solve problems which are with us still; [69] and he probably thought that he was simply developing the teaching of St Paul to its logical and practical conclusion.

To this day, bishops are still required to condemn Marcionism in the *scrutinium* preceding their consecration; and an indirect tribute to the importance of Marcion in the history of the New Testament canon stands in the canons of the Council of Florence and Trent, both of which state explicitly that 'one and the same God is the author of the books of the Old Testament and of the New Testament' — a formula which has its origin in the controversy with Marcion.

---

[67] Cf. O. Cullmann, 'The plurality of gospels as a theological problem,' in his collection of essays, *The Early Church,* London, 1956.

[68] Cf. J. Bligh, 'The Church and Israel according to St John and St Paul,' *Studiorum Paulinorum Congressus Internationalis Catholicus,* Rome, 1963, pp. 151-156.

[69] See the two recent collections of essays on the relation between the two Testaments: Anderson, *The Old Testament and Christian Faith,* and Westermann, *Essays on Old Testament Interpretation.*

*How did St Paul arrive at the view of Judaism expressed here?*

St Paul is appealing to the Jewish Christians to draw from their own experience a lesson which he had drawn from his. He is contrasting the two phases in his own religious life, before and after conversion. Looking back on his Jewish days, he sees himself as a man whose mind was trapped in this lower world, and whose standing before God was not much better than that of the pagans whom, at the time, he had despised. Then the heavens were opened for him and he knew God for the first time; or rather, God took the initiative and made himself known. He sent forth his Son, to open up a route of direct access to himself — an escape hatch through the solid dome of the heavens. To return to the law would be like turning away from the opening of the heavens. It would mean returning to the service of the stars and the angels that rule them — powerless 'powers' who have nothing to give but come back again and again with ever repeated demands.

*Is it likely that this view of Judaism was acceptable to the other Jewish Christians?*

Another way of putting this question is to ask whether during the public ministry Jesus had prepared Peter and the other disciples to accept such an interpretation of Judaism and the law. Probably he did so in the discourse on Inner Purity, of which the evangelists preserve only fragments (Mt 15:1-20 and parallels). The discourse may have been an elaboration on the lesson of Jeremiah that what God wants of the Jews is circumcision, not of the foreskin, but of the heart (Jer 4:3-4):

> Thus says the Lord to the men of Judah and to the inhabitants of Jerusalem:
>     'Break up your fallow ground,
>         and sow not among thorns.
>     Circumcise yourselves to the Lord,
>         remove the foreskin of your hearts.'

St Mark understood Christ's sermon to imply that for the disciples all foods are clean (cf. Mk 7:19), hence that the parts of the ceremonial law which distinguish between clean and unclean foods are obsolete. It is easy to generalize the idea and say that all the ceremonial laws of Judaism were symbolic and preparatory. The Jews had first to learn to keep themselves pure and clean in the material world, in order to pass on from there to spiritual purity and cleanliness. This generalization is made in the Epistle attributed to Barnabas; he infers from

Jer 4 : 3-4 that God never wanted the Jews to circumcise their bodies
at all, but they were misled by a wicked angel and circumcised their
foreskin instead of their hearts. [70] It is unfortunate that we are not
better informed about the teaching of our Lord on this subject. Very
little has been preserved of his synagogue sermons.

In his public teaching, as recorded in the fourth gospel, Jesus told
the Jews that despite all their searching of the Scriptures they had
not yet come to know God (cf. Jn 5 : 37-38; 8 : 55).

## Is St Paul christianizing a Jewish midrash in 4:8-9?

Vv. 8-10, taken by themselves, could be an exhortation to a proselyte to Judaism not to 'return' to the superstition and idolatry from
which he 'came to' Judaism ('proselyte' is from *proselthein*, to 'come
to'). The prototype of all proselytes was Abraham, and his migration
from Ur of the Chaldees was the prototype of all conversions. Philo
explains: [71]

> 'He said to him, I am the God who brought thee out of the land of the
> Chaldeans, to give thee this land to inherit' (Gen 15:7). These words
> indicate not only a promise, but also the confirmation of an old promise.
> The good bestowed in the past was his departure from Chaldean sky-lore,
> which taught the creed that the world was not God's work, but itself
> God, and that to all existing things the vicissitudes of better and worse
> are reckoned by the courses and ordered revolutions of the stars, and that
> on these depends the birth of good and ill. The even tenour, the uniformly
> ordered motion of the heavenly bodies have induced weak-minded people
> to adopt this fantastic creed. Indeed, the name 'Chaldean' when in-
> terpreted corresponds to even tenour or levelness.

It is probable that St Paul borrows and adapts to his own purpose
many of the themes of Jewish missionary preaching. The above passage
of Philo shows that Jewish teachers warned proselytes that they should
no more think of returning to idolatry than Abraham thought of returning to Ur of the Chaldees after he had been called by God. Since
St Paul has proposed the faith of Abraham as a type of Christian
faith, he can compare defection from the Christian faith to a return
to the astrology of Abraham's Chaldean forefathers.

Thus, whereas Philo accuses the Gentiles of worshipping God's
servants instead of God himself, [72] and prides himself on *not* mistaking

---

[70] Cf. *The Epistle of Barnabas*, IX, 4.
[71] Philo, *Who is the heir?*, 96-97 (Loeb, IV); cf. *The Migration of Abraham*, 178-
179 (Loeb, IV).
[72] Cf. Philo, *The Decalogue*, 61 (Loeb, VII).

the angels of the planets for God, [73] St Paul transposes the argument and accuses the Jews of worshipping God's servants, while he himself recognizes the angels for what they are. It was inevitable, therefore, that the question should arise, How can the true *gnôsis* (saving knowledge) be recognized? The Jews thought they had it. St Paul claims that he has it. Later Gnostics profess that they have it. Who is right? In 3:1-5, St Paul applies Christ's own criterion: 'By their fruits you shall know them.'

*Why does St Paul object to the observing of days and months and seasons and years?*

St Paul probably has in mind the sabbath, the weekly fast days, [74] new moon celebrations, [75] the great feast-days (Passover, Pentecost, Tabernacles, Dedication), sabbatical and jubilee years. The context suggests that he has two objections to the observance of a regular calendar.

(1) If v. 10 at the end of the section is compared to v. 1 at the beginning, it appears that in St Paul's view counting the days, weeks, months and years is just what a minor does when looking forward to the day of his liberation from guardians and stewards, or what a schoolboy does when he is looking forward to the day of his liberation from the tyranny of his pedagogue. This is one of the main differences between childhood and adulthood. A child regards his status as provisional: he is growing up, learning, preparing, and, as it were, climbing up a ladder. He looks forward to the time when he will get to the top of the ladder and start walking along on the level, as a free adult. St Paul seems to imply that Israel's condition under the law was like that. He is obviously right in so far as Messianic expectation was an important part of Jewish religion. The Jews were all convinced that they would not remain for ever under the rule of idolatrous pagans; one day God would send his Messiah and bring this period of intense expectation to an end. St Paul is saying that the period of waiting *is* at an end; the Messiah has already come; Israel has already been liberated; Christian Jews are already reigning with Christ.

What is not so easy to understand is how St Paul could regard the observance of a religious calendar as an expression of the Messianic expectation of Israel. He seems to have in mind Jews like the author

---

[73] Cf. Philo, *The Special Laws*, 13, 20, 31 (Loeb, VII).
[74] Cf. Didache, 8:1.
[75] Cf. Filson, *A New Testament History*, p. 46.

of the Book of Daniel who have calculated the date when the Messiah should come (cf. Dan 9 : 24-27), and use the feasts of the year as a means of marking off days, weeks, months and years until the day comes. But perhaps he simply means that a Jew living from one feast day to the next is too much like a schoolboy living from one holiday to the next.

(2) St Paul disliked the idea of Christians observing a regular calendar because this, he thought, would make their actions dependent on the movement of heavenly bodies and hence of angels, from whose control they have been delivered by Christ. If, for example, St Paul regarded the moon as either identical with, or at least moved by, an angel, he will naturally have found it repugnant that Christians should watch for the new moon and celebrate the next day as a feast. This does far too much honour to the moon-angel. Again, the fixing of the day of the Passover required careful observation of the first full moon after the Spring Equinox. Why should Christians allow the pattern of their religious lives to be dictated by the moon?

Each of these two objections leads to obvious difficulties. If looking forward to a day of liberation is a mark of childhood, are not Christians as childish in this respect as the Jews are? And if observance of the Jewish calendar is condemned, how can the Church preserve any order in her liturgical life? These two difficulties will be discussed below. But first a note on St Paul's surprising omission to mention the sabbath in 4 : 10.

## Why does St Paul not mention the sabbath in 4:10?

It is remarkable that in v. 10, when St Paul is speaking of Jewish practices, he does not refer explicitly to the observance of the sabbath. [76] The two most characteristic observances of the Jews were circumcision and the sabbath, and the Judaizers must surely have insisted on both. Irenaeus brackets the sabbath with circumcision as a second 'sign' of the special relationship between Israel and God. [77] The Scriptural justification for this view is Exod 31 : 13-17:

A  *13* You shall keep my sabbath, for this is *a sign* between me and you throughout your generations, that you may know that I, the Lord, sanctify you.   B  *14* You shall keep the sabbath because it is holy for you;

---

[76] According to Philo, *The Special Laws*, II, 56 (Loeb, VII), some people called the sabbath *kairos* ('turning-point'?). This is the third of the words used by St Paul in v. 10: 'days, months, *kairoi*, years.' But to judge by its position, he does not intend it to mean 'sabbaths'.

[77] Cf. Irenaeus, *Adv. Haer.*, IV, 27.

everyone who profanes it shall be put to death; whoever does any work on it shall be cut off from among his people.    C    *15* Six days shall work be done,    **B¹** but the seventh is a sabbath of solemn rest, holy to the Lord; whoever does any work on the sabbath day shall be put to death.    **A¹**  *16* Wherefore the people of Israel shall keep the sabbath, observing the sabbath throughout their generations, as a perpetual co_ venant.  *17* It is *a sign* for ever between me and the people of Israel that in six days the Lord made heaven and earth, and on the seventh day he rested and was refreshed.

Ezekiel too describes the sabbath as a covenant-sign, intended to remind the Jews of their 'holiness' by bringing home to them that they are a people set apart and dedicated to God the creator of heaven and earth (Ezek 20:6-16):

**A**   *6* On that day I swore to them that I would bring them out of the land of Egypt into the land that I had searched out for them, a land flowing with milk and honey, the most glorious of all lands.  *7* And I said to them, Cast away all the detestable things your eyes feast on, every one of you, and do not defile yourselves with the idols of Egypt; I am the Lord your God.  *8* But they rebelled against me and would not listen to me; they did not every man cast away the detestable things their eyes feasted on, nor did they forsake the idols of Egypt.    **B**    Then I thought I would pour out my wrath upon them and spend my anger against them in the midst of the land of Egypt.  *9* But I acted for the sake of my name, that it should not be profaned in the sight of the nations among whom they dwelt, in whose sight I made myself known to them in bringing them out of the land of Egypt.  *10* So I led them out of the land of Egypt and brought them into the wilderness.    **C**   *11* I gave them my statutes and showed them my ordinances, by whose observance man shall live.  *12* Moreover I gave them my sabbaths, as a sign between me and them, that they might know that I the Lord sanctify them.    **D**   *13* But the house of Israel rebelled against me in the wilderness:    **C¹**   they did not walk in my statutes but rejected my ordinances, by whose observance man shall live; and my sabbaths they greatly profaned.    **B¹**   Then I thought I would pour out my wrath upon them in the wilderness, to make a full end of them.  *14* But I acted for the sake of my name, that it should not be profaned in the sight of the nations, in whose sight I had brought them out.    **A¹**   *15* Moreover I swore to them in the wilderness that I would not bring them into the land which I had given them, a land flowing with milk and honey, the most glorious of all lands,  *16* because they rejected my ordinances and did not walk in my statutes, and profaned my sabbaths; for their hearts went after their idols. [78]

St Paul explicitly condemns the adoption of circumcision as a Christian rite. It is, therefore, puzzling that he should avoid explicit

---

[78]  Compare C and C¹ with Levit 18:5, quoted in Gal 3:12. On the sabbath see also Levit 19:3; 26:2; Neh 13:19-20; Isa 56:2-4; 58:13.

mention of the sabbath. There may be an allusion to it in the word
'days' in v. 10, but this is uncertain, and even if it is admitted, the
absence of any *explicit* comment on sabbath observance remains a
puzzle.

A possible explanation of St Paul's silence on this point is that the
sabbath had already gained widespread acceptance among the Gentiles
in general (pagans as well as Christians) and was therefore no longer
a distinguishing mark of the Jews. Listen to Philo: [79]

> We may fairly say that mankind from east to west, every country and
> nation and state, shew aversion to foreign institutions, and think that
> they will enhance the respect for their own by shewing disrespect for
> those of other countries. It is not so with ours. They attract and win the
> attention of all, of barbarians, of Greeks, of dwellers on the mainland and
> islands, of nations of the east and the west, of Europe and Asia, of the
> whole inhabited world from end to end. For who has not shewn his high
> respect for that sacred seventh day, by giving rest and relaxation from
> labour to himself and his neighbours, freemen and slaves alike, and beyond
> these to his beasts?

If this passage could be taken literally, no further explanation of
St Paul's silence would be required; but it probably contains a good
measure of exaggeration. [80] We may conjecture, therefore, that in the
church of Antioch it had been the custom from the very beginning
for Christians, both Jew and Gentile, to meet for the liturgy on the
sabbath, and that St Paul did not wish to upset this custom.

### Are Christians better off without visible 'signs'?

In place of circumcision of the body, Christians have spiritual
circumcision (the cleansing of the whole man in baptism) and 'the
stigmata of Christ' (a mortified life). They should be distinguished
from other people because they manifestly walk according to the Spirit
and produce the fruits of the Spirit — charity, joy, peace, and the
rest. This is fine in theory, but perhaps it takes insufficient account
of the bodily condition of Christians in this world. [80a]

If a Christian is in no way outwardly distinguished from his non-
Christian neighbours, he can get away with conduct which is sub-Christian. If, on the other hand, he is known to be a Christian, everyone
expects him to live up to Christian standards. It is therefore good for

---

[79] *On Moses*, II, 19-21 (Loeb, VI).
[80] Further, there is a hint in Philo on *The Decalogue*, 96 (Loeb, VII), that observance of the seventh day was also a part of the worship of Apollo.
[80a] See further below, p. 492.

Christians to be known as such, and to be easily identifiable as such. Some kind of covenant-sign seems desirable. Until very recently Coptic Christians had a cross tatooed on their wrist — a primitive device, but no doubt effective.

Since the time of St Augustine, theologians have spoken of the 'character' impressed on the Christian soul by Baptism. This may render Christians immediately recognizable to angels, but psychologically it is ineffective: it does not remind the bearer that he is a Christian, for he never sees it. Perhaps St Paul went too far in reacting against Jewish practices. There is still much to be said for the wearing of some covenant-sign which will remind the wearer that he is a Christian, even if it does not identify him in the eyes of others as a Christian.

### Does Paul condemn Adventism in 4:10?

If St Paul means that watching the passage of days, weeks, months and years in expectation of a future day of liberation is a mark of childhood and immaturity, it is hard to see how Christians are any less 'childish' in this respect than the Jews were. Just as the Jews of St Paul's day were on the look out for the coming of the Messiah, so (or more so) were St Paul and his converts on the look out for the return of Christ. St Paul's argument in 4:1-10 takes no account of the interim-state of Christians. The Jews are awaiting liberation, the Christians the completion of their liberation; the Jews await the day when they will enter into their inheritance, the Christians look forward to receiving the whole inheritance of which so far they have only an earnest. [81] The Jews expected the Messiah to come once and complete his task in one stage; according to the Christian view, Christ has already come and has begun man's liberation, but he will come again to complete it. For the Christian the present interim may be adulthood in comparison with the past, but it is childhood in comparison to the future kingdom of God. In Gal 4:1-10, St Paul loses sight of the eschatological hope which is so strong in the Thessalonian Epistles. In the parallel passage in Rom 8, he gives a more balanced view: we already possess the Spirit, and yet for this very reason we groan and long the more intensely for the fulfilment and completion of this gift by the redemption of our bodies.

In 4:10, St Paul is condemning Adventism in the sense of calculating the date of the End and marking off the years to its arrival,

---

[81] St Thomas makes this point in Gal, 414 B.

but he is not discouraging Christians from looking forward to the Parousia as the day of their final liberation. In the heat of his controversy with the Judaizers, he has lost sight of the future.

The psalmist says in psalm 90 (vv. 10 and 12):

> The years of our life are threescore and ten,
>     or fourscore if we are strong...
> Teach us to count our days,
>     that we may arrive at wisdom of heart.

There is no reason why a Christian should not make this prayer his own.

### Does St Paul leave room for a Christian calendar?

If the Jewish calendar is to be condemned because it enslaves men to the heavenly bodies, it would seem that Christians cannot follow any calendar at all, since every calendar is a means of bringing order into human life through observation of the regular movements of the heavenly bodies. [82]

At the time when St Paul was writing, the Church probably had only a rudimentary calendar of her own. St Paul seems to have regarded this situation as a mark of Christian freedom from ceremonial law and of the superiority of Christianity over Judaism. He may also have been influenced by an idea found in the writings of Philo, that men of virtue need no feast days: 'Rejoicing in the virtues, they make their entire life the celebration of a feast.' [83] Origen is dependent on this passage, [84] when he attempts to explain and justify Gal 4 : 10-11 : [85]

> As one of the Greek wise men rightly said, 'a feast is nothing but doing one's duty.' [86] In fact, he who is doing his duty is really keeping a feast; for he is always praying, continually offering bloodless sacrifices to God. For this reason also St Paul seems to me to have said very finely: 'Do

---

[82] Cf. Philo, *The Special Laws*, I, 90 (Loeb, VII): 'Who else could have shown us nights and days and months and years and time in general except the revolutions, harmonious and grand beyond all description, of the sun and the moon and the other stars?' Also S. Freud, 'Civilization and its Discontents,' *Complete Works*, XXI, p. 93: 'Man's observation of the great astronomical regularities not only furnished him with a model for introducing order into his life, but gave him the first points of departure for doing so.'

[83] Philo, *The Special Laws*, II, 46 (Loeb, VII).

[84] This is pointed out by H. Chadwick, *Origen: Contra Celsum*, Cambridge, 1953, p. 467.

[85] *Contra Celsum*, VIII, 21 (trans. by Chadwick, pp. 467-468).

[86] From Thucydides, *Histories*, I, 70. The Corinthians are denouncing the Athenian way of life: 'They toil all their life long . . . their only holiday is to do their duty.' It is a left-handed compliment.

you observe days and months and times and years? I am afraid for you lest by any means I have bestowed labour on you in vain.'

This may well be an accurate exegesis of St Paul's meaning: Christians have no need of special feast days on which to celebrate special religious rites, because every day they offer their own bodies to God as a living sacrifice, holy and pleasing to him — and this is real worship (cf. Rom 12:1).

But on this point as on the last, St Paul modified his position a little in the Epistle to the Romans. He there acknowledges that there are differences of opinion within the Church on this matter: 'One man prefers this day to that; another man counts all days alike; let each be fully at ease in his own opinion' (Rom 14:5). But he goes on to add that the strong (i.e., those who share his own view that all days are alike) must make some concession to the weak (i.e., to the 'scrupulous' who distinguish one day from another). This means, in effect, that the church of Rome would do well to accept some regular days of fasting and abstinence. There is no sign that at the time of writing Galatians St Paul was ready to make any such concession.

If regular fasts and feasts are a concession to the 'weak', St Paul's view must have been that ideally the Church should have no fast days or feast days, or as few as possible. For the perfect Christian, every day is Good Friday, every day is Easter, every day is Pentecost. [87] But the Church soon found that most Christians are incapable of living on this high plain of spirituality; they need a time for fasting and a time for feasting. So the formation of a Christian calendar began. St Paul's ideas were soon forgotten, and the Christian calendar became far more complex than the Jewish. Periodically a reform is carried out and the number of feast days is reduced. But in no time fresh additions are made by pious prelates. These are largely ignored by the laity, perhaps not entirely through lack of piety. It *is* a mark of immaturity to live from one feast day to the next. Adults prefer a more regular rhythm of work with fewer interruptions for obligatory rejoicing. According to Abelard's hymn *O quanta qualia*, the blessed in heaven, who of course have attained perfect maturity, enjoy a perfectly regular routine:

Illic ex sabbato succedit sabbatum,    There sabbath follows sabbath, in
perpes laetitia sabbatizantium.    endless sabbatical joy.

---

[87] See the amplification of this theme in Origen, *Contra Celsum*, VIII, 22; also St Jerome, PL 26, 404 CD. This justifies the celebration of the Christian Passover every day; cf. J. Bligh, 'Do this in commemoration of me,' *The Way* 5 (1965), pp. 154-159.

But on earth this simply would not do. [88] The Corinthians' assertion
about the Athenians, that 'their only holiday is to do their duty,' needs
to be compared with the words of Pericles in his Funeral Oration: [89]

> We have provided for the spirit many relaxations from toil: we have
> games and sacrifices regularly throughout the year, and homes fitted out
> with good taste and elegance; and the delight we find in these things
> day by day drives away sadness.

In reacting against the judaizing tendency, St Paul himself tended
towards the opposite mistake of over-spiritualizing the practice of
Christianity.

---

[88] It is one of the threats of cybernation. Cf. K. Cragg, *The Privilege of Man,*
London, 1968, p. 14.
[89] Thucydides, *Histories,* II, 38.

# SARAH AND AGAR: PAUL AND HIS OPPONENTS

The sixth section falls into two disparate parts, each of which has a symmetrical structure. The first, 4:11—4:20, is Paul's personal appeal to the Galatians to adhere to the gospel as he preached it to them; the second, 4:21—4:30, contains the allegory of Sarah and Agar, a final argument from Scripture. Here is the whole text:

**A** *4:11* I fear that I may have laboured in vain for you. *12* Be like me, because I became like you, brethren, I beseech you — **B** and you did me no harm. **C** *13* You know that it was in sickness of body that I preached the gospel to you on the former occasion. *14* My sickness was your temptation; yet you did not despise me or reject me; **D** on the contrary, you received me as an angel of God, as Christ Jesus. *15* Where, then, is your fervour gone? For I testify to your credit: you would have plucked out your eyes and given them to me, if possible. *16* Have I, then, become your enemy by speaking the truth to you? **E** *17* They are courting you dishonourably; they want to exclude you, so that you will court them. *18* It is an honour to be courted honourably — at all times, and not only when I visit you. **F** *19* My children, I am in travail with you again, until Christ is formed in you. *20* I wish I could visit you now and adapt my tone to you, for I am perplexed about you. **E¹** *21* Tell me, you who want to be under the law, do you not hear what the law says? *22* It is written that Abraham had two sons, one by the slave-girl, and one by the free woman. *23* The son of the slave-girl was born according to the flesh, but the son of the free woman in fulfilment of a promise. *24* These are allegorical statements. For the two women are two covenants — one is from Mount Sinai and bears children who are slaves. She is Agar. *25* Mount Sinai, though situated in Arabia, goes with the present Jerusalem, which is a slave and the mother of slaves. **D¹** *26* But the heavenly Jerusalem is the free woman. She is the mother of us all. *27* For it is written: 'Rejoice, O childless one, who hast not borne, break forth and cry, thou who hast not been in labour; for more numerous are the children of her who is desolate than of her who has the husband.' **C¹** *28* But we, brethren, are, like Isaac, children of promise. *29* But just as of old he who was born according to the flesh sought to exclude him who was born according to the Spirit, so now. **B¹** *30* But what does the Scripture say? It says: 'Reject the slave-girl and her son, **A¹** for the son of the slave-girl shall not share the inheritance with the son of the free woman.'

In **A¹** St Paul gives the reason for the fear expressed in **A**: if the Galatians judaize and so become 'sons of the slave-girl', they will lose the inheritance and Paul's missionary labours on their behalf in Christ's cause will have been brought to nothing.

In B he says: 'When I came to you first, you did not reject me,' and implies: 'Do not reject me now!' In B¹ he urges the Galatians to reject his rivals, the judaizing teachers.

In C he speaks of the bodily sickness he suffered through persecution at the hands of the Jews in Galatia; in C¹ he points out that these sufferings were prefigured in the persecution of Isaac by Ishmael.

D and D¹ both speak of a reversal of feelings — from joy to disillusionment in D, from desolation to joy in D¹.

In E St Paul tells the Galatians that they are being wooed by two suitors, one proposing an honourable alliance, the other a dishonourable union. In E¹ he describes the two unions into which Abraham entered, the one with a freeborn woman, the other with a slave-girl.

F, the centre of the section, has obvious links with the beginning — in both places St Paul refers to his labours and to his presence among the Galatians. The link with the end is less strong: Paul speaks of himself as the mother of the Galatian Christians in F, by contrast to the mother of slaves in A¹.

*How was this section composed?*

Commentators have been puzzled by the position of the personal appeal. It seems out of place when the argument from Scripture is still incomplete. One suggested explanation is that St Paul regarded his argument as being already complete at v. 10, and therefore began his personal appeal in vv. 11-20, when suddenly a further argument from Scripture occurred to him, which he thereupon added as an afterthought (vv. 21-30). [1] But the Epistle is written with much greater care than this explanation supposes. 4:10 would have made a very abrupt end to the argumentative part of the Epistle. And the allegory, far from being an afterthought, is the climax of St Paul's discussion of the question, Who are the heirs of Abraham? The Judaizers are identified with Agar and her offspring, and Paul's final word on the situation which they have created is: 'Send away the slave-woman and her offspring!'

Probably the allegory of Sarah and Agar was the climax of St Paul's discourse at Antioch, and was immediately followed by the exhortation to stand firm and defend the liberty of Christ's disciples (i.e., by the substance of 5:1—5:13a [2]).

[1]  Cf. e.g. Burton, Gal, and Schlier, Gal, ad loc.
[2]  See pp. 235-236 and 414-415.

But the personal appeal in 4:11 20 is obviously not a part of the discourse at Antioch. It refers to the circumstances of the first evangelization of Galatia by St Paul. [3] It must, therefore, be an insertion, written by St Paul when he was incorporating the Antioch-discourse into the Epistle. Thus in the present section, the second half was composed first, and the first was skilfully added to form with it the symmetrical pattern of 4:11—4:30. (It is therefore advisable to study 4:21-30 first and then return to vv. 11-20.)

## *Why does St Paul insert his personal appeal just here?*

When St Paul used the 'allegory' at Antioch, he interpreted Agar as the Sinai-covenant and Sarah as the Abraham-covenant. When he came to adapt the discourse for the instruction of the Galatians, he saw that a further identification was possible, highly appropriate to the situation in the Galatian churches. He could identify himself with Sarah, the mother of the free, and the judaizing teachers with Agar, the mother of slaves. Then the closing command: 'Send away the slave-woman' would mean: 'Send away the judaizing teachers' — and, by implication, remain faithful to me, your true mother. [4]

The purpose of the inserted passage, 4:11-20, is, therefore, to remind the Galatians that Paul is their spiritual mother and thus to insinuate the identification: Sarah = Paul. In v. 19 he says: 'My children, I am in travail with you again, until Christ is formed in you,' and to prepare for this highly emotional statement, he reminds the Galatians of the intense affection they had for him, and he for them, when he first evangelized them: 'you received me as an angel of God, as Christ Jesus....you would have plucked out your eyes and given them to me.'

The inserted passage also contains allusions to the sufferings inflicted on St Paul by the Jews when he preached in Galatia. These exemplify his statement towards the end of the allegory that 'just as of old he who was born according to the flesh sought to exclude him who was born according to the spirit, so now.' However, an allusion to these sufferings would have been equally effective if placed after the allegory. Its presence does not, therefore, explain why the insertion was made before the allegory.

---

[3]  See above, pp. 7-17.
[4]  At Antioch, the meaning was: 'Send away the people from James'. It is unlikely that St Paul meant to insinuate the identification: Agar = Peter. The name 'Cephas' would rather suggest that Peter = Abraham. Cf. Isa 51:1-2, and J. Massingberd Ford, ' "Thou art 'Abraham' and upon this Rock",' HJ 6 (1965), pp. 289-301.

*The First Subsection, 4:11-20*

# PAUL'S PERSONAL APPEAL

**A**   *4 : 11* I fear that I may have laboured in vain for you.   **B**   *12* Be like me, because I became like you, brethren — and you did me no harm. **C**   *13* You know that it was in sickness of body that I preached the gospel to you on the former occasion.   **D**   *14* My sickness was your temptation, yet you did not despise me or turn away in horror.   **E**   You received me as an angel of God, as Christ Jesus.   *15* Where, then, is your fervour gone? For I testify to your credit: you would have plucked out your eyes and given them to me, if it were possible.   **F**   *16* Have I, then, become your enemy by speaking the truth to you?   **E¹**   *18* It is an honour to be courted honourably — at all times, and not only when I visit you.   **D¹**   *17* They are courting you dishonourably; they want to exclude you, so that you will court them.   **C¹**   *19* My children, I am in travail with you again, until Christ is formed in you.   **B¹**   *20* I wish I could visit you now and adapt my tone to you,   **A¹**   for I am perplexed about you.

*What is St Paul worried about in v. 11?*

He says he fears that his labours have been wasted. This does not mean that he is thinking back over the persecutions he suffered in Galatia, and telling himself that if the Judaizers now have their way, he might as well have stayed in Antioch. He is not worried over any personal loss. No doubt he would have said that he would receive his 'crown' whether the Galatians fell away or not (cf. 2 Tim 4 : 8). His fear is altruistic (the Greek means literally: 'I fear as to you, lest I have laboured in vain in your regard'). He is concerned about the loss which the Galatians will suffer, if they have themselves circumcised: Christ will give them no further help (cf. 5 : 2).

One of St Paul's admirable qualities is that he cares about success. He does not console himself with the thought that he has done his best, that his intentions were good, even if they did not issue in success, and so on. He *wants* men to accept the faith and to persevere in it, for their own sake, and for Christ, whose servant he is.

*What is the sequence of thought in vv 12-16?*

Through the brevity and ambiguity of his language, and through the omission of connecting particles, St Paul has made it difficult for the reader to follow him here. The text is probably to be filled out thus: 'Be like me, brethren, <free from the law>; for I became like you

$<$when I preached to you — I adopted the Gentile way of life$>$; and $<$at that time [5] $>$ you did me no harm $<$— far from it! $>$. You remember that I was ill when I preached to you; my illness was a trial to you, but you did not despise me or turn away from me. On the contrary, you welcomed me as an angel of God $<$or even$>$ as Christ Jesus himself. What then $<$has become of$>$ your enthusiasm $<$at that time$>$? I swear that $<$so great was your love,$>$ you would have made any personal sacrifice for me — even your eyes! $<$Is it possible,$>$ then, that I have now become your enemy — and simply by telling you the plain truth?'

*What are the limits of missionary adaptation?*

One of St Paul's missionary principles was that an apostle should adopt the way of life of the people he hopes to convert. He explains this in some detail in 1 Cor 9:19-22:[6]

**A** *19* Although at liberty to serve no one, I have made myself the slave of everyone, in order to gain more conversions. **B** *20* With Jews I have lived as a Jew, to convert Jews. **C** *21* As they live under the law, I have lived under the law, though I am not under the law, to convert some men of the law. **C¹** With men who live outside the law, I have lived as one outside the law — not that I am an outlaw before God; I am an in-law of Christ. **B¹** *22* With the scrupulous I have been as one who is scrupulous, to convert some of the scrupulous. **A¹** I have been all things to all men, in order to save at least a few. [7]

Only by becoming like a man, sharing his way of life, and even his mood, is it possible to win his confidence and gain him for the gospel. [8] St Paul became like the Galatians in order to win them to faith in Christ, not in order to win them over to the Jewish way of life.

The difficulty with the principle of missionary accommodation is to know how far it should be pushed. In modern terms, must a priest become a worker in order to convert workers? Some would

---

[5] The Greek could mean: 'You have not offended me.' Then St Paul will be assuring the Galatians that in spite of his severe tone (cf. v. 20) he is not personally offended (cf. 2 Cor 7:2). But this rendering makes the transition from v. 12 to v. 13 difficult; and in the sixth section (p. 378) this phrase is linked to 4:30a, the point being: 'you did not reject me then . . . do not reject me now—reject the Judaizers instead.'

[6] The chiastic analysis is from Lund, *Chiasmus in the New Testament*, p. 147.

[7] Daube, *The New Testament and Rabbinic Judaism*, pp. 336-346, attempts to show that this maxim was taken over by St Paul from Jewish missionary practice.

[8] St Jerome the presbyter, PL 26, 405, takes the occasion of this verse to attack the arrogance of bishops 'who, as if placed on some lofty pedestal, scarcely deign to appear as mortals or speak to their fellow servants.'

say Yes. Must a priest be a married man and wear ordinary clothes?
Again, some would say Yes. Must a missionary steep himself in the
language and culture of the people to whom he is sent? Most people
would say Yes. Must a priest become a plumber to convert plumbers,
and a carpenter to convert carpenters? At this most people will smile.
St Paul did not become a tent-maker to convert tent-makers. Nor
did he steep himself in Greek literature and culture. Probably he was
not married. [9] But his example is not necessarily to be regarded as
a living law for missionaries. The missionaries of today are not recommended to follow the whirlwind methods of Paul or of St Francis
Xavier, but to build more slowly and solidly. They are told to study
the language, culture, customs and traditions of the peoples to whom
they are sent; and in some cases they even prepare for the work by
taking degrees in anthropology. [10]

At the present day, the Church's missionary appeal to the workers,
who are the mass of the population (both in missionary and non-
missionary countries), cannot be said to meet with great success. It is
questionable how far the clergy should become like the workers in
order to gain them. Bishops no longer engage in the pioneering work;
and priests have their Canon Law, which like the Mosaic law, creates
barriers for their protection. Either they must break through this
fence, or they must train lay apostles. The second alternative is being
followed with success in America.

*What was the illness mentioned in v.* 13?

As to the nature of St Paul's illness, the immediate context
offers two clues. V. 14 suggests that it was some malady which might
easily have made him an object of contempt or of loathing. Malaria
is, therefore, unlikely, in spite of Professor Ramsay's advocacy. [11]
It would awaken compassion, but not contempt or superstitious
horror. [12] Many commentators diagnose epilepsy — which puts St

---

[9] Some authors have reasoned that he would not have ventured to lay down the
law about marriage as he does in 1 Cor 7 if he had had no experience of
marriage; others argue that if he had had experience of marriage he would not
have spoken about marriage in the way he does in 1 Cor 7. Pope Paul VI in his
encyclical *Humanae Vitae*, § 26, recommends the apostolate of like to like, and
in particular of married couples to married couples.

[10] Cf. McKenzie, *The Power and the Wisdom*, p. 274: 'Historians now generally
agree that if the Roman Curia had permitted the gospel to be proclaimed in
China in the eighteenth century with certain adaptations to Chinese culture, the
country would have become substantially Catholic.'

[11] Cf. Ramsay, Gal, pp. 422-428.

[12] The Greek word (*exeptusate*) implies spitting as a gesture to ward off the evil
influence of the disease or the demon producing it. Hence Job 17:6, 'I am one
before whom men spit.'

Paul in good company, for Julius Caesar, Cromwell and Napoleon were epileptics. If the Galatians saw St Paul fall down in a fit, they might well conclude that he was being buffetted by an angel of Satan (cf. 2 Cor 12:7), hence that he was a demoniac, hence that he could not be, as he claimed to be, a messenger of God. [13]

Secondly, the violent expression used in v. 15, 'you would have plucked out your eyes and given them to me,' has given rise to the conjecture that the sickness, whatever it was, affected St Paul's eyes. Two other pieces of evidence have been adducted to confirm the conjecture that his eyes were bad. Gal 6:11 is usually taken to mean that he added a postscript in his own hand in large letters; [14] and in Acts 23:5, after reviling the High Priest as a whitewashed wall, St Paul apologizes, saying: 'Brethren, I did not know it was the High Priest.'

These two lines of argument can be combined, because epilepsy can affect a man's eyesight. [15] But perhaps they should both be rejected. If St Paul was capable of sewing the seams of tents, his eyesight must have been moderately good. And the structural links of vv. 13 and 14 suggest that the 'weakness of the flesh' was simply the physical weakness caused by the stoning at Lystra, after which he was dragged out of the city and left for dead (cf. Acts 14:19). [16] In the structure of 4:11—4:20, the sickness which St Paul suffered when he first preached in Galatia is linked to the travail he feels over them at the time of writing — which suggests that the sickness too was brought upon Paul by his missionary work. And in the structure of 4:11—4:30, the link is with 4:29, which again speaks of the persecution of Christians by Jews. St Paul seems, then, to mean that his feeble physical condition after the stoning was a spiritual temptation to the Galatians, [17] because they could not help asking themselves whether this wreck of a man really could be, as they had believed, a special messenger from God. Would not God have protected his ambassador? This is not the only place where St Paul allows us to see that his sufferings and imprisonments caused some people to doubt his apostleship (cf. Col 1:24-25). [18]

It is likely enough that St Paul's eyes were blackened and bloodshot after the stoning. But v. 15 is not to be taken literally. It may

---

[13]  Cf. Lightfoot, Gal, pp. 190-191; Schlier, Gal, p. 149.
[14]  The inference is unwarranted. See below, pp. 489-490.
[15]  Cf. Schlier, Gal, p. 150.
[16]  This is the view of Chrysostom, PG 61, 659 C.
[17]  In v. 19 St Paul adds that the spiritual weakness of the Galatians is a physical trial to him.
[18]  Cf. Jerome, PL 26, 407 CD.

be simply a rhetorical hyperbole. [19] In ancient literature lovers often say to each other: 'I love you more than my eyes.' However, it is one thing to say: 'I love you more than my eyes,' and another to say: 'I would gouge (or dig) out my eyes and give them to you.' The latter is so gruesome that it would ruin any love scene in poetry or drama or real life. Is it possible, then, that at the back of St Paul's mind is the thought: 'So great was your fervour, you would have done anything I said: you would have circumcised yourselves — or made eunuchs of yourselves (cf. 5 : 12) — or even plucked out your eyeballs, if I had given the word'? [20]

*How many visits has St Paul made to Galatia* (v. 13)?

The adverbial phrase 'on the former occasion' (in Greek, *to proteron*) has been taken as meaning 'on the former of my two visits'. [21] But the verb to which it is attached is not 'to visit' but 'to evangelize'. The previous occasion, when St Paul evangelized the Galatians by word of mouth, is compared in the subsection 4 : 11—4 : 20 to the present occasion, when he is evangelizing them all over again by this letter (the counterpart of v. 13 is v. 19). No inference can be drawn, therefore, as to the number of *visits* he has made to Galatia. According to the chronology worked out in the Introduction (pp. 1-16), he had in fact revisited them twice between the occasion when he first evangelized them and the date of writing the Epistle.

*'As an angel of God, as Christ Jesus'* — *Why does St Paul use these phrases?*

A strong point in favour of the theory that St Paul's illness was epilepsy is that epilepsy was popularly attributed to demons (cf. Mk 9 : 14-27). If v. 14a means 'when you saw me in a fit, you did not turn away from me as from one possessed by a demon,' v. 14b is joined on by way of antithesis: 'far from rejecting me as one possessed by a devil, you received me as an angel of God — indeed as Christ Jesus himself.' But probably the connection between the two sentences is much looser. St Paul is not writing chronologically here.

---

[19] Cf. G in G on 4 : 15. Chrysostom, PG 61, 659 D, interprets the passage in this sense.

[20] Cf. Chrysostom, PG 61, 668 CD; J. Bligh, 'Comment on Gal 4 : 15,' in *Studia Evangelica* IV (TU 102), Berlin, 1968, pp. 382-383.

[21] Cf. Lightfoot, Gal, ad loc.

He does not mean that as soon as he arrived in Galatia, he threw a fit and nevertheless the Galatians received him as an angel or even as Christ himself.

What happened was that when he arrived among them and worked miracles (cf. 3:5), for example, the cure of the cripple at Lystra (Acts 14:8-12), there was a great outburst of popular enthusiasm. The ignorant Lycaonians at first identified St Paul as Hermes, the messenger of the gods (14:12) — until he explained that he was an apostle of Christ, and that Christ lived in him and worked these miracles (cf. Gal 2:20—3:5). They then believed him and welcomed him joyfully as a messenger from God, indeed as Christ Jesus himself.

The 'temptation' or 'trial' mentioned in v. 14a occurred *after* this, when the Jews stoned Paul and left him for dead. The sight of his sorry condition might have caused his converts to abandon their new faith in Paul as a messenger of God, and in Christ, the Lord whom he served. But they resisted the temptation and continued to see Christ in him. St Paul may even mean that their faith was strong enough to enable them to find in his sorry condition a confirmation of their faith — here was Christ crucified in his members!

## Does v. 16 *refer to 'the truth' spoken in this Epistle?*

Many commentators think that v. 16 refers to warnings given to the Galatians during his second or third visit, [22] or perhaps even during his first. [23] But the structure of the subsection shows that St Paul is referring to the possible effects of this Epistle. He says three times, at the beginning (v. 11), at the middle (v. 16), and at the end (v. 20), that he is worried about his present relationship to the Galatians. Has all his labour been in vain? Will they take the Epistle amiss? If only he could revisit Galatia and adapt his tone to their mood and attitude!

However, while the main reference of v. 16 is to the possible effects of the letter, a reference to the truth preached on St Paul's first visit is not to be excluded. If the corresponding vv. 11 and 20 are to be connected with the centre of the passage, so too are the corresponding vv. 13 and 19.

---

[22] Cf. e.g. Lightfoot, Gal, ad loc.
[23] Thus Viard, Gal, ad loc. Viard thinks that St Paul's adversaries had said that Paul had proved himself no real friend but an enemy, by concealing the obligation to submit to circumcision.

In the section 4:11—4:30 (p. 378), v. 16 is linked to the quotation from Isa 54:1, perhaps to suggest that St Paul is like Isaiah in having made enemies by announcing God's word. 4:11 is almost certainly a deliberate reminiscence of Isa 49:4, where the prophet says: 'I have laboured in vain; I have spent my strength for nothing and vanity.'

The thought expressed in v. 16 may have been put into St Paul's head by his experience at Antioch. Unfortunately we do not know how successful he was there in adapting his tone to the mood of his hearers. [24]

## How is v. 18 relevant?

In vv. 15-18, St Paul uses the language of love-making. The office of an apostle is to woo a bride for Christ. V. 18 is deliberately ambiguous, so that the Galatians can apply it both to themselves and to St Paul. Applied to the Galatians themselves, it reminds them that it is an honour for a woman to be wooed, provided the suitor's intentions are honourable — as his were, and the Judaizers' were not. They must not succumb to the blandishments of every suitor, but discern the intentions of each. Applied to St Paul, the sentence means: 'It is all very fine to be made a fuss of when present, but demonstrations of affection become meaningless if they are forgotten or renounced as soon as the suitor departs.' In either case, v. 18 is a mild reproach to the Galatians for being so inconstant.

St Jerome has a valuable comment on this verse, in which he generalizes from St Paul's experience: [25]

> Even now we see the same thing happening in churches. If there is present in a church a preacher distinguished for his eloquence and by his way of life, one who stimulates and arouses his hearers to virtue, we see the whole populace busy, fervent and active in almsgiving, fasting, chastity, care for the poor, burying the dead, and so on. But when he departs, we see their vigour gradually fail; deprived of their spiritual food, they grow thin and pale and languid; their previous activities perish. Therefore, as the harvest is great and the labourers few, let us pray the Lord of the harvest to send workers to reap — men who will gather in the standing corn of the Christian people and store it in barns, and not allow it to go to waste.

[24] See above, pp. 127 and 233-234.
[25] St Jerome, PL 26, 410-411.

O

*Is St Paul fair to his adversaries in vv. 17-18?*

It was shown above that St Paul is probably less than fair to St Peter and Barnabas in his account of the Antioch incident. [26] Here again, he attributes low motives to his adversaries. Whereas he himself has courted the Galatians for honourable motives, to betroth them to Christ (cf. 2 Cor 11:2), his adversaries are courting them for no good purpose at all. They would like to shut the Galatians out of Christ's presence, [27] so that they will bestow their affection elsewhere — namely, upon the judaizing teachers. In a word, these teachers are seeking to put themselves in the place of Christ.

No doubt the Judaizers would have indignantly repudiated this interpretation of their motives. But in St Paul's view they were deceiving themselves, just as he had deceived himself in the days when he was a persecutor of the Christians (cf. 1:13-14 and 2:3-5 in the second section, p. 121-122).

*Why does St Paul compare himself to a pregnant woman (v. 19)?*

In vv. 17-18 St Paul implied that in evangelizing the Galatians he was acting as proxy (*proxenos*), wooing the Galatians as a bride for Christ — somewhat as Abraham's servant woos Rebekah for Isaac in Gen 24. [28] In v. 19, he makes a violent change of imagery. He is no longer a proxy or a lover, but a pregnant mother forming children in her womb: 'I am in travail over you again,' he says, 'until Christ is formed in you.' So long as the Galatians have not clearly understood the gospel, they are like embryonic fetuses. The same unattractive metaphor had been used by Philo: [29]

> Just as the eyes of the body often see dimly and often clearly, so the distinguishing characteristics which things present sometimes reach the eye of the soul in a blurred and confused, sometimes in a clear and distinct form. When the vision thus presented is indistinct and ill-defined, it is like the embryo not yet fully formed in the depths of the womb; when it is distinct and definite, it bears a close analogy to the same embryo when fully shaped, with each of its parts inward and outward elaborated, and thus possessed of the form suited to it.

[26] See above, pp. 231-232.
[27] The verb 'to exclude' in v. 17 belongs to the imagery of the bridal feast; cf. Mt 25:10-12.
[28] This incident is allegorized by Philo in his treatise *On Mating with the Preliminary Studies*, 111 (Loeb, IV).
[29] Philo, *On Mating*, 135-136. St Jerome, PL 26, 411C, aptly quotes Num 11: 11-12: 'Did I conceive all this people? Did I bring them forth that thou shouldst say to me, "Carry them in your bosom, as a nurse carries the suckling child"?'

St Paul feels that the image of Christ which he conveyed to the Galatians has been confused and blurred by the preaching of the Judaizers. He is therefore labouring to make it clear again, like a mother forming the fetus within her. [30] (Theodoretus remarks that 'this verse shows up the folly of the Novatianists, who close the door of penance.' [31])

As was pointed out above, the reason why St Paul introduces this particular image is that he wishes to insinuate the identification of himself with Sarah and of the Judaizers with Agar, to prepare the way for v. 30: 'Send away the slave-woman.'

### What means are available for the renewal of a church?

In this section we see St Paul faced with the problem of how to renew a church which has fallen from its first fervour. He confesses that he is at a loss what to do about it (v. 20).

What he actually does is, first, to remind the Galatians of their previous fervour. It is a device he has learned from lovers (about whom he is quite well informed). The memory of the scenes of their first love can bring back the echo of the emotions then felt and undo something of the hardening effects of time. But it is a device of limited use. One cannot recall the spirit of a former time (say 'the Dunkirk spirit') at will. Religious conversion is accompanied by emotions which cannot be prolonged throughout the Christian life. It is remarkable that St Paul does not remind the Galatians of their almsgiving, their fasting, their chastity, their care for the poor, and so on, but only of their emotional attachment to himself. He was an emotional man, and perhaps set too much store by warm personal feelings.

However, he does not rely on memory alone. He seeks to remove the cause of the Galatians' falling-away by showing up the falsity of the Judaizers' doctrine, and labours to preach the gospel to the Galatians all over again (v. 19). [32] The renewal of the church can come about only by a renewal of the preaching of the gospel. The word

---

[30] Another interesting parallel in Philo is *Who is the Heir?*, 60. Commenting on Exod 18:4, Philo says it is impossible to escape from Pharaoh's bondage 'unless Eliezer is born in the soul'. St Paul has christianized the idea by substituting the law for Pharaoh and Christ for Eliezer. Whereas for Philo Moses liberates Israel from slavery in Egypt, for St Paul Christ liberates Israel from slavery to the Mosaic Law.

[31] Cf. Theodoretus, PG 82, 490 B.

[32] If St Paul had not first corrected their faith, it would have been of little use to remind them of their first fervour. So long as a man thinks his first fervour was a by-product of misconceptions, he does not wish a renewal of it.

itself must be heard, in which is 'the power of God unto salvation' (Rom 1 : 16). But the word is not heard unless preachers arise such as St Jerome described;[33] and preachers are sent in response to the prayers of those who see the need of them.

One of the most potent means now available for the inner renewal of the Church is the retreat movement. In a retreat, men are given a chance to listen again, in silence and recollection, to the word of the gospel.

*The Second Subsection, 4:21-30*

## SEND AWAY AGAR!

**A**  *4 : 21* Tell me, you who want to be under the law, do you not hear the law?  *22* For it is written that Abraham had two sons, one by the slave-girl, and one by the free woman.  **B**  *23* But while the son of the slave-girl was born according to the flesh, the son of the free woman was born in fulfilment of a promise.  *24* These are allegorical statements.  **C**  For the two women are two covenants.  **D**  The one is from Mount Sinai and bears children into slavery.  **E**  She is Agar.  **F**  *25* Mount Sinai, though situated in Arabia, goes with the present Jerusalem,  **G**  a slave and the mother of slaves.  **F¹**  *26* But the heavenly Jerusalem  **E¹**  is the free woman,  **D¹**  and she is the mother of all of us.  **C¹**  *27* For it is written: 'Rejoice, O childless one, who hast not borne, break forth and sing, thou who hast not been in labour; for more numerous are the children of her who is desolate than of her who has the husband.'  **B¹**  *28* But you, brethren, like Isaac, are children of promise.  *29* But just as of old the one born according to the flesh sought to dispossess the one born according to the spirit, so now.  **A¹**  *30* But what does the Scripture say? It says: 'Reject the slave-girl and her son, for the son of the slave-girl shall not share the inheritance with the son of the free woman.'

*What is the purpose of this passage?*

In the discourse at Antioch, this passage was the final demonstration from Scripture that the law of Moses has no place in the Gentile churches and must be excluded from them. Christians must no longer look to the law-observing church of Jerusalem as their mother-church. Their true mother is the heavenly Jerusalem. It is implied that Jewish (law-observing) Christianity is an inferior form of Christianity,

---

[33]  See above, p. 387.

which must lead its own life apart. There is no room in the Gentile churches for the law of Moses (Agar) or for those who observe the law (sons of Agar) — whether these are Christians or not. St Paul's last word on the controversy as to who are the heirs of Abraham is: 'Send away the slave-girl (the law) and her son (those who observe the law), for the son of the slave-girl shall not share the inheritance with the son of the free-woman (Christians who do not observe the law).'

The argument is drawn from the law and the prophets, represented by Genesis and Isaiah. [34] The argument from the law is typological: in the household of Abraham there arose a crisis which prefigured the crisis that has now arisen in the Church, which is the household of 'the Issue of Abraham'. The solution which God authorized in the earlier crisis is equally applicable to the latterday crisis: 'Send away the slave-girl and her son!' [35] The typological correspondences are remarkable:

| | |
|---|---|
| In the household of Abraham there was a son born according to the flesh (Ishmael) and a son born according to the spirit (Isaac). | In the household of the Issue of Abraham there are now sons of Abraham according to the flesh (those who rely on circumcision and the law) and sons of Abraham according to the spirit (those who rely on faith in Christ). |
| Ishmael was the son of a slave-girl (Agar), and Isaac was the son of a free woman (Sarah). | The sons according to the flesh are sons of a covenant of slavery (the Sinai covenant), the sons according to the spirit are sons of a covenant of freedom (the covenant with Abraham and his Issue). |
| For a while, Sarah and Agar, Isaac and Ishmael lived together in the same household; then Ishmael began to persecute Isaac, hoping to dispossess him of his inheritance. | For a while the Isaacs and the Ishmaels have lived together in the Church; but now the Ishmaels are trying to dispossess the Isaacs of their inheritance. |
| Abraham dealt with the situation by sending away the slave-woman and her son and excluding them from the inheritance. | The same solution must be applied in the church of Antioch: Jewish Christians who insist on observing the law must be sent away. |

[34] Cf. Chrysostom, PG 61, 663 A: 'You see how Sarah forecast the future for us through actions (dia pragmatôn) and the prophet through words (dia rhêmatôn).'

[35] The words quoted in v. 30 are spoken by Sarah to Abraham in Gen 21:10, but God turned Sarah's request into his command by saying in 21:12: 'whatever Sarah says to you, do as she tells you, for through Isaac shall your descendants be named.' The Targum inferred that Sarah had spoken prophetically. Cf. Lightfoot, Gal, ad loc.

It is quite incorrect to say that St Paul has imposed on the story of Sarah and Agar a meaning that is wholly alien to it. [36] He has observed a typological correspondence which is as remarkable as that between the brazen serpent and the cross of Christ (cf. Jn 3:14). With great ingenuity he has cast it into a symmetrical pattern. The analysis on p. 390 shows that he is chiefly interested in the fate of Agar (and her antitype) — she appears at the beginning and end along with Sarah, but she alone is at the centre. The centre of the subsection brackets together Agar-Sinai-Jerusalem. The lesson of the whole structure is that these have no standing in the Church. Agar must be sent away, the law given at Sinai is obsolete, the earthly Jerusalem is not to remain the centre of the Church.

Within this typological argument, St Paul has inserted an argument from prophecy. Isaiah spoke of two Jerusalems (the earthly and the heavenly) under the figure of two women; and he described these two women in terms which fit Sarah and Agar. The heavenly Jerusalem, like Sarah, who corresponds to the Abraham covenant, was for a long time childless, [37] while the earthly Jerusalem, like Agar, who corresponds to the Sinai covenant, had offspring. But, Isaiah prophesied, the time would come when the heavenly Jerusalem would have far more children than the earthly Jerusalem — and the prophecy, says St Paul, is now being fulfilled as the Christian faith spreads far and wide in Gentile lands.

*Does St Paul treat the story of Sarah and Agar as a type or as an allegory?*

An allegory is an extended metaphor. It is a story in which each of the terms (or the more important ones) can be decoded so as to disclose a deeper meaning than the surface-meaning. For example, the parable of the Cockle in the Wheat (Mt 13:24-30), narrates an incident in the life of a farmer and his household; but it is possible to decode the narrative with the following startling results:

A man (Christ) sowed in his field good seed (Jewish Christianity, adhering to the law). While everyone was asleep (while Peter, James and John were unaware), an enemy (Paul) came and oversowed bad seed (the gospel of freedom from the law) among the wheat, and made off. So the servants (the rulers of the church of Jerusalem) went to the owner (Christ) and

[36] Thus G. V. Jones, *The Art and Truth of the Parables*, London, 1963, p. 107.
[37] Gal 4:27 seems, therefore, to imply a pessimistic view about the salvation of the Jews of the period from Moses to Christ. If they were all sons of Agar, they have no part in the inheritance promised to Abraham (cf. v. 30). On the salvation of the saints of the Old Testament see above, pp. 205-207.

said, 'How does the crop come to contain weeds?' He answered: 'An enemy has done this.' The servants asked him: 'Do you want us to go out and collect the weeds' (to excommunicate the Gentile Christians)? But he said: 'No. In collecting the weeds you might root up the wheat as well. (If you excommunicate the Gentile Christians, a large number of Jewish Christians will go with them.) Let them both grow till the harvest...'

Read as an allegory, this story looks like the composition of a prophet or churchman who disapproved of Gentile Christianity but took the view that it ought to be tolerated in order to preserve unity among all true Jewish Christians. [38] St Matthew himself did not interpret the story in this way (cf. Mt 13 : 36-43); he allegorizes only the beginning and end. But he does treat it as an allegory. The story in its literal or superficial sense is not meant to be a historical narrative.

A 'type', on the other hand, is an historical event which prefigures another historical event. The story of the setting up of a brazen serpent in Num 21 : 8-9 is not an allegory but a type, because the author means that Moses did in reality set up a brazen serpent.

In Gal 4 : 25, St Paul describes the story of Sarah and Agar as allegorical. If he is using the word 'allegory' correctly, he is saying that the story of the two women does not describe events which actually took place in the past, but is a prophetic description, in an extended series of metaphors, of events which were taking place in his own day.

The Antiochene exegetes, Theodore of Mopsuestia and John Chrysostom, and most later commentators take the view that St Paul has misused the word 'allegory'. Thus Chrysostom says: 'He has incorrectly described as allegory what is in fact a type.' [39] This is probably true, [40] but the point should not be too easily conceded. There is a good deal to be said in favour of the view that St Paul meant exactly what he says in v. 25: 'These statements are allegorical.'

---

[38]  The parable may originally have been used by Jesus in a more general discussion of the problem of evil. Cf. Dubarle, *The Biblical Doctrine of Original Sin*, p. 139. But in St Matthew's gospel, the parable is applied to the problem of evil within the Church.

[39]  Chrysostom, PG 61, 662 B. Theodore insists several times that the narrative is historical fact (Gal, pp. 73, 74, 79, 86), and takes the occasion of v. 24 for a general diatribe against Alexandrian exegesis. St Paul, he says, speaks of past time, 'but they do the exact opposite, treating all the history in the Bible as if it were no different from a succession of dreams in the night. They say that Adam was not Adam—especially when they chance to be giving a "spiritual" discourse on Scripture, for they describe their stupidity as "spiritual interpretation"!—and paradise was not paradise, and the snake was not a snake.' The example is not a happy one; cf. Dubarle, *The Biblical Doctrine of Original Sin*, p. 222, n. 1.

[40]  Philo does not always reject the historicity of the passages which he allegorizes. Cf. *The Special Laws*, I, 287, II, 29 (Loeb, VII).

In the first place, St Paul was quite capable of using the word 'type' when he thought it appropriate. In 1 Cor 10:11, for example, he says that the punishments inflicted on the Israelites in the desert befell them 'typically' — they were real events, but foreshadowed later events (the punishment of Christian sinners); and in Rom 5:14 he describes the first Adam as the 'type' of the one who was to come. Secondly, St Paul may have shared the view which is expressed by Philo, that the story of Abraham's dealings with Agar and Ishmael is too shocking to be taken literally, and therefore *must* be understood allegorically. Since the excavations at Nuzu in north eastern Iraq in 1925-1931, scholars have known that when Sarah offered Agar to Abraham and he accepted, they were following the custom of the age. One of the tablets discovered at Nuzu records a contract containing the following stipulation:

> Furthermore, Kelim-ninu has been given in marriage to Shennima. If Kelim-ninu bears [children], Shennima shall not take another wife; but if Kelim-ninu does not bear, Kelim-ninu shall acquire a woman of the land of the Lullu as wife for Shennima, and Kelim-ninu may not send the offspring away. [41]

But Philo and St Paul did not know the Nuzu tablets and could not excuse Abraham on the grounds that by the moral standards of his day he was doing no wrong. [42] Judged by the standards of their own day, the conduct attributed to Abraham was shocking. First he had sexual relations with his wife's maidservant, and then, when his wife became jealous, he cruelly dismissed the slave-girl and her illegitimate child into the desert, where only a miracle could save them from death. Rather than attribute such reprehensible conduct to the patriarch, Philo chose to read the story as a pure allegory. He says at the end of his treatise *On Mating with the Preliminary Studies*: [43]

[41] Quoted by F. L. Moriarty, *Introducing the Old Testament*, Milwaukee, 1949, p. 10, from Pritchard, ANET, p. 220.
[42] St Augustine explains the morality of Abraham's conduct by an argument which, if valid, would allow the same remedy to be applied when a Christian marriage proves infertile (PL 35, 2133 D): 'How did it come about that the one woman was "desolate" and the other "possessed the man" if not because Abraham transferred his activity of procreating offspring to the slave-girl Agar who was fertile, from his wife Sarah who was barren?—but Sarah permitted this and took the initiative. For it is an ancient rule of justice, which the same apostle commends to the Corinthians, that "the wife has not power over her own body; and likewise the man has not power over his body, but the woman" (1 Cor 7:4). These (conjugal) debts, like other debts, are in the power of those to whom they are owed. He who does not defraud this power (or right), preserves the laws of conjugal chastity.' The fallacy in this way of thinking is the supposition that the wife may alienate her right over the husband's body. If Sarah cannot transfer her marital right to Agar, Abraham has no duty or right to approach her.
[43] Philo, *On Mating*, 180 (Loeb, IV).

When you hear that Agar is afflicted or maltreated by Sarah, do not suppose that it is an ordinary case of female jealousy. For *the story is not about women;* it is about two stages in the development of the mind, the one in which the mind exercises herself in preliminary studies, the other in which she contests for the palm of virtue.

Before his conversion, St Paul may have held much the same view himself. As a Christian missionary, he found the new way of decoding the allegory which he sets forth in 4 : 21-30. If it was commonly held in the Jewish schools that Gen 16-17 is not history but allegory, St Paul as a Christian may still have shared this misconception (just as he probably thought that the earth was flat), and this may account for his use of the word 'allegory' in v. 25. Such a view is not incompatible with the doctrine of inspiration, for St Paul is not formally teaching that the narrative is unhistorical; rather, he is diverting attention from the literal sense and disclosing a deeper sense.

But the Antiochenes must be allowed to have the last word here. Theodore of Mopsuestia scores a good point against the allegorists when he says that the comparison of past and present in v. 29 implies the historicity of the ancient story: 'Just as of old the one born according to the flesh sought to dispossess the one born according to the spirit, so now.' [44] It is therefore better to describe St Paul's argument as typological.

## *What cogency has a typological argument?*

A typological argument is a species of argument from prophecy. Prophecies can be given either in words or in actions. [45] The prophets themselves sometimes enacted their prophecies (cf. e.g. Ezek 4-5), and God can so dispose that the actions of men of one generation prefigure, without their knowing it, the events of a later generation. The Jews believed that just as God had intervened in their history in the past, so he would intervene again in the future. His past interventions set the pattern or 'type' in their minds so that they would recognize future interventions as his. [46]

---

[44]  Cf. Theodore of Mops., Gal, p. 74, lines 9-14.
[45]  Cf. Chrysostom, quoted above, p. 391, n. 34; A. Farrer, 'Typology,' *Expository Times* 67 (1955), pp. 229-231; J. Marsh, *Saint John*, Harmondsworth (Pelican), 1968, pp. 56-58.
[46]  Cf. J. Moltmann, *Theology of Hope*, London, 1967, p. 175: 'It is generally acknowledged that historical understanding nowadays is always analogical understanding and must therefore always remain within the realm of what is understandable in terms of analogy.'

Since God alone can foresee the future, he alone can prophesy, whether through types or through the words of his prophets. He is therefore able to make his actions recognizable as divine actions by foretelling or prefiguring them.

St Paul was able to show that the situation which had arisen in the church of Antioch had been prefigured with surprising accuracy in the narratives of Gen 16-17. Any Jew who recognized that the hand of God was at work in the events narrated in Gen 16-17 should be able to recognize the same hand at work in the church of Antioch. If the solution which God had approved in the ancient story seemed shocking and, taken by itself, inexplicable, the explanation of it could be found in the antitype. [47] For the church of Antioch to send away the slave-woman and her offspring was no injustice, since the authorities at Jerusalem had themselves approved of the freedom of the Gentile churches.

### What is meant by 'hearing the law' (v. 21)?

The Greek verb 'to hear' (*akouein*) can also mean 'to obey'. Accordingly, v. 21 can mean: 'You who want to be under the law — why not obey the law?' Then v. 30 (its counterpart) adds: 'The law bids you send away the slave-woman and her son.'

But probably St Paul had in mind a technical rabbinic sense: 'to hear' a passage in a certain way is to 'interpret' it in this way. [48] Hence to miss the true meaning of a passage is to fail to 'hear' it. As St Jerome remarks, [49]

> he 'hears the law' who does not stop at its surface but sees into its marrow; he fails to 'hear the law' who, like the Galatians, attains only the outer bark (*corticem*).

This sense suits the present passage better: if St Paul's hearers take the story of Sarah and Agar literally, they are failing to hear the true allegorical sense of the passage — a veil lies over their minds (cf. 2 Cor 3:12-18).

---

[47] Jewish readers found it difficult to explain why God should have prescribed such a remedy as the brazen serpent for a people who were still prone to idolatry and who were forbidden, for that reason, to make any graven image. The Wisdom of Solomon 16:7 attempts an explanation: 'He who turned towards it (the Serpent) was saved, not by what he saw, but by Thee, the Saviour of all.' The reason why God prescribed such a dangerous remedy became evident when the type was fulfilled.

[48] Cf. Daube, *The New Testament and Rabbinic Judaism*, pp. 55-62.

[49] St Jerome, PL 26, 414 B.

*Did Ishmael 'persecute' Isaac (v. 29)?*

When St Paul says that 'the son born according to the flesh began to persecute the son born according to the spirit,' he is doubtless alluding to Gen 21: 9-10:

> But Sarah saw the son of Hagar the Egyptian, whom she had borne to Abraham, playing <with her son Isaac [50] >. So she said to Abraham, 'Cast out the slave-woman with her son; for the son of this slave-woman shall not be heir with my son Isaac.'

The word 'playing' (*metsaheq*) puzzled the rabbis. Why should the boy's playing provoke Sarah's enmity? As St Jerome says, 'a simple game between infants does not deserve expulsion and rejection.' [51] The Midrash Rabbah gives a collection of explanations offered by various rabbis: [52]

> AND SARAH SAW THE SON OF HAGAR THE EGYPTIAN, etc. (xxi, 9). R. Simeon b. Yohai said: R. Akiba used to interpret this to his [Ishmael's] shame. Thus R. Akiba lectured: AND SARAH SAW THE SON OF HAGAR THE EGYPTIAN, WHOM SHE HAD BORNE UNTO ABRAHAM, MAKING SPORT. Now MAKING SPORT refers to nought else but immorality, as in the verse, *The Hebrew servant, whom thou hast brought unto us, came in unto me to* make sport *of me* (Gen xxxix, 17). Thus this teaches that Sarah saw Ishmael ravish maidens, seduce married women and dishonour them. R. Ishmael taught: This term SPORT refers to idolatry, as in the verse, *And rose up to* make sport (Ex xxxii, 6). This teaches that Sarah saw Ishmael build altars, catch locusts, and sacrifice them. R. Eleazar said: The term sport refers to bloodshed, as in the verse, *Let the young men, I pray thee, arise and* sport *before us* (II Sam ii, 14). R. Azariah said in R. Levi's name: Ishmael said to Isaac: 'let us go and see our portions in the field'; then Ishmael would take a bow and arrows and shoot them in Isaac's direction, whilst pretending to be playing. Thus it is written, *As a madman who casteth fire-brands, arrows, and death; so is the man that deceiveth his neighbour, and saith: Am I not in sport* (Prov xxii, 18f.)? But I say: This term sport [mockery] refers to inheritance. For when our father Isaac was born all rejoiced, whereupon Ishmael said to them, 'You are fools, for I am the firstborn and I receive a double portion.' You may infer this from Sarah's protest to Abraham: FOR THE SON OF THIS BONDWOMAN SHALL NOT BE HEIR WITH MY SON, WITH ISAAC (xxi, 10). WITH MY SON, even if he were not Isaac; or WITH ISAAC, even if he were not my son; how much the more, WITH MY SON, WITH ISAAC!

---

[50] This phrase is absent from the Hebrew but present in the LXX.
[51] St Jerome, PL 26, 419 B.
[52] Midrash Rabbah, LIII, 11 (trans. by H. Freedman and M. Simon, *Midrash Rabbah*, I, London, 1939, pp. 469-470).

This last explanation is doubtless the one which St Paul had in mind. It is explained at greater length in the Palestinian Targum on Gen 22:1:[53]

> It came about, after these things, after Isaac and Ishmael had quarrelled... that Ishmael said: 'It is for me to inherit from my father, for I am his first-born son,' but Isaac said: 'It is for me to inherit from my father, for I am the son of Sarah his wife, whereas you are the son of Agar, my mother's servant.' Ishmael replied: 'I am more just than you, for I was circumcised at thirteen years and if I had wished to refuse, I would not have let myself be circumcised; but you were circumcised at eight days; if you had had knowledge of it, perhaps you would not have submitted to circumcision?' Isaac replied: 'See I am thirty-six years old, and if the Holy One, blessed is he, demanded of me all my members, I would not refuse.' At once these words were heard by the Master of the universe, and at once God tested Abraham (viz. by demanding the sacrifice of Isaac, as is described in Gen 22:2). [54]

It is probable that St Paul understood the 'playing' of Gen 21:9 in the light of this midrash, as meaning 'mocking' or 'jeering' at Isaac's claim to be heir of Abraham. [55] This will explain why he says in 4:29 that Ishmael 'persecuted' Isaac — he tried to drive him out of his inheritance. It also explains why Sarah was provoked to say: 'Cast out this slave-woman with her son, for the son of this slave-woman shall not share the inheritance with my son Isaac.'

St Paul, then, accuses the Judaizers of doing the same as Ishmael had done: they are mocking the true heirs, saying: 'You are fools, we are the first-born, and receive a double portion.' St Paul replies: 'On the contrary, you will be excluded from the inheritance, like Ishmael.'

### Does St Paul regard Isaac as Abraham's son according to the flesh?

The present passage gives us three reasons for thinking that in St Paul's view Isaac was born *to* Abraham but not *of* Abraham, that is to say, Abraham did not generate Isaac physically by intercourse with Sarah.

[53] This was pointed out by R. Le Déaut, 'Traditions targumiques dans le Corpus Paulinien?' *Biblica* 42 (1961), pp. 37-43.
[54] Translated from the French version given by Le Déaut, art. cit., pp. 38-39. Cf. *Midrash Rabbah* on Genesis, LV, 4 (trans. Freedman and Simon, I, pp. 484-5).
[55] St Jerome shows knowledge of this midrash in his comment (PL 26, 419 B): 'The apostle, a Hebrew of the Hebrews, educated at the feet of Gamaliel ... understood that it was not a simple game. Perhaps Ishmael, being the elder and circumcised at a time when he could understand and feel what was done to him, claimed the right of primogeniture; and the Scripture calls the wrangling of the small boys a "game".' (Without the midrash, this comment would be as obscure as the text which it is meant to explain.)

The first indication is in v. 23: 'The son of the slave-girl was born *according to the flesh,* but the son of the free woman *through the promise.'* Unless there is some strong reason to the contrary, this should be taken to mean that Ishmael was not born through a divine promise, and Isaac was not born according to the flesh. The second indication is in v. 27. The heavenly Jerusalem resembles Sarah in having many children although she has not a husband but is *desolate* (*erêmos*). The third is that in v. 29 where Ishmael and Isaac are contrasted as 'the one born according to the flesh' and 'the one born according to the spirit'. Again, unless there is some strong reason to the contrary, this should be taken to imply that Isaac was not born of sexual intercourse ('according to the flesh').

There is good evidence that some of St Paul's Jewish contemporaries believed that Isaac and others of the patriarchs were born without male intervention. In his treatise *On the Cherubim,* Philo gives four examples of women who were caused to conceive by God alone. He interprets them allegorically as standing for virtues:[56]

> Man and woman, male and female of the human race, in the course of nature come together to hold intercourse for the procreation of children. But it is not permissible for the Virtues, whose children are many and perfect, to have intercourse with mortal man. Yet if they do not receive the seed of generation from another, they will never of themselves conceive. Who then is he that sows good seed in them but the Father of all, the unbegotten God who begets all things? He, then, is the one who sows; but his own offspring, the fruit which he sowed, he gives away. For God begets nothing to himself, in as much as he has no need of anything; he begets all for him who needs (or, prays) to receive.
>
> I will give as warrant for my words one whom none can gainsay, Moses, the holiest of men. For he shows us Sarah conceiving at the time when God visited her in her solitude (cf. Gen 21:1); but she brings forth her child not to the One who visited her, but to the one who seeks wisdom, and his name is Abraham.
>
> He (Moses) teaches this even more clearly in the case of Leah, for he says that God opened her womb (Gen 29:31), and to open the womb belongs to the husband. She conceived and brought forth her child not to God — for he alone is all-sufficient to himself — but to the one who endures toil for the sake of the good, namely Jacob.
>
> Thus Virtue receives the divine seed from the Creator, but brings forth to one of her lovers — to the one who is preferred above her other suitors.
>
> Again, Isaac the all-wise besought God, and through the power of the One besought, Rebecca (who is Steadfastness) became pregnant (Gen 25:21).

---

[56]  Philo, *On the Cherubim,* 43-47 (Loeb, II, slightly revised).

And without supplication or entreaty, Moses, when he took Zipporah, the winged and soaring Virtue, [57] found her pregnant through no mortal agency at all (Exod 2:22).

The idea that these four women conceived by divine generation is not derived from their allegorical equivalence to the virtues. Rather, it is derived from an ultra-literal interpretation of phrases in Genesis and Exodus. Philo himself may not be the inventor of it. [58] If it was possible for Philo to hold such views, the same was also possible for St Paul.

However, there is a reason to the contrary in Rom 4:19-20:

He (Abraham) did not falter in his faith, although he saw that his own body was already like one dead — he was a hundred years old — and that the womb of Sarah was dead. When he heard God's promise, he was not torn by unbelief but was strong in faith (*enedynamôthê têi pistei*), for he gave glory to God and was fully convinced that God can do what he has promised. That is why *it was reckoned to him as justice*.

The phrase here translated 'he was strong in faith' can be taken to mean that thanks to his faith he became capable of intercourse (his impotence was taken away). Abraham's saving faith, according to this interpretation of Gen 15, was not a purely internal assent to God's word. His acceptance of God's promise was embodied in physical action — just as Christian faith is embodied in the actions of receiving the sacraments of Baptism and Eucharist.

So the *prima facie* meaning of vv. 23, 27 and 29 should be rejected.

## Why does St Paul introduce the two Jerusalems here?

After St Paul has said: 'the two women represent two covenants,' we might expect him to continue: 'One is Agar, the mother of slaves; the other is Sarah, the mother of the free; Christians who are released from the law, being free, are sons of Sarah; all who remain under the law are sons of Agar. The free sons of Sarah must cast out the slavish sons of Agar who would like to enslave them.' Why, then, has St Paul complicated his argument by introducing the two Jerusalems — and Mount Sinai too?

He knew that Sarah had been treated by Jewish teachers as a figure of Jerusalem [59] — both Sarah and Jerusalem, 'the daughter of

[57] *Zippor* in Hebrew means 'a bird'.
[58] Cf. M. Dibelius *Botschaft und Geschichte*, Tübingen, 1953, I, p. 31. The idea reappears later in the Midrash Rabbah, Gen LIII, 6 (Soncino Version, I, p. 466) in a saying of R. Huna.
[59] See below on Isa 54:1, pp. 401-403.

Zion', could claim to be 'mother of the sons of Abraham'. Hence he must explain that when he says: 'We are sons of Sarah,' he does *not* mean: 'We are sons of the earthly Jerusalem.' The earthly Jerusalem has renounced control over the Gentile churches (cf. 2 : 9). He says, therefore, 'We are sons of the *heavenly* Jerusalem,' and brackets the earthly Jerusalem with Mount Sinai — which is easily done, since Mt Zion shares with Mt Sinai the dubious title of 'mountain of the law' (cf. Isa 2 : 2). In the allegory, the earthly Jerusalem goes with Mt Sinai; spiritually, there is no difference or distance between them, for they are both at the beginning, not at the end, of Israel's journey. [60] The city of the free-born sons is the heavenly Jerusalem, to which Christians look forward as their home. Thus St Paul christianizes this piece of Jewish typology by saying: 'Sarah does stand for Jerusalem — but for the *heavenly* Jerusalem.' The contrast between Sinai and the heavenly Jerusalem is further developed in Heb 12 : 18-24.

*What is the context of Isa 54:1 (quoted in v. 27)?*

The quotation in v. 27 comes from the work of Second Isaiah (chapters 40-45), written during the Exile. The prophet had meditated deeply on the promises made to Abraham and his Issue, and on their apparent frustration: How has it come about that the seed of Abraham, which according to the divine promise should be as glorious as the stars and as numerous as the sand on the seashore, is in fact reduced to a small remnant of exiles at Babylon? What has become of the justice of God? Has he been unfaithful to his covenants? (St Paul was not the first Jew to ponder these questions.) Isaiah gives his answer in 48 : 18-19, where the Lord says:

> O that you had hearkened to my commandments!
>     Then your peace would have been like a river,
>         and your righteousness like the waves of the sea;
>     your *seed* would have been like the sand,
>         and your descendants like its grains. [61]

In 51 : 1, the prophet begins a song of consolation, to reassure the exiles: they must not be dismayed over their small numbers, for God will again make them a great and mighty nation. Let them remember how God increased the seed of Abraham in the past:

---

[60] Cf. H. Sahlin, 'The New Exodus of Salvation according to St Paul,' in A. Fridrichsen et al., *The Root of the Vine*, London, 1953, p. 86.

[61] Cf. also Isa 41 : 8; 43 : 5; 44 : 3, and the valuable commentary on Isaiah II and III by D. R. Jones, in *Peake's Commentary on the Bible*, ed. 2, London, 1962, ss. 447-457.

> Hearken to me, you who pursue deliverance,
>> you who seek the Lord;
> look to the rock from which you were hewn,
>> and to the quarry from which you were digged.
> Look to Abraham your father,
>> and to Sarah who bore you;
> for when he was but one I called him,
>> and I blessed him and made him many.

What God has done in the past he will do again in the future: he will comfort Zion and multiply the seed of Abraham (51:3—52:12). In the famous chapter 53, the greatest of the Servant Songs, he explains how this change in the fortunes of Israel is to come about: through the vicarious suffering of his Servant (vv. 10-12):

> When he makes himself an offering for sin,
>> he shall see his offspring (or, *seed*)...
> By his knowledge shall the righteous one, my servant,
>> make many to be accounted righteous;
>>> and he shall bear their iniquities.
> Therefore I will divide him a portion (or, *inheritance*) with the great,
>> and he shall divide the spoil with the strong;
> because he poured out his soul to death
>> and was numbered with the transgressors...

Thus 'the divine intention revealed in the call of Abraham, frustrated by Israel's sin and punishment, will be fulfilled in the righteous servant.' [62] As a result of his obedience in suffering, the servant will live again to see the fulfilment of the promise: a numerous 'seed' in possession of a great 'inheritance'. Chapter 54, from which St Paul quotes in v. 27, describes first the 'seed' (vv. 1-10), then the inheritance, which is a new Jerusalem (vv. 11-17).

In the verse which St Paul quotes, Isaiah describes the new Jerusalem in terms which show that he is thinking of Sarah, the mother of the promised seed. The Hebrew, translated literally, probably means:

> Cry out, thou childless one that hast not borne,
>> break forth in cries and rejoice, thou that hast not been in travail!
> For more numerous the children of the desolate
>> than the children of the woman ruled by a husband.

The first couplet is reminiscent of Gen 11:30: 'Now Sarah was barren, she had no child.' In the second couplet, the prophet may be comparing the condition of Israel in exile to that of Sarah during the period of Agar's triumph. [63] Sarah was then childless and desolate,

---

[62]  D. R. Jones in *Peake's Commentary*, 456f.
[63]  Cf. Burton, Gal, p. 264.

while Agar had the husband and had her child Ishmael. The meaning of Isaiah's prophecy will then be that just as Sarah had her period of sorrow and desolation, but this was followed by a period of rejoicing in a great posterity, so it will be with Israel: the daughter of Zion is now in exile and desolate, but soon she will have a 'seed' more numerous than that of the Gentile nations which for the time being enjoy God's favours. According to this interpretation, [64] the daughter of Zion will no longer be desolate when the numerous children are given to her. At present she is like a woman separated from her husband; but her husband (the Lord) will take her back. This agrees well with what follows (54:6-7):

> For the Lord has called you
>> like a wife forsaken and grieved in spirit,
> like a wife of youth when she is cast off,
>> says your God.
> For a brief moment I forsook you,
>> but with great compassion I will gather you.

54:1b is a prophecy of the future. In the Hebrew there is no verb (*rabbim beney shomemah mibbeney be'ulah*); a prophetic perfect must be supplied, hence in English a future: 'The sons of her who is now desolate *will be* more numerous than the sons of her who now has a husband.'

## How did St Paul understand Isa 54:1?

St Paul recognized that Isaiah had seen in Sarah a type of the new Jerusalem, mother of the promised 'seed' (described in Isa 54:11-17). He understood the second couplet as a contrast between two distinct women (not between two stages in the life of one woman), and between two Jerusalems. The women are Agar and Sarah, and they correspond to the old Jerusalem and the new heavenly Jerusalem.

In the light of the fulfilment, he can see that Isaiah's words are being fulfilled in an ultra-literal sense. The old Jerusalem remains 'under a husband', that is, subject to the law. [65] The new Jerusalem, being 'desolate', is not subject to the law of a husband, but is free. St Paul sees the children of the heavenly Jerusalem becoming more numerous than the children of the earthly Jerusalem, *while the*

---

[64] For a different view, see J. Skinner, *Isaiah XL-LXVI*, Cambridge, 1929, p. 151: 'Zion, addressed as a barren and desolate woman, is comforted with the assurance that her children are more numerous than those she formerly had as the "married wife" of Jehovah.' Viard, Gal, p. 101, follows this view.

[65] Cf. Rom 7:2: 'A married woman is subject to the law of her husband so long as he lives.'

*heavenly Jerusalem remains free of the law.* 'The children of the one who *is* desolate (free from law) *are* more numerous than the children of the one who is "subject to a husband" (under the law).' [66] In scholastic language, Isaiah meant: 'the children of the desolate woman will be more numerous *sensu diviso*' (for she will not be desolate when her children become numerous). St Paul sees that the prophecy has come true *sensu composito*: the desolate woman remains 'desolate' in the sense of 'free from law' while her children are becoming numerous. [67]

## Why does St Paul introduce the quotation from Isaiah?

The structure of the subsection (p. 390) links the quotation to v. 24b: 'The two women are two covenants.' Probably, therefore, one reason why he introduces the passage is to show that he is not the first to treat Sarah and Agar allegorically — Isaiah had done it before him.

But there are further reasons. The quotation is linked to the preceding verse by the phrase '*For* it is written.' The prophecy supports both halves of v. 26. 'The heavenly Jerusalem is the free woman,' for Isaiah described her as 'desolate' by contrast to one who is 'ruled' by a husband; 'and she is the mother of all of us (i.e., of our great multitude [68] )' — as Isaiah foretold when he said that the children of the new Jerusalem would be more numerous than those of the old.

But what is most important of all: by interpreting Gen 16-19 in the light of Isa 54, St Paul is able to draw from the law and the prophets together the conclusion that the earthly Jerusalem is not the mother of the Gentile Christians and that the heavenly Jerusalem is not subject to law. He is resuming Isaiah's meditation on the promise made to Abraham and his Issue, and is showing that the fulfilment is coming about exactly as Isaiah foretold — or rather, that Isaiah foretold the fulfilment more exactly than he realized.

## How can the heavenly Jerusalem be both a mother and free?

If the heavenly Jerusalem is now producing numerous offspring, this must be because she is reunited with the Lord, her husband. But

---

[66] The Hebrew for this phrase ('subject to a husband') is *be'ulah*, which is a past participle meaning 'ruled over'.

[67] See above, pp. 252-253, on St Paul's treatment of Gen 18:18: 'all the Gentiles will be blessed in you.'

[68] On the text and translation here, see G in G, pp. 183-184.

if she has a husband, must she not be in subjection to him as her
'living law'? [69] And in that case, how can she be free?

St Paul would probably reply that the Church, espoused to the
Lord Jesus, is guided by 'the law of Christ' (cf. 6:2), but is not
*subject to* this law as an exterior discipline. Because the heavenly
Jerusalem is united to her spouse in perfect love, his will is her will.
He imparts to her his own Holy Spirit, who becomes an interior law
guiding the life of the heavenly Jerusalem — as was foretold by
Isaiah (44:2-5):

> Fear not, O Jacob my servant,
> Jeshurun whom I have chosen.
> 3  For I will pour water on the thirsty land,
>    and streams on the dry ground;
>    I will pour my Spirit upon your *seed,*
>    and my blessing on your offspring...
> 5  This one will say, 'I am the Lord's',
>    another will call himself by the name of Jacob,
>    and another will write on his hand, 'The Lord's' [70]
>    and surname himself by the name of Israel.

V. 3 refers to the Jews, 'the seed of Abraham', and v. 5 to the
Gentiles who will share in the blessing promised to Abraham. Together
they will make up the new Jerusalem, [71] ruled by the will of God, and
yet 'free' because the Spirit is an interior law.

Further, the heavenly Jerusalem, like Sarah, will be both a mother
and 'free' because all her children will be born, not according to the
flesh, but after the pattern of the virgin birth of Jesus — 'not of blood,
nor of the will of flesh, nor of the will of man, but of God' (Jn 1:13). [72]
The last two chapters of the Apocalypse describe the marriage of the
heavenly Jerusalem and the Lamb.

## How numerous were the Gentile Christians in St Paul's day?

Since Isaiah prophesied that the children of the heavenly Jerusalem
would far outnumber those of the earthly city, and St Paul quotes
the prophecy in confirmation of his claim that 'the heavenly Jerusalem....is mother of *all of us*,' his words in vv. 26-27 seem to imply
that already, at the time of writing, the Gentile-Christian sons of

---

[69] Cf. Rom 7:2-3, and Philo, *On Abraham,* 5; *Moses,* I, 162 (Loeb, VI).
[70] This may be a reference to religious tattooing, on which see Gal 6:17, and
Philo, *The Special Laws,* I, 58 (Loeb, VII); and above, pp. 373-374.
[71] Cf. Ps 87.
[72] Cf. C. K. Barrett, *The Gospel according to St John,* London, 1955, ad loc.

Sarah outnumbered the Jewish sons of Agar. If the Epistle was written, as some suppose, in A.D. 49, when St Paul had completed only one missionary journey and founded only four or five small churches, the claim seems absurd; and even if, as is more likely, it was written as late as A.D. 57, the claim still sounds quite extravagant. Apart from the population of Palestine (2-3 millions?), there were about a million Jews in Alexandria and probably fifty thousand at Rome. Where in the world was there a Gentile Christian community of these proportions in St Paul's lifetime? He has perhaps a tendency to magnify his missionary successes (cf. Rom 15:19), but surely not to this extent.

It seems best to suppose that he has in mind the situation at Antioch. The Jews have had a synagogue there for generations and have attracted a certain number of proselytes and 'God-fearers' (cf. Acts 15:20-21). Now the gospel has come, and at once it has won far more adherents than the synagogue ever gained (cf. Acts 11:26). St Paul evidently saw in this situation the presage of a glorious future — the beginning of the fulfilment of Isaiah's prophecy. He means that the heavenly Jerusalem has *begun* to produce her numerous offspring and is already filled with the joy of a woman blessed with children; [73] the church of Antioch, predominantly Gentile, reveals the shape of things to come.

By the time of St Jerome, the apostle's prophetic cry of triumph had been vindicated: [74]

> I do not feel it necessary to speak of the multiplication of the Christians and the fewness of the Jews, when the standard of the Cross is resplendent throughout the world, and when the odd Jew seen in our cities is conspicuous for his rarity.

There is a touch of 'triumphalism' here. But St Jerome caught it from St Paul (cf. also Col 1:6).


### Does St Paul regard Judaism and Jewish Christianity as doomed?

Lightfoot's comment on 4:30 contains a striking tribute to St Paul's prophetic vision:

> The law and the gospel cannot co-exist; the law must disappear before the gospel. It is scarcely possible to estimate the strength of conviction and depth of prophetic insight which this declaration implies. The Apostle

---

[73] In the sixth section v. 27 is linked to vv. 14-15 which describe the joy of the new-born church in Galatia. Cf. Jn 16:21.

[74] Jerome, PL 26, 418 C. The last sentence, 'et vix rarus atque notabilis in urbibus Judaeus appareat,' is doubtless meant to remind us of Virgil's 'apparent rari nantes in gurgite vasto.'

thus confidently sounds the death-knell of Judaism at a time when one-half of Christendom clung to the Mosaic law with a jealous affection little short of frenzy, and while the Judaic Party seemed to be growing in influence and was strong enough, even in the Gentile churches of his own founding, to undermine his influence and endanger his life. The truth which to us appears a truism must then have been regarded as a paradox.

The tribute is justified, though not by Gal 4:30 alone. All St Paul says in this text is that there is no room in the Gentile churches of Antioch and Galatia for Agar (the Sinai covenant and the law of Moses) and her offspring (those who seek justification in the law), and that the offspring of Agar will not share in the inheritance promised to the seed of Abraham. This does not necessarily imply that non-Christian Judaism is doomed to extinction. As St Jerome points out, a promise was also made to Ishmael — though in his case by an angel; [75] and in fact Judaism has survived the centuries and is still a power in the world today. Nor does 4:30 necessarily imply that Jewish (law-observing) Christianity was destined to wither away — though in fact it very soon did. Gal 4:30 is compatible with the view that Jewish Christianity (observing the law, but not seeking justification from it) should and will continue its own separate existence in the spirit of the agreement recorded in Gal 2:9. St Paul probably regarded Jewish Christianity as an inferior form of Christian life — a kind of spiritual teenage, half-way between the restraints of childhood and the freedom of adulthood. From Rom 11:26, we learn that he looked forward to the day when 'all Israel' would be converted, and this through jealousy of the spiritual wealth granted to the Gentile churches. He may perhaps have expected that when this happened, all Israel would abandon the ceremonial law, though he does not say so. If he hoped or expected that the conversion of all Israel would take place within a generation, he was ready to sound the death-knell of Judaism. But this cannot be inferred from Gal 4:30 alone.

### What was St Paul's attitude to Jerusalem and Rome?

The famous prophecy common to Isa 2:1-5 and Micah 4:1-3 pictures Jerusalem in the Messianic Age as the religious centre of the world: [76]

> It shall come to pass in the latter days
> that the mountain of the house of the Lord

---

[75] Cf. Gen 16:10 and Jerome PL 26, 414 D. M. Barth, 'Was Paul an Anti-Semite?' JES 5 (1968), p. 99 remarks: 'Paul fails to mention that according to the Genesis story God also protected and multiplied Ishmael.'

[76] Isa 2:1-4:6 is a chiasm. The counterpart of 2:1-5 is 4:2-6. See Lund, *Chiasmus in the New Testament*, pp. 64-67.

shall be established as the highest of the mountains,
   and shall be raised above the hills;
and all the nations shall flow to it,
   and many peoples shall come and say:
'Come, let us go up to the mountain of the Lord,
   to the house of the God of Jacob;
that he may teach us his ways
   and that we may walk in his paths.'
For out of Zion shall go forth the law,
   and the word of the Lord from Jerusalem.

No doubt many of the earliest Jewish Christians took this to mean that Jerusalem was destined to remain the geographical and administrative centre of the Church. If the apostles shared this view, it is easier to understand why they remained so long in Jerusalem and were so slow to embark on missions to the Gentiles. [77]

St Luke, though he never quotes this prophecy, gives an interpretation of how it has been fulfilled. At the beginning of Acts, he describes how visitors who had flocked to Jerusalem from all the nations heard the apostles preach on the day of Pentecost (cf. Acts 2:1-11). Then in the rest of the book he shows how the gospel radiated out *from Jerusalem* through Judaea and Samaria to the end of the earth (cf. Acts 1:8), that is to say, he shows how it was transplanted from Jerusalem to Rome [78] and was dejudaized in the process. The geographical structure of Acts points to Rome as the future centre of the Church. [79]

St Paul was convinced that the Gentile churches were not to look to the earthly Jerusalem as their mother (cf. Gal 2:9; 4:25-26). The 'Jerusalem above' is their mother (v. 26). This does not mean that the heavenly Jerusalem is already on earth in the form of the Church. [80] The members of the Church on earth are sons of the heavenly Jerusalem, destined one day to be gathered into her. They belong to her, though she is not yet present (cf. Heb 12:18-24; Apoc 21:2). The church of Antioch, and those of Galatia, like the church of Philippi, are colonies (cf. Phil 3:20) and as such are dependent on a mother-city. But the city in question is neither Jerusalem nor Rome; it is the heavenly Jerusalem. St Paul is here in agreement with St John: salvation is to come forth from the Jews, but Christian worship 'in spirit and truth' is not tied to Jerusalem or to any other mountain (cf. Jn

---

[77] See above, pp. 167-168. For a different explanation see J. Héring, *The Second Epistle of St Paul to the Corinthians*, London, 1967, pp. 110-111.
[78] Cf. H. Conzelmann, *The Theology of St Luke*, London, 1960, pp. 27-94.
[79] Cf. J. C. O'Neill, *The Theology of Acts*, London, 1961, pp. 70 and 170-174.
[80] As Schlier thinks, Gal, p. 159.

4:21-22). St Paul recognizes the authority of St Peter, but does not regard it as being tied to one place — any more than is his own. [81]

*Is v. 31 out of place?*

After the triumphant v. 30, which draws the practical conclusion and rounds off the allegory, v. 31 sounds lame and superfluous. It contains one step in the argument towards the conclusion which has already been reached. It spoils the effect of the conclusion. And there is nothing corresponding to it at the beginning of the subsection (cf. vv. 20-21). If it belongs to the section containing the allegory, it ought to come after v. 28. But almost certainly it belongs to the next section and was inserted to make the transition. Section seven begins and ends with the concepts of freedom and slavery (see p. 411).

---

[81] Cf. P. Benoit in H. Bouësse et A. Mandouze, *L'Evêque dans l'église du Christ*, Bruges, 1963, pp. 56-57.

# HORTATORY SECTIONS OF THE EPISTLE

In the third main division, St Paul turns his attention from the initial justification of the sinner by faith and baptism towards his final justification and admission to the kingdom of God. The message of these last two chapters is that entry into the promised inheritance does not depend on faith alone but on works rendered possible by the Spirit of Christ given to believers in and through their faith. It depends on works done in and through us, not by the law of Moses, but by the Spirit of Christ; or in other words, it depends not on 'works of the law' inspired by fear, but on works of Christ who inspires love. The centre of this long symmetrical structure does, however, specify a law, namely, the law by which all men, including Christians, will be judged: those who have been guilty of the works of the flesh listed in 5:20-21 will not inherit the kingdom. Thus it transpires that the Abraham-covenant too has its law, and the sanction for breaking it is exclusion from the promised blessings. The following analysis will bring out the points of correspondence.

A    We are Christ's freedmen and must resist slavery, 4:31—5:1.
B    Circumcision would cut us off from the source of power, 5:2-6.
C    Condemnation of the Judaizers, vindication of Paul, 5:7-12.
D    Christian freedom is freedom to serve others, 5:13-15.
E    Spirit and flesh are in conflict, 5:16-18.
F    The works of the flesh, 5:19-21a.
G    *Who will inherit the kingdom?* 5:21b.
$F^1$    The harvest of the Spirit, 5:22-23.
$E^1$    The spirit is victorious over the flesh through Christ, 5:24-25.
$D^1$    Christians must exercise charity in judgment and in generosity, 5:26—6:11.
$C^1$    Condemnation of the Judaizers, vindication of Paul, 6:12-14.
$B^1$    Circumcision is useless, 6:15-16.
$A^1$    Christ's freedman warns the troublemakers, 6:17-18.

Here, for comparison, are the matching passages.

A  *4:31* So, brethren, we are sons, not of the slave-girl, but of the free woman. *5:1* Christ has freed us in order to remain free. Stand firm, then, and do not submit again to the yoke of slavery.

$A^1$  *6:17* From now on let no one disturb me! For I bear in my body the stigmata of Jesus. *18* The grace of our Lord Jesus Christ remain with your spirit, brethren. Amen.

B  *5:2* See, I, Paul, declare to you that if you have yourself circumcised, Christ will give you no help.

$B^1$  *6:15* For neither circumcision nor its absence makes any difference, but only creation anew. *16* Upon

411

*3* Once again I solemnly assure every man who has himself circumcised, that he is obliged to fulfil the whole of the law. *4* You are cut off from the power of Christ, any of you who justify yourself by means of the law; you are banished from his grace. *5* For it is by the Spirit through faith that we receive the justification that is our hope. *6* For in Christ Jesus neither circumcision is of any avail nor its absence, but only faith working through charity.

C *5:7* You were running well; who has put obstacles in your way? Do not let anyone persuade you not to obey the truth! *8* Such persuasion is not from the one who calls you. *9* A little yeast leavens the whole mass. *10* I have confidence in you in the Lord that you will not think otherwise. But he who is upsetting you will bear the condemnation, whoever he may be. *11* But as for me, brethren, if I am still preaching circumcision, why am I still being persecuted? For in that case the scandal of the cross would have lost its power. *12* Would that those who are making trouble among you would go further and castrate themselves!

D *5:13* For you have been called to freedom, brethren — only do not let your freedom become an incitement to the flesh. But serve one another in charity. *14* For the whole law is fulfilled in obeying this one precept: 'You shall love your neighbour as yourself.' *15* But if you rend and devour one another, beware lest you be destroyed by one another.

all who walk by this rule be peace and mercy, and upon the Israel of God.

C¹ *6:12* Those who desire the approval of the world of flesh — they are the ones who urge you to be circumcised — but only that they may avoid being persecuted for the cross of Christ. *13* For those who practise circumcision do not even keep the law themselves; but they want you circumcised so that they can make your flesh a subject for their boasting. *14* For my part, heaven forbid that I should boast of anything except the cross of our Lord Jesus Christ, by which the world is crucified to me, and I to the world.

D¹ *5:26* Let us not be eager for vain glory, provoking one another, envying one another. *6:1* Brethren, if a man falls into some misdeed, you who are spiritual must put him right, in a spirit of gentleness, with an eye on yourself, lest you too be tempted. *2* Bear one another's burdens, and so you will fulfil the law of Christ. *3* For if anyone thinks he is something whereas he is nothing, he is deluding himself. *4* Let each man examine his own conduct; then he will be able to claim superiority only over himself, not over his neighbour. *5* For each will bear his own burden. *6* But a man who is being instructed in the word must give his teacher a share in all his goods. *7* Do not deceive yourselves: God is not mocked. For whatever a man sows, that he will reap. *8* If he sows for his flesh, from his flesh he will reap destruction; but if he sows for the spirit, from the Spirit he will reap eternal life. *9* Let us not weary of doing what is right; in due time we shall reap our harvest, if we do not weaken. *10* Therefore while we have time, let us do good to all men, but especially to our kindred in the faith. *11* Look at these large letters which I have written with my own hand.

E *5:16* What I mean is: walk by the Spirit and you will not fulfil the lust of the flesh. *17* For the flesh lusts against the spirit, and the spirit against the flesh (for these are opposed to each other), to prevent you from doing whatever you want. *18* But if you are led by the Spirit, you are not under the law.

E¹ *5:24* Those who belong to Christ Jesus have crucified the flesh with its passions and its lusts. *25* If we live by the Spirit, let us also walk by the Spirit.

F *5:19* It is plain what are the works of the flesh: fornication, impurity, licentiousness; *20* idolatry, sorcery; enmities, strife, jealousy, fits of anger, quarrels, dissensions, intrigues, *21* envy; drunkenness, orgies, and things like these.

F¹ *5:22* But the harvest of the Spirit is charity, joy, peace, patience, kindness, goodness, fidelity, *23* gentleness, self-control — against such things as these there is no law.

G *21b* I warn you as I warned you before, that those who do such things will not inherit the kingdom of God.

# FAITH AND LIBERTY

**A** *4 : 31* Therefore, brethren, we are sons, not of the slave-girl, but of the free woman. *5 : 1* Christ has freed you in order to remain free. Stand firm then, and do not submit again to the yoke of slavery. **B** *2* See! I, Paul, declare to you that if you have yourselves circumcised, Christ will give you no help. *3* Once again, I solemnly assure every man who has himself circumcised that he is obliged to fulfil the whole of the law. *4* You are cut off from the power of Christ, any of you who justify yourselves by means of the law; you are banished from his grace. **C** *5* For it is by the Spirit through faith that we receive the justification that is our hope. *6* For in Christ Jesus neither circumcision is of any avail nor its absence. **D** but only faith working through charity. **E** *7* You were running well; who has put obstacles in your way? **F** Do not let anyone persuade you not to obey the truth! **E¹** *8* Such persuasion is not from the one who calls you. **D¹** *9* A little yeast leavens the whole mass. **C¹** *10* I have confidence in you in the Lord that you will not think otherwise. **B¹** But he who is upsetting you will bear the condemnation, whosoever he may be. *11* But as for me, brethren, if I am still preaching circumcision, why am I still being persecuted? For in that case the scandal of the cross would have lost its power. **A¹** *12* Would that those who are making trouble among you would go further and castrate themselves! *13* For you have been called to freedom, brethren — only do not let your freedom become an incitement to the flesh.

Reasons were given above (pp. 235-236) for thinking that this section is a revised version of the closing section of the discourse at Antioch, and that the original ending has been re-used by St Paul at the end of the whole Epistle. If these passages are reunited, the following symmetry is obtained.

**A** *4 : 31* Therefore, brethren, we are sons, not of the slave-girl, but of the free woman. *5 : 1* Christ has freed us to remain free. Stand firm, then, and do not submit again to the yoke of slavery. **B** *2* See! I, Paul, declare to you that if you have yourselves circumcised, Christ will give you no help. [*3*] *4* You are cut off from the power of Christ, any of you who justify yourselves by means of the law; you are banished from his grace. **C** *5* For it is by the Spirit through faith that we receive the justification that is our hope. *6* For in Christ Jesus neither circumcision is of any avail nor its absence, **D** but only faith working through charity. **E** *7* You were running well; who has put obstacles in your way? **F** Do not let anyone persuade you not to obey the truth! **E¹** *8* Such persuasion is not from the one who calls you. **D¹** *9* A little yeast leavens the whole mass. **C¹** *10* I have confidence in you in the Lord that you will not think otherwise. *6 : 16* Upon all who walk by this rule be peace and mercy, and upon the Israel of God. **B¹** *17* From now on let no one disturb me! For I bear in my body the stigmata of Jesus. A¹ *18* The grace of our Lord Jesus Christ be with your spirit, brethren. Amen.

The correspondences restored by this reconstruction are as follows. In C¹ St Paul calls down a blessing upon all who walk by the rule or 'canon' which he has defined in C, namely, 'in Christ Jesus neither circumcision is of any avail nor its absence.' In B and B¹ he speaks of himself: in B¹ he says that he bears the marks of belonging to Christ, and as one who belongs to Christ, he utters a threat to use the power of Christ which is at his command [1]; in B he says that those who bear the mark of circumcision are cut off from Christ's power. In A¹ he prays that the 'grace' or free gift of Christ may remain with the brethren; in A he tells the brethren that Christ has given them the gift of freedom and they must defend it.

In the structure of the original Antioch discourse, this reconstructed passage was the Epilogue, balancing 2 : 14—3 : 4, which was the Prologue. The correspondences between these two passages were as follows :

*4 : 31* Therefore, brethren, we are sons, not of the slave-girl, but of the free woman.

*5 : 1* Christ has freed us in order to remain free.

*5 : 2* See, I, Paul, tell you: if you return to the Jewish way of life, Christ will give you no help. [*3*] *4* You are cut off from Christ, any of you who seek justification in the law; you are banished from grace. [2]

*5 : 5* For it is by the Spirit through faith that we receive the justification that is our hope.

*5 : 6* For in Christ Jesus neither circumcision is of any avail nor its absence, but only faith working through charity.

*5 : 7* You were running well. Who has stopped you? Do not let any-

*2 : 15* We by our birth are Jews and not sinners of Gentiles.

*2 : 19* Through the law I died to the law, in order to live to God; I am crucified with Christ crucified.

*2 : 17* If through seeking to be justified in Christ, we turn out to be sinners ourselves — has Christ become a servant of Sin? Heaven forbid! *18* For if I rebuild what I have torn down, I make myself a sinner. [2]

*3 : 2* Was it by doing the law that you received the Spirit or by hearing the faith? Cf. also 2 : 16.

*2 : 20* The life that I now live while in the flesh, I live through faith in God and Christ who loved me and delivered himself for me.

*2 : 14* When I saw that they were not walking steadily according to

---

[1]   On 6 : 17 see below, pp. 496-497.
[2]   There is the same pattern in both passages: If you do A for the sake of B, the result will be not-B.

one persuade you not to obey the truth. *8* Such persuasion is not from the one who calls you.

*5 : 9* A little yeast leavens the whole mass. [3]

*5 : 10* I have confidence in you in the Lord that you will not think otherwise. *6 : 16* All who walk by this canon, peace be upon them and mercy —

*6 : 16b* and upon the Israel of God.

*6 : 17* From now on, let no one vex me, for I bear in my body the stigmata of Jesus. [4]

*6 : 18* The grace of the Lord Jesus Christ be with your spirit brethren, Amen.

the truth of the gospel, I said to Peter.... *3 : 1* Who has bewitched you?

*2 : 20* I live, but not I — Christ ferments within me. [3]

*3 : 3* Are you so foolish?....*4* Have all your sufferings taught you nothing? *2 : 14* I saw that they were not walking according to the truth of the gospel.

*2 : 14* How can you compel the Gentiles to judaize?

*3 : 1* Who has cast his spell upon you — you before whose eyes Jesus Christ was placarded crucified?

*2 : 21* I do not set aside the grace of God. For if justification comes from the law, Christ died for nothing.

## *What is the purpose of the seventh section?*

In the Antioch discourse this was St Paul's final appeal to the Jewish Christians not to return to the Jewish way of life. It contains a severe warning: if they return to Judaism, they will cut themselves off from the grace of Christ. St Paul lays down a canon for their future guidance, pronounces a blessing on all who accept it, jokes a little at St Peter's expense (St Paul casts a spell to counter Peter's witchcraft!), and ends with a blessing. If this reconstruction is correct, St Paul tried hard to maintain friendly relations with Peter (cf. 6: 1).

In the structure of the Epistle, section seven is the beginning of the 'moral section', in which St Paul exhorts the Galatians to defend their liberty and to resist two contrary temptations: on the one hand, they must not submit to the slavery of a legalistic religion again (5: 1); and on the other hand, they must not make their liberty an excuse for libertinism (5: 13). The Jews at Antioch had no need of this latter warning, which is developed at some length in the eighth section.

The seventh and eighth sections both present a choice. In the seventh, both Jews and Gentiles are presented with the choice between the law and freedom, that is, between Judaism and Christianity. In

---

[3]   *Zuma*, the Greek word for 'yeast' is derived from *zeô* 'to ferment'.
[4]   The vocabulary used here is paralleled in magical papyri. See G in G, p. 224.

the eighth, the Gentiles are confronted with the radical choice between two ways of life — the life of the Spirit or the life of the flesh.

*The First Subsection, 5:1-6*

## CHRISTIAN LIBERTY AND JEWISH SLAVERY

**A**   *5 : 1* Christ has freed us in order to remain free;   **B**   stand firm, then, and do not submit again to the yoke of slavery.   **C**   *2* See! I, Paul, declare to you that if you have yourselves circumcised, Christ will not help you.   [*3*]   **D**   *4* You are cut off from the power of Christ,   **E**   all who seek justification in the law;   **D¹**   you are banished from his grace. **C¹**   *5* For it is by the Spirit through faith that we receive the justification that is our hope.   **B¹**   *6* For in Christ Jesus neither circumcision is of any avail, nor its absence,   **A¹**   but only faith made effective through (Christ's) charity. [5]

*Why are Christians under an obligation to preserve their freedom?*

In v. 1, St Paul gives only one reason. He says: 'Christ has truly made you free; he has freed you in order that you may remain free [6] — that is why you must stand firm and refuse to take up again the yoke of slavery.' He bases the Christian's obligation on the will of Christ. Since it is Christ's will that those whom he has redeemed should remain free, any Christian who returns to the law is failing in his duty; he is like a follower of Moses going back to Egypt. [6a]

The remoter context suggests a further reason. The Christian enjoys the freedom of a son of God, and it is the Father's will that his sons should no longer be under the law as a pedagogue. They must now get used to living as adults (cf. 3 : 26—4 : 5).

St John Chrysostom adds a further reason. Christ liberated his disciples at great cost to himself; he paid the ransom-money. [7] They are therefore indebted to him as their benefactor. To return to the law would be to set his gift at nought, or to throw it away as valueless. This argument might be developed by saying that through his sacrifice Christ 'acquired' us as his 'own people' [8] and as his 'servants' (cf.

---

[5]   On the ambiguity of the Greek here, see G in G, p. 193.
[6]   Cf. G in G, p. 186.
[6a]  Cf. Rabbi H. A. Cohen, quoted above, p. 51, n. 8.
[7]   Cf. Chrysostom, PG 61, 663 D.
[8]   Cf. 1 Pet 2 : 9 (based on Exod 19 : 5).

Gal 6:16); hence to go back to the law is to desert one's rightful Lord and Master. — This third argument is quite in line with St Paul's thinking (cf. Rom 6:16-23), but he does not use it in Galatians — at least in the text as it stands. There was a hint of it in the Antioch discourse, since the prologue of it included the verse: 'I do not set aside God's free gift (redemption); for if justification is from the law, Christ died for nothing.'

## Was St Paul justified in calling the law a 'yoke of slavery'?

What St Paul's previous argument has implied, he now states openly: that the law is a 'yoke of slavery'. No doubt this statement was, as it still is, extremely offensive to the Jews, who regard the law as a precious gift bestowed on Israel by God.

Christ himself said something similar, but he was careful to make it plain that he was attacking not the law itself, properly understood, but rather the scribes and Pharisees who expounded the law and overloaded it with their traditions (Mt 23:2-4):

> Since the scribes and Pharisees have occupied the chair of Moses, you must heed and do all they say to you. But do not imitate what they do, for they do not obey their own teaching. They bind heavy and unbearable burdens and pile them on other men's shoulders, but themselves never stir a finger to move them.

In Galatians, St Paul neglects to make this distinction. He speaks as if the law itself were a yoke of slavery, and does not distinguish between the law itself and the 'traditions' of the Pharisees. Writing in a different mood, and addressing himself to a different problem, in Romans (9:4) he reckons possession of the law as one of the privileges of Israel. It is easy to see how he incurred charges of inconsistency.

## Why does St Paul name himself in v. 2?

(1) In the Antioch discourse, St Paul said to the Jewish Christians: 'Look! I, Paul, hereby inform you that if you follow the Jewish way of life, or if you continue to rely on your circumcision and seek justification from the law, you are cut off from Christ's grace and will receive no further strength from him!' To judge from the counterpart in 6:17, he meant: 'I, Paul, who bear in my body the scars of my sufferings on the mission — I, Paul, who have proved myself an apostle by preaching the gospel and suffering for the gospel.'

He is tacitly contrasting himself with St Peter, who by his example is teaching the Jewish Christians not to obey the truth (cf. 5:7; 2:14). He is quietly reminding the church of Antioch that he too, Paul, is an apostle and servant of Christ.

It is much less likely that St Paul is alluding to his own Jewish past. He does not mean: 'I, Paul, who used to be so excessively zealous for the law, tell you that if you observe the law, Christ will not help you.' Nor is he drawing a lesson from his own post-conversion experience of the law. In vv. 2-4, he does not mean: 'Whenever, since my conversion, I have returned to the practice of the law, I have found myself cut off from Christ's influence.' On the occasions when he returned to the observance of the law (e.g. when visiting Jerusalem), he did not seek justification from it.

(2) In the context of the Epistle, 5:2 means: 'I, Paul, the apostle of Christ.' But the counterpart in this seventh section gives it a further point: 'I, Paul, who am said to be preaching circumcision (v. 11)! I tell you the exact opposite: If you have yourselves circumcised, you are cut off from Christ.' [9]

*What are the consequences of judaizing according to St Paul?*

(1) At Antioch, when Barnabas and the other Jewish Christians decided to withdraw, they probably did so in order to remain in Eucharistic communion with St Peter. St Paul now tells them that if they continue in this course of action, they are cut off from Christ and banished from his grace. He does not say that they are to be expelled from the Church or excluded from the Eucharist, since they are forming a church of their own and celebrating their own Eucharist. But he does imply that their Eucharist will be ineffectual: they are cut off from the power of Christ, for they are departing from the true gospel (cf. 2:14).

(2) In the Epistle, St Paul adds a warning to the Galatians that if a man has himself circumcised, he incurs an obligation to fulfil the whole of the law. (It would have been appropriate for St Paul to tell the Galatians whether they must expel such a man and exclude him from the Eucharist; but he has not revised this section to this extent.) Henceforth, he must seek justification from the law — a hopeless undertaking, of course — for Christ will not help him. [10]

---

9   Cf. Lagrange, Gal, ad loc.
10  Neither the apostolic decretal of Acts 15:23-29 nor Didache 6:1-2 goes so far as to prohibit circumcision.

P

*Was St Paul justified in threatening these dire consequences?*

(1) At Antioch, St Paul implied that those who were returning to the observance of the law were doing so in order to seek justification through the law. He tells them that this is a tragic mistake: the result will be the exact opposite of what they intend. They do not please God by returning to the law; they displease him to such an extent that they are banished from his grace. In the language of moral theology, he is telling them that their present conduct is *materially* a grave sin, and that if, after his solemn apostolic warning (v. 2), they persist in this line of conduct, they will be committing a *formally* grave sin.

St Paul does not regard the conduct of the Jewish Christians as excusable by reason of their good intentions. They are acting *as if* the law were still binding, and are obscuring in their own minds and in the minds of others the true demands of the gospel. [11] For the common good of the Church, St Paul could not leave them in good faith. He had to show them the error of their ways. What they were doing was directly contrary to the intention of God when he sent his Son into the world (cf. 4:4). To oppose God in this way with their eyes open would be gravely sinful and would deserve the dire penalties which St Paul threatens.

(2) Re-addressing his words to the Galatians, St Paul tells them that it is impossible to please God by submitting to circumcision. As a religious act, circumcision is the rite whereby a man accepts the yoke of the Mosaic law. It is absurd for the Galatians to say: 'We wish to undergo circumcision as a religious rite, without however accepting the yoke of the law.' If they submit to circumcision, they are formally consigning themselves to the condition of slavery which Christ came to abolish. They are rejecting Christ, and betaking themselves to another master whom Christ came to supplant. They must know, therefore, that for the future if any Christian submits to circumcision, he is committing a formal act of apostasy.

St Paul does not say what is to be done if any members of the Galatian churches have already had themselves circumcised without realizing the implications of what they were doing. Once again, he has omitted a distinction which seems to us of great importance. If there were such members of the Galatian churches, they must have wondered whether St Paul meant that they could not repent and be reinstated. Here, then, is a point at which St Paul's theology, as expressed in his Epistles, *required* development. He did not leave a

---

[11] On 'the truth of the gospel' see below, pp. 427-428.

complete and perfect system, to be passed on unrevised and unde-
veloped from one generation to another for ever.

*Why does St Paul insist that judaizing Christians must fulfil the whole
of the law?*

The Galatians surely knew that to submit to circumcision was to
take upon oneself the yoke of the law of Moses — presumably the
judaizing teachers had told them this (cf. Acts 15 : 5). Why then does
St Paul insist? Probably what he means is: 'If you cut yourself off
from the justification that comes through faith in Christ, you must
look elsewhere for justification, and you will find that the only way
left is the way of the law; but this means fulfilment of the *whole* of
the law, as I explained above (3 : 10). [12] Therefore be warned: if you
commit yourself to the Jewish way of life, you are setting yourself
the impossible task of fulfilling the whole of the law. If you will not
trust Christ to help you, you will be left in your own weakness to
carry a burden which even the Jews themselves cannot endure.'

From 4 : 10 and 5 : 3 we learn that some Gentile Christians wished
(a) to be circumcised, and (b) to observe the Jewish calendar. St Paul
is replying: 'You cannot stop there — you must also observe the
food laws, the law of tithes, the laws of purification, and so on.' If
the Galatians wished to adopt *only* circumcision and the Jewish calendar, a possible explanation of their selection might be that the
persons in question were Gentile Christian slaves, who had been
told by Jewish visitors that if they and their Christian masters submitted to circumcision and observed the Jewish law, at the next
sabbatical year their masters would be required to liberate their Christian slaves. [13] It is curious to reflect that if St Paul had allowed his
Gentile churches to accept the Jewish calendar *in toto,* the conscience
of Christendom would have been quickened much sooner to the iniquity
of slavery. It was left to the apostles to decide which parts of the
Jewish law were to remain binding and which were not; [14] it is perhaps
to be regretted that they did not retain more of the social legislation
contained in the Old Testament. [15]

However, the above hypothesis has little probability. If the Galatian sympathizers were slaves bent on escaping from their servile

---

[12] Chrysostom elaborates the point convincingly in PG 61, 644 B: if a man
respects a part of the law, he respects the law itself, and must therefore obey
all its parts. Cf. Jas 2 : 10.
[13] Cf. Exod 21 :2; Deut 15 :12; Philo, *The Special Laws,* II, 79-85 (Loeb, VII).
[14] See above, p. 232.
[15] Cf. J. Bligh, 'Eschatology and Social Doctrine,' HJ 3 (1962), pp. 262-267.

condition, St Paul would probably have included some special word for slaves, and some judgment upon their motives. Moreover, his argument in 5:3 would probably not have deterred such slaves; they would reply: 'We will willingly adopt the Jewish food laws and any other customs you choose to mention, if we can thereby escape the social stigma of slavery. What you call "slavery to the law of Moses" is almost complete freedom by comparison with our present wretched condition.' According to St Paul, there is no difference *before God* between slave and free, once they have been baptized (cf. 3:28), but the social disabilities of slaves remain. One wonders whether Christian slaves were satisfied with this doctrine. If a man is hungry, a fine sermon which will satisfy his spiritual hunger is a poor substitute for a square meal. St Paul's whole contention that obedience to the law is as bad as slavery is a little tactless, if the churches of Antioch and Galatia included even a small proportion of slaves.

The most likely explanation of St Paul's insistence on fulfilment of *all* that is written in the Book of the law is that the judaizing teachers attached far more importance to circumcision than to any other ceremonial observance — and indeed paid no more than lip-service to most of the law's demands. [16] Their own observance of the law, judged by St Paul's high Pharisaic standards, was inadequate (cf. 6:13). Once again, St Paul is retorting an argument of his adversaries: they say: 'Paul has not explained to you the full demands of the gospel'; he replies: 'They have not explained to you the full demands of the law.'

## *Is Heb 12:14-17 dependent on Gal 5:4?*

Heb 12:14-17 is one of the rigoristic passages in Hebrews which seem to deny the possibility of repentance after grave post-baptismal sin:

> Strive to live at peace with everyone and to attain the sanctity without which no one will see the Lord. See that none of you fails to respond to God's grace. See that no poisonous weed grows up to disturb you and infect your whole community. See that none of you is a fornicator, or a materialist like Esau, who for the sake of one meal sold his right as first-born. Afterwards, as you remember, when he wished to receive the blessing due to the heir, he was rejected; he was given no chance for repentance, although he begged for it with tears.

The community addressed is urged to root up the weeds growing among the corn lest the whole church be infected (cf. Gal 5:9). The

---

16   See above, Introduction, p. 34.

readers are warned against selling their right to an inheritance for the sake of a meal — which is just what they would do if they adopted the Jewish food laws (cf. Gal 5:4). The following verses (Heb 12:18-24) contrast Christianity with Judaism; and the meals in question are treated as a threat to peace (12:14). It is therefore a reasonable conjecture that the author of Hebrews had Gal 5:2-4 in mind when writing the above passage, and therefore that the rigorism of v. 17 derives from a strict interpretation of Gal 5:4. Both authors are warning vacillating Christians that, as a general rule, apostates prove intractable and do not repent. Philo makes the same observation about apostates from Judaism: 'It is difficult, or rather it is impossible, for an apostate to be corrected.' [17]

*Is justification transferred to the future in v. 5?*

V. 5 is not easy to construe. The RSV has: 'For through the Spirit, by faith, we wait for the hope of righteousness' — which seems to project justification not only into the future but into the further reaches of the future: in the present the Holy Spirit enables us to wait — for the hope which is to come in the future, and for the righteousness which will fulfil this hope in a remoter future. The NEB brings the hope into the present: 'For to us, our hope of attaining that righteousness which we eagerly await is the work of the Spirit through faith.' But this still projects justification into the future.

Earlier statements in Galatians, particularly 2:16—3:4 (and still more the parallels in Rom 5:1, 9), speak of justification as something which happens to the believer here and now, in the present, as soon as he believes. These earlier statements can be harmonized with 5:5 by recognizing that St Paul uses the verb 'to be justified' both of first justification and of last justification. [18] When a sinner believes in Christ, God initiates a process of justification which is completed only at the Judgment. The man receives, to start with, as a free gift, or a pure grace, the 'first instalment' of the Spirit which strengthens him and enables him to run his course. If with the aid of the Spirit he perseveres to the end in obedience to the truth, his justification will be completed by the spiritualization of his whole person, body included (cf. 1 Cor 15:44), and by his 'justification' in the juridical sense, before the tribunal of God. [19]

[17] Quoted by Spicq, *L'Epître aux Hébreux*, I, p. 57, from *Rewards and Punishments*, 49 (Loeb VIII).
[18] See above, pp. 201 and 205.
[19] Cf. Mt 25:37, where the sheep at God's right hand are called 'the just'.

Gal 5:5 contains a good example of the studied ambiguity of language which St Paul uses to express the ambiguity of the Christian's interim position: we are justified, but only in principle; and we have the Holy Spirit, but only the first instalment. The compound verb which he uses (*ap-ek-dechometha*) contains the idea of *receiving from* another (*apo-dechesthai*) and of *eagerly awaiting* some future event (*ek-dechesthai*). Through faith we here and now *receive* the first instalment of the justifying Spirit, and we *look forward* to the completion of this gift at the resurrection of our bodies (cf. Rom 8:23). In v. 5, then, justification is not transferred wholly to the future — there is still an allusion to our present reception of the Spirit — but whereas in the earlier chapters of the Epistle the emphasis has been on first justification, from this point onwards St Paul begins to devote his attention to the final justification.

## Is v. 6a consistent with v. 2?

In v. 6a St Paul says: 'In Christ Jesus neither circumcision nor its absence is of any avail; what counts is faith working through charity.' From this it might seem to follow that a Gentile Christian who has himself circumcised will neither gain nor lose by it; what matters is that he should live in faith and charity. But this conflicts with v. 2, where St Paul said that a Gentile who has himself circumcised cuts himself off from Christ.

According to the reconstruction given on p. 414, this little anomaly was not present in the original Antioch discourse; it was introduced as a result of the revision of v. 2 and the insertion of v. 3 for the benefit of the Galatians. At Antioch, St Paul was telling the Jewish Christians that as Christians they must set no store by their circumcision: 'In Christ Jesus', that is to say, in the Church, there are uncircumcised Gentile Christians and circumcised Jewish Christians; both are running the same course; no one runs faster for being circumcised or slower for being uncircumcised; what matters is faith and the charity that draws its energy from faith.

In the Epistle, there is no real contradiction, because, by the law promulgated in vv. 2-4, any Gentile Christian who has himself circumcised thereby ceases to be 'in Christ Jesus'. Hence he is no exception to the dogma laid down in v. 6. And even the appearance of inconsistency vanishes once it is realized that the verb 'is of no avail' means, *not* 'is of no effect', but 'is of no avail towards our final justification.' St Paul is reassuring the Galatians that by remaining uncircumcised they will be no worse off than the Jewish Christians who

are circumcised — and no better off, either. The dogma is for Jew
and Gentile alike.

*What connections does St Paul make between faith, hope and charity?*

The three theological virtues of faith, hope and charity are all
named in vv. 5-6. St Paul is quite fond of this triad, which is probably
not of his own invention. [20] But he does not attempt to systematize
them as later theologians have done — for example, by saying that
faith generates hope, and hope charity, or that faith generates charity
and from the two proceeds hope.

The relationships sketched in vv. 5-6 are extremely complex. Faith
generates hope in us; but this hope is already fulfilled in so far as we
already possess the first instalment of the Spirit received in or through
faith; and in so far as our hope remains unfulfilled, it is a hope to
receive the blessings of final justification through faith. This faith,
which is generated in us by Christ's charity, generates charity in us,
because faith is self-committal to the will of Christ — which is the
law of charity. — If this explanation is becoming confused, that is
because faith, hope and charity form a unity. They are three parts
of the believer's response to the gospel. They defy systematization
because they are not sufficiently distinct from one another.

*In v. 6 does St Paul abandon his doctrine of justification by faith
alone?*

The Greek phrase used by St Paul at the end of v. 6 (*pistis
di'agapês energoumenê*) can mean either 'faith working through charity'
or 'faith energized by charity'. The first alternative is preferred by
most commentators, but comparison of v. 6 with its counterpart at
the beginning of the Antioch discourse shows that the second is not
to be excluded:

| | |
|---|---|
| *2 : 20* I live by faith in God and in Christ who loved me (*agapê-santos*)... | *5 : 6* In Christ Jesus neither circumcision is of any avail nor its absence, but only faith energized through love (Christ's love — cf. 2 Cor 5 : 14). |

As usual, it is best to suppose that St Paul wishes to profit by the
ambiguity of his language.

---

[20] Cf. A. M. Hunter, *Paul and His Predecessors*, London, ²1961; J. Bligh,
'Salvation by Hope,' *The Way* 8 (1968), p. 270.

But if the first alternative is admitted at all, the question arises whether St Paul is quietly modifying his doctrine of justification by faith alone and by modifying it *abandoning* it (since even the smallest modification destroys the 'alone'). There was no suggestion in 2:16 that a man is justified by faith only if his faith blossoms into works of charity.

The difficulty is no difficulty to those who accept the distinction between first justification and last. First justification is by faith alone, but final justification depends, in normal cases, [21] on faith working through charity. At the Judgment God will not simply ask: 'Did you believe the gospel?' He will ask: 'Did you commit the works of the flesh (5:19-21a)? Or did you cooperate with the Spirit in producing a spiritual harvest (5:22-23a)?' The man who has committed the works of the flesh, even though he believed the gospel, 'will not inherit the kingdom of God' (5:21b). Even at the end of the sixth section, therefore, St Paul had not said his last word on the question, Who is the heir of Abraham? Up to that point he insisted on faith; now, as his attention moves forward from first justification to last, he adds that faith must express itself in charity. [21a]

*The Second Subsection, 5:7-12*

## FAITH, CONFIDENCE AND PERSUASION

**A**  *5:7* You were running well. Who has put obstacles in your way? **B**  Do not let anyone persuade you not to obey the truth!  **C**  *8* Such persuasion is not from the one who calls you.  **D**  *9* A little yeast leavens the whole mass.  **E**  *10* I have confidence in you  **F**  in the Lord **E¹**  that you will not think otherwise.  **D¹**  But he who is upsetting you will bear the condemnation, whosoever he may be!  **C¹**  *11* But as for me, brethren, if I am still preaching circumcision, why am I still being persecuted?  **B¹**  For in that case the scandal of the cross would have lost its power.  **A¹**  *12* Would that those who are upsetting you would go further and castrate themselves!

The links between the corresponding sentences are as follows. Between A and A¹ the connection is concealed by the translation. In the Greek, *enekopsen* ('put obstacles') in v. 7 is from the same root as *apokopsontai* ('castrate') in v. 12. Perhaps St Paul intends v. 7 to

---

[21]  In the case of infants and others who die shortly after their baptism, there is no room for works of charity. But such persons will not be condemned for want of them, since *nemo tenetur ad impossibile*.

[21a]  Turner, *Grammatical Insights*, p. 112, remarks on Gal 5:6 that 'it is the very gospel insisted on by St James.' See above, p. 209.

mean: 'Who has taken away the manhood and strength in which like a giant you exulted to run your course?' In B and B¹ the reader is warned that if he abandons the truth, the cross, which is a scandal to reason and yet a source of energy to the believer, will cease to 'energize' him. C and C¹ shows that St Paul, the 'one who called' the Galatians, does not believe in circumcision, whatever his adversaries may say about him. The proverb used in D can have various applications. Taken in connection with D¹, the 'yeast' stands for the evil influence of those who are upsetting the Galatians. According to E and E¹, Paul has confidence in the Galatians that they will have confidence in him.

The corresponding part of the closing section of the Antioch discourse formed two overlapping patterns, thus:

**A**  *6* but only faith working through charity.   **B**  *7* You were running well. Who has put obstacles in your way?   **C**  Do not let anyone persuade you not to obey the truth!   **B¹**  *8* Such persuasion is not from the one who calls you.   **A¹**  *9* A little yeast leavens the whole mass.

**D**  *9* A little yeast leavens the whole mass.   **E**  *10* I have confidence in you in the Lord that you will not think otherwise.   *6:16* And all who walk by this rule,   **F**  peace be upon them and mercy   **G**  and upon the Israel of God.   **F¹**  *17* From now on, let no one disturb me,   **E¹**  for I bear in my body the stigmata of Jesus.   **D¹**  *18* The grace of our Lord Jesus Christ be with your spirit, brethren. Amen.

Here, the leaven is the grace of the Lord Jesus Christ which is at work transforming the spirit of the whole mass of believers — so long as they place their trust in the spiritual stigmata which mark them as belonging to Christ, and not in circumcision which is the mark of those who belong to the law.

*What does St Paul mean by 'truth' in v. 7?*

Of the two doctrines which are competing for acceptance and obedience, St Paul describes the one (his own) as 'the truth'. The whole context and the verb which immediately governs this noun show that the truth in question is not so much an affirmation as a precept. The 'truth' which must be 'obeyed' is imperative-and-prohibitive rather than affirmative and categoric. 'Justification is by faith alone' has the appearance of an affirmation; but in fact it is equivalent to a hypothetical imperative: 'If you wish to be saved, do not submit to circumcision and the law.' Similarly the doctrine of the Judaizers can be cast in the categoric form 'Circumcision is necessary for salvation,' but this is equivalent to: 'If you wish to be saved, you must be circumcised and live by the law of Moses (cf. Acts 15:1).

In English, we do not usually describe an imperative sentence as true or false. But there are two senses in which a sentence can be called true: first, if it corresponds to the mind of Christ, it can be called true Christian doctrine, even though Christ himself did not explicitly formulate it; and secondly, if the action prescribed or forbidden in the apodosis is in reality conducive to the end specified in the protasis.

The 'truth', therefore, which St Paul teaches is not simply something to be believed. It is also something to be done; and the doing of it is obedience. That is why he can speak of 'doing the truth' (cf. Eph 4:15) and of 'obeying the truth' (cf. Rom 2:8) — phrases which sound strange in English. [22]

In all its three occurrences in Galatians, the word 'truth' means 'practical truth' (2:5; 2:14; 5:7). 'The truth of the gospel' which St Paul preaches is a way of life, not simply a set of theological propositions to which the hearer must give intellectual assent. Such an assent is necessary, as a beginning; it then remains to walk consistently along the lines marked out by the practical propositions which have been accepted in the act of assent. The hearer of the gospel is not called upon simply to assent to the proposition that 'Justification is by faith alone'; the response required of him is one which commits him to the line of conduct which this concealed imperative requires: '*I* do wish to be saved, and therefore *I* will not submit to circumcision and the law.' That is what is meant by saying that the act of faith is an act of *personal commitment* or *engagement*. The 'truth' is not an impersonal theological proposition; it is an imperative addressed by Christ through his apostle to me: 'If *you* wish to be saved, etc.' And acceptance of this truth is an act of obedient submission made by *me* to Christ. No one will make this act of submission unless he first accepts the apostle as an apostle. I must first accept St Paul as an apostle, before I can accept his teaching as the 'true' doctrine of Christ. But having satisfied myself on this point, I accept his doctrine as the doctrine of Christ, and in committing myself to it, I am committing myself not to Paul but to Christ, for the word of command or prohibition comes, not from Paul, but from Christ. Christ responds to the believer's faith by granting the Holy Spirit, by leading him 'from faith to faith'; then the witness of the Holy Spirit supersedes the witness of the apostle. [23]

---

[22]  See the valuable essay of Prof. W. D. Davies, 'Torah and Dogma,' HTR 61 (1968), pp. 87-105, in which he calls for a less kerygmatic and more halakic interpretation of Christianity.

[23]  Cf. Rom 1:17; Jn 4:42.

*What connection does St Paul make between obedience and persuasion?*

In vv. 7-10, St Paul plays upon the various meanings of the Greek verb *peithesthai* — to be persuaded, to be won over, to comply, to yield, to obey, to trust, to have confidence in.

In v. 7b he says: 'Do not allow yourselves to be persuaded not to comply with the truth,' or in other words: 'Do not obey those who would persuade you (by word or example) not to obey the truth.' Then in v. 8 he adds a warning which can mean *either*: 'Such persuasion does not come from the one who is calling you,' that is to say, 'The Jewish visitors from Jerusalem and St Peter himself are not acting as God's mouthpiece in this matter,' *or*: 'Such obedience does not come from the one who is calling you,' that is to say, 'Your concession to the Jewish visitors may look like virtue, but in fact it is not the Holy Spirit who moves you to make them.' [24] In v. 10, St Paul uses another sense of the same verb: '*I have confidence in* you in the Lord that you will not think otherwise than as I do.'

This is not idle punning. It is true that St Paul is already writing playfully (see below on 6:17); but he is at the same time disclosing his ideas about the obedience which ecclesiastical authorities can expect of their 'brethren' (cf. 5:11) — whom he never calls their 'subjects'. The relationship between those in authority and the others must be one of mutual confidence. St Paul expects his hearers to trust him; he expects them to allow themselves to be persuaded and then to obey. He looks for obedience, but intelligent obedience. That is why he does not simply lay down the law for them, but first persuades them that what he is requiring of them is according to the mind of Christ. St Paul's hearers are to obey because they have been persuaded. They too have the Spirit, since they are 'in Christ' (cf. v. 10), and therefore St Paul can expect them to recognize the truth and wisdom of what the Spirit has enabled him to say.

The passage is an object lesson for the ecclesiastical authorities of later times. If they wish to declare any type of action gravely sinful, they should take great pains to explain why they are sure that such is the mind of Christ. They do not fulfil their whole duty by laying down the law; they must still use all their powers of persuasion to show the brethren that they are right. [25] And they must be very

---

[24] The phrase in v. 8, 'the one who is calling you,' contains the same ambiguity as the similar phrase in 1:6.
[25] Cf. J. L. McKenzie, 'Authority and Power in the New Testament,' CBQ 26 (1964), p. 418: 'For a practical demonstration of the power of love in action one can usefully study the letters of Paul. The efforts he makes to explain his

careful not to impose grave obligations where no grave obligations exist, for by so doing they would render intelligent obedience impossible.

### 'A little yeast' (v. 9) — Why does St Paul suddenly change his imagery here?

The reason why St Paul suddenly thinks of yeast and forgets about his race-track imagery is that he has before his mind the opening passage of the Antioch discourse where he said: 'It is no longer I who live, but Christ lives (or ferments) within me' (2:20). The noun yeast (*zumê*) is from the verb 'to ferment' (*zeô*). The power of Christ contained in the gospel quickly transforms the mass of mankind. But false doctrines, too, work quickly and unobtrusively. [26] V. 9 is probably a warning: the judaizing error must be rejected quickly, before it corrupts the whole Church. In the second subsection it is linked to the threat: 'He who is upsetting you will bear the condemnation.'

### Do vv. 7a and 10b refer principally to St Peter?

The parallel to v. 7a in the first half of the Antioch discourse is 3:1: 'Who has bewitched you?' (*tis hymas ebaskanen*). As was shown above, this was a half-playful allusion to the influence of St Peter's example. In 5:7a, therefore, St Paul may again be alluding to St Peter when he asks: 'Who has put obstacles in your way?' (*tis hymas enekopsen*). It was in fact the example of St Peter that had caused the Jewish Christians at Antioch to stop running along the course marked out for them by St Paul. V. 7 is probably meant to suggest that St Peter has again become a stumbling-block to Christ, this time to Christ in the person of his Jewish disciples (cf. Mt 16:23).

V. 10b, 'He who is upsetting you will bear the condemnation, whosoever he may be,' was probably not a part of the Antioch discourse (see p. 236). If St Paul introduced it in writing the Epistle, he probably had in mind the leader of the judaizing movement in Galatia

---

position to his churches offer an interesting contrast to many communications from modern church offices.' It should, however, be added that the reasons given by St Paul for the positions which he adopts are not always fully convincing, and he would expect obedience even from those not fully convinced. Cf. 1 Cor 11:16.

[26] St Jerome, PL 26, 430 C, illustrates v. 9 from the history of Arianism: 'Arius of Alexandria was one spark; because he was not promptly stamped out, his flame devastated the whole world.'

— not, therefore, St Peter himself. [27] But on the other hand, v. 10b harks back to 1:7-9, where St Paul declared anathema anyone, however exalted, even an angel from heaven, who should preach a gospel at variance with his own. In the structure of the second section (see p. 121), 1:8-9 is linked to 2:6-9, where St Paul speaks of 'those who seem to be pillars' of the Church, namely James, Cephas and John. There is, therefore, some reason to suspect that the phrase 'whoever he may be' includes, in St Paul's mind, 'even Peter'. If so, in this seventh section, St Paul's reference to himself in 5:2 is balanced by an obscure reference to St Peter in 5:10 (see p. 414).

*What are the implications of v. 11?*

V. 11 comes as a surprise: 'If I am still preaching circumcision, why am I still persecuted?' St Paul cannot have said this at Antioch, for everyone there knew that he did not preach circumcision; and besides, he was not being persecuted.

The verse is intelligible only on the supposition that the Judaizers in Galatia were saying that elsewhere St Paul was teaching the necessity of circumcision. [28] In other words, they were charging him with inconsistency. St Paul replies by charging *them* with inconsistency. Why do the Jews go on persecuting him? It is because they know that he is *not* preaching circumcision in the Gentile churches, but forbidding it. Their actions refute the charges they are making.

The retort is not entirely successful. The Judaizers could reply: 'We are not "persecuting" Paul; we are showing up his inconsistency; we are denouncing him here in Galatia not because he preaches circumcision elsewhere but because he did not preach it here.' However, v. 11 is only a debating point, thrown in hurriedly.

*Why is the cross a 'scandal'?*

In 5:11 St Paul implies that if he preached circumcision, the cross would cease to be a stumbling-block to the Jews. It seems, then, that

---

[27] St Jerome, PL 26, 431 A, argues that v. 10 cannot refer to St Peter because 'Paul would not speak ill of the Prince of the Church in such an insolent fashion, nor did Peter deserve to be held guilty of upsetting the Church.'

[28] Cf. Rom 3:1-2. They may also have argued that if Peter was preaching Judaism when he ate with the Jews, Paul was preaching circumcision when he circumcised Timothy. E. Haenchen, *Die Apostelgeschichte*, Ed. 11, Göttingen, 1957, pp. 427-428, thinks that in Acts 16:3 St Luke unwittingly preserved an unreliable tradition. But on the contrary, Acts 16:3 helps us to understand how the accusation arose which St Paul rejects in Gal 5:11.

what offends the Jews is the doctrine that the cross of Christ has
made circumcision unnecessary or rather irrelevant to justification and
salvation (cf. 5:6). This is surprising. One would have thought that
the essential scandal of the cross was that God had sent his Messiah
and the chosen people had rejected him, or that God had sent his
own Son and men had executed him as a criminal.

It is, however, a historical fact that the Jews were willing to
tolerate Christianity as a sect within Judaism so long as its members
obeyed the law. The Jews were remarkably tolerant of dissident
opinions; but they reacted quickly and violently against anyone who
broke the law or called in question the privilege of Israel as God's
chosen people. [29] The gospel of the cross, as preached by St Paul,
meant that the law was obsolete, and salvation was open to Jews and
Gentiles on the same terms.

If St Paul had preached the necessity of circumcision, the cross
would have lost its power to shock the Jews, but it would also have
lost its power to help the believer, since according to vv. 2-4 the
believer who has himself circumcised is thereby cut off from the
power of Christ.

St Paul does not say that the cross is a 'scandal' to the Gentiles.
The Gentiles have no cause to be shocked if he preaches that the law
is obsolete and that the privileges of Israel are now open to all
mankind. In 1 Cor 1:23 St Paul says that Christ crucified is 'to the
Jews a scandal, and to the Gentiles folly.' As this passage casts
valuable light on the notion of 'the scandal of the cross', it deserves
to be quoted:

> The Jews ask for signs (*sêmeia*),
> and the Greeks seek wisdom (*sophian*);
> but we preach Christ crucified —
> to the Jews a scandal (*skandalon*),
> and to the Gentiles folly (*môrian*).
> But to those who are called, both Jews and Greeks,
> Christ the power of God (*dynamin* [30])
> and the wisdom of God (*sophian*).

The Greeks (or Gentiles) ask for 'wisdom' and God gives them in
the gospel what looks like 'folly' but is in fact the wisdom of God;
the Jews ask for 'signs' (manifestations of power) and God gives them
a 'scandal' which looks like weakness but is in fact the power of God.
Just as folly is opposed to wisdom, so a 'scandal' is opposed to a
'sign' (the 'sign' guarantees faith, the 'scandal' tends to overthrow it).

---

[29] Cf. Baum, *The Jews and the Gospel,* pp. 230-231; Schmithals, *Paul and
James,* p. 37.
[30] *Dynamis* and *sêmeion* are almost synonymous in some of their uses.

To say that the cross is a 'scandal' means, therefore, that it is a manifestation of God's power which appears to the unbeliever to be a manifestation of weakness.

St Paul is using a deliberate oxymoron when he suggests that 'the scandal of the cross might lose its power.' In place of 'scandal' we might have expected its opposite, 'power': 'If I were to preach circumcision, the *power* of the cross would be cut off.' St Paul writes instead: 'the scandal of the cross would be cut off.' The cross would neither *seem* a scandal to the unbelieving Jew, nor *be* a source of power to the believer.

To the believer the cross still seems a scandal, in so far as it is an affront to his natural wisdom. His own reason would never have led him to imagine that God would redeem sinners in this way. Only faith, submission to the teaching authority of God's apostles, makes it possible to believe that the 'folly' of God is greater than human 'wisdom', and the 'weakness' of God is greater than human 'power'.

*Does v. 12 contain an allusion to ritual castration?*

V. 12 may mean either 'Would that these disturbers of the peace would cut themselves off [31] (from the Christian community)', or 'Would that these disturbers of the peace would castrate themselves!' Theodore of Mopsuestia adopted the second view, offering this paraphrase: 'If they think that a frivolous excision of flesh is something good, let them cut off their genitals completely and gain still greater advantages!' [32] Probably St Paul intended both senses. It is his custom, when saying something offensive, to cover his tracks by using words which need not necessarily bear the offensive meaning. [33] According to Aristotle, sophisticated insolence of this kind is the mark of a witty man. But few critics would call St Paul witty. [34]

---

[31]  Cf. Mt 5:29-30.
[32]  Theodore, Gal, p. 93. Bring, Gal, p. 243, agrees: 'This combination of circumcision and castration must have seemed to the Jews as pure blasphemy. . . . St Paul does not hesitate to use the most violent and offensive words.'
[33]  M. Barth, 'Was Paul an anti-Semite?' JES 5 (1968), pp. 78-104, attempts to show that St Paul himself never said anything offensive or hurtful to the Jews; the offensive meanings have always been read into his words by interpreters who have misunderstood him. It is true that he never says anything which is *necessarily* offensive. Barth is right in his judgment (p. 96) that Paul 'stands in the tradition of the prophets like Jeremiah who had to say in God's name cruel words to their own people.'
[34]  An American pupil of mine (Rev. J. K. Mott) once wrote a dialogue between a TV interviewer and St Paul, which ended something like this: 'One last question, Paul: is there anything in your life that you now regret?' Answer: 'I guess I took myself too darn seriously.'

The parallel in the conclusion to the Antioch discourse (6:17) contains an allusion to religious branding and tatooing. St Paul means that Jewish circumcision is not so very different from the ritual self-castration and the branding of stigmata practised by the pagan priests of Cybele in Phrygia and Galatia. Rituals which attach great significance to a surgical operation on the male member belong to a primitive stage of religion, which is now dead and buried, or ought to be. [35]

From the point of view of moral theology, there is of course no comparison between circumcision and self-castration, since circumcision does not frustrate the reproductive faculty. Quite the contrary, according to Philo. [36]

---

[35] H. von Campenhausen, who regards this 'bloody wisecrack' as the starting-point of Christian humour, denies that there is any allusion to ritual castration in v. 12. See his much too ponderous article, 'Ein Witz des Apostles Paulus und die Anfänge des christlichen Humors,' in *Neutestamentliche Studien für Rudolf Bultmann* (Beiheft zur ZNTW, 21), 2. Aufl., Berlin, 1957, pp. 189-193. St Jerome spends a whole column excusing this wisecrack—cf. PL 26, 432C-433D; and St Thomas gives two highly improbable interpretations: (1) 'May they become spiritual eunuchs' (cf. Mt 19:12), and (2) 'May their marriages be infertile'—lest they beget children to inherit and perpetuate their error.

[36] Cf. Philo, *The Special Laws*, I, 7 (Loeb, VII). As a matter of topical interest, here are Philo's views on birth-control (*The Special Laws*, III, 36): 'Those who sue for marriage with women whose sterility has already been proved with other husbands, do but copulate like pigs or goats, and their names should be inscribed in the lists of the impious as adversaries of God. For while God in his love both for mankind and all that lives spares no care to effect the preservation and permanence of every race, those persons who make an art of quenching the life of the seed as it drops, stand confessed as the enemies of nature.'

# TWO WAYS: FLESH AND SPIRIT

If the seventh section was the conclusion of the Antioch discourse, the eighth will be the beginning of the second half of the framework which St Paul compiled for the benefit of the Galatians. But it may not have been composed explicitly for the Epistle. It contains important ideas which St Paul must have used again and again in his oral preaching. Here is the text.

**A** *5 : 13b* But serve one another in charity. *14* For the whole law is fulfilled in obeying this one precept: 'You shall love your neighbour as yourself.' **B** *15* But if you rend and devour one another, beware lest you be destroyed by one another. **C** *16* What I mean is: walk by the Spirit and you will not fulfil the lust of the flesh. *17* For the flesh lusts against the spirit, and the spirit against the flesh (for these are opposed to each other), to prevent you from doing whatever you want. **D** *18* But if you are led by the Spirit, you are not under the law. **E** *19* It is plain what are the works of the flesh: fornication, impurity, licentiousness; *20* idolatry, sorcery; enmities, strife, jealousy, fits of anger, quarrels, dissensions, intrigues, *21* envy; drukenness, orgies, and things like these. **F** I warn you now as I warned you before, that those who do such things will not inherit the kingdom of God. **E¹** *22* But the harvest of the Spirit is charity, joy, peace, patience, kindness, goodness, fidelity, *23* gentleness, self-control. **D¹** Against such things as these there is no law. **C¹** *24* Those who belong to Christ Jesus have crucified the flesh with its passions and its lusts. *25* If we live by the spirit, let us also walk by the spirit. **B¹** *26* Let us not be eager for vain glory, provoking one another, envying one another. *6 : 1* Brethren, if a man falls into some misdeed, you who are spiritual must put him right, in a spirit of gentleness, with an eye on yourself, lest you too be tempted. **A¹** *2* Bear one another's burdens, and so you will fulfil the law of Christ.

The analysis is as follows.

A   Love is the fulfilment of the law, 5 : 13b-14.
B   Do not carp at one another, 5 : 15.
C   Flesh and spirit are in conflict; follow the Spirit, 5 : 16-17.
D   Then you will not be under law, 5 : 18.
E   The works of the flesh, 5 : 19-21a.
F   *The law of Christ*, 5 : 21b.
E¹   The harvest of the Spirit, 5 : 22-23a.
D¹   Law does not prohibit these things, 5 : 23b.
C¹   Crucify the flesh and walk by the Spirit, 5 : 24-25.
B¹   Be gentle in fraternal correction, 5 : 26—6 : 1.
A¹   Love is the fulfilment of the law of Christ, 6 : 2.

The only parts which have special reference to the Galatian situation are B and B[1]. Reasons will be given below for thinking that 5:15 and 6:1 were inserted at the time when the Epistle was written.[1] For the rest, the section is a warning that Christian freedom does not mean the end of all obligations; it does not mean that the flesh is released from all restraints and permitted to follow its own lusts. St Paul is not preaching libertinism.

Such warnings were needed. The language used by St Paul in attacking the Jewish law was perhaps at times intemperate and ill-chosen. He seemed to be attacking not only the ceremonial laws of Judaism, but all laws in general. When he told the Gentiles that they were no longer 'under law' (cf. 5:18), he was sowing the seeds of misunderstanding. We can with great difficulty sort out, more or less satisfactorily, what he was getting at in his various statements about the law. But when we have done so, we have to admit that he spoke with regrettable obscurity on this important matter. He says that the Christian is 'not under law', then adds that he is obliged to fulfil the law of Christ (6:2) — and this under pain of exclusion from the kingdom of heaven (5:21). Is not a Christian who obeys the law of Christ for fear of exclusion from the kingdom 'under the law of Christ'? Vv. 18-23 seem to imply that a Christian is not 'under the law' so long as he willingly follows the guidance of the Spirit. But then what did St Paul mean in 4:4 when he said that Christ 'became under the law'? Surely something else, for he did not abandon the guidance of his own Spirit.[2] And for the ordinary Christian, does it make sense to say that he is not 'under the law' until he breaks the law? How is it possible to break a law if one is not under it?

Our reverence for St Paul should not deter us from admitting that his statements about law are confused and misleading. The Church, like any other society, must have its law, and her members are subject to this law. Ask an ordinary Christian of today whether he is 'under a law', and he will reply that he is: he has been taught that certain types of action have been forbidden by Christ (either personally or through the authentic interpreters of the moral tradition which he founded) under the severest of penalties; and he has been taught that he has positive obligations in charity, omission to fulfil which will be punished with the same severity. He holds these precepts and pro-hibitions in reverence as a law to which he is subject. He does not resent the law or find it irksome, but it remains a law and he remains its subject. On this matter, the Church no longer uses the language

---

[1]   See below, pp. 437-438 and 469.
[2]   Cf. St Jerome, PL 26, 442 A.

of St Paul, [2a] which was called forth by his controversy with the Judaizers, and was not above criticism even then.

In the present section, he is attempting to forestall misunderstanding and criticism of his doctrine of freedom from law. He shows that the Christian *has* obligations to fulfil. He has been freed from slavery to the law of the Jews in order that he may become the slave of his neighbour (v. 13). He has been freed from the law of Moses, but must still fulfil the law of Christ (6:2). He must no longer seek justification through the practice of specifically religious acts of ritual; he must seek it through the service of his neighbour. If 'religion' means the attempt to win God's favour by the performance of a series of ritual acts laid down in a 'law' or code of ceremonial, this Epistle is an attack on religion. Its message is that truly religious actions, the acts by which God's favour is preserved (not won), are works of charity done in the service of one's neighbour. This is the law of Christ. As St James puts it in his Epistle (1:27): 'religion that is pure and undefiled in the sight of God our Father means this: to assist orphans and widows in their loss, and keep oneself untarnished by the world.'

*The First Subsection, 5:13-16*

## FREEDOM TO SERVE

A   *5:13* You have been called to freedom, brethren,   B   only, do not turn your freedom into an occasion for the flesh.   C   But serve one another in charity,   D   *14* for the whole law is fulfilled in obeying one precept: 'You shall love your neighbour as yourself.'   C¹   *15* But if you bite one another and rend one another, beware or you will be ruined by one another. B¹   *16* What I mean is: walk by the spirit,   A¹   and you will not fulfil the lust of the flesh.

V. 15 was probably added at the time when this passage was incorporated in the Epistle. Without it, the centre would be better balanced:

---

[2a] Cf. Paul VI, *Humanae Vitae*, 4: 'Let none of Christ's disciples deny that the interpretation of natural moral law falls within the competence of the Teaching Authority of the Church. For, as our predecessors have frequently declared, there is no doubt that when Christ Jesus communicated his divine power to Peter and the other apostles and sent them to teach all nations his precepts, he made them reliable guardians and interpreters of all law concerning morality, that is, not only of evangelical law but also of natural law. For natural law too declares the will of God, faithful observance of which is necessary for man's eternal salvation.'

C    But serve one another in charity,
D    *for the whole law is fulfilled in obeying one precept:*
C¹  'You shall love your neighbour as yourself.'


*What kind of liberty is St Paul referring to in v. 13?*


When St Paul says: 'You have been called to freedom,' he certainly means 'to freedom from law' (cf. 4:5), but he also means 'to freedom from sin'. The assurance of freedom in A is matched and explained by the assurance of power over the lust of the flesh in A¹. The end (A¹) and the centre (D) both contain the verb 'to fulfil': a man fulfils either the law of charity or the lust of the flesh. The implication is that the lust of the flesh is another law, antagonistic to the law of charity; in Rom 7:23 it is called 'the law of Sin in my members'. The freedom proclaimed in A includes, therefore, besides freedom from the law of Moses, freedom from the law of the flesh or the tyranny of lust. Before a man is called to freedom in Christ, he is the slave of Sin (or concupiscence) lodged in his own members, because he finds himself unable to hold out for long against temptation. Sooner or later, he will succumb to the imperious demands of the flesh. Christ liberates the believer from this slavery by communicating to him the power of the Spirit. Strengthened in this way, the Christian is able to resist the law of Sin, though not always without a struggle. The liberty which he enjoys is, in the language of St Augustine, 'liberty not to sin' (*posse non peccare*), not inability to sin (*non posse peccare*).

The central part of this subsection adds the further explanation that Christian freedom is liberation of the *spirit* (from the tyranny of the flesh) so that we can *serve* one another, not liberation of the *flesh* (from the control of the spirit) so that we can *tear* one another to pieces. In the whole section there is a further point of contrast: instead of rending one another's flesh (v. 15), Christians must crucify their own (v. 24).

Thus Christian freedom does not consist in *indifference* in regard to the Two Ways of living; it is not a psychological condition of readiness for good and bad conduct alike. Psychologically, the more a Christian is possessed by the Spirit, the less he is capable of doing the works of the flesh. As his liberty is perfected, he approaches more and more closely to the liberty of Christ who was unable to sin, yet was perfectly free because he had complete mastery over his own acts. St Thomas quotes Aristotle's dictum that 'a man is free who is the cause of his own act' (*liber est qui est causa sui*) and thus explains how charity unites freedom and service:[3]

> Charity, as regards its moving cause, possesses liberty, because it works *a se* (from within). Hence St Paul says (2 Cor 5:14): 'The charity of Christ urges me' — that is, to work spontaneously. But charity is also a servant in that it disregards its own advantage and adapts itself to the advantage of others.

### *What does St Paul mean by 'the flesh' and 'the spirit'?*

'Flesh' and 'spirit' are the names of the two conflicting principles of conduct active in each man. St Paul does not identify the man with either flesh or spirit; nor does he say that the two together make up the man (like the body and soul in Plato's philosophy). Rather, the man himself, the 'I', is distinct from the flesh and the spirit, since he can align himself with either. The exhortation to 'walk by the spirit' (v. 16) cannot be addressed to the spirit itself, for the spirit needs no exhortation to walk its own way. St Paul pictures the 'I' tugged this way and that by two principles which are at war within him.[4] It approves the promptings of the spirit (cf. Rom 7:16), and yet finds itself coerced like a slave by the promptings of the flesh. What the man really wants to do (cf. Gal 5:17) is to obey the law of the spirit, but as he cannot always hold out against the solicitations of the flesh, he is not always able to do what he wants.

What St Paul offers us here is a simple, unscientific metaphysic of man, designed to render intelligible our experience of moral conflict and moral failure. A man who is in the grip of some gross fleshly lust (say sodomy) sometimes says that he cannot understand his own actions. The vice in question is disgusting and revolting to him; he does not wish to hear it even mentioned — and yet he finds himself succumbing to it again and again. St Paul's 'anthropology' (to give it a rather pompous name) is an analysis of the components which a man must have if such moral conflicts are to be possible. There is the principle of misconduct and moral weakness, which he calls 'the flesh'; and there is the principle of right conduct (or justice) which he calls 'the spirit'. In the unredeemed man these two are always at war, like the python and the mongoose, and in the end the flesh, like the mongoose, always wins.

The distinction between flesh and spirit is not derived from a comparison of man with the other animals. It would be inexact to say

---

[3]   St Thomas, Gal, 429 D.
[4]   Cf. Marcus Aurelius, *Meditations*, XII, 3: 'Thou art formed of three things in combination—body, spirit, mind (*sômatikon, pneumatikon, nous*).'

that flesh is the element which man has in common with the animals, and spirit is what distinguishes him. The 'flesh' does urge men to rend and devour one another like wild animals, but some of the works of the flesh are proper to men, for example, idolatry, poisoning and jealousy, while on the other hand some of the fruits of the spirit are not wholly wanting in the animal kingdom.

Nor does St Paul's distinction exactly correspond to the Stoic distinction between sense and passion. The Stoics are fond of pointing out that in a bad man reason does not make war on the passions but on the contrary becomes the slave of the passions. St Paul does not say that the spirit becomes the slave of the flesh; he regards the two principles as irreconcilable enemies.

Prejudice in favour of St Paul should not conceal from us that the Stoic anthropology had certain advantages. The Stoics argued that because all men share in reason, each man is *by nature* a political and social being or 'community-man' (*koinônikos*);[5] hence no man must live for himself, but each must serve others.[6] St Paul does not argue that the Christian as a sharer in the (human) spirit is obliged to serve all other men, or that as a sharer in the Holy Spirit he has an obligation *for that very reason* to serve those who are not sharers (cf. 6:10). Thus the Stoic anthropology leads to a more universalistic morality than does St Paul's.

## How is it possible for a Christian not to walk by the spirit?

In the unredeemed man, spirit fights an unequal struggle against the flesh and succumbs. In the Christian, the spirit receives powerful reinforcements from the Holy Spirit, whose presence alters the balance of power. How, then, is it possible for a Christian still to succumb — so that he still needs to be warned against biting and rending his neighbour?

The answer is that the believer receives only a first instalment of the Spirit. The balance of power is affected, but the flesh remains strong and rebellious. The Christian is still able to follow the promptings of the flesh. What he must do is to align himself with the Holy Spirit reinforcing his own spirit and 'do to death the practices of the

---

[5]   Cf. Gal 6:6, and Marcus Aurelius, II, 1; III, 4; IV, 4, 33, etc. This sound insight of natural morality is taken up by St Thomas, *Summa Theologica*, I-II, q. 94, a. 2, to which Pope Paul VI refers in *Humanae Vitae*, 10.

[6]   Cf. Philo, *The Unchangeableness of God*, 19 (Loeb, III): 'Do not think that all else is an appendage to you, but that you are an appendage to all else.'

body.'[7] He has been given sufficient strength, but it still remains to do the job. V. 16 contains a promise and a reassurance to the Christian who has been disappointed by his own past failures: 'If you walk by the Spirit, rest assured, you will not fulfil the lust of the flesh. Believe that you have the Spirit, act on this belief, and you will find that you *have* the Spirit.' John L. McKenzie has a fine parable to illustrate this point — drawn, no doubt, from his own experience of physical illness:[8]

> The Spirit is power, and each Christian is endued with power from on high. But if he does not know he has it and is afraid to use it, the Spirit will assert itself in him more slowly; or it will be more difficult for him when the Spirit does assert itself. He is like a man who cannot convince himself that he has really recovered from a long illness; the mere effort of getting out of bed fatigues him so much that he feels he must crawl right back in.

*Why is there no mention of the love of God in 5:14?*

The ten commandments serve as a principle of classification for all the particular laws: the latter can be grouped together according to their subject matter under the several commandments. This arrangement is used in the legal codes of Exodus, Deuteronomy and Leviticus,[9] and likewise by Philo in his four books on *The Special Laws*.

The ten commandments can be further reduced to two. The first table (prohibiting false gods, graven images, and blasphemy, and enjoining observance of the sabbath) can be summed up in the commandment: 'You shall love the Lord your God with your whole mind,' etc.; and the second table can be summed up in the commandment: 'You shall love your neighbour as yourself.' There is thus no difficulty in understanding Christ's saying: 'Upon these two commandments depends the whole of the law and the prophets.'[10] The implications of these two are set forth in greater detail in the ten commandments, and the practical applications of the ten commandments are set forth in the particular laws.

But in Gal 5:14 St Paul says that the whole law is summed up in the one precept: 'You shall love your neighbour as yourself.'

---

[7]   Rom 8:13. This passage shows that although St Paul does not simply identify the flesh with the body, he does not always take the trouble to distinguish them.

[8]   *The Power and the Wisdom*, p. 146.

[9]   Cf. A. Guilding, 'Notes on the Hebrew Law Codes,' JTS 49 (1948), pp. 43-52.

[10]  Cf. Mt 22:34-40; Mk 12:28-34.

Either he has found some way of bringing the laws of the first table under this precept, or he is using 'the law' in the restricted sense of 'the second table'. The same difficulty is presented by the parallel passage in Rom 13: 8-10:

> The man who loves his neighbour has fulfilled the law. For 'You shall not commit adultery,' 'You shall not kill,' 'You shall not steal,' 'You shall not covet,' and all the other commandments are summed up in this precept: 'You shall love your neighbour as yourself.' He who loves his neighbour does him no harm; that is why love fulfils the whole of the law.

St Jerome saw this difficulty, and could only suggest that the ceremonial law of the Old Testament had a spiritual or symbolic meaning which is fulfilled in a life of Christian charity. [11] This view could find support in Rom 12: 1: 'Offer your own bodies to God as a living sacrifice, holy and pleasing to him — this is *real* worship' (as contrasted with the figurative worship of the Old Testament). [12]

Alternatively, one might say that both in Gal 5: 14 and Rom 13: 8-10 St Paul is speaking to believers and means that one who already believes in God has only to fulfil the precept of charity and he has fulfilled the whole of the law. [13]

Neither of these explanations is fully satisfactory. The first means in effect that a Christian's only obligations to God are fulfilled in the exercise of charity towards his neighbour. This would seem to imply a denial of the duty to pray and take part in public worship. The second is not exactly what the text says.

Probably the best solution is to say that St Paul is here using 'the law' in a restricted sense. What he means is: 'the law of the second table.' The reasons are two: first, in Rom 13: 8-10 he quotes only the laws of the second table; and secondly, the well-known dictum of R. Hillel was probably not intended either to spiritualize the ceremonial law or to presuppose a 'law of faith': a pagan came to him and said that he would become a proselyte if Hillel could teach him the whole of the law while he stood on one foot. Hillel replied: 'Do not do to your neighbour what you hate to have done to you. That is the whole law, entire; the rest is explanation. Go and learn!' [14] Hillel was not the first Jewish teacher to sum up the law in a nutshell. There is a homily of R. Simlai in which he starts from the six hundred

---

[11] Cf. St Jerome, PL 26, 437 A-C.
[12] Cf. Philo, *The Special Laws*, I, 260, 272, 277 (Loeb, VII).
[13] This appears to be the meaning of Lagrange's very brief comment: 'Paul ne parle de l'amour de Dieu qui était bien le principal. C'est qu'il est supposé par la foi chrétienne elle-même, avant toute conception de vie pratique.' Viard, Gal, p. 113, says much the same: 'L'amour de charité à l'égard du prochain ne peut qu'être l'expression d'une foi vivante qui inclut déjà l'amour pour Dieu.'
[14] Cf. Daube, *The New Testament and Rabbinic Judaism*, p. 251.

and thirteen commandments given by Moses, then shows that David summed them up in eleven (Ps 15), Isaiah in six (Isa 33:15), Micah in three (Mic 6:8), Isaiah in two (Isa 56:1), and Amos in one: 'Seek me and live' (Amos 5:4). In all such rabbinic attempts to express the essence of morality, the 'law' means simply 'the rule of moral conduct'. [15]

It is therefore superfluous to ask whether 'the whole law' of which the Golden Rule is a summary is the law of Moses or the law of Christ. In regard to the essence of morality there is no discrepancy between the teaching of Moses and the teaching of Christ, between the teaching of the rabbis and the teaching of the apostles. Christ could express the substance of his teaching in words taken from the old law; [16] and in Gal 5:14 St Paul is dependent on the same moral tradition as Hillel in the anecdote quoted above.

Some Christian commentators have thought they discerned an essential difference between St Paul and Hillel in that the latter added: 'the rest is explanation — *go and learn!*' [17] But neither Christ nor St Paul meant that the man who knows the Golden Rule has no need of any further instruction. [18] The value of the Golden Rule is that it helps the learner to recognize the unity of inspiration underlying the plurality of commandments, laws and regulations. [19] The Christian too must 'go and learn' how the principle works out in various relationships and situations. He can find a brief explanation in the Sermon on the Mount (which comments on the decalogue) and further explanations in the Christian moral tradition founded on the decalogue as expounded in the Sermon on the Mount. Attempts to rewrite moral theology on the basis, not of the decalogue, but of the precept of charity are therefore misguided, since the decalogue is but the first unfolding of the precept of charity and a necessary link between the precept of charity and the detailed teaching of the Sermon on the Mount.

### Why does St Paul change his imagery in v. 15?

In the first half of the subsection (p. 437), St Paul has spoken of freedom, service and love. In the second half, we expect him to

---

[15]  Cf. G. F. Moore, *Judaism in the First Centuries of the Christian Era*, Harvard, 1950, I, p. 85.
[16]  Cf. Mt 22:34-40.
[17]  Cf. T. W. Manson, *The Teaching of Jesus*, Ed. 2, Cambridge, 1955, p. 305: 'For Hillel the commentary is every whit as essential as the Golden Rule.'
[18]  Cf. Moore, *Judaism*, I, p. 88.
[19]  In a paperback, *Our Divine Master* (Scripture for Meditation, No. 3), London, 1969, I have shown how the teaching of Jesus on every human relationship

speak by contrast of tyranny, hatred and slavery. He does speak of
hatred, but under the figure of 'biting and rending one another'. His
reason for introducing this metaphor may be to suggest that the man
who obeys the guidance of the spirit is truly human, while the man
who follows the promptings of the flesh behaves like a wild animal.
But a more probable explanation is that he has in mind the warning
of Christ: 'Beware of false prophets! They come to you clad in
sheep's clothing, but beneath it are ravening wolves' (Mt 7:15). False
prophets have arisen and have provoked a sharp controversy in Galatia.
The two parties, believing each other to be wrong, are not conducting
a dialogue in a spirit of gentleness (cf. 6:1); they are biting and rending
one another like wolves. [20] There is a warning here that *odium
theologicum*, though it masquerades as love of truth, is in reality a
work of the flesh; and since the dispute between the Judaizers and the
disciples of Paul was over the interpretation of the Old Testament,
there is a special warning for students of the Scriptures. St Jerome
saw the point and commented wisely: [21]

> We interpret the Scriptures. We employ many changes of style. We try to
> make our writings worth reading. If these things are done, not for Christ,
> but to make us remembered in time to come, and to win us the admiration
> of the people, the whole work becomes useless, and we will be like a
> sounding drum or a noisy cymbal.

As is well known, St Jerome himself was far from setting a good
example of how Christians should engage in religious controversy; [22]
and even St Paul exposes himself to criticism. In this Epistle he
anathematizes his opponents, attributes bad motives to them, and
suggests they should castrate themselves. If he were alive today and
wrote book reviews, few editors would dare to print them. It is a pity
St Paul was such an irascible man. If the Church has been less tolerant
than Judaism of dissentient opinions and doctrines, this is due in part
to the example of St Paul thundering his anathemas at the Judaizers.
A milder policy is recommended in the parables of the Dragnet and
of the Cockle. [23]

Throughout the history of the Church there has been much rending
and devouring of Christians by Christians. Anathemas, once uttered,

(ruler and ruled, husband and wife, master and slave, Jew and Samaritan, etc.)
is an application of the principle 'You shall love your neighbour as yourself.'
[20] Cf. St Paul's use of this metaphor in Acts 20:29.
[21] St Jerome, PL 26, 453 A; cf. 445 A and 452 D.
[22] There is a delightful outburst in PL 22, 544: 'Knowledge of the Scriptures is
the one art of which every Tom, Dick and Harry thinks he is master. Talkative
old women, garrulous old men, word-spinning sophists—the lot: they grab hold
of it, tear it to shreds, and teach without having learned.'
[23] See above, pp. 392-393.

make reconciliation almost impossible. It is sad that St Paul's warnings in vv. 15 and 26 and in 6:1 have not received more attention.

In the third main division (p. 411), there is a link between v. 15 and 6:10: 'Let us do good to all men, and especially to our kindred in the faith.' Theodore of Mopsuestia draws out of the word 'especially' a warning against persecuting non-Christians:[24]

> I should like to bring this text to the attention of those who think that men who do not share our faith ought to be indiscriminately maltreated. They would do well to remember that it is not fitting for us to *do* to a man all that he deserves to *suffer* (*non omne quod quis pati dignus est, hoc et nobis decet facere*).

An evil-doer deserves to be punished according to the *lex talionis* (cf. 5:15), but it is not fitting for Christians to apply such rigour.[25]

In Europe of the Middle Ages, when heresy and sedition often went hand in hand, the spirit of toleration was not in evidence. The Fourth Lateran Council in 1215 A.D. decreed as follows:[25a]

> Secular authorities are to be urged, and if necessary compelled by ecclesiastical censure, to swear publicly that they will honestly strive, to the best of their ability, to exterminate (or banish?) from their realms all heretics who have been denounced by the Church.

The Declaration of Vatican II on Religious Liberty is strikingly different in tone. It begins thus:

> The Vatican Synod declares that the human person has a right to religious freedom. This freedom means that all are to be immune from coercion on the part of individuals or of social groups and of any human power, in such wise that in matters religious no one is to be forced to act in a manner contrary to his own beliefs....The right to this immunity continues to exist even in those who do not live up to their obligation of seeking the truth and adhering to it. Nor is the exercise of this right to be impeded, provided that the just requirements of public order are observed.

It is a remarkable fact that in the New Testament the principle of religious toleration is put forward by a Jew — Gamaliel in Acts 5:35-39.

[24] Theodore, Gal, pp. 106-107.
[25] The *lex talionis* is not really the Golden Rule in reverse (though cf. Deut 19:16-19). It is permissive, not prescriptive, and aims at *limiting* private vengeance and self-help. Cf. Porteous, *Daniel*, p. 91.
[25a] Translated from J. D. Mansi, *Amplissima Collectio Conciliorum*, Paris and Leipzig, 1903, t. 22, p. 987 (not included in Denz).

*The Second Subsection, 5:16-18*

# FLESH *VERSUS* SPIRIT

**A**  *5 : 16* Walk by the Spirit, and you will not fulfil the lust of the flesh.
**B**  *17* For the flesh lusts against the spirit, and the spirit against the flesh
**C**  (for these are opposed to each other)   **B¹**   to prevent you from doing
whatever you want.   **A¹**  *18* But if you are led by the Spirit, you are
not under (the) law.

*To which 'law' does v. 18 refer?*

V. 16 is really a conditional sentence. The imperative is the
protasis: 'If you walk by the Spirit, you will not fulfil the lust of the
flesh.' In this form the sentence is clearly parallel to v. 18:

| | | |
|---|---|---|
| If you walk by the Spirit, | = | If you are led by the Spirit, |
| you will not fulfil the lust | = | you are not under the law (i.e. |
| of the flesh. | | the tyranny, of the flesh). |

One sense of v. 18 is, therefore, that if the believer will ally himself
with the Spirit and make war on the flesh, he will find that he is no
longer subject to 'the law of sin in his members' (Rom 7: 23).

However, in the eighth section (p. 435), the parallel to v. 18 is
v. 23b: 'Against such things as these there is no law,' where 'law'
must mean 'a law (such as the decalogue) which prohibits the works
of the flesh.' If 'law' also has this meaning in v. 18, the sense can
only be: 'If you are led by the spirit, you are not *under* law,' [26] for
you are identifying yourself with the law of the Spirit (cf. Rom 8: 2),
and a man is not *under* a law which is within him. To be *under* a law
implies lack of identification; it implies that the law is something
separate, an exterior constraint. St John Chrysostom has a valuable
comment here: [27]

> He who has the Spirit extinguishes by means of the Spirit all evil desires.
> But the man who is rid of all evil desires has no need of the law's assistance,
> for he has risen far above its injunctions.

---

[26] A reason for thinking that St Paul intends the preposition 'under' to be
emphatic is that in the corresponding v. 23b there is another preposition which
must be emphatic: 'There is no law *against* these things (the fruits of the
Spirit)'—they are just the things enjoined by the law which says 'You shall love
your neighbour as yourself.'

[27] Chrysostom, PG 61, 672 C. Cf. St Thomas, Gal, 416 C; S. Lyonnet, 'Liberté
du chrétien et loi de l'Esprit selon saint Paul,' *Christus* 4 (1954), pp. 6-27.

*The Third Subsection, 5:18-23*

# THE TWO WAYS

**A**  *5 : 18* But if you are led by the Spirit, you are not under the law.  **B**  *19* It is plain what are the works of the flesh: fornication, impurity, licentiousness;  *20* idolatry, sorcery; enmities, strife, jealousy, fits of anger, quarrels, dissensions, intrigues,  *21* envy; drunkenness, orgies, and things like these. **C**  I warn you now as I warned you before, that those who do such things will not inherit the kingdom of God.  **B¹**  *22* But the harvest of the Spirit is charity, joy, peace, patience, kindness, goodness, fidelity,  *23* gentleness, self-control.  **A¹**  Against such things as these there is no law.

Early Christian preachers and writers used for the imparting of ethical instruction certain literary forms which are hardly ever used in the Church today — (1) the *Haustafel* or list of duties for the various members of a household (husbands, wives, parents, children, masters, slaves), [28] (2) lists of virtues and vices, [29] and (3) the 'Two-Ways'-form, in which the way to salvation is contrasted with the way to perdition. A Two-Ways-text always incorporates lists of virtues and vices; but it is not simply a more elaborate form of virtue-and-vice catalogue, since it is built up out of sentences rather than of lists.

In this subsection, St Paul sets forth two contrasting lists, one of vicious actions ('the works of the flesh') and the other of virtues ('the harvest of the spirit'). But in several ways the passage resembles a Two-Ways text. It is worthwhile comparing it with earlier and later specimens of this literary form. The comparison may enable us to judge how far St Paul has taken the trouble to integrate his moral theology and his dogmatic theology into one system.

*What is the origin of the 'Two-Ways'?*

It is impossible to say where this literary form first made its appearance — whether in Greece, among the Jews, or in Iran. In Greek literature, a very early example is found in Hesiod: [30]

Badness can be got easily and in shoals: the way to her is smooth, and she lives very near. Before Goodness, however, the gods have placed the sweat

---

[28] Examples in the New Testament are Col 3 : 18—4 : 1; Eph 5 : 22—6 : 9; 1 Pet 2 : 18—3 : 7.

[29] Cf. e.g. Mk 7 : 21-22.

[30] Hesiod, *Works and Days*, 287-292, translated by H. G. Evelyn-White, *Hesiod* (Loeb), London, 1914, p. 25 (slightly revised). The last line is a deliberate paradox: *rêidiê dê epeita pelei, chalepê per eousa.*

of our brows: long and steep is the path that leads to her, and rough at first; but when the top is reached, she is then easy, hard though she is.

Among the Jews, the image of the Two Ways occurs in Jer 21:8-9, but not in connection with a body of moral instruction:

> Thus says the Lord: 'Behold, I set before you the way of life and the way of death. He who stays in this city shall die by the sword, by famine, and by pestilence; but he who goes out and surrenders to the Chaldeans who are besieging you shall live.'

As a device for setting forth moral instruction, the Two Ways is used for the first time in the Bible at Deut 30:15-19:

> See, I have set before you this day life and good, death and evil.
> If you obey the commandments of the Lord your God, by loving the Lord your God, by walking in his ways, and by keeping his commandments and his statutes and his ordinances,
>> then you shall live and multiply,
>>> and the Lord your God will bless you in the land which you are entering to take possession of it.
> But if your heart turns away, and you will not hear, but are drawn away to worship other gods and serve them,
>> I declare to you this day that you shall perish;
>>> you shall not live long in the land which you are going over the Jordan to enter and possess.
> I call heaven and earth to witness against you this day, that I have set before you life and death, blessing and curse; therefore choose life, that you and your descendants may live.

In this passage, the fundamental decision presented to the reader or hearer is: Will you follow Yahweh or Baal, the law of Yahweh or the licentiousness of Baal? In 1 Kgs 18:21, Elijah presents the same choice in similar imagery though without actually mentioning two ways: [31]

> How long will you go limping with two different opinions? If the Lord is God, follow him; but if Baal, then follow him.

---

[31] This passage is quoted in the introduction to the Two Ways in *The Apostolic Constitutions*, VII, 1. If St Paul had wished to transpose Elijah's exhortation into the terms of his own theology, we might have expected him to say: 'Behold I set before you two ways, the way of Moses (the works of the law) and the way of Christ (faith in the gospel); choose the way of Christ and you will live.' Or perhaps: 'I set before you two ways, the law of Moses and the law of Christ; follow the law of Christ and you will live.' There is a faint suggestion of this in Gal 2:14, where he says that Peter, Barnabas and the other Jews at Antioch were not walking steadily according to the truth of the gospel. But in the moral section of the Epistle he contrasts the way of Christ (i.e. the way of the Spirit), not with the way of Moses, but with the way of the flesh. The reason may be that he shrinks from identifying the law of Moses with the way of the flesh; or it may be that the eighth section, 5:13-6:2, was composed by St Paul long before the judaizing crisis blew up. It began as an exhortation to Gentiles to abandon idolatry and its vices (cf. Acts 14:15), and has been imperfectly adapted to fit into the Epistle.

In Iran, the Two Ways are related to a system of theology and cosmology in the teaching of Zoroaster (about 600 B.C.). The supreme God, Ahura Mazda, creates two spirits, the good spirit presiding over the realm of light, and the evil spirit presiding over the realm of darkness. The two spirits are in constant conflict with each other in the soul of every man. He can side with either against the other. [32] It is easy to see how these opinions were arrived at. The man who wonders at the beauty and order in nature is quickly led to the con- clusion that it was created by a good God (Ahura Mazda). None of his works is more wonderful than man. Yet not a few men are thoroughly corrupt and vicious, and in every man there are strong impulses to evil. The hypothesis that man was made by a good God requires some adjustment to make it square with the fact of moral evil. A very natural supposition is that some other power, more or less independent of God, and hostile to him, has either had a hand in the creation of man or has somehow won control over him. [33] The defect of such a system is that it cannot explain the origin of the evil spirit or why his activities are tolerated by the good God who is master of all. But those who acccept the system may find this defect a small one by comparison with the advantage of being able to explain the presence of evil in such a splendid creature as man.

The Iranian version of the Two Ways is the most complete and systematic, and may well be the source upon which the Jewish and Christian users of this form are ultimately dependent.

## Was the 'Two-Ways' borrowed by Christians from Jewish teachers?

Two very early Christian writings which contain elaborate exposi- tions of the Two Ways are the *Didache* and *The Epistle of Barnabas*. The dating of both is disputed; probably both were written before A.D. 125. Soon after the publication of the *Didache* in 1883, the suggestion was put forward that both texts depend on a lost Jewish version of the Two Ways. [34] This hypothesis was rejected by certain scholars of note, who held that 'Barnabas' was the originator of the Two Ways. [35] But the discovery of the Dead Sea Scrolls has shown

---

[32] Cf. L. W. Barnard, 'The Problem of the Epistle of Barnabas,' CQR 158 (1958), p. 224, for some quotations from the Zoroastrian poems called the *Gathas*. See also A. Dupont-Sommer, *The Jewish Sect of Qumran and the Essenes*, London, 1954, pp. 118-130.

[33] See above, pp. 439-440, on St Paul's anthropology.

[34] Cf. C. Taylor, *The Teaching of the Twelve Apostles with Illustrations from the Talmud*, Cambridge, 1886.

[35] Cf. e.g. R. H. Connolly, 'The Didache in relation to the Epistle of Barnabas,' JTS 33 (1932), pp. 237-253.

that the Two Ways was used by Jewish teachers long before the time of Barnabas — that is to say, the literary form used in the *Didache* and in *The Epistle of Barnabas* was used more than a century earlier at Qumran. [36] But in content and vocabulary the two Christian documents are not descendants of the Qumran text.

The Qumran text is in the *Manual of Discipline*. [37] Its resemblance to the Zoroastrian doctrine is obvious. The theology of Qumran was certainly affected by Iranian influences.

*The Two Ways*

From God most wise comes all that is and will be. And before they come to be, He has established their whole plan, and when they do come to be according to the ordinances concerning them, it is by His glorious plan that they accomplish their work. Change is not possible. In His hand are all the decrees concerning all things. And He supports them in all their concerns. It was He who created man to rule the world and appointed two spirits by which he would walk up to the time of His visitation. These are the spirits of truth and of wickedness. In the fountain of light is the birth of truth, but from the source of darkness is the birth of wickedness. [20] In the hand of the Prince of Lights is the dominion of all the sons of righteousness; in the ways of light they walk. And in the hand of the Angel of Darkness is all the dominion of the sons of wickedness; and in the ways of darkness they walk. And it is through the Angel of Darkness that any of the sons of righteousness go astray. And all their sins and their iniquities and their guilt and their deeds of transgression are under his dominion according to the mysterious decree of God until his end. And all their afflictions and their seasons of tribulation are under his hostile dominion; and all the spirits of His party attempt to make the sons of light stumble. But the God of Israel and His faithful Angel give help to all [25] the sons of light. And he created the spirits of light and of darkness; and on them He founded all operation....all work and on their ways....[Of them] God loves the one all [IV, 1] the ages of eternity and with all its activities He is ever pleased. He abhors the fraternity of the other and hates all its ways for eternity.

*The Way of Light*

And these are their ways in the world. To illumine the heart of man and to make straight before him all the ways of justice in truth and to

---

[36]  Cf. L. W. Barnard, 'The Epistle of Barnabas and the Dead Sea Scrolls: Some Observations,' SJT 13 (1960), pp. 45-59.

[37]  *The Manual of Discipline*, III, 15—IV, 23, translated by E. Sutcliffe, *The Monks of Qumran*, London, 1960, pp. 164-166. The cross-headings were inserted by the present writer. For another Jewish Two-Way text see Philo, *The Sacrifices of Cain and Abel*, 20-32 (Loeb, II)—a highly entertaining passage in which the two ways are personified as an attractive courtesan and a modest free-born wife.

strike fear into his heart by the judgments of God; and the spirit of
humility and patience and abundant mercy and eternal goodness and
prudence and understanding and wisdom with strength trusting in all the
works of God and relying on the abundance of His kindness, and the
spirit of knowledge in every plan of action, and zeal for just judgments
and [5] holy intention with a strong determination, and abundance of
kindness for all the sons of truth, and glorious purity with abhorrence of
all impure idols, and humble conduct with all prudence and reticence
about the true secrets of knowledge. These are the foundations of the
spirit of the sons of truth in the world.

And the visitation of all who walk therein is for healing and abundance
of peace with length of days and fruitful seed with all blessings for ever
and perpetual joy in everlasting life with a crown of glory and a resplendent
robe in eternal light.

## The Way of Darkness

And to the spirit of wickedness belongs ambition and slackness in the
service of righteousness, wickedness and falsehood, pride and haughtiness,
lying and deceit, cruelty [10] and abounding hypocrisy, impatience and
great folly, and the passion of arrogance, abominable deeds in the spirit
of harlotry, and impure ways in the service of uncleanness, and a blasphemous tongue, blindness of the eyes and heaviness of hearing, stubbornness
and self-will to walk in all the ways of darkness and evil craftiness.

And the visitation of all who walk therein brings many afflictions at
the hand of all the angels of destruction, eternal ruin in the wrathful anger
of the God of vengeance, perpetual trembling and eternal obloquy with the
shame of destruction by fire in the regions of gloom, and all their times
in their generations shall be in the mourning of sorrow and bitter mis-
fortune in the ruin of darkness till their destruction without remainder or
escape.

## The Two Ways and their End

[15] In these (spirits) are born all the sons of man, and in their separate
parties all their hosts have their inheritance in their generations, and in
their ways they walk and every deed and action of theirs is in these
separate parties according to the inheritance of each man, whether great
or little, for all the periods of eternity. For God has set (these spirits) each
separately up to the last time, and He has put perpetual enmity between
their divisions. An abomination to truth is the conduct of wickedness, and
an abomination to wickedness are all the ways of truth; and there is a
passionate strife in all their behaviour, for they cannot walk in harmony. [38]

And God in the mysteries of His providence and in His glorious wisdom
has set a term to the existence of wickedness, and in the epoch of His

---

[38]  Cf. Gal 5 : 17.

Q

visitation He will annihilate it for ever, and then shall the truth come forth to victory throughout the world. For it (the world) will have wallowed in the ways of vice in the dominion of wickedness until [20] the time of judgment definitely decreed, and then will God purify by His truth all the works of man and will refine for Himself the construction of man bringing to an end every spirit of wickedness from the midst of his flesh and cleansing him with the spirit of holiness from all wicked conduct.

The last paragraph of this quotation is of particular interest as showing that the men of Qumran, no less than St Paul, looked forward to the day when God's elect, the sons of light, would no longer be subject to the influence of the evil spirit but wholly possessed by the Spirit of God.

There are good reasons for thinking that St Paul was directly acquainted with the thought and writings of Qumran. In particular, it has been shown that in 2 Cor 6:16—7:1 'Qumran ideas and expressions have been reworked in a Christian cast of thought.' [39] This passage contains the idea of disjunction which is expressed in the Two Ways:

Do not be misyoked with unbelievers. For what partnership can justice have with wickedness, or what fellowship can light have with darkness? What agreement can there be between Christ and Belial? What part can a believer have with an unbeliever? And what compromise is possible between the temple of God and worship of idols?...

If this paragraph were a non-pauline interpolation into the Epistle, [40] it would not of course be evidence that St Paul was influenced by Qumran. It must be admitted that it fits rather awkwardly into its context, but probably it is not an interpolation. It is part of the symmetrical structure of Second Corinthians (matching 2:5-11). Probably, like Gal 5:13—6:2, it is a passage composed originally for another purpose and re-used in the composition of the Epistle. If so, it *is* by St Paul, and it *is* evidence of his direct dependence on Essene thought. [41] If St Paul's literary remains were more extensive, we might have found much more evidence of this dependence. [42]

---

[39] J. A. Fitzmyer, 'Qumrân and the Interpolated Paragraph in 2 Cor 6:14-7:1,' CBQ 23 (1961), p. 279.

[40] As Fitzmyer thinks likely (art. cit., p. 280).

[41] W. Jaeger, *Early Christianity and Greek Paideia,* Harvard, 1961, pp. 8-10, thinks that Christian missionaries borrowed the Two Ways from Pythagorean and other Greek sources. But the Qumran parallel is closer and nearer at hand.

[42] Another example is Col 1:12, on which see Fitzmyer, art. cit., p. 274. According to J. Murphy-O'Connor in RB 72 (1965), p. 56, Eph 4:22-24 is a deliberate christianization of the Qumran Two-Spirits passage. D. Flusser, 'A New Sensitivity in Judaism and the Christian Message,' HTR 61 (1968), p. 123, observes that Rom 12:8-21 contains several motifs known from the scrolls.

In many ways, the best example of an early Christian Two-Ways text is the beginning of the *Didache*. In the only surviving manuscript of the Greek text, dislocations have occurred, which various editors have dealt with in various ways. Two simple transpositions give a convincing chiastic pattern:

A    The Two Ways (1 : 1).
B    The Way of Life (1 : 2-3a & 2 : 2-7).
C    Meekness (1 : 3b-4).
D    Almsgiving (1 : 5-6).
E    Peacemaking and Purity of Heart (3 : 1-3).
F    Good Companion & Honesty (3 : 4-5).
G    *Meekness* (3 : 6-10).
F¹   Good Companions & Payment of Teachers (4 : 1-2).
E¹   Purity of Heart & Peacemaking (1 : 4a & 4 : 3-4).
D¹   Almsgiving (4 : 5-8).
C¹   Meekness (4 : 9-14).
B¹   The Way of Death (5 : 1-2).
A¹   Exhortation to follow the Way of Life (6 : 1).

The text is too long to reproduce in full, but here are the beginning and end:

A    There are two ways, the one of life and the other of death, and there is a great difference between the two ways.

B    The way of life is this: first, you shall love the God who made you, and secondly, you shall love your neighbour as yourself. Whatever you do not wish to happen to you, do not do to another. The explanation (in Greek, the *didache*) of these words is as follows [1 : 3b—2 : 1a] : you shall not kill, you shall not commit adultery, you shall not corrupt boys, you shall not fornicate, you shall not steal, you shall not practise magic, you shall not use poison, [42a] you shall not slay a child in the womb or kill one just born, you shall not covet your neighbour's goods. You shall not swear false oaths, you shall not bear false witness, you shall not slander, you shall not bear a grudge. You shall not be divided in mind or double-tongued, for duplicity is a lethal snare. Your speech shall not be false, or empty, but carried into effect. You shall not be greedy or rapacious or hypocritical or ill-tempered or arrogant. You shall not plan mischief against your neighbour. You shall not hate any man, but some you will correct, some you will pity, for some you will pray, and some you will love more than yourself.

                .      .      .      .      .      .      .      .      .      .      .
                .      .      .      .      .      .      .      .      .      .      .
                .      .      .      .      .      .      .      .      .      .      .

---

[42a] To judge from its position, *pharmakeia* (use of drugs or poisons) may here refer to drugs inducing sterility (i.e., contraceptives—the 'cup of sterility' is mentioned in the Talmud). But this sense is not likely in Gal 5 : 2, where the same word *pharmakeia* (translated above as 'sorcery') occurs between 'idolatry' and 'enmities'.

B¹  The way of death is this: first of all it is wicked and fraught with a curse: acts of murder, adultery, lust, fornication, theft, idolatry, magic, poisoning, plunder, false witness, hypocrisy, duplicity, trickery, arrogance, baseness, self-will, greed, foul speech, jealousy, boldness, pride, flattery — persecutors of the good, [43] haters of truth, lovers of falsehood, who ignore the reward of justice, not adhering to the good or to just judgment, watchful not for good but for evil, men far from kindness and patience, lovers of what is worthless, seekers of repayment, without pity for the beggar, without sympathy for the oppressed, without knowledge of the one who made them, slayers of children, destroyers of God's creation, who turn aside the petitioner and crush the oppressed, who take the side of the rich and condemn the poor unjustly, given up to every kind of sin. May you be preserved, my children, from all such.

A¹  Let no one lead you astray from this way of teaching — for such a one teaches you apart from God.

A remarkable feature of this text is that the author has stripped away all mention of the two spirits or two angels who preside over the two ways. Here for comparison is the beginning of the Two Ways in the Epistle of Barnabas:

> There are two ways of teaching and of power, the way of light and the way of darkness; and there is a great difference between the two ways. Over the one are appointed light-bearing angels of God; over the other angels of Satan. The One is Lord from eternity to eternity; the other is the ruler of the present lawless age.

And here is the beginning of the Latin *Doctrina Apostolorum*: [44]

> There are two ways in the world, the ways of life and of death, of light and of darkness. Over these are appointed two angels, the one of justice, the other of iniquity. But there is a great distance between the two ways.

Perhaps the author of the *Didache* felt a scruple about allowing even a mitigated form of cosmological dualism to stand in a work of instruction for Christians. But others did not. The *Shepherd* of Hermas, which enjoyed great popularity in the early Church, includes the following: [45]

> 'I commanded you,' said he, 'in the first Command, to observe faith and fear and self-control.'
>
> 'Yes, sir,' I said.
>
> 'But now,' said he, 'I want to show you their capabilities also, so that you may understand what capability and effectiveness each of them possesses. For their effects are twofold. So they relate to right and wrong. So put your faith in what is right, and not in what is wrong. For uprightness has a

---

[43]  For a similar but less awkward change of construction, see Rom 1:29.

[44]  The Latin text was published by Joseph Schlecht, *Doctrina XII Apostolorum*, Freiburg im Breisgau, 1900.

[45]  *Mandatum* 6, translated by Edgar J. Goodspeed, *The Apostolic Fathers*, London, 1950, pp. 131-132 (slightly revised).

straight way, but wrong-doing a crooked one. But follow the straight and level way, and leave the crooked one alone. For the crooked way has no paths, but broken ground and many obstacles, and it is rough and thorny. So it injures those who follow it. But those who follow the straight way walk smoothly and without stumbling, for it is neither rough nor thorny. So you see that it is better to follow this way.'

'I am pleased,' said I, 'to follow this way.'

'You shall do so,' said he, 'and whoever turns to the Lord with his whole heart will follow it.'

'Now hear about faith,' said he. 'There are two angels with man, one of uprightness and one of wickedness.'

'How, then, sir,' said I, 'am I to know their operations, for both angels live with me?'

'Listen,' said he, 'and you will understand them. The angel of uprightness is sensitive and modest and gentle and quiet. So when this one comes up into your heart, he immediately talks with you about uprightness, purity, reverence, self-control, and every upright act and every glorious virtue. When all these things occur to your mind, know that the angel of uprightness is with you. These then are the works of the angel of uprightness. Put your faith in him and in his works. [46] Now observe what are the works of the angel of wickedness. First of all, he is ill-tempered and bitter and foolish, and his acts are wicked, destroying the servants of God. So when he comes up into your heart, know him by his works.'

'I do not understand, sir,' said I, 'how I am to recognize him.'

'Listen,' said he. 'When ill-temper comes over you, or bitterness, know that he is in you; then the desire for much business, and extravagance in many kinds of food and drink and many drinking-parties and exquisite and superfluous delicacies, and the desire for women, and covetousness and a great arrogance and ostentation and everything like them and akin to them — when these things come up into your heart, know that the angel of wickedness is in you. So when you recognize his actions, shun him, and do not put your faith in him, because his works are wicked and harmful to the slaves of God. Here you have the operations of both the angels. Understand them, and trust the angel of uprightness. But shun the angel of wickedness, for his teaching is wicked in all he does. For even if a man is a believer and the thought of this angel comes up into his heart, that man or that woman is sure to commit a sin. But again, even if a man or woman is very wicked, and the doings of the angel of uprightness occur to his mind, he must necessarily do something good. So you see,' said he, 'that it is good to follow the angel of uprightness, and to bid the angel of wickedness goodbye. This command tells what relates to faith, in order that you may believe what the angel of uprightness does, and through doing it may live to God. [46] But believe that the doings of the angel of wickedness are bad; so if you do not do them, you will live to God.'

---

[46] The author appears to be contriving a moralistic interpretation of 'The just man will live by faith' (Hab 2 : 4; Gal 3 : 11). Cf., however, Rom 14 : 23.

*What are the characteristics of Two-Ways texts?*

From the examples given above, the following characteristics can be collected:

1. There must be a catalogue of virtues and a catalogue of vices. These may take the form of two contrasted characters.
2. The two catalogues are connected with two ways, which are described in contrasting terms as rough and smooth, broad and narrow, steep and level, etc.
3. Each 'way' is associated with a spirit or angel.
4. Each way is associated with a conflicting element in man's make-up, spirit and flesh, good and bad inclination (*yetser*), etc.
5. There is a description of the destination to which each way leads, i.e. a statement of the sanctions of good and bad action.
6. On each side there is a summary statement, followed by particular examples.
7. The distinction between the sons of light and the sons of darkness may be connected with a doctrine of predestination.

*Was this form of instruction used by John the Baptist?*

We have very little information about the preaching of John the Baptist (cf. Lk 3:18), but we do know that 'the way' was an important concept in his preaching. Christianity inherited from John's movement the title of 'The Way' (cf. Acts 9:2). Christ himself describes John's teaching as 'the way of justice',[47] and may have referred to him as the 'angel' of this way (Mt 11:9-10):

> Why did you go out? To see a prophet? Yes, I tell you, and more than a prophet. This is he of whom the Scripture says: 'See, I am sending my *angel* ahead of you, to prepare your *way* before you.'

John certainly announced as imminent the outpouring of the Spirit which, according to the Qumran text quoted above, 'will bring to an end every spirit of wickedness from the midst of man's flesh.' Although, therefore, positive evidence is wanting, it is likely enough that St John the Baptist contrasted his way with a second way, the way of death. If St John the evangelist was a disciple of the Baptist before he began to follow Jesus, some of the ethical dualism of the fourth gospel may come from the Baptist.[48]

---

[47] Mt 21:32; cf. the *Doctrina Apostolorum*, quoted above, p. 454.
[48] Cf. A. Wikenhauser, *Das Evangelium nach Johannes*, Regensburg, 1948, pp. 141-144.

*Was this form used by Christ himself?*

'There is a great difference between the two ways,' says the author of the *Didache*; but he does not stop to explain the difference in general terms, whether metaphorical or literal. [49] Christ, however, does so in the Epilogue of the Sermon on the Mount (Mt 7: 13-14):

> Enter by the narrow gate. For the gate that leads to destruction is wide, the road is broad, and many go that way; but the gate that leads to life is narrow, the road is difficult, and those who find it are few.

Here is clear evidence that Jesus did use the imagery of the two ways. [50] The surprising thing is that this text occurs in such an inconspicuous and insignificant position in the Sermon on the Mount. The body of the Sermon on the Mount describes two ways of life, but not under the image of two ways. It explains Christian morality in a series of antitheses which set the teaching of the Pharisees alongside the teaching of Christ for purposes of comparison. But the whole sermon is not organized as a Two-Ways text and has practically none of the characteristics listed above (p. 456). We know that Christ preached regularly in the synagogues (cf. Jn 18: 20), but we have very little information about what he said or about the literary forms into which he cast his preaching. Mt 7: 13-14 is evidence that he sometimes used the image of Two Ways. From the fourth gospel we learn that he spoke of 'light' and of 'darkness' and of the 'sons of light' (Jn 12: 36) — hence probably of the 'sons of darkness' too. But evidence is lacking that he connected the two ways with two conflicting spirits external to man, or with two conflicting impulses inherent in human nature.

In Mk 7: 21-22, Christ uses a catalogue of vices, but it is not matched by a catalogue of virtues, nor is it connected with the image of a way.

The parable of the Pharisee and the Publican (Lk 18: 9-14) contains something like a Two-Ways text in the 'prayer' of the Pharisee. First he gives a brief catalogue of the Publican's vices, then a brief catalogue of his own good works: 'O God, I thank thee that I am not like the rest of men, greedy, unjust, adulterous — like this tax-gatherer here. I fast twice a week, and I pay tithes of my whole income.'

---

[49] An interesting attempt to fill up this obvious lacuna is made in the *Apostolic Constitutions* (compiled about A.D. 375). The two ways 'admit of no admixture (for there is a great difference between them)—rather they are entirely separate. The way of life is natural (*physikê*); but the way of death is a foreign import *epeisaktos*)—it is not according to the will of God, but is due to the hostile design of the alien (i.e. the devil).' For the Greek text see J. Rendel Harris, *The Teaching of the Apostles*, London, 1887, pp. 25-33.

[50] Cf. P. Gaechter, *Das Matthäus Evangelium*, Innsbruck, 1964, p. 243.

From the scanty evidence at our disposal, perhaps we can venture to say that Christ made occasional use of the imagery of the Two Ways, but did not combine it with a Two-Spirit theology, and pointed out (in the parable) the spiritual dangers attendant upon its misuse.

*How far does Gal 5:16-25 share the characteristics of Two-Ways texts?*

1. There are two contrasting catalogues, the works of the flesh (vv. 19-21a) and the harvest of the spirit (vv. 22-23a).
2. The image of the Two Ways is not explicitly used, but is implied in the phrases 'Walk by the spirit' and 'If you are led by the Spirit.'
3. The Holy Spirit is mentioned, [51] but not the 'spirit of wickedness' or the powers of darkness or Beliar (contrast 2 Cor 6: 14—7: 1). But the 'Flesh' itself tends to become a demonic power in the thought of St Paul.
4. The two ways of life are linked with two conflicting elements in man's physical constitution — the flesh and the spirit.
5. The destinations to which the two ways lead are not described in detail, but v. 23 shows that those who follow the way of the flesh are not allowed to enter the kingdom. Their final abode is not described. The same verse implies that those who follow the guidance of the Spirit will enter the kingdom.
6. There is a summary-statement on the side of the spirit (v. 14), but not on the side of the flesh. (The same is true of the Sermon on the Mount; cf. Mt 7: 12.)
7. There is no suggestion that each man's destination is predetermined. On the contrary, the implication of the whole passage is that the Christian, after receiving the Holy Spirit in baptism, is still free to choose his way — whether he will be guided by the Spirit or not.

The peculiarities which distinguish the Two-Ways of Galatians from other specimens of this form are the result of its adaptation to the special context in which St Paul is using it. He endeavours to link it to the major themes of the Epistle:

1. An attempt is made to link it to the discussion of whether a Christian is subject to law. The man who follows the way of the spirit is not *under* the law (v. 18), but he does fulfil the law of Christ, which is the law of charity. It is implied that those who do the works of the flesh are under the law, that is, under its curse.

---

[51] 'If you are led by the Spirit' (v. 18) probably means 'by your own spirit clothed with and strengthened by the Holy Spirit.'

2. The two ways are linked to the question, Who is the heir?, by means of the central verse (21b): the one way leads into the inheritance, the other does not.

3. The two ways are thoroughly christianized: the way of the Spirit is the way along which the Spirit of Christ leads the believer into the kingdom of Christ; and this way involves 'crucifixion' of the flesh (v. 24) — hence assimilation to Christ crucified.

4. Among the 'works of the flesh' prominence is given to just those which are threatening to destroy the unity of the church in Galatia — strife, jealousy, quarrels, dissensions.

The Epistle does not, of course, give a complete account of St Paul's theology. The Two-Ways text leaves behind a number of questions to which no answer is supplied in this Epistle:

1. How does it come about that in the unredeemed man the flesh is as a rule so much stronger than the spirit? To this, St Paul gives his answer in Rom 5. The devil led Adam into sin; sin largely destroyed the strength of the spirit (in Adam and in his posterity); and the flesh thus gained the upper hand. [52]

2. How does it come about that the flesh remains so strong even in the baptized Christian? Why does he receive only a first instalment of the Spirit? To this St Paul offers no answer at all. He might consider the question impertinent (cf. Rom 9:20).

3. How far are the impulses of the flesh to be attributed to the external influence of Beliar? When St Paul uses such language (e.g. in 2 Cor 6), does he mean it to be taken literally?

4. *How* does a man ally himself with the Holy Spirit against Beliar? Is this simply a way of exhorting him to avoid impurity, idolatry, quarrelling, etc., and to practise patience, kindness, fidelity, etc.?

5. If exclusion from the inheritance is the penalty for doing the works of the flesh, is admission to the inheritance the reward for producing the harvest of the spirit? Or is the harvest its own 'absolute' or 'katalectic' reward, as the Stoics would say? [53] St Thomas discusses this question and answers it with a neat scholastic distinction: 'Works of virtue are to be desired for their own sake *formaliter*, but not *finaliter*.'[54] He explains that although these works are from one point of view 'fruits', from another they are

---

[52] See further below, pp. 464-465.
[53] Cf. Marcus Aurelius, *Meditations*, IX, 41, and Antigonus of Socho, in *Pirqe Aboth*, I, 3: 'Be not like servants who minister to their master upon the condition of receiving a reward; but be like servants who minister to their master without the condition of receiving a reward.'
[54] St Thomas, Gal, 434 A.

blossoms: 'They are called "blossoms" in respect of future beatitude, because just as blossoms give hope of fruit, so from works of
virtue comes hope of eternal life and beatitude.' [55] To judge from
Rom 6: 21-23, St Paul would avoid calling eternal life a 'reward':
the wages of sin is death; but eternal life is not the wages of
justice. [56]

### Could the Two Ways still be used in Christian preaching?

The aim of a Two-Ways text is to convince the reader or hearer
that the choices and decisions of his life are not unrelated to one
another. Whether he is aware of it or not, underlying his particular
decisions there is a radical decision to choose one or other of the two
possible ways of life. The human race divides basically into two classes
of men, the sons of light and the sons of darkness, the sons of God
and the sons of Belial, those who walk according to the spirit and
those who drift according to the flesh. (The older a man is, the more
clearly he recognizes this truth, when it is pointed out to him.) A
preacher who uses the two ways, challenges his hearer to re-examine
his own fundamental choice, to commit himself wholeheartedly to the
way of light, and for the future to live it out consciously, deliberately
and consistently. Psychologically, the argument is powerful, partly
because 'opposites juxtaposed illuminate each other' (*opposita iuxta
se posita magis exsplendescunt,* as the grammarians say), and partly
because it invites the reader to draw the conclusion from the whole
of his own moral experience.

The Two Ways is a device which belongs to *kerygma* quite as
much as to *didache.* [57] It makes a strong appeal to the conscience of
the unconverted man (cf. Rom 2: 15). When the two ways are set
forth vividly, there is something in every man which inclines him
toward choosing the way of life, namely, his conscience. It is the duty
of the preacher to call upon this ally lurking in the breast of every
hearer and to encourage him with the promise of divine assistance:
'Hitherto you have not found the strength to follow perseveringly the
way of life; but now new strength is offered to you from God: believe
in Christ, and he will give you his Holy Spirit.'

There are, however, certain disadvantages in the use of this device
for the preaching of the gospel. First, this form carries with it the

---

[55] St Thomas, Gal, 433 D.
[56] The Epistle to the Romans contains descriptions of the Two Ways: the Way
of Death in 1:19—2:16 is balanced by the Way of Life in 12:1—15:13.
[57] Cf. C. H. Dodd, *The Apostolic Preaching and Its Developments,* London, 1936,
pp. 6-7.

danger of spiritual conceit. The preacher and the hearer are encouraged to identify the actual way of life of their own community with The Way of Life, and to assume that all who are not members are following the way of death. The danger is obvious enough in the Dead Sea Scrolls, and is further illustrated by the Pharisee in Christ's parable, who congratulates himself on following the way of life, and takes it for granted that the publican is on the road to perdition. St Paul himself sails close to the wind when denouncing the pagans in Rom 1 : 29-31. It is difficult to read such a passage with the emphasis required by its emotive language without feeling mightily superior to the persons denounced, and without forgetting that no man walks in either way with perfect consistency. As Elijah said, all go limping.

Secondly, we now find it difficult to take literally the Two-Spirit theology with which the Two Ways are usually associated. The Iranian belief that an evil spirit took a hand in man's creation is rejected as pure mythology; but we are no longer sure how far we should take St Paul's account of original sin literally. Darwin and his followers have at length convinced us that man, in so far as he is an animal, is evolved from the animal kingdom. We can, therefore, no longer marvel that his conduct often resembles the behaviour of beasts or that his beastly instincts are so difficult to control. The wonder is not that there is so much evil in man, but rather that there is so much good. To explain the good and the evil in his conduct, we no longer feel any need to postulate the constant intervention of 'spirits' good and bad. Take an animal and give him the power of reason, and what else can you expect but a mixture of reason and unreason in his conduct? To expect that he should always follow the path of reason is to ask too much of such a hybrid creature.

## Are the Two Ways to be linked with the Two Cities of 4:25-26?

There is no structural link between the two Jerusalems in 4 : 25-26 and the Two Ways described in 5 : 19-23. Since the way of the flesh is not the way laid down by the law of the earthly Jerusalem, St Paul would certainly not accept as a legitimate development of this thought the suggestion that while those who follow the way of the spirit are citizens of the heavenly Jerusalem, those who follow the way of the flesh belong to the earthly Jerusalem. Hence, if the two ways are to be connected with two cities, some pagan city must be set over against the heavenly Jerusalem. St Augustine chose Babylon — an excellent choice, since Jerusalem is the city of peace (*shalôm*) and Babylon is the city of confusion (*balal*). He restated the doctrine of the Two Ways in the imagery of two cities (or citizenships, *civitates*). In this

form it was popular throughout the middle ages and deeply influenced
St Ignatius of Loyola, through whose *Spiritual Exercises* it continues
to influence large numbers of Christians to this day

The origin of St Augustine's doctrine of the Two Cities is a matter
of dispute. The occurrence of two cities in Gal 4 and two ways in
Gal 5 may have had something to do with it.

Some critics have thought that St Augustine derived the idea of
the Two Cities directly from the Scriptures. [58] But the Scriptural
passages which he quotes as containing the idea are not necessarily
the *source* of the idea. [59] Others have suggested that Augustine took
over the idea from the Manicheans, who described in dualistic terms
a kingdom of light and a kingdom of darkness. This conjecture should
not be rejected simply because St Augustine's doctrine of the Two
Cities is not dualistic (i.e., does not presuppose a dualistic metaphysic
in which good and evil spring from two independent principles). [60]
Just as the Two-Ways probably originated in the dualistic system of
Zoroaster, and was corrected by Jewish and Christian users, so too
it is possible that the image of the Two Cities was first developed
by the dualistic Manicheans, and corrected by St Augustine and other
Christian writers. [61] There is no room here to discuss this historical
problem. [62] It will suffice to show that in working out the contrast
between the two cities St Augustine made some use of Gal 5. In one
of the best known passages of his *City of God*, he writes: [63]

> Two loves, then, have given origin to these two cities (or citizenships [64]):
> self-love going so far as contempt of God has made the earthly city, love
> of God going so far as contempt of self has made the heavenly city. The
> one glories in itself, the other glories in the Lord. For the one seeks glory
> from men, the other finds its greatest glory in God, the witness of con-
> science. The one raises up its own head in its own glory; the other says
> to God: 'Thou art my glory, thou raisest up my head.' The one is ruled
> by lust of power in its princes and over the nations it subjugates; in the
> other rulers and subjects *serve one another in charity* (Gal 5:13), the rulers
> by giving counsel, the subjects by obeying.

---

[58] Cf. J. W. C. Wand, *St Augustine's City of God*, London, 1963, p. xiv; G.
Bardy in *Oeuvres de saint Augustin*, 33 (Bibliothéque augustinienne) Bruges,
1959, p. 59.
[59] E.g. Pss 86:3; 47:2-3, 9; 45:5-6, quoted in the *City of God*, XI, 1.
[60] Cf. Bardy, op. cit., p. 59.
[61] See the quotation from Tichonius in Bardy, op. cit., p. 64.
[62] Cf. J. Ratzinger, 'Herkunft und Sinn der Civitaslehre,' in *Augustinus Magister*,
Paris, 1954, pp. 965-979.
[63] *City of God*, XIV, 28.
[64] The Latin *civitas* means not only 'a city' (e.g. Rome) but also 'citizenship' and
concretely the whole body of citizens wherever they may be (e.g. the Roman
citizens scattered throughout the colonies, municipalities, etc., of the Roman
Empire).

It is unlikely that St Ignatius of Loyola had read Augustine's
*City of God* at the time when he composed the *Spiritual Exercises*.
Knowledge of Augustine's thought was mediated to him, however,
through certain medieval writers who made excerpts from the works
of Augustine. There is a remarkably close resemblance between the
meditation on the Two Standards and the following passage from a
Florilegium compiled by a certain Werner of Küssenberg, a Benedictine
abbot who died in 1174: [65]

> Of St Augustine: He composed a work *On the City of God,* where he
> treats of two cities, namely Jerusalem and Babylon, and their kings; the
> king of Jerusalem is Christ, the king of Babylon is the devil. These two
> cities, he says in the same work, are built for themselves by two loves: the
> city of the devil was constructed by love-of-self growing as far as contempt
> of God; the city of God by love-of-God growing as far as contempt of
> self....Between these two cities there is constant war, discord and battle;
> each marks out his own soldiers — Christ his, and the devil his, so that
> they recognize their king and follow him. The soldiers of Christ follow
> *their* king, and the soldiers of the devil follow theirs.

Either from this text, or from some later writer dependent on Werner,
St Ignatius developed his meditation on the Two Standards, which
has been described as the central point of the whole *Exercises*, [66]
and the characteristically Ignatian 'Rules for the Discernment of
Spirits.' These latter are strongly reminiscent of the passage quoted
above from the *Shepherd* of Hermas (see pp. 454-455).

### Is v. 21b consistent with 3:18?

In v. 21b, at the centre of the section, St Paul promulgates a
severe law. In effect he says: 'You shall not commit fornication,
impurity, licentiousness, idolatry, and the rest; or else you will not
inherit the kingdom.' [67] His adversaries might well protest at this
point: 'Did you not say in 3:18 that if the inheritance depends on
law, it no longer depends on the promise?'

St Paul would presumably answer that in v. 21b he has simply
made explicit a condition which was implied in the promise from the
beginning: from the nature of the case, those who commit the works
of the flesh cannot enter the presence of God. But the ritual law of

---

[65] Cf. F. Fournier, 'Les "Deux Cités" dans la littérature chrétienne,' *Etudes* 123
(1910), pp. 644-665. For Werner's Latin text see Fournier, p. 658, or PL
157, 1144.
[66] Cf. H. Rahner, *Notes on the Spiritual Exercises,* Woodstock College Press,
Woodstock (U.S.A.), 1956, p. 323.
[67] Cf. Apoc 21:8.

the old covenant was not implicit in the original promise; it was something 'added' (3:19), for disciplinary reasons.

It turns out, then, that this is our condition: we cannot, strictly speaking, earn the inheritance by our good works, but we can lose it by bad works or by the omission of good works which the law of charity demands. The dependence of the inheritance both on the divine promise and on man's fulfilment of the law of charity is less clear in St Paul than it is in Mt 25:34, where Christ is pictured as saying to the elect at the Last Judgment: 'Come ye *blessed of my Father;* inherit the kingdom prepared for you; for I was hungry and *you gave me to eat,*' etc. Here the inheritance is stated to be dependent both on the Father's blessing (*eulogia,* cf. Gal 3:9, 14) and on charitable service of one's neighbour. Final justification does not depend on faith alone. On the day of judgment, even charismatic faith will be no claim to justification, in the absence of good works (cf. Mt 7:22-23).

*Why does the flesh lust against the spirit and vice versa (5:17)?*

In a dualistic system, the answer to this question would be that flesh is by nature corrupt and prone to evil. But St Paul is not a dualist. [68] He accepts the teaching of Genesis that man, as originally created, was good. But he does not necessarily mean that the instinctive desires of the flesh which now so often prevail over the spirit were not present in the flesh of unfallen man. These instincts are not in themselves evil. Unfallen man could still be described as 'good' through and through, if the spirit was then strong enough to keep the impulses of the flesh under control and prevent them from breaking out into sinful actions. It is not even necessary to suppose that unfallen man always found it easy to control the desires of the flesh. God was under no obligation to create the best of all possible worlds or the most perfect of all possible men. It is conceivable that he created man imperfect and intended him to pass through a period of trial before attaining his perfection. Neither in Genesis nor in the Epistles of St Paul is it said that the struggle between the flesh and the spirit is simply a consequence of sin. [69] If man is in fact descended from brutes 'according to the flesh', it may have been God's will that the animal impulses should remain within him to test him and give him the opportunity to develop spiritual strength (cf. 2 Cor 12:9). A passage from Epictetus will illustrate this point: [70]

---

[68]  Cf. Whiteley, *The Theology of St Paul,* pp. 39-41.
[69]  Cf. Dubarle, *Original Sin,* pp. 188-191.
[70]  Epictetus, *Discourses,* I, 6.

What do you think would have become of Heracles if there had not been a lion, as in the story, and a hydra and a stag and a boar and unjust and brutal men, whom he drove forth, and cleansed the world of them? What would he have done, if there had been nothing of this sort? Is it not plain that he would have wrapped himself up and slept? Nay, to begin with, he would never have been a Heracles at all, had he slumbered, all his life, in such ease and luxury; and if by any chance he had been, of what good would he have been? What use would he have made of his arms and his might and his endurance and noble heart as well, had he not been stimulated and trained by such perils and opportunities?

On the supposition that the spirit and the flesh (Heracles and the wild beasts) were already in conflict before the Fall, the effect of sin must have been to infect the spirit of man with weakness (i.e., with 'death'); as a result, the previous balance of power was altered. The spirit could no longer control the flesh, which therefore appeared so much the stronger and the more unruly. Thus the flesh became sinful, not through some corrupting infection of itself, but through the failure of the spirit to keep it in control.

In Gal 5 : 17, St Paul does not explain why the flesh and the spirit are at enmity. Perhaps he would have accepted the explanation just proposed. If even in unfallen man there was a state of tension between spirit and flesh, these two must be by nature antagonistic — a positive and negative, created to check each other. Yet there is no doubt which of the two *ought* to prevail — and the more completely the better. The one is naturally subordinate to the other, but is not naturally acquiescent.

In the light of modern evolutionary ideas, one might say that in general [71] the 'works of the flesh' are the works of the animal in us. The man whose spirit is strengthened by the Holy Spirit becomes progressively less beast-like and more human, humane, and God-like. Even without the aid of evolutionary ideas, Epictetus saw this clearly: [72]

> By reason of this lower kinship some of us fall away and become like wolves, faithless and treacherous and mischievous, others like lions, savage and brutal and untameable, but the greater part of us become foxes and the most god-forsaken creatures in the animal world. For a foul-mouthed and wicked man is no better than a fox or the meanest and most miserable of creatures. Look to it then, and beware lest you turn out to be one of these god-forsaken creatures.

The Holy Spirit, strengthening our human spirit, is therefore the power of God unto civilization.

---

[71] See above, pp. 439-440.
[72] Epictetus, *Discourses*, I, 3; cf. Freud, *The Future of an Illusion*, p. 11 (Complete Psychological Works, Vol. XXI), and Knight, *Christian Theology of the O.T.*, pp. 163-164.

*Why does St Paul speak of the 'works' of the flesh but of the 'fruit' of the Spirit?*

Let Theodore of Mopsuestia reply: [73]

He did well to use 'works' of the flesh, because those things are done by us; but in speaking of the Spirit he wrote 'fruit' because it is through grace and through the cooperation of the Spirit that we attain these fruits. Alone by ourselves we cannot achieve the works of virtue, just as we cannot produce the fruits of the earth, however hard we work, unless God deigns to give them.

This comparison with the fruits of the earth shows how fitting it is to pray for the fruits of the Spirit. A Christian might well use the prayer of the Athenians quoted by Marcus Aurelius with the comment: 'Either pray not at all (cf. Mt 6:32), or in this simple and frank fashion': [74]

Rain, rain, O dear Zeus, upon the corn-lands of the Athenians and their meads.

We plough, but God produces the harvest, whether of corn or of virtues. The same philosopher makes the interesting suggestion that it is more fitting to pray for things which are already in our power than for things which are not: [75]

Who told thee that the gods do not cooperate with us even in the things that are in our power? Begin at any rate with prayers for such things and thou wilt see. One prays: 'How may I lie with that woman!' Thou: 'How may I not lust with her!' Another: 'How may I quit of that man!' Thou: 'How may I not wish to be quit of him!' Another: 'How may I not lose my little child!' Thou: 'How may I not dread to lose him!' In a word, give thy prayers this turn, and see what comes of it.

*Why is the first list longer than the second?*

St Thomas raises the question why St Paul did not make his second list (nine fruits) as long as his first (fifteen works). He replies, almost with a sigh: 'The answer is: he did not do so because the vices are more numerous than the virtues.' [76]

*'Charity, joy, peace' — How are these three related to one another?*

St Thomas divides the fruits of the Spirit into those which perfect a man interiorly and those which perfect him exteriorly, then sub-

---

[73] Theodore, Gal, p. 101.
[74] Marcus Aurelius, *Meditations*, V, 7.
[75] Marcus Aurelius, *Meditations*, IX, 40. Cf. however, Jn 4:49.
[76] St Thomas, Gal, 435 A.

divides the first group into those which perfect him interiorly with regard to what is good, namely, charity, joy and peace, and those which perfect him interiorly with regard to what is evil, namely, patience and longanimity. [77] Thus charity, joy and peace form a group apart. St Thomas explains that the first interior movement of the soul towards good is *love;* this movement finds its perfection and completion in *joy,* which arises in the presence of that which is loved, and in *peace,* which comes from possession of that which is loved.

But all this is too scholastic and monastic. Recently, a young nurse on 'Woman's Hour' said that the joy of being a nurse is to be a member of a team which moves smoothly and efficiently into action when an injured person is brought in, each member of the team pouring out his skill and care to make the sick person well. [78] Here is joy springing from charity expressed in action. If the Good Samaritan found himself surprised by joy after leaving a certain man at the inn, and if he slept soundly at Jericho that night, his joy and his peace were 'fruits of the Spirit'.

*Have Christians a monopoly of the Spirit (5:24)?*

In 5 : 24, St Paul says that Christians have crucified the flesh and its desires. Hence they are committed to the way of the Spirit. He does not say, but the whole context suggests, that the same is not true of the Jews (cf. Eph 2 : 3), and still less of the pagans. This eighth section might easily give the impression that Christians alone live according to the spirit of charity. But this is not true. The nurse quoted in the last paragraph went on to say that she had no religious belief; and an American priest who entertained the present writer at his presbytery for a few weeks spoke three or four times about the most charitable man he had ever met — a prison governor who spent all his private income on the after-care of prisoners, and yet practised no religion at all. To the priest in question, this man was a theological puzzle. From our reading of St Paul we are led to believe that such an unselfish way of life can only be the expression of a firm faith (cf. Gal 5 : 6).

Here a great difficulty presents itself: religious faith and practice often fail to produce the expected fruits of the Spirit, and the fruit of the Spirit is quite often found unsupported by religious faith. If

[77] St Thomas, Gal, 434 B.
[78] The same Woman's Hour included a letter from a male listener who complained that many of the items in this programme were far too good to be wasted on women.

Christianity consists in living according to the spirit of charity, it would seem that some of the best Christians do not believe in Christ. The explanation of this paradox is to be found in the Christology of Colossians: Christ is creator as well as redeemer, the source of natural as well as of supernatural charity. But Christians who have his supernatural revelation should be ashamed if they are outdone by those who are without it. Their charity ought to be a commendation of the gospel; but this requires their cooperation (cf. Phil 2:12-13).

*How does St Paul connect Christian morality with the Cross and Resurrection?*

With the aid of the distinction between the flesh and the spirit, St Paul is able to show how Christian morality brings the life of the Christian into conformity with Christ crucified, that is, into conformity with Christ who *was* crucified and *is* now risen. [79]

In so far as the Christian crucifies his own flesh by abstaining from the works of the flesh (v. 20), by 'doing to death the practices of the body' (Rom 8:13), or in other words by 'crucifying the flesh with its passions and its lusts' (v. 24), he takes on the likeness of Christ crucified.

Out of the death of the flesh rises the harvest of the spirit (v. 22). Therefore, in so far as the Christian produces the harvest of the spirit, he is conformed to Christ risen from the dead. The risen Christ, who has become 'a life-giving Spirit' (1 Cor 15:45), enables those who believe in him both to do to death the practices of the body and to produce the harvest of the Spirit. They have only to set to work to produce this harvest, and they will find that they can do it: they will 'experience the power of Christ's resurrection' (i.e., of Christ in his risen state) and will find the promise of their baptism fulfilled: 'if we have been united with him in a death like his, we shall also be united with him in his resurrection' (i.e., in his risen life). [80]

In this world, therefore, the life of a Christian is, or should be, on the one hand a long drawn out crucifixion of the flesh, but on the other a participation in Christ's risen life. To adapt a phrase of St Augustine's, the Christian life is *quaedam prolixitas mortis et resurrectionis.*

---

[79] On the meaning of 'Christ crucified' (*estaurômenos*) see above, p. 228.
[80] In the two texts quoted here, Phil 3:10 and Rom 6:5, *anastasis* means, not the act of rising from the dead, but the life of one who has risen from the dead; i.e., *anastasis* = 'risen life'.

*The Fourth Subsection, 5:24—6:2*

## THE LAW OF CHRIST

It was conjectured above that 6 : 1 (like 5 : 15) was inserted by St Paul when he incorporated this section into the Epistle. If this verse is omitted, 5 : 24-25 with 6 : 2 form a symmetrical pattern.

A  *5 : 24* Those who belong to Christ Jesus    B   have crucified the flesh C   with its passions and its lusts.   D   *25* If we live by the spirit,   E   let us walk by the spirit.   D¹  *26* Let us not be puffed up with empty conceit,   C¹ trying to outdo one another (*allelous*), jealous of one another (*allelois*).   B¹  *6 : 2* Bear the burden of one another (*allelôn*), [81] A¹  and in this way you will fulfil the law of Christ.

*What is the mark of a true Christian according to St Paul?*

The mark of 'those who belong to Christ' is that they fulfil the law of Christ, by crucifying the flesh with its passions and lusts. This is St Paul's restatement of the words of Christ: 'If anyone wishes to come after me, let him deny himself and take up his cross and follow me' (Mt 16 : 24); and 'whoever does not carry [82] his cross and come after me, cannot be my disciple' (Lk 14 : 27). V. 24 is, therefore, of great importance as the middle term linking St Paul's dogmatic statements about Christ's death with his moral instruction about the conduct expected of Christians. Indeed his fondness for the antithesis 'flesh/spirit' may spring from the discovery that it solves the preacher's problem of making a smooth transition from dogmatic statements to moral exhortation. [83]

To 'crucify the flesh with its passions and lusts' does not mean, in the first place, to practise corporal austerities. The second half of the subsection (C¹) shows what kind of passions and lusts St Paul has

---

[81]  This use of the same word in different cases is a trope called *ptôsis* by the Greek rhetoricians.

[82]  The Greek verb here is *bastazein*, as in Gal 6 : 2 and 6 : 5. This word is used in other connections, but in the mind of any regular reader of the gospels it is strongly associated with cross-bearing. By using the same word of the followers of Christ, St Paul not only shows that in exercising charity they are imitating Christ carrying his cross, but conversely he also shows that Christ carrying his cross was fulfilling his own law, because he was bearing the burden of the sins of others.

[83]  It is a notable weakness of many otherwise excellent sermons of St John Chrysostom that a violent break occurs between the end of the dogmatic section and the opening of the moral section.

chiefly in mind — envy and jealousy and the desire to excel. 'The flesh' is active in relations with other people which bring out the selfishness in every man.

The Christian who is filled with the Spirit, or alive with the Spirit, or seething with the Spirit, [84] cannot be puffed up with a vain desire of glory. He must not display his religious 'works' so as to stir up a spirit of selfish competition; and he must not be jealous of another's spiritual good. If others behave in this way, their conduct is a burden which the Christian must accept as his cross — the 'carrying' of it is part of the 'crucifixion of his flesh'. By carrying the cross (of his neighbour's vexatious conduct) a Christian fulfils the law of Christ. [85] St John Berchmans was entirely in the spirit of this passage when he said: 'My greatest mortification is community life' (*mea maxima mortificatio vita communis*). Impatience with one's neighbour's faults is refusal to bear the cross — not conscious refusal, of course; for the most part, the impatient man has simply failed to recognize the cross presented to him as the cross which God wishes him to carry. St Paul is trying to remedy such ignorance in vv. 25-26.

The verse inserted within this subsection (6:1) has itself a symmetrical structure:

A  Brethren, if a man falls into some misdeed,   B  you who are spiritual
C  must put him right   B¹  in a spirit of meekness,   A¹  with an eye
on yourself, lest you too be tempted.

The faults of our neighbour are our cross. But St Paul does not bid us accept the cross and carry it in silence. [86] What he enjoins is even harder: 'Correct the man — but in a spirit of gentleness.' The natural impulse of the flesh is to bite and devour the offender (v. 15). To remain silent and say nothing is already a victory for the spirit. But St Paul, following the instructions given by Christ in Mt 18:15, bids those who claim to be 'spiritual men' to prove it by correcting the offender 'in a spirit of meekness', that is, with gentleness, courtesy and good humour, in restrained language, and without passion.

He also suggests three considerations which may help the corrector to be gentle. First, he calls the brother who has fallen a 'man', not a brother. The suggestion is that man is frail, and to err is human.

[84] In v. 25 St Paul is again playing with *zeô/zaô*. See above, pp. 416 and 430.
[85] By teaching this law, Christianity civilizes men. Cf. Freud, *The Future of an Illusion*, p. 6: 'It is remarkable that, little as men are able to exist in isolation, they should nevertheless feel as a heavy burden the sacrifices which civilization expects of them in order to make a communal life possible.'
[86] The faults which St Paul has in mind involve doctrinal error, which must be checked. There is evidence in Didache 11:4—12:1 that there was perplexity in the early Church as to how one could reconcile Christ's prohibition against

Secondly, he uses a verb which implies that the offender has been caught unawares by temptation [87] — with the implication that he would not have fallen had he been on his guard. And thirdly, he tells the corrector to bear in mind his own frailty — suggesting that here too the rule applies: 'Treat others as you would wish to be treated in similar circumstances.' St Paul might have added: 'Correct others in a spirit of gentleness, *bearing in mind your own past sins.*' It is surely significant that Christ gave his apostles power to forgive sins immediately after he had forgiven them for deserting him in his passion. In Jn 20:22, first they are reconciled ('Receive the Holy Spirit'); then they receive power to absolve ('Whose sins you shall forgive...').

The structure of the eighth section suggests a further motive for gentleness in correcting others. A slave is less than a man. Therefore when a Christian is freed from the slavery of Sin by the gift of the Spirit, he begins to be truly human. The works of the flesh are sub-human; the fruits of the spirit alone are worthy of man. To show self-control and therefore gentleness in correcting others is a proof of strength. It is more human and more masculine. This motive (a strong and effective one) was used by the Stoics, [88] but that is no reason why a Christian preacher should not use it. Every Christian should respect the human nature which God wonderfully created and still more wonderfully restored. He shows respect for it by doing nothing unworthy of it. St Leo the Great, who was no less a Christian for his Stoicism, appeals to this motive in a famous Christmas sermon: *Agnosce, O Christiane, dignitatem tuam :* 'Recognize, O Christian, your dignity!'

*Is the word 'spiritual' used ironically in 6:1?*

6:1 can be read as meaning: 'You who pride yourselves on being "spiritual men" should give evidence of your spirituality by correcting others in a spirit of gentleness.' But more probably the note of irony is absent. Those who follow the way of the flesh are 'fleshly men' (*sarkikoi*); those who follow the way of the spirit are 'spiritual men' (*pneumatikoi*).

There is an obvious danger that anyone who calls *himself* a 'spiritual man' will become, if he has not already become, a priggish,

---

judging others (Mt 7:1) with his warning to beware of false prophets (Mt 7: 15): how was it possible to recognize a false prophet without passing judgment upon him?

[87] Cf. Chrysostom, PG 61, 673 D.

[88] Cf. Marcus Aurelius, *Meditations*, XI, 10.

pompous, and self-important person. Thus the word easily lends itself to ironic use. But there is no clear instance of an ironic use in St Paul's Epistles. In 1 Cor 2:15 and 3:1 it is used in a purely descriptive sense.

### *Does St Paul's theology take sufficient account of post-baptismal sin?*

In 6:1 St Paul touches lightly on the question of post-baptismal sin. It is surprising how little he has to say on this extremely important topic. [89] The reason may be that his own theology of baptism made post-baptismal sin an anomaly: it ought not to occur in fact, and when it does, it conflicts with theological theory. Just as the death of Christians took the people of Thessalonica by surprise, so too the committing of sin and the frequency of sin within the Gentile churches probably took St Paul by surprise; and it is questionable whether he modified his position sufficiently to render the presence of sin in the Church intelligible.

The history of the Church in the next few centuries suggests that bishops and other theologians who inherited St Paul's legacy were not satisfied with his position. At least, they adjusted the practice of the Church so as to reduce the discrepancy between theory and practice. For St Paul, baptism, administered at the very beginning of a man's Christian life, makes him a full and perfect Christian, in the sense that there is no higher degree to which he can later be promoted. He has died to sin and to the world; he has the Holy Spirit; he ought not to sin, and he is able not to sin. But in practice, the baptized Christian remained subject to the temptation and fell into sin. This was not, and is not, a wholly exceptional and paradoxical situation, but rather the normal thing. If the administration of baptism at the very outset of Christian life rested on the expectation that after baptism a man would normally lead a sinless life, once this expectation had been proved false it was reasonable for Church authorities to change their practice in regard to the administration of baptism. They introduced the catechumenate. Henceforth, the first step in Christian life was no longer baptism but admission to the catechumenate; [90] baptism, administered after two or three years of probation in this grade, implied that the catechumen had now learned to follow Christ, that he had already abandoned his sinful past, and that he was now

---

[89] St Thomas, Gal, 399 A, records an attempt to apply 2:17 to post-baptismal sin. But this does not fit the context.

[90] Cf. the Council of Elvira, in Mansi, *Concilia*, t. II, cols 5-19, and above, pp. 318-319.

capable of leading the sinless life to which, according to St Paul's theology, the sacrament of baptism commits the recipient.

These developments were forced upon the Church by the discrepancy which existed between St Paul's theology of baptism and of the Spirit and the realities of Church-life which this theology was supposed to explain. The Church could not simply repeat the doctrine and continue the practice of St Paul, because they did not square with each other satisfactorily. Some adjustment was necessary, either in the theological doctrine or in the sacramental practice.

In later centuries, the Church restored baptism to its original position as the sacrament of admission to the Christian life and reduced the catechumenate to a mere vestige. Post-baptismal sin was dealt with by developing the system of private penance. But this solution too has its disadvantages. It leads to a devaluation of baptism: this sacrament, administered in infancy, seems to make no difference; the Christian's hope of salvation is placed in the forgiveness of God mediated through penance rather than in the forgiveness granted in baptism and probably lost. And secondly, not all Christians by any means have the courage to confess their sins (particularly sins of the flesh) with that degree of 'integrity' which the moral theologians declare to be necessary; [91] then they fear that they have not used this sacrament worthily and lose the peace in God which, according to St Paul's theology, a Christian should habitually enjoy (cf. Rom 5:1-5). In other words, St Paul bequeathed to the Church a problem to which as yet no fully satisfactory solution has been found.

### What is 'the law of Christ'?

In the structure of the eighth section (p. 435) and of the third main division (p. 411), 6:2, in which occurs the first and only mention of 'the law of Christ', is linked to the precept 'You shall love your neighbour as yourself.' As the *Didache* shows (see p. 453), this positive precept implicitly forbids all the works of the flesh catalogued in vv. 19-20. V. 21b expresses the sanction attached to this law.

The 'law of Christ' might be described as a repromulgation by Christ of the moral parts of the Mosaic law (cf. Mt 19:17-22). But Christ 'promulgated' the law in a new sense: his 'Finger' rewrites it

---

91 Jn 20:23 shows that the Church has power to forgive all post-baptismal sin; it does not, explicitly at least, impose on the faithful the obligation to confess all post-baptismal sins. Nor does Mt 18:15-20 require that all post-baptismal sin be brought to the knowledge of the Church. But see above, p. 300.

in the hearts of those who believe. Since all who believe in him are one with him (3:28), his law is a self-imposed law, not an external restraint. Moreover, the law which Christ repromulgates is in reality the law written in man's nature by the Logos at creation (cf. Rom 2:15) and obscured by sin.

It follows that God has attached the supernatural sanction (of admission to or exclusion from the kingdom) to observance of the law written from creation in man's heart. It also follows that the law of Christ is in agreement with the best intuitions of philosophers and of non-Christian religions. Their formulations of the laws of man's nature may be of value to Christians. A third corollary is that, since the task of the Church is to teach the law of Christ, it is the task of the Church to expound the law of our nature, for the two are essentially one. Nor is the Church's teaching for Christians only. It is for all men, to help them become truly men. When Christ gave his teaching on marriage, he cut away the ground beneath the feet of Hillel and Shammai by going back to the law of creation (cf. Mk 10:2-9). [92]

The law of charity (v. 14), which turns out in 6:2 to be 'the law of Christ', is in fact the law on which all civilization is based.

## Why has St Paul delayed so long before mentioning the 'law of Christ'?

After so much talk about liberation from law, it comes as a shock to find in 6:2 that Christians are required to fulfil a law after all. Why did not St Paul say to the Galatians from the beginning: 'You are to obey not the law of Moses but the law of Christ, and the law of Christ does not require circumcision or abstinence from certain types of food or observance of regular feast days, but only charity to your neighbour'? Or why did he not simply distinguish between the ceremonial precepts and the moral precepts of the law of Moses, and say that Christ had cancelled the ceremonial precepts?

The reason may be that Christ himself did not declare the Mosaic law obsolete in whole or in part; on the contrary, he said that not the slightest part of it would pass away until the whole passed away — which of course implied that when any part of it passed away the whole would go with it. Thus St Paul's view is that the whole body of Mosaic legislation is obsolete; what it leaves behind is the 'law' of the patriarchal days — the unwritten code of behaviour of men who, like Abraham, believed God and were justified.

---

[92]  Cf. J. A. T. Robinson, *Honest to God*, London, 1963, p. 110, and above, pp. 436-437.

What St Paul omits to say is that the unwritten tradition of the patriarchs was put into written form by Moses. It was overlaid with religious practices, but there was probably little in the oral tradition of the patriarchs that did not become written in the Torah. St Paul does not make it clear that when he rejects written law, he is retaining its substance on other grounds. There is, however, a hint of this in v. 14.

Further, for St Paul 'law' really means 'written law'. That is why he speaks as if there was no law in the patriarchal period, and why he is so reluctant to describe the law of Christ as law. 'Law' is external, it is written, it exercises constraint. In these three respects the 'law of Christ' is not a law at all. [93] It is better called the spirit of charity. A man who has this spirit knows what he ought to do, wants to do it, and does it. Thus the 'law' of Christ is a life-giving law and does impart justice (cf. 3:21).

What St Paul has been saying throughout the Epistle is that Christians have been freed from ritual law in order to devote themselves, unhindered and unimpeded, to works of charity. This is one of the ideas expressed in the parable of the Good Samaritan: the Samaritan, who is not impeded by the ritual laws of the Jews, is free to obey the promptings of charity, whereas the priest and the levite are not. The Mosaic law had created some purely artificial notions of 'defilement' which, though originally useful, had ended by becoming a real impediment to works of charity and mercy, both corporal and spiritual. That is why Christ raised the question what defiles a man (cf. Mk 7:15-23).

## How do Christians 'bear one another's burdens'?

In the light of the two preceding verses, 6:2 means: 'Be patient with the faults of others and be patient in correcting them; in this way you will fulfil Christ's precept of charity.' St Jerome presses the words even further, and takes them to mean: 'Share in your neighbour's penance.' To show that the neighbour's 'burden' is the weight of sins he carries, Jerome quotes Ps 38:4: 'My iniquities have gone over my head; they weigh like a burden too heavy for me.' He continues: [94]

---

[93] E. Bammel, 'Nomos Christou,' TU 88, pp. 120-128, remarks (p. 128) that the phrase 'the law of Christ' was coined 'in an almost playful manner'. But it is difficult to discern the slightest trace of humour in the urgent warnings of 6:1-10. St Paul is not smiling here any more than when he coins the phrase 'the law of Sin' in Rom 7:23.

[94] St Jerome, PL 26, 455-456.

This burden our Saviour bore for us, teaching us by his example what we ought to do. He 'carries our iniquities and grieves on our behalf' (Isa 53:4-5) and invites those who are oppressed by the burden of their sins and of the law to take up the light burden of virtue, saying: 'My yoke is sweet and my burden light' (Mt 11:30). He, therefore, who does not despair of his brother's salvation but stretches out a hand to the petitioner, and, so far as he can, weeps with the weeper, is weak with the weak, and deems as his own the sins of others — *he* by his charity fulfils the law of Christ.

Taken in this way, 6:1 is specially addressed to the presbyters of the Church. It is they in particular who must not only be patient in correcting, but must also share in the sinner's penance — in his contrition, his confession, and his satisfaction. When a priest hears the confession of a sinner, he should not listen as a detached and impersonal judge, but should share in and help to deepen the penitent's sorrow. The liturgy of penance makes him pray with and for the penitent. And he should make some vicarious satisfaction to aid the penitent in his repentance. [95]

More generally, a Christian 'bears his neighbour's burden' whenever he helps him in his needs. Here again, St Jerome's comment is excellent: [96]

He too bears his brother's need who helps a poor brother oppressed by the burden of poverty and thus wins friends by the unjust mammon (Lk 16:9). After the resurrection Christ will address him thus: 'Come to me, you who are blessed by my Father; enter into possession of the kingdom prepared for you from the beginning of the world. For I was hungry and you gave me to eat; I was thirsty and you gave me to drink' (Mt 25:34-35).

The quotation from St Matthew is extremely apt, being complementary to Gal 5:19-21. Just as the Christian who fails in charity proves himself unworthy to inherit the kingdom of God (5:19-21), so the Christian who loves Christ in his neighbour proves himself worthy to enter the kingdom.

## Is Christ proposed as a model for imitation in 6:2?

'Jesus is "the man for others", the one in whom love has completely taken over,' says the Bishop of Woolwich. [97] But it is not too easy for the modern Christian to see Christ's life and death in this light. It would have been easier to see his death as a death *for others,* if, for example, he had denounced the institution of slavery

[95] Cf. Col 1:24.
[96] St Jerome, PL 26, 456 B.
[97] J. A. T. Robinson, *Honest to God*, p. 76.

and had been put to death as an upsetter of social peace, or if he had
sold himself into slavery and died in the galleys or the mines. But in
as much as he deliberately provoked his enemies and almost forced
them to put him to death by the fierce denunciations of Mt 23, and
in so far as he was put to death for maintaining his own claim to be
the Son of God (cf. Jn 19: 7), his death seems less admirable and is
less clearly a 'death for others'.

For St Paul, this difficulty did not exist. Christ voluntarily delivered himself to death by crucifixion — perhaps even courted crucifixion — in order to come under the curse of the law and so release
his fellow-Jews from the curse of the law (cf. 3 : 13-14). Furthermore,
his death was a death for all men, because by his death he bore away
the sins of the world. 6: 2 might be paraphrased: 'Bear one another's
burdens, and in this way you will fulfil the law which Christ fulfilled
in his death, for he then bore the burden of other men's sins.' Christ
in his death was the law of charity incarnate. [98]

It is probably true to say that the model of charity which most
Christians nowadays keep before their mind is not the crucifix but the
parable of the Good Samaritan — something which Christ *said*, not a
description of a particular act of charity which he *did*. For the Fathers,
there was no difficulty here: they read the parable of the Good Samaritan as an allegorical description of Christ's saving work. Just as
the Samaritan bore the expenses of the injured man's cure, so Christ
bore the expenses of the cure of mankind injured by sin. Taken in
this way, the parable is an interpretation of Christ's death. But most
modern scholars will not take it in this way; they regard the patristic
exegesis as an illicit allegorization of Christ's parable. [99] A discussion
of the principles of parable-exegesis would be out of place here. [100]
Suffice it to point out that the patristic exegesis had the great practical
advantage of helping the ordinary Christian to see that Christ *did*
exemplify his own teaching, and in particular that his death was the
supreme example of his own law of charity. It was then above all that
he gave himself for others and bore the burdens of others.

[98] The 'law of Christ' can mean 'the law which Christ was (and is)'—if 'of
Christ' is read as a defining genitive. Christ was and is a 'living law' (*nomos
empsychos*—cf. Philo, *On Abraham*, 5 [Loeb, VI]). Similarly in Rom 7:2, St
Paul may mean that the husband is the wife's 'living law' (if 'the law of the
husband' means 'the law which is her husband').
[99] Cf. C. H. Dodd, *The Parables of the Kingdom*, London, 1935, pp. 11-13.
After quoting St Augustine's allegorical exegesis (*Quaest. Evangeliorum*, II,
19), he adds: 'To the ordinary person of intelligence . . . this mystification
must appear quite perverse.'
[100] See my review of J. Jeremias, *The Parables of Jesus*, London, ²1963, in HJ
6 (1965), pp. 485-486.

# THE CHRISTIAN COMMUNITY

The eighth and ninth sections overlap, i.e., the end of the eighth section is used as the beginning of a new symmetrical structure. Here is the text.

**A** *5 : 22* The harvest of the Spirit is charity, joy, peace, patience, kindness, goodness, fidelity, *23* gentleness, self-control. Against such things as these there is no law.    **B** *24* Those who belong to Christ Jesus have crucified the flesh with its passions and its lusts.    **C** *25* If we live by the Spirit, let us also walk by the Spirit.    **D** *26* Let us not be eager for vainglory, provoking one another, envying one another. *6 : 1* Brethren, if a man falls into some misdeed, you who are spiritual must put him right, in a spirit of gentleness, with an eye on yourself, lest you too be tempted. *2* Bear one another's burdens, and so you will fulfil the law of Christ. *3* For if anyone thinks he is something whereas he is nothing, he is deluding himself.    **E** *4* Let each man examine his own conduct; then he will be able to claim superiority only over himself, not over his neighbour. *5* For each will bear his own burden.    **F** *6* But a man who is being instructed in the word must give his teacher a share in all his goods. **G** *7* Do not deceive yourselves: God is not mocked. For whatever a man sows, that he will reap.    **H** *8* If he sows for his own flesh, from his flesh he will reap destruction;    **H¹** but if he sows for the spirit, from the Spirit he will reap eternal life.    **G¹** *9* Let us not weary of doing what is right; in due time we shall reap our harvest, if we do not weaken.    **F¹** *10* Therefore while we have time, let us do good to all men, but especially to our kindred in the faith. *11* Look at these large letters which I have written with my own hand.    **E¹** *12* Those who desire the approval of the world of flesh — they are the ones who urge you to be circumcised — but only that they may avoid being persecuted for the cross of Christ. *13* For those who rely on circumcision do not even keep the law themselves; but they want you circumcised so that they can make your flesh a subject for their boasting. **D¹** *14* For my part, heaven forbid that I should boast of anything except the cross of our Lord Jesus Christ, by which the world is crucified to me, and I to the world. *15* For neither circumcision nor its absence makes any difference, but only creation anew.    **C¹** *16* Upon all who walk by this rule be peace and mercy, and upon the Israel of God.    **B¹** *17* From now on let no one disturb me! For I bear in my body the stigmata of Jesus. **A¹** *18* The grace of our Lord Jesus Christ be with your spirit, brethren. Amen.

## *What is the purpose of this section?*

The general subject of the ninth section is: relationships within the Christian community. St Paul gives his doctrine with the aid of three antitheses, neighbour and self, spirit and flesh, sowing and reaping. The Christian must serve not his own interests but his neighbour's; he may judge himself but not his neighbour; he may boast of his superiority over his former self but not of his superiority over his neighbour. He must not follow the promptings of his flesh, but live in the strength of the Spirit and according to the guidance of the Spirit. Now is the time of sowing; the time of harvesting will come later. If he scatters his wealth generously now, he will reap a harvest in eternal life. If he spends his wealth on his own flesh, he will reap a harvest of ruin.

The links are as follows:

A     The harvest of the Spirit, 5 : 22-23.
B     Christians have crucified the flesh, 5 : 24.
C     Let us follow the Spirit, 5 : 25.
D     Condemnation of vainglory and harsh criticism, 5 : 26—6 : 3.
E     Let each judge himself, 6 : 4-5.
F     Be generous to your teachers, 6 : 6.
G     Sow now for a harvest later, 6 : 7.
H     *The harvest of the flesh, 6 : 8a.*
H¹    *The harvest of the Spirit, 6 : 8b.*
G¹    Sow good seed for the harvest later, 6 : 9.
F¹    Be good to all; I, Paul, am your teacher! 6 : 10-11.
E¹    The Judaizers themselves do not keep the law, 6 : 12-13.
D¹    Let us glory in the cross of Christ, 6 : 14-15.
C¹    A blessing upon those who follow the Spirit, 6 : 16.
B¹    I bear the stigmata of Christ in my body, 6 : 17.
A¹    The grace of Christ be with your spirit, 6 : 18.

In the second half of this section, which corresponds in the overall pattern (see p. 39) to the opening section of the Epistle,[1] St Paul speaks several times of himself. There is a delicate hint that he would welcome financial assistance (compare F with F¹), an assurance that he does not wish to boast, and a rather mysterious reference to the 'stigmata of Jesus' which he bears in his body (see on 6 : 17).

*The First Subsection, 5:26—6:3*

## FRATERNAL CORRECTION

A   *5 : 26* Let us not be eager for vainglory,   B   provoking one another, envying one another.   C   *6 : 1* Brethren, if a man falls into some misdeed, D   you who are spiritual   E   must put him right   D¹   in a spirit of gentleness,   C¹   with an eye on yourself, lest you too be tempted.

---

[1]   The correspondences are set out in parallel columns below, pp. 488-489.

B¹  *2* Bear one another's burdens, and thus you will fulfil the law of Christ.    A¹  *3* For if anyone thinks he is something whereas he is nothing, he is deluding himself.

*Is this passage particularly relevant to the situation in Galatia?*

In the overall pattern of the Epistle, 5:13—6:10 corresponds to 1:11—2:19. Accordingly, 5:26—6:3 is a commentary on the events narrated in the autobiographical section of the Epistle rather than on the contemporary situation in Galatia.

V. 26, 'Let us not be eager for vainglory, provoking one another, envying one another,' is the principle on which St Paul behaved towards the other apostles after his conversion. He kept away from Jerusalem and the churches of Judaea, so as to provoke no invidious comparisons between his own learning and zeal and their lack of these things.

6:1 is probably a comment on the dispute at Antioch. Peter was 'caught unawares' [2] in a misdeed, and Paul 'put him right'. That he did so 'in a spirit of meekness or gentleness' is not evident on the usual assumption that his discourse to Peter ended with the thunderbolt, 2:21: 'If justice is from the law, Christ died for nothing.' If Paul immediately after saying that wrapped his cloak about him and stormed out of the assembly, his conduct did not square with his excellent advice in 6:1. But if, as has been maintained above, the discourse continued till about 5:13, it did end on a kind and friendly note, even though some plain speaking had gone before.

6:2 is relevant to the dispute at Antioch, in so far as St Paul was there defending 'the truth of the gospel' — performing a task which really belonged to Peter. Hence Paul might claim that he was bearing Peter's burden. But 6:2 is more obviously relevant to the agreement mentioned in 2:10 — that Paul would collect alms for the poor of Jerusalem who were the other apostles' burden.

The wording of 6:3, 'If anyone thinks he is something whereas he is nothing,' is strongly reminiscent of 2:6, which can bear the translation: 'From those who thought they were something...' There is, therefore, a tacit contrast between St Peter (in 6:3) and St Paul (in 5:26): Paul was not seeking vainglory, but the glory of God (cf. Jn 12:43); Peter was enjoying a prestige which perhaps he did not fully deserve.

---

[2]  The Greek word (*prolêmphthêi*) is difficult to translate; it both accuses and excuses. See above, p. 471.

These verses (5 : 26—6 : 3) are also applicable to the situation in Galatia, though a little less easily. The beginning (5 : 26) and the end (6 : 3) can be taken as a diagnosis of the psychological roots of the Galatian crisis: the Judaizers wish to establish a reputation as teachers and seek to do this by contrasting themselves with St Paul and his uncircumcised, non-observing converts. They think that they are something, and look down on St Paul as if he were nothing. Thus pride leads to theological disagreement, theological disagreement generates *odium theologicum,* and this odium threatens to disrupt the churches. But the intervening verses seem too mild after the severity of 5 : 2-3. It is doubtful whether St Paul means that a Galatian who has succumbed to the propaganda of the Judaizers to the extent of having himself circumcised is simply to be 'put right in a spirit of gentleness'. However, in the case of a Galatian who had merely succumbed to the extent of adopting Jewish feasts and fast-days, the advice would be fitting enough. At this point of his exhortation (6 : 1), St Paul may be afraid that if the fickle Galatians allow themselves to be persuaded by the Epistle, they may react too violently against the Judaizers and their followers. [3]

St Paul is recommending the spiritual men of Galatia to adopt the principle of conduct on which he himself claims to have acted in the dispute at Antioch. He could do this because the Galatian crisis was in essence a repetition of the Antioch incident. Discreetly and indirectly, he is proposing himself as a model for imitation. This he can venture to do, because his own life is conformed to the pattern of Christ's crucifixion (cf. 6 : 14-15).

*The Second Subsection, 6:2-5*

## SELF-CRITICISM

The second subsection overlaps with the first. Whereas the first dealt with fraternal correction, the second deals with the complementary topic of self-criticism and self-correction.

A  *6 : 2* Bear one another's burdens, and thus you will fulfil the law of Christ.  **B**  *3* For if anyone thinks he is something whereas he is nothing, he is deluding himself.  **C**  *4* Let each man examine his own conduct,

---

[3]  For this pattern of events see 2 Cor 2 : 5-8, with Lightfoot's comment, Gal, p. 54.

**B**¹ then he will be able to claim superiority over himself, not over his neighbour.   **A**¹  5 For each will bear his own burden.

The gospels treat sin as a social phenomenon and give rules for fraternal correction, punishment, and forgiveness of sinners (Mt 18; Jn 20); but they say remarkably little about self-examination and self-accusation. St Paul does something to fill this lacuna. 6:1c and 6:4 taken together mean that a man's first duty, before he begins to correct others, is to examine his own conduct and, it is implied, to correct anything which he finds amiss. ⁴ If he will do this, two advantages will follow, one for himself and one for others. For himself, he will be cured of any false belief in his own superiority; if he thought he was something, he will find that he is nothing. ⁵ At best, he will be able to boast that his conduct is not as bad as it used to be (v. 4). He may find here a source of encouragement, but not a reason for looking down on others. Secondly, if each man will devote his critical faculties to the correction of himself rather than of his neigbour, he will bear the burden of his own faults and thus lessen the burden which his own conduct imposes on others. He will also relieve others of the burdensome duty of correcting him. ⁶

There is no hint in vv. 4-5 that a Christian who finds himself guilty of some secret or purely interior sin is bound to bring it to the knowledge of church authorities in confession. On the contrary, the suggestion rather is that a man who takes himself to task for his sins, whether secret or not, thereby relieves the church authorities of the obligation to 'set him right'. The rulers of the early Church did not urge specific confession of all grave post-baptismal sins as a grave obligation. ⁷

---

⁴   In his self-examination, the Christian must employ an external standard or law of some kind. Philo, *The Decalogue*, 98 (Loeb, VII), says that the sabbath is the time for self-examination: 'God commanded that they should apply themselves to work for six days but rest on the seventh and turn to the study of wisdom, and that while they thus had leisure for the contemplation of the truths of nature they should also consider whether any offence against purity had been committed in the preceding days, and exact from themselves in the council-chamber of the soul, with the laws as their fellow-assessors and fellow-examiners, a strict account of what they had said or done in order to correct what had been neglected and to take precaution against repetition of any sin.' On the 'uses' of law, see above, pp. 297-300.

⁵   In the days before his conversion Paul was keen to outshine his contemporaries in the practice of Jewish perfection; cf. 1:14.

⁶   St Jerome, PL 26, 457 CD, noticing the apparent contradiction between v. 2 and v. 5, referred v. 5 to the Day of Judgment: we shall then be judged, not by comparison with others, but each according to his own works. This interpretation is not to be excluded. It is always rash to say that St Paul's ambiguous words are intended to mean one thing and not another. But the meaning given above fits the context better.

⁷   See above, p. 300.

*How is v. 5 to be harmonized with v. 2?*

Charity consists in bearing the burdens of others — being patient with their defects, assisting them in their repentance, aiding them in their needs — but it is not a part of charity to provide burdens for other Christians to carry. On the contrary, a Christian should lighten the burdens of others by *not* being a burden to them, financially or otherwise, if he can help it.

One of the burdens which the advance of science is making steadily heavier is the burden of old age. For old age *is* a burden, and it must be carried either by the aged person himself or by others. Apart from the financial burden, there is the social burden which an old person becomes if he or she feels useless or neglected and sinks into self-pity and peevishness. Such persons can impose heavy burdens on the patience of those with whom they live. Many an aging mother has made a saint of her unmarried daughter — but gets no more credit for this than Nero gets for throwing early Christians to the lions.

The present subsection is full of excellent advice for the aged — but it is advice which needs to be absorbed in middle age, for it is in middle age that a man takes out the insurance, spiritual as well as financial, which will save him from becoming a burden when he is older. A strong faith and a lively hope, sustained through middle age, will make a gentle old man, like Symeon, through whom the Holy Spirit can speak words of kindness and peace to younger generations (cf. Lk 2: 25-35).

*The Third Subsection, 6:6-11*

## GENEROUS GIVING

The third subsection is identical with the central portion of the section. For the analysis of it, see F and F¹ above, p. 478.

*What is the sequence of thought in vv. 6-11?*

St Paul has a gentlemanly dislike for talking about money. Vv. 6-11 are obscure because he finds it distasteful to say plainly what he wants. [8]

---

[8]   Cf. C. H. Dodd, *New Testament Studies*, pp. 71-72.

R

Having said in v. 5 that each man must (as far as possible) bear his own burden, St Paul adds: '*But* a man who is being instructed in the word should share with his instructor in all good things.' [9] Catechumens or neophytes undergoing regular instruction should contribute to the support of their instructors; they must not shrug off their responsibility on the ground that 'each man must bear his own burden.' The apostle or catechist has a right to 'be a burden' to those whom he teaches (cf. 1 Thes 2:6), or as we say nowadays 'to be supported' by them. [10] The principle that converts undergoing instruction should make some payment has been abandoned, and perhaps not wisely, for what is given away is rarely valued by the receiver, and it is not good to encourage people to receive without thought of making any return. [11]

In v. 7, St Paul adds, rather abruptly: 'Do not deceive yourselves; God is not mocked.' This undoubtedly is a reproach. It is a probable conjecture that St Paul had asked the Galatians to contribute to the fund for the relief of the poor in Jerusalem and they had shown themselves unresponsive. [12] This view is based on 1 Cor 15:1-2:

> In regard to the collection for God's poor, you should follow the same instructions which I gave to the churches of Galatia. That is to say, on the first day of the week, each of you should set aside and save up whatever he can well afford, so that the collection will not have to be made when I come...[13]

One reason why St Paul overcame his reluctance and organized this collection was that he had been asked to do so by the pillar-apostles

---

9  The Greek can also mean that the disciple should participate in all his teacher's virtues by imitating them. St Thomas, Gal, 438 D, takes v. 6 in this sense. The phrase 'in all good things' then adds an important qualification, which St Thomas explains thus (439 A): 'The evil conduct of prelates does not excuse us. For they are an example to their subjects only in so far as they imitate Christ. . . . In 1 Cor 11:1 the Apostle says: "Be imitators of me, as I am of Christ"—as if to say: "Imitate me in the things in which I imitate Christ."' Perhaps St Paul also means that the neophyte may have something valuable to say to the person instructing him. This does happen!

10  Unfortunately the Greek does not show whether the instruction in question is given before or after baptism, or whether it is begun before and continued after. Cf. C. F. D. Moule, *The Birth of the New Testament*, London, 1962, p. 129, who observes that in any case 6:6 seems to imply a lengthy period of instruction.

11  Cf. Marcus Aurelius, *Meditations*, XI, 25: 'Socrates refused the invitation of Perdiccas to his court, *That I come not*, said he, *to a dishonoured grave*, meaning, that I be not treated with generosity and have no power to return it.'

12  Cf. Lightfoot, Gal, p. 55: 'The messenger who had brought him word of the spread of Judaism among the Galatians, had also, I suppose, reported unfavourably of their liberality. They had not answered heartily to his appeal.'

13  'Planned giving' is not, after all, a recent innovation. According to McKenzie, *The Power and the Wisdom*, p. 191, 'almsgiving in the New Testament is a personal encounter.' But it was on the way to being institutionalized even in

in Jerusalem (cf. 2 : 10). [14] He probably felt that the Galatians' reluctance to cooperate was an affront to himself, but he refrains from saying so. Instead, he says: 'God is not mocked,' and adds a warning couched in an agricultural metaphor borrowed from the psalmist. He uses the same imagery in the same connection in 2 Cor 9 : 5-9:

> I have thought it necessary to urge the brethren to go ahead of me and see that your promised donations are collected in good time. Then they will be waiting for me as the fruit of your generosity and not of my 'rapacity'. However, I will say this: the man who sows sparingly will reap sparingly, while the man who sows with an open hand will reap a generous harvest. Each of you should make up his mind what he will contribute, and do so without sadness and without any sense of compulsion. God loves a cheerful giver. And he is able to furnish you with all his gifts in such abundance that besides having your own needs fully satisfied, you will always have enough left over for good works of every kind. You will be like the man of whom the Scripture says: *He sowed his wealth broadcast, he gave it to the poor; the memory of his almsgiving will live for ever.*

The quotation with which this passage ends is from Ps 112 : 9; it shows that 'sowing' in 6 : 8 is a metaphor for spending money. [15] He who spends his money on his own flesh, that is, on his own physical comfort, or to promote his own glory, will reap from the flesh a harvest of ruin; but he who spends his money in a spiritual manner, for the support of the poor and of the ministers of the gospel, [16] will reap a harvest of eternal life.

V. 8 is an assertion of the Justice of God. It may be compared with Job 4 : 7-8, where similar imagery is used:

> Think now, who that was innocent ever perished?
> Or where were the upright cut off?
> As I have seen, those who plough iniquity
> and sow trouble, reap the same.

Whereas Eliphaz tried to maintain that this principle of retribution holds good even within the limits of this life, St Paul says that the harvest of the spiritual sower is 'eternal life'. No doubt he means that the harvest of the fleshly man is 'eternal ruin'.

The particular relevance of v. 9 can only be guessed at. Perhaps at St Paul's first appeal the Galatians had contributed generously to

---

St Paul's lifetime. Did the Gentile donors ever receive an acknowledgement from Jerusalem? If not, their lack of enthusiasm is understandable.

[14] See above, pp. 171-173.

[15] Literally, the Greek of v. 8 means: 'He who sows into his own flesh,' St Jerome, PL 26, 460 B, feels it necessary to point out that this cannot refer to a man's intercourse with his own wife.

[16] Cf. *Didache*, 13 : 3-7.

the relief fund, but had grown tired of making regular contributions. If so, the agricultural metaphor is not really suited to what St Paul wishes to say, for a farmer does not continue sowing his field week by week until harvest time.

In v. 10, St Paul lays down the important principle that while Christians have obligations towards all men, they have special obligations towards 'their kindred in the faith' (who include the poor of the church of Jerusalem — they, like the Galatians, are sons of Abraham by reason of their faith). This is not a falling-away from the precepts of love for all men as taught by Christ in the parable of the Good Samaritan (cf. Lk 10: 25-37). Rather, it is a rule for the application of Christ's teaching in circumstances where the money available is limited and the needs of others are many and great. Nowadays such problems confront us in political as well as in private life: How important is foreign aid? Should a hospital in Bombay be given priority over a hospital in Liverpool? Unfortunately, St Paul's simple principle in 6: 10 does not provide a solution to such questions, but it does show that our obligation to all men are not equal. [17]

Most editors regard v. 11, 'See with what large letters I have written to you in my own hand,' as the beginning of a new section in the Epistle. But the analysis of this section (p. 478) shows that it is linked with what precedes and not with what follows. There is first of all a link with 6: 10: St Paul implies by the juxtaposition that his own laborious letter-writing is an example of persevering effort for others. [18] But there is a more interesting link between v. 11 and its counterpart in the first half of the section, namely, 6: 6: 'He who is being instructed should share with his instructor in all good things.' Since St Paul has been labouring all through this Epistle, which he has written out with his own hands in block letters, [19] to instruct the Galatians in the true faith, by the principle stated in 6: 6 the Galatians ought to contribute to his support. The very obscurity of this hint shows how anxious he was to avoid the accusation of 'rapacity' (cf. 2 Cor 9: 5).

*Why does St Paul say 'while we have time' in 6:10?*

This may be a relic of the eschatological motive, which is also used, in a rather perfunctory way, in Rom 13: 11-12:

[17] Cf. St Thomas Aquinas, *Summa*, 2a 2ae, 26, a. 9.
[18] St Jerome, PL 26, 462 A, remarks that v. 10 may go with what precedes—so that by 'kindred in the faith' St Paul means 'the teachers' who should receive a share in all the goods of those whom they instruct.
[19] Cf. G in G, p. 216, and below, pp. 489-490.

Remember the time! It is already the hour for you to arise from sleep. Salvation is even closer to us now than when we first believed. Night is far advanced; day is at hand.

But such phrases can be used without any reference to the Parousia, simply as a reminder that life is soon over (cf. Job 14:1), and our few opportunities of doing good must be seized before they slip away. It is not a specifically Christian idea. St Jerome has this interesting comment: [20]

> Titus, the son of Vespasian, who overthrew Jerusalem in retribution for the shedding of Christ's blood and then enjoyed a triumph at Rome, is said to have been so good a man that one day when he remembered late in the evening, during supper, that he had done no good deed during the day, he exclaimed: 'My friends, I have wasted the day!'....If he who had no law, no gospel, no teaching of our Saviour, or of the apostles, spoke and acted in this way, what should we do?

V. 10 has a parallel in Jn 9:4-5, where, immediately before curing the man born blind, Jesus says: 'We must do the works of him who sent me while daylight lasts. Night is coming, when no one can work. So long as I am in the world, I am the light of the world.' This text presents several obvious difficulties, which are best solved by adopting Bultmann's conjecture that in the original form of the logion, v. 5 stood before v. 4, thus:

> So long as I am in the world,
> I am the light of the world.
> Work while the daylight lasts;
> night is coming when no one can work.

In this form, the words are a repetition to the disciples of Christ's warning to the Jews (cf. Jn 7:34; 8:21; 13:33) that their opportunity for belief is limited; they must use it, for soon it will be too late. [21]

In Gal 6:10, St Paul is extending this doctrine: just as the opportunity (*kairos*) for believing is of limited duration and must be grasped when it comes, so too the opportunities for works of charity are given intermittently, and must be grasped before it is too late (cf. Jn 5:7). But his formulation of the idea, it must be admitted, is disappointingly negative — as if it were sufficient to wait patiently for an opportunity to turn up. Pelagius (whose commentary on Galatians is not in any bad sense 'Pelagian') introduces an element of

---

[20] St Jerome, PL 26, 462 B. He goes on to tell the famous story of St John in his old age at Ephesus. Criticized for constantly repeating 'Little children, love one another,' he replied 'with a sentence worthy of John: "It is the Lord's command; and if it alone is obeyed, it is enough."' ('Respondit dignam Ioanne sententiam, quia praeceptum Domini est, et si solum fiat, sufficit.')

[21] Cf. R. Bultmann, *Das Evangelium des Johannes*, Göttingen, 1956, p. 252, n. 1.

active choice: 'It is now the end of the sowing season; let us make haste to sow all the fields, and especially those which are most fertile.' [22] Great Christians like Ignatius of Loyola and General Booth have not been content to sit back and wait for opportunities; they have prayed for them and have gone to look for them. If the Salvationists had not gone into the slums of Victorian London, they would not have seen Christ hungry, thirsty, cold and naked. At the Day of Judgment, according to Mt 25:37-38, some Christians will say: 'Lord, when did we see you hungry, thirsty and naked?' Maybe he will reply: 'Of course you didn't! You hid yourself away in large and comfortable country houses.' [23]

## The Epilogue and its Parallels in the Prologue

| 6:11-18 | 1:1-13 |
|---|---|
| *11* Look at these large letters which I have written with my own hand. | *1-2* Paul....and all the brethren who are with me, to the churches of Galatia. |
| *12* Those who desire the approval of the world of flesh — they are the ones who urge you to be circumcised — but only that they may avoid being persecuted for the cross of Christ. *13* For those who rely on circumcision do not even keep the law themselves, but they want you circumcised, so that they can make your flesh a subject for their boasting. | *10* Am I now seeking the favour of men or of God? Or am I trying to please men? If I were still trying to please men, I should not be a servant of Christ. |
| *14* For my part, heaven forbid that I should boast of anything except the cross of our Lord Jesus Christ, by which the world is crucified to me and I to the world. *15* For neither circumcision nor its absence makes any difference, but only creation anew. | *4* who offered himself for our sins, to redeem us from the present evil age, according to the will of God our Father, *5* to whom be glory for ever and ever. Amen. |
| *16* Upon all who walk by this rule (or *canon*) be peace and mercy, | *6* I am astonished that you are so quickly abandoning the one who called you in the grace of Christ, in favour of another gospel, *7* which |

---

22 Pelagius, Gal, p. 341.
23 According to Mt 9:32-37, it was after Christ had travelled up and down the land, through towns and villages, that his heart was touched with compassion for the spiritual condition of the people.

is not another gospel, but certain persons are upsetting you and would like to overturn the gospel of Christ. *8* But even if we ourselves or an angel from heaven should preach to you a gospel other than the one we preached, let him be *anathema*! *9* As we said before, so now I repeat: if anyone is preaching to you a gospel other than the one you received, let him be anathema!

and upon the Israel of God. *17* Henceforth let no one disturb me!

*11* For I inform you, brethren, that the gospel preached by me is not according to man. *12* I did not receive it from men, nor was I instructed by man, but by a revelation of Jesus Christ. *13* For you have heard how I formerly conducted myself in Judaism — how I went to excess in persecuting the Church of God.

For I bear in my body the stigmata of Jesus.

*1* An apostle not from men nor through man, but through Jesus Christ and God the Father who raised him from the dead.

*18* The grace of our Lord Jesus Christ be with your spirit, brethren. Amen.

*3* Grace to you and peace from God our Father and from the Lord Jesus Christ.

## *Did St Paul write the whole Epistle with his own hand (6:11)?*

Most commentators think that 6:11 refers only to the closing paragraph of the Epistle. Lightfoot, for example, says: 'At this point the Apostle takes the pen from his amanuensis, and the concluding paragraph is written with his own hand.'[24] But St John Chrysostom is almost certainly right in thinking that it refers to the whole Epistle.[25]

Within the ninth section (p. 478), 6:11 is linked with 6:6: 'a man who is being instructed in the word must give his teacher a share in all his goods'; and what is still more remarkable, its counterpart in the prologue of the Epistle is 1:2: 'Paul....and all the brethren who are with me greet the churches of Galatia.' In spite of having many brethren with him, who might have done the writing for him, St Paul

---

[24] Cf. Lightfoot, Gal, ad loc. Similarly Lagrange, Burton, Schlier, Lyonnet, Bring, Viard, etc.
[25] Cf. Chrysostom, PG 61, 678 A.

preferred to write the letter with his own hand. In 1:1-2, he emphasizes that he received his apostleship *directly* from God. In 3:19 it is a proof of the inferiority of Judaism that God gave the law through angels and by the hand of Moses. Since St Paul is claiming to be the father or mother of the Galatians, it is fitting that he should instruct them directly, and not by the hand of an amanuensis. (If this was St Paul's view, it is unsatisfactory to explain the stylistic differences between the various pauline Epistles by supposing that in some cases he merely gave a few ideas to some member of his curia to be worked up into an Epistle. This is the way of an emperor, rather than a father, and not of all emperors, either.)

St Paul may have used large letters simply for the sake of emphasis, or perhaps because his eyes were weak, or perhaps because when a father writes a book for the instruction of his little boy, he uses big letters. [26]

*The Fourth Subsection, 6:12-14*

## THE WRONG KIND OF BOASTING

**A** *6:12* Those who desire to win the approval of the world of flesh — they are the ones who urge you to be circumcised,    **B** but only that they may avoid being persecuted for the cross of Christ.    **C** *13* For those who urge circumcision    **D** do not keep the law themselves;    **C¹** yet they want you circumcised,    **B¹** so that they can make your flesh a matter for boasting.    **A¹** *14* For my part, heaven forbid that I should boast of anything — except the cross of our Lord Jesus Christ.

*Is St Paul fair to his opponents in this passage?*

St Paul is here contrasting the motives of the Jewish propagandists with his own. Their motive in preaching circumcision, he says, is a desire for social prestige — they wish to win the approval of the unconverted Jews at Jerusalem. The authorities in Jerusalem were willing to tolerate the Christian belief that Jesus was the Messiah, provided it was combined with a proper respect for the law, and

---

[26] Cf. G in G on 6:11, and III Enoch 45:1-2, quoted by J. Jeremias, *The Central Message of the New Testament*, p. 26. Turner, *Grammatical Insights*, p. 94, offers the conjecture that 'St Paul had actually been crucified at Perga in Pamphilia by Jews'—this would explain his ungainly handwriting and give added meaning to Gal 3:1; 6:12-13; 2 Cor 4:10. However, St Luke knows nothing of this (cf Acts 13:13); crucifixion was not a punishment which Jews

hence for the privilege of Israel as the chosen people. [27] The Judaizers, therefore, according to St Paul's diagnosis of their motives, urge circumcision upon Gentile converts for the sake of peace with the unconverted Jews, or rather, in order to win for themselves the prestige of having brought some Gentiles under the wing of the Shekinah. They have no real belief in the law, in spite of what they say, for they do not keep it strictly themselves. Their real motive must be that they wish to be able to boast at Jerusalem that after scouring land and sea, they have made such and such a number of proselytes. St Paul expresses this rather crudely and satirically by saying: 'They want you circumcised in order that they may boast of your flesh' — which is as much as to say: 'They collect foreskins like red Indians collecting scalps, so that they can return in triumph to Jerusalem — like David with his two hundred foreskins of the Philistines! (cf. 1 Sam 18 : 27).' This is St Paul's retort to the Judaizers' charge that he is rejecting circumcision in order to please the Gentiles. The truth is, he says, that they are insisting on it in order to please the Jews. It is a debating point, and perhaps not to be taken too literally. The Judaizers may have felt it their duty to make a few concessions for the sake of peace with the Jews, for after all 'Blessed are the peacemakers.'

Having accused his adversaries of a desire to boast, St Paul seems to realize, in v. 14, that he is exposing himself to a counter-attack. His opponents might retort that he too is not averse to boasting of his missionary successes. [28] He too desires to be held in honour by the Gentile churches as a successful missionary. To forestall this charge, he protests that he has no boast except in the cross of Christ, thanks to which his converts are a 'new creation'. [29] He implies that there is no discrepancy between his real and his ostensible motives: he is crucified to this world (hence does not desire its praise) and he really wants his converts to obey the law which he preaches, namely 'the law of Christ' (which he does observe himself).

Probably St Paul also wishes his reader to see in vv. 12 and 14 a contrast between the circumcision of the flesh advocated by the Judaizers and the crucifixion of the flesh advocated by himself. The point is more clearly made in Col 2 : 11: Jewish circumcision ought to be a symbol of circumcision of the heart, that is, of purification of

inflicted on Jews; and Paul's battle with wild beasts at Ephesus (I Cor 15 : 32) is generally agreed to have been metaphorical.
[27] See above, pp. 431-433, and Acts 8 : 1-3, where persecution hits the non-observing 'Hellenists' but not the law-observing apostles. Cf. E. Hirsch, 'Zwei Fragen zu Galater 6,' ZNTW 29 (1930), p. 195, and W. Schmithals, 'Die Häretiker in Galatien,' ZNTW 47 (1956), p. 27.
[28] Cf. Rom 15 : 19; Gal 2 : 8-9; Acts 15 : 12.
[29] He is already forestalling this charge in 1 : 1 and 1 : 10.

the whole man. But purification of the whole man is effected by baptism. Hence circumcision is a material symbol of the spiritual reality ('creation anew') which the Christian possesses thanks to his baptism. Thus the contrast in vv. 12 and 14 is between the Judaizers who glory in the material symbol and St Paul who glories in the spiritual reality (cf. Phil 3:3).

The question whether one who has the spiritual reality has any further need of the material symbol had been discussed by Philo. He maintained the conservative view that it is laudable to conform to established customs and refrain from condemning material rites on the strength of a higher spirituality. There is much good sense in what he says:[30]

> We should take thought for good repute (*euphêmia*) as a great matter and one of much advantage to the life we lead in the body. And this good repute is won as a rule by all who cheerfully take things as they find them and interfere with no established customs, but maintain with care the constitution of their country...
>
> It is true that receiving circumcision does indeed portray the excision of pleasure and all passions and the putting away of the impious conceit, under which the mind supposed that it was capable of begetting by its own power: but let us not on this account repeal the law laid down for circumcising. Why, we shall be ignoring the sanctity of the temple and a thousand other things, if we are going to pay heed to nothing except what is shewn us by the inner meaning of things. Nay, we shall look on all these outward observances as resembling the body, and their inner meanings as resembling the soul. It follows that exactly as we have to take thought for the body, because it is the abode of the soul, so we must pay heed to the letter of the laws.

The Judaizers may have argued in just this way — and there is force in the argument. Modern theologians explain the necessity of sacraments in much the same way, namely, by pointing out that man is not a disembodied soul, and that material signs correspond to the material nature of his bodily component. [31]

St Paul could certainly have been kinder to his adversaries here. All in all, this much quoted passage, though it sounds so pious, reveals, on closer examination, a less attractive side of St Paul's personality. 'Heaven forbid that I should boast of anything except the cross of our Lord Jesus Christ' is embedded in a passage where St Paul is in fact boasting that his own motives are good while those of

---

[30] The Loeb translation gives 'for fair fame' for *euphemia*. I have altered this because, as Cicero observes, an assonance of f's is *foedum*. The text is Philo, *The Migration of Abraham*, 88-92 (Loeb, IV).

[31] Cf. B. Leeming, *Principles of Sacramental Theology*, London, 1963, pp. 590-614, and see above, pp. 373-374.

his adversaries are bad, and that he has the spiritual reality of which they have only a material symbol. He describes himself as 'crucified to the world' with a note of self-approval, enhanced (unconsciously no doubt) by the contrast which he sees in others. However, we must remember that it was a part of his apostolic office to set an example and invite others to imitate him (cf. 4 : 12).

*The Fifth Subsection, 6:14-18*

# FINAL CANON

A  *6 : 14* For my part, heaven forbid that I should boast of anything — except the cross of our Lord Jesus Christ,    B  by which the world is crucified to me and I to the world.  *15* For neither circumcision nor its absence makes any difference, but only creation anew.    C  *16* Upon all who walk by this rule be peace and mercy    D  and upon the Israel of God.    C¹  *17* From now on let no one disturb me,    B¹  for I bear in my body the stigmata of Jesus.    A¹  *18* The grace of our Lord Jesus Christ be with your spirit, brethren. Amen.

*Who are the Israel of God?*

At the centre of this last subsection, St Paul wishes to say: 'Peace upon Israel, the true Israel, that is the men who walk according to the rule or canon laid down in v. 15.' He might have expressed this by saying: 'Upon all who walk by this rule be peace and mercy, for they are the Israel of God.' But he wished, apparently, to keep the fine liturgical phrase 'Peace upon Israel', which occurs in Psalms 125 : 5 and 128 : 6, and in the last of the Eighteen Benedictions of the synagogue liturgy:[32]

> Bestow Thy peace upon Israel Thy people and bless us, all of us together. Blessed art Thou, O Lord, who makest peace!

He therefore placed the two phrases 'those who walk by this rule' and 'the Israel of God' in apposition, linking them by an explanatory 'and'. So the sense is: 'Upon all who walk by this rule be peace and mercy, *that is*, upon the Israel of God.'

That 'the Israel of God' means the Christian Church and not the whole Jewish nation, is clear from three parallel passages where St Paul expresses himself in similar terms. In 1 Cor 10 : 18, when com-

---

[32]  Cf. Schlier, Gal, p. 209; W. Förster, *Palestinian Judaism in New Testament Times*, Edinburgh-London, 1964, p. 229.

paring the Eucharist with Jewish sacrifices, he says: 'Consider Israel according to the flesh: are not those who eat the victims of its altar thereby united with the altar?' The implication is that the Church is 'Israel according to the spirit' — though St Paul never actually uses the phrase. In Phil 3:3 he says: 'We are the true circumcision, we who worship in the Spirit of God, who glory in Christ Jesus (cf. Gal 6:14), and do not place our confidence in the flesh.' And in Rom 2:28-29 he says: 'The true Jew is not a man who is outwardly such, nor is the true circumcision that which is visible in the flesh; the real Jew is he who is such inwardly, and true circumcision is that of the heart — spiritual, not literal, circumcision.' The blessing, therefore, contains a final reassurance to the Galatians that they are already the true Israel; they have no need of the fleshly symbols, since they have the spiritual realities.

The structure of the subsection suggests that the Church is the Israel of God because it has the true circumcision (crucifixion of the flesh and creation anew in baptism). But the structure of the whole Epistle reveals a further reason. 6:16b in the Epilogue corresponds to 1:11-13 in the Prologue. [33] Philo mentions in several places that 'Israel' means 'the man who saw God,' and St Paul too was doubtless familiar with this etymology. The Church is the true Israel because some of its members, including St Paul, have seen God in the Risen Christ. Because some have seen him, all can say: '*We* have seen with our eyes, we have beheld, and our hands have touched....the Word of Life.' [34] Theodoretus was on the right track when he wrote: 'He calls the faithful "the Israel of God" in as much as they see God through faith — for that is what the word means.' [35]

### What is meant by 'creation anew' in v. 15?

The Greek phrase (*kainê ktisis*) can be taken either actively as meaning 'God's act of re-creating us (in baptism)', or passively as meaning 'our new life resulting from God's act of re-creating us.' Both senses fit the context, but the second is the one chiefly intended. The distinction between circumcised and uncircumcised belongs to the old aeon and is of no further account. What is of importance to Christians is that they have died out of the old aeon, through union with Christ's crucifixion, and have been born into the new aeon where

---

[33]   See above, p. 489.
[34]   1 Jn 1:1. C. H. Dodd, *The Johannine Epistles,* London, 1946, ad loc, points out that the 'we' here may stand for the whole Christian community.
[35]   Theodoretus, PG 82, 504 B.

they experience the power of the Holy Spirit. 'Creation anew' means either this spiritual death-and-resurrection, or the new existence to which this spiritual death-and-resurrection grants access.

The origin of the phrase is in Ps 103:30: 'Thou sendest forth thy spirit, and there is a fresh creation; thou dost repeople the face of the earth.'[36] In St Paul's mind, the new creation may also have been connected with Dan 7. The story of 'creation' in Gen 1-3 includes, besides the sheer act of creation, the placing of man among the animals as their ruler, the marriage of man and woman, and the beginning of human history. In Dan 7, man is reinstated as ruler over the beasts (cf. Gen 1:28; Ps 8:6-7) when the Son of Man receives dominion over every race and tribe and tongue, including those symbolized by the lion, the bear, the leopard, and the beast with ten horns.[37] Christ, the fulfilment of this prophetic vision, is, in St Paul's thought, the new Adam; he receives the Church as his bride; a new aeon is inaugurated, and human history begins again (cf. 1:4 in the Prologue). But there is only a passing allusion to all this in 6:15.

*Is 'canon' a technical term in v. 16?*

The word 'canon' originally meant a rod, measuring-rod, or ruler. Then it came to mean 'a measured area' (e.g. in 2 Cor 10:16), or 'a line marked out by a ruler'. In 6:16 it is used metaphorically of a rule of faith and of conduct. In later ecclesiastical use, it means the decision of a synod or council on some matter of faith or morals, usually in the form: 'If anyone says..., let him be anathema.'

For St Paul neither 'canon' nor 'anathema' has become a technical term. But the technical meanings of these words grew straight from the pauline uses. In the structure of the whole Epistle, 6:16 containing the canon matches 1:6-9 containing the anathema.[38] The language of 'orthodoxy' and 'heresy' is already in formation. Though St Paul does not use the word 'orthodoxy', he comes close to it in 2:14, where he says that Peter and Barnabas were not walking straight (*orthopodein*) according to the truth of the gospel.'[39]

---

[36] The above is the Knox Version. Jas 1:18 is also dependent on this psalm. Cf. St Thomas, Gal, 442 C.
[37] See the excellent treatment of Dan 7 in E. W. Heaton, *The Book of Daniel*, London, 1956, pp. 169-190; see also W. Künneth, *The Theology of the Resurrection*, London, 1965, pp. 161-173, and my review of this book in HJ 7 (1966), pp. 233-235; and J. P. M. Sweet, 'The Theory of Miracles in the Wisdom of Solomon,' in C. F. D. Moule, *Miracles,* London, 1965, pp. 115-116.
[38] See above, pp. 488-489.
[39] Cf. H. D. Betz, 'Orthodoxy and Heresy in Primitive Christianity,' *Interpretation* 19 (1965), p. 308.

*What does St Paul mean by 'the stigmata of Jesus' (v. 17)?*

To the modern reader, v. 17 may easily suggest that St Paul had mystical wounds in his hands, feet and side, like those which St Francis of Assisi later had as a result of his intense contemplation of the Passion of Christ. Then v. 17 will be a plea for peace and quiet, so that he can devote himself to this contemplation without distraction. But this is not at all what St Paul means.

Literally, 'stigmata' are marks made by branding. Cattle and slaves bore the brand of their owner. Secondly, the devotees of some pagan religions had themselves tatooed or branded as a mark of their devotion to the pagan gods. [40] Thirdly, there was a temple of Heracles in Egypt where a slave could escape from civil slavery by receiving the 'sacred marks' of Heracles and becoming a slave of Heracles — after this his human owner could not touch him. Hence the 'stigmata' could also be a guarantee of freedom. [41]

St Paul's meaning in v. 17 can be gathered from its structural links, which are four:

1. In the subsection 6:14-18 (p. 493), it corresponds to 6:14-15: 'The world is crucified to me, and I to the world. For neither circumcision nor its absence makes any difference, but only creation anew.'

2. In the ninth section 5:22—6:18 (p. 478), it corresponds to 5:24: 'Those who belong to Christ Jesus have crucified the flesh with its passions and lusts.'

3. In the third main division 5:1—6:18 (p. 411), it corresponds to 5:1: 'Christ has made us truly free; stand firm, then, and do not submit again to the yoke of slavery.'

4. In the overall pattern 1:1—6:18 (p. 39), it corresponds to 1:1: 'Paul, an apostle....through Jesus Christ.' And through 1:1 it has an indirect link with 1:10 (the counterpart of 1:1 in the first section): 'If I were still seeking to please men, I should not be the slave of Christ.'

These links show, first, that the 'stigmata' are the spiritual counterpart of circumcision; secondly, that they mark St Paul as the servant and apostle of Christ; and thirdly, that they are a spiritual badge of freedom.

The 'stigmata', then, must be St Paul's metaphorical description of the 'circumcision of heart' or 'new creation' which he and the other

---

[40] Cf. Philo, *The Special Laws*, I, 58 (Loeb, VII).
[41] For the ancient evidence see G in G, pp. 221-222.

Christians receive through faith and baptism. But since the stigmata in question mark Paul not only as a servant but also as an apostle of Christ, he is probably thinking also of the scars left on his body by the persecutions he underwent during his missions to the Gentiles. [42]

## Why must the Galatians leave St Paul alone?

V. 17 should not be read as a pathetic plea for a little peace and quiet. It is not written in a spirit of self-pity. On the contrary, it is a good-humoured threat. St Paul is parodying a magical charm used for winning friends and influencing people. [43] He means: 'Anyone who vexes me further had better watch out. I bear the spiritual tatoo, not of Osiris, but of Christ. Anyone who vexes me will have to reckon with someone more powerful than Osiris!'

In its original position, at the end of the Antioch discourse, this was the counterpart of 3 : 1: 'Foolish men, who has bewitched you?' 6 : 16 is a bit of pauline magic to undo the spell cast by St Peter.

Since the expression is playful, it is unsafe to infer from v. 17 that at the time of writing St Paul had already decided to go to Rome and the Western Mediterranean — though probably he had.

*Excursus*

# THE 'SPIRIT' IN SECTION 9

St Paul wrote in block letters TO PNEUMA (cf. 6 : 11). But a modern editor or translator cannot do this. He must decide whether to write 'the spirit' or 'the Spirit'. Sometimes the decision is difficult, and sometimes both alternatives are unsatisfactory in that they determine what St Paul left indeterminate.

In the ninth section, 'THE SPIRIT' occurs at the beginning (5 : 22), in the middle (6 : 8), and at the end (6 : 18) — a sure sign of its importance. [44] At the end it clearly refers to the human 'spirit': 'The grace of our Lord Jesus Christ be with your spirit, brethren.' But at the beginning and middle, the word is ambiguous. In 5 : 22, since 'the harvest of THE SPIRIT' stands in contrast to 'the works

---

[42] Cf. Lightfoot, Gal, ad loc., and above, p. 490, n. 26.
[43] See the magical papyrus quoted in G in G, p. 224.
[44] The word *pneuma* also occurs in 5 : 25 and 6 : 1, and in eleven other passages in this Epistle: 3 : 2, 3, 5, 14; 4 : 6, 29; 5 : 5, 16, 17 (twice), 18.

of the flesh', it is reasonable to argue that as the flesh is a constituent of human nature, so too is the spirit — hence it should have a small s. But on the other hand, as the fruits listed are produced in the believer by the Spirit of God, a capital is equally appropriate. In the middle, since there is the same contrast of 'flesh' and 'spirit', it is reasonable to write: 'If he sows for his flesh....if he sows for the spirit.' But then in the last clause it is not satisfactory to write 'from the spirit he will reap eternal life,' since eternal life comes not from any part of man's own nature but from the Spirit of God.

In 5:25 capitals are more appropriate: 'If we are alive with (or seething with) the Spirit, let us also walk by the Spirit (i.e., let us obey the guidance of the Spirit of God).' And in 6:1 a small letter is clearly indicated: 'you who are spiritual must put him right in a spirit of gentleness.'

In this section, then, the word 'SPIRIT' is as ambiguous as the word 'law'. St Paul's thought and expression are lacking in precision. When we ask exactly what he meant in any particular verse, we may be asking a question to which there is no answer. A theologian of today who is unwilling to acquiesce in St Paul's ambiguities may legitimately try to define more precisely the meaning of such words in each context. But when he does so, he is developing St Paul's thought rather than analysing it.

### Is St Paul here using 'the Spirit' in a specifically Christian sense?

Whenever 'THE SPIRIT' is written with a capital S, the modern reader thinks of the Third Person, consubstantial with the Father and the Son. But in St Paul's usage 'the Spirit' probably retains very much the same sense as it had in the Old Testament.

The writers of the Old Testament did not speak about the Son of God at all, because they were entirely unaware that God had a Son of his own nature, consubstantial with himself. But they did speak about 'the holy Spirit' or 'the Spirit of God'. At the very beginning of Genesis, we read: 'The Spirit of God was moving over the face of the waters' (Gen 1:2). Often the Spirit seems to be pictured as an extension of the divine personality, filling the whole of heaven and earth, for example in Ps 139:7:

> Whither shall I go from thy Spirit,
> or whither shall I flee from thy presence?

And in the Wisdom of Solomon (1:7): 'The Spirit of the Lord has filled the universe.' Sometimes, even in the Old Testament, the Spirit is described in almost personal terms, as when Isaiah (63:10) says that the Israelites rebelled against God 'and grieved his holy Spirit' (for only a person can be grieved). [45] But such expressions were not understood to mean that the Holy Spirit is a distinct person. They were indirect ways of speaking about God himself, adopted out of reverence, to safeguard the notion of his transcendence. [46] They imply that while God remains aloof in his high heaven, dwelling in light inaccessible, he is nevertheless present and active among his people — through his Spirit. In Haggai 2:4-5, the Lord says:

> Work, for I am with you, says the Lord of hosts, according to the promise that I made to you, when you came out of Egypt: My Spirit abides among you; fear not.

'My Spirit abides among you' means the same as 'I am with you.' The Lord of hosts is the Spirit, and the Spirit is the Lord of hosts — there is no distinction of persons here. There is not the least hint of interaction between the Lord and his Spirit. God is active among his people, but it is a one-way action — God acts through his Spirit.

In the ninth section, taken by itself, there is nothing which goes beyond the Old Testament conception of the Spirit. 5:25 has a close parallel in Ps 143:10: [47]

> Teach me to do thy will,
> for thou art my God!
> Let thy good Spirit lead me
> on a level path!

But the statement made about the Spirit in this section must of course be read in the light of what has been said about the Spirit earlier in the Epistle. St Paul has asserted that God has a Son, and that the Spirit sent forth by God is the Spirit of his Son. Because the Father and the Son are one God (cf. 3:20), they send forth the one divine Spirit — who can now be called either, as in the Old Testament, 'the Spirit of God (the Father)', or, as in Gal 4:6, 'the Spirit of his Son.'

This important development in the doctrine of the Spirit is not explicit in the ninth section. But if it is kept explicitly in mind in reading the passage, it casts valuable light on St Paul's thought. The 'new creation' in 6:15 is a fresh intervention of the Spirit of God the Father, as at the beginning of the old aeon: [48] but as the Spirit is also the Spirit of the Son, the effect of the new creation is to conform

---

[45] Cf. Ps 143:10.
[46] Cf. Wainwright, *The Trinity in the New Testament*, p. 30, n. 4.
[47] Cf. Ps 42:3; Deut 31:6; Phil 2:13.
[48] Cf. Ps 103:30, quoted above, p. 495.

the lives of believers to the pattern of the Son of God: the Spirit of love, obedience and self-sacrifice in which he lived and died takes possession of them and produces the same harvest of good in them. The life and especially the death of Christ is a manifestation of the Holy Spirit: in Christ we see a man who 'walks by the Spirit'. Christ revealed the Holy Spirit by following his guidance: his human will was in perfect conformity with the inspirations of his own divine Spirit.

Curiously, no New Testament writer says that Christ 'revealed' the Holy Spirit. St Matthew, St Luke, St John and St Paul say that the Father 'reveals' the Son, and that the Son 'reveals' the Father, but none of them says that either the Father or the Son 'reveals' the Holy Spirit. They do not use the word 'reveals' in this connection. Both St John and St Paul speak of the Holy Spirit, not so much as one who *is* revealed, but rather as one who reveals. St John says that the Spirit will lead us into all truth (cf. 16:13) and St Paul says in 1 Cor 2:10 that God has revealed to us the mystery of the cross 'through the Spirit'.

As was shown above (p. 219), it is almost impossible to distinguish between faith and the HOLY SPIRIT: the man who has faith has the Holy Spirit, and the man who has the Holy Spirit has faith. Only the man who has faith, and hence only the man who has the Holy Spirit, is able to recognize Jesus as the Son of God and God as the Father of Jesus. Therefore only the man who already has the Spirit is able to recognize the death of Jesus as a manifestation or revelation of the Spirit. It is a revelation 'from faith to faith' (Rom 1:17). The Holy Spirit takes *secret* possession of the believer, strengthens and elevates his mind and will, but himself remains in the background — somewhat as the thinking ego always remains in the background of our thought. Whenever I think, it is *I* who think. Even when I think of myself, I can still distinguish between the thinking 'I' and the 'me' which is the object of my thought. I cannot turn round quickly and catch the thinking 'I'. Nor can I turn round quickly and see the Holy Spirit. He does not reveal himself to our introspection. We learn what he is like when we turn our thoughts to the cross of Christ as a revelation of the love of the Father and of the Son for each other and for mankind.

The cross, placarded before the believer's eyes, reveals to him that the Holy Spirit is a Spirit of love or charity and thus corrects the image of the Spirit conveyed by the Old Testament. Some of the cruder stories in the historical books might easily give the impression that the Spirit of God is fierce, violent and terrible. When Dalilah disclosed the riddle of the lion and the honey, Samson's wrath blazed out, 'and the Spirit of the Lord came mightily upon him, and he went down to Ashkalon and killed thirty men of the town.' [49] In Gal 5:25, when St Paul describes the Spirit by his 'fruits', he is correcting the Old Testament image in the light of Christ's life and death. He is setting forth a thoroughly Christian doctrine of the Spirit, though he does so without making any dogmatic statement about the Spirit which a non-Christian Jew would feel obliged to repudiate.

*How could St Paul tolerate the ambiguity of the word* 'SPIRIT'?

In modern usage, there are four distinct meanings of SPIRIT.

1. It can mean a constituent of man's natural being — his spirit as opposed to his body or his flesh.
2. It can mean a natural affection or disposition of the human will, as for example, when we say that Augustus treated his vanquished enemies in a spirit of clemency.
3. It can mean an infused, supernatural affection of the human will, as for example, when we pray for a spirit of patience or charity.
4. It can be the name of the third divine person.

But these four senses do not provide a satisfactory system of classification for St Paul's uses of the word. As was shown above (p. 497), as often as not a pauline usage will not fit into any of our pigeon-holes. Another example is Gal 3:3, 'Having begun with the SPIRIT, will you now end with the flesh?', where St Paul is undoubtedly speaking of the gift of the Spirit received through faith and baptism (sense 3 — or perhaps sense 4); yet, as SPIRIT here stands in contrast to 'flesh', the first sense cannot be excluded. Again, the clearest example of sense 4 in Galatians is 4:6: 'God sent forth the Spirit of his Son into our hearts, crying "Abba, Father".' But in some ways it would be better to classify this under the third head.

Not only the individual occurrences, but the very ambiguity of this key term presents a problem. How could St Paul tolerate such a degree of ambiguity? *We* feel that his thought here stands in great need of clarification; why did he not feel the same himself?

One reason may be that we have some 'clear and distinct ideas' about the metaphysics of transient action which St Paul had not. In

---

[49]   Jud 14:19; cf. 1 Sam 11:5-7.

the language of traditional metaphysics, if substance A produces an effect on substance B, it does this by producing an accidental modification in substance B. Thus if a hot iron bar A is placed close to a cold iron bar B, A produces the accident of heat in B. Or if a wise man A gives a lesson to an ignorant boy B, A produces the accident of knowledge in B. Similarly, we think, if the Holy Spirit acts upon the soul of the believer, this can only be by producing in the believer the accident which we call 'the gift of the Spirit' (sense 3 above): the uncreated Holy Spirit produces the created gift of a holy spirit, a spirit of holiness.

But St Paul did not think in this way. [50] He regarded the SPIRIT, whether of God or of man (1 Cor 5: 1), as an extension of his personality, capable of penetrating the spirit of another and of becoming, in some sense, 'one spirit' with the spirit of another.

It cannot be said that our way of considering the mystery of transient action is better than St Paul's. In our way of thinking it remains a complete mystery how one substance can produce an accident in another. In St Paul's way, it remains a complete mystery how one substance can enable another to surpass its own powers while remaining distinct from it.

Secondly, St Paul saw resemblances between the spirit of man and the Spirit of God (cf. 1 Cor 2: 11), and used the same word *pneuma* to keep these in sight. In man, *pneuma* is a principle of knowledge, scrutinizing his own being and ranging out over other beings, and a principle of love or hatred towards other beings; in God, too, it is a principle of knowledge scrutinizing all being, and a principle of love, though this love may sometimes take the form of anger.

St Paul teaches that the human spirit is now invited or 'called' into union with the Spirit of God through faith in Christ. If the call is accepted, the human 'spirit' begins to produce the harvest which of its nature it ought to produce — charity, joy, peace, etc. In a sense, these are fruits of the human spirit. Yet they are also fruits of the Holy Spirit, since without the guidance and assistance of the Holy Spirit, the human spirit would not have produced them.

Probably St Paul looked at the matter in this way. Man at his creation, before the Fall, had a certain 'spirit' in him, received from God, for 'the Lord formed man of dust from the ground and breathed

---

[50] The scholastic metaphysic is often called the handmaid of theology; but she is sometimes not very helpful.

into his nostrils the breath of life' (Gen 2:7). This breath of life is a kind of emanation from God. Man consists of his body, formed from the dust of the earth, and his spirit, received from God. This spirit, received from God through Christ (cf. Col 1:15), was a spirit of charity, like the Spirit in God himself. It was defiled and almost extinguished by sin, but not entirely, for even fallen man does 'some' charitable act (as the theologians rather grudgingly admit). [51] When God pours out the Spirit upon believers, he gives them, again through Christ, much more of the spirit that is already in them. The re-creation or 'new creation' of man through the Holy Spirit (cf. Gal 6:15) is a renewal of the original creation, but it is also more than a renewal, since God's grace is far greater than man's sin (cf. Rom 5:15-17).

### Is the personality of the Holy Spirit revealed in Galatians?

St Paul does not, of course, attempt to set forth a complete exposition of his beliefs in Galatians (or in any other Epistle). If, therefore, we can find no clear statement or hint of the personality of the Holy Spirit, it will not follow that this doctrine was completely unknown to him.

When one scrutinizes the Epistle, it is hard to find any text which goes beyond what some have called 'Binitarianism'. The text which can most easily be read in a Trinitarian sense is at the centre of the fifth section (p. 330), where we find as counterparts:

> God sent forth his own Son.
>
> God sent forth the Spirit of his Son
> into our hearts, crying: 'Abba, Father.'

Here the Father and the Son are clearly two distinct persons, and the parallelism between the Son and the Spirit of the Son *suggests* that the Spirit is a third person. [52] But the text need not necessarily be read in this sense. Since the Father and the Son know and love each other perfectly, they are perfectly united in one SPIRIT, and this SPIRIT is communicated to those who adhere to the Son through

---

51   See above, p. 467.
52   St Thomas Aquinas has a good theological note here (Gal, 417 A): 'The Holy Spirit is common to the Father and to the Son and proceeds from both, and is given by both. That is why, wherever it is said that the Father sends the Holy Spirit there is mention of the Son, as in Jn 15:26: "whom the Father will send in my name"; and similarly when the Spirit is said to be sent by the Son, there is mention of the Father—hence "whom I will send you from the Father". And here too, when St Paul says "God (the Father) sent the (Holy) Spirit," immediately there is mention of the Son—"the Spirit of his Son".'

faith. Just as Old Testament writers can speak of God (the Father) as 'sending forth his Spirit' (cf. Ps 103:30) without intending to imply that the Spirit is a distinct person, so too St Paul may be speaking of God (the Father) as 'sending forth the Spirit of his Son' without intending to imply that the Spirit is a distinct person. If the Old Testament writers could think of the Spirit as an extension of the one divine person known to them, St Paul could think of the Spirit as an extension of the two persons of the Father and the Son. [53] At all events, the idea that the Holy Spirit is a third divine person was far less clear in the mind of St Paul than it is in the minds of Christians today. The efforts of later theologians to clarify his thought on this matter, while laudable in some respects, have had the disadvantage of obscuring one important lesson of this Epistle: that what we need to make us sons of God is 'the Spirit of his Son'. If the Spirit is too sharply hypostatized as a third person, it ceases to be clear why possession of *the Spirit* assimilates us to *the Son*. This brings us to a question which intelligent students often ask:

*What advantage is there in knowing that the Holy Spirit is a person?*

Perhaps it is of no practical importance at all to know that the Holy Spirit is a person. Christ our Lord said that it was the Father's will that we should honour the Son as we honour the Father (cf. Jn 5:23), but he did not say that it was the Father's will or his own that we should honour the Holy Spirit as we honour himself and the Father. For centuries the Church did not worship the Holy Spirit or address prayers directly to him. The controversy over the personality of the Holy Spirit, which occurred in the second half of the fourth century, was little more than an epilogue to the great controversy over the consubstantiality of the Father and the Son. [54] The heresy, known as Macedonianism, which denied that the Holy Spirit was a third divine person, did not create anything like so great a crisis as was caused by Arianism, which denied the full divinity of Christ. [55] Even after the condemnation of Macedonianism, the Holy Spirit did not move right into the focus of the Church's worship.

Since neither Christ himself, nor St Paul, nor St John thought it important to emphasize that the Holy Spirit is a person, this cannot be regarded as one of the central affirmations of our faith. There

---

[53] Cf. Whiteley, *The Theology of St Paul*, pp. 127-129.
[54] Cf. Wainwright, *The Trinity in the New Testament*, p. 199.
[55] Arianism was condemned at Nicaea in 325, and Macedonianism at Constantinople I in 381.

may even be certain *dis*advantages in giving it much emphasis. If we think of the Holy Spirit first as the Spirit of the Father, whereby he knows and loves his creatures, and secondly as the Spirit of the Father and the Son, whereby they know and love each other and their creatures, then to be filled with this Holy Spirit will obviously mean being drawn into this relationship between the Father and the Son — to be drawn into the likeness of the Son and into his loving obedience to the Father — thus it will mean sharing in the 'family life' of God. The theological doctrine defined at the Council of Constantinople has the disadvantage of making it less easy for us to understand how possession of the Holy Spirit draws us into the shared life of the Father and the Son.

The Holy Spirit *is* a person, as Christ himself implied (cf. Jn 14:16; 14:26; 15:26) and the Council of Constantinople made explicit. But he is a person who acts and prays in us and through us, not a person whom we confront in our prayers, like the Son and the Father. He prefers to be hidden in us and amongst us. If we insist on bringing him round to the front, and placing him in our thoughts alongside the Father and the Son, we may find it harder to keep hold of the truth that he is within us.

If we try to enter, by what might be called 'sympathetic contemplation', into the love which the Son has for the Father, and into the love which the Father has for the Son, particularly at the moment of his death — if, that is to say, we turn to the Father and say: 'Father, fill me with the love which you had for your Son at the moment of his death,' and then turn to the Son and say: 'Lord Jesus, fill me with the love which you had for your Father at the hour of your death', and if the prayer is granted, then that love *is* the Holy Spirit, and to be filled with this Holy Spirit is to share in the life of the Trinity. It is to become personally involved in the pattern of love which unites the divine persons. There is an analogy in human family life: an adopted child becomes a member of the adopting family by becoming personally involved in the pattern of love, reverence, fidelity, affection, which holds the family together.

It is questionable whether it really helps to turn directly to the Holy Spirit and say: 'Holy Spirit, fill me with your love for the Father and the Son.' We have seen no instance of this love, but we have seen the Son's love for the Father, particularly in his passion and death. [56]

---

[56] Through this love Christ completely fulfilled the law, for he loved God with his whole heart and soul and mind, and his neighbour more than himself. Cf. Althaus, *The Theology of Martin Luther*, p. 203.

It is through the contemplation of Christ, the visible image of the invisible God, that we find our way into the life of the Trinity. The Holy Spirit is content to remain hidden within us and almost behind us, unobtrusively raising our minds and hearts to the Son and the Father.

So what advantage is there in knowing that the Holy Spirit is a distinct divine person? The answer seems to be: Very little. But once the question had been explicitly raised, there was no doubt how it had to be answered. Our Lord's words at the Last Supper were clear enough, on this as on other subjects — or should have been; it was only the aberration of heretics which forced the Church to try and make the matter clearer.

## What effects does St Paul attribute to the Spirit?

In the Old Testament, the Spirit of God is often given intermittently, for example to Samson and to Saul, to enable them to perform something beyond their normal powers. The craftsman Bézalel was filled with the Spirit of God 'to work in gold and silver and bronze' and construct the Ark of the Covenant (cf. Exod 35:31-32). But there are other texts in which the holy Spirit is understood as a permanent possession guiding men in the paths of holiness and justice. The best known is in the *Miserere* (Ps 51:10-12):

> Create in me a clean heart, O God,
>     and put a new and right spirit within me.
> Cast me not away from thy presence,
>     and take not thy holy Spirit from me.
> Restore to me the joy of thy salvation,
>     and uphold me with a willing spirit.

In the New Testament too, the Holy Spirit produces on the one hand extraordinary, intermittent effects, such as prophecy, speaking with tongues, and miraculous cures, and on the other hand less conspicuous but more permanent ethical effects, such as charity, joy and peace. The Spirit is still thought of as a *power* coming forth from God, taking possession of certain men, enhancing their natural powers, and enabling them to know, to say and to do things which ordinarily they could not have known, said or done. The Holy Spirit is a power that raises men into the sphere of the divine. [57]

---

[57] Cf. M. E. Boismard, 'La révélation de l'Ésprit-Saint,' *Revue Thomiste* 55 (1955), p. 10.

The extraordinary gifts or 'charismata' were given to the early Church for the double purpose of confirming believers in their faith and of commending the gospel to unbelievers. At Pentecost, the sound of the rushing wind attracted a large crowd of unbelievers, and the gift of tongues enabled the disciples to address all in their own languages and convert many. Similar charismata were recognized as a seal of divine approval upon the conversion of Cornelius, of the Samaritans, and of the Galatians (cf. 3: 1-3). In all these instances the outpouring of the Spirit was a 'Confirmation' for the Church of the rightness of what had been done by the apostles in extending the Church to include Samaritans and Gentiles. St Paul shows us the importance of the charismata in the spread of the gospel when he says in 1 Cor 14: 24-25 (speaking of the Corinthian liturgy):

> If all are prophesying and some unbeliever or some visitor comes in, he is convicted by all, he is shown his worth by all; the secrets of his heart are laid bare, and he will fall on his face and adore God, confessing that truly God is among you. [58]

These two purposes of the extraordinary charismata can be summed up in St Paul's word 'edification' or 'up-building' (*oikodomê*). They build up the Church by gaining new members and confirming the old ones.

When the extraordinary charismata died out, or were extinguished (cf. 1 Thes 5: 19), there remained the less conspicuous gifts. For the most part, the Holy Spirit now acts in unobtrusive ways. The main purpose for which he was sent was, and is, to remedy human weakness, to strengthen our will and understanding, [59] so as to enable us to live the sinless and charitable life which God expects of his sons. The effect of the Holy Spirit upon the moral life of believers can easily escape notice, because true holiness is not obtrusive. Christ himself did not attract attention during the hidden life. [60] The people of Nazareth were amazed when he came forward one day and said: 'The Spirit of the Lord is upon me, because the Lord hath anointed me, to bring good tidings to the afflicted' (Isa 61: 1; Lk 4: 18-19).

---

[58] Cf. 1 Thes 1:4-5.
[59] St John speaks mainly of the effect of the Holy Spirit on the disciple's understanding; he uses the title 'Spirit of Truth' and speaks of the Spirit as leading the disciples into all truth (cf. Jn 16:13). St Paul, on the other hand, speaks mainly of his influence on the will and on conduct (cf. Rom 8:26)—but not exclusively; in the list of the fruits of the Spirit he includes 'faith' (5:22), and in 1 Cor 13:13 he probably means that faith, hope and charity are all charismata.
[60] Cf. J. H. Newman, 'Christ hidden from the World,' in *Parochial and Plain Sermons*, IV, London, 1900, p. 242-243.

The normal effect of union between the human spirit and the Spirit of God is to cleanse the human spirit of the defilement it has contracted through sin (cf. 2 Cor 7:1) and to make it bear the fruit which of its own nature it *ought* to have produced. Thus, for example, according to St Paul, the Holy Spirit enables the mind of the believer to see in the Old Testament what was there before his eyes all the time waiting to be seen; the gift of the Holy Spirit is like the removal of a veil (cf. 2 Cor 3:15-16). Or it can be compared to an illumination which intensifies the natural light of the understanding. The Holy Spirit also strengthens a man's *will* in such a way that he now effectively wills what in some sense he has willed all the time (cf. Rom 7:15-25). That is why to the recipient the gift of the Holy Spirit is largely or even wholly imperceptible. What the Holy Spirit does is to enable his spiritual powers to function normally or supernormally. When his powers are simply functioning normally, he cannot tell by introspection whether he is being aided by the Holy Spirit. If, like St Paul himself, he has been converted as an adult, the contrast between his conduct before and after conversion may convince him that he is now aided by the Holy Spirit (cf. Gal 6:4). But the man who was baptized in infancy is not able to make this reassuring comparison; the cradle-Christian may be unable to discern the influence of the Holy Spirit in his life. Such a man should look back over his past and reflect that whatever good there has been in it is probably much more due to the Holy Spirit than he has ever been inclined to think. The assistance of the Holy Spirit is so unobtrusive that we can easily take to ourselves alone the credit for what he has enabled us to do. But this is a costly mistake. St Paul repeats again and again that the man who boasts of his own justice will not receive the justice that comes from God through the Holy Spirit.

The dove is a useful image of the Holy Spirit in so far as the Spirit, like a bird, comes down from above, that is, comes to us from God, and in so far as the dove is a gentle, simple and innocent bird. But that about exhausts the usefulness of the dove image. The Holy Spirit also has the title 'Paraclete', which some people imagine is another kind of bird. In fact, of course, it is a Greek word meaning either 'Advocate' or 'Comforter'. The Holy Spirit is a Comforter because he diffuses in our hearts charity, joy and peace. He enables us to share in the love of the Father and of the Son, to find joy in the knowledge that we are loved by them, and to find peace through his strength enabling us to do their will. St Paul sums up the tone or atmosphere of the Christian life in a short phrase which is very hard to translate: *kauchômetha en Theôi* — 'We are full of joy and confidence in God' (Rom 5:11). That should be the Spirit in which Christians live. The Holy Spirit is given to us in order that we may live in a spirit of love, at peace with God, at peace with ourselves, at peace with the world in which he has put us. As the Father is content to be the Father and not the Son, and as the Son is content to be the Son and not the Father, so the Spirit teaches us to be content to be what we are, the sons and daughters whom God has adopted into his family.

## Why does St Paul speak so often of the Spirit?

One has only to glance at a Concordance to see that the Spirit is a constantly recurring theme in St Paul's Big Four Epistles (Rom, 1-2 Cor, Gal). As has just been pointed out, he used this word to explain and describe the difference which acceptance of the gospel makes to a man's life. It was, therefore, an essential part in his technique of commending the gospel. The man who believes, he says, receives the Spirit of God, enabling him to live a life of charity, joy and peace, very different from the life of those who follow the promptings of sinful flesh. Since somewhere in every man's breast there lurks a desire for the life of charity, joy and peace, the offer of the Holy Spirit should find some response in the heart of every man.

'Spirit' is an appropriate word with which to express the change effected in a believer, because while his body and physical appearance are unaffected, he is changed through and through. [61] The strength of the Spirit does not remedy the weakness of the body, which still remains subject to sickness and death (cf. Rom 8:10); but it does strengthen the human spirit. St Paul adds that at the resurrection of the dead the influence of the Holy Spirit will be extended to our bodies, for, he says, 'God will raise up our mortal bodies through his Spirit dwelling within us' (Rom 8:11). In this life the Holy Spirit affects the body only through the human spirit, in so far as it enables the human spirit to put to death the practices of the body (cf. Rom 8:13). At the resurrection, it will directly affect, transform and transfigure the body, which will then become 'a spiritual body' (1 Cor 15:44). [62] Here, no doubt, we have one reason why St Paul adds that in this life we have only 'the first-fruits' of the Spirit (Rom 8:23) or an 'earnest' or 'first instalment' of the Spirit (2 Cor 1:22; 5:5) — though he also means that at present even our spirit is not completely

---

[61]  Jn 9:8-9 expresses this pictorially.
[62]  Cf. Ezek 37:1-14.

impregnated with the Holy Spirit. It is subject to the powers both of
the old evil age and of the new Christian age, 'just as a man who has
come out of the cold into a warm room is subject both to the cold
which has numbed his hands and to the heat which is thawing them
out.' [63]

*Is St Paul's doctrine of the Spirit thoroughly integrated with the rest
of his thought?*

Many theological connections which we might have expected St
Paul to make, are not made in his extant letters. [64] For example, since
the Spirit of God is mentioned in the account of creation in Gen 1:2,
we might expect him to say that the outpouring of the Holy Spirit
upon Christians is the 'new creation'. He probably had this connection
in his mind in Gal 6:15, but he has not made it explicit.

Again, since the promise of the new covenant in Jer 31:31-34
includes a promise of the Holy Spirit, we might expect him to say
that the Holy Spirit is the spirit of the new covenant promised by the
prophets. There are possible allusions to this identification in 2 Cor
3:3, but Jer 31:31-34 is not nearly as prominent in the pauline
passages about the Spirit as one might expect. [65] The reason may
perhaps be that St Paul found Jer 31:34 altogether too individualistic:

> No longer shall each man teach his neighbour and each his brother saying,
> 'Know the Lord,' for they shall all know me, from the least of them to the
> greatest, says the Lord.

In St Paul's view, the gifts of the Spirit are given to *some* for the
benefit of *all* members of the body. Jer 31:34 strongly suggests that
the man who has the Spirit has no need of his fellow-men to instruct
him, but is sufficient to himself — an idea which St Paul would not
wish to encourage among his converts (cf. 6:1-6). [66]

St Paul makes a very clear connection between faith and reception
of the Spirit (cf. Gal 3:2; 3:14; 5:5), but a less clear link between

---

[63] Whiteley, *The Theology of St Paul*, p. 127.
[64] Cf. McKenzie, *The Power and the Wisdom*, p. 141: 'Paul's theology of the
Spirit is the most elaborate of all the New Testament writers; but it is un-
structured and not altogether logically consistent.'
[65] It is quoted at length in Heb 9:8-12, but as a proof that the Old Covenant
was defective.
[66] The reason why St Peter in his discourse on the day of Pentecost quoted Joel
2:28-32 rather than Jer 31:31-34 may be that the gift of the Spirit promised
in the Jeremiah-passage was to manifest itself in righteous conduct, whereas St
Peter wanted a text which spoke of extraordinary manifestations: 'Your sons
and daughters shall prophesy, and your young men shall see visions and your
old men shall dream dreams.'

Baptism (and the Eucharist) and reception of the Spirit. Theologians have never been quite comfortable about these connections. When St Paul speaks of our present possession of the Spirit as a first instalment, he implies the possibility of receiving the Spirit in greater and greater abundance or fullness; but he does not say that the various sacraments are the means through which God communicates his Spirit in ever greater abundance. Later theologians have said this, [67] but unfortunately St Paul left it unsaid.

Again, we might have expected St Paul to link the gift of the Spirit with the Messiahship of Jesus, since there are two passages in Isaiah which point to such a connection (11:1-3 and 61:1). But St Paul makes no use of these texts. [68] He is not a systematic thinker, and we have, after all, only an incomplete record of what he did think. He thought more than he said, he said more than he wrote, and not all that he wrote has survived. Galatians is a good introduction to his thought, but that is all.

---

[67]  There is a hint of it in Jn 6:63 (see my comment in HJ 5 [1964], p. 10) and
        in 1 Cor 10:3-4 (cf. Galot, *La Rédemption*, p. 355).
[68]  They are used in Lk 4:18 and Acts 10:38-40.

# EPILOGUE

The reader may perhaps have noted with surprise that in writing the Foreword I mentioned faith in Paul before faith in Christ. I did so deliberately, because the first act of faith which an apostle had to ask for was an act of faith in himself; and in the Epistle to the Galatians St Paul is appealing to his readers not to lose their faith in him — not to allow the propaganda of the Judaizers to undermine their confidence in him as an apostle sent by God to bring them a message of salvation. He saw that the Galatians' faith in Christ would stand or fall with their faith in himself; if they ceased to believe that he was a true apostle, they would begin to doubt the correctness of his gospel (and *vice versa*). That is why he devotes so much of the Epistle to self-justification and self-commendation.

The modern reader of the Epistle must face the same twofold decision which St Paul placed before the Galatians: Do I believe in Paul as an apostle chosen and commissioned by God? And do I believe in Christ as the Son of God? To study Galatians and evade these personal, existential questions is a waste of effort. The Epistle, when read or heard read, *is* the gospel. It announces God's offer of justification and salvation through faith in Christ, and calls upon the hearer to believe and be saved. It is idle for a Christian, or for anyone else, to study what St Paul is saying as if it were a message for others but not for oneself. Nor should anyone evade half of the challenge by saying: 'My faith in Christ is not based on Paul's witness; therefore, while listening to what he says about Christ, I will shelve the question of his own self-evaluation.' The reader is called upon to face both questions, or both halves of the question: 'Do I believe that Paul was a vessel of election, predestined from his mother's womb (cf. 1 : 15), that his vision on the road to Damascus was a true divine intervention, and that he was sent by God to carry to the Gentiles the gospel of his Son?'

If the answer is an emphatic Yes, certain important consequences will follow, which I shall mention in a moment. But first let me point out the dangers of the answers 'No' and 'Don't know'. If any Christian decides to base his faith and understanding of Christ exclusively on the gospels, he soon finds himself involved in difficult literary problems, and may easily conclude that the mind of Christ is unknowable. After much reading, he may feel that the Quest of the Historical Jesus is hopeless, and yet, so long as the problem remains unsolved, the Church has no clear message to offer — only when the scholars have completed their research will we know what the gospel is, and so on. This is a paralyzing state of mind for anyone whose life is dedicated to the preaching of the gospel. The advantage of giving an emphatic Yes to St Paul's appeal for faith in his apostolic authority is that he gives us a Christian interpretation of the Old Testament, an interpretation of the mind of Christ himself, and a gospel to preach. Certainly there are some areas of uncertainty in St Paul's theology, but the substance of his message is clear and simple. If we have faith in him as an apostle, we shall take his interpretation of the gospel as authentic, loyal and true; and at once we have a gospel to preach. If we associate ourselves with him as Timothy did, and Titus, and the others whose names are written in the Book of Life (cf. Phil 4:3), we become sharers in his divine mission to the Gentiles.

We may feel disinclined to commit ourselves in this way to pauline Christianity, on account of certain defects in St Paul's character which alienated some of his contemporaries and can still alienate some of his readers today. Perhaps in certain parts of the commentary I have spoken too freely of those defects. I am well aware that if we let our critical reason loose upon the writings of St Paul we can find ways of devaluating his message until it may seem hardly worth preaching. As the work of the extreme form-critics has shown, there is almost nothing in the gospels themselves which cannot be made to look questionable under the assaults of critical reason when it is unleashed. It is as 'fleshly' as the flesh, and can generate agnosticism and cynicism which shatter the preacher's confidence and reduce him to silence. Just as the first disciples had to decide whether to put their faith in Christ as their Master, and having decided, had to accept what he taught even in face of reason's criticisms (cf. Jn 6:68), so the student of the pauline Epistles must decide whether to take Paul as his master; if he decides to do so, he must believe resolutely that the Apostle's message, simple as it is, truly contains the power of God unto salvation. In Jn 7:17, Jesus says that if anyone will try living according to his doctrine, he will learn, in his own experience, whether it is from God. The same applies to the teaching of St Paul, which, for those who accept his apostolic authority, is an authentic interpretation of the work and teaching of Christ. When he hands it over to us, in this short Epistle, it may look as small and insignificant as a mustard seed; but if accepted and used, it reveals, like the mustard seed, amazing potentialities. Justification is a mystery and a work of faith from start to finish.

So let us turn a blind eye to the few defects which we can observe in this great apostle, and consider instead some of his admirable qualities. I said at the beginning that I cannot expect the reader to agree with me about every one of the questions which I have raised.

There are, however, two controversial questions on which I sincerely hope, for Paul's sake, that my arguments will carry conviction, namely, Where does the Antioch-discourse end? and, Did St Paul write the whole Epistle with his own hand? If he concluded his public protest at Antioch with the thunderbolt, 'If justification comes from the law, Christ died for nothing,' his abruptness and severity fell short of his own teaching (cf. 6:1); but if, as I have argued, he continued to reason with his brothers and concluded with a magical spell to counter the fascination of Peter's example, he spoke in a friendly, gentle and conciliatory spirit. And if he wrote the whole Epistle in large letters with his own hand (6:11), like a Roman father writing out a primer for his little son, the whole physical format of the Epistle will have consoled the Galatians and taken the sting out of the rather sharp rebuke which he administered at the corresponding place in the beginning of the Epistle (1:6).

The gentle and affectionate side of Paul's nature does not appear too evidently in Galatians. But while interpreting this controversial writing, we should bear in mind some of his sayings in Philippians — for example (4:8): 'Devote your minds to all that is true, and venerable, and just, and holy, and lovable, and seemly, and good, and praiseworthy.' He did so himself (4:9), thanks to Christ, in whom he found the inspiration and the strength to live on these heights of gentleness, refinement and peace. It is the same Paul who writes to the Galatians. He is not to be pictured as an argumentative clergyman delighting in controversy as some delight in hunting or shooting. He found conflict painful and engaged in controversy with distaste, when forced to do so in order to preserve the gospel in its purity. For only the pure gospel, he believed, can form true Christians (cf. 4:19) and build up a really Christian community: 'If a word of encouragement in Christ, if an appeal made in love, if fellowship in the Spirit, if tenderness and compassion have any power with you, bring my joy to completion, by being all of one mind, united in one love, living by one soul, sharing one mind' (Phil 2:1-2). The tone is different in Galatians, but the purpose is the same: the true gospel, rightly understood, releases the power of the Spirit, the fruits of which are charity, joy and peace, in a Christian community or church.

Whoever studies Galatians with sympathy cannot fail to recognize above all St Paul's profound reverence for the cross of Christ, which renders all the ritual law, the Jewish ceremonial, and the animal sacrifices of the temple, at one blow, obsolete. In Paul's mind, the cross has a once-and-for-all finality which lifts it out of the stream of time. It becomes, along with the resurrection, the centre of a complex event, the 'new creation', which gradually spreads as time goes on. The cross is the great revelation of the constant and enduring love of Christ who 'delivered himself for me' (2:29); and at the same time it is the supreme demonstration of obedience, since Christ offered himself according to the will of the Father (1:4). St Paul does not pretend to 'explain' the mystery of the cross; he is content to show it forth as a revelation of the love of Christ and of God his Father, who is not a harsh task-master (like the angels of the law), but a fatherly God of peace and mercy (6:16), generous and gentle, severe only to the unbelieving and the disobedient (cf. Rom 11:22). This God, the gracious Father of our Lord Jesus Christ (cf. 1:16), Paul too strove to reveal both in his care for his 'little children' (4:19) and in his preaching. In his own life, he had experienced conversion to Christ as liberation from a state which, looking back, he described as slavery; he had passed over, through association with Christ's death and resurrection, into a new relationship with God characterized by grace, peace and victory over sin. These were the blessings which he sought to extend to the Gentiles.

As most men are not scholars, their religious convictions must of necessity be simple. The greatness of the Epistle to the Galatians is that it preaches so insistently the basic truths of the Christian faith: that in the cross of Christ God has provided the expiation of our sins and the well-spring of holiness; there we see, and thence we receive, the Spirit of sonship. Through faith in Christ, God draws us to hope and to love and so to fulfil the law of Christ. Faith, hope and charity are the principal manifestations of his Spirit, indeed of Christ himself living and working within us, like leaven secretly fermenting. By assimilating these few truths, and by experiencing the power of Christ in his own life, a man learns what it means to be a Christian. He comes to value his privilege, desires to pass it on to the next generation, and shares the indignation of Paul when he sees others 'setting aside the grace of God' (2:21).

Along with the essential simplicity of the message, we must also admire the immense sweep of St Paul's thought — from Abraham to Moses, from Moses to Christ's death, and from the resurrection to the consummation. Paul offers an understanding of the whole human panorama, and discloses the secret councils of God. If the word were not so closely associated with dualism, we might well call Paul a 'Gnostic'. He offers divinely revealed knowledge of man's situation before God and of the appointed Way to salvation; whoever accepts this knowledge or *gnosis* by faith will be saved by it from the present evil age (1:4). Galatians is a wonderful Epistle, in which St Paul

s

sums up his deepest convictions and the lessons of his own incomparable experiences. He expresses them in words and sentences constructed with great human skill under the inspiration of the Holy Spirit (cf. 1 Cor 2:13). So great is his mastery of his literary skills and techniques that he pours out, without any apparent effort after style, sentence after sentence of such strength and vigour that his formulations have never been surpassed.

Let me end with an autobiographical comparison. When I was a student at Oxford, I studied patiently, phrase by phrase, for purposes of examination, the *Res Gestae* of the emperor Augustus, in which he recorded for posterity the principal events of his career. Several years later, when I was in Rome for my Biblical studies, I found myself one afternoon at the *Ara Pacis* by the Tiber, where the text of the *Res Gestae* is inscribed in stone. There, for the first time, I read through it as a human document, and I will confess that I read it through tears of admiration and compassion and love. So too here: having examined the Epistle to the Galatians phrase by phrase, and pulled it apart, and criticized it, we must now return to it and read it again as a whole. Those of us who fully accept Paul's claims must make it our task to propagate his teaching *in faith*, that is, believing in face of the criticisms of our own destructive reason, that this message *is* the power of God unto salvation, and *can* steadily recreate a new and reunited human family. Here, then, is the Mustard Seed.

1  ¹ PAUL, an apostle — not from men, not through man, but through Jesus Christ and God the Father who raised him from the dead — ² I and all the brethren with me greet the churches of Galatia: ³ grace to you and peace from God our Father and the Lord Jesus Christ, ⁴ who gave himself for our sins, to rescue us from the present evil age, according to the will of God our Father, ⁵ to whom be the glory for ever and ever. Amen.

⁶ I am astonished that you are so quickly deserting the one who called you in the grace of Christ and going over to another gospel, ⁷ which is not another gospel, but certain persons are shaking you and would like to turn Christ's gospel upside down. ⁸ But if anyone, even ourselves or an angel from heaven, preaches to you a gospel other than the one we preached, let him be anathema! ⁹ We warned you before,

and now I say it again: if anyone preaches to you a gospel other than the one you received, let him be anathema! [10] For am I now seeking the favour of men or of God? Or am I trying to please men? If I were still trying to please men, I should not be a servant of Christ. [11] For I inform you, brethren, that the gospel which was preached by me is not according to man. [12] Nor did I receive it from any man, nor was I taught it by any man; I received it through a revelation of Jesus Christ.

[13] For you have heard the way of life I once followed in Judaism — how I was going to extremes in persecuting the Church of God and making havoc of it, [14] how I was making greater progress in Judaism than many of my contemporaries among my own people, and showing greater zeal for the traditions of my forefathers. [15] But when he who had set me apart from my mother's womb and graciously called me was pleased [16] to reveal his Son to me, that I might preach him to the Gentiles, there and then, instead of consulting flesh and blood [17] or going up to Jerusalem to those who had been made apostles before me, I went off to Arabia. From there I returned to Damascus. [18] Then, three years later, I went up to Jerusalem to see Peter, and I stayed with him for fifteen days. [19] But not one of the other apostles did I see — unless you count James the brother of the Lord. [20] I declare before God that what I am writing is the truth. [21] Then I went into the countries of Syria and Cilicia, [22] but I remained unknown by sight to the Christian churches in Judaea, [23] though they kept hearing: 'The man who once persecuted us is now preaching the very faith which he formerly tried to destroy.' [24] And they gave glory to God because of me.

**2** [1] Then after fourteen years, I again went up to Jerusalem with Barnabas, taking Titus with me too. [2] I went up in obedience to a revelation, and I laid before them the gospel which I preach to the Gentiles, but privately before those held in regard: Was I perhaps running or had I run my course in vain? [3] But even my companion Titus, Greek as he is, was not compelled to be circumcised. [4] But on account of intruders — false brethren who had wormed their way in to spy on the liberty we have in Christ Jesus, in order to enslave us. [5] But not for a moment did we yield to their demand — in order that the truth of the gospel might remain with you. [6] As for those held in regard — what they once were makes no difference to me, God is no respecter of persons — those held in regard laid down no further requirements. [7] On the contrary, seeing that I had been entrusted with the gospel of the uncircumcised, as Peter had been with that of the circumcised ( [8] for he who had made Peter's apostleship to the circumcision effective had made mine effective among the Gentiles), [9] and recognizing the grace that had been given to me, James, Cephas and John, the ones regarded as pillars, gave to me and to Barnabas the right hand of fellowship, with the understanding that we should preach to the Gentiles and they to the Jews. [10] Only (they said) we should remember the (Jewish) poor — and this I took care to do.

[11] But when Cephas came to Antioch, I resisted him face to face, because he was self-condemned. [12] For before the arrival of certain persons from James, he had been taking his meals with the Gentiles; but after their arrival, he began to draw back and set himself apart, fearing those of the circumcision. [13] The other Jews played the hypocrite along with him — so much so that even Barnabas was swept along with them by their hypocrisy. [14] But when I saw that they were not walking steadily according to the truth of the gospel, I said to Cephas in the presence of them all: 'If you, who were born a Jew, live as a Gentile and not as a Jew, how can you compel the Gentiles to judaize?

[15] 'We by our birth are Jews and not sinners of Gentiles, [16] but knowing that no man is justified from works of the law, but through faith in Jesus Christ, we too put our faith in Jesus Christ, in order to be justified from faith in Christ,

and not from works of the law, for from works of the law *no flesh will be justified.* ¹⁷ But if through seeking to be justified in Christ we have turned out to be sinners ourselves — has Christ become a servant of Sin? Heaven forbid! ¹⁸ For if I rebuild what I tore down, I make myself a sinner. ¹⁹ For it was through the law that I died to the law, in order that I might live to God. I am crucified with Christ crucified. ²⁰ It is no longer I who live, but Christ is alive within me. So far as I now live, while in the flesh, I live through faith in God and in Christ who loved me and offered himself for me. ²¹ I do not set aside the grace of God; for if justice comes through the law, Christ died for nothing.'

3   ¹ O foolish Galatians, who has bewitched you — you before whose eyes Jesus Christ was placarded crucified? ² I would have you tell me this one thing: Was it after doing the law that you received the Spirit, or after hearing the faith? ³ Are you really so foolish? Having begun with the Spirit, will you now end with the flesh? ⁴ Have your great experiences been useless, or worse than useless?

⁵ He then who bestowed the Spirit upon you and worked wonders in you — was it because you observed the law or because you heard the faith? ⁶ It was the same with Abraham: *he believed God and it was reckoned to him as justice.* ⁷ Recognize, then, that those who rely on faith — they are the sons of Abraham. ⁸ Because the Scripture foresaw that God would justify the Gentiles through faith, she announced to Abraham the good news that *all the nations will be blessed in you.* ⁹ So then, those who rely on faith are sharers in the blessing with faithful Abraham. ¹⁰ For all who rely on the works of the law are under a curse; for it is written: *Cursed is every man who does not abide by all the things written in the book of the law so as to do them.* ¹¹ That no one is justified by the law is certain, for *the just man will live by faith;* ¹² but the law is not concerned with faith, but <with works, for it says: > *He who does them will live by them.* ¹³ Christ re-

deemed us from the curse of the law, by becoming for our sake a curse (for it is written: *Cursed is every man who is hanged upon a tree*), [14] in order that the blessing promised to Abraham might be extended to the Gentiles in Jesus Christ, in order that we might receive the promised gift of the Spirit through faith.

[15] Brethren, I speak in human fashion: once a covenant has been ratified, even a human covenant, no one sets it aside or adds conditions to it. [16] Now the promises were made to Abraham *and to his Issue*. It does not say *and to his issues*, in the plural, but uses the singular *and to his Issue* — and this is Christ. [17] What I mean is this: when the covenant had been ratified by God, the law, made four hundred and thirty years later, does not invalidate it, so as to render the promise void. [18] For if from the law comes the inheritance, it is no longer from the promise. But to Abraham it was by way of promise that God made the gift. [19] What then was the purpose of the law? It was added on account of sins, until the Issue should come, to whom the promise had been made. It was drawn up by angels by the hand of a mediator. [20] Now a mediator does not mediate between one party, and God is one. [21] Is then the law opposed to the promises? Heaven forbid! For if a law had been given with power to give life, truly justice would come from the law. [22] But the Scripture has delivered up all to sin, in order that the promised blessing may be given to all through faith in Jesus Christ. [23] But before the coming of faith we were locked up in custody until the faith should be revealed. [24] So the law was our pedagogue to Christ, that we might be justified through faith. [25] Now that faith has come, we are no longer under a pedagogue. [26] For you are all God's sons through faith in Jesus Christ. [27] For when you were all baptized in Christ, you put on Christ. [28] There is no longer Jew or Greek, there is no longer slave or free, there is no longer male and female; for you are all one, in Christ Jesus. [29] But if you belong to Christ, then

you are the Issue of Abraham, and heirs according to the promise.

**4** ¹ What I mean is this: so long as the heir to a property is a minor, he is no different from a slave, though he is the lord of all. ² He is subject to guardians and stewards until the date fixed by his father. ³ So too with us: so long as we were minors, we were subject to the elements of the world, enslaved to them. ⁴ But when the fullness of time arrived, God sent forth his own Son, who was born of a woman, and became subject to the law, ⁵ in order to redeem those under the law, in order that we might receive the status of sons. ⁶ And as proof that you are his sons, God sent forth the Spirit of his Son into our hearts, crying: 'Abba, Father!' ⁷ So then you are no longer a slave but a son, and if a son, then also an heir, thanks to God. ⁸ Formerly, not knowing God, you were the slaves of beings who by nature are not gods; ⁹ but now that you have come to know God, or rather to be known by God, how can you turn back to the weak and grasping elements? ¹⁰ Do you wish to be enslaved to them all over again, observing days and months and seasons and years?

¹¹ I fear that I may have laboured in vain for you. ¹² Be like me, because I became like you, brethren, I beseech you — and you did me no harm. ¹³ You know that it was in sickness of body that I preached the gospel to you on the former occasion. ¹⁴ My sickness was your temptation, yet you did not despise me or reject me; on the contrary, you received me as an angel of God, as Christ Jesus. ¹⁵ Where, then, is your fervour gone? For I testify to your credit: you would have plucked out your eyes and given them to me, if possible. ¹⁶ Have I, then, become your enemy by speaking the truth to you? ¹⁷ They are courting you dishonourably; they want to exclude you, so that you will court them. ¹⁸ It is an honour to be courted honourably — at all times, and not only when I visit you. ¹⁹ My children, I am in travail with you again,

until Christ is formed in you. [20] I wish I could visit you now and adapt my tone to you, for I am perplexed about you.

[21] Tell me, you who want to be under the law, do you not hear what the law says? [22] It is written that Abraham had two sons, one by the slave-girl, and one by the free woman. [23] The son of the slave-girl was born according to the flesh, but the son of the free woman in fulfilment of a promise. [24] These are allegorical statements. For the two women are two covenants — one is from Mount Sinai and bears children who are slaves. She is Agar. [25] Mount Sinai, though situated in Arabia, goes with the present Jerusalem, which is a slave and the mother of slaves. [26] But the heavenly Jerusalem is the free woman. She is the mother of us all. [27] For it is written: *Rejoice, O childless one, who hast not borne, break forth and cry, thou who hast not been in labour; for more numerous are the children of her who is desolate than of her who has the husband.* [28] But we, brethren, are, like Isaac, children of promise. [29] But just as of old he who was born according to the flesh sought to exclude him who was born according to the Spirit, so now. [30] But what does the Scripture say? It says: *Reject the slave-girl and her son, for the son of a slave-girl shall not share the inheritance with the son of the free woman.*

[31] Therefore, brethren, we are sons, not of the slave-girl, but of the free woman. 5 [1] Christ has freed you in order to remain free. Stand firm, then, and do not submit again to the yoke of slavery. [2] See! I, Paul, declare to you that if you have yourselves circumcised, Christ will give you no help. [3] Once again, I solemnly assure every man who has himself circumcised that he is obliged to fulfil the whole of the law. [4] You are cut off from the power of Christ, any of you who justify yourselves by means of the law; you are banished from his grace. [5] For it is by the Spirit through faith that we receive the justification that is our hope. [6] For in Christ Jesus neither circumcision is of any avail nor its absence, but only faith working through charity. [7] You were running well; who has

put obstacles in your way? Do not let anyone persuade you not to obey the truth! [8] Such persuasion is not from the one who calls you. [9] A little yeast leavens the whole mass. [10] I have confidence in you in the Lord that you will not think otherwise. But he who is upsetting you will bear the condemnation, whosoever he may be. [11] But as for me, brethren, if I am still preaching circumcision, why am I still being persecuted? For in that case the scandal of the cross would have lost its power. [12] Would that those who are making trouble among you would go further and castrate themselves! [13] For you have been called to freedom, brethren — only do not let your freedom become an incitement to the flesh.

But serve one another in charity. [14] For the whole law is fulfilled in obeying this one precept: *You shall love your neighbour as yourself.* [15] But if you rend and devour one another, beware lest you be destroyed by one another. [16] What I mean is: walk by the Spirit, and you will not fulfil the lust of the flesh. [17] For the flesh lusts against the spirit, and the spirit against the flesh (for these are opposed to each other), to prevent you from doing whatever you want. [18] But if you are led by the Spirit, you are not under the law. [19] It is plain what are the works of the flesh: fornication, impurity, licentiousness; [20] idolatry, sorcery; enmities, strife, jealousy, fits of anger, quarrels, dissensions, intrigues, [21] envy; drunkenness, orgies, and things like these. I warn you now as I warned you before, that those who do such things will not inherit the kingdom of God. [22] But the harvest of the Spirit is charity, joy, peace, patience, kindness, goodness, fidelity, [23] gentleness, self-control. Against such things as these there is no law. [24] Those who belong to Christ Jesus have crucified the flesh with its passions and its lusts. [25] If we live by the spirit, let us also walk by the spirit. [26] Let us not be eager for vainglory, provoking one another, envying one another.   6   [1] Brethren, if a man falls into some misdeed, you who are spiritual must put him right, in a spirit of gentleness, with an eye on yourself, lest you too be tempted. ² Bear one another's burdens, and so you will fulfil the law of Christ.

³ For if anyone thinks he is something whereas he is nothing, he is deluding himself. ⁴ Let each man examine his own conduct; then he will be able to claim superiority only over himself, not over his neighbour. ⁵ For each will bear his own burden. ⁶ But a man who is being instructed in the word must give his teacher a share in all his goods. ⁷ Do not deceive yourselves: God is not mocked. For whatever a man sows, that he will reap. ⁸ If he sows for his own flesh, from his flesh he will reap destruction; but if he sows for the spirit, from the Spirit he will reap eternal life. ⁹ Let us not weary of doing what is right; in due time we shall reap our harvest, if we do not weaken. ¹⁰ Therefore, while we have time, let us do good to all men, but especially to our kindred in the faith. ¹¹ Look at these large letters which I have written with my own hand!

¹² Those who desire the approval of the world of flesh — they are the ones who urge you to be circumcised, but only that they may avoid being persecuted for the cross of Christ. ¹³ For those who rely on circumcision do not even keep the law themselves; but they want you circumcised so that they can make your flesh a subject for their boasting. ¹⁴ For my part, heaven forbid that I should boast of anything except the cross of our Lord Jesus Christ, by which the world is crucified to me, and I to the world. ¹⁵ For neither circumcision nor its absence makes any difference, but only creation anew. ¹⁶ Upon all who walk by this rule be peace and mercy, and upon the Israel of God. ¹⁷ From now on let no one disturb me! For I bear in my body the stigmata of Jesus. ¹⁸ The grace of our Lord Jesus Christ be with your spirit, brethren. Amen.

# INDEX OF BIBLICAL REFERENCES

| | | | |
|---|---|---|---|
| 10:1-48 | 109-111 | 1:4 | 289n, 331 |
| 10:38-40 | 511n | 1:8 | 82n |
| 10:44-48 | 323n | 1:9 | 123 |
| 11:1-10 | 106n | 1:16 | 390 |
| 11:2 | 33 | 1:17 | 204 |
| 11:24 | 33, 406 | 1:19—2:16 | 460n |
| 11:27-30 | 145 | 1:20-21 | 321 |
| 13:3 | 8n | 1:20—2:29 | 173n |
| 13:13 | 490n | 2:6 | 232n |
| 13:38-39 | 12, 20 | 2:17-20 | 365n |
| 13:48-52 | 15 | 2:20 | 314 |
| 14:8-12 | 386 | 2:28-29 | 494 |
| 14:14-18 | 15 | 3:1-2 | 431n |
| 14:15 | 448n | 3:2 | 30 |
| 14:22 | 224 | 3:8 | 86n |
| 14:23 | 65 | 3:9-20 | 258 |
| 14:27-30 | 74n | 3:19 | 264 |
| 15:1 | 33, 244 | 3:20 | 295 |
| 15:1-2 | 155 | 3:21 | 344 |
| 15:1-5 | 26 | 3:22 | 204 |
| 15:1-35 | 148-52 | 3:23 | 271n |
| 15:2 | 156 | 3:25 | 207n, 295 |
| 15:5 | 421 | 3:26 | 117n |
| 15:9 | 185 | 3:28 | 205, 219 |
| 15:10 | 232 | 4:1-3 | 208 |
| 15:12 | 148n, 491n | 4:9-12 | 242, 278 |
| 15:24 | 184 | 4:11 | 342 |
| 15:25-29 | 419n | 4:13 | 254, 273 |
| 15:35 | 1 | 4:19-20 | 399-400 |
| 15:39-41 | 36 | 5:1 | 118, 423 |
| 16:3 | 431n | 5:1-5 | 473 |
| 16:4 | 211n | 5:8 | 80n |
| 18:13 | 17 | 5:9 | 423 |
| 20:34 | 170n | 5:11 | 508-09 |
| 21:20 | 33, 162 | 5:19 | 196, 213n |
| 21:20-21 | 169 | 6:1 | 173n |
| 21:22-23 | 161 | 6:3 | 222 |
| 22:3-21 | 97-98 | 6:6 | 325 |
| 22:16 | 214 | 6:7 | 73n, 272 |
| 22:17-21 | 136, 139 | 6:11 | 219n |
| 23:1 | 31, 92 | 6:15 | 173n, 209 |
| 23:5 | 384 | 6:16-23 | 418 |
| 26:2-26 | 98-100 | 6:17 | 316n |
| 26:17 | 136 | 7:2 | 403n |
| | | 7:4 | 213 |
| *Romans* | | 7:7 | 117 |
| 1:1 | 55 | 7:7-25 | 173n |
| 1:1-11 | 250 | 7:9 | 339 |

# INDEX OF AUTHORS

# INDEX OF SUBJECTS